An Introduction to TEACHING AND SCHOOLS

Charles B. Myers
Peabody College
Vanderbilt University

Lynn K. Myers
Harpeth Valley Elementary School
Nashville, Tennessee

Teacher—one who makes a difference in the lives of others

Holt, Rinehart and Winston, Inc.
Fort Worth   Chicago   San Francisco   Philadelphia
Montreal   Toronto   London   Sydney   Tokyo

Editor-in-Chief   Ted Buchholz
Acquisitions Editor   Jo-Anne Weaver
Developmental Editor   Sue Hull
Project Editor   Michele Tomiak
Manager of Art and Design   Guy Jacobs
Production Manager   Ken Dunaway
Copyeditor   Wanda H. Giles
Text Design   Rita Naughton
Cover Design   Pat Sloan
Cover Photograph   Larry Wilson

Copyright © 1990 by Holt, Rinehart and Winston, Inc.

All rights reserved. No part of this publication may be reproduced or transmitted in any form or by any means, electronic or mechanical, including photocopy, recording or any information storage and retrieval system, without permission in writing from the publisher.

Requests for permission to make copies of any part of the work should be mailed to: Copyrights and Permissions Department, Holt, Rinehart and Winston, Inc., Orlando, Florida 32887.

Address editorial correspondence to: 301 Commerce Street, Suite 3700, Fort Worth, Texas 76102

Address orders to: 6277 Sea Harbor Drive, Orlando, Florida 32887 1-800-782-4479, or 1-800-433-0001 (in Florida)

Printed in the United States of America

ISBN 0–03–002513–3

0 1 2 3 071 9 8 7 6 5 4 3 2 1

Holt, Rinehart and Winston, Inc.
The Dryden Press
Saunders College Publishing

To Jeff, Mark, and Brian

Acknowledgments

Teachers of many types have had a direct impact on our professional lives and on the writing of this text. They include our parents and children, our own elementary and secondary school teachers in Columbia and Wrightville, Pennsylvania, particularly Elmer Kreiser, Dorothy Broom, Mary S. Groff, Dorcas Bortz, and John Filby; our college instructors, especially Jack Allen, Kenneth Cooper, Robert P. Thompson, and Earline Kendall; our cooperating teachers when we student taught, Neil Everhart and Mary Miller; our teaching colleagues, especially Pauline Maderia, Sarah Rowan, Debbie Ladd, Marty McSwiney, and Joe Myers; our students from Grade 1 through graduate school. In various ways, all influenced this book and specific elements of its content.

We also acknowledge the unique, expert, and gracious participation of the contributing authors—Jane Stallings, Terry Deal, Carolyn Evertson, Ann Neely, Penny Brooks, Jeanne Plas, Doug Simpson, Brian Hansford, and Alene Harris. We asked each of these well-known specialists and widely published scholars to explain major aspects of their respective areas of expertise at a level addressed to beginning teacher education students, within the limits of our specifications, and with the understanding that we would make revisions when doing so would help the book as a whole. They provided concise, focused ideas at a level appropriate for our readers and at the same time allowed us a latitude with their creative work that was truly admirable.

Several of our professional colleagues gave their talent and time in reviewing the manuscript in part or in whole: Malcolm Allred; Jane Applegate, Kent State University; Frederick J. Baker, California Polytechnical Institute; John A. Beineke, University of Evansville; David Byrd, Southern Illinois University; Alex M. Cuthbert, Virginia Polytechnical Institute and State University; Susie Edmond, Saginaw Valley State University; Philip Fitch, Point Loma College; Ann Harris; Douglas D. Hatch, University of Southern Florida; Louis Hill, Youngstown State University; Lindy Hoover, Youngstown State University; Randy L. Hoover, Youngstown State University; Susan Booth Larson; Jerry C. Long, University of Montana; Jane McCarthy, University of Houston; John M. McIntyre, Southern Illinois University; Bill M. Morrison, Central Connecticut State University; Robert Reed, Bowling Green State University; Steve Ross, Northern Georgia College; Dorothy Sheldon, Central Washington University; Richard D. Shepardson; Clyde Slicker, Rhode Island College; Peter A. Soderbergh, Louisiana State University; Phillip Stewart, University of Cincinnati; Jack Stewart, Columbus College; and Gene Sullivan, University of Michigan at Flint.

We would also like to thank the people who helped us bring this project into its final form: Susan Hull, who helped us develop the manuscript; Christy Edgin and Sheryl Bransford, who patiently typed and retyped; Wanda Giles, who copyedited and gave us food for thought; Michele Tomiak, who saw the book through production; and finally, Jo-Anne Weaver, our editor at Holt, who enthusiastically led us through the entire process.

Preface: About This Text

Why We Wrote This Text

From time to time most teachers consider writing texts that they think will be more appropriate for the students they teach than the book they are already using, and the two of us are no exceptions. Unlike many others, we were challenged to put our thoughts to work, and this text is the result. It all started several years ago when two representatives from Holt, Rinehart and Winston, Roger Macquarrie and Earl McPeek, visited Charles Myers at Peabody College, Vanderbilt University, and began a conversation by saying something like, "We hear you have mentioned doing a text for the introductory course in teacher education. How would you like to do it with Holt?"

At that time, Charles was (and still is) teaching the introductory course at Vanderbilt University. Lynn Myers was teaching first grade in an inner-city school in the Metropolitan Nashville Schools and was supervising Vanderbilt students completing their practica and student teaching in her classroom. The Holt representatives' question prompted several weeks of personal reflection and introspection for us and for Jane Stallings, who was coteaching the introductory course with Charles. Prominent among the questions were: How would such a text improve upon those already available? How should it address beginning education students? Could it explain the current changes in teaching and schools in both an introductory and an understandable way? In what ways would it better prepare practica students and student teachers for teaching in classrooms such as those in Lynn's urban school? How could we make it an interesting, substantive, realistic, and appropriate book for beginners? Could it connect beginning students with live classrooms in their very first professional course?

Obviously, we decided we could and would take up the challenge. We became primary authors—a college instructor with secondary school experience and a practicing elementary school teacher with classroom supervisory responsibility for college practica students. Jane Stallings agreed to author a chapter and to collaborate, consult, and advise on others. We asked seven of our colleagues to contribute in their individual areas of expertise. They and their areas are listed in the About the Authors section.

Our Goals for This Text

We intend this text to do the following:

1. introduce you quickly and understandably to teaching and what happens in classrooms and schools;
2. help you become actively aware of real classrooms and schools early in your teacher-education program;
3. provide you with substantial information and ideas on which you can build intellectually as you pursue your studies;

4. show you the scholarly, research-oriented nature of teaching and learning and help you to formulate research questions of your own;
5. enable you to develop your own mental pictures—or concepts—of the general ideas presented in the fifteen text chapters, along with the many smaller concepts embedded in each.

Each goal is explained further below.

Quick, Understandable Introduction. In our own teaching of the first course in teacher education, including our discussions with students, we have been constantly struck by two observations: Many texts are very general and vague. Others concentrate on foundations of education. Neither type explains what is happening in classrooms now. They seem to stress abstractions instead of current teaching, schools, and students. In contrast, we want you to get into teaching and classrooms quickly and actively, and we want you to do so in a way that is understandable even with little or no previous study of the subject.

We think this text provides that introduction, and from its beginning. Chapter 1 presents a focused analysis of teaching and schools today. Chapter 2 teaches you several ways in which classrooms can be analyzed when you observe them. Chapter 3 describes recent classroom effectiveness research so that you can use it to interpret the teaching and classroom activity you observe. Chapter 4 provides two perspectives for understanding K–12 students. Chapter 5 describes schools in terms of their goals and purposes. Chapter 6 explains schools as cultures. And so our book proceeds.

This is not to say that we ignore the foundations of education. Chapters 7 through 10 concentrate on them. However, we hope we have added something and that you can understand the meaning of the ideas in these chapters for today's teachers, students, and schools when you get to them, not just afterward.

Involvement in Real Classrooms and Schools. Often education texts and courses describe teaching, classrooms, and schools as if they are far off and unavailable to the students reading the texts and taking the courses. This is not really the case. Most college campuses are within short distances of real, active K–12 schools. So we decided to structure this text to take advantage of the schools close to you as learning sites and to prepare you to make use of them. Case studies of teaching, lessons, classrooms, students, and schools appear frequently throughout the book and every chapter begins with a Snapshot of such a scene. These illustrations are based on actual observations and are intended as examples of what you can look for during your own visits to schools. Chapter 2 and sections of several subsequent chapters teach you how to observe and to understand what you see. Videotapes of classroom episodes and school scenes are also available to supplement or substitute for your visits to schools.

Substantial Information and Ideas. Although this text is introductory, it is not just a superficial survey of fifteen topics. It has substance. We selected the content and wrote the text knowing that you would be starting your study of each topic but that we would supply enough substance for you to develop a depth of understanding as you read. We think that as you finish each chapter, you will be knowledgeable about the ideas presented. We also think you will know enough to use that knowledge as you continue in your study of this book and in later professional studies. You will not only be getting information but meaningfully questioning and thinking about what you are reading.

Scholarly, Research Orientation. The field of education has changed rapidly in recent years, and it will continue to do so. New ideas are generated constantly, and researchers are digging deeper into all facets of the field and coming up with novel, complex explanations of what they are studying. As a result, learning to teach now requires that you understand new research and become skilled at applying it in your classroom. Therefore, we have tied the content of this text to up-to-date research findings and have included sections of chapters that ask you to consider research questions. We did this to help you begin to develop a research's mind set, a perspective that you can use throughout your teaching career to stay informed and current.

Conceptual Organization. You, as a beginning student, can understand this text, with its substantial depth and research orientation, because it is organized conceptually. In each chapter we draw at least one mental picture for a rather broad aspect of education which is that chapter's focus; we drew each of those pictures with beginning students in mind. As you read a chapter, the general concepts, as well as smaller supporting ones, should gradually build into a clear image of the subject. At the end of a chapter, you will not know all that there is to know on the subject, but you should have learned to understand the main ideas and be able to use your new learning to push on. The concepts or mental images that you should be able to develop in each chapter are listed in a later section explaining the table of contents.

Some Assumptions

In writing this text, we made two important sets of assumptions that have influenced what we cover and how we present it. One of those deals with the nature of teaching and schools and what we know about them. The other concerns you, the student who uses this text.

The Nature of Teaching and Schools

Teaching is a complex, challenging process that requires well-educated, skilled professionals who must make important decisions almost constantly. Schools are complicated, dynamic organizations that must function effectively if students are to learn.

We now know enough about teaching to assert that it is more than a craft that can be learned by watching others do the right things and then copying them. There is a knowledge base to the field of professional education, a multitude of skills to effective classroom performance, and a constant need for teachers to decide what to do and how to do it.

We also know that this idea of teaching is rather new and not always shared by the public, by politicians, or by some teachers. People often think anyone can teach, that teaching is not hard (except for controlling "bad" students), and that knowing the subject that one teaches is the only important prerequisite to teaching. Analyses of teaching have demonstrated that this is simply invalid.

Schools are not static institutions. They are living organizations made up of interacting individuals. Schools constantly change, and transactions within them consistently fluctuate. Some are more effective—better—than others, and we can characterize their effectiveness and goodness. Building and maintaining quality schools requires intelligence, skills, dedication, and vigilance by all involved.

The Nature of Beginning Teacher-Education Students. We assume that you, as a reader of this text, may know fairly little at this point about teaching in schools. Of course, you have some idea about the topic, but your learning has probably been rather unsystematic so far. You know enough, however, to have decided you want to know more. We also realize that you may or may not have had courses in a major outside education and undergraduate general education courses.

We also assume that you are intelligent and that you are capable of serious professional study. We realize that you probably do not know for sure whether you want to teach, but we would guess that you are at least probing the question seriously.

We subscribe to the idea that becoming a teacher is a developmental process, with somewhat noticeable stages, and we have written this text with that in mind. For instance, most people who actually become teachers start with a general concept of teaching based on their personal experiences as students; they later pick up more ideas from teachers they know, start to inquire purposefully about teaching, engage in systematic study through coursework and classrooms, practice the skills of teaching, take responsibility for their own classrooms, get their first real jobs, and so on. All along the way, they ask questions: Is this for me? Should I change to another major? Will I be any good at teaching?

From our perspective, the first stages of the process of becoming a teacher (some would say developing into a teacher) are rather intellectual, while the later stages stress the development of skills or the gaining of expertise. This text concentrates on that early part—the part that explores basic questions: What is teaching? What are schools really like? What do teachers actually do day after day? Would I fit in? Would I be good at it? Would I like it? We cannot answer all of these questions for you, but we think we provide enough information and questions that you can start answering them for yourself.

Pilot Testing

Over the past few years every chapter of this text has been used in our own classes and/or with our practica students. After each use, we made adjustments in response to student suggestions and our own reactions. We believe the various revisions helped make the text more useful and easier to use.

Features

We have incorporated a number of design features into this text in order to accomplish the following:

1. to teach the goals listed above;
2. to make the content as clear and understandable as possible; and
3. to help you apply ideas and issues to real teaching and real school situations.

Chapter Introductions

Each chapter begins with a brief introduction that sets the chapter focus and describes its contents.

Snapshots

A Snapshot—a short word picture that illustrates and applies to the real world of teaching the major ideas of the chapter—immediately follows each chapter introduction. It helps you visualize situations that reflect the points to be covered. Each begins with general questions that stimulate and direct your thinking. Each is accompanied by one or more pictures showing the situation or circumstance that is described.

Key Concepts

Key concepts are highlighted throughout the text in several ways—as subheadings, as marginal notations, and as boldface and italicized items in the text. These show you the important ideas being presented and help guide your reading and thinking.

Analyses

Fourteen chapters contain an Analysis section in which you are asked to use ideas presented in the chapter to study an episode or event of relevance. They enable you to apply your learning by analyzing a practical case study. Questions are provided to guide your thinking.

Educational Research

Thirteen of the fifteen chapters also contain an Educational Research section, which describes specific aspects of educational research related to the chapter focus. These sections give you a glimpse of the nature of research, specific research efforts, conclusions from some of those efforts, and ways in which the conclusions have affected teaching practice and schools.

Case Studies

Case studies are scattered throughout the text. Some of these are parts of chapter sections that have already been described—Snapshots and Analyses—and others are located within the narrative. Some study actual people and events; others use composites, and some are created material. All are based on real situations, although several have been modified to illustrate particular points. They illustrate realistic situations and conditions and give you a chance to apply your learning to settings teachers and other educators often face.

Chapter Ending Items

Chapters end with summaries, study questions, and bibliographies. These enable you to review, probe, and extend what you have learned from each chapter.

Involvement in Schools

Much of the text sets the stage for meaningful school observations. For example, in Chapter 2, you are taught observation systems that you can use to analyze classroom instruction. You may learn the concepts and practice the skills in this chapter. Later you will observe on your own.

Videotapes

Videotapes accompany this text. They portray teaching, schools, and teachers that illustrate ideas and techniques described in the book; and they provide episodes of teaching that can be analyzed as supplements to or substitutions for classroom observations.

Active Learning

Throughout the text, we try to involve you actively in the learning process. From time to time, we ask you questions, suggest that you read professional journals along with the course, direct you to analyze case-study situations, challenge you to formulate or reflect upon your own ideas, and urge you to continuously reformulate your ideas about teaching in schools. We believe the last two chapters of the text are realistic portrayals of the job of teaching now and in the future; in them, we ask you to raise serious questions about the profession of teaching and your place in it.

And Finally, An Exchange of Professional Ideas

Because of many of the ideas we already expressed, and particularly because we know that being a teacher is a continuous process of learning and improving, we want to invite you to join in an exchange of professional ideas. Our addresses are below. Write to us about your ideas, hunches, reactions, beliefs, opinions concerning this text, your teacher-education experiences, and teaching in schools in general. We will use your contributions as best we can, not only to improve this text, but when it is appropriate, to compile and disseminate your contributions to others.

We hope we can build a sizable network of teacher-education students, teachers, and professors who have used this text and want to share their ideas.

Charles B. Myers
Box 330, Peabody College
Vanderbilt University
Nashville, Tennessee 37203

Lynn K. Myers
Harpeth Valley Elementary School
7840 Old Harding Road
Nashville, Tennessee 37221

Brief Contents

CHAPTER 1   Teaching and Schools in America Today: The Current Scene and Future Directions   1

2   Inside Classrooms: Analyzing Real Teaching   46

3   Teaching Effectiveness: Classroom Practices and Characteristics That Enhance Learning   81

4   Human Development: Students Are Alike, but Not the Same   121

5   Equity and Excellence: Teaching All Students   166

6   The School: A Culture   206

7   The Schools in Historical Context: From Ancient Greece to the Twentieth Century   243

8   Philosophical Beliefs and Teaching: Ideas That Guide What Teachers Do   282

9   Theories of Learning: Ideas from Educational Psychology That Guide Teaching   325

10   Approaches to Teaching: A Look at Five Models of Instruction   358

11   Content: Knowledge, Skills, and Affective Learning   399

12   The Curriculum and Lessons: Designs for Learning   438

13   The Act of Teaching: From Planning to Evaluation   476

14   The Professional Teacher: The Life and the Work   517

15   Teaching the Next Generation: Is It for You?   561

APPENDIX   The Teacher-Student Interaction Observation System   598

GLOSSARY   607

INDEX   623

Concepts to Be Learned

We have mentioned that each chapter of this text is organized around general concepts that explain the topic on which the chapter focuses. Within the context of those general concepts are several lower-level, but important, supporting concepts that explain chapter subtopics and help clarify the bigger ideas.

As you read each chapter, you should be able to form in your mind a mental picture of what is being described. The image may be vague at first; but as you proceed, it should become clearer. At the end of a chapter, you should have your own idea of what was described. For example, after reading Chapter 1, you should have an idea of the context and influences on teaching and schools today; after Chapter 5, you should see which goals and objectives have guided teaching and schools in recent decades; and after Chapter 6, you should look upon schools as cultures.

If this process is successful, when you finish this text and the course in which it is being used, you should have a conceptual framework that you can use to guide your further study. That framework should supply you with background knowledge, help you formulate questions, and enable you to interpret new ideas. It should give you a set of intellectual images that will help explain ideas that you will confront later. For example, when you study teaching, you will be able to compare what you see with ideas about "effective teaching" (Chapter 3); when you look at students, you will be able to think of them in terms of developmental stages and clusters of personal characteristics (Chapter 4); and when you observe teachers, you will be able to do so in terms of the roles various individuals play in schools (Chapter 6).

The general and supporting concepts for each chapter are listed below. These are the ideas that should develop as mental pictures in your head by the time you finish and think about each chapter you read. Look them over now as you prepare to use this text. They should provide a preliminary guide for your reading. Do not be concerned, however, if some of the statements seem unclear. Many contain terms that you will not understand until you read the chapters.

Chapter 1: Teaching and Schools in America Today: The Current Scene and Future Directions

General Concepts
- Teaching and schools in America are changing rapidly, especially since the pressures for reform of the 1980s.
- The changes involve different expectations of schools, shifts in priorities, and new insights into the nature of teaching and learning.

Supporting Concepts
- Studying teaching and schools today means raising appropriate questions more than finding simple answers.
- General purposes of schools include citizenship education, academic

- achievement, vocational training, college preparation, and personal and social development.
- Virtually all Americans of school age attend school, although many drop out and some are not served as well as they could be.
- School curricula are rather common across schools.
- Teachers vary greatly, but many share common characteristics and interests.
- Reform agendas for schools in recent years include accountability, professionalization of teaching, school and teaching effectiveness, equality of education, and changes in content.
- Schools of the future will be different from those of today and will reflect changes in broader society.

Chapter 2: Inside Classrooms: Analyzing Real Teaching

General Concepts
- Classrooms have characteristics that set them apart from all other settings; although there are similarities among classrooms, each is also unique.
- Classroom teaching and learning can be studied and analyzed through the use of observation systems.

Supporting Concepts
- Recent studies of classrooms provide data that can be used to improve teaching.
- Knowledgeable and guided classroom observation provides understanding about teaching and learning for beginning teacher-education students.
- One type of classroom activity that can be observed analytically is student on-task/off-task behavior.
- Firsthand, guided study of classrooms is often more productive for teacher-education students than reading books about teaching.

Chapter 3: Teaching Effectiveness: Classroom Practices and Characteristics That Enhance Learning

General Concepts
- Teachers often have a very significant influence on the students they teach, but some teachers are much more influential than others.
- Recent research has identified teaching practices that are more effective in producing learning than others.

Supporting Concepts
- Teachers who seem to be particularly influential with teenage students generate enthusiasm for learning, create a sense of excitement, make learning pleasant, explain things, are approachable, instill student confidence, and show that they care about students.
- How teachers use time is an important variable in how well students learn.
- Teachers who plan, organize, and manage their classrooms and instruction will usually produce more learning than those who do not.
- A brisk teaching pace, withitness, overlapping, set classroom routines, student alerting and accountability techniques, lesson variety, and structured use of space often characterize effective classrooms.

- Teachers are executive managers of all classroom elements and have so many things to do that they are sometimes thought of as ringmasters.
- There are a variety of useful approaches to handling student misbehavior, although none is foolproof.
- Students achieve more in the classrooms of teachers who actively supervise them.
- Teacher expectations, rewards, and praise affect student learning.
- Much more remains to be learned about classroom effectiveness.

Chapter 4: Human Development: Students Are Alike, but Not the Same

General Concepts
- Although students are similar, each is unique and must be understood to be taught properly.
- Because students are so different, teachers categorize them according to certain characteristics; although the practice is often useful, it can harm children and must be done carefully.
- Categorizing students is an artificial procedure followed by schools and teachers; students are not born in categories.

Supporting Concepts
- Children tend to develop through common progressions, which some describe as stages.
- Dialectical theory describes development as a series of four types of interactions between individuals and their environment—inner biological, individual psychological, cultural-social, and outer physical.
- Perceptual development involves a process of becoming less captive, more self-initiating, more systematic, more specific, and more able to ignore irrelevant information.
- Piagetian theory of cognitive development consists of four stages—sensorimotor, preoperational, concrete operational, and formal.
- Social-emotional development consists of four periods—infancy, early childhood, middle childhood, and adolescence.
- Teachers often categorize children on the bases of intelligence, learning ability or disability, and the presence of a handicapping condition.
- No matter how students are categorized, they are apt to be more similar to other students than they are different from them.
- Even average and normal students have distinguishing and exceptional characteristics.

Chapter 5: Equity and Excellence: Teaching All Students

General Concepts
- The concepts of equity and excellence have guided schooling in America in recent decades.
- American schools attempt to provide an equal and excellent education for all students in terms of their potential.
- American schools have still not succeeded in reaching the goals of equal and excellent education for all.

Supporting Concepts
- Goals for American schools have shifted several times during the twentieth century, from training the mind to "life adjustment" to a relative balance between the two ideas.
- Virtually every child in America attends school, and schools try to serve all of them appropriately.
- U.S. courts and legislative mandates require schools to provide equal education regardless of race, gender, or handicapping condition.
- Special efforts to meet the needs of particular students include racial desegregation, compensatory education, bilingual education, multicultural education, gender-related education, mainstreaming, programs for handicapped students, and programs for gifted and talented students.

Chapter 6: The School: A Culture

General Concepts
- Schools are organizational cultures with people who follow certain patterns of behavior, possess common values and beliefs, and pursue particular goals.
- Key cultural characteristics of all schools are shared values and beliefs, heroes and heroines, rituals and ceremonies, stories and legends, and informal players.
- School cultures include subgroups, which must work together if the school is to be effective.

Supporting Concepts
- Looking at schools as cultures helps explain their commonalities.
- When people enter organizational cultures for the first time, including new teachers in schools, they need to learn how things are done in that culture in order to be accepted and to feel comfortable.
- Subcultures that operate in schools have positive and negative influences on the general institutional culture.
- Students, teachers, administrators, and service workers all have their subcultures within schools, and each of these subcultures has subdivisions within it.

Chapter 7: The Schools in Historical Context: From Ancient Greece to the Twentieth Century

General Concepts
- American schools developed from traditions of Western Europe that include religious and civic purposes for schooling.
- Americans think of schools as a community responsibility and as a service available to and appropriate for all children.
- Because of the democratic and republican form of U.S. government, common schools are needed to educate the citizens of the United States.

Supporting Concepts
- Ideas from the Greeks and Romans, and from the Middle Ages, the Renaissance, and the Enlightenment form the roots of American schools today.

- American colonial religious and political traditions formed the basis of common schools in America.
- Over the last 200 years, civic purposes for schools in the United States have gradually overshadowed religious ones.
- The history of schools in America is one of gradual expansion of schools to serve all school-age children.

Chapter 8: Philosophical Beliefs and Teaching: Personal Ideas That Guide What Teachers Do

General Concepts
- Philosophical beliefs are answers that people provide for fundamental questions, and beliefs of this kind relating to education inform the ways teachers teach.
- All teachers have philosophies of education that they have developed over time and have revised as they find it appropriate to do so.

Supporting Concepts
- Forming an educational philosophy involves engaging in a set of intellectual activities that teachers use to think clearly, logically, ethically, and comprehensively about educational concerns.
- The process of philosophizing includes classification, justification, interpretation, and systematization.
- Philosophies, including those about education, involve questions about the nature of reality (metaphysics), the nature of knowledge (epistemology), and the nature of values (axiology).
- Two of the oldest philosophies that still affect teaching are idealism and realism.
- Pragmatism and existentialism are modern philosophies that affect teaching, but they rest on ideas and attitudes with long histories.
- Some contemporary philosophies that also affect teaching are reconstructionism, futurism, behaviorism, perennialism, evangelicalism, Marxism, and essentialism.

Chapter 9: Theories of Learning: Ideas from Educational Psychology That Guide Teaching

General Concepts
- Learning theories help explain how people learn and guide how teachers teach.
- Teachers tend to select learning theories as their guides on the basis of their personal style of teaching and the characteristics of the students they teach.

Supporting Concepts
- Behavior theory (including association and reinforcement approaches), cognitive theory, and Piagetian theory are currently widely relied upon and useful theories of learning.
- Behavior theory emphasizes connections between ideas and experiences, as well as consequences of behavior.

- Cognitive theory attempts to explain the dynamics of thought processes.
- Piagetian theory is both cognitive and developmental.

Chapter 10: Approaches to Teaching: A Look At Five Models of Instruction

General Concepts
- Models of instruction are designs for teaching based on particular theories of learning and philosophies of education and are intended to accomplish specific learning goals.
- Teachers tend to pursue models of instruction that are consistent with their own ideas about teaching and learning.

Supporting Concepts
- Models of instruction bring together theories of learning, philosophies of education, and classroom practices.
- Research data indicate that certain models of instruction are effective in reaching the learning goals for which they are intended.

Chapter 11: Content: Knowledge, Skills, and Affective Learning

General Concepts
- The content taught in schools can be thought of as having three dimensions—knowledge, skills, and affective learning.
- All three dimensions need to be taught to all students, in all subjects, at all grade levels.

Supporting Concepts
- Teachers select content on the basis of its availability, the values of society, their knowledge of their students, and their understanding of teaching and learning processes.
- The knowledge dimension of content is more than just the information students should know; it includes facts, concepts, and generalizations.
- Knowledge has structure, and knowing the structure of knowledge makes it more understandable and easier to teach.
- Skills, such as thinking, reading, and writing, are things people are able to do, and learning them involves both understanding and proficiency.
- Problem solving and developing concepts are examples of two types of thinking skills that can be taught across grade levels and subjects in schools.
- Values, feelings, and sensitivities can and should be taught in schools, along with knowledge and skills.
- Exploring feelings and analyzing values are two examples of teaching strategies that teach affective learning.

Chapter 12: The Curriculum and Lessons: Designs for Learning

General Concepts
- The school curriculum is a framework developed by educators to integrate all the dimensions of content into a teachable pattern.
- Students learn more in school than the content planned for them in the prepared curriculum; some of this is called the hidden curriculum.

Supporting Concepts
- Units of instruction and lesson plans are usually focused subsections of the school's curriculum.
- Curriculum development involves organizing goals, content, teaching strategies, activities, and materials into an arrangement that produces learning.
- Teachers organize curricular frameworks and choose content for their lessons as a matter of personal judgment and in accordance with their views of the roles of schools.
- Curriculum designs vary and range from those that are very content centered to those that are very student centered.

Chapter 13: The Act of Teaching: From Planning to Evaluation

General Concepts
- Teaching is a complex act in which teachers take all the ideas and elements affecting education available to them and formulate them in a personal way to produce learning in their students.
- Teaching is a multifaceted process that begins with thorough planning and ends with lesson evaluation. Teaching can be thought of as a process of communication between the teacher and students.

Supporting Concepts
- In planning lessons, teachers usually develop mental images of what they expect to happen and then fit the pieces together.
- Teaching is a dynamic, interactive process that requires teachers to play many roles.
- Lesson evaluation is an integral step in the act of teaching.
- Beginning teachers usually need to devote quite a bit of time and effort to planning lessons. Those with experience seem to be able to streamline the process.

Chapter 14: The Professional Teacher: The Life and the Work

General Concepts
- Teachers are a diverse group who have similar professional goals and perform similar work.
- The job of teaching revolves around a number of contexts in which it takes place—the nature of classrooms and schools as workplaces, the characteristics of students, relationships between teachers and their students, interactions among teacher colleagues, teachers' associations with administrators and parents, and the roles and responsibilities teachers assume when they close the classroom door.
- Job conditions of teachers vary greatly, but most teachers seem to balance out the good and the bad.

Supporting Concepts
- Teaching is a complex job with many responsibilities.
- Most teachers, including those just finishing their first year on the job, are satisfied with their work.

- The needs of the students each teacher faces greatly affect the job of teaching.
- Students who experience particularly harsh living conditions have special problems and present special challenges for their teachers.
- Teachers often list a feeling of doing worthwhile and respected work as the most positive aspect of teaching.
- Teachers see day-to-day frustrations and specific deterrents to doing their work, as well as persistent negative elements of teaching.
- Teachers join professional groups to share common concerns, marshal professional power, and influence educational and political decisions.

Chapter 15: Being a Teacher of the Next Generation: Is It for You?

General Concepts
- During the next generation, the most significant educational reform will occur in classrooms, with teachers and students, rather than in legislatures and among policy boards.
- Teachers are the most critical variable in the education process.
- Teaching in the next generation will be influenced by many professional and societal conditions, including the continued professionalization of teachers, international competition, changing technology, poverty, and the changing nature of the American family.

Supporting Concepts
- Continuing reform agendas in education will include back to basics, greater professionalization of teachers, more effective schools and teaching, more equitable education, and changes in content.
- Because teaching is becoming more complex, teachers in the future will have to increase their competence in a wide variety of ways.
- Attracting highly capable people to teaching in the future will be hard.
- Teacher salaries have improved in recent years.
- Deciding where to teach is a decision based on personal preferences and values.
- Many states have pledged to improve teacher compensation and job conditions.

About the Authors

Charles B. Myers is a professor and former chair of the Department of Teaching and Learning, George Peabody College for Teachers, Vanderbilt University. He teaches the introductory courses for both undergraduate and master's degree students preparing to teach in elementary and secondary schools, teaches the course Teaching Social Studies in Secondary Schools, and coordinates pre–student teaching practica and internships in schools. In 1982, Professor Myers was recognized by the college as the faculty member who made the greatest contribution outside the classroom to student-faculty relations.

Dr. Myers has taught in junior and senior high schools in Harrisburg, Pennsylvania, and Nashville, Tennessee. At the college level, he has taught at Rider College in New Jersey and Armidale College of Advanced Education, New South Wales, Australia, and at Vanderbilt. He received his undergraduate education at the Pennsylvania State University in secondary education and social studies and his master's and Ph.D. degrees from Peabody College in American history and the teaching of history and the social sciences.

In addition to this text, Professor Myers has written and served as general editor for a number of elementary and secondary school texts including *The Taba Program in Social Science—People in Change*; a sixth-grade social studies text, *People, Time and Change*; and a high school issues-oriented text, *The Environmental Crisis*.

Professor Myers has held a number of national positions in teacher-education and social studies–education organizations. He writes, speaks, and conducts workshops for teachers on teacher education, social studies, and the teaching of thinking and valuing skills.

Lynn K. Myers is a third-grade teacher at Harpeth Valley Elementary School in the Metropolitan Nashville Public Schools in Tennessee. She teaches basic subjects in a self-contained classroom. She also supervises classroom practica, student teaching, and internship experiences for college teacher-education students. For most of her teaching career, she taught first and second grades at Fall-Hamilton Elementary School, an inner-city school that serves a high proportion of children from economically disadvantaged homes. She has been designated a Career Ladder III teacher, the highest level in the Tennessee career ladder system.

Ms. Myers received her undergraduate education in elementary education at Rider College in New Jersey, Millerville State College in Pennsylvania, and Peabody College. She completed her master's degree in early childhood education and reading education at Peabody and has pursued further study at the Educational Specialist level in reading.

In addition to writing this text, Ms. Myers has served as a consultant and evaluator of elementary school language arts, social studies, and reading texts and supplemental materials. She has also been an evaluator of computer program software designed for elementary instruction.

Ms. Myers is active locally and nationally in reading education and teacher professional development efforts. She has developed a recognized system for student behavior management.

Contributing Authors

Although Charles and Lynn Myers are the primary authors of this text, a number of other experts in teacher education wrote chapters, parts of chapters, and initial drafts of chapters in their areas of expertise. Often their contributions were edited so that the chapters would fit together in an overall sense, but each contributing author prepared a valuable part of the manuscript. Those authors and their contributions are as follows:

Jane Stallings, chair of the Curriculum and Instruction Department and director of the Houston Center for Effective Teaching, University of Houston, is best known for her work in classroom research that links observed instructional strategies with student behavioral outcomes. Findings from her research have formed the basis for a staff development program called The Effective Use of Time for Teachers and Students. Her publications include *Learning to Look: A Handbook for Observation and Models of Teaching*, "A Self-Analytic Approach to Staff Development and School Improvement" and "Beyond Time on Task." Professor Stallings wrote Chapter 10 and prepared the initial draft and supplied most of the content for Chapter 3. Chapter 2 is also based substantially on her work. We have earlier acknowledged her help in developing the original text as a whole.

Terrence E. Deal, professor of education at Peabody College, Vanderbilt University, is an expert in school and organizational cultures. His publications include the national best-selling book, *Corporate Cultures* (with Allan Kennedy). His most recent book, *Modern Approaches to Understanding Organizations* (with Lee Bolman) looks at organizations from four perspectives: human resource, structural, political, and symbolic. Professor Deal wrote the substantive parts of Chapter 6.

Carolyn M. Evertson, professor of education at Peabody College, Vanderbilt University, is an expert and researcher on effective teaching and classroom organization and management. She is a fellow in the American Psychological Association. She has written widely on effective teaching and has co-authored *Classroom Management for Elementary Teachers, Classroom Management for Secondary Teachers* (both with Edmund Emmer and others); and *Learning from Teaching* and *Student Characteristics and Teaching* (both with Jere Brophy). Professor Evertson collaborated with Ann Neely in writing the planning and organization components of Chapter 13.

Ann Neely, assistant professor of the practice of education and the assistant dean for undergraduate affairs of Peabody College, Vanderbilt University, is an expert in teacher planning. Her publications include two articles that relate directly to her contribution here: "Integrating Planning and Problem Solving in Teacher Education" and "Teacher Planning: Where Has It Been? Where Is It Now? Where Is It Going?" Professor Neely collaborated with Carolyn Evertson in writing the planning and organization components of Chapter 13.

Penelope H. Brooks, professor of psychology, Peabody College, Vanderbilt University is a developmental psychologist with special interests in mental retardation and cognitive development. Her recent publications include *The Cognitive Curriculum for Young Children* (with H. Carl Haywood and Susan Burns). Professor Brooks wrote Chapter 4.

Jeanne M. Plas, associate professor of psychology, Peabody College, Vanderbilt University, is an expert in the training of school, community, and clinical psychologists. Her publications include *Working Up a Storm: Anger, Anxiety, Joy, and Tears on the Job* (with Kathleen Hoover-Dempsey). Professor Plas wrote Chapter 9.

Douglas J. Simpson, professor of education and dean of the School of Education, Texas Christian University, is a philosopher of education. His publications include *The Teacher as Philosopher* (with Michael Jackson). Professor Simpson wrote Chapter 8.

Brian Hansford, a member of the faculty of education, department of behavioural studies, in the University of New England, Armidale, New South Wales, Australia, is an expert in classroom dynamics and communication. His publications include *Teacher and Classroom Communication.* Professor Hansford wrote the teaching section of Chapter 13 and the classroom climate section of Chapter 3.

Alene Harris, a research assistant professor of special education at Peabody College, Vanderbilt University, is a specialist in classroom management and the analyzing of teaching. Her writing includes a study of effectiveness in teacher training programs. Professor Harris collected data for and wrote a number of the case studies that appear throughout the text. She also reviewed much of the manuscript from the perspective of a secondary school classroom teacher of seventeen years.

Contents

Preface: About This Text   vii

Concepts to Be Learned   xvii

About the Authors   xxv

CHAPTER 1   **Teaching and Schools in America Today: The Current Scene and Future Directions**   1

Introduction   2
Snapshot   2
A Study of Teaching and Schools   5
The Contemporary Scene   6
     Schools Today   7
         Why We Have Schools   8
         Who Goes to School   9
         What Is Taught in Schools   12
         What Else Happens in Schools   13
         Who the Teachers Are   15
         Current Issues concerning Schools and Teaching   19
Americans' Perceptions of Schools   20
Analysis   23
Reform in the 1980s   25
     Waves of Reform   25
     Directions of Change   27
National Studies and Reports   30
     A Nation at Risk   30
     Beyond the Commission Reports: The Coming Crisis in Teaching   32
     Teachers for the 21st Century   33
     Tomorrow's Teachers   33
Effects of the Reports   34
The Years Ahead   36
     Prediction One   36
     Prediction Two   37
     Prediction Three   37
     Prediction Four   37
     Prediction Five   37
     Prediction Six   37
     Prediction Seven   38
     Prediction Eight   38
Educational Research: Teaching and Schools   39
Conclusion   41

CHAPTER 2 Inside Classrooms: Analyzing Real Teaching 46

Introduction   47
Snapshot   47
What Happens in Classrooms   51
    Common Characteristics   51
    Differences   52
    Perceptions of Classrooms   53
        Goodlad's Observations   54
        Carew and Lightfoot's Observations   54
        Lortie's Observations   55
        Morine-Dershimer's Observations   55
Studying Classrooms Closely   55
    Systematic Study   56
    Classroom Observation and Analysis   57
An Illustration   59
Analysis   63
Analytical Observation Systems   64
    The Student On-Task/Off-Task Behavior Observation System   64
    Explanation   64
        Off-Task Behaviors   65
        Activities   66
        Numbered Observation Sweeps   67
    Directions   67
    Summarizing the Off-Task Seating Chart Data   69
    Calculating Off-Task Rates   71
Analysis   71
Conclusion   74
Educational Research: What We Know about Studying Classrooms   74

CHAPTER 3 Teaching Effectiveness: Classroom Practices and Characteristics That Enhance Learning   81

Introduction   82
Snapshot   83
Characteristics of Effectiveness   85
The Influence of Teachers on Students   86
Early Studies of Classroom Effectiveness   88
    Time as a Variable   88
Effective Teaching Practices   89
    Learning Time   90
    Time as a Teaching Technique   93
    Classroom Organization and Management   94
    Classroom Climate   94
        Minimizing Problems   96
        Handling Misbehavior   99
        Grouping   104
    Active Teaching Strategies   105
    Expectations and Rewards for Student Performance   108

Analysis   112
Conclusion   113
Educational Research: Much More to Learn   114

CHAPTER 4 Human Development: Students Are Alike, but Not the Same   121

Introduction   122
Snapshot   122
The Nature of Growth and Development   125
Perceptual-Cognitive-Moral Domains of Development   128
   Perceptual Development   128
   Cognitive Development   129
   Piagetian Stages of Development   129
      Sensorimotor Stage   130
      Preoperational Stage   130
      Concrete Operational Stage   131
      Formal Operational Stage   133
   Development of Moral Reasoning   134
Social-Emotional Domains of Development   136
   Infancy and Early Childhood   136
   Middle Childhood   139
   Adolescence   144
Categories of Students   146
   Categories Based on Intelligence   147
   Categories Based on Learning Difficulties   150
   Categories Based on Behavior Disorders and Emotional Disturbance   152
   Categories Based on Sensory Handicaps   153
   Analysis   154
   The Physically Handicapped Category   156
   The Average Category   158
Educational Research: Using Research Data for Educational Decisions   158
Conclusion   161

CHAPTER 5 Equity and Excellence: Teaching All Students   166

Introduction   167
Snapshot   167
Goals and Purposes   171
   Goals for Schools during the First Half of the Twentieth Century   171
   Goals for Schools at Midcentury   173
   Current Goals for Schools: Equity and Excellence   175
   An Emphasis on Equity   178
   The Legal Mandate for Equity   179
   The Legal Mandate for Equity Applied to Students with Handicaps   182
Schools and Differences among Students   184
   Categorizing Students and Targeting Instruction   184
Efforts to Serve All Students   185
   Racial Desegregation   185

Compensatory Education   187
Analysis   190
Bilingual Education   193
Multicultural Education   195
Gender-related Aspects of Education   196
Educating Students with Handicapping Conditions   197
Educating Gifted and Talented Students   199
Educating Average Students   200
Likenesses and Differences among Students—A Reminder   200
Educational Research: From Experimentation to Common Practice   201
Conclusion   203

CHAPTER 6   The School: A Culture   206

Introduction   207
Snapshot   207
Culture and Cultures   211
    The Culture of Organizations   211
    Understanding Cultures   213
The School as a Culture   215
    Back to Laurie Renfro   217
Differences among Schools   218
A Close Look at Four Schools   219
    Observation Number One: A Day at Ridgefield High   219
    Observation Number Two: George Washington Carver Comprehensive High School   221
    Observation Number Three: The Ensworth School   223
    Observation Number Four: Life at Fall-Hamilton Elementary   226
Subcultures within Schools   229
Analysis   231
School Culture and Effectiveness   232
Schools from a Cultural Perspective   233
    Laurie Renfro's Primary Task   234
    Carson's Primary Task   234
Conclusion: Carson Junior High—Ten Years Later   237
Educational Research: An Ethnographic Approach   238

CHAPTER 7   The Schools in Historical Context: From Ancient Greece to the Twentieth Century   243

Introduction   244
Snapshot   244
Early Schooling—From Ancient to Modern Times   246
    The Greeks—500–146 B.C.   246
    The Romans—146 B.C.–A.D. 476   250
    The Middle Ages—A.D. 500–1500   251
    The Renaissance—A.D. 1300–1500   252
    The Reformation and the Rise of the Middle Class—A.D. 1500–1700   253

The Enlightenment—1700–1800   254
American Schools of the Past   259
  Colonial Schools   259
  Analysis   263
  Schools of the New American Nation   267
  Toward Free Public Schools   268
  What the Schools Taught   271
  American Colleges and Universities   273
  The Schooling of Women and Minority Group Members   274
Educational Research: A Historical Approach   276
Conclusion   279

CHAPTER 8 Philosophical Beliefs and Teaching: Ideas That Guide What Teachers Do   282

Introduction   283
Snapshot   283
Philosophical Beliefs and Teaching   287
  The Nature and Value of Educational Philosophy   288
    Clarification   288
    Justification   289
    Interpretation and Systematization   291
  Systematic Views of Education   293
    Historical Philosophies   294
      Idealism   295
      Realism   297
    Modern Philosophies   302
      Pragmatism   302
      Existentialism   305
    Contemporary Philosophies   309
      Reconstructionism   310
      Futurism   311
      Behaviorism   312
      Perennialism   312
      Evangelicalism   313
      Marxism   314
      Essentialism   315
Educational Research: A Philosophical Perspective   316
Analysis   318
Conclusion   320

CHAPTER 9 Theories of Learning: Ideas from Educational Psychology that Guide Teaching   325

Introduction   326
Snapshot   326
The Nature of Learning   328
  The Need for Learning Theory   329
General Theories   331
  Behavior Theory   331

Association Theory 331
Reinforcement Theory 334
Reinforcement and Learning 336
Reinforcement and Classroom Conduct 338
Cognitive Theory 340
Piagetian Theory 343
Learning Theories and Teaching Styles 345
Analysis 347
Conclusion 349
Using a Learning Theory: A Case Study from the Future 350
Educational Research: Experiments on Learning 352

CHAPTER 10 Approaches to Teaching: A Look at Five Models of Instruction 358

Introduction 359
Snapshot: Mastery Learning 359
Mastery Learning 361
Educational Theory behind the Model 362
The Model in Practice 362
Assessing the Model's Effectiveness 363
Snapshot: Cooperative Learning 366
Cooperative Learning 367
Educational Theory behind the Model 368
The Model in Practice 369
Assessing the Model's Effectiveness 371
Snapshot: Instructional Theory into Practice 373
Instructional Theory into Practice (ITIP): Madeline Hunter 375
Educational Theory behind the Model 376
The Model in Practice 376
Assessing the Model's Effectiveness 378
Snapshot: The Cognitive Oriented Curriculum 379
The Cognitive Oriented Curriculum 381
Educational Theory behind the Model 382
The Model in Practice 384
Assessing the Model's Effectiveness 385
Snapshot: Direct Instruction 386
Direct Instruction 388
Educational Theory behind the Model 389
The Model in Practice 389
Assessing the Model's Effectiveness 391
Conclusion 393

CHAPTER 11 Content: Knowledge, Skills, and Affective Learning 399

Introduction 400
Snapshot 400
The Nature of Content 403
Information as Part of Content 403
Deciding What to Teach 405

Knowledge as Subject Matter   405
The Structure of Knowledge   406
    Disciplines   406
    Levels of Abstraction   408
    Teaching the Structure of Knowledge   410
Educational Research: Teaching and Learning History   413
Skills as Content   415
    Thinking   415
    Teaching Thinking   417
    Thinking about Thinking   420
    Other Skills Taught in Schools   421
    Analysis   422
    Teaching Skills   425
Affective Learning as Content   426
    Teaching Values, Feelings, and Sensitivities   427
Conclusion   433

CHAPTER 12 The Curriculum and Lessons: Designs for Learning   438

Introduction   439
Snapshot   439
The Curriculum   441
    Bases for Selecting Content   442
    The Process of Selection   443
    Making Content Choices   444
Curriculum Organization   446
    Curriculum Frameworks   447
        Subject-centered Curricula   447
        Student-centered Curricula   451
Educational Research: Middle Schools   458
Units of Instruction   459
    Expressive Arts—Art   460
    Mathematics   461
    Reading—Language Arts   461
    Social Studies   461
    Physical Education/Health   462
    Science   463
    History   463
    English   464
Lesson Plans   466
Analysis   468
The Hidden Curriculum   470
Conclusion   472

CHAPTER 13 The Act of Teaching: From Planning to Evaluation   476

Introduction   477
Snapshot   477
Planning   479

        Approaches to Planning   481
            The Rational-Choice Approach to Lesson Planning   481
            The Lesson-Image Approach to Lesson Planning   482
            Factors Affecting Teacher Planning   483
            Before, During, and After the Lesson   484
            Teacher Influence on Planning   485
            External Influences on Planning   488
            Organizational Influences on Planning   490
            Student Influences on Planning   494
            Circular Influences on Planning   496
            Analysis   497
            Conclusions about Planning   498
    Teaching as Process   498
        The Teacher's Challenge   500
    Teaching as Communication   501
        Verbal Communication   501
        Nonverbal Communication   504
        Impeding Classroom Communication   506
        Educational Research: Communication Apprehension   508
        Conclusions about Teaching as Communication   510
    Evaluation   511
    Conclusion   512

CHAPTER 14   The Professional Teacher: The Life and the Work   517

Introduction   518
Snapshot   518
Professionals Who Educate   521
    Images of Teachers   522
    Beginning Teachers   524
    Reasons for Teaching   524
The Job of Teaching   525
    In Classrooms   525
    With Students   529
    In the General School Environment   531
    Among Professional Peers   532
    As Employees   534
    With Parents   534
    Behind the Classroom Door   535
Analysis   537
The Needs of Students   539
    Poverty   539
    Discrimination   541
    Physical, Emotional, and Intellectual Disability   541
    Family Stress   542
    Child Abuse   543
    Drug and Alcohol Abuse   544
    Vandalism, Delinquency, and Violence   544
    Addressing Student Needs   545

Job Conditions   545
    Educational Research: Assessing the Condition of Teaching   546
    The Positives   548
    The Negatives   550
    Teaching—On Balance   551
Teachers as a Professional Group   551
    Unions   552
    Specialized Professional Organizations   554
    Teachers and Group Membership   555
Conclusion   555

CHAPTER 15 Teaching the Next Generation: Is It for You?   561

Introduction   562
Snapshot   562
Education Reform Extended   563
    Pursuing Reform: The Next Steps   563
The Importance of Teachers   567
    Teacher Influence on Students   568
    Effective Teaching   568
    Competencies of Future Teachers   568
        Knowledge   570
        Intelligence and Insight   570
        Organizing Ability   570
        Technical Skills   570
        Confidence   571
        Ability to Handle Complexity   571
Teacher Supply and Demand   571
    Influencing the Equations   575
    A Look Ahead   577
Where to Teach   578
    Regions of the Country   578
    Types of Communities   579
    Types of Schools   580
Salaries and Compensation   581
Conditions Ahead   586
    The Continued Professionalization of Teaching   586
    America and International Competition   587
    Changing Technology and the Media   588
    Poverty   590
    Changing Families   591
    Teaching in the Years Ahead—As We See It   592
Do You Want to Be a Teacher?   593
Analysis   593

APPENDIX The Teacher-Student Interaction Observation System   598

Explanation   599
Directions   599
Data Recorded and Codes   600

Analyzing the Teacher-Student Interaction Seating Chart Data 601
Analysis   603

GLOSSARY   607

INDEX   623

CHAPTER 1

Teaching and Schools in America Today: The Current Scene and Future Directions

INTRODUCTION

This chapter provides an overview of the contemporary scene of teaching and schools in America and suggests ways in which you can begin your study of that scene. The overview includes sketches of current conditions, explanations of how things got this way, and predictions about trends for the future. All along, you are asked to think about what is being described and to formulate questions that will guide your study.

After a quick glimpse at two classes in the Snapshot, the chapter begins with suggestions for approaching your study of teaching and schools. This is followed by a look at schools today, which includes consideration of purposes for schools, students, subjects taught, life in schools, teachers, and current issues. Next, Americans' perceptions of schools are described.

About halfway through the chapter, focus changes to the education reform movement of the 1980s. First, the movement is described generally, and then several effects of it are surveyed.

The chapter's last section shifts from current times to the years ahead. Several predictions about schools and teaching in the future are described, and you are asked to think of how the predicted circumstances are likely to affect you.

The Snapshot presents two pictures, taken ten years apart, of a teacher and his classes of sixth-grade students. You are asked to compare the two pictures and to think about the differences between them.

The Analysis section describes the release of the best-known education reform report of the 1980s. You are asked to reflect upon its impact and the thrust of what it said. The Educational Research section provides an overview of contemporary research in education and sets the stage for more detailed investigations that follow in subsequent chapters.

SNAPSHOT

The Snapshot for this first chapter provides pictures of two classes taught by the same teacher ten years apart.[1] The first is from 1988, the second from 1978. During these ten years, the teacher has changed teaching styles. As you read, consider:

- What seem to be the most important elements of each picture?
- How is the teaching of the two classes different?
- How is it similar?
- How would you account for the differences? For the similarities?
- What recollections from your own elementary and secondary schooling does the Snapshot raise?

FALL-HAMILTON SCHOOL—1988

It is 10:30 A.M., October 14, 1988. Leonard Rucks is teaching English to his

third-period class. Today is a review day. Mr. Rucks has planned for the students to review the paragraphs they wrote yesterday, which he evaluated last night. When that is finished, he will drill the students on several spelling, punctuation, and grammar rules that a number of the students do not seem to understand. He wants the class to be ready for the competency test that he will administer next week before the end of the report card period.

The test is part of a statewide achievement testing system that is required of all sixth graders in the state. One is administered each report card period. Students who do not score 75 percent for the year will not be passed on to seventh grade. The tests are new. Last year's sixth graders were the first to take them. There are similar tests in mathematics. Before last year, virtually all sixth graders passed every year, but last year 15 percent failed one of the two tests and are now repeating the grade.

Mr. Rucks is a "taskmaster." He expects all students to be in their seats before the bell rings, and he tolerates no nonsense. He follows a school-system-adopted matrix of English skills that must be mastered, and he keeps everyone on task almost all the time. He assigns homework four days a week, and he calls parents if it is not done. He assigns paragraph writing twice a week. He is a personable teacher, friendly and fair, but he expects a lot from his students.

Mr. Rucks teaches five classes of English. Each is ability grouped based on grades and test scores in English from last year. Sometimes students get moved to other classes if they are ahead of or behind everyone else. This third-period group is about average, but the ability range is rather broad. A few students are not doing well and will probably fail for the year. But they are still trying. Two have failed both report card periods so far. They already know they will probably repeat sixth grade in a "transitional" class, but the more they master this year, the less they will have to repeat.

Mr. Rucks is a Career Ladder teacher this year. He attended special workshops last summer and is being evaluated for a Career Ladder promotion that will give him a chance to make $7,000 more each year. He has developed his Career Ladder plans and is being observed periodically by his principal and other evaluators who visit his class. He is being assessed according to state and school system guidelines and in terms of his own plans. How well his students behave in his classes and how well they perform on the tests are two of the criteria on which he is being evaluated. The evaluation puts pressure on Mr. Rucks, and sometimes he distrusts the process. But he decided to participate because he wants the extra money and because he is tired of being paid the same base salary as some other teachers he considers unsatisfactory. He knows he is good, and he intends to show it.

WHARTON SCHOOL—1978

It is 1:30 P.M., January 14, 1978. Leonard Rucks is teaching sixth-grade English to one of the classes that he shares with three other teachers in an interdisciplinary mini-school. The school is racially and economically integrated. All classes are heterogeneously organized. The other teachers in the mini-school teach science, mathematics, and social studies, respectively. The same four teachers plan together and share the same students so that they can get to know each student better. This enables them to adjust their content and levels of expectation to fit the needs of each student. They are very happy with the fact that they have not failed a student for five years.

Mr. Rucks is singing a ballad to the class, a historical ballad from the period in England that the students are studying in social studies. He hopes to have the students feel what life was like in 1688 in Europe. The students are very attentive. They love Mr. Rucks. They know he cares about them. He is very animated and always upbeat. When students do not do well on tests, he is always encouraging and tells them he knows they will do better next time. Happy faces abound in Mr. Rucks' class.

Although Mr. Rucks provides some full-class direct instruction, much of his instruction is provided to small groups and to individuals. The classroom is organized into learning centers and individual study desks. Students often work alone on programmed study sheets, which they take to Mr. Rucks for evaluation. Visitors tend to think Mr. Rucks' classes are disorganized, but they are not. Students are simply working at their own level and at their own speed. He knows where each student is in terms of his or her own abilities.

Tests are infrequent in Mr. Rucks' classes except for the weekly spelling tests. Mr. Rucks assesses informally and continuously. He believes this type of evaluation is less threatening to students than formal evaluation, and he believes it is just as effective. The students' self-concepts are important to him. He wants them to believe they are successful.

Mr. Rucks and his mini-school partners run their classes as they see fit. Their principal has confidence in them and rarely "interferes." Although the principal is welcome in their classes, he rarely comes unless invited to a special class presentation. He rates their teaching performance from what he hears "as he walks the halls and talks to students and parents." He knows the mini-school is a happy learning environment.

A STUDY OF TEACHING AND SCHOOLS

During the past decade, teaching and schools in America have been scrutinized, criticized, eulogized, and "reformed." Nine major national reports on reforming schools appeared in 1983 alone, and many more have appeared since. Change has been the order of the day, and the impact of that change on students and teachers has been widespread, noticeable, and significant. Some of the specific changes that have occurred have been long in coming. Some have been rapid. Some have been consistent with each other. Some have been at cross purposes. Some have been relatively easy to implement. Some have been traumatic. Some seem to have been successful. Some have already failed.

Reform-generated changes have resulted in shifts in how teachers such as Leonard Rucks teach. In Leonard's case, he has become more demanding and precise in what he expects his students to learn, more structured in how he deals with his class, and more focused on academics. In the 1970s, positive student self-concepts were predominant classroom goals; in the 1980s, academic performance was a higher priority.

So, what do all these changes mean? What are schools and teachers in America like today? Why and how did they get this way? What ideas, principles, and assumptions guide them? What will they be like in the future? These are the questions addressed in this text.

Formulating Questions

However, be forewarned that the text raises more questions than it answers. It does so because there are no simple answers in the study of teaching and schools in America. There is no "secret formula." To understand teaching and schools, you will need to reflect upon what you already know, gather the information presented in this book, and seek complementary information elsewhere. Then, you will need to use that information to formulate your own tentative answers to these questions and many others like them. These answers will become your own initial ideas about teaching and schools. Once you develop and refine them, you will be able to use them as bench marks for further study and a more sophisticated understanding as your learning continues through the years.

Tentative Answers

To begin, pause for a few minutes and consider the following questions. Do so seriously. Jot down your thoughts.

- What were predominant characteristics of your own K–12 learning?
- What types of things occurred in your K–12 education that you now consider especially informative,

  challenging,

  enjoyable,

  sad,

  frightening,

  depressing?
- What good things did your teachers do?
- What bad or harmful things did they do?
- Of the students who went to school with you, which do you think benefited the most? Which benefited the least? What made the difference?
- If you do teach, in what ways do you hope to be like your own teachers?
- How do you expect to be different from them?

Sources of Information

In addition, plan to read professional material that will keep you informed as you pursue your studies. For example, subscribe to the newspaper *Education Week*, which is published weekly during most of the year, and read regularly one or two current education journals such as *Phi Delta Kappan*, which has been particularly up to date in its coverage during the last few years.[2]

THE CONTEMPORARY SCENE

The General Purposes of American Schools

Schooling in America has always rested on the democratic and republican foundations on which the nation is based. To state the point simply, the founders of the United States believed that the people of America should govern themselves, either directly or through elected representatives; and that principle has guided America throughout its history. Because of that principle, all Americans need to be educated adequately so that they can understand the issues of the day, make informed judgments, and select appropriate leaders. They need to be educated well enough to get along with others and to be able to provide for their own economic well-being. This is the point made years ago by Thomas Jefferson when he said, "If a nation expects to be ignorant and free, in a state of civilization, it expects what never was and never will be." (Jefferson, 1816)[3]

Schools are the primary mechanism through which formal education occurs. They are the institutions that society uses to train its children politically, socially, and economically. Because the United States has a republican form of government, its schools are expected to teach citizens to be active and effective members of society. Because it is a democracy, the schools are expected to reach *all* citizens.

Schools for Everyone

In comparison with other cultures, America has been unique in trying to educate *all* its citizens. To be sure, that goal has not always meant what it does today, and it has not yet been attained. It is, however, closer to reality today than ever before. Over the years, women, slaves, poor people, those with limited abilities, those who could not get to a school, and those whose parents chose not to send them to school were neglected. But by the 1960s, all Americans of school age were expected to be in school, and nearly all of them were.

Learning for Everyone

In recent years, Americans have realized that having most children *in schools* is not enough to accomplish what Jefferson had in mind. Children not only have to be in school, they have to be *learning*. In essence, this is the common theme of the reports of the 1980s on schools. These reports say that schools should be expected to *be successful in educating all the children* of America and that the people who operate the schools are to be accountable in this regard.

This expectation has put greater pressure on teachers such as Leonard Rucks. It requires Leonard to teach academics more precisely and to show that his students are actually learning what is expected of sixth graders. As a result, how teachers teach and what students learn has been modified in recent years, and both continue to change. At the same time, perceptions of teaching, teachers, and schools have been noticeably transformed in the eyes of teachers themselves, students, parents, and the general public. In short, teaching and schools are very different today from the way they were only a few years ago.

Schools Today

This study of teaching and schools in America begins by looking at schools today. First, it is important to note that schools and what happens in them are not static. Like all social institutions, schools are always in transition. The two pictures of Leonard Rucks presented in the Snapshot at the beginning of this chapter highlight some of the changes that have occurred in recent years. As you read about schools today, think of how they were different in the past and how they will be different in the future. This look at schools addresses the following questions:

- Why do we have schools?
- Who goes to school?
- What is taught in schools?
- What else happens there?
- Who are the teachers?
- What are some of the current issues?

Why We Have Schools

General purposes of schools in America have been mentioned already. Schools are expected to educate citizens politically, socially, and economically. But specifically what does this mean? What does it mean today?

Citizenship Education

Because the United States is a democratic republic, all its citizens have the opportunity to participate in the decisions of the national, state, and local governments. In fact, for the system to work properly, a significant percentage of the citizens must participate actively in the government, must understand what they are doing, and must act responsibly. They must also get along with each other peacefully and positively. In other words, they must be *good citizens*.

But people are not born good citizens. Good citizenship is taught. It involves knowledge about government, people, relationships among people, and issues of the day. It involves positive values toward the goals of society, toward the system of government, toward other people, toward other nations, and toward active personal involvement in public affairs. It involves *skills* of effective participation.

Amercian schools are expected to teach the knowledge, values, and skills of citizenship. Although they do not function in this role alone, they have the broadest and most formal responsibility of any institution to do so. In a sense, the schools' general civic mission is to transform self-centered young children into responsible, understanding, thoughtful decision makers.

Schools educate citizens through virtually every facet of their operation—when they teach reading, listening, thinking, geography, history, government, current events, vocational studies, and so forth; when they teach proper behavior, set dress codes, provide for peer social interaction; and when they train students for active participation in peer groups, club activities, sports, school government, and community projects. In fact, because the role of citizen is so broad and involves so many facets, it is impossible to separate the times when schools and teachers are educating for citizenship from those when they are educating for other purposes.

Academic Achievement

Most people think of the academic purpose of schools as their central reason for being. As they see it, students go to schools to develop their intellects, to become *learned*; that is, to learn information and ideas, to develop insights, and to put those ideas and insights to use as they explore new information.

The academic purpose of schools is reflected in how schools are organized. School days are divided by subjects—reading, arithmetic, social studies, science, language arts, music, art, English I, world history, physics, algebra I, computer science, and Spanish III.

In a sense, however, academic achievement is an *intermediate* purpose rather than an end in itself. It helps students to be better citizens, to be more successful economically, and to be more satisfied and successful social human beings.

Vocational Preparation or Training

Schools are also expected to train students for jobs. But how they do this in today's world is a matter of debate. The debate usually centers on the degree to which the education is directed toward specific jobs rather than toward more general skills that are useful for a variety of occupations. For example, should a high school student be trained as a sales clerk in a clothing store as part of his or her senior year, or would that class time be better spent on business math and accounting? Or, should a person who is weak in reading and mathematics be taught auto repair instead of additional reading and mathematics?

Most prospective employers in recent years have favored more education in the "basic skills" and the "core academic subjects" rather than specific job training. They point out that if students are educated adequately in the "basic subjects," they can be provided specific training on the job—something that is difficult to do if trainees are not prepared academically. Employers also note that the rapidity of change in business and industry requires that employees be retrained often, frequently for jobs that did not exist when they were in school.

College Preparation

For many students, the primary purpose of school, especially high school, is preparation for college. In this context, schools prepare students for more schooling, and that, in turn, prepares them for jobs. Along the way, students also learn to be good citizens, but their main objectives are getting into college, being prepared to perform well while there, and graduating into a profession. From one perspective, the college preparation purpose of schools is a combination of the academic achievement purpose and the vocational preparation purpose.

The college preparation purpose of schools is more narrow than the other purposes mentioned here because not all students intend to go to college and because it is not easily identifiable as a purpose for elementary schools. However, because the typical highest-achieving students and the children of the most influential parents see high school learning as college preparation, that purpose for schools is the basis of many decisions by school leaders. Probably the two most often-mentioned measures of apparent success for schools are the numbers of graduates who enter prestigious colleges and how well they do in their studies there.

Personal and Social Development

In addition to all the above purposes, schools are expected to develop students into good individual and good social human beings—human beings who feel good about themselves, who are capable of interacting with others in positive ways, and who are inclined to do so. This combined personal and social development purpose parallels the citizenship education purpose of schools but is less tied to civic responsibility and active political participation. This purpose stresses the fundamental worth and dignity of all people, even those not likely to become leaders. It teaches caring, sharing, and interpersonal understanding. It expects schools to instill in their students the American values of the importance of each individual, equality of treatment and opportunity, and potential for individual success within the American system.

In summary, we have schools for a variety of reasons. Those reasons are derived from the beliefs and traditions of America. When viewed generally, they are consistent with each other rather than contradictory. Often they overlap.

But Americans expect very much from their schools, maybe too much. Different people have different priorities and ask that schools emphasize different goals. Those priorities constantly change, and schools usually cannot adjust fast enough. As a result, although most Americans agree on the importance of schools and on their general reasons for being, they tend to be dissatisfied with the schools' effectiveness and are quick to suggest how schools can be better.

Who Goes to School

Percentage of School-Age Children in School

In the United States, almost everyone of school age is enrolled in school. For example, in 1984 about 40 million or approximately 97 percent of all school-age children were attending elementary or secondary schools. Of those, about 89 percent were in public schools; 9 percent were in religiously affiliated schools,

Table 1–1: Gender, Racial, and Ethnic Characteristics of School-Age Children

Gender	Race and Ethnic Origin	
Male 51.4%	White, predominately Anglo	71.2%
	Black	16.2%
Female 48.6%	Hispanic	7.1%
	Asian and Pacific Islander	2.5%
	Native American	.9%

primarily Catholic parochial schools; and 2 percent were in other private schools (Bureau of Census, 1985).[4] Table 1–1 shows the percentage of the 40 million students when they are categorized by gender, race, and ethnic background (Office of Civil Rights, 1986).[5]

Table 1–2 lists the family income breakdown for students in public schools for 1985 (Stern & Williams, 1986).[6]

Economic Characteristics

Table 1–2: 1985 Annual Family Income for Students in Public Schools

under $15,000	33%
$15,000–$34,999	41%
$35,000–$49,999	15%
over $50,000	11%

In 1983, 21.3 percent of American school children lived below the poverty line—17 percent of whites, 37 percent of Hispanics, and 47 percent of blacks (Stern and Williams, 1986).

An idea of the family situation of today's school students is illustrated by three graphic analyses by educational researchers in the mid 1980s.

Social Characteristics

For every 100 children born around 1985:

- Twelve were born out of wedlock (and most of these will not know a father).
- Forty will have their parents divorce before they reach age 18.
- Five have parents who were already separated by the time of their birth or soon thereafter.
- Two will have one parent die before they reach age 18.
- Forty-one will reach age 18 still living with both parents.

In 1985 only 7 percent of American households consisted of the American ideal—two parents and two or more children. Many households were made up of one or two older adults with no children, although children may have lived with them earlier before growing up and moving away (Hodgkinson, 1985, p. 8).[7]

In 1984, 23 percent of all children lived in a household without a father, and 60 percent of black children lived with a single parent (Stern and Williams, 1986).

Data such as these are changing constantly, and many of those changes are significant for schools. For example, during the 1980s:

Changing Demographics

- The number of school-age children increased as children of the "baby boomers" moved through the grades.
- By the middle of the decade, 25 percent of school children lived below the poverty line, and that percentage has been increasing.
- Each year, more students come to school from single-parent homes.
- More young children are attending daycare and preschool programs.
- More states and school systems are making kindergarten compulsory.
- Because of more achievement testing, more students are expected to fail in school and drop out.

What Is Taught in Schools

Typically, American students have studied a relatively common pattern of content as they proceed through the elementary school grades. In kindergarten, they are introduced to school and their school peers and are instructed at a readiness level in basic subjects—prereading skills, letter recognition, colors, numbers, rules of social behavior, and following directions.

Kindergarten

Often classes are relatively flexible with play- and naptime scheduled regularly. Lately, however, kindergartens have become more structured and more seriously academic in orientation. Kindergarten has not been mandatory in many states, and many children attend for only half-days. But in recent years, a higher percentage of students has enrolled in kindergarten than earlier, and more of them are attending for a full school day.

Primary Grades

Most primary grades are still organized by grade level as self-contained classes with twenty to thirty students per teacher. Most primary level instructional time is devoted to direct teaching or reading, writing, spelling, and arithmetic, with smaller amounts of time for social studies, science, art, music, and physical education. "Basic skills" have received increasingly more attention in recent years, and students, even in these early grades, are expected to demonstrate that they have learned minimum amounts of content in the "basic" fields before they can pass to the next grade.

Upper Elementary Grades

The upper elementary or middle grades are either self-contained or departmentalized, based on local school preference. Typical class sizes are between twenty-four and thirty. Subjects taught are usually an extension of those at the primary levels. Basic subject content and skills are still stressed, but proportionally more time is provided for social studies, science, art, and music. Often, time is set aside for interdisciplinary studies and the study of student-interest-generated topics. One approach to this latter type of study is "discovery time" or, as it is called in many schools, *exploratory*.

Increasingly, elementary schools provide before-school and after-school daycare for children to accommodate single-parent families and families in which both parents work outside the home. Schools, especially those serving poor communities, often begin the day by providing breakfast to the children. Nearly all schools serve hot lunches.

Middle Schools or Junior High

Middle schools and junior high schools usually include grades 6 or 7 through 8 or 9. Ideally, these schools are designed to fit the special student characteristics of preadolescents. Most are departmentally organized, but interdisciplinary classes are prevalent. Most provide a common curriculum with students grouped according to an ability ranking of some kind. At each successive grade level, the instruction is usually more content (and less student) focused.

High School

High schools usually include grades 9–12, although some do not begin until grade 10. Students usually follow discernible subject paths or tracks according to their assessed ability or by their election of particular subjects. Typical high school courses of study are

College Prep Students	General Studies Students
English/language arts—4 years	English/language arts—4 years
Mathematics—2 or 3 years (algebra, geometry, trigonometry, calculus)	General mathematics—1 or 2 years
	Science—1 or 2 years

Science—2 or 3 years
Social studies—2 or 3 years
Foreign language—2 years
Health/physical education—3 or 4 years
Computer science
Electives

Social studies—2 or 3 years
Foreign language—elective
Computer science—elective
Health/physical education—3 or 4 years
Computer science
Electives

Vocational Students

English/language arts—4 years
General mathematics—1 year
Science—1 or 2 years
Social studies—2 or 3 years
Health/physical education—3 or 4 years
Data processing
Selections from
    Business education
    Commercial education
    Industrial education
    Trades
    Agriculture education
    Home education

The 1970s

Over the past twenty years, American schools have followed two distinct patterns in what is taught. During the 1970s, the emphases were on developing curricular flexibility, individualizing instruction, grouping students, teaching the "whole child," developing racial and ethnic identity, and enhancing the student's "self-concept." These emphases grew out of the philosophy of the 1960s that stressed the recognition of individual differences and the tailoring of learning to the different needs of the students. They were reactions to earlier times in which schools were more achievement oriented and, according to some educators, "less humane."

The 1980s

The 1980s, particularly after 1983, saw a shift "back to the basics" and a more achievement-oriented set of educational assumptions. Students were expected to be more serious about learning. More "basic" academic subjects were required. There was less time for electives and vocational subjects. Those who did not achieve what was expected were more likely not to pass. Students who failed subjects were prohibited from participating in school sports and in other extracurricular activities.

What Else Happens in Schools

The School Culture

Schools are more than just places to learn. They are cultures in which children, youth, and a few adults live for a major part of five days a week, for approximately forty weeks a year. In that environment, students learn more than just the academic content of the subjects taught, and they learn from more than just the teachers employed to teach them. They learn from the school environment itself, from their peers, and from the social and personal interactions that take place in the school society. In that environment, they grow, develop, and mature—physically, intellectually, emotionally, socially, and personally. They participate in classes, teacher conferences, lunchtime discussions, intramural and interscholastic sports, class parties and trips, debates, newspaper writing assignments, chorus and band, and hallway conversations. They learn about and sometimes become involved in fights, protection rackets, drug experimentation, and gang rivalries. They develop close friendships, lifetime attachments, love affairs, and bitter enemies.

Age-Grouped Societies

Schools are age-grouped societies made up primarily of students but under the direction of a few institutionally imposed adult authorities. They have their own rules and folkways, their own social class distinctions, their own leaders, their own followers, and their own "underclass." In a sense, schools are at least two societies in one. They reflect the broad society from which their students come, but they also are societies of their own.

Subgroups

Students function in schools as individuals and as members of many subgroups. For example, at a given time, a hypothetical high school student, Mark David, could be all of the following: student, sophomore, class vice-president, hall monitor, wrestler, track star, "big man on campus," "a macho hunk," son of Doctor Kenneth David, brother of Tim and Sherry David, "class activist," and driver of the best-equipped Pontiac Fiero. He also could be an average-achieving student, a member of Ms. Underwood's fifth-period physics class, a good writer,

Mark David and Cassie Holloran.

a smooth talker, a secure personality, a teacher's pet, the "steady" of Cassie Holloran, a friend of the principal, and a member of the "in group" of the school.

Personal and Social Development

Through the course of the typical thirteen years of school, students learn from all events in their school lives. Some of those events are positive and stimulating; some are negative and inhibiting; some are bland and unimportant. Whatever those events are, they help transform the four- or five-year-old who enters preschool or kindergarten into a seventeen- or eighteen-year-old young adult. In that transition, students pass through a long sequence of personal modifications in which they actually become different people over and over again.

At age 17, the hypothetical Mark David described above is a different human being from anyone else. Much of what he is and what he will become was determined by what happened to him in school.

Who the Teachers Are

In January 1986, a United States spaceship exploded on takeoff at Cape Canaveral, Florida, killing all seven people aboard. One of those killed was Christa McAuliffe, a teacher from Concord High School, Concord, New Hampshire. She was one of the first "civilians" chosen for such a mission and was selected through a nationwide competition among teachers. President Ronald Reagan had established that selection process when he announced more than a year earlier that a teacher would be the first "civilian" in space.

How Teachers Are Perceived

Although the selection of a teacher probably rested on political motives, the fact that a teacher was designated illustrates to some extent the unique way in which teachers are perceived in American society, probably in all societies. More significant, however, was the reaction of the American public to the tragedy. The focus of news reports and the theme of most conversations about that explosion were consistently portrayed in terms of "the teacher and the other astronauts," and Christa McAuliffe became a name and a personal hero with whom many Americans seemed to identify. Christa McAuliffe's death was considered to be so traumatic for so many Americans that special media programs and special consultation services were established in communities nationwide to help people, especially students and young people, cope with it.

The events that surrounded the death of the teacher in space illustrate very poignantly the degree of attachment that most people develop with some of their own schoolteachers and with teachers in general. Teachers individually, and as a group, are usually viewed as good, caring people who devote their time and energies to helping others. They are usually thought to be more honest, more "proper," more sensitive, and more "well meaning" than people in other professions. They are not usually thought to be the most intelligent professional group, but they are considered to be among the most dedicated.

Of course, nearly everyone remembers some teacher who does not fit the ideal. But, when people are asked which person had the greatest impact on their lives other than a member of their family, a teacher is mentioned 58 percent of the time, much more often than any other professional (Csikszentmihalyi & McCormack, 1986, p. 417).[8]

In spite of this feeling, however, Americans seem to express a curious ambivalence about teachers. They respect them and acknowledge their value but

Teachers Today

do not accord them the same status as they do physicians, attorneys, and several other professionals.

So who are the K–12 teachers of America? According to a National Education Association survey in 1987, about two-thirds were female. Ninety percent were white, 7 percent were black, and 3.4 percent represented other minorities. Virtually all teachers are college graduates, and just over half also have a master's degree. Most became teachers through teacher preparation programs at state colleges and universities, although some attended liberal arts colleges and became certified to teach later. The average teacher has been teaching fifteen years and is 41 years old (National Education Association, 1987).[9]

Patterns of who become teachers have fluctuated over time. Years ago, nearly all teachers in America were women and, except in racially segregated minority schools, all teachers were white. Then, toward the middle of this century, more men and minority group members entered teaching. Many were the first of their families to attend college, and they saw teaching as a step upward, socially and

Changing Patterns

economically. Many of these teachers were returning World War II and Korean conflict veterans who attended college under the G.I. Bill of Rights of the 1940s and 1950s.

The population boom of the 1950s increased K–12 school enrollments so greatly that during the fifties and sixties teaching was an easy field in which to get a job. Nearly everyone with a college degree who wanted to teach was hired, and more than 20 percent of all those entering college said they wanted to teach.

Then, by the early 1970s, the baby boom had run its course, and school enrollments dropped significantly. Few teachers were hired, and many were laid off. Fewer college students entered teacher education programs, and job opportunities in teaching dried up.

At about the same time, employment opportunities expanded in other fields for women and blacks, two groups who traditionally gravitated toward teaching, in part because of discrimination against them in other professions. This situation had little impact on teaching while jobs in teaching were scarce, but it had tremendous impact by the mid-1980s.

Recently, the children of the "baby boom children" of the 1950s have reached school age. These children are expanding school enrollments, especially in the southern and western regions of the country. At the same time, because fewer teachers were hired over the past two decades, more of those in the classroom are older, and greater percentages of them are retiring. (Figures 1–1, 1–2, and 1–3 show trends in numbers of teachers employed, school enrollment, and student–teacher ratios, respectively.) Because of this and because many of the people who traditionally would have entered teaching are now attracted to other accessible fields, a shortage of competent teachers has developed in most subject

Figure 1–1. Number of teachers employed in K–12 public schools: 1960–1989. (Source: Snyder (1988), pp. 1, 39, and 67.)[10]

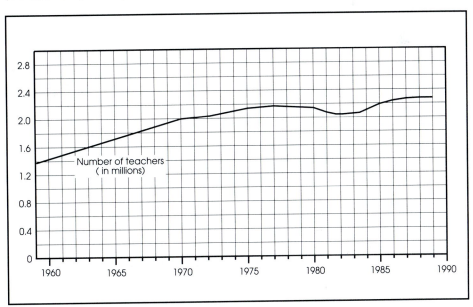

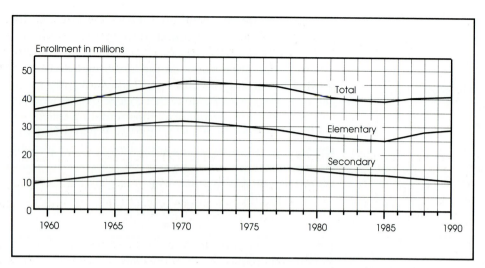

Figure 1–2. Enrollment in public schools: 1960–1990. (Source: Snyder (1988), pp. 10, 39, and 45.)

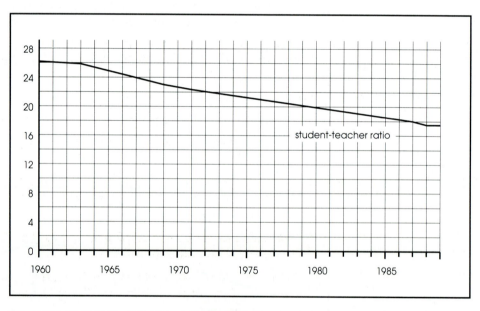

Figure 1–3. Student–teacher ratios: Fall 1960–Fall 1988. (Sources: Snyder (1988), pp. 39 and 67; NEA, *Rankings of the States* (1986, 1987, and 1988).)[11]

areas and across most regions of the country. As a result, in many regions of the country people not prepared as teachers are being offered positions in classrooms by school systems that cannot attract qualified applicants.

Generalizations about Teachers

Because of these trends, current teachers in the United States as a whole are older than their counterparts of a decade or two ago. Lower percentages of college graduates enter teaching than before. Proportionally more academically strong women and minority group members are attracted away from teaching than previously. A greater percentage of teachers shifts to other professions after teaching only a few years. A higher percentage of untrained and noncertified teachers staffs classrooms. In short, the nature of teachers in K–12 schools in America today is in the midst of significant change.

Current Issues concerning Schools and Teaching

Prominent issues concerning schools and teaching today include the following:

- Which purposes of schools are most important—civic, academic, vocational, college prep, or social and personal development? What is the proper balance among them?

- How equal is education for all students in the same class, across all classes in a school, across all schools, and across all school systems? How important is it that education be equal? How can it be made more equal?

- What standards should be set for students to be graduated from school and to pass from one grade to the next? What should be done to or for the students who cannot meet the standards?

- Which subjects should be required of all students? Which subjects are more important than others?

- Should American schools be changed because American industry cannot compete with that of other nations, such as Japan? If so, how should they be changed?

- What should be done to improve the performance of poor, minority, and non-English-speaking students in American schools?

- What changes should be made in the pay and working conditions of teachers? Should student performance and individual evaluations of teachers be bases for determining teacher pay?

- Who should be certified to teach? Who should decide? What criteria should be used?

- Should teachers be evaluated more thoroughly? What should be done once evaluation data are collected?

- How should America address the increasing teacher shortage? Should less-qualified people be hired to fill empty classrooms?

- Should religion be taught or practiced in public schools?

- Should taxes for schools be increased?

- Should taxes be used to support private schools? Should private schools that are tax exempt be required to take minority students, handicapped students, and students of any religious preference?

- Should schools provide sex education and AIDS education? If so, what should be taught? At which grade levels?

- Should public schools be required to teach *all* handicapped students, regardless of cost?
- Should students be required to attend only certain schools, or should they be free to choose among all schools in a city or school system?

Each of these issues and many others like them are worthy of significant discussion, but because this chapter is intended only as an introduction, they will not be discussed at this point. As you continue your study, however, think about these and other issues concerning schools and teaching. Make a list of issues to guide your thinking. Use the issues to stimulate questions, challenge your answers, and develop your ideas.

AMERICANS' PERCEPTIONS OF SCHOOLS

For approximately two decades, American attitudes about K–12 public schools have been reported each September in an annual Phi Delta Kappa/Gallup Poll. Data reported in that poll in recent years are presented below (Gallup, 1986; Gallup & Clark, 1987; Gallup & Elam, 1988).[12]

The Rating of Schools

In 1988, when those interviewed were asked to rate their local public schools on an A to F scale, 40 percent graded the schools A or B, and 14 percent said D or F. That rating was consistent with those of the previous four years. However, the rating of 42 percent in 1984 constituted a dramatic shift from earlier years toward a more positive view of schools. For example, the combined A and B grade in 1983 was 31 percent, in 1980 was 35 percent, and in 1973 was 31 percent.

The dramatic shift in perception that occurred in 1984 happened just one year after the issuing of the first wave of major reports about schools. Ironically, however, most of the reports were critical of the conditions of schools, and the reforms they suggested had not yet been implemented. Apparently, the reports caused people to think better of their schools, even though the schools themselves had not changed significantly.

A more specific breakdown of responses for 1988 for the question *What grade would you give the public schools here—A, B, C, D, or Fail?* is shown in Table 1–3A. Responses to the same question from 1977 to 1987 for the total national sample are shown in Table 1–3B.

Table 1–3A: American Citizens' Rating of Public Schools

1988	Total National Sample %	Adults with No Children in School %	Public School Parents %	Nonpublic School Parents %
A	9	8	13	8
B	31	29	38	25
C	34	34	36	37
D	10	10	8	21
FAIL	4	4	4	4
Don't know	12	15	1	5

Table 1-3B: Total National Sample for 1977-1987

	1977 %	1978 %	1979 %	1980 %	1981 %	1982 %	1983 %	1984 %	1985 %	1986 %	1987 %
A	11	9	8	10	9	8	6	10	9	11	12
B	26	7	26	25	27	29	25	32	34	30	31
C	28	30	30	29	34	33	32	35	30	28	30
D	11	11	11	12	13	14	13	11	10	10	9
FAIL	5	8	7	6	7	5	7	4	4	4	4
Don't know	19	15	18	18	10	11	17	18	13	15	14

Interestingly, some of the patterns in the responses to poll questions have been consistent over the years. Respondents tend to rate the public schools they know best higher than other schools. They rate their local schools higher than they rate schools nationally—in 1988, 40 percent rated local schools A or B, but only 23 percent rated schools nationally that high. Parents who have children in public schools rate their local schools higher than do people without children in the schools. Parents rate their *own* children's schools significantly higher than the local schools in general.

Opinions of Teachers

In 1987, 49 percent of Americans rated local public school teachers A or B, and 64 percent of those with children in public schools did so. The 49 percent figure was up significantly from 39 percent in 1981. In 1986, 49 percent believed that teacher salaries should be higher, 14 percent said they should be lower, and 10 percent said they were about right. In 1986, the public thought that teacher beginning salaries should be almost $5,000 above their actual amount at that time—over $21,000 instead of $16,500. In 1988, 89 percent favored increased pay for teachers who "proved themselves particularly capable."

Opinions about Tests and Student Promotion

When asked in 1986 whether students in local schools should be given national tests and whether the test scores should be compared with those of students in other communities, 81 percent said "yes" and 14 percent said "no." In 1986, 72 percent said standards for promotion from one grade to another should be more strict; and 70 percent had the same opinion about requirements for high school graduation.

Opinions about School Problems

When asked what were the biggest problems facing public schools in 1988, poll respondents listed "use of drugs" most often, with "lack of discipline" a distant second. The response marked the third successive year in which drug use was seen as a greater problem than "lack of discipline." Prior to 1986, discipline was considered the major problem in sixteen of the seventeen years the poll was used. Matters involving the curriculum and teachers were mentioned no more than 11 percent of the time, respectively, in 1988. Table 1–4 shows the items mentioned and the percentage of the time each was listed.

On the question of raising taxes to help raise standards of education, in 1988 64 percent supported raising taxes and 29 percent did not. Although Americans in the 1980s were generally supportive of public schools, they were also supportive of education reform. They seemed to be saying that schools are good generally but can be improved; and they endorsed, at least generally, efforts, including higher taxes, to make schools better.

Table 1–4: 1988 Poll Results on Major School Problems

	National Totals %	No Children in School %	Public School Parents %	Nonpublic School Parents %
Use of drugs	32	34	30	29
Lack of discipline	19	20	15	25
Lack of proper financial support	12	10	17	11
Difficulty getting good teachers	11	10	11	13
Poor curriculum/poor standards	11	11	11	14
Parents' lack of interest	7	7	7	8
Moral standards	6	6	7	2
Large schools/overcrowding	6	4	10	9
Pupils' lack of interest/truancy	5	6	4	5
Drinking/alcoholism	5	5	6	6
Low teacher pay	4	3	7	5
Integration/busing	4	4	3	3
Teacher's lack of interest	3	3	3	8
Crime/vandalism	3	3	2	1
Lack of needed teachers	2	1	3	2
Lack of respect for teachers/other students	2	2	1	2
Fighting	1	2	1	1
Lack of proper facilities	1	1	3	3
Mismanagement of funds/programs	1	1	1	1
Problems with administration	1	1	1	1
Communication problems	1	1	*	*
Parents' involvement in school activities	1	1	*	*
Lack of after-school programs	1	*	1	1
Too many schools/declining enrollment	1	*	1	*
School board politics	1	1	1	1
There are no problems	2	2	4	3
Miscellaneous	5	4	6	4
Don't know	10	12	4	5

* Less than one-half of 1 percent.
Figures add to more than 100 percent because of multiple answers.*

ANALYSIS

This analysis section consists of two elements. It describes the release of a document entitled *A Nation at Risk* in 1983, and it presents the substance of that report. The document announced that American schools were in deep trouble, and it recommended that immediate changes be made. Many experts believe its release marked a watershed point for American education. As you read, consider:

- Why do you think the United States government commissioned this report?
- Why do you think it is considered to be so important?
- Based on what you know about schools and teaching since 1983, what has been its impact?
- If American schools are (were) weak, why and how did they get that way?
- What is good about American schools? Why is this the case?
- What are the purposes of elementary and secondary schools in America?

A NATION AT RISK

In April 1983, Terrel Bell, Secretary of Education of the United States, released a report of the National Commission on Excellence in Education entitled *A Nation at Risk: The Imperative for Educational Reform*.[13] He had appointed the commission twenty months earlier and charged it with the responsibility of reporting to the people of the United States on the quality of education in America (National Commission, 1983).

A Watershed

The *Nation at Risk* document represented a major event in the history of schooling in America. It reflected what many Americans felt about their schools, particularly high schools. It focused those sentiments into a condensed set of statements that made the condition of schools a national topic of concern. It started a nationwide series of reforms in schooling in America that continues today.

The release of the report was described by Chris Pipho, an expert on educational reform, as follows:

> When the National Commission on Excellence in Education called for educational reform in *A Nation at Risk*, it fell in at the head of a parade that had already begun to take shape. Just as Sputnik became a symbol around which the math and science reformers of the late fifties rallied, the report of the National Commission and the dozen or so other major reports that followed transformed 1983 into a watershed year for American education. It was the year we discovered the term "mediocrity," and the national reports were soon followed by hundreds of reports from state-level task forces and blue-ribbon commissions.
>
> All this activity gave the media something to report, the public something to identify with, and state policy makers a cause to champion that was above

ordinary political bickering. That many of the reports had a consistency among them, that they called for a broad range of reforms, and that they came with such rapidity combined to move public opinion. Suddenly the parade was moving under the unifying banners of more rigorous standards for students and more recognition and higher standards for teachers. . . . (Pipho, 1986, p. K1)[14]

The report said in part:

> Our nation is at risk. Our once unchallenged preeminence in commerce, industry, science, and technological innovation is being overtaken by competitors throughout the world. This report is concerned with only one of the many causes and dimensions of the problem, but it is the one that undergirds American prosperity, security, and civility. We report to the American people that while we can take justifiable pride in what our schools and colleges have historically accomplished and contributed to the United States and the well-being of its people, the educational foundations of our society are presently being eroded by a rising tide of mediocrity that threatens our very future as a Nation and a people. What was unimaginable a generation ago has begun to occur—others are matching and surpassing our educational attainments.
> If an unfriendly foreign power had attempted to impose on America the mediocre educational performance that exists today, we might well have viewed it as an act of war. As it stands, we have allowed this to happen to ourselves. . . . We have, in effect, been committing an act of unthinking, unilateral educational disarmament.

Rising Tide of Mediocrity

Educational Disarmament

The report described the risk as follows:

Well-Educated Competitors

> The world is indeed one global village. We live among determined, well-educated, and strongly motivated competitors. We compete with products but also with the ideas of our laboratories and neighborhood workshops. America's position in the world may once have been reasonably secure with only a few expectionally well-trained men and women. It is no longer.
>
> The risk is not only that the Japanese make automobiles more efficiently than Americans and have government subsidies for development and export. It is not just that the South Koreans recently built the world's most efficient steel mill, or that American machine tools, once the pride of the world, are being displaced by German products. It is also that these developments signify a redistribution of trained capability throughout the globe. Knowledge, learning, information, and skilled intelligence are the new raw materials of international commerce and are today spreading throughout the world as vigorously as miracle drugs, synthetic fertilizers, and blue jeans did earlier. If only to keep and improve on the slim competitive edge we still retain in world markets, we must dedicate ourselves to the reform of our educational system for the benefit of all—old and young alike, affluent and poor, majority and minority. Learning is the indispensable investment required for success in the "information age" we are entering.
>
> Our concern, however, goes well beyond matters such as industry and commerce. It also includes the intellectual, moral, and spiritual strengths of our people which knit together the very fabric of our society. The people of the United States need to know that individuals in our society who do not possess the levels of skills, literacy, and training essential to this new era will be effectively disenfranchised, not simply from the material rewards that accompany

Slim Competitive Edge

A High Level of Shared Education

> competent performance, but also from the chance to participate fully in our national life. A high level of shared education is essential to a free, democratic society and to the fostering of a common culture, especially in a country that prides itself on pluralism and individual freedom.
>
> For our country to function, citizens must be able to reach some common understandings on complex issues, often on short notice and on the basis of conflicting or incomplete evidence. Education helps form these common understandings, a point Thomas Jefferson made long ago in his justly famous dictum:
>
> > I know no safe depository of the ultimate powers of the society but the people themselves; and if we think them not enlightened enough to exercise their control with a wholesome discretion, the remedy is not to take it from them but to inform their discretion.
>
> Part of what is at risk is the promise first made on this continent: All, regardless of race or class or economic status, are entitled to a fair chance and to the tools for developing their individual powers of mind and spirit to the utmost. This promise means that all children by virtue of their own efforts, competently guided, can hope to attain the mature and informed judgment needed to secure gainful employment and to manage their own lives, thereby serving not only their own interests, but also the progress of society itself. . . . (National Commission on Excellence in Education, 1983)

Common Understanding

The Progress of Society

REFORM IN THE 1980s

A Nation at Risk and other reports and studies of the 1980s made the conditions of the schools a matter of national concern and initiated a reform movement that has led to substantial changes in the nature of schools and teaching since 1983. Those reports and studies and the actions that followed them can be explained by dividing the reform movement along two dimensions. There have been, first, three somewhat successive *waves* of reform; and, second, five *strands* or directions of change. Each of the two dimensions is outlined below. A few representative reports and subsequent activities are described on later pages.

Waves of Reform

National Alarm

The first wave of reform lasted for about three years beginning in 1983 and consisted of a succession of national reports that sounded nationwide alarms that the schools of America were in trouble. The second wave was made up of two parts: state-level reform efforts that were begun to change the schools, and a "second generation" of national reports that proposed specific, direct solutions to correct problems and suggested who should take those actions. The third wave involved school system, school building, and classroom-level efforts to do what the reports and state-level regulations said should be done.

The first-wave reports, following the lead of *A Nation at Risk*, were public calls to action. They were national in scope, general in nature, and in the form of printed documents released as media events. Those reports attracted citizen and political leader attention to "the weakened condition of our schools" and the "tide of mediocrity." They insisted on immediate emergency action and suggested, in a general way, what the action should be. First-wave reports included:

- *A Nation at Risk*
- *Academic Preparation for College*
- *High School*
- *A Place Called School*
- *Horace's Compromise*
- *First Lessons*
- *Beyond the Commission Reports: The Coming Crisis in Teaching*[15]

(Complete citations for each are listed in the Notes section at the end of this chapter.)

State Actions

The second-wave state-level reports were more specific sets of recommendations and plans for legislative or regulatory action to change conditions. Some actually had been issued before *A Nation at Risk,* but others surfaced later. Many have included annual updates of actions already taken. These plans produced the most significant activity of the reform movement. They told schools, teachers, and state agencies what should be done, and many have the force of law to require compliance.

Because these actions are so numerous and are still continuing, it is difficult to describe them adequately here, but the following information should provide an illustration. In the spring of 1987, the excerpt below appeared in the newspaper *Education Week.* It was part of an article that described recent education reform action by the Indiana state legislature.

Student Testing. The Indiana Statewide Test for Educational Progress will be expanded to cover grades 1, 2, 3, 6, 8, 9, and 11. Student achievement in language arts, mathematics, social studies and science will be tested each spring.

Students scoring in the bottom 16 percent on the test will be required to attend summer school, with the state picking up the full cost of remediation and transportation. Students will be retested at the end of the summer. If they fail to move out of the bottom 16 percent, they will be retained in their current grade.

School districts that promote such students would lose a proportionate amount of state tuition support.

School Accreditation. Beginning with the 1988–89 school year, schools will be accredited not only on the basis of "inputs," such as curriculum offerings and the length of the school day and year, but also on the basis of "outcomes," including student test scores, graduation rates, and the results of locally developed evaluations of teachers.

Schools that comply with existing "input" standards and perform at or above average for demographically similar schools on the new "outcome" standards will be accredited by the state board for a five-year period. Sub-par schools will be placed

An Introduction to Teaching and Schools   27

on probation. If the state board determines that improvements have not been made after three years of probationary status, it could ask the state legislature to approve the appointment of a state manager. In the case of low-achieving school districts, the board could ask lawmakers to force them to consolidate with other districts.

Merit Schools. Schools that demonstrate year-to-year improvements in student academic achievement would become eligible for financial rewards. . . . (Mirga, 1987, p. 11)[16]

"Second Generation Reports"

Parallel to this state activity, several "second generation" national commissions proposed actions to address the problems that the earlier commissions noted. Frequently, they spelled out steps to be taken and targeted the groups that should act. For example, the Carnegie Task Force on Teaching as a Profession, among a number of recommendations, proposed a national teacher-certification board and national standards for evaluating teacher knowledge and ability. It followed those ideas with efforts to establish the certification board and to develop a national teacher evaluation plan. Similarly, the Task Force and the Holmes Group outlined new ways to prepare teachers and formed organizations to do so.

"Second-wave" reports include:

- *A Nation Prepared: Teachers for the 21st Century* (Carnegie)
- *Tomorrow's Teachers* (Holmes)
- *A Call for Change in Teacher Education*
- *Who Will Teach Our Children?* (California)
- *Improving Teacher Education: An Agenda for Higher Education and the Schools*
- *Time for Results: The Governors' 1991 Report on Education*
- *The Nation's Report Card*
- *The Redesign of NCATE*

Local Implementation

(Complete citations are listed in the Notes section at the end of this chapter.)[17]

Much of the third wave is only now being pursued. It involves the work by schools and teachers to implement the changes that have been recommended and legislated. If successful, these efforts will produce the results that the reports say are needed. The five directions of reform described next show the thrust of most of these efforts. However, the best way to understand them is to monitor the developments occurring nationally and in your local schools and state at the present time. Recent issues of *Education Week* and *Phi Delta Kappan* should provide information of national scope. Ask your instructor for the best sources of information locally and at the state level.

Directions of Change

The five strands or directions of educational change generated by the education reforms of the 1980s seem to be

1. back to basics and accountability,
2. greater professionalization of teaching,
3. more effective schools and teaching,
4. more equitable education for all students (not just equal amounts of schooling), and
5. changing the content or subject matter taught.

Each is elaborated upon below.

"The Basics"

The idea of teaching "the basics" is not at all new, but reform agendas seem to push harder in this direction than similar recent efforts. *A Nation at Risk*, several other national reports, and most state actions specify subjects to be required for high school graduation, and basic academic subjects predominate—

Accountability

language arts, mathematics, science, and social studies. Tests are being mandated in most of these areas for many, if not all, grade levels. Students must know certain ideas, information, and skills to pass to the next grade and to graduate. Teachers must educate them effectively, or they will not pass.

Professionalization of Teaching

According to those who support the thinking of many of the reports, teaching is being made more "professional" by the use of more evaluations and higher standards to assess who can become teachers as well as who can remain in the classroom. College preparation programs are becoming longer, more selective, and more demanding. Larger numbers of marginal applicants are being turned away. Practicing teachers are being evaluated more often and more thoroughly. Teachers are being paid better and respected more.

An increasing number of critics, however, challenges the notion that these movements produce greater teacher professionalization. They question how taking authority from teachers by subjecting them to more outside laws and commissions produces stronger professionals. In a way, a major aspect of education reform is at a crossroads that can be illustrated by two questions about how to produce improvements: Should there be more laws and rules that tell teachers what they must do? Should teachers be given more freedom and support to do what they think is best? (See Darling-Hammond, 1988 and Meek, 1988.)[18] More will be said about this in later chapters.

Effectiveness

Schools and teaching are being scrutinized more closely than ever to determine which teacher characteristics are most influential with students and which techniques are most effective in instructing them. Characteristics of schools such as clear and common purposes, an ethos of achievement, a team spirit among staff, and quality leadership have been found to be good for student learning. Teacher characteristics such as good verbal ability, enthusiasm for subject matter, intelligence, and concern for students impress and influence students positively. Classroom techniques such as effective use of time, high time-on-task ratios, proper questioning, and appropriate wait-time are said to produce high student achievement.

Equal Education

The need to provide better education to poor, minority, non-English-speaking, and handicapped students has been reiterated as a dramatically high priority for schools and teachers. However, of all the reform ideas, this goal is furthest from being achieved. Concerns are being expressed, plans tried, and resources marshalled, but significant results are still elusive. America has still not discovered how to educate children out of poverty but thinks it can be done and is still trying.

In addition to the return to "the basics," reform agendas include the teaching of certain content that most or all students are expected to master. Reading, writing, spelling, literature, most areas of common mathematics, natural science, biology, health, history, civics, and geography are usually among the subjects specified. And virtually everyone agrees that thinking skills must be developed. Also, most want more and better teaching of values, although there is much disagreement over which values warrant the most attention.

Content

Something to Think About

The following is an excerpt from a news item in *Newsweek* magazine (May 25, 1987). Shawn Doherty wrote the article, which is used with permission.

Fighting Over a Principal

A schoolboard tries to fire an innovative educator

When a bushy-bearded city slicker named Dennis Littky took over as principal of Thayer High School in Winchester, N.H., six years ago, the locals wagered on how long he'd last. The 250-year-old mill town had the region's highest welfare load, and the Thayer High kids were reputed hellions. That summer Littky hired a dropout to paint murals over graffiti on school walls, replaced study halls with new math and science requirements, and met individually with all 200 students to plan their schedules. By 1985 reading scores had jumped two and one-half grades. Today the dropout rate is half what it was in 1980, and more than half the kids go on to college—up from 10 percent when Littky took over. Last week, as parents watched their children dance at the spring prom, Thayer High seemed a happy place. So why is the school board trying to fire Dennis Littky?

Board members have a list of reasons. Littky permits class discussions of homosexuality and birth control. Board member Bobby Secord even heard Eddie Murphy's "Boogie in Your Butt" booming out of a classroom one day. "He runs things too loosely," says Secord, a local businessman who was Thayer's 1967 prom king but sends his two children to a nearby Christian school. The 42-year-old Littky, who received PhD.'s in education and psychology from the University of Michigan and ran a nationally acclaimed middle school on Long Island, also wears Khakis to school, lets kids call him "Doc" and chooses to live in a mountaintop log cabin without running water or electricity. ("I wanted to learn how to cut down trees and relax," he explains.) "He's the highest-paid individual in town and, instead of setting a dignified example, he acts like a tramp," complains former state legislator Elmer Johnson, a leader of the oust-Littky campaign.

. . . Mostly, however, the battle is a clash between old and new values. "Us old-timers resent liberal newcomers coming in and telling us how backwards we are," says Johnson, who lives in the same farmhouse he was born in 67 years ago.

However radical it seems to local eyes, Littky's transformation of Thayer does meet a call by a 1983 Reagan administration commission for a return to basics in public schools. Littky has imposed stiffer discipline and toughened academic standards at Thayer, and his efforts have been hailed by the National Education Association and the Carnegie Foundation. Theodore Sizer, a champion of new teaching methods and a Brown University education professor, named Thayer one of a dozen schools to participate in his national program of educational reform. The school board, however, yanked Thayer out of the program.

'Human Beings': For all his devotion to basics, Littky's style is reminiscent of the experimentalism of the '70's—and that is what has exercised many townspeople. Instead of lecturing from textbooks, Thayer teachers helped students excavate an 18th-century town and build a log cabin. Writing teachers assign journals. (One mother was so outraged to find vomit and child murder among the topics in her daughter's writing class that she organized a campaign to protest.) In a required course for seniors called Life After Thayer, kids discussed everything from sex to balancing checkbooks—though the board recently ordered teachers to get its approval before broaching sexual topics. Littky also won grants for an apprentice program that places students in beauty parlors, restaurants and garages; the board cut the program in half. "Thayer will never send the most kids to college or get the best test scores," Littky argues. "But our kids learn to think and become decent human beings."

In the clash of personalities and power, the kids are often forgotten. "Dennis has given these youngsters hope," says Brown's Sizer. Most of Thayer's students support Littky, who knows each of them by name and attended every basketball game this season. "Littky puts us before anything," says Terri Racine. "He's opened doors for us." Terri knows that better than most. She got pregnant during her Junior year and only Littky's support kept her in school after she had the baby. That semester Terri was elected class president, made the honor roll and undertook a special writing project about the town's attitudes toward teenage pregnancy. Littky's critics distributed her paper door to door to illustrate the immorality corrupting Thayer. But this fall Terri begins college—and that's why Dennis Littky thinks his job is worth fighting for.

Update—After two school board elections, Littky supporters won control of the school board and renewed his contract for another year.

- What do you think are implications of situations such as this for changes in schools in the years ahead?
- Think of this situation as you read the recommendations of various commissions that are reported on the succeeding pages. Which recommendations are most likely to cause conflict?

NATIONAL STUDIES AND REPORTS

A few of the reports and studies mentioned are described below. As you read about each, consider the extent to which the ideas expressed have affected teaching and schools as you think of them.

A Nation at Risk

As noted already, *A Nation at Risk* (1983) was the most influential of the reports of the 1980s. The fact that it was so influential resulted from several circumstances:

1. It was a report of the federal government addressed to the people of America, rather than a report of educators for other educators.
2. It was one of the first of the reports to be released.
3. The hearings at which testimony about the condition of schools was taken received much media attention.
4. The document itself is short, succinct, and easy to read.
5. Its assessment of schools and its recommendations reflected current public sentiment. That is, Americans in general agreed with it and the timing was right for action.

As you have read, the report said that American schools suffered from mediocre performances and that this "rising tide of mediocrity" threatened the future of the nation and its people. It announced that because of these conditions, America was *at risk*. It documented its position by quoting statistics about trends on academic achievement of school students. It cited, as *indicators of risk*, lower standardized test scores, lower SAT scores, higher illiteracy rates, lower graduation requirements, and the offering of more remedial courses in colleges.

Indicators of Risk

To correct these problems, it recommended changes in five areas:

Content

That high school graduation requirements be strengthened and that all students be required to take the *Five New Basics* of (a) 4 years of English; (b) 3 years of mathematics; (c) 3 years of science; (d) 3 years of social studies; and (3) one-half year of computer science. That college-bound students also take 2 years of foreign language.

Standards and Expectation

Recommendations

That schools, colleges, and universities adopt more rigorous and measurable standards and higher expectations for academic performance and student conduct. That four-year colleges and universities raise their requirements for admission.

Time

That more time be devoted to learning the New Basics, including more effective use of the existing school day, a longer school day, and a lengthened school year.

Teaching

That new teachers meet higher standards in teaching ability and in their academic discipline; teachers' salaries be increased; teachers be evaluated more effectively; teachers have eleven-month contracts; there be career ladders for teachers; people other than currently certified teachers be hired in areas of teacher shortage; incentives be used to attract outstanding college students to teaching; and master teachers design training programs for teachers and supervise new teachers.

Leadership and Fiscal Support

That citizens hold educators and elected officials responsible for providing the leadership necessary to achieve these reforms, and that citizens provide the fiscal support and stability needed to bring them about. (National Commission on Excellence in Education, 1983)

Beyond the Commission Reports: The Coming Crisis in Teaching

Partly as a response to some of the earlier reports, the RAND Corporation issued a report in 1984 on the status of the teaching profession. It had the effect of shifting some of the focus of the reform effort from schools to teachers and teacher preparation. The report was based on several studies done by the RAND Corporation for the National Institute of Education and the Ford Foundation.

The report stated:

Teacher Shortages

> . . . dramatic changes in our nation's teaching force will soon lead to serious shortages of qualified teachers unless policies that restructure the teaching profession are pursued. Until teaching becomes a more attractive career alternative, the problems of attracting and retaining talented teachers will undermine the success of other reforms intended to upgrade educational programs and curricula. (Darling-Hammond, 1984, p. v)

According to RAND data, the "high educated and experienced teaching force" of the 1970s and the first years of the 1980s was dwindling as increasing numbers of teachers retired and younger teachers left teaching for other jobs. It said there would be insufficient numbers of new teachers and that the newer recruits would be less qualified academically than those being replaced. It noted that the most academically able teacher recruits tended to leave teaching after only a short time.

The report explained the situation in terms of demographic trends and supply-demand imbalances. Academically talented women and minority group members, who in the past were restricted to teaching as a profession, were choosing other professions that offer greater financial rewards, more opportunities for advancement, and better working conditions. Teachers' salaries were considerably below those of most occupations that require a college degree. Other nonpecuniary rewards for teachers were dwindling: Teachers were increasingly viewed as "bureaucratic functionaries" rather than professionals, they lacked input into professional decision making, and they had inadequate administrative support. Teacher dissatisfaction and attrition were increasing, particularly among the most highly qualified.

Salaries and Working Conditions

The RAND report, then, called for action to avoid the predicted crisis and proposed what needed to be done.

> Unless major changes are made in the structure of the teaching profession, so that teaching becomes an attractive career alternative for talented individuals, we will in a very few years face widespread shortages of qualified teachers. We will be forced to hire the least academically able students to fill these vacancies, and they will become the tenured teaching force for the next two generations of American school children. (Darling-Hammond, 1984, p. vi)

It listed two elements of the problem: salaries, and working conditions that affect teachers' abilities to do their jobs effectively. It said that a greater degree of professionalism needed to be injected into teaching, including new career structures for teachers, improved preparation, professionally enforced standards of practice, and more decision-making responsibility.

Teachers for the 21st Century

In 1986, the Task Force on Teaching as a Profession of the Carnegie Forum on Education and the Economy issued a report entitled *A Nation Prepared: Teachers for the 21st Century*, which continued the focus on teachers and teacher preparation. It called for restructuring schools and overhauling teacher education. The report advocated

Overhauled Teacher Education

- establishing a national board of standards for those becoming teachers;
- restructuring school responsibilities so that local teachers would control their schools;
- restructuring the teaching force, with a new level of teachers who would be in charge of other teachers;
- raising teachers' salaries and expanding career opportunities so that teaching would be competitive with other professions;
- tying incentives for teachers to schoolwide student performance; and
- increasing the number of minority teachers.

The report said that recent reforms in education had been intended to reverse the decline in the performance of schools and that future success in schools depended on creating a profession of well-educated teachers prepared to assume new powers and responsibilities to redesign schools for the future. To produce these teachers, it proposed

- requiring a bachelor's degree in the arts and sciences as a prerequisite to the professional study of teaching;

National Board of Professional Teaching Standards

- a new master's degree professional program of study for all teachers that would include internships and residences in schools, probably requiring two years of study; and
- a National Board for Professional Teaching Standards to certify new teachers.

The group consisted of fourteen political, business, and educational leaders, including the presidents of the National Education Association and the American Federation of Teachers. Both organizations endorsed its recommendations and the Carnegie Foundation pledged to finance some of the suggested efforts. In 1987, the foundation funded efforts to begin implementing the teacher certification board idea. That process has been a multiyear effort, and its actual impact has yet to be realized.

Tomorrow's Teachers

Deans of Research Universities

Between 1983 and 1985, the Holmes Group, which consisted of deans of schools of education from research-oriented universities, developed a rather precise new plan for the education of teachers. In 1986, it released the plan as *Tomorrow's Teachers* and invited handpicked universities from various parts of the country to subscribe to its principles and commit themselves to implementing the plan on their campuses. By January 1987, only months after publication, ninety-four of the universities invited to participate had chosen to do so.

In general, the Holmes plan has many characteristics similar to those of the Carnegie recommendations, but initially it was less flexible. At least on paper, participating universities had to agree to proceed with the plan as outlined, including the stipulation that they eliminate undergraduate teacher education majors. In its implementation, however, the plan has become more flexible.

Three Tiers of Teachers

The plan envisions the establishment of a three-tier teacher licensing system and different levels of preparation for each. The top two levels, Professional Teacher and Career Professional, are renewable and could carry tenure. The lower level, Instructor, is temporary and nonrenewable. The professional levels entail examinations, performance assessments, and other specific requirements.

According to the plan, teachers prepared at Holmes Group institutions complete master's degrees and presumably qualify for the professional levels. They study the subject matter that they teach more deeply than had been the case in typical programs, and usually their professional studies are noticeably more sophisticated.

Doctors and Nurses

Some observers of the reform movement equate participants in the Holmes Plan with the members of the medical profession. The Professional levels are the doctors—highly trained, carefully selected, well paid, and decision makers. The instructors are the nurses—less highly trained, less select, modestly paid, and followers of doctors' directions.

EFFECTS OF THE REPORTS

Schools—A Public Issue

The reports of the 1980s did two things. First, they focused the public's attention on schools by suggesting and demonstrating that schools were generally not good enough and had to be made better; second, they set up actions to change the situation. As a group, they stimulated movements toward (1) higher expectations of teacher education, and both higher expectations and accountability on the part of students, schools, and teachers; (2) more emphasis on "the basic" subjects; (3) greater focus on academic achievement; (4) new designs for educating teachers; (5) rebuilding confidence in schools; and (6) modifying the political environment in which schools operate.

Redefining the Purposes of Schools

This happened, of course, in a historical context. The schools of the 1980s simply could not do everything expected of them and do it well. They could not teach *everything* to *all* students regardless of their capabilities, socioeconomic status, and the family backgrounds of their enrollment. Therefore, the reports said, the purposes of schools should be focused on academics and that they should truly educate all students academically. They also said that education should be a higher state-level and national priority.

A Shift from the 1970s

This was a shift in direction from expectations for schools in the 1970s. In the early seventies, schools were criticized because their curricula were too academic—"too traditional," "too factual," and boring; because student interests and needs were not addressed; and because "average," "below-average," minority, urban, and non-English-speaking students were not adequately served. Efforts to respond to these criticisms and the trade-offs involved in doing so sowed the seeds of discontent of the eighties. In essence, during the 1970s, the curriculum was made more interesting and often less academic, but at the expense of serious learning.

Historical Context

When placed in this historical context, the reports of the 1980s and the reactions to them are not surprising. Americans have always had the dream that *all* citizens can be educated to their maximum and that the schools should be the primary institution to bring this about. That dream is part of the ideal of America as a republican and democratic society. The authority to govern rests with the people; therefore, the people must be educated in order to govern themselves effectively.

As noted earlier in this chapter, America has tried from its beginnings to provide schools for more of its people than other nations. By the 1960s, nearly all school-age Americans were in school, and they usually had opportunities to study a broad array of subjects. But recently, prospective employers, political leaders, parents, and the general public have begun to ask whether students in school are *learning enough* and whether they are learning the right things. For most people both answers were "no," and that prompted the reports and set into motion the reform activity that followed.

Learning Enough?

At this point, definitive judgments about the effects of the reforms in education cannot be made. Nevertheless, it should be helpful to your study if you begin formulating your tentative judgments about whether and how they have improved teaching and schools. Although your knowledge may still be very limited, and your judgment will have to be tentative, consider the following questions before you continue your reading:

Questions to Ask

- In what ways has the education reform movement of the 1980s changed teaching and schools?
- Which aspects of the reform are good?
- Which are bad?

Something to Think About

In 1987, as American schools were going about the process of reassessing their purpose and adjusting their programs and standards in response to education reform agendas, a fifteen-year-old girl in Detroit gave the following response as her definition of the American dream:

To go to school and fenisch my Schooling without getting prenant. (*Newsweek*, 1987, June 29, p. 19)

- What do you think are some of the implications of this type of student perspective for educational reform agendas and priorities?

THE YEARS AHEAD

Everyone knows that change is a fact of contemporary life. It is rapid and occurs at an accelerating rate. People must prepare for it and adjust to it. The future will be dramatically different from today.

If you begin teaching this year or in a few years and do not change professions, you will teach students as yet unborn. You will teach information as yet unknown. You will prepare students for jobs that have not yet been created and for a world environment that does not now exist. You will use teaching devices and techniques not yet invented.

Some of the views of schools and teaching, and of the society in which schools will operate only a few years from now, early in the twenty-first century, appear below. As you read these ideas, think of the following questions:

- Do you agree with these predictions?
- What are their implications?

More Questions to Ask

- Will you be prepared?
- Will you be able to adjust?
- What are your predictions?

Prediction One

Electronic Teaching

Much of what students now learn in school will be learned at home through computers, television, and other electronic devices. Students will learn primarily from computerized learning programs and will talk to their teachers electronically rather than sitting in their classrooms.

Students learning at home from television lesson and computer.

Prediction Two

Early Learning

Schooling will begin earlier. Small children will learn at home or in daycare centers almost from infancy. They will be exposed to sophisticated electronic recordings and video tapes, which will teach them sounds, shapes, and elements of their environment at much earlier ages than now occurs. They will be tested in evaluation centers so that specific learning programs can be written for them. These programs will help them learn material and develop skills that are particularly difficult for them and will enable them to forge ahead in their areas of strength. These children will arrive at kindergarten or first grade with a computer printout of their previous learning, which will be fed into the schools' learning management system.

Prediction Three

Continuous Learning

Learning will be continuous, and it will occur everywhere. Students who attend school will learn not only in the classroom but also on the bus traveling to and from school, through the public address system while they have lunch, and through their headsets while they exercise. Adults will learn through audio cassettes that they play in their cars, through educational cable television channels, through rented or borrowed video cassettes, and through telephone lectures piped into their home speaker systems. Electronic and print correspondence courses will be available on virtually every topic, for people of all ages.

Prediction Four

Without Grade-Level Distinctions

Grade-level distinctions in schools will disappear as learning becomes more individualized and computer managed. The amount of school time devoted to full class instruction will decline. Teachers will monitor and guide student progress more and instruct less.

Prediction Five

Differentiated Teacher Roles

The roles that teachers play will become more differentiated. Some will be "lead teachers" or "master teachers" who direct teams of assistants. Some will develop and refine curriculum packages, with only occasional contact with students. Some will record or present in-person lectures for classes. Some will specialize in student evaluation. Some will guide small group discussions. Some will counsel individual students. Some will train new teachers. All will be skilled in media and electronic instruction. Teacher salaries will vary greatly according to type of job performed, level of skill, and position of responsibility among the other teachers.

Prediction Six

Different Teacher Education

The education of fully certified teachers will consist of four or more years of "pre-education" study in the liberal arts and sciences, at least one subsequent year of professional study, a one-year internship operated jointly by a college and a school system, and one or more years of apprentice teaching under a mentor teacher. Teachers will be employed for twleve months and will continue on-the-job training throughout their entire professional lives. The nature of the specific functions that teachers perform will change substantially every ten to twenty years.

Prediction Seven

Larger "Underclass" in Need of Education

More students will be poor, urban, minority, and undereducated. More will have been born to teenage parents. More will come from undereducated families, whose adults are unable to understand, support, or supplement the instruction of the school. More of these students will not find jobs or be fully employed most of their adult lives. More of them will be members of a social and economic underclass that year after year will become further separated from the educated, "successful" segment of society.

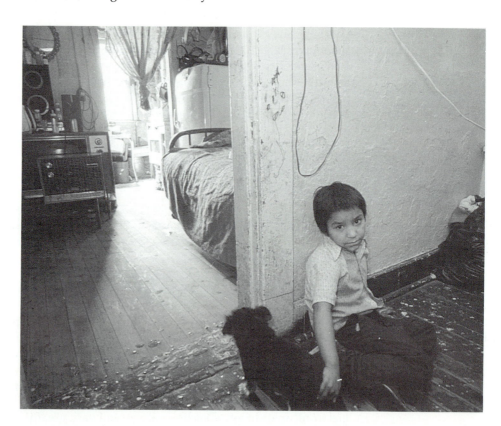

Prediction Eight

The Future Environment

The world outside the school will change radically, and those changes will have a significant impact on schools, students, and teachers. Everyone will be pressured by further urbanization, pollution, water and power shortages, population growth, prohibitive medical costs, international militarism, information overload, and similar conditions. Social priorities and values will be turned on end. But schools and teachers will still be expected to educate students for successful, productive lives in that future environment.

EDUCATIONAL RESEARCH

Teaching and Schools

The Educational Research sections of chapters in this text introduce you briefly to aspects of educational research consistent with each chapter focus. This first section is rather general; the others will be more specific.

Research is a careful and thorough search or investigation of something. It is intended (1) to discover new knowledge, (2) to correct interpretations of current knowledge, and (3) to revise previously accepted conclusions in light of new knowledge. Much of the research on teaching and schools that is useful to educators today is relatively new.

Research Questions

For centuries, teachers seemed to have practiced their profession based on hunch, common sense, tradition, repetition from the examples of other teachers, and trial and error. And for a long time, the practice seemed to have worked. Then, as research became more sophisticated in other fields, educators began to ask research questions about what they do. They asked: Why do we teach this way? Is it the most effective way? How to students learn this content most efficiently? Why do some learn it while others do not? What is the most practical way to organize this school?

Knowledge Base

Answers to these types of questions over the past twenty-five to thirty years have provided a pool of information, called a *knowledge base*, about schools and teaching, and that knowledge base has become the intellectual "stuff" that educators need to know to improve teaching and schools. The knowledge base is growing, evolving, and becoming more sophisticated each year. All educators need to understand it and use it in their work if they are to be successful.

The 1970s marked a significant change in the nature of research on teaching and schools. Until then, much of the research was rather uncomplicated and tended to focus on the process of teaching, often on specific teacher behaviors. Typical types of questions included: What is the teacher doing? Why is the teacher doing that? Is he or she lecturing, asking open questions, monitoring seatwork?

"What Is Happening?" Questions

In the last decade, however, research on schools and teaching has expanded to include a greater number of studies than ever before, and those studies are using more probing questions and substantially different investigative approaches. These increases in number, in complexity, and in variety of approaches have, of course, produced more and more useful information about teaching and schools. For example, one of the approaches, *process–product research,* compares what happens in the classroom with student outcomes. Instructional processes, such as the specific methods a teacher uses, what students do during the course of a school period, how time is divided among classroom activities, and the amount of homework assigned, are compared with such products as how much the students learn as measured on achievement tests.

Process–Product Research

This process–product research has led to documented conclusions that school characteristics, teacher traits, and the specific nature of teaching make a difference in what students learn. It has shown that some schools are better than others, that some specific school environments produce more learning than others, that some types of teachers influence students more significantly than others, and that some teaching techniques are more effective than others.

Rutter Study

For example, British researcher Michael Rutter and his colleagues reported, after intensively studying twelve London schools, that the nature of a school environment, or its *ethos*, is a factor in how well students learn. In *Fifteen Thousand Hours* (1979),[19] he concluded that students in some schools performed better on tests and behaved better than expected in terms of their socioeconomic backgrounds. In those schools, the principals established clear guidelines and monitored teacher work closely. The teachers expected high student performance and rewarded hard work. Rutter drew a connection between the student test performance and behavior on one hand, and the school conditions on the other.

Other process–product researchers have found that certain types of teaching methods contribute significantly to student learning. Some of those methods are (1) particular classroom management techniques, (2) direct and structured learning strategies, (3) a clear focus of instruction, (4) flexible instructional planning, (5) variation in teaching methods, and (6) a warm, enthusiastic, accepting teacher personality (Ornstein, 1985).[20]

Coleman and Jencks Studies

But the idea that schools and teaching make a difference in what students learn has not always been accepted. Two widely read and influential books of the 1960s and early 1970s, James Coleman's *Equality of Educational Opportunity* (1966)[21] and Christopher Jencks' *Inequality: A Reassessment of the Effect of Family and Schooling in America* (1972)[22] concluded in general terms that schools did not make much difference in what children learned. Coleman's conclusion stated, in essence, that the ability of the child to learn depends more on his or her socioeconomic background than on what happens in the classroom. Jencks said, "The character of a school's output depends largely on a single input, namely the characteristics of the entering children. Everything else . . . is either secondary or completely irrelevant." (Jencks, *et al.*, p. 256)

Schools and Teachers Can Make a Difference

These two studies led many educators to conclude that what happened in schools did not make much difference in terms of student learning, but that conclusion was erroneous. Schools and teachers might have to work against tremendous odds sometimes, but process–product research has shown (1) that they can make a difference and (2) that some ways of doing things are more effective than others. Some schools and teachers are more effective than others, and the differences between the effective and the ineffective ones can be identified. With that knowledge, the less effective can be made better.

Other Research Approaches

As noted above, process–product research is only one of the approaches to studying schools and teaching that have proven useful in recent years. Among the others are ethnographic, cognitive, sociolinguistic, and behavioral approaches. Each approach provides a perspective that illuminates different dimensions of teaching and schools. At this point, it is not important for you to understand all of the approaches mentioned, but it is important to realize that research on teaching and schools is continually producing information about what is and should be happening in schools. That information is important to all educators.

In the next two chapters, the Educational Research sections focus on research on classroom teaching. The Chapter 2 section looks closely at the ways in which researchers study classrooms and teaching. The Chapter 3 section reports on studies of the types of teaching that have been found to be more effective than others.

CONCLUSION

Constant Change

Teaching and schools in America today are a product of long-term policies and conditions, and to the extent that they are, they reflect a continuity with schools of the past. Although conditions always change, the reasons why we have schools, students, subjects, life in schools, teachers, and some of the issues of the day are more like those of some years ago than they are different. Because of that continuity, schools have to be studied and understood in terms of their historical context.

On the other hand, circumstances surrounding teaching and schools have changed radically during the recent years of education reform. Expectations of students, schools, and teachers have been modified, and what happens in classrooms must be adjusted to conform to those expectations. Teaching is changing and will continue to change, especially during the next decade or two, as reform agendas are implemented, modified, and discarded.

Predictions for the future do not describe a return to more complacent times. Expectations and conditions in schools and in the worldly environment that surrounds schools will force constant adjustments and redirections. Teachers will need to strive constantly to keep up and to do what is needed to teach well.

Prospective teachers need to understand teaching and schools in the contexts of the past and present, and they must also prepare for the schools of the future. They need to ask continuously:

- What is happening in schools and the profession of teaching?
- In what directions are things moving?
- What does this mean for me as a potential teacher?

SUMMARY

The study of teaching and schools in America should involve formulating questions about the subject and using those questions as guides for investigation. Although simple answers are rare, systematic study makes the topics understandable and provides direction for further inquiry.

Schools in America are intended to provide citizenship education, academic achievement, vocational training, college preparation, and personal and social development. Virtually all school-age children and youth attend school. The curriculum is rather consistent across schools. The culture of schools affects students' and teachers' lives. Teachers are a rather varied lot of human beings, but many share similar general characteristics. Americans tend to be satisfied with schools, but they are more scrutinizing lately.

The education reform movement of the 1980s raised questions about schools, set directions for improvement, and started processes for change that are now being implemented. *A Nation at Risk* and other reports were most instrumental in reform developments. Reform agendas include "back to basics" and accountability, greater professionalization of teaching, more effective schools and teaching, more equitable education for all students, and changes in content. As a whole, the reform movement has, to some extent, redefined the purposes of schools.

Teaching and schools in the years ahead will be different from the teaching and schools of today. Some of the predictions are more electronic teaching, more early learning, more continuous learning, fewer grade-level distinctions in schools, increased differentiation among teacher roles, different and more demanding patterns of teacher education, a greater need to educate poor children, and a radically different social environment in which schools will operate.

STUDY QUESTIONS

1. Review the five agendas of education reform noted in this chapter. Which of these do you think are most likely to be accomplished? Which are least likely to be accomplished? Why do you think so in each case?

2. In terms of your own priorities, which goals of education and which reform agendas will be most in need of being satisfied during the 1990s and the early twenty-first century? Why do you think so?

3. When your own children attend K–12 schools during the next twenty years, what are the most important things you expect them to learn? Are these things also the most important for all children? If not, what are the differences and why do they exist?

4. Make a list of the ways in which teaching in K–12 schools will be different in the year 2020 from teaching today. Explain and justify each item on your list. Decide whether each change is good or bad for students and teachers. Explain why you think so.

BIBLIOGRAPHY

Apple, M. W. (1982). *Education and power.* Boston: Routledge and Kegan Paul.

Bush, R. N. (1987). Teacher education reform: Lessons from the past century. *Journal of Teacher Education, 38*(3), 13–19.

Carnegie Task Force on Teaching as a Profession. (1986). *A nation prepared: Teachers for the 21st century.* New York: Carnegie Forum on Education and the Economy.

Csikszentmihalyi, M., & McCormack, J. (1986). The influence of teachers. *Phi Delta Kappan, 67*(6), 415–419.

Education Week. Subscription Office, P.O. Box 6987, Syracuse, NY 13217. (Newspaper on contemporary issues affecting schools and teaching, published 40 times a year—weekly during the school year.)

Good, T. L., Biddle, B. J., & Brophy, J. E. (1975). *Teachers make a difference.* New York: Holt, Rinehart and Winston.

Hodgkinson, H. L. (1985). *All one system: Demographics of education—Kindergarten through graduate school.* Washington, DC: Institute for Educational Leadership.

Jackson, P. (1968). *Life in classrooms.* New York: Holt, Rinehart and Winston.

National Commission on Excellence in Education. (1983). *A nation at risk: The imperative for educational reform.* Washington, DC: United States Department of Education.

Phi Delta Kappan. (1986, November). pp. 197–227. (Several articles on the National Governors' Association report *Time for Results.*)

Phi Delta Kappan. September Issue. (Each year the September issue contains results of the Phi Delta Kappan/Gallup poll of the American public's attitudes toward public schools.)

Pipho, C. (1986). States move reform closer to reality. *Phi Delta Kappan, 68*(4), K1–K8.

Stern, J. P., & Williams, M. F. (Eds.). (1986). *The condition of education: A statistical report, 1986 edition.* Washington, DC: Center for Educational Statistics. United States Government Printing Office.

NOTES

1. The two episodes described in this Snapshot are composites based on classes of several teachers known by the authors of this text.

2. The Subscription Office of *Education Week* is P.O. Box 6987, Syracuse, NY 13217.

3. Jefferson, T. (1816, January 6). Letter to Colonel Yancey. Cited in H. A. Washington (Ed.). (1854). *The writings of Thomas Jefferson* (Vol. 6, p. 517). Washington, DC: Taylor and Maury.

4. Bureau of Census. (1985). School enrollment—social and economic characteristics of students: 1984, October (advance report). Washington, DC: United States Government Printing Office.

5. Office of Civil Rights. (1986). *Elementary and secondary civil rights survey, 1984. National summaries.* Washington, DC: Office of Civil Rights.

6. Stern, J. P., & Williams, M. F. (Eds.). (1986). *The condition of education: A statistical report, 1986 edition.* Washington, DC: Center for Educational Statistics. United States Government Printing Office.

7. Hodgkinson, H. L. (1985). *All one system: Demographics of education—Kindergarten through graduate school.* Washington, DC: Institute for Educational Leadership.

8. Csikszentmihalyi, M., & McCormack, J. (1986). The influence of teachers. *Phi Delta Kappan, 67*(6), 415–419.

9. National Education Association. (1987). *Status of the American public school teacher: 1986.* Washington, DC: National Education Association.

10. Snyder, T. D. (1988). *Digest of education statistics, 1988.* Washington, DC: National Center for Education Statistics.

11. National Education Association, (1986, 1987, 1988). *Rankings of the states.* Washington, DC: National Education Association.

12. Gallup, A. M. (1986). The 18th annual Gallup poll of the public's attitudes toward the public schools. *Phi Delta Kappan, 68*(1), 43–59; Gallup, A. M. & Clark, D. L. (1987). The 19th annual poll of the public's attitudes toward the public schools. *Phi Delta Kappan, 69*(1), 17–30; Gallup, A. M. & Elam, S. M. (1988). The 20th annual Gallup poll of the public's attitudes toward the public schools. *Phi Delta Kappan, 70*(1), 33–46.

13. National Commission on Excellence in Education. (1983). *A nation at risk: The imperative for educational reform.* Washington, DC: United States Department of Education.

14. Pipho, C. (1986). States move reform closer to reality. *Phi Delta Kappan, 68*(4), K1–K8.

15. National Commission on Excellence in Education. (1983). *A nation at risk: The imperative for educational reform.* Washington, DC: United States Department of Education; The College Board. (1983). *Academic preparation for college: What students need to know and be able to do.* New York: The College Board; Boyer, E. (1983). *High school: A report on secondary education in America.* New York: Harper & Row; Sizer, T. (1984). *Horace's compromise: The dilemma of the American high school.* Boston: Houghton Mifflin; Goodlad, J. L. (1983). *A place called school: Prospects for the future.* New York: McGraw-Hill; Bennett, W. J. (1986). *First lessons: A report on elementary education in America.* Washington, DC: United States Department of Education; Darling-Hammond, L. (1984). *Beyond the commission reports: The coming crisis in teaching.* Santa Monica, CA: RAND.

16. Mirga, T. (1987, May 13). Indiana lawmakers approve reform bill. *Education Week, 6*(33), 11–12.

17. Carnegie Task Force on Teaching as a Profession. (1986). *A nation prepared: Teachers for the 21st century.* New York: Carnegie Forum on Education and the Economy; Holmes Group. (1986). *Tomorrow's teachers: A report of the Holmes group.* East Lansing, MI: Holmes Group; National Commission for Excellence in Teacher Education. (1985). *A call for change in teacher education.* Washington, DC: American Association for Colleges for Teacher Education; California Commission on the Teaching Profession. (1985). *Who will teach our children?* Sacramento, CA: California Commission on the Teaching Profession; Commission for Educational Quality of the Southern Regional Education Board. (1985). *Improving teacher education: An agenda for higher education and the schools.* Atlanta, GA: Southern Regional Education Board; National Governor's Association. (1986). *Time for results: The governors' 1991 report on education.* Washington, DC: National Governor's Association; National Academy of Education. (1987). *The nation's report card: Improving the assessment of student achievement.* Cambridge, MA: National Academy of Education.

18. Darling-Hammond, L. (1988). The futures of teaching. *Educational Leadership, 46*(3), 4–10; Meek, A. (1988). On teaching as a profession: A conversation with Linda Darling-Hammond. *Educational Leadership, 46*(3), 11–17.

19. Rutter, M., Maughan, B., Mortimore, D., Ouston, J., & Smith, A. (1979). *Fifteen thousand hours: Secondary schools and their effects on children.* Cambridge, MA: Harvard University Press.

20. Ornstein, A. C. (1985). Research on teaching: Issues and trends. *Journal of Teacher Education, 36*(6), 27–31.

21. Coleman, J., Campbell, E., Hobson, C., McPartland, J., Mood, A., Weinfield, F., & York, R. (1966). *Equality of educational opportunity.* Washington, DC: United States Government Printing Office.

22. Jencks, C. S., Smith, M., Ackland, H., Bane, M. F., Cohen, D., Gintis, H., Heyns, B., & Michelson, S. (1972). *Inequality: A reassessment of the effect of family and schooling in America.* New York: Basic Books.

CHAPTER 2

Inside Classrooms: Analyzing Real Teaching

INTRODUCTION

Chapter 2 differs from Chapter 1 in its treatment of teaching and schools in two distinct ways. First, whereas Chapter 1 is primarily introductory in general, this chapter zeroes in directly on teaching and what happens in classrooms. Second, Chapter 2 does not present descriptions of classrooms for you to read. Instead, it instructs you in ways to observe classes so that you can look at video tapes and go into local classrooms to learn from the real thing. This approach puts you where the important action is—where teachers teach and students learn—and involves you actively in what goes on there. It helps you formulate your own ideas about teaching rather than read about those of others.

The chapter provides instruction in several ways of thinking about what happens in classrooms. The first involves your own recollections about schools and requires no expertise. The second is a little more structured because it is guided by four commonsense questions, but it is still a rather nonexpert approach. The third consists of learning to use an observation system developed by educational researchers. For those interested in developing more expertise, a fourth way of analyzing teaching appears in the appendix of the text.

The chapter Snapshot presents pictures of a few minutes in two actual classrooms. Both were recorded by a trained observer. The two descriptions are intended to start you thinking about specific classroom activity. The two Analysis sections serve as exercises for practicing your observation skills. The Educational Research section describes how some researchers analyze teaching and classrooms.

SNAPSHOT

The Snapshot for this chapter describes classroom activity of a few minutes' duration in two classrooms on a typical school day. One class is second grade, the other is eleventh-grade mathematics. As you read, consider:

- What are the teachers and students doing?
- Why are they doing these things?
- What learning is taking place?
- What do these episodes tell you about these teachers? About these students? About these classrooms?
- What knowledge did you use to answer the above questions, and how did you gain that knowledge?

A SECOND GRADE

It is 9:13 A.M., and school has been in session for more than an hour.[1] Ms. Myers has completed her direct teaching of reading to two of her four reading groups. The Green Group has just assembled before her at the reading table in the front of the room. The class consists of twenty-three students today. Four are absent.

The seven students of the Red Group, who had their reading lesson first, are in the process of completing their worksheets. Two have already placed their work in the basket on Ms. Myers' desk and are beginning to read their books as Ms. Myers instructed and as the assignment written on the board reminds them to do. Two others are talking and laughing while they stand at Ms. Myers' desk. John is getting a drink on the way back to his seat. Karrie is not quite finished but is working diligently. Tana is not nearly finished and is staring across the room at the bulletin board.

The five students of the Blue Group, who just finished the reading lesson, have returned to their regular seats and are writing their names on worksheets that will assess their ability to apply the reading skills that were just taught in directed reading. Vicki has already begun the first exercise. Shasta cannot find her pencil.

The six students of the Yellow Reading Group are at the listening center listening to a tape of *Sleeping Beauty*. After they finish the tape, they will complete a worksheet on which they will list the story's events in sequence. They will then write a short report about the story's characters and plot.

The five students seated before Ms. Myers open their books as the teacher directs. While they do so, she scans the room quickly, looking over their heads to check on the other students. She wants to know whether everyone is "on task" or at least appears to be. She tells the two at her desk to return to their seats and start the assignment quickly. She warns them that she will remove their names from the Good Helper list on the bulletin board if they do not respond promptly. She calls Tana by name and tells her to finish quickly. She notices that Karrie has not finished yet and that John is at the water fountain. She does not say anything to either of them but makes a mental note to check on them specifically on her next "visual sweep of the room."

Ms. Myers returns her attention to the reading group before her. She says, "Mary, please read the new words for today." Mary reads the five new words from the chart, sounding out each. Ms. Myers compliments her. She then asks Mark to read the first page. When Mark finishes, she asks Candice to say in her own words what the story is about. She praises Candice for her insight. Then she asks Jason to read the next page.

When the last reading group is finished, Ms. Myers moves among the students to see how much of the morning work each has completed. She tells the children who have completed all assignments to put a star by their names on the "completed work chart" on the wall and lists the names of those not finished on the chalkboard. She suggests to them that they try to find time during the day to complete their work and says they may put a star by their name when they do. At the end of the week children who complete all the week's work will receive a reward.

ELEVENTH GRADE ALGEBRA II

At the five-of bell, Ms. Bassler enters the classroom.[2] Bob and Tim are already seated; others trickle in. Cathy enters and explains that she cannot come for a make-up test today as planned; she asks if she may take it tomorrow and

the teacher agrees. John enters and asks Ms. Bassler if she would like him to erase the board, but she says no because the problems at the top are part of today's work.

As the bell rings, the last of the seventeen students hurry to their seats; seven are absent today, taking AP tests. Fred and Cari go to the board and begin to put up problems from last night's homework. Other students get out their papers and books. Ms. Bassler checks the board work and pronounces it correct.

Ms. Bassler then reads the correct answers for last night's homework, and the students check their own papers. Fred frantically searches through his book but cannot find his work. When Peter asks the teacher to explain how one problem should be done, she does so and then continues on with the checking. As she reads, two students fill in answers to some problems they had not completed.

Ms. Bassler finishes reading the answers for the thirty problems and asks whether any students have questions. Several hands go up, and she answers the questions, using the board to illustrate each. At one point, she asks whether anyone worked a certain problem differently and got a correct answer. Marcia explains her different approach and receives praise for good thinking.

After dealing with questions about homework, Ms. Bassler reviews yesterday's lesson about inverse functions and works two examples. She asks Elizabeth whether she understands. She says she does. The teacher then tells Elizabeth that she had a conversation with her father last night, and she goes back to working an example.

After explaining the examples, Ms. Bassler gives the whole class a problem to work. All students copy the problem. Brad looks puzzled; Peter raises his hand. The teacher goes to Peter and gives help. Tom also raises his hand, and she goes to him.

When no more hands are raised, Ms. Bassler again goes to the board and reviews the process. She writes a new problem on the board. She makes an error in her example but catches her error and corrects herself.

Ms. Bassler now introduces today's lesson on finding first identities. After a brief explanation, she asks for a volunteer to build on what she has just demonstrated and find the second identity. Janie responds and is correct in her work. Ms. Bassler praises her. She then gives the class some tips on how to remember identities for exponents and for logarithms.

Ms. Bassler now refers to the problems she had written on the board before class and asks the class to give the answers for the first five. Students answer in chorus and the teacher leads a brief checking procedure for each response. Tom corrects the teacher on an error she makes, and she praises him for being observant.

Ms. Bassler next leads the students in working the second five problems dealing with the other identity. Students correctly answer all ten problems.

A student messenger comes to the door and hands the teacher a note. This student was once in the class but dropped it. Ms. Bassler teasingly asks if he wants to rejoin. He looks at all the problems on the board, declines, and leaves. Ms. Bassler and the class remind each other about class at the beginning of the year. Ms. Bassler admits she was hard and congratulates the students for sticking with the course.

Ms. Bassler goes to the board and works a problem from page 378 in the text. She assigns the remaining problems on the page as classwork and leaves the room to make a phone call in response to the note brought by the student messenger. The students all work on their assignment. At first some ask others for help, and they give further explanations to each other. Then all settle at their own desks and work quietly and individually.

Ms. Bassler returns and asks if anyone needs help. Several students raise their hands, and she goes individually to each and guides the work.

Ms. Bassler assigns homework problems for tomorrow and calls for all of today's homework to be turned in. Fred now says that he lost his. Ms. Bassler says she believes him; he may turn in a piece of paper with an explanatory note on it and submit the paper if he finds it. As she says this, the P.A. interrupts with an announcement about awards.

The bell rings, and students begin to leave the room. Ms. Bassler stands at her desk and continues to help students who come up to her for last-minute help.

WHAT HAPPENS IN CLASSROOMS

Classrooms Are Unique Places

Classrooms are places where students, teachers, learning materials, and ideas interact. In good classrooms, the interaction is purposeful, planned, and controlled by the teacher. If it is successful, students learn.

People read, talk, listen, question, respond, smile, frown, laugh, cry, gesture, day-dream, and sleep in classrooms. As they do, personalities and ideas intertwine, often meshing, sometimes clashing.

Classrooms are places where children, adolescents, and teenagers live a major part of their lives, where they have to be even if they want to be somewhere else. In them, students study, grow, develop, mature, think, and learn. Classrooms are where *students* struggle, achieve, give up, fail, and try again.

Classrooms are also places where teachers practice their profession and apply their skills, where they inform, question, motivate, cajole, joke, understand, sympathize, and scold. Classrooms are places where *teachers* struggle, achieve, give up, fail, and try again.

Common Characteristics

Classrooms have common characteristics. In fact, throughout the United States they are surprisingly the same.

The hallmark of most elementary school classrooms is perpetual activity. The students interact constantly in a friendly, flexible, yet energized atmosphere under the patient and subtle direction of the teacher. Students participate as a total class, in small groups, and individually. They listen to teacher explanations, work problems at their seats, engage in "hands-on" experience at study centers, read assignments, write answers to questions, and complete worksheet exercises.

Elementary Classrooms

Elementary teachers such as Ms. Myers constantly manage a multitude of classroom events. They lead students through carefully paced sequences of experiences, with frequent changes in activities in order to maintain interest. They respond to correct student ideas with praise and other forms of encouragement. They monitor student progress and guide learning by asking questions and giving directions.

Secondary Classrooms

Because there is so much activity in elementary classrooms, successful teachers have well-developed plans of operation, consisting of rules and procedures, rewards and punishments, and patterns of communication with students that all understand. They use these devices to maintain classroom control, order student work, sustain learner interest, and stimulate learning.

Most secondary school classrooms are usually more "ordered," more focused on the content to be learned, and more noticeably purposeful than elementary classrooms. Some of these types of differences are reflected when Ms. Bassler's lesson described in the Snapshot is compared with that of Ms. Myers. In the more academic subjects, teachers frequently stand at the front of the class or sit next to a podium from which they read lecture notes, follow along in the textbook, or study their teaching plans. Students typically sit at their desks, which are usually in rows facing the teacher, listening to the teacher, taking notes, socializing with each other, or daydreaming.

In secondary schools learning is overwhelmingly cognitive, and teaching is most often focused on the class as a group rather than on individual students. Teachers present facts and ideas, and successful students learn them, either by rote memory or through some higher level of thinking. In the process, students come to know and understand new information. When they have learned the information, students demonstrate what they have learned by answering questions, doing problems, completing exercises, writing papers, and passing tests.

Even when the subject matter involves more skill development than cognitive and verbal learning, common patterns are still present. Usually classroom instruction is still teacher-dominated; teacher-student questioning cycles still follow a pattern; and a common routine of teacher instruction, student practice, and student demonstration of skill and knowledge learned is obvious.

Differences

But classrooms are also very different, and to some degree each classroom is unique. The differences result from variations in student age, abilities, and personalities; in teacher characteristics, styles of teaching, and personal philosophies; in the ways classes are organized, students grouped, and lessons conducted; in the family, school, and community cultures that envelop the classroom; and in the political, psychological, social, ethnic, racial, and economic ideologies and norms on which the classroom operates.

Besides the obvious differences in physical appearance of classrooms and the differences in the individual human beings who constitute a class, classrooms are also different in ways such as the following:

- the extent to which students are actively involved in their learning;
- the amount and types of interpersonal interaction;
- the level of abstraction and understanding at which learning takes place;
- the ways in which students are grouped for instruction;
- the type of social stratification within the classroom culture;
- the amount of creativity;
- the level of tolerance of conflict, noise, and confusion;

- the ways in which subject matter is organized and integrated;
- the ways in which space and instructional materials are used;
- the styles in which information and materials are presented;
- the ways in which student behavior is managed;
- the ways in which students are questioned and feedback is provided;
- the degree of emotional support and physical contact;
- the extent to which parents are involved; and
- the level at which special needs of students are recognized and met.

Perceptions of Classrooms

What is most important about classrooms is, of course, what happens to the students in them. If the right things happen, students learn what they should learn. What are the right things? What "should" happen in classrooms? What "should" students and teachers do? How "should" students learn?

These questions might seem simple. A casual observer, for example, might respond:

> Teachers should tell students what they need to know; assign them worksheets, exercises, and reading; make them do homework; ask them questions; correct them when they are wrong; compliment them when they are right; make them behave; give them tests; and assign them grades.

What Observers See in Classrooms

That might be the start of an appropriate answer, but, of course, there is much more to it. What people see in the classrooms depends to a great extent on what they already know about classrooms, teachers, and students and on what biases and purposes they have as they observe. More knowledgeable and experienced observers tend to see more and understand more of what they see. But even the experts observe from their own particular perspectives.

Even if you are very much a beginner in your study of teaching and classrooms, you are already an expert of sorts. You have some knowledge, and you have formed some perspectives about teaching. That knowledge and those perspectives will influence what you see in the classrooms that you observe. If you are like most people in the early stages of teacher preparation programs, your view of teaching and what happens in classrooms comes very much from a student's point of view.

Let's check on your perspectives. Think about one of your high school classes and teachers—not just a single class on one single day, but a year-long class such as history, English, math, or science. Then consider the following:

- What are some of the things that happened in that class?
- What did the teacher do regularly?
- What did you and the other students do?
- Why do you think things occurred as they did?

Compare your thinking with that of other students in this education class.

Now, raise the same questions about a class or teacher from your elementary schooling. After that, apply the same questions to one of your college classes. Then consider:

- In what ways are your perceptions of the three classes similar to those of other students in this class?

- In what ways do your perspectives reflect the fact that much of your contact with teaching has been as a student?

- How might the views of more experienced and trained classroom observers be different from yours?

- How might your perspectives change as you continue your study of teacher education?

Four Researchers' Perceptions

Below are quotations from educational researchers who study classrooms. Their statements are reflections drawn from their classroom observations. Each comment reflects the particular researcher's perspective. As you read the comments, note the differences and identify the perspectives. Compare their comments to the way you responded to the questions above.

Goodlad's Observations

I stood in the open doorway of a classroom in one of the junior high classes located side by side down a long hallway. The day was a warm one and the doors of three of the classrooms were open. Inside each, the teacher sat at a desk, watching the class or reading. The students sat at table-type desks arranged in rows. Most were writing, a few were stretching, and the remainder were looking contemplatively or blankly into space. In one of two other rooms with closed doors, the students were watching a film. It appeared to be on the cause and prevention of soil erosion. In the other, the teacher was putting an algebraic equation on the chalkboard and explaining its components to the class. In visits to several other academic classes that day, I witnessed no marked variations on these pedagogical procedures and student activities. . . .

Writers and speakers reinforce our own memories of classrooms like these with references to cells, each with thirty or so students, desks or tables in rows, a teacher at the front, and pupils looking toward the teacher. A snapshot of such a scene would freeze in time a teacher lecturing and questioning and students in various poses of listening and responding (Goodlad, 1984, pp. 93–94).[3]

Carew and Lightfoot's Observations

Classrooms are not isolated and autonomous settings. Rather, each class and its inhabitants are in constant interaction with the social contexts in which they are embedded. The influences of family life, social class, ethnic and racial history, political and social ideologies reach the school directly each day through students and parents, teachers and administrators. The streets children negotiate to get to school, the people who live and work along the way, the houses or apartments where families live, the nature and quality of the social networks within the community are all important influences on the social, psychological, and educational forces at work in the classroom. Classroom life, therefore, is very much shaped and constrained by the norms, values, and traditions of the school; and likewise, the school is an integral part of the community which surrounds it. Each of these social systems—classroom, school, community—has its own structural arrangements, cultural idioms, and functional purposes, but each is also greatly influenced and sustained by the others (Carew & Lightfoot, 1979, p. 53).[4]

Lortie's Observations

The teacher therefore must "motivate" students, within the constraints described, to work hard and, if possible, to enjoy their efforts. He cannot count on voluntary enthusiasm; the teacher must generate much of the positive feeling that animates purposeful effort. All this, moreover, must be accomplished within a group setting and with persons who (in many cases) have not yet acquired the capacity for sustained effort. . . .

. . . control must be maintained, work must be ordered, and the students' interest must be aroused and sustained. These objectives must be met within a group over which the teacher presides; although there are dyadic contacts, a simple bit of arithmetic discloses that teachers can hardly spend more than a few minutes with each child in the course of a working day. Most of their teaching behavior, therefore, must be addressed to groups of children. Thus the teacher, willy-nilly, must successfully perform the emotional (or "expressive") tasks involved in sustained leadership. The tasks set for students must be accomplished, but this also entails coping with the emotional needs individual children bring to the classroom. The teacher must handle these various aspects of leadership in a visible situation where inconsistencies are quickly observed by students (Lortie, 1975, p. 152).[5]

Morine-Dershimer's Observations

In general, these six classrooms [those studied by Morine-Dershimer] exhibited certain basic similarities in language use, many of which would tend to indicate that they were fairly typical of classrooms observed in prior studies. Questions were primarily known information questions, although "real" questions were asked fairly often. Pupils answered most questions by providing non-personal information. Pacing of lessons, and extended development of question cycles through repeated or probing questions, increased as the school year progressed. Language use reflected more businesslike procedures in September and January and more informal procedures in December (Morine-Dershimer, 1985, pp. 78–79).[6]

STUDYING CLASSROOMS CLOSELY

Until recently, most educators had not analyzed what happens in classrooms very closely, very precisely, or very scientifically. Instead, they tended to hold one of two oversimplified conceptualizations of teaching: (1) the teacher as "born artist" or (2) the teacher as "craftsperson." Either of these conceptualizations made systematic and thorough study of classrooms relatively unimportant.

The first of these conceptualizations rested on a combination of two assumptions about teaching: (1) that teachers were "born, not made" and (2) that teaching was an "art, not a science." This view of teaching included the belief that some people possessed an intrinsic talent for teaching. Somehow they knew instinctively how to teach; they were innately skilled. They did not need to be

The Nature of Classroom Teaching

taught to be teachers. They were born artists. They only needed to learn the content they would teach to their students.

The second conceptualization rested on the assumption that teaching was a craft, much like those of the Middle Ages, such as carpentry and shoe-making. This view of teaching included the belief that people became teachers by watching other "master teachers" teach and by practicing the same techniques as an apprentice under the guidance of the "master." When the apprentices became good enough at the trade, they left the tutelage of the master for their own classrooms.

With these mind-sets, teacher educators of the past tended to think of the task of preparing new teachers as a very general three-step process:

1. Recruit intelligent, dedicated, compassionate young people.

2. Teach them some "subject matter" and a sufficient supply of "tricks of the trade" of teaching.

3. Send them to perform their art or practice their craft in student teaching and then on the job.

If these new teachers succeeded in the classroom, they were judged to have become "classroom artists," "skilled craftspersons," or some combination of both. They were expected to get better over the years, but that improvement would come from practice rather than from any systematic study of their effectiveness.

Although there is some validity to both of these ideas of the nature of teaching, educational researchers now know that they can study classrooms systematically. They can look for specific events and interactions, analyze what they see, determine which teaching is most effective, and develop ways to help teachers improve their performance.

Systematic Study

The study of almost any phenomenon is usually most productive if the people doing the study approach their task with some background knowledge and then do the study in an organized way. To do this, they begin with some general ideas about what they are looking at so that they can decide what it is that they see. Then they observe, analyze, and interpret the phenomenon under study very systematically.

Observing

One way of observing systematically is through a three-step process of (1) formulating questions to be answered, (2) brainstorming about the kind of data expected, and (3) constructing a system for gathering and categorizing the expected data. Such efforts at the start of an investigation provide guides for the analysis. They tell the investigator what to look for, what to record, how to record it, what to emphasize, and so forth. They help to assure that the correct and appropriate data are collected.

Analyzing and Interpreting

Once data are collected, they must be analyzed and interpreted. They must be made understandable and useful. Investigators must formulate them into meaningful conclusions and explain them in ways that others can understand. These tasks require skill, as well as knowledge of both the data collected and the general phenomenon being studied.

The importance of skilled, systematic observation, analysis, and interpretation of data can be illustrated by a look at the way many coaches and players on athletic teams analyze what they do. They first record their games on videotape and then analyze those tapes over and over again. Because they are knowledgeable, they know what to look for; but nevertheless, they look at the plays repeatedly, from different angles, and in slow motion. Several people look at each tape and interpret them from their individual perspectives. They compare notes and draw conclusions. Then they prepare for the next game in the hope of playing better and being successful. For purposes of comparison, think of how much more meaningful and valuable this type of analysis of a football game would be compared with off-the-cuff observations of a person attending a football game for the first time.

Classroom Observation and Analysis

The same principles apply to classroom observation and analysis. Knowledgeable, prepared observers see more in classrooms than the uninformed and unprepared. They know what to look for, where to focus attention. They are able to understand more of what they see and can record their data more meaningfully than the unprepared observer. Unprepared or unskilled classroom observers tend to miss or to misinterpret much of what happens in classrooms and to become confused because they see so much that they do not understand. They may also fail to see all that is going on.

Knowledgeable Observers

In other words, just as with other types of analyses, raw data collected on classrooms do not mean much in themselves. They have to be interpreted for meaning, and they have to be made useful. To do this, classroom observers must understand both classrooms and the observation process. They not only need to be knowledgeable in a general sense, so that they know where to begin and what to look for; but as they proceed, they must develop that knowledge and increase their sophistication so that they can attach appropriate meaning to the data they collect. In the end, they need to understand the data well enough to provide useful information to the teachers they observe.

The Value of Classroom Observation

One of the national experts on the observation and analysis of classrooms, Jane Stallings, has described the value of systematic classroom observation on a number of occasions. The next three sections of this chapter are based primarily on her ideas. (See, for example, Stallings, 1977, especially pp. 4–5).[7]

For Teachers

Systematic observation can help *classroom teachers* teach in ways that are consistent with the social, emotional, and cognitive development of children. For example, if a child is observed to be shy and introverted, the teacher might organize groups so that this child can work among friendly, nonaggressive children. If a child is observed to enjoy tinkering with machines and examining objects to see how they work, the teacher might direct that child to a good selection of exploratory materials in the classroom.

Systematic observation can also increase teachers' awareness of their own behavior and, when appropriate, can lead to changes. For example, observation can tell teachers how much they talk, how well they listen to student ideas, and what nonverbal messages they transmit.

For Students of Teaching

For *students in the process of becoming teachers*, classroom observation enables them to compare and contrast teaching styles. These students can learn a great deal from observing a master teacher handle difficult problems such as fights between children. Recording the observation in a precise way provides students with a concrete reference instead of just a general impression of how the teacher handled the fight. Also, students can compare different teacher behaviors with those recommended in a textbook. By doing this, they can better decide which techniques they prefer. But whatever the students decide, their knowledge and repertoire of teaching techniques will increase as a result of observing others teach in the classroom.

It is also helpful for education students to observe children in classroom settings, so that they see whether the child behaviors described in textbooks are identifiable in the classroom. For example, a student teacher could observe a third-grade classroom where most of the children are likely to be eight years old and look for behaviors that Jean Piaget identifies with that age. Piagetian developmental theory describes children between ages seven and eleven as being in the *concrete* operational stage—that is, the stage at which they are able to think while manipulating objects and to understand and transfer meaning to symbols that represent these objects—as they do in the process of reading. Piaget says that children of this age begin to solve problems in their heads and that they have less need than younger children to manipulate objects physically in order to draw meaning from them.

The observer of eight-year-olds, then, could see how many of the children in the classroom behave in the ways Piaget describes for children in the concrete operational stage. For instance, the observer can ask whether most of the children use counting sticks, blocks, weights, or measures to solve problems in mathematics or whether they solve the problems without such aids. With such observations and comparisons, student teachers are likely to develop a good understanding of child growth and development.

For Supervisors

School administrators, who must evaluate teachers' performances each year, can use systematic observations in making judgments about teachers' proficiencies. For example, they can use their observations to identify and study relationships between teaching practices and children's achievement test scores. The administrator can also use the observation as a training device by discussing it with the teacher. Such discussions of the observations are likely to be more helpful in providing feedback about classroom teaching techniques than are general, unsupported statements about the teacher's behavior.

Systematic observation also provides more accurate and more precise pictures of classroom activity than more general and casual looks at teachers and students. This is particularly important because teachers have little time to reflect on or analyze their own behavior; and often their perceptions of their behavior and its effect on children differ widely from those of objective outside observers. John Goodlad (Goodlad & Klein, 1974) pointed this out in a study of elementary teachers when he said

> . . . there seemed to be a considerable discrepancy between teachers' perceptions of their own innovative behavior and the perceptions of observers. The teachers [in the study] sincerely thought they were individualizing instruction, encouraging inductive learning, involving children in group processes [although the observers reported they were not doing so]. (Goodlad & Klein, 1974, p. 78).[8]

Becoming a Skilled Classroom Observer

Most of the remainder of this chapter is intended to help you develop your skills as a classroom observer. The next few pages illustrate a general, beginning-

An Introduction to Teaching and Schools **59**

level way of studying classrooms. Later pages provide instruction in the use of a more sophisticated observation system that highlights a specific aspect of classroom activity. An additional observation system is presented in the appendix.[9]

AN ILLUSTRATION

Let's assume you are going to observe a classroom and report to your instructor what you see. You have not been provided with guiding questions or an observation form. You want to conduct the observation systematically, and you want to be able to draw some meaningful conclusions about what you see. Let's also assume that you have never done an observation and report before and that you want to keep the whole effort simple.

Questions you might use for the observation are:

- What is the teacher doing?
- Why is he or she doing it?
- What are the students doing?
- Why are they doing it?

Formulating Questions

Before you proceed, however, let's look at the questions more closely. The four questions differ in at least two ways. One difference is the focus of the questions. Questions 1 and 2 focus on the teacher, Questions 3 and 4, on the students.

The other difference is less obvious. Questions 1 and 3 ask for *actions* of the teacher and students, respectively. Answers to them will be *descriptions* of what the people in the classroom do.

On the other hand, Questions 2 and 4 ask observers to make *inferences* about the actions they see. They ask observers to *infer* the *reasons behind* the actions, to determine what motivated the teacher and students to do what they did. These *reasons* for actions cannot be seen. Observers have to provide them. To answer Questions 2 and 4, observers must draw on their backgrounds and understanding of the situation to a much greater extent than for Questions 1 and 3.

Collecting Data

Now, let's consider what kind of data you could expect these questions to generate. Some of the *actions* you might see are as follows:

Question One

What is the teacher doing?

standing	saying "yes"	giving directions
talking	giving instructions	collecting homework
pointing	writing on the chalkboard	frowning
laughing	telling Joe to sit down	shouting

2: Inside Classrooms: Analyzing Real Teaching

Principal informally observing a teacher.

Reasons that you might infer for the actions you see are listed below:

Question Two: Teacher

Why is she doing this?

Action	Reason
standing	She wants attention.
	She wants to be seen by all students.
	She is standing because she always stands when she lectures.
	She probably has not made a conscious decision to stand.
talking	She is presenting information to the students.
	She wants to tell them about the child in the play rather than take the time to have them read it.
	She wants everyone to get the same ideas about the play.
writing on the chalkboard	She want to emphasize certain ideas so that the students can see what is most important.
	She wants to hold student attention.
	She wants to reinforce some points that she

mentions so that the students are more likely to remember them.

Question Three

What are the students doing?

sitting/listening	writing	copying from chalkboard
reading	laughing	copying from another
sleeping	whispering	student
walking to the trash can	answering	

Question Four: Students

Why are they doing this?

Action

Most are sitting in their seats listening to the teacher.

Reason

Most want to hear what the teacher is saying.

They are interested in the lesson.

Some unusual teacher behaviors are difficult to interpret.

2: Inside Classrooms: Analyzing Real Teaching

Two are reading books.	They want to learn about the characters in the play.
	Two are not very interested in this play.
	They are more interested in their other subjects. (We do not know why.)
	The teacher has not stopped them.
One is sleeping.	One is tired or bored.
One is taking a piece of paper to the trash can.	One is not concentrating and is restless.
	He is not paying attention.
	She wanted to interrupt the boredom.
	This child seems to be immature.
Two are whispering to each other.	Two are not interested in the lesson.
	One wanted to ask the other a question.
	The teacher often does not notice whispering.

Organizing Data

Now, let's consider ways of gathering and organizing the data that you expect to find. One such way is a chronological log as follows:

Time	Teacher		Students	
	Action	Reason	Action	Reason
9:03	Standing	Wants attention	Most listening	Interested, want to learn
	Tells whole class what Bob did in the play	Wants everyone to know what Bob did and why he did it	Most listening	Interested in play
			Two reading other material	Not interested in play
	Explains why Bob did it	Wants everyone to know what Bob did and why he did it	Most listening	Interested
			One sleeping	Bored, tired
			One taking paper to trash can	Bored, restless, immature
			Two whispering, not on subject	Not interested, distracted, bad
9:08	Watching students read	Wants them to practice reading	Most reading	Following teacher's directions
	Ignoring sleeping student	Willing to let him sleep	One sleeping	Tired
			Two daydreaming	Bored, short attention span
9:13	Asking questions about reading	Checking for understanding	One answering	Was called on
			Most listening to answer	Interested
			One sleeping	Tired
9:18	Giving directions for next activity	Transition to spelling	Most taking out paper	Following teacher's directions
			One sleeping	Tired

At this point, you should have some idea about planning for and conducting a systematic observation of a classroom. Let's see if you have.

Look at the two descriptions of classrooms presented in the Snapshot at the start of this chapter. If you were to observe in these classrooms, using the four questions above,

1. What data would you record?
2. How would you gather and categorize those data?

Now, go ahead and practice using the four questions on each of the two Snapshot classrooms.

1. Record responses to all four questions for each class.
2. Organize the data chronologically for each class.

Interpreting Data and Concluding

A word of caution is in order here. In this illustration, you have only been asked to *begin* a process of observing in classrooms. You were not asked to *interpret* data gathered in classrooms or to *draw conclusions* from them. This hypothetical illustration and the descriptions of classrooms in the Snapshot are too superficial to enable interpretation or conclusions. Also, you probably do not have the appropriate background knowledge to provide meaningful interpretations at this time. The purpose of this exercise is limited to developing your beginning *observation* skills. Practice on the skills of *interpreting* and *concluding* will be deferred until later study.

ANALYSIS

If you have access to K–12 classrooms or videotapes of classes, this would be a good time to practice your classroom observation skills and to see how much more analytical you can be now as compared to when you made the student-based reflections earlier in this chapter. To begin, simply make a list of the four guiding questions already listed above and repeated here.

- What is the teacher doing?
- Why is he or she doing it?
- What are the students doing?
- Why are they doing it?

Then arrange to view a class. While doing so, record your observations in the form of answers to each of the questions, and see what happens.

Once you have done this and feel that you know what you are doing, you can add a second level of sophistication to your observing skills by interjecting the element of time. To do this, continue to record responses to the same four questions, but do so every five minutes. Follow these steps:

> 1. Select a seat in a classroom (or choose a videotape) that will enable you to see the teacher and as many students as possible.
> 2. When you are settled comfortably, note the time and immediately scan the class, making mental notes of what the teacher and students are doing at that specific moment.
> 3. Answer all four questions based on what you just saw.
> 4. Repeat the same scan-and-record process every five minutes for a full period, a complete lesson, or for as long as you wish.
> 5. Review your notes, noticing not only what occurred each time you scanned the class but also how events changed over the time you observed.

ANALYTICAL OBSERVATION SYSTEMS

This section of the text provides instruction in the use of an analytical classroom observation system that focuses on student on-task and off-task behavior. The observation system described is used currently by educational observers to determine what happens in classrooms. It was developed by Jane Stallings.

Although the On-Task/Off-Task Behavior System is not difficult to use and our purpose for you to learn it is relatively elementary, the system can be used by experts to produce significant, useful information for experienced teachers, teacher supervisors, and educational researchers. Once you learn the system, you should be able to make frequent and continued use of it with increasing sophistication throughout your teaching career. The system is described, explained, and illustrated on the next few pages; and then, an Analysis section provides an exercise so you can practice using it.[10] (A second observation system, one on teacher-student verbal interaction, is explained and illustrated in the appendix of this text. Once you learn the first system, you might want to try that one as well.)

The Student On-Task/Off-Task Behavior Observation System

The Student Time On-Task/Off-Task Observation System provides data on what individual students in a class are doing. Each student who is doing what the teacher wants is considered to be *on task* and each student who is doing something other than what the teacher wants is *off task*. The form on which the observer records the observation data is the Student Off-Task Seating Chart, which is actually a seating chart prepared by the observer to conform to the seating arrangement of the class being observed. If the class is organized with desks in traditional rows, and the teacher is instructing the whole group, the chart might look like the one shown in Figure 2–1 below. (Note that the codes to be used by the observer are listed on the sheet for easy reference.)

Explanation

The purpose of the Student Off-Task Seating Chart is to record a sample of all students' off-task behavior and nonproductive use of time during a scheduled period. Three types of data are recorded on the Seating Chart:

1. the off-task behavior,

```
                    STUDENT OFF-TASK SEATING CHART

   Teacher: _____    School: _____

   Date: _____ Time: _____ to _____ Number of Sweeps: _____
                   (beginning)  (end)
                         (front of classroom)
                           ┌─────────┐
                           │ Teacher │
                           └─────────┘
        ┌──────┐   ┌──────┐   ┌──────┐   ┌──────┐
        │      │   │      │   │      │   │      │
        └──────┘   └──────┘   └──────┘   └──────┘

        ┌──────┐   ┌──────┐   ┌──────┐   ┌──────┐
        │      │   │      │   │      │   │      │
        └──────┘   └──────┘   └──────┘   └──────┘

        ┌──────┐   ┌──────┐   ┌──────┐   ┌──────┐
        │      │   │      │   │      │   │      │
        └──────┘   └──────┘   └──────┘   └──────┘

        ┌──────┐   ┌──────┐   ┌──────┐   ┌──────┐
        │      │   │      │   │      │   │      │
        └──────┘   └──────┘   └──────┘   └──────┘
                                              Sweep in Which
   Student Off — Task Codes    Activity Contest   Activity Occurred
   C  =  Chatting              I  =  Instruction
   D  =  Disruptive            O  =  Organization
   P  =  Personal Needs        Q  =  Question/Answer
   U  =  Uninvolved            R  =  Oral Reading
   W  =  Waiting               S  =  Seatwork
   Z  =  Sleeping              C  =  Cooperative Group
                               G  =  Game
```

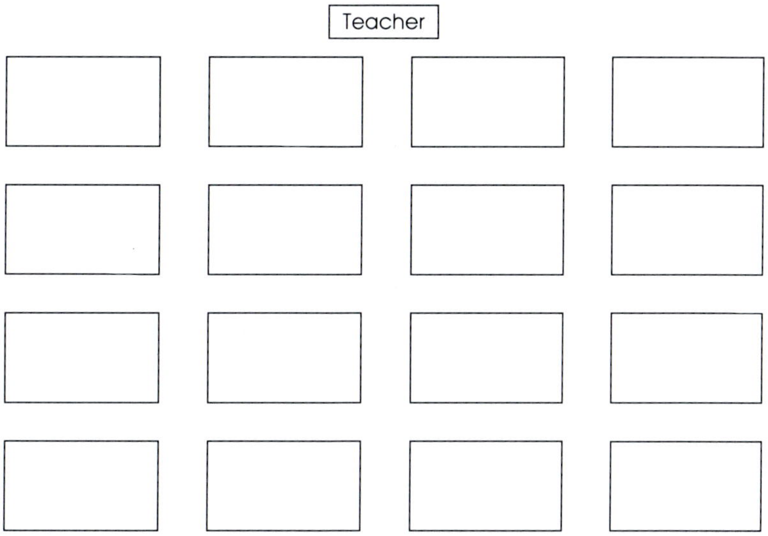

Figure 2–1. Example of a student off-task seating chart. (Source: Jane Stallings: Houston Center for Effective Teaching, University of Houston.)

2. the activity in which the students should have been involved, and
3. the time the off-task behavior occurred.

Nothing is recorded for students who are on task.

Off-Task Behaviors

    C Chatting—Low-volume talking or whispering, passing notes between students.

Sometimes students are hard to motivate.

- **D** Disruptive—Bothering a number of students, such as loud talking, throwing things, pushing or fighting.
- **P** Personal needs—Sharpening pencils, going to the restroom, getting a drink, getting papers or books.
- **U** Uninvolved—Doing something other than assigned tasks but not bothering anyone else.
- **W** Waiting—Sitting with hand up for the teacher's help before being able to proceed, for materials to be passed, for the teacher to review one's work, and other times when the student is "stuck" until receiving the teacher's attention. (Note: This does *not* include raising a hand in volunteer response to the teacher's questioning and waiting to be called on. Such behavior is *on* task.)
- **Z** Sleeping.

Activities

The following activity codes are used to record how students *should* be involved:

- **I** Instruction—Listening to the teacher's explanation of content or subject matter.

O   Organizing—Listening to the teacher make assignments or explain organizing procedures; getting paper and books out.

Q   Question/Answer—Listening to the teacher question students, answering a question, listening to another student answering such a question, as in drill and practice; also includes students writing on the board.

R   Reading Orally—Participation as a member of a reading group that is reading aloud.

S   Seatwork—Working at seats on silent reading or written assignments.

C   Cooperative Group—Working on a cooperative group task.

G   Games—Playing academic games.

Numbered Observation Sweeps

A number of sweeps or observation records are made of students' behavior at equal intervals, such as every five minutes, during one class period. In order to know *when* the off-task behavior occurred, the number of the sweep is entered with each off-task behavior recorded. For example, if a student is *chatting* during *instruction* at the time of the *fourth sweep*, it is recorded C/I④. The record of when the off-task behavior occurred helps the teacher to know whether students are

Directions

1. Prepare for the observation by developing a box-type seating chart for the class to be observed. The boxes need to be large enough so that several entries can be made in each.

2. Enter the teacher's name, beginning time, date, school, and the number of sweeps planned on the form.

3. As the period starts, immediately begin making the first scan, or visual sweep, of the room, going clockwise from the door you entered. Record one of the following symbols for each student *who is off task:*
   C = Chatting P = Personal needs W = Waiting D = Disruptive U = Uninvolved Z = Sleeping
   Record nothing for the students who are on task.

4. Make a slash mark beside each symbol just recorded (for example, C/).

5. Write in the space following each slash mark the symbol that shows what the student was supposed to be doing. (A notation of "C/I," for example, means that a student was chatting instead of listening to instruction.

6. Place the numeral ① beside each entry to indicate that the off-task behavior occurred during the first sweep. Make the marks small enough so that several entries can be made in each box.

7. Watch the clock and make visual sweeps of the classroom, repeating Steps 3 to 6 every five minutes for the length of time you had planned.

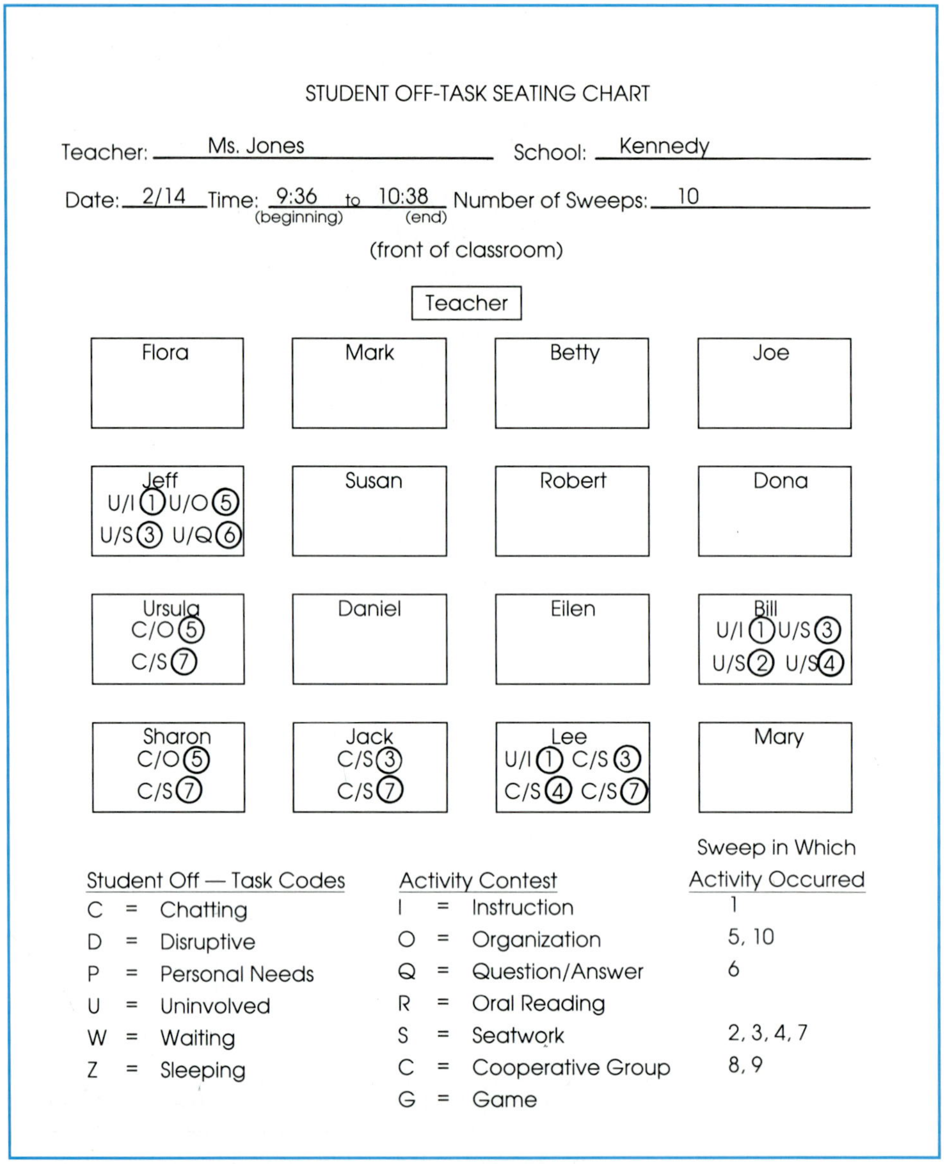

STUDENT OFF-TASK SEATING CHART

Teacher: __Ms. Jones__   School: __Kennedy__

Date: __2/14__ Time: __9:36__ to __10:38__   Number of Sweeps: __10__
                  (beginning) (end)

(front of classroom)

[Teacher]

Flora	Mark	Betty	Joe
Jeff U/I ① U/O ⑤ U/S ③ U/Q ⑥	Susan	Robert	Dona
Ursula C/O ⑤ C/S ⑦	Daniel	Eilen	Bill U/I ① U/S ③ U/S ② U/S ④
Sharon C/O ⑤ C/S ⑦	Jack C/S ③ C/S ⑦	Lee U/I ① C/S ③ C/S ④ C/S ⑦	Mary

Student Off — Task Codes		Activity Contest		Sweep in Which Activity Occurred
C = Chatting		I = Instruction		1
D = Disruptive		O = Organization		5, 10
P = Personal Needs		Q = Question/Answer		6
U = Uninvolved		R = Oral Reading		
W = Waiting		S = Seatwork		2, 3, 4, 7
Z = Sleeping		C = Cooperative Group		8, 9
		G = Game		

Figure 2–2. Example of a partially completed student off-task seating chart. (Source: Jane Stallings: Houston Center for Effective Teaching, University of Houston.)

At each repeat of Step 6, make the circled number match the sweep number.

8. Record the time when you stop.

A sample seating chart that has been completed by an observer appears in Figure 2–2.

Summarizing the Off-Task Seating Chart Data

Notice in Figure 2–2 that each notation for a time when a student was observed to be off-task has three elements:

1. the symbol for the off-task behavior (one of six possible),
2. the symbol for the activity in which the student should have been involved (one of seven possible), and
3. the number of the sweep (from one to ten).

With these data the observer can analyze:

1. how often students are off task;
2. which students are off task the most;
3. which type of off-task behavior is the most frequent;
4. during which activities in the lessons the greatest number of students are off task; and
5. which time during the class the greatest number of students are off task.

Armed with these data, the teacher can make changes that may lead to an increase of time that students spend on specified tasks.

The data about a class as a whole can be summarized so that the material is easy to understand. A Summary Chart of off-task behaviors (see Figure 2–3)

SUMMARY CHART
OFF-TASK BEHAVIORS

Teacher: Ms. Jones School: Kennedy
Date: 2/14 Time: 9:36-10:08

BEHAVIORS	Chatting	Disruptive	Personal Needs	Uninvolved	Waiting	Sleeping
No. of Sweeps = 10	9	0	0	9	0	0

ACTIVITIES	Instruction	Organizing	Question/Answer	Oral Reading	Seat-Work	Cooperative Groups	Games
	3	3	1	0	11	0	0

Figure 2–3. Example of a summary chart of off-task behaviors. (Source: Jane Stallings: Houston Center for Effective Teaching, University of Houston.)

can be developed for a teacher; and the data, such as that from Figure 2–2, can be recorded each time the teacher is observed. To do this, the observer in the example would record in the appropriate box on the line marked "Observation" the number of times each behavior occurred and the number of times each activity occurred.

From the information recorded on the Seating Chart in Figure 2–2 and on the Summary Chart in Figure 2–3, respond to the following:

- How many times was it possible for an individual student to be off task during this observation? (Multiply the number of students by the number of sweeps.)
- How many off-task behaviors were recorded?
- Which students were off task most often?
- Which type of off-task behavior was most frequent?
- During which type of activity were students off task most often?
- When during the class period were students off task most often?

Something to Think About

During her first week as a student teacher in a junior high school, a college senior was observing in several teachers' classes to get a "feel" for the school as a whole before she started her own teaching. As she watched in one eighth-grade history class, she compiled an informal Student Off-Task Behavior Seating Chart. At the end of the class, her data showed the following:

Of the 31 students,

- 16 participated as expected for at least 8 of the 10 sweeps.
- 3 slept for at least 7 sweeps.
- 4 chatted for 5 of the 10 sweeps (in 2 different conversations).
- 5 were uninvolved for 4 or more of the sweeps.
- 3 were disruptive for at least 3 of the sweeps.

As the class left the room, the teacher approached the student teacher and said, "Well, that was a rather typical class. I noticed you were taking notes. What does that mean?"

If you were the observing student teacher, how would you respond? Why would you respond in this way?

Calculating Off-Task Rates

The number of times students are off task compared to the total number of times they could have been off task is called the Off-Task Rate for the class. This rate can be found by dividing the total number of off-task behaviors of all students by the total opportunities that all students had to be off task. The total number of opportunities to be off task is determined by multiplying the number of students in the class by the number of sweeps. If the formula is stated in the form of a fraction, it looks like this:

$$\text{Total number of instances of off-task behavior of all students} \div \text{Number of opportunities for all students to be off-task} = \text{Off-task rate}$$

What is the Off-Task Rate for the class recorded in Figures 2–2 and 2–3?

Limited Data

At this point you have reviewed data from one classroom observation. If you were the supervisor of this teacher and chose to use this system with her class, you would observe a number of times, summarize all your data, formulate some conclusions about the data, and talk with the teacher about what you believe the data mean. In the process, the two of you would probably discuss ideas about changes in the teacher's teaching.

Limited Experience

With the limited data presented in "Something to Think About," you do not now have enough information to determine why the student behavior recorded for this class is occurring. Also, you do not have the amount of observation or teaching experience necessary to develop recommendations for the teacher. With that additional experience, however, you should be able to develop into a skilled classroom observer.

ANALYSIS

This section contains two parts: an outline of the seating arrangement of a middle-school English class and a description of what each person in the classroom is doing at five specific times during a lesson. The teacher is teaching the whole class. The sweeps are at five-minute intervals.

Now that you have learned about the Student On-Task/Off-Task Observation System, record the student behavior that is described.

1. Make a Student Off-Task Seating Chart for the class, as in Figure 2–2.

2. Fill in the seating chart based on the class descriptions during the five sweeps.

3. Make and complete a Summary Chart as in Figure 2–3 and record the data from your seating chart.

4. Respond to the questions listed in the section on summarizing off-task seating chart data.

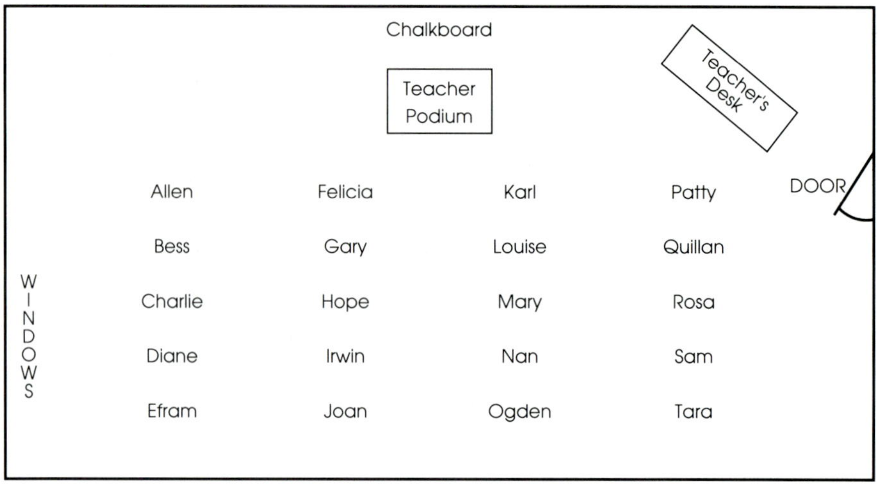

```
                    Chalkboard

                    ┌─────────┐
                    │ Teacher │              ┌──────┐
                    │ Podium  │              │Teacher's│
                    └─────────┘              │  Desk  │
                                             └──────┘
                                                      DOOR
         Allen    Felicia    Karl    Patty

         Bess     Gary      Louise  Quillan
  W
  I      Charlie  Hope      Mary    Rosa
  N
  D      Diane    Irwin     Nan     Sam
  O
  W      Efram    Joan      Ogden   Tara
  S
```

Figure 2–3A. Ms. Lloyd's English class.

SWEEP #1

As the 9:05 bell rings, Ms. Lloyd closes the door of her seventh-grade English class and directs her students to copy the homework assignment from the side chalkboard onto their six-weeks calendars, to take out their red grading pens, and to exchange last night's grammar papers for in-class checking.

    Allen opens his English folder to his calendar and begins to copy. Bess searches noisily through her purse for a red pen as Charlie quietly studies the chalkboard in dismay. Diane tries to hand her paper to Efram, who leans back and stares out the window. Joan walks up the row and hands her paper to Felicia, while Gary and Hope discuss whether the assignment means up to or through page 67. Irwin sharpens his pencil. Karl, Louise, and Mary all copy from the board. Nan offers an extra red pen to Ogden, who ignores her as he and Tara comment on pictures of his new Great Dane puppy, Atilla. Patty combs her hair. Quillan copies from the board. Rosa cannot see the board clearly and copies from Quillan's calendar. Sam searches for his calendar, cannot find it, and asks the teacher for another.

SWEEP #2

At 9:10 students check last night's homework. Ms. Lloyd asks various students to identify prepositional phrases in sentences and to tell which words they modify.

    Allen checks Diane's paper while Bess still searches for a red pen. Charlie raises his hand to volunteer for the next sentence, and Diane checks Charlie's paper. Efram did not have the assignment and therefore has no paper to grade; he sits and pokes at a rip in his book cover. Felicia explains #6. Gary places a red check beside #6, while Hope marks a red X on Gary's paper. Irwin's pencil breaks, and he gets up to sharpen it. Joan stares at Efram. Karl, Louise, and Mary raise their hands to volunteer for #7. Nan watches

Sam and Rosa's conversation. Ogden looks at the paper before him. Patty and Quillan both raise hands to ask questions. Rosa asks Sam whether #4 had three prepositional phrases, and Sam says it did. Tara tries to get Sam's attention to show him the photos of Atilla.

SWEEP #3

At 9:15 Ms. Lloyd has finished collecting the graded homework papers and begins to introduce the adverbial use of a prepositional phrase.

In the first row, Allen and Bess take notes as the teacher lectures, Charlie and Efram stare intently at the teacher, and Diane takes a mirror from her purse and examines a cut on her lip. In the second row, Felicia and Gary study an example the teacher has written on the board; and Hope, Irwin, and Joan take notes. In the third row, Karl, Louise, Mary, and Nan all take notes, while Ogden tries to see who now has his puppy pictures. In the fourth row, Patty stares at the teacher; Quillan looks at pictures of Atilla; Rosa squints hard at the board, then copies notes from Quillan's paper; and Sam and Tara take notes.

SWEEP #4

At 9:20 Ms. Lloyd has finished her explanation of adverbial phrases, and students are working in class on the first five sentences of a twenty-sentence assignment. Ms. Lloyd walks around the room and looks over each student's shoulder.

In the first row, the teacher works with Efram to help him get started; all other students in the first two rows work independently on the assignment. In the third row, Karl, Louise, Nan, and Ogden pick out prepositional phrases, while Mary and Rosa discuss Atilla's photos. In the fourth row, Patty and Sam both are stuck and have their hands raised for help; Quillan and Tara are finishing the fifth sentence.

SWEEP #5

At 9:25 Ms. Lloyd has distributed a teacher-made crossword puzzle to students for review practice of *ie* and *ei* spelling words. Students may work on either grammar or spelling until the period ends. Ms. Lloyd has finally confiscated the puppy pictures, and she continues to walk around the room and look over shoulders.

In the first row, Allen, Bess, and Charlie work silently on the spelling puzzle; Diane works on spelling and asks Irwin how to spell several words; Efram stares out of the window. In the second row, Felicia and Hope continue on the grammar, and Gary and Irwin work on spelling; Joan stops to sharpen her pencil. Everyone in row three tries to fill in the spelling puzzle, and the teacher looks over Louise's shoulder. In the fourth row, Patty checks back in her folder notes on prepositions, Quillan and Rosa compare spelling puzzle answers thus far, and Sam and Tara work independently on their puzzles.

CONCLUSION

Now you should be ready to observe in classrooms with some sense that you know what you are doing. You are not a skilled observer, of course, and you have learned only one analytical observation system, but you should be able to recognize and understand classroom events that you would not have understood before you read this chapter. So, if you have not already done so, go try it. If you do so in a local classroom, make sure the teacher understands and agrees to what you will be doing. Use the four guiding questions and the observation system to learn more about real classrooms and more about what teachers and students do as they teach and learn. As you do this, you will refine your observation skills, you will gradually see more subtleties in classroom activity, and you will develop deeper understandings about what is going on.

Remember, however, that at this point you do not know much about what are good and bad classroom practices. Do not be quick to judge what you see. Observations can tell you what is happening, but only background knowledge about teaching and learning will enable you to judge appropriately what is good classroom practice and what is not. Chapter 3 begins to provide that background.

The Educational Research section that follows describes the ways in which educational researchers use classroom observations in their work and how the data generated are used to formulate conclusions about classroom effectiveness. The description includes references to small-scale, teacher-conducted research in their own classrooms, as well as more complex endeavors.

EDUCATIONAL RESEARCH

What We Know about Studying Classrooms

The Effectiveness of Teaching

As mentioned in Chapter One, the study by Coleman et al., *Equality of Educational Opportunity* (1966),[11] included comparisons of different factors that help determine how much students in a particular school learn. The study asserted that teachers are not *as significant* in determining how well students learn *as other factors,* such as family background and the economic conditions in which the students live. This assertion led some readers of the study to jump to the conclusion that teachers and what they do in the classroom *are not very effective* in educating students.

But Coleman's findings did not justify such a conclusion. His investigation was a classic *input-output* study. Students were assessed when they entered school and again when they completed their studies. The data that were collected showed that student backgrounds and the abilities they brought with them to school were more significant in determining what they learned than were the characteristics of the teachers who taught them and the ways those teachers taught. The data did not say teachers were ineffective, and they did not compare different types of teaching.

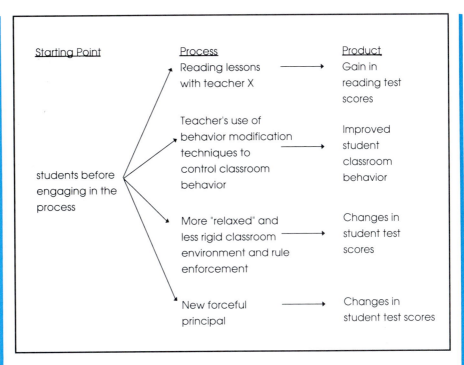

Figure 2–4. A schematic representation of process–product research designs. Students enter the school and are affected by some process, which produces a change in them. The change is the product.

A Closer Look at Classrooms

However, the Coleman data prompted other researchers to look at schools and classrooms more closely and to look at them in different ways. Some of these researchers have used *process-product* instead of input-output research designs. For example, they looked at different teachers, different teaching styles and techniques, different classroom environments, and different school organizations (the processes of teaching); and they compared what they saw with how much the students in the various settings learned (the product of the teaching). They found that some of the things that teachers and schools do produce more student learning than others, and they found that these things can be identified and classified.

Conclusions about Effectiveness

These process-product findings mean that teachers and schools can make a difference in what their students learn. They mean that schools, classrooms, and teachers can be observed and analyzed in ways that lead to conclusions about the effectiveness of schools and teaching. They mean that the knowledge and skills used by the more effective schools and teachers can be taught to those that are less effective. Results from many of these studies are now being used to change classroom practices, to change policies that govern schools, and to change the ways in which teachers are educated.

"Should Do" Formulas

Often the direction of these changes appears in the form of policy statements about what teachers and schools *should do*. For example,

"Teachers should plan thoroughly." "Teachers should monitor student work closely." "Teachers should have high expectations of students and communicate them clearly and consistently." "Schools should have clearly established sets of purpose that are agreed to by all of the staff." "Principals should be instructional leaders."

There is a potential danger, however, if this use of should-do ideas is pursued uncritically, and, unfortunately, many schools and teachers have suffered because of it. Those who have suffered have tended to adopt should-do principles as rigid *formulas* to be followed rather than as flexible guides to be applied sensitively to local circumstances. For example, a number of schools and teachers have incorrectly concluded from Stallings' research that there is a specific formula on the "best" percentage of classroom time to be used for interactive instruction. They then assume that that percentage is the *correct* percentage for all classes, all teachers, and all contexts. Similar errors have been made in the misuse of findings on classroom organization and management from Evertson, Brophy, and others. (See, for example, Brophy, J. (1979). Teacher behavior and its effects. *Journal of Educational Psychology, 71*, 733–750; Brophy, J. E. (1983). Classroom organization and management. *Elementary School Journal, 83*(4), 265–286; Emmer, E., Evertson, C., & Anderson, L. (1980). Effective classroom management at the beginning of the school year. *Elementary School Journal, 80*(5), 219–231; Evertson, C., & Emmer, E. T. (1988). Effective management at the beginning of the school year in junior high classes. *Journal of Educational Psychology, 74*(4), 485–498.)

One of the reasons for this use of research findings as rigid formulas is the desire of educators for quick and simple solutions to problems. They want to improve their instruction, and they fall for easy fixes.

All Designs Have Weaknesses

Another, and related, reason for the frequent misuse of research data lies in the nature of research itself. All research leaves more questions unanswered than it answers. Just as Coleman's input-output design left some dimensions of classroom instruction unexplored, so do process-product designs, as well as all other designs. The simple truth is all research designs have weaknesses as well as strengths. No research can "prove" how all teachers should teach.

Guides Rather than Formulas

Nevertheless, should-do statements, if considered to be guides rather than formulas, can be used effectively in schools and classrooms. This happens when school leaders and teachers apply research findings to a school or classroom, not as proven fact, but in the form of a new, small-scale, local research study. In other words, when teachers try to follow a should-do idea in their classrooms to determine *whether* it works or not, those teachers are using research findings appropriately. They are doing a small-scale experiment of their own. They are testing the idea to see if it works for them in their setting.

For example, if a teacher decides to follow the research conclusion that *frequent positive feedback to students produces greater and quicker learning*, he or she can follow the practice and see how it works. If it does, that teacher has produced one more bit of evidence that the conclusion is valid, at least in that teacher's present classroom. In addition, the teacher can now use the technique with some confidence.

The Process-Product Sequence of Investigation

Researchers who study classrooms follow the same basic pattern. They arrange for certain kinds of teaching, or they find classrooms where that kind of teaching is already being done. Next, if they are using a process-product design, they observe those classrooms, using instruments such as those presented earlier in this chapter. Then they assess student achievement. Finally, they compare the observation data with the achievement data. When they find classroom activities and teacher behaviors (processes) that lead to increased levels of student achievement (product), they designate these activities and behaviors as *effective*.

Some of the specific things contemporary classroom researchers are looking at are the following:

- the *academic content* covered—in the text, in a teacher's lecture, on the test, during a typical period, or during a whole school day;
- teacher expectations of students;
- the ways teachers communicate expectations;
- student *academic engaged rate* (time spent actively on academic learning);
- the teacher's organizational and managerial plans and style;
- the pace and sequencing of lessons;
- time spent on *active teaching*, rather than on procedural or managerial tasks;
- student *time on task*;
- the relative value and appropriateness of whole class, small group, and individualized instruction;
- the effects of grouping for instruction;
- the teacher's *structuring of lessons*;
- the cognitive level of questions;
- teacher reactions to student responses;
- the ways in which teachers *monitor* seatwork and follow up homework assignments;
- teacher instructional objectives; and
- student socioeconomic status.

The Educational Research section of the next chapter describes some of these studies and reports on their findings.

SUMMARY

Classrooms differ from other places. In many ways classrooms are similar, yet each is also unique. To a great extent, perceptions of classrooms and what happens in them varies depending on the point of view of the observer.

Classrooms have been studied more closely in recent years than in the past. That study has led to the accumulation of data that can be used to change classroom practice and improve teaching.

Classroom observers can better understand what they see if they approach their task with a set of guidelines about what to look for, a list of questions to ask, and background knowledge about both teaching and the process of observing. The guidelines and questions can be rather simple; for example, they may focus on what is happening and why it is happening. They can also be more complex and may focus on specific classroom phenomena, such as student on-task/off-task behavior and teacher-student verbal interaction.

Student on-task/off-task behavior can be calculated and reported by use of a classroom seating chart and the Stallings Student On-Task/Off-Task Observation System. Similarly, the Stallings Teacher-Student Interaction Observation System described in the Appendix can supply data on classroom verbal interaction.

Those studying schools and teaching can learn best by observing classrooms with specific skills that make observation much more effective as a teaching tool than simply reading books about teaching or unguided classroom visits.

STUDY QUESTIONS

1. Make a list of things that can be observed in classrooms that would likely indicate that something is wrong. Make a similar list of things that would likely indicate that the class is functioning well. Defend your reasons for including each item on each list.

2. What are the advantages and disadvantages of guided classroom observations for
   - a teacher education student who is doing the observing?
   - a teacher education student being observed?
   - an experienced practicing teacher?
   - a school supervisor or principal?

3. How could classroom observation data be misused? What safeguards should be established to avoid such problems?

4. Lawyers, medical doctors, engineers, and other professionals seem to be more willing to analyze and critique their own and each other's professional performance than teachers are. Even professional athletes video tape performances and criticize what they see in order to improve. Do you agree that some teachers are more reluctant to do self-studies than others? If so, why do you think they might have such a reluctance?

BIBLIOGRAPHY

Barr, R. (1987). Classroom interaction and curricular content. In D. Bloome (Ed.), *Literacy and schooling.* Norwood, NJ: Ablex.

Barr, R., & Dreeban, R. (1983). *How schools work.* Chicago: University of Chicago Press.

Carew, J., & Lightfoot, S. L. (1979). *Beyond bias: Perspectives on classrooms.* Cambridge, MA: Harvard University Press.

Denham, C., & Lieberman, A. (Eds.). (1980). *Time to learn.* Washington, DC: National Institute of Education.

Duckett, W. (Ed.). (1983). *Observation and the evaluation of teaching.* Bloomington, IN: Phi Delta Kappa.

Evertson, C. E., & Green, J. L. (1986). Observation as inquiry and method. In M. C. Wittrock (Ed.), *Handbook of research on teaching: Third edition.* (pp. 162–213). New York: Macmillan.

Flanders, N. (1970). *Analyzing teacher behavior.* Reading, MA: Addison-Wesley.

Goodlad, J. I., & Klein, M. F. (1974). *Looking behind the classroom door* (2nd ed.). Worthington, OH: Charles A. Jones Publishing.

Green, J., Harker, J., & Wallat, C. (Eds.). (1988). *Multiple perspectives analysis in classroom discourse.* Norwood, NJ: Ablex.

Lortie, D. C. (1975). *School teacher: A sociological study.* Chicago: University of Chicago Press.

Morine-Dershimer, G. (1985). *Talking, listening, and learning in elementary classrooms.* New York: Longman.

Stallings, J. A. (1977). *Learning to look.* Belmont, CA: Wadsworth Publishing Company.

Stubbs, M., & Delamont, S. (Eds.). (1976). *Explorations in classroom observation.* London: John Wiley.

NOTES

1. Lynn Myers is one of the authors of this text. The class episode reported here is drawn from her teaching at Fall-Hamilton Elementary School, Nashville, Tennessee.
2. Shirley Bassler is a teacher at Father Ryan High School, Nashville, Tennessee. This class episode was recorded during one of her classes by Alene Harris, a trained classroom observer and a contributing author of this text.
3. Goodlad, J. I. (1984). *A place called school: Prospects for the future.* New York: McGraw Hill.
4. Carew, J., & Lightfoot, S. L. (1979). *Beyond bias: Perspectives on classrooms.* Cambridge, MA: Harvard University Press.
5. Lortie, D. C. (1975). *School teacher: A sociological study.* Chicago: University of Chicago Press.
6. Morine-Dershimer, G. (1985). *Talking, listening, and learning in elementary classrooms.* New York: Longman.
7. Stallings, J. A. (1977). *Learning to look.* Belmont, CA: Wadsworth.

8. Goodlad, J. I., & Klein, M. F. (1974). *Looking behind the classroom door* (2nd ed.). Worthington, OH: Charles A. Jones Publishing.

9. One of the first observation systems used widely for the analysis of teacher–student interactions was the Flanders Interaction Analysis System. See Flanders, N. (1970). *Analyzing teacher behavior*. Reading, MA: Addison-Wesley. For a comprehensive discussion of classroom observation and analysis see Evertson, C. E., & Green, J. L. (1986). Observation as inquiry and method. In M. C. Wittrock (Ed.), *Handbook of research on teaching: Third edition* (pp. 162–213). New York: Macmillan.

10. For additional information on these and other observation systems developed by Stallings, see Stallings, J. (1983). *The Stallings observation system*. Unpublished manuscript, Vanderbilt University, Peabody Center for Effective Teaching, Nashville, Tennessee, or contact Jane Stallings, Houston Center for Effective Teaching, University of Houston, Houston, Texas.

11. Coleman, J., Campbell, E., Hobson, C., McPartland, J., Mood, A., Weinfield, F., & York, R. (1966). *Equality of educational opportunity*. Washington, DC: United States Government Printing Office.

CHAPTER 3

Teaching Effectiveness: Classroom Practices and Characteristics That Enhance Learning

Jane Stallings developed an initial detailed outline for this chapter and prepared the first draft for much of it. The Snapshot and beginning pages of the chapter were written by her. Much of the chapter as a whole is based on her ideas, insights, and suggestions. Brian Hansford wrote the section entitled "Classroom Climate."

INTRODUCTION

Chapter 3 is a survey of some of the teacher characteristics and classroom practices that educational researchers have found to be effective in producing learning. The teacher characteristics discussed are primarily personality traits and ways of interacting with students. The classroom practices are of four types: learning time, classroom organization and management, active learning, and expectations and rewards for student performance. The chapter is intended to provide knowledge about teachers and classrooms that you can use to analyze the teaching you observe as well as to decide how you will teach if and when you become a teacher.

Before you start the chapter, however, a caution is in order. Teaching effectiveness as described here is not all there is to successful classroom performance. Many factors determine how much and how well students learn. Other factors are discussed later in this text, in Chapter 6 for example; and still others remain for your study in future courses.

The Snapshot and the first few pages of chapter narrative provide illustrations and an overview of effective classroom practices. The Analysis section asks you to compare what you read with general conclusions about classrooms made by a contemporary researcher. The Educational Research section cautions that much is still unknown about classroom effectiveness.

Before you proceed, however, pause for a moment to complete the following exercise in order to place what you are about to read into a personal frame of reference.

1. Think about your classroom teachers from the past. Who was the best teacher you have had? (The person might have been an elementary or high school teacher, a college professor, or a Sunday school teacher.)

2. Now think of the characteristics that made that person so special that you remember him or her more than others. If appropriate, include among your list of characteristics two types: (1) personal characteristics and (2) teaching practices the person used in the classroom.

3. Write five characteristics of your best teacher on a piece of paper.

4. Compare your list with those of others in the class.

5. Keep your list and, as you read, compare it with the ideas described in this chapter. You will be asked to look at the list again at the end of the first main section of the chapter and in the Conclusion.

SNAPSHOT

The Snapshot for this chapter describes short segments of two classes: sixth-grade reading and ninth-grade social studies.[1] As you read, consider two things:

- In what ways is the instruction in the two classes different from classroom instruction you have experienced?

- Which elements of the instruction seem to you to represent characteristics of "effective teaching"? Why do you think so?

SIXTH-GRADE READING

Ms. Sweeny: Terry, what does Langston Hughes mean by the line in the poem, "Life ain't been no crystal stair"?

Terry: That life has not always been perfect. There are problems sometimes.

Ms. Sweeny: That's a good way to say it, Terry. What did the author say to make you think that?

Terry: The mother in the poem said the stair of life had tacks in it and flat places.

Ms. Sweeny: Good analysis, Terry. But what in the world is a tack in life? Can you tell us, Joe?

Joe: Something that kind of tears you up.

Ms. Sweeny: That's right, Joe. Have you ever had a tack in your life?

Joe: (Looks thoughtful and utters softly) When I didn't make the football team last fall.

Ms. Sweeny: That was a very big tack, Joe, but you didn't give up. Did anyone encourage you to hang in there like this mother did with her son?

Joe: Yeah, my big brother.

This interaction is taking place in a sixth-grade remedial reading classroom in an inner-city middle school. The class has just read Langston Hughes' poem "Mother to Son," and the teacher is preparing them to read Hughes' short story "Thank You, Ma'm." The teacher and students have read some passages aloud. With each reading the teacher asks thought-provoking questions that relate the students' background experiences and feelings to the characters in the story.

The teacher also explains some of the new words in the story to be read, each time checking for the students' understanding by asking them to use the words in the context of the story and in their own lives. For example:

Ms. Sweeny: The author says one of the characters is a "purse snatcher." What is a purse snatcher, Billy?

Billy: A person who takes someone's purse very quickly.

Ms. Sweeny: Right, a purse snatcher steals purses quickly. This story has two characters: an old woman and a purse snatcher—one who took something quickly.
Now I want you to feel what it would be like to be an old lady going home from work late at night and have someone run past and grab your purse. Visualize it and write a few words.

[All of the children look pensive and then write.]

Ms. Sweeny:	How did you feel?
Several students:	Scared, angry, tired, lonely.
Ms. Sweeny:	Read the next three pages to yourselves now, and see how the old lady surprises the purse snatcher. How would you feel if you were the purse snatcher? What would you do?

The teacher uses focusing questions to guide the students' silent reading. Student interpretations of passages are solicited and respected. Toward the end of the period she asks the students to write two paragraphs comparing how "Thank You, Ma'm" by Hughes is similar to and different from a Hemingway short story they read during the previous week.

NINTH-GRADE SOCIAL STUDIES

In a rural midwestern school, a social studies teacher of current events is preparing to show a videotaped discussion of a tax-reform proposal involving state and federal politicians. He tells the students to think about how the tax reforms that will be discussed would affect them and their families. He gives the students a structured overview chart showing the major issues of the tax reform being proposed. The chart also has the names of the politicians who participated in the discussion. The students are asked to listen and record statements and points of view on each issue made by each discussant.

At the end of the tape, students are given five minutes to analyze which issues were covered and what the contrasting points of view were. Next, students meet in predetermined small work groups to collaborate on a report of issues covered. Each group is asked to develop its own point of view and some defenses of it. The teacher provides the groups with other sources of information (for example, newspaper and journal articles). After twenty minutes of group work, the recorders for each group make summary statements.

An argument develops about who would gain and who would lose if the tax reform is enacted. The teacher makes certain that all points of view are heard. All students have a chance, but they must back up opinions with facts.

The assignment for the following week requires a person from each group to interview an adult family member, a banker, an educator, someone representing the medical profession, and someone from the armed forces. The interview is to focus on how the person being interviewed thinks the tax reform will affect him or her and the work that person does. The goal of the assignment is to learn about different points of view on a critical issue and to estimate how well people seem to be informed on the issue.

The stated goal of this teacher is to create knowledgeable, thinking people who can thrive in a democracy. Above the classroom door he has a sign: "You can fool some of the people all of the time; and all of the people some of the time; but you can't fool all of the people all of the time. Don't be fooled! Knowledge is Freedom!"

CHARACTERISTICS OF EFFECTIVENESS

All of the students in the classrooms described in the Snapshot were deeply involved in their lessons. That involvement resulted from the excellent preparation and planning by the two teachers. In each case, the teacher's expectations and objectives for the class were clearly specified on the chalkboard or in folders passed out in advance.

Preparation

In the sixth-grade reading class, the teacher listed on the chalkboard the pages that would be covered and the written assignment to be completed during the 55-minute class period. For extra points, there was a riddle to be solved by those who entered class early. All needed materials were in stacks on the first desk of each row. When the bell rang at the start of the class, the teacher called for answers to the riddle while a student monitor took the roll with a seating chart. Materials were passed down the rows, and the lesson began within three minutes.

Grouping

In the ninth-grade social studies classroom, copies of the tax-reform proposals were on the work tables. A question on the chalkboard asked: "How will tax reform affect teenage paychecks? See pages 48 and 63." Students entering the room started quickly thumbing through the materials. The room had five tables to which the students had been assigned so that high, medium, and low achievers were represented at each table. Each table of students formed a collaborative work group to carry out group assignments. The facilitator at each table took the roll and checked missing members on the roll sheet.

Variety

Although the students being served in both classrooms described above were very different in age, cultural background, and subject matter, the two teachers were using similar instructional strategies. Many of their strategies have been identified through classroom research as being effective in keeping students involved in their studies and learning the required subject matter. Each teacher planned a variety of interesting activities for each class period, so that the students would read, write, speak, listen, speculate, and visualize other times and places. When students are encouraged to engage in a variety of learning activities, they are more likely to stay involved in their lessons and are more likely to integrate their learning into useful intellectual patterns. When the teacher structures the content to be learned into patterns that the students can recognize, the students can more easily store the learning in long-term memory and retrieve the information in new situations.

Involvement

Both teachers involved their students in thought-provoking discussions. They used strategies that required all of the students to think and to participate. Their comments on students' contributions were low key, specific, and supportive.

Nevertheless, the extent to which the teachers described in the Snapshot were effective with students depended on more than the techniques they used in the classroom. The teachers also had to be perceived positively by their students and had to be influential with them. If this were not the case, the students would have simply "turned them off." Therefore, before attention in this chapter goes to specific elements of classroom effectiveness, it is first directed toward teacher characteristics that researchers say have positive influences on students.

THE INFLUENCE OF TEACHERS ON STUDENTS

A mid-1980s study of the influence of teachers on students reported a number of results about (1) the extent to which teachers have an impact on students and (2) the types of teacher characteristics that seem to generate the strongest impact (Csikszentmihalyi & McCormack, 1986).[2] Although the study focused on teenage students and their teachers, its data and conclusions are enlightening for other school levels as well. The information described below is drawn primarily from that study.

Time Students Spend with Teachers

American teenage school students spend approximately three hours a day (weekends and vacations are factored in) with teachers. In contrast, they spend about two hours with other adults, including their parents, and about four hours with peers. Much of the time with other adults involves diverse activities (watching television and shopping, for instance), and comparatively little direct discussion or passing of information from the adult to the teenager occurs. Therefore, teachers have sufficient time and contact to make more of a significant influence on teenagers than do other adults, all else being equal.

The Influential 9 Percent

As a result, teachers—at least some teachers—have significant impact on their students. In the Csikszentmihalyi and McCormack (1986) study, when teenagers were asked who or what influenced them to become the kinds of people they are, 58 percent mentioned one or more teachers, 88 percent said peers, and 90 percent listed parents. But further analysis of the responses shows that only a limited number of teachers with whom the students had contact actually produced the influence noted. The teenagers reported that only 9 percent of all their teachers had the impact that they mentioned. Ninety-one percent left no such mark.

Sorting out what distinguishes the teachers who have powerful influence over students from those who do not is, of course, important to improving teaching effectiveness. Psychological and sociological theories suggest that influential teachers are those who are seen by students as having (1) control over resources that they desire, (2) power to reward or punish, (3) expertise in a particular area of knowledge, and (4) status and power in a general sense. But teenagers interviewed in the Csikszentmihalyi and McCormack study indicated that these teacher traits were not by themselves enough to influence them so significantly. Instead, these teenagers said the influential teachers also

1. *generated enthusiasm* for learning through their personal involvement with the subject matter and skill in teaching it,
2. *communicated a sense of excitement* about learning the material,
3. *made learning pleasant* instead of a chore,
4. *explained things* in original or unusual ways,
5. *were especially approachable*—easy to talk to and ready to listen,
6. *instilled student self-confidence,* and
7. *showed that they really cared* about the students.

Teacher's Attitude Is Critical

In sum, the critical characteristics seemed to be the teachers' attitudes toward teaching, toward the subject matter, and toward student success in learning. The influential teachers exhibited enthusiasm, dedication, and energy that showed that they believed learning what they are teaching is worth the time and effort. Students in the study often described learning under these teachers as follows: "You learn a lot because it doesn't seem like work; it's something you really *want* to do." (Csikszentmihalyi & McCormack, 1986, p. 419)

Making Learning Meaningful and Worthwhile Is Important

This information about teacher influence seems to highlight a dimension of teaching effectiveness that has not often been stressed in older studies or in much of the classroom effectiveness literature. Older studies have said that effective teachers are enthusiastic, accessible, caring, and friendly; and more recent classroom effectiveness literature (such as most of that reported later in this chapter) has added precision to those earlier ideas by identifying specific teaching strategies that produce more learning than others and by indicating how teachers can produce greater gains in student achievement. Now, information such as that reported in this study adds to those ideas the belief that the most influential teachers are the ones who, in addition to being entertaining and caring and in addition to using the most effective techniques, also *make what they teach meaningful* and enable students to see its *inherent worth* to their own lives.

More than Entertainers and Technicians

This means that especially influential teachers are those who teach so that students are *intrinsically* motivated to learn. Students come to math class because they want to learn math. They enjoy it and believe it is valuable to them personally. Teachers who have this effect on students do not just entertain and care about students *in addition to* their teaching, and they are not just effective or efficient in a technical way. They are teachers whose strengths are tied directly to what they teach. They might use extrinsic gimmicks to motivate students, and they probably use efficient teaching techniques; but most importantly, they make students want to learn what they teach. In a sense, they infect the students with their enthusiasm for learning.

At this point, before your attention is redirected to effective classroom approaches and techniques, pause and look at the list of characteristics you noted for your best teacher during the Introduction to this chapter.

- How closely do your characteristics match the points noted so far?

EARLY STUDIES OF CLASSROOM EFFECTIVENESS

Despite a widespread concurrence about the qualities of good teaching, precise research into what makes classroom instruction effective is a rather recent phenomenon. During the 1970s and 1980s, research into effective teaching focused primarily upon classroom organization, time management, classroom interaction, teacher planning, and teacher expectations. Researchers found that some of the characteristics generally valued in good teaching, such as being well organized, can be evaluated relatively easily; but others, such as being caring and interesting, are harder to measure. As would be expected, the characteristics that are easier to measure have been researched more thoroughly than the others. So far, data from the research have contributed significantly to the understanding of effective teaching, but much remains to be discovered.

Time as a Variable

Several large-scale research studies conducted during the 1970s and funded primarily by the federal government assessed the effectiveness of compensatory education programs such as Head Start, Follow Through, bilingual education, and special education. At that time, the government was funding many different models of education for these programs, and no one knew which of the strategies would be most effective in helping the targeted children learn to read, write, and compute. Because so little was known about effective instruction, most of these studies were correlational in nature. That is, they were designed to look for relationships between different phenomena. In several studies, data collected from observing a large number of classrooms were compared to student test data, using a process–product design. These studies typically sought to determine what kind of instruction would be most effective for these special and economically deprived children.

The Use of Time Was a Significant Variable

For example, when researchers found classrooms in which students were making unexpected gains in mathematics, they analyzed what the teachers of the high performers were doing that was instructionally different from the teachers of comparable students who were not achieving so well in mathematics. The findings of these different studies were quite consistent. The *use of time* in the students' instruction was a significant variable affecting how well the students performed. Although all the school districts studied had comparable amounts of time *allocated* for schooling, the districts, schools, and teachers *used* the time very differently.

Additional studies of the use of time for instruction followed quickly. Because these studies looked at *time* as the variable to be studied, their results were easy to compare. Time is a universal. It is a factor in all instruction; it is constant (one minute equals one minute everywhere); and it is easily measured, quantified, and analyzed. (See, for example, Stallings, 1975.)[3]

Findings from studies such as these indicate that student academic achievement is *not* tied to the mere length of the school day or the length of a class period. Longer school days or longer class periods did not produce greater student achievement in either elementary or secondary schools. How the available time was *used* was the important factor.

EFFECTIVE TEACHING PRACTICES

Studies on teacher effectiveness such as those described above indicate that what teachers do in classrooms does make a difference in what students learn. They also show, to some degree, which teacher behaviors or practices appear to contribute most effectively to student learning. This section of the chapter describes some of the teacher practices found to be effective in recent studies. They are divided into four categories:

- learning time,
- classroom organization and management,
- active teaching strategies, and
- teacher expectations and rewards for student performance.

Classrooms Are Unique

As you read about effective classroom practices, it is important to remember that (1) classrooms and their occupants possess characteristics that set them apart from other types of group meetings, and (2) many of those characteristics are in place before the students and teachers arrive at the classroom door. Those characteristics or elements affect teaching and learning.

One researcher, Walter Doyle (1977, 1980, 1986),[4] says that classroom environments contain the following elements:

The Classroom Environment

- *Multidimensionality:* Large numbers of events and tasks occur because of the number of people present, the goals to be accomplished, the schedules to be met, the resources to be used, and so forth.
- *Simultaneity:* Many things happen at the same time.
- *Immediacy:* The pace of things is rapid.
- *Unpredictability:* Many classroom events happen unexpectedly.
- *Publicness:* Events occur in the open and are witnessed by all present.
- *History:* Classes meet day after day, and classmates and teachers develop common experiences, routines, and norms, which guide future events.

Classrooms Are Not Alike

It is also important to remember that all classrooms are not alike and that their differences have an impact on the effectiveness of specific teaching practices. Some strategies work better at lower grade levels, and some are better with older students; some are more successful with lower socioeconomic status students, some with learners from more affluent backgrounds; some are appropriate with one type of teacher objectives and not others (Brophy & Good, 1986).[5]

In addition to these two reminders concerning the nature of classrooms, you need to keep in mind several other cautions regarding what will be said about effective classroom practices.

1. The effective practices reported here do not include all effective classroom strategies.

2. The extent to which each practice is effective varies from classroom to classroom, school to school, and teacher to teacher.

3. A preponderance of the studies that have led to the conclusions reported here were conducted at elementary grade levels, in basic skill subjects, and with low socioeconomic status students.

4. Many of the studies seem to overemphasize direct instruction and slight more interactive approaches.

5. In most cases, the primary criterion on which the effectiveness of the practice studied was judged is student academic achievement. Certainly there are other bases for deciding which classroom strategies and teaching methods are best; for example, the extent to which they enhance student self-concepts, peer group interactions, and the more affective outcomes from learning.

6. Research on effective classroom practice is relatively new and continuing. Data generated in the years ahead may require modification of present conclusions.

7. The general context in which learning takes place influences how much students learn just as significantly as what happens in classrooms. For example, student socioeconomic status, intellectual abilities, physical conditions, and grade levels also make a difference.

Therefore, it is important not to overgeneralize from what is reported.

Learning Time

Both common sense and research studies indicate that students of teachers who efficiently channel available classroom time to learning tasks usually learn more than students of teachers who do not. However, the actual amount of time used by different teachers for learning varies greatly, and many teachers do not realize how often they fail to use time for this purpose.

Teacher Awareness of Use of Time

In one study of how varied teachers' use of time is, reading teachers of grades seven through twelve were divided into two groups (Stallings, Needels, & Stayrock, 1978).[6] One group consisted of teachers whose students showed about average achievement gains in reading, and the other was made up of teachers whose students showed unusually high achievement. The observers studied how each group of teachers used time. The teachers of the average-achieving classes spent only 12 percent of class time on active instruction. They spent 26 percent of the time on management chores, such as taking roll, passing out papers, making assignments, and grading papers. Their students were doing seatwork for 50 percent of the time and were off task 12 percent of the time. The teachers of the students making greater gains provided active instruction for 50 percent or more of the time, four times as much as the other group. They spent only 12 percent of class time on management. Students in the high-achieving classes were on task 9 percent more of the time than those in the average classes.

The diagrams in Figure 3–1 illustrate how two teachers observed by an author of this text used a 50-minute class period in eighth-grade English. The subject matter being taught and the student ability levels were comparable.

Academic Learning Time

Academic learning time is the class time students spend engaged in academic tasks that they can perform at high success rates. It is derived from three other measures: *allocated time,* the time designated for students to work on academic tasks; *engaged time,* the portion of allocated time during which students actually engage in academic tasks; and *student success,* a measure of student success or failure at the academic tasks (Berliner, 1979; Fisher et al., 1980).[7]

Generally, classes with large proportions of academic learning time yield higher levels of academic achievement than other classes. In essence, students learn more if they are *engaged* in *quality* instruction at which they can *succeed.*

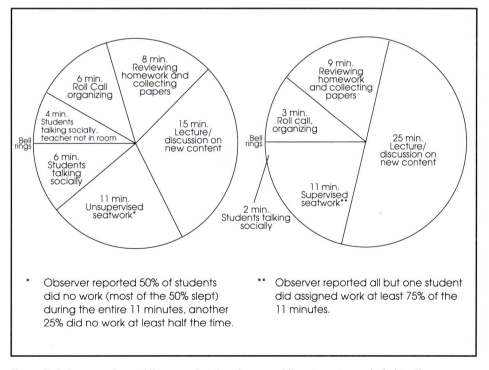

Figure 3–1. A comparison of the ways two teachers used the same amount of class time.

This means that effective teachers need to engage students in academic learning, not just provide the time for the learning to take place. It means that the activities and subject matter must be set at the appropriate level of difficulty, the instruction must be paced appropriately, and the students must experience continuous progress. (See Denham & Lieberman, 1980.)[8]

Allocated Time

One of the first studies to illustrate the importance of academic learning time was a study designed to look at beginning teachers in California in 1978 (Fisher et al., 1978).[9] That study analyzed how teachers of second- and fifth-grade children used school time. The investigators first found that although most children spent six hours of the day at school, they spent only four and three-quarters hours in the classroom. The researchers considered this—what is left after time is subtracted for lunch, for students passing in the halls from one class to another, and for recess—the time allocated for instruction.

Exposure to Instruction

Having defined the real allocated instruction time, they looked more closely at how teachers used it: They found that the time different teachers actually spent providing instruction varied from two to four hours. Some children were exposed to instruction for only one-third of the school day. Not surprisingly, the children who received more instruction achieved more in reading and mathematics.

Moreover, the researchers also found that the amount of time during which instruction was provided in classrooms was also *not equal* to the time in which students were actually learning. At times, teachers were providing instruction, or *opportunities* for children to learn, but they were not learning. These non-learning times occurred, for example, when students were not listening, not responding, not reading, or otherwise not involved in their work.

Engaged Time

Of the two to four hours of instructional time available to students in the study, students generally were *engaged* in their studies from one and one-half to three and one-half hours for the total school day. As might be expected, students who were engaged in their studies longer made more academic gain.

Maximizing engagement rates, however, is not simply a matter of making teachers aware of how they are using time. It also depends on the teacher's ability to organize and manage the classroom as an efficient learning environment in which academic activities are appropriate to the students' levels of development, lessons are conducted smoothly, transitions are brief and orderly, and students take little time to be inattentive or to behave otherwise inappropriately (Brophy & Good, 1986). Several techniques for accomplishing this set of optimal circumstances are described later in this chapter.

Optimal Error Rate

Related to academic learning time is the concept of *optimal error rates*, the rate of correct and incorrect student responses that lead to the highest student achievement. Some research indicates that when the purpose of instruction is to teach new knowledge or to review recently learned information, the most effective classrooms are those in which teacher questions yield a minimum of about 75 percent correct responses and in which seatwork yields about 90 percent correct answers for most students (Brophy & Evertson, 1976; Brophy, 1979; Rosenshine, 1983).[10]

Continuous Progress

The concept of *continuous progress* is also related to academic learning time. If students are to learn efficiently, they need to be engaged in lessons suited to their level of achievement, appropriate to the subject matter being taught, and paced at a rate that they can keep up with. Usually, the best lessons are those that permit the greatest number of students to progress continuously, in relatively small increments, with high rates of success, with a minimum of confusion, and without loss of momentum from step to step (Brophy & Good, 1986).

Time as a Teaching Technique

Wait-Time

The discussion above indicates that teachers can use the teaching time available to them in a variety of ways, from least to most efficient; that is, they can maximize academic learning time. But time can also be used effectively in another sense. It can be used as a teaching technique in and of itself. One such use of time is *wait-time*. Wait-time occurs when teachers are questioning students, as in recitation or in discussion. It is the time between the end of a teacher's question and the time when a student is called upon to respond. It is the time when a teacher can logically expect students to be thinking about the question because they might be designated to supply the answer.

Teacher waiting before calling on a student.

Teachers usually wait about eight-tenths of a second between asking a question and calling on a student. But when they wait about three full seconds instead (some researchers say three to five seconds), a number of positive things happen: the student who responds talks longer, more of the other students offer a greater number of unsolicited but appropriate responses, fewer students fail to respond, students demonstrate increased confidence in their answers, more of the students whom the teachers consider academically "slow" respond, and the student answers involve higher levels of thought (Berliner, 1985; Gage, 1984; Gage & Berliner, 1984).[11]

Apparently there are no negative effects of using three-second wait-time. Interestingly, it may be a bit difficult for the teacher at first, as teachers who try a longer wait-time than they have been accustomed to using report that the three-second pause seems as if it is much longer.

Classroom Organization and Management

In study after study over the last two decades, the areas of greatest concern for new and experienced teachers alike are classroom organization and management. These areas are often problem areas for teachers, and students simply do not learn effectively if classrooms are not organized and managed well.

But successful organization and management are not simple processes of setting down rigid rules and insisting on conformity to them. *Classroom organization* must be a well-developed, flexible plan of operation which has limits but which also tolerates exceptions and variations when goals and circumstances warrant them. *Classroom management* must be a thoughtful implementation of the plan by the teacher, who makes on-the-spot judgments about when to apply which rules and procedures and how to communicate those decisions to students. In short, successful classroom organization and management are multifaceted processes that establish a classroom order that can be maintained while class goals, contexts, and events continuously shift (Doyle, 1979, 1984, 1986).[12] The two classes and teachers described in the Snapshot for this chapter exemplify classroom organization and management in a number of ways that you can observe.

Classroom Climate

Although the physical setting and the types of instructional activities used in many classrooms seem surprisingly similar, classrooms differ widely, and a number of those differences can be attributed to *classroom climate*—that is, the psychological and social feeling or atmosphere that exists in each classroom. Some teachers create an atmosphere in their classrooms that is supportive, comfortable, friendly, and relaxed; others oversee threatening, competitive, and tense climates. It is difficult to describe precisely what creates a particular classroom climate, but research data suggest that a great number of interacting factors are involved. (See Hansford, 1988, pp. 166–187.)[13]

The paragraphs that follow, which show the use of four variables through which classroom climate can be looked at, describe some of these factors. In these paragraphs, classroom climate variables are clustered into four major groups—ecology, milieu, social system, and culture. (See Anderson, 1982.)[14] All

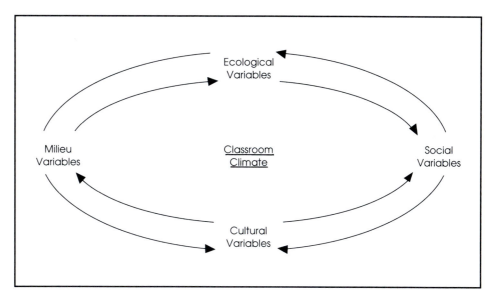

Figure 3–2. Variables involved in classroom climate.

four clusters mentioned interact with each other and have both positive and negative effects on classroom climate as a whole. (See Figure 3–2.)

Ecology
- *Ecology,* as used here, refers to the physical aspects of a classroom—the things that make it up. It includes, for example, the classroom space as a whole, displays on the walls, chalkboards, the equipment present, and the learning resources.

Milieu
- *Milieu* means that part of a classroom setting that stresses the "feeling" or "interpersonal atmosphere." It includes the aspect of the setting that some observers call teacher and student "morale." The idea can be illustrated as follows: When both teachers and students have a high degree of satisfaction with what happens in their classrooms, a positive climate develops; and when they are unhappy, threatened, or "burned out," the climate has a noticeably different "feel" to it.

Social System
- The *social system* relates to the informal and formal rules guiding interpersonal relationships in classrooms and in schools generally. Included under the heading are student-teacher relationships, principal-teacher interactions, teacher-parent associations, and so forth. An important variable in this aspect of classroom environment is the way in which communication between teachers and students is developed; for example, how well the teacher communicates information to students and helps them understand rules and policies; and how extensively students are involved in or consulted on policy and rule formulation.

Culture
- *Culture* refers to the values, belief systems, and norms existing in classrooms and schools. Variables included under this heading are expectations; teacher commitment; clarity of goals; and teacher use of praise, criticism, and rewards.

A positive classroom climate is not developed or maintained by chance. It arises from careful planning and thought, and many of the day-to-day actions of teachers and students affect it, both positively and negatively. Clearly the way teachers praise and criticize students is involved, as is the extent to which students perceive teachers as being impartial, credible sources of information, and predictable, trustworthy people.

A good deal of power is vested in teachers; classroom climate is therefore greatly influenced by the teachers' use of that power and their willingness to delegate some aspects of power to students. Although learning can and does take place in very oppressive classroom climates, in those classrooms where there is a positive socioemotional climate, teachers and students are happier and less stressed, and there is greater student desire for participating in learning.

Minimizing Problems

Preplanned Management Plan

Research indicates that some organization and management practices are more effective than others in keeping students attentive to academic tasks and engaged in them. Successful classrooms generally have an organization and management plan developed ahead of time by the teacher, communicated to the students at the start of the school year, and maintained consistently throughout the year. They are classrooms in which efficient routines and procedures are clear and consistently followed, in which teacher and students clearly understand expectations about student behavior and consequences of inappropriate behavior, and in which the rules and procedures are enforced and reinforced (Kounin, 1970; Emmer, Evertson, & Anderson, 1980; Evertson & Emmer, 1982).[15]

Classroom Structures

Effective classroom organization and management require that the teacher start off the school year right, and starting the school year right involves the establishment of successful *classroom structures* from the first day. That means announcing thoughtfully formulated rules and procedures, demonstrating them, enforcing them, and developing them into routines. To accomplish this, teachers must know what their management plan will be, teach it to the students, and watch over them closely (some researchers say "hover over them") until they have learned and accepted the system (Brophy & Good, 1986; Doyle, 1986).

The Teaching of Routines

One group of investigators looked intensively at how third-grade teachers who were known to be effective planners began their school year (Emmer, Evertson, & Anderson, 1980; Evertson & Emmer, 1982). They found that these teachers not only planned thoroughly before school started, but they spent significant amounts of time during the first weeks of the year introducing rules and procedures and establishing schedules and routines. The researchers noted that the teachers actually *taught* these organizational elements as part of their classroom instruction; they did not just present them to the students as arbitrary rules of behavior. The effective teachers told the students what was expected of them, but they also explained their expectations clearly, modeled the procedures, responded to questions, and allowed time for practice.

Setting the Stage for Teaching

In addition to developing management plans, establishing classroom structures, and following teaching routines, teachers considered to be successful classroom managers have also been found to be teachers who have set the stage for teaching in order to prevent behavior problems. In addition to the practices mentioned above, such efforts include arranging for well-paced lessons geared to student abilities and interests; setting up efficient routines for taking care of procedural tasks; and creating a classroom climate that is task oriented, pleasant, and purposeful. Although these efforts do not focus directly on student behavior, they make classes successful because they minimize distraction from academic learning and keep students actively engaged in productive classroom work, thus minimizing the amount of trouble that they might cause (Kounin, 1970).

Withitness

Many successful classroom managers have also been found to possess a characteristic called *withitness*. They seem to know what is happening in the classroom all of the time and often can predict what is about to occur before it does. They can cut short small behavior problems before they escalate by constantly monitoring their classrooms from a position that allows them to see all of their students. Their students know these teachers are "with it"; that is, they know they can detect and deal with inappropriate behavior quickly and appropriately. The students know that if they act up, they will get caught (Kounin, 1970; Brophy, 1983).[16]

Overlapping

Often successful classroom managers are teachers who can do more than one thing at a time. They have the ability to *overlap* what they do. For example, they can monitor the entire class with frequent eye contact while conferring with an individual student and can keep their instruction flowing without disruption while taking care of routine management chores or correcting a single student's behavior (Kounin, 1970; Brophy, 1983).

Brisk Pace

Successful classroom managers usually maintain a *brisk pace*. As a result, students tend to stay on task and are unlikely to lose momentum and motivation. These teachers have all necessary materials in place before they need them, know what they expect to do without consulting their notes, avoid giving confusing directions, and rarely have to repeat or backtrack in their instructions. Without disrupting the lesson, they watch for inattention and deal with it through eye contact, gestures, verbal cues, approaches to the inattentive students, and questioning (Brophy, 1983).

Student Alerting and Accountability Techniques

Successful classroom managers also keep their students alert and accountable for their academic work through the use of certain techniques of presentation and questioning. For example, they mix the presentation of information with some questions. They state the question and look over the entire class before calling on a student to answer. This encourages all to listen and to think about the question because anyone might be designated to answer. They call on students in rather random order, but they get to everyone frequently. They intersperse individual responses with choral responses when those will work. They call on volunteers and on those whose hands are not up. They ask students to comment on other student responses. They ask follow-up questions (Kounin, 1970; Brophy, 1983).

Lesson Variety

Also, successful classroom managers provide for variety in their lessons. They have whole group, small group, and individual activities; they present short lectures; they conduct recitation sessions; and they assign and monitor seatwork. They provide time to explain ideas and directions and provide feedback on academic content. They use different types of materials. They use the techniques listed earlier, but they avoid monotony (Brophy, 1983).

Successful classroom managers are sensitive to student inattention; and they monitor student work for signs of confusion and lapses of concentration. They

A teacher doing several things at the same time.

arrange desks to direct student attention. To avoid boredom, they vary activities, teach lessons of appropriate length, and provide for transitions that minimize wasted time (Brophy, 1983).

Structuring Space

Finally, successful managers structure physical classroom space to accommodate different types of learning activities, to make sure that all students are visible and can be reached for independent help, and to minimize traffic flow problems and congested areas (Emmer, Evertson, & Anderson, 1980; Brophy, 1983; Good & Brophy, 1986; Evertson & Emmer, 1982; Smith & Geoffrey, 1968).[17]

Teacher as Ringmaster

This long list of things that successful classroom managers do to minimize classroom behavior problems has been thought of by some researchers in terms of *teacher as ringmaster*. Like circus ringmasters, effective teachers constantly manage people, time, space, content, and materials. They make decisions and communicate directions virtually all the time. They do all of this within an overall system that includes

- attention to individual characteristics and differences;
- preparation of the classroom as an effective learning environment;
- organization that maximizes student engagement in learning;
- development of workable housekeeping procedures and rules of conduct; and

techniques of group management, motivation, and conflict resolution (Brophy, 1983).

Handling Misbehavior

To this point, the discussion of effective classroom organization and management has dealt with approaches to teaching and techniques that tend to prevent misbehavior in the classroom. The focus now turns to approaches and techniques for handling misbehavior when it does occur.

Violent Behavior

Although traumatic when they occur, severe types of disruptive behavior in schools, such as physical violence, theft, robbery, and vandalism, are rare in most schools. When they do occur, they usually happen in corridors, lunchrooms, and outside school buildings rather than in classrooms. If a teacher is present when they happen, the teacher must, of course, take appropriate action (1) to protect others, (2) to stop the behavior, and (3) to report the incident to school and/or legal officials. The teacher's action should be cautious, sensitive, responsible, commonsensical, and forthright. The people involved should be turned over to other authorities.

The focus of the discussion here, however, is on the more typical instances of classroom misbehavior—tardiness, class cutting, inattention, talking, name-calling, mild forms of verbal aggression, pushing, punching, neglecting academic work, and refusing to follow directions. These types of disruptive and uncooperative acts happen frequently in classrooms, and teachers are expected to deal with them as part of their responsibility.

The Classroom Context

Probably the key to understanding what should be done when classroom misbehavior occurs is to think of it in the context of what is expected in classrooms. Teachers are expected to teach; students are expected to learn. Therefore, teachers plan classroom activities in order to accomplish certain learning purposes, and they arrange what they and the students do based on those plans. When student behavior does not inhibit the accomplishment of the teacher's purposes, difficulties normally do not arise. Problems do occur when student behavior is at cross purposes with teacher expectations. This then constitutes *misbehavior* (Doyle, 1986; Kounin, 1970; Emmer, Evertson, & Anderson, 1980; Evertson & Emmer, 1982).

Sometimes the misbehavior is limited to a single student whose actions are inappropriate; other times, it is more widespread. Even a small degree of disruptive behavior is likely to be visible to other students, and this, in turn, means that it may spread to others in the class.

When misbehavior occurs, then, the teacher's tasks are (1) to prevent it from spreading, (2) to extinguish it, and (3) to get the class back on track. Teachers who are considered effective classroom managers of misbehavior intervene quickly and with the smallest possible amount of disruption to the normal flow of events.

Specific Interventions

Some effective *specific interventions* are nonverbal signals such as direct eye contact, frowns, gestures, and teacher movement toward the misbehaving student or students. Others are verbal *"soft imperative" suggestions or questions* such as "It's time to settle down." "Why don't you get your book out quietly?" Others include praise, manipulation of privileges, isolation, seat changes, and detention (Erickson & Mohatt, 1982; Borman, Lippincot, Matey, & Obermiller, 1978; Doyle, 1986).[18]

Cognitive Behavior Modification Systems

In addition to specific interventions, several general approaches to dealing with disruptive or uncooperative students have been found to be effective in some classrooms. One of these approaches is based on *cognitive behavior modification techniques*. This approach starts with the principle that appropriate behavior should be rewarded and inappropriate behavior discouraged and ignored. It applies the principle to classes as a whole, rather than to individual misbehaving students. It includes components that encourage students to think about their behavior and to control themselves, rather than only respond to external rewards and punishments assigned by the teacher.

Effective cognitive behavior modification techniques tend to be more than simple rewards and punishments. In addition, they stress teaching students to think about their behavior and accept responsibility for it. They teach students self-monitoring and self-control skills. Often they involve formal contracts with stipulated performance standards. Students are expected to do certain things to receive particular rewards; they are punished for unwanted behaviors. Since they know the consequences of their behavior ahead of time, they tend to see the system as a fair bargain (Brophy, 1983).

Counseling and Therapy-Based Systems

The Teacher Effectiveness Training Approach

Another effective approach to dealing with disruptive and uncooperative behavior is based on ideas from counseling and psychotherapy. One such system is called *Teacher Effectiveness Training*.[19] This system, developed by psychologist Tom Gordon (1974), focuses on interpersonal conflict situations and provides a schema to analyze the conflict based on who *owns* the problem. (See Figure 3–3.) For instance, when a conflict occurs between a teacher and a student, it is analyzed to determine whether the problem is *owned* by the teacher (the teacher is experiencing the primary frustration), whether it is *owned* by the student (the

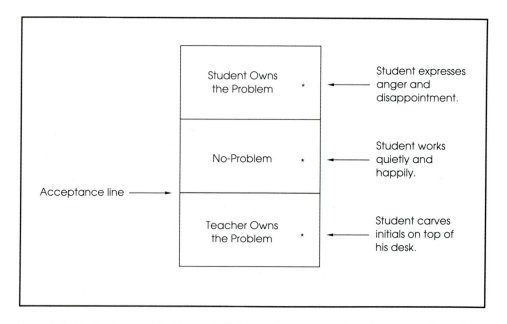

Figure 3–3. Gordon's schematic representation of problem ownership and the acceptance line for student behavior.

student is experiencing the primary frustration), or whether the problem is actually *shared* by both.

Once the ownership of the problem is determined, Teacher Effectiveness Training provides interpersonal devices that the teacher can use to overcome the problem in such a way that neither the teacher nor the student "loses." The process involves a number of steps and includes two specific techniques—"active listening" and "sending *I*-messages" (Gordon, 1974; Brophy, 1983).

Reality Therapy

Another counseling-based system with a significant number of followers is William Glasser's *reality therapy*; he discusses it in his books *Reality Therapy* (1965) and *Schools without Failure* (1969).[20] This system provides guidelines for both general classroom management and for solving problems with individual students.

In its most recent form, Glasser's system for dealing with individual problem students involves ten steps to "good discipline," which he describes as nonpunitive, constructive, and no-nonsense. It holds students responsible for their behavior; sets fair and reasonable rules; requires consistent, fair, and firm enforcement; and assumes a positive, problem-solving stance by the teacher (Glasser, 1969).

Assertive Discipline

A third counseling-based system, called *Assertive Discipline*,[21] was developed by Lee and Marlene Canter (1976) around principles from assertiveness training. This approach includes the following key ideas:

1. Teachers should insist on appropriate, responsible student behavior.
2. They should not consider firm control of the classroom to be stifling or inhumane.
3. They should communicate behavior expectations to students clearly and follow up consistently.
4. Principals and parents should provide support.
5. Teachers should be assertive and not feel guilty about it.

According to the Canters, assertive teachers are positive, firm, consistent, and caring—caring about themselves to the point that they are not taken advantage of by students and caring about students to the point that they prevent them from behaving in ways that are harmful to their classmates or to themselves. These teachers are in charge of the classroom, not meek or wishy-washy; but they are calm and supportive, not hostile, abusive, or threatening. They build an environment that fosters student self-control (Charles, 1989).[22]

Common Elements of Effective Behavior Management

Although much research on the effectiveness of approaches such as these remains to be done, teachers who are applying the various strategies with apparent best results appear to be doing some things in common. They assume an instructional role in helping teach students to deal with their inappropriate behavior, rather than rejecting them, punishing them, or referring them to the office. They look for causes of the misbehavior; and they use long-term, solution-oriented approaches to problems, rather than quick attempts at extinguishing the behavior. So far, each of the approaches has its disciples and its particular desirable effects, but none has been shown to be superior to the others (Brophy, 1983; Doyle, 1986).

Too Many Variables

When you consider your own approaches to dealing with classroom behavior problems, it is important to remember that no approach or set of techniques works for all teachers or with all students. There are just too many variables involved. For example, the level of intellectual and social development of students has major implications for what is effective and what is not. In this regard, Brophy and Evertson (1976) identified four stages of student development, illustrating that different approaches fit students at different developmental stages.

Stage 1 (Kindergarten through Grades 2–3). Most children of this age are compliant and oriented toward pleasing their teachers, but they need to be socialized into the student role. They require a great deal of formal instruction, not only in rules and expectations but in classroom procedures and routines.

Stage 2 (Grades 2–3 through Grades 5–6). Students have learned most school rules and routines, and most remain oriented toward obeying and pleasing their teachers. Consequently, less time must be devoted to classroom management.

Stage 3 (Grades 5–6 through Grades 9–10). Students enter adolescence and become oriented toward peers. Many become resentful or at least questioning of authority, and disruptions resulting from attention seeking, humorous remarks, and adolescent horseplay become common. Classroom management once again becomes more time-consuming, but in contrast to Stage 1, the task facing teachers is not so much one of instructing willing but ignorant students about what to do as it is motivating or controlling students who know what to do but are not always willing to do it. Also, individual counseling becomes more prominent, as the relative quiet and stability that most

A well-behaved class of first-grade students lined up to go to lunch.

A fifth-grade class "somewhat in line" to go to physical education class.

students show in the middle grades give way to the adjustment problems of adolescence.

Stage 4 (Grades 9–12). Most students become more personally settled and more oriented toward academic learning again. As in Stage 2, classroom management requires less teacher time and trouble, and classrooms take on a more businesslike, academic focus.

Although no single formula works all of the time, researchers have identified several common principles that can guide teachers as they deal with misbehavior. Those include

- respect for student individuality;
- willingness to try to understand students' problems;
- reliance on instruction and persuasion rather than force; and
- recognition that students have responsibilities as well as rights and that if they misbehave, they must suffer the consequences (Brophy, 1983).

Something to Think About

A group of high school students was having a discussion in a current events class. The topic was "life in school," and the conversation turned toward a particular teacher in the school and her relationships with students. The following dialogue took place:

Teacher: In which classes in this school would you expect everyone to behave properly nearly all of the time?
Carie: Ms. Daley's.
Teacher: What do others think?

[Virtually every other student in the class agrees with Carie.]

Teacher: Why is this the case?
Carie: It's hard to explain [long thoughtful pause]. Well, to act up in Ms. Daley's class is about like kicking a newborn puppy. It's something you just wouldn't do. No one would. She would be so hurt, and you would be so sorry.
Jeff: If someone would do something really wrong in Ms. Daley's class, the other kids would stop him. They would take her side.
Teacher: But why?
Don: We respect her.

- Can you visualize Ms. Daley? What would cause students to think of a teacher in this way?
- Why are only a few teachers perceived in this way?

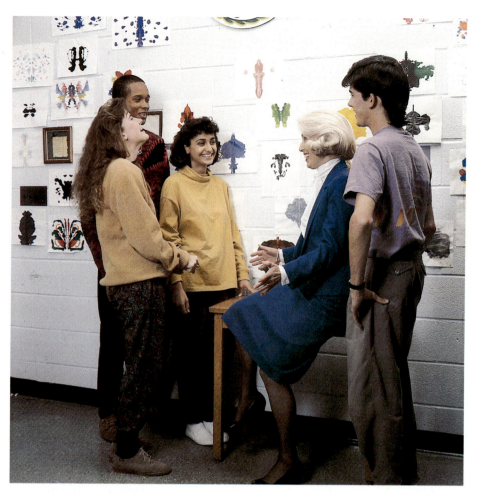

Shirley Daley and her students.

Grouping

We now turn from dealing with disruptive behavior to the classroom organization practice of grouping students. In some studies, various arrangements for grouping students have been found to be effective; but in general the results are mixed, primarily because there are too many other factors that influence what happens within and among the groups.

For example, teachers often group students by academic ability so that they can teach to different achievement levels with a variety of students at different times in the same class. There is some evidence that this leads to positive student achievement, particularly in directly taught skill subjects such as reading and mathematics (Becker, 1977).[23] But teaching different groups in the same classroom requires different types of classroom organization and management plans, as well as different teaching skills, than whole-group instruction. It presumes self-directed study by the students. It has considerable impact on the students' self-images, their motivation, and their perceptions of each other. (See Peterson, Wilkinson, & Hallinan, 1984.)[24]

Differential Instruction

Apparently many teachers teach differently to "lower" than to "higher" groups. For example, certain studies of language classes showed that teachers emphasized different instructions with different subgroups in a class. The lessons for "low" student groups placed greater emphasis on pronunciation, grammatical errors, and understanding single words; the lessons for "high" groups stressed "getting the meaning" and often ignored pronunciation and grammatical errors (Green & Smith, 1982; Good, 1979).[25]

Another study reported that low-achieving students often receive more negative feedback, are given more directives, and are allowed fewer choices than higher-achieving students. Higher achievers are the objects of greater expectations, are given more opportunities to demonstrate what they have learned, and are permitted more choices (Weinstein, 1982).[26]

Grouping Practices and Classroom Organization

Teachers who work effectively with multiple groups in the same classroom usually have successful classroom organization and management strategies that keep most of the students on task most of the time. They can handle several purposeful student activities at once because they have taught the students the appropriate routines. When student behaviors that require attention occur, they can signal what is to be done, as well as what is acceptable and what is not. These teachers make it clear when students can ask questions and whom they can ask. They do not allow interruption of certain focused small-group instruction sessions. The students know the norms and understand (Brophy & Good, 1986; Good & Brophy, 1984; Doyle, 1986).[27]

Cooperative Learning

One approach to grouping that has received significant attention is *cooperative learning,* an instructional design that stimulates peer interaction and student-to-student cooperation in the process of fostering successful learning by all. Teams-Games-Tournaments, Student Teams Achievement Divisions, and Jigsaw are three versions of cooperative learning. (See Slavin 1980a, 1980b, 1981.)[28] The general idea of cooperative learning is that students are organized into teams that include students of different abilities. Each team is expected to work together so that all students in each group learn the material being studied. In addition to individual grades, students receive group grades. Cooperation *in* a team is stimulated by competition *among* teams. In effect, all students are rewarded if they help each other learn.

A number of cooperative-learning efforts have been studied to determine effects of the approach on academic achievement, race relations among students, and the development of mutual concern among students. Results seem to indicate positive effects on all three points for Teams-Games-Tournaments and for Student Teams Achievement Divisions but were more ambiguous for Jigsaw (Brophy, 1983). More will be said about cooperative learning in Chapter 10.

Other forms of grouping that encourage and reinforce student cooperation generally seem to have positive effects on student learning. For example, students engaged in peer tutoring (students provide resource help to each other) are involved in academic learning more of the class time than those in traditional classes. Also, classroom problem-solving lessons in which different students possess parts of information needed to solve the problem seem not only to motivate the students to cooperate but also to achieve.

Active Teaching Strategies

Students achieve more in classrooms in which their teachers actively teach and actively supervise them than in classrooms in which teachers leave them alone to work on their own for long periods of time. They learn more in classrooms in which the teachers follow a pattern of (1) presenting information and developing concepts through lectures and demonstrations, (2) elaborating and reinforcing ideas through feedback to students, and (3) preparing for seatwork through demonstrations and presentations of examples (Brophy, 1983; Soar & Soar, 1983; Good, 1979; Good, Grouws, & Ebmeier, 1983; Rosenshine, 1983).[29] Look back at the chapter Snapshot for the first three chapters of the book to refresh your memory about how the teachers interacted actively with their students.

Teacher-Provided Content

Students learn more when the teacher personally provides the content to them instead of expecting them to pick it up on their own from their readings and assignments. The teacher talks a great deal when this occurs, but the talk deals with academic rather than procedural, managerial, or behavioral matters. Also, the teacher presentations are brief, not extended lectures; and they involve questioning, recitation, and feedback on student ideas (Brophy & Good, 1986).

Teacher Presentations

The most effective teacher presentations are structured or organized in a way that the students can follow easily. Some elements of this type of presentation are initial overviews of content to be covered, advanced organizers, outlines, noticeable transitions, special emphases on the main points, summaries at the end of each subpart, and reviews of the main ideas at the end. Students also seem to learn more from well-paced presentations with a degree of *redundancy*—the main points and key concepts are repeated several times (Brophy & Good, 1986).

Seatwork

Several studies indicate that teachers who use active teaching techniques while students are engaged in seatwork have better-managed classes and greater student achievement than teachers who schedule long periods of independent, unsupervised seatwork. The effective teachers explain the seatwork with examples before the students start, demonstrate and model what is to be done, lead the students in guided practice, circulate among the students and monitor the work conscientiously, inspect individual papers frequently, provide timely and precise feedback, hover over the students, and usher the work along. For these teachers, seatwork is not a passive experience for the students or for themselves. It is not a relaxed, slow, inconsequential activity. It is serious, important classroom business, and students are kept on task (Brophy & Good, 1986; Doyle, 1984; Emmer, Evertson, & Anderson, 1980; Evertson & Emmer, 1982; Rosenshine & Stevens, 1986).[30]

Effective Teaching Functions

A number of specific things that many teachers do in their classrooms, called *teaching functions*, have been found by researchers to be noticeably effective strategies in helping students to learn and remember new information and to develop basic skills. Some functions that are especially useful when the learning is primarily memory level, when the students are young, and/or when the material is new to the students, are

- structuring the learning experience;
- reviewing and checking student work daily and reteaching if necessary;
- proceeding through lessons in small steps but at a rapid pace;
- giving detailed and repeated instructions and explanations;
- using a high frequency of questions and involving students in overt, active practice;

- providing feedback, particularly in the initial stages of learning new material;

- providing *prompts* (such as "Look at the 'e' at the end of the sentence. What does that tell you about the way the 'a' sounds?") during initial learning, enabling the students to respond to the prompt and in turn providing feedback;

- setting levels of difficulty that provide for a success rate of 80 percent or higher on initial learning;

- dividing seatwork assignments into small segments or devising ways to provide frequent monitoring;

- providing for continued student practice (overlearning) so that they have a success rate of 90 to 100 percent;

- conducting weekly and monthly reviews and reteaching if necessary; and

Teacher monitoring seatwork.

- offering praise if the answer is correct and providing correction if the response is incorrect (Anderson, Evertson, & Brophy, 1979; Rosenshine, 1983; Hawley & Rosenholtz, 1984; Bennett, 1982).[31]

Mental Linkages

Teaching strategies that produce student understanding, rather than simple recall, are usually considered more effective than others because student understanding is almost always thought to be a worthy instructional goal. But as cognitive psychologists point out, if students are to understand new ideas, they need to be able to link them to their previous knowledge and experience. Naturally, then, teachers who help students make these linkages are more effective at teaching for understanding than those who do not. These teachers help students recognize new ideas, see how they relate to ideas they already possess, and assist them in storing the ideas mentally in a way that associates the ideas with previous knowledge and that enables them to be recalled easily for a long time. (See Bransford, 1979.)[32]

Checking for Understanding

Checking for understanding is an important specific teaching technique in this context. (See Rosenshine, 1983.) If students do not understand, they are less likely to remember ideas or know how and when to use them again. To facilitate understanding, programs such as Madeline Hunter's Instructional Skills include steps that require teachers to check for students' understanding regularly before proceeding with instruction. (See Chapter 10 for more information on the Hunter model.) If students do not understand, the teacher is directed to restructure the task and provide different examples and experiences to build the required background knowledge.

Questioning

Questioning is also a significant aspect of active teaching, and when and how teachers use questioning significantly determines what students learn. For example, basic-skills instruction requires a large amount of drill and practice, and drill and practice is accomplished best with fast-paced questions that have right and wrong answers and can be answered quickly and correctly. On the other hand, instruction at higher cognitive levels requires thought-provoking questions that stimulate students to conceptualize, generalize, and evaluate ideas. They usually cannot be answered quickly and rarely have one correct response.

So far, research on questioning indicates that the more effective teacher questioners are not those who rely on one particular type of questioning. Instead, they use a variety of types of questions. They also fit questioning to their instructional purposes and adjust the level of their questions both to the conceptual level of the content they are teaching and to the intellectual abilities of their students (Brophy & Good, 1986).

Expectations and Rewards for Student Performance

Teacher Expectations

A number of years ago Rosenthal and Jacobson conducted a study of the relationship between teacher expectations and student performance and reported their findings in *Pygmalion in the Classroom* (1968).[33] They found that students whose teachers expected them to perform well did so, and students who were expected to be low achievers, in fact, were.

Other researchers have looked at the same phenomenon and have found that some teachers behave toward low achievers in ways that communicate that they expect less of them. For example, Brophy and Good (1974)[34] report that teachers act differently toward students whom they perceive as high or as low achievers in the following ways: slow students are seated farther from the teacher than high achievers, are called on to answer questions less often, are provided less wait-time to answer, are criticized more openly for incorrect responses, are praised less frequently for correct responses, are smiled at less often, receive less eye contact, are given less demanding work, are interrupted more frequently, and receive less instruction (Brophy & Good, 1974). (Also see Hamilton, 1983.)[35]

Self-Fulfilling Prophecy

The point that teacher expectations of students are reflected in actual student performance is significant, but it takes on even greater importance when the relationship is explored more thoroughly. Researchers who have done so believe that the relationship is not just a correlation. There is evidence that teacher expectations actually *cause* students to achieve or not achieve, at least to some degree. In some cases, students scored higher on tests after being changed from teachers who thought they were "slow" academically to teachers who thought they were stronger academically. The reverse happened when students were shifted from teachers who held high expectations for them to those who had lower expectations. In essence, the students' performances fulfilled the teachers' prophecies (Brophy & Good, 1974).

Something to Think About

Some years ago Charles Myers, one of the authors of this text, approached one of his ninth-grade homeroom students, Gary, who had just received his midyear report-card grades. The grades showed that Gary had failed both science and mathematics every report-card period since the beginning of the year, and Myers expressed his concern.

Gary said he was not worried because he could pass on to tenth grade even if he failed both subjects. Although Myers knew Gary was correct about passing the grade even with two failures, he instead told Gary that if he failed the two subjects, he would have to repeat the grade and remain in junior high another year.

After some doubt, Gary accepted Myers' story as if it were correct. Then, the two developed a plan for Gary to try to pass science. (Gary felt math was hopeless.)

Near the end of the school year, Ms. Baxter, Gary's science teacher, told Myers that Gary was going to pass science because of a surprising turnaround in the quality of his work since midyear. She had asked Gary about this change, and Gary said he and Mr. Myers had a special plan that would help him pass. Ms. Baxter asked Myers to explain.

Myers described what happened, including the fact that he had lied to Gary in order to force him to take science seriously. He said that Gary still did not know he lied and asked Ms. Baxter not to reveal that he had.

Ms. Baxter was shocked. She stated, "But you deliberately lied to a student."

Myers replied, "Yes, I did, and it worked. Gary is studying science and learning as a result."

> - What does this episode have to say about expectations of students and their performance?
> - Should Myers have lied to Gary as he did?

Peer Perceptions

Teacher expectations of students affect not only what teachers do to students and how those students perform; they also affect peer perceptions of classmates. In at least one study, the way in which students were perceived by their classmates was influenced by the level of questions the teacher asked of them rather than by their actual achievement. In that study (Morine-Dershimer & Tenenberg, 1981),[36] a group of teachers was trained to ask higher-level questions of low-achieving students that elicited ideas, hunches, or opinions, rather than rote answers. When students in the class were asked to select from the class roster the names of those who made good contributions to the class discussion, low-achieving students' names were checked. In classrooms where teachers asked low-achieving students only simple questions, these students were not rated as making significant contributions (Morine-Dershimer, 1982).[37]

If teachers do not believe that students can take part in a higher-level discussion, those students are not given a chance. The behavior, then, carries over from teacher to classmates. In the case of high-achieving students, high achievement is reinforced; similarly, low-achieving students' low achievement is reinforced.

Rewards and Academic Achievement

Teachers reward appropriate student performance as a regular function of their classroom responsibilities. They do so to make students feel good about themselves, to motivate them to further and more complex study, and to direct or redirect their behavior. They do so to maintain desired classroom activities and an appropriate classroom atmosphere, as well as to provide feedback to students about their performance. (See Brophy, 1981; Morine-Dershimer, 1982; Brophy & Good, 1986.)[38]

Numerous rewards and incentives can be used effectively to reinforce academic learning. They include smiles, compliments, breaks from school work, a homework-free day, names of achievers on bulletin boards, parties, and so forth. Generally, when rewards are used appropriately, they increase learning across a wide spectrum that includes grade levels, types of school, student socioeconomic status, and types of community. For instance, studies have shown that when teachers use rewards to train students in the basic classroom learning skills of attending to what is occurring, staying on task, complying with directions, and talking with the teacher, those behaviors occur more consistently. More importantly, at least in the primary grades, the use of such rewards leads to increases in student achievement (Cobb, 1972; Cobb & Hope, 1972).[39]

Reward Structures

But to be effective, rewards must fit the context in which they are used—the classroom and school setting, the peer group culture, the instructional goals, and the type of student population. They need to be offered within a set of rules and arrangements that let the students know what to expect. The rewards cannot be arbitrary, whimsical, or unfair. Students must perceive them as valuable. For instance, praise from a highly respected, demanding teacher has more value than praise from a teacher who is not respected; and praise is received differently

Classroom bulletin board that reinforces student academic performance.

by an academically motivated high achiever than by a cynical, alienated student who is about to drop out.

Reward structures themselves are of different types, and the types vary in effectiveness depending on the context in which they are used and the purposes for which they are used. Structures can be classified as individual or group, and as competitive or cooperative. *Competitive reward structures,* such as grading on a curve, have the result that when some students receive a reward, the chances of rewards for others are diminished. *Cooperative reward structures* function so that the good performance of one student can increase the likelihood of rewards for the other students. *Individual reward structures* are most effective when there are fixed criteria for reinforcement and when the probability of one receiving an award is unrelated to the probability of another's receiving a reward. Some studies indicate that low-achieving students respond to cooperative reward arrangements better than competitive ones (Slavin, 1978, 1980a, 1980b, 1981; Johnson, Johnson, & Scott, 1978).[40]

Praise

Praise, as a specific reward, is often effective in directing behavior and encouraging academic performance, but it too must be used appropriately. It seems to be most effective when it is focused on specific student achievements, so that the relationship between the student behavior and the praise is explicit. It is more effective with younger children, with lower achievers, and with students from lower socioeconomic backgrounds (Brophy, 1981; Brophy & Evertson, 1976; Soar & Soar, 1983).

ANALYSIS

This Analysis section consists of descriptions of nine common patterns of classroom activity. The descriptions are drawn from the conclusions about classrooms in J. L. Goodlad's *A Place Called School* (Goodlad, pp. 123–124).[41] That report was based on a study that investigated more than 1000 classrooms in 38 schools between 1973 and 1983. As you read, consider the questions below. Also remember that the descriptions are broad generalizations about many classrooms and would not be valid for all classes and all teachers.

- Why do you think these classrooms possessed the characteristics described?

- How would you compare the classroom practices described here with the characteristics of classroom effectiveness you just studied? Which seem consistent with what you have learned? Which do not?

- Think about the classroom practices described here that are not consistent with your understanding of classroom effectiveness. Why do you think they persist?

- In what ways do you think these classroom practices will change in future years as more data about classroom effectiveness are accumulated and disseminated to teachers and school administrators? Why do you think so?

- Which of the classroom practices will continue? Why do you think so?

PATTERNS OF CLASSROOM LIFE

1. The dominant pattern of classroom organization is whole-group instruction with twenty to thirty or more students and one teacher. Most of what goes on is intended to maintain orderly relationships.

2. Students usually work alone within a class setting and are recognized because of individual, rather than group, accomplishments.

3. The teacher is the central classroom figure in determining class activities and tone. The teacher is also virtually autonomous with respect to classroom decisions—selecting materials, determining class organization, and choosing instructional procedures.

4. For most of the time while teaching, teachers face the whole class, monitor seatwork, or check on what the students have learned. On rather rare occasions students learn directly from one another or initiate interaction with teachers. When students work in groups, they usually do the same thing side-by-side as directed by the teacher.

5. Teachers tend not to respond to the work students do in overtly positive or negative ways. Praise, correction of student performance, and guidance in how to do better the next time are infrequent. Classrooms tend not to be strongly positive or strongly negative places to be. Enthusiasm, joy, and anger are kept under control.

6. Students generally engage in a rather narrow range of classroom activities—listening to teachers, writing answers to questions, and taking tests and quizzes. They receive relatively little exposure to audiovisual aids, field trips, or guest lecturers. Except in the arts, physical education, and vocational education, they engage in little hands-on activity. Acting out, role play, dance, and manipulation of materials are rarely used.

7. Variety of teaching techniques is greatest in the lower elementary grades and least in the secondary school years.

8. Large percentages of the students are passively content with classroom life, feel positive about peers and teachers, and say they like all subjects and classroom activities. The activities they like most involve physical movement and are activities in which they seldom engage—those that involve drawing, making, shaping, moving, and interacting. These are regarded as the easiest and the least important. They also happen to be electives at the upper-grade levels and are not required for college admission.

9. Even in the early elementary years students appear not to have time to finish their lessons and do not seem to fully understand what the teacher wants them to do. A significant percentage see themselves as not getting sufficient teacher help with mistakes and difficulties.

CONCLUSION

Early in this chapter, you were asked to list characteristics exhibited by the people you remember as your best teachers. Most of the chapter described some of the characteristics of effectiveness that have been reported in recent research studies. It is now time to get your list out again and make additional comparisons.

- In what ways is your list compatible with the research findings?
- Are there any incongruities?

More than likely, there is some parallel between your list and the research findings. But there probably also are significant mismatches. The extent to which there is lack of congruence illustrates the fact that good teaching is not merely the sum of a fixed list of proven effective classroom practices. Good teaching is more than that.

Research Is Incomplete

Some of the incongruity between your ideas of good teaching and the research findings can be explained by a point that was mentioned earlier: researchers have studied some areas of classroom effectiveness but have neglected others. They simply have not had much to say, so far, about the effect on learning of the care that a teacher has for his or her students, of the teacher's love of subject matter, or of his or her sincere interest in students. These characteristics of good teaching are hard to study and difficult to document. But, despite the lack of documentation, you know intuitively that they are important.

Teaching Is Complex

Another reason for the incongruity has to do with the complexity of teaching. There are so many things for teachers to do, so many purposes to be pursued and goals to be achieved, so many student personality and character traits to be accommodated, so many classroom environmental influences to be managed, so many out-of-school influences to be overcome, and so many other intangibles that are not even recognized.

This complexity is illustrated in the writings of two scholars of the teaching process. Berliner (1985)[42] notes in one of his papers about teaching that

> researchers have found that teachers make about 10 significant decisions per hour (McKay and Maraland, 1978).[43] These are not decisions about whether Johnny can go to the bathroom. Rather, they are decisions about whether Johnny should stop fractions and go on to decimals, or whether Jane should be moved into the fast mathematics group. These complex, professional decisions take place in environments where teachers have about 1,500 distinct interactions per day with different children on different issues, in classes where 30 students need to be supervised all the time, all day long (e.g., Jackson, 1968).[44] (Berliner, 1985, p. 5.)

Gage (1978, 1984)[45] describes teaching as part science and part art. For him, the science part is the part that can be studied and analyzed for its underlying principles—the rules that, when discovered, will guide most teachers toward more effective practice. The part that is art is the part of teaching that extends beyond the underlying principles that can be studied.

According to Gage, a complete science of teaching is not attainable because good teaching will never be limited to an identifiable set of rigorous laws to be followed by all teachers. He says that teaching is more than science. It is also the artistry that involves the teacher's judgment and insight in day-to-day classroom situations, the teacher's decisions on when to apply generalizations generated by research and when to ignore them, and the teacher's ability to make practical assessments of how the multitude of variables present at any moment in a classroom should be manipulated in order to produce significant learning.

In summary, more is known about positive teacher characteristics and effective teaching practices today than ever before, and researchers and practicing teachers are providing new knowledge every day. That new knowledge has helped and will continue to help teachers to teach better. Even though teaching will continue to get better, there is nonetheless no perfect formula for good teaching.

Abstract Theory

Unscientific Personal Experience

EDUCATIONAL RESEARCH

Much More to Learn

Until the type of research described in this chapter became available, educators who wanted to know the most effective ways of teaching and organizing classes needed to rely on either theories from educational psychology or personal experiences of other teachers. But many of those theoretical ideas were developed outside real classrooms and were often found to be incorrect for many situations and impractical to apply in others. At the same time, many of the experience-based recommendations from practitioners proved to be unsystematic, incapable of being generalized, and contradictory.

Body of Knowledge

However, recent research on teacher characteristics and classroom effectiveness as described in this chapter has changed that situation. We now have the beginnings of a body of knowledge about techniques, strategies, and approaches to teaching that work better in more circumstances than others do. Therefore, educational researchers are now at the point at which they know that teachers do make a difference in terms of what students learn, and they know that certain practices are more productive than others. Many of those practices have been identified in the main part of this chapter.

Limits to What Is Known

But at the same time, all educators—researchers, college instructors, teachers, and education students—must be careful not to inflate what is known about classroom effectiveness, and they need to guard against the temptation to latch onto a few practices as panaceas for a multitude of classroom teaching difficulties. These cautions are necessary because research also points out limits to what is known about teaching.

Consider the following five points.

First, the data from research are far from complete, and the principles being formulated do not apply all of the time. Students and teachers vary; classroom conditions and school environments vary; interactions among students, teachers, and principles vary. As a result, scientific rules and generalizations about classrooms are rarely precise and without exception.

Cautions

Second, many assessments of the effectiveness of classroom practices and techniques in recent years have used student gains in achievement as their predominant criterion for success. But academic success, however important, is not the only goal of schools. For example, nearly all teachers and schools also want to socialize students and promote their affective and personal development. They want to keep poorly achieving students in their classes rather than have them drop out, even though having them in class lowers the achievement scores of the class and takes teaching time away from more immediately successful students.

Third, although teacher performance affects student performance, the link between the two is not a simple cause-effect chain. There are many variables and intervening complexities that both hinder and help the relationship—variables, for example, in the students themselves, such as their health, home environment, relationships with peers, ability to see or hear clearly, and general interest in the subject matter.

Fourth, events occur in classrooms with astonishing rapidity, and they occur among a group of twenty to thirty or more individuals simultaneously. In this context, teachers engage in hundreds of interchanges with students each day. Of necessity, many of these interchanges are spontaneous and intuitive, not theoretically based. They are not easily anticipated, predicted, or studied. Good teachers just seem to do these things well, often without thinking about them.

Fifth, teachers do not work in isolation, and sometimes the results of instruction do not show up immediately or evenly. A student may work at a particular mathematics operation for days or weeks before grasping it to the point of being able to do it correctly every time. In the meantime, explanations from another teacher, classmates, and parents may have stimulated the understanding. While studying the history of a particular period in grade nine, a student may develop insight into a novel from last year's English class. It is certainly possible that a student who has been to Europe and seen the Bastille will have a different level of understanding of the French Revolution than do classmates who have not had the same experience.

The point here is a simple one. Just as research is telling us more and more about schools and teaching, it is also telling us that we do not have all the answers. There is indeed much more to learn.

SUMMARY

The degree of influence that teachers have over students and the classroom strategies and techniques that they use affect what students learn. Teachers spend more time with students than other adults, and many students report that teachers have influenced them significantly. However, only certain teachers seem to have this influence.

Early studies of classroom effectiveness looked at how teachers used time. Their methods, which varied greatly, affected learning. Many recent studies have investigated learning time, classroom organization and management, active teaching strategies, and teacher expectations and rewards for student performance. In each dimension, certain classroom practices have been found to be more successful in producing learning than others.

To a great extent, characteristics that make teachers influential with students and classroom strategies that appear to produce the most learning seem to be consistent across the country. But caution must be exercised not to generalize too sweepingly about "the best ways to teach" because no two teachers, students, or classrooms are exactly alike, and research data are still limited.

STUDY QUESTIONS

1. In what ways is teaching an art, and in what ways is it a science? Why do you think so?

2. Look again at your list of characteristics of your best teachers. Which of these do you think *all* students would think are positive qualities of teachers? Which characteristics would raise some disagreement? How do you account for the difference?

3. Of all the characteristics of effective classrooms mentioned in this chapter, which five do you think are the most important? Justify your selection.

4. What standards besides student achievement should be used to assess classroom effectiveness? Which are, or might be, more important than student achievement? Explain your thinking.

BIBLIOGRAPHY

Berliner, D. C. (1985). Laboratory settings and the study of teacher education. *Journal of Teacher Education, 36*(6), 2–8.

Brophy, G. (1986). Teacher influences on student achievement. *American Psychologist, 41*(10), 1069–1078.

Brophy, J. E. (1983). Classroom organization and management. *Elementary School Journal, 83*(4), 265–286.

Brophy, J. (1981). Teacher praise: A fundamental analysis. *Review of Educational Research, 51*(1), 5–32.

Brophy, J. (1979). Teacher behavior and its effects. *Journal of Educational Psychology, 71*(6), 733–750.

Brophy, J., & Evertson, C. (1976). *Learning from teaching: A developmental perspective.* Boston: Allyn and Bacon.

Brophy, J. E., & Good, T. L. (1986). Teacher behavior and student achievement. In M. C. Wittrock (Ed.), *Handbook of Research on Teaching: Third edition* (pp. 328–375). New York: Macmillan.

Charles, C. (1989). *Building classroom discipline: From models to practice* (3rd ed.). New York: Longman.

Cooper, H. M., & Good, T. L. (1982). *Pygmalion grows up.* New York: Longman.

Csikszentmihalyi, M., & McCormack, J. (1986). The influence of teachers. *Phi Delta Kappan, 67*(6), 415–419.

Denham, C., & Lieberman, A. (1980). (Eds.). *Time to learn.* Washington, DC: National Institute of Education.

Doyle, W. (1986). Classroom organization and management. In M. C. Wittrock (Ed.), *Handbook of research on teaching: Third edition* (pp. 392–431). New York: Macmillan.

Gage, N. (1978). *The scientific basis of the art of teaching.* New York: Teachers College Press, Columbia University.

Gage, N. L. (1984). What do we know about teacher effectiveness? *Phi Delta Kappan, 66*(2), 87–93.

Good, T., & Brophy, J. (1984). *Looking at classrooms* (3rd ed.). New York: Harper & Row.

Hamilton, S. F. (1983). The social side of schooling: Ecological studies of classrooms and schools. *Elementary School Journal, 83*(4), 313–334.

Jackson, P. W. (1986). *The practice of teaching.* New York: Teachers College Press.

Jackson, P. (1968). *Life in classrooms.* New York: Holt, Rinehart and Winston.

Kounin, J. S. (1970). *Discipline and group management in classrooms.* New York: Holt, Rinehart and Winston.

Lortie, D. C. (1975). *School teacher: A sociological study.* Chicago: University of Chicago Press.

Morine-Dershimer, G. (1985). *Talking, listening and learning in elementary school classrooms.* New York: Longman.

Rosenshine, B. (1983). Teaching functions in instructional programs. *Elementary School Journal, 83*(4), 335–351.

Rosenshine, B., & Stevens, R. (1986). Teaching functions. In M. C. Wittrock (Ed.), *Handbook of research on teaching: Third edition* (pp. 376–391). New York: Macmillan.

Rosenthal, R., & Jacobson, L. (1968). *Pygmalion in the classroom: Teacher expectations and pupils' intellectual development.* New York: Holt, Rinehart and Winston.

Slavin, R. E. (1981). Student team learning. *Elementary School Journal, 82*(1), 5–17.

Smith, D. C. (1983). (Ed.). *Essential knowledge for beginning educators.* Washington, DC: American Association of Colleges for Teacher Education.

NOTES

1. The segments of classes described in this Snapshot were observed by Jane Stallings.
2. Csikszentmihalyi, M., & McCormack, J. (1986). The influence of teachers. *Phi Delta Kappan, 67*(6), 415–419.
3. Stallings J. (1975). Implications and child effects of teaching practices in Follow Through classrooms. *Monographs of the Society for Research in Child Development, 40*(7–8), 50–93.
4. Doyle, W. (1977). Paradigms for research on teacher effectiveness. In L. S. Shulman (Ed.), *Review of Research in Education, 5,* 163–199; Doyle, W. (1980). *Classroom management.* West Lafayette, IN: Kappa Delta Pi; Doyle, W. (1986). Classroom organization and management. In M. C. Wittrock (Ed.), *Handbook of research on teaching: Third edition* (pp. 392–431). New York: Macmillan.
5. Brophy, J. E., & Good, T. L. (1986). Teacher behavior and student achievement. In M. C. Wittrock (Ed.), *Handbook of research on teaching: Third edition* (pp. 328–375). New York: Macmillan.
6. Stallings, J., Needels, M., & Stayrock, N. (1979). *The teaching of basic reading skills in secondary schools, Phase II and Phase III.* Menlo Park, CA: SRI International.
7. Berliner, D. C. (1979). Tempus educare. In P. Peterson & W. Walberg (Eds.), *Research on teaching: Concepts, findings, and implications.* Berkeley, CA: McCutchan; Fisher, C., Berliner, D., Filby, N., Marliare, R., Cahen, L., & Dishaw, M. (1980). Teaching behaviors, academic learning time, and student achievement: An overview. In C. Denham & A. Lieberman (Eds.), *Time to learn.* Washington, DC: National Institute of Education.
8. Denham, D., & Lieberman, A. (1980). (Eds.). *Time to learn.* Washington, DC: National Institute of Education.
9. Fisher, C., Filby, N., Marliare, R., Cahen, L., Dishaw, M., Moore, J., & Berliner, D. (1978). *Teaching behaviors, academic learning time and student achievement: Final report of Phase III-B, Beginning teacher evaluation study.* San Francisco: Far West Laboratory.
10. Brophy, J., & Evertson, C. (1976). *Learning from teaching: A developmental perspective.* Boston: Allyn & Bacon; Brophy, J. (1979). Teacher behavior and its effects. *Journal of Educational Psychology, 71,* 733–750; Rosenshine, B. (1983). Teaching functions in instructional programs. *Elementary School Journal, 83*(4), 335–351.
11. Berliner, D. C. (1983). Developing concepts of classroom environments: Some light on the T in classroom studies of ATI. *Educational Psychologist, 18*(1), 1–13; Gage, N. L. (1984). What do we know about teacher effectiveness? *Phi Delta Kappan, 66*(2), 87–93; Gage, N. L., & Berliner, D. C. (1984). *Educational psychology* (3rd ed.). Boston: Houghton Mifflin.

12. Doyle, W. (1979). Making managerial decisions in classrooms. In D. L. Duke (Ed.), *Classroom management* (78th yearbook of the National Society for the Study of Education, Part 2). Chicago: University of Chicago Press; Doyle, W. (1984). How order is achieved in classrooms: An interim report. *Journal of Curriculum Studies, 16*(3), 259–277.

13. Hansford, B. (1988). *Teachers and classroom communication.* Sydney, Australia: Harcourt Brace Jovanovich.

14. Anderson, D. J. (1982). The search for school climate: A review of the research. *Review of Educational Research, 25,* 368–420.

15. Kounin, J. S. (1970). *Discipline and group management in classrooms.* New York: Holt, Rinehart and Winston; Emmer, E., Evertson, C., & Anderson, L. (1980). Effective classroom management at the beginning of the school year. *Elementary School Journal, 80*(5), 219–231; Evertson, C., & Emmer, E. T. (1982). Effective management at the beginning of the school year in junior high classes. *Journal of Educational Psychology, 74*(4), 485–498.

16. Brophy, J. E. (1983). Classroom organization and management. *Elementary School Journal, 83*(4), 265–286.

17. Good, T. L., & Brophy, J. E. (1986). *Educational Psychology* (3rd ed.). New York: Longman; Smith, L. M., & Geoffrey, W. (1968). *The complexities of an urban classroom.* New York: Holt, Rinehart and Winston.

18. Erickson, F., & Mohatt, G. (1982). Cultural organization of participation structures in two classes of Indian students. In G. Spindler (Ed.), *Doing the ethnography of schooling.* New York: Holt, Rinehart and Winston; Borman, K. M., Lippincott, N. S., Matey, C. M., & Obermiller, P. (1978, March). Characteristics of family and classroom control in an urban Appalachian neighborhood. Paper presented at the annual meeting of the American Educational Research Association, Toronto.

19. Gordon, T. (1974). *Teacher effectiveness training.* New York: Peter H. Wyden.

20. Glasser, W. (1965). *Reality therapy: A new approach to psychology.* New York: Harper & Row. Glasser, W. (1969). *Schools without failure.* New York: Harper & Row.

21. Canter, L., & Canter, M. (1976). *Assertive discipline: A take-charge approach for today's educator.* Seal Beach, CA: Canter and Associates.

22. Charles, D. M. (1989). *Building classroom discipline: From models to practice* (3rd ed.). New York: Longman.

23. Becker, W. C. (1977). Teaching reading and language to the disadvantaged—What we have learned from field research. *Harvard Educational Review, 47*(4), 518–543.

24. Peterson, P. L., Wilkinson, L. C., & Hallinan, M. (Eds.). (1984). *The social contexts of instruction: Group organization and group process.* Orlando, FL: Academic Press.

25. Green, J. L., & Smith, P. (1983). Teaching and learning: A linguistic perspective. *Elementary School Journal, 83*(4), 353–391; Good, T. (1979). Teacher effectiveness in the elementary school: What we know about it now. *Journal of Teacher Education, 30*(2), 52–64.

26. Weinstein, D. E. (1982). Training students to use elaboration learning strategies. *Contemporary Educational Psychology, 7*(4), 301–311.

27. Good, T., & Brophy, J. (1984). *Looking in classrooms* (3rd ed.). New York: Harper & Row.

28. Slavin, R. E. (1980a). Cooperative learning. *Review of Educational Research, 50*(2), 315–342; Slavin, R. E. (1980b). Effects of student teams and peer tutoring on academic achievement and time on task. *Journal of Experimental Education, 48,* 252–257; Slavin, R. E. (1981). Student team learning. *Elementary School Journal, 82*(1), 5–17.

29. Soar, R. S., & Soar, R. M. (1983, February). Context effects in the teaching–learning process. In D. C. Smith (Ed.), *Essential knowledge for beginning educators*. Washington, DC: American Association of Colleges for Teacher Education; Good, T., Grouws, D., & Ebmeier, M. (1983). *Active mathematics teaching*. New York: Longman.

30. Rosenshine, B., & Stevens, R. (1986). Teaching functions. In M. C. Wittrock (Ed.), *Handbook of research on teaching: Third edition* (pp. 376–391). New York: Macmillan.

31. Anderson, L., Evertson, D., & Brophy, J. (1979). An experimental study of effective teaching in first-grade reading groups. *Elementary School Journal, 79*(4), 193–223; Hawley, W., & Rosenholtz, S. J. (1984). Good schools: What research says about improving student achievement. *Peabody Journal of Education, 61*(4), 1–178. Bennett, D. (1982). Should teachers be expected to learn and use direct instruction? *Association for Supervision and Curriculum Development Update, 24,* 5.

32. Bransford, J. D. (1979). *Human cognition*. Belmont, CA: Wadsworth.

33. Rosenthal, R., & Jacobson, L. (1968). *Pygmalion in the classroom. Teacher expectations and pupils' intellectual development*. New York: Holt, Rinehart and Winston.

34. Brophy, J., & Good, T. (1974). *Teacher–student relationships: Causes and consequences*. New York: Holt, Rinehart and Winston. Also see Cooper, H. M., & Good, T. L. (1982). *Pygmalion grows up*. New York: Longman.

35. Hamilton, S. F. (1983). The social side of schooling: Ecological studies of classrooms and schools. *Elementary School Journal, 83*(4), 313–334.

36. Morine-Dershimer, G., & Tenenberg (1981). *Participant perspectives on classroom discourse*. Final report to National Institute of Education. Executive Summary, April (Ed 210 107).

37. Morine-Dershimer, G. (1982). Pupil perceptions of teacher praise. *Elementary School Journal, 82*(5), 421–434.

38. Brophy, J. (1981). Teacher praise: A fundamental analysis. *Review of Educational Research, 51*(1), 5–32.

39. Cobb, J. A. (1972). Relationship of discrete classroom behaviors to fourth-grade academic achievement. *Journal of Educational Psychology, 63*(1), 74–80; Cobb, J. A., & Hops, H. (1972). *Survival skills in the educational setting: Their implications for research and implementation*. Report No. 13. Eugene, OR: Oregon University Department of Education.

40. Slavin, R. E. (1978). Student teams and comparisons among equals: Effects on academic performance. *Journal of Educational Psychology, 70*(4), 532–538; Johnson, D., Johnson, R., & Scott, L. (1978). The effects of cooperative and individual instruction on student attitudes and achievement. *Journal of Social Psychology, 104,* 207–216.

41. Goodlad, J. L. (1983). *A place called school: Prospects for the future*. New York: McGraw-Hill.

42. Berliner, D. C. (1985). Laboratory settings and the study of teacher education. *Journal of Teacher Education, 36*(6), 2–8.

43. McKay, D. A., & Marland, P. W. (1978, February). *Thought processes of teachers*. Paper presented at the annual meeting of the American Educational Research Association, Toronto.

44. Jackson, P. (1968). *Life in classrooms*. New York: Holt, Rinehart and Winston.

45. Gage, N. (1978). *The scientific basis of the art of teaching*. New York: Teachers College Press, Columbia University.

CHAPTER 4

Human Development: Students Are Alike, but Not the Same
PENELOPE H. BROOKS

INTRODUCTION

Chapter 4 describes the human beings who are students in K–12 classrooms, and it does so from two perspectives. First, it chronicles how students grow and develop from birth through the high school years. Then it describes the categories that educators often use to characterize students whose special conditions influence how they should be taught—"gifted," "retarded," "handicapped," and so forth.

As a brief overview necessarily paints pictures of students with a very broad brush, students may appear to fit a common pattern when in fact they do not. Every human being is unique. The chapter title emphasizes this fact.

When teachers know how children develop and what causes the changes they experience, they can understand them better and anticipate certain events in their lives. As a result, teachers can better design the physical and social environments of classrooms. They can teach better. Therefore, this chapter summarizes both the cognitive and social-emotional nature of children at four different periods—infancy, early childhood, middle childhood, and adolescence.

The first part of the chapter is about normative development. Then, because no one is exactly "normal," the second half of the chapter looks at differences in students and how those differences affect teaching.

The intricacies of the weave between development and the role of environment are illustrated in the Snapshot and the Analysis sections. In all three case studies presented, parents, peers, and teachers had significant influence on the students involved—so also did the traits and the ages of the students. From these case studies, you can see how students are the same, and how subtle, often chance, interactions affect their lives.

The Educational Research section describes a particular situation in which research data are used to influence policy decisions. The situation involves the issue of whether mildly retarded and other mildly handicapped students should be taught in special classes or in regular classrooms.

SNAPSHOT

The Snapshot for this chapter consists of short case studies of two students.[1] As you read each, consider:

- What special needs do these two children seem to have?
- What could or should their teachers and schools do, or have done, to help them?
- What would you do if you taught the two?

CASE STUDY: WILLIAM, SIXTH GRADE

On the first day of school that year, William appeared to have wandered into the sixth grade by mistake. He was small, frail, thin, and pale. He slipped almost unnoticed into the classroom, sat at the back, and never spoke. When the teacher walked toward him, he seemed to cower; and when she asked if he would rather be called Bill, he whispered that he would rather be called William.

William was the second son of a wealthy physician. He had an older brother who was a high school football star, an honors student, and president of his class. William grew up in the care of a sitter. His parents entered him into nursery school when he was three years old, but he cried so much that his parents took him out and put him back with the babysitter. Discipline at home was strict. He spent a great deal of time in his room alone, playing with his dog and his pet turtle and talking to himself.

His family was quite proud of his older brother's accomplishments. They talked of his feats on the football field and took William to the brother's games. William did not appear interested in his brother's activities.

William's parents tried to help him develop other interests. He and his father joined the Boy Scouts, and his father became a scout leader. His father bought him a trumpet, but William did not care about learning to play. Other attempts failed—his father took him fishing and let him experiment in his workshop. William was not interested in doing those things by himself, and his father did not have the patience to work with William and tolerate his mistakes. By sixth grade, William's parents quit investing time and energy on encouraging him because they thought it was wasted.

In class William was so quiet that it was easy to forget he was there. He was two grade levels behind in reading and writing. Before the fourth grade, teachers thought he was not trying. In the fourth grade he was tested for learning disability and diagnosed as severely learning disabled. He was sent

to a resource room daily for an hour of reading help. Although he worked diligently at the tasks the teachers gave him to do, his improvement was not sufficient to show up noticeably on achievement tests.

William's fifth-grade teacher decided that the previous teachers had been too lenient with him because of his family's prominence in the community. She insisted that he complete his work correctly; if not, he was kept in during recess or after school. His parents supported her efforts because they wanted him to eventually get into a good college.

William's performance still did not improve. By the beginning of sixth grade, he was still very shy. He sat quietly at his desk, rarely completed his work, and did not interact with the other children even at recess. His intelligence test (IQ) scores were high, but he showed absolutely no motivation to do anything.

CASE STUDY: SHERRY, ELEVENTH GRADE

Sherry had been classified as "gifted" in the fifth grade. She performed well in all her classes and scored high on tests. Learning seemed to come easily to her. She was active socially at school but was also a serious student.

But by junior high (grades 7–9), Sherry's academic performance was only adequate, mostly C's; and her school behavior was punctuated with mischievous acts and attempts to get out of class to engage in extracurricular activities that were only mildly interesting to her. The pattern continued in high school. Sherry was extremely popular with her peers but an enigma to her teachers because she tried to get by with minimal effort in class. She seemed to know just how frequently and seriously she could avoid assignments and violate school rules and policies without major consequences. For example, she left the school premises when she thought she would not get caught. If

about how children come to have emotional problems, teachers, as people essentially untrained in psychology and psychiatry, need to avoid guessing at the causes of emotional problems and blaming parents' behaviors, home environments, or recent traumatic events. (See Gilfand, Jenson, & Drew, 1982.)[25]

Categories Based on Sensory Handicaps

Students with a *sensory handicap* are usually *hearing impaired* or *visually impaired*. That is, their hearing or sight is considered below the normal range. Although some students are completely deaf or blind, schools more often encounter milder forms of these and other sensory impairments.

Hearing-impaired Students

Students with mild or moderate hearing loss may adapt quite well in a classroom if they wear a hearing aid. Students with serious hearing impairment

Deaf students using manual communication.

communicate with sign language, speech and lip-reading, or a combination of both (known as *total communication*). The particular form of communication they use is a product of their parents' preferences and the special training they have had. Most students with severe hearing impairment cannot succeed in a regular classroom without a lot of extra help, and their teachers must possess special skills. Even under optimal conditions, many hearing-impaired students experience delays in reading achievement.

Significantly hearing-impaired students often experience interpersonal problems because they cannot communicate readily with the students and other people who make up their school environments. Although sign language is a real language, just like spoken English or Spanish, few hearing individuals know it, and it is therefore not as useful to the hearing impaired as it could be. In some classes, however, enterprising teachers have used the teaching of sign language as a device for the social integration of the hearing-impaired student in regular classrooms. They and the hearing-impaired student teach the others the sign language so that all can communicate. The hearing students learn a new skill and usually have fun doing so. Frequently, the sign-language skill and the value orientation developed by the hearing students who engage in this process are retained for a lifetime. (See Skinner & Shelton, 1985.)[26]

Visually Handicapped Students

Visually handicapped students also use a variety of communication modes, depending on their degree of handicap. Mildly impaired students may have their vision corrected with glasses and may need large print to read. Seriously impaired students most frequently use Braille as their primary method of reading, but they may also make use of sighted "readers," who read to them, or of "talking books"—audiotapes of novels, scholarly works, or texts. Like hearing-impaired students, they have to make many difficult adjustments in order to learn in ordinary schools. They also are especially vulnerable to being isolated socially by other students, a situation that often results in loneliness, lack of achievement, feelings of inadequacy, and other emotional consequences.

As in the case of hearing-impaired students, the integration of visually handicapped students into regular classrooms poses special challenges for teachers. They must adjust their teaching so the handicapped student can learn and must orient the classmates of visually handicapped students to these students' special needs. Showing them how to do things and knowing when and how to offer help are two areas of such training. (See Warren, 1984.)[28]

ANALYSIS

This Analysis section describes interaction between two junior high school students and football teammates.[27] One is deaf, and the other is not handicapped. As you read, consider

- In what ways was James like other students?
- Why do you think the coaches kept James on the team?
- In what ways did contact with James help Chris?

caught, she would think of an excuse that seemed to satisfy the teacher. She and her boyfriend often held hands in the classes they had together. On one occasion she sat in his lap when an important visitor came to observe the classroom. For her junior year she signed up for only one solid academic class—required English. The others were classes in which she could make a C almost without trying—commercial art, recording studio, office aids.

Sherry's parents were divorced and remarried. Her stepfather bought her a car so that she would not have to rely on her mother for transportation. Her mother, who also worked outside the home, had a great deal of difficulty setting and enforcing rules.

Sherry's life was very socially oriented. She was a cheerleader and a member of a high school sorority and other clubs. While in high school she maintained a C average, but she failed algebra once and had to take it in summer school. She saw very little of her parents because she was constantly on the go.

When the time comes to take college entrance exams, Sherry will have very little knowledge of the information tested and will probably perform so poorly that she will not be accepted by any of the colleges to which she intends to apply. She is not concerned, however. She is not sure she wants to go to college anyway, and studying all the time does not appeal to her.

THE NATURE OF GROWTH AND DEVELOPMENT

As William and Sherry's cases show, children do not grow and change in a conveniently predictable way. They are not like balloons, which gradually expand in a consistent, even, and symmetrical fashion. Rather, periodic examinations seem to show growth and change at uneven rates and in spurts. Furthermore, it seems that a child may have qualitative differences during growth; the little person at age three or seven may seem like someone else at nine or twelve. An obstinate, oppositional child at age three may be a thoughtful, cooperative student at twelve; a small, frail child at five may be a handsome, well-proportioned adolescent at sixteen; an unmotivated, borderline-passing high school teenager may become a successful engineer or businessperson as an adult.

Gradual, Continuous Change

Experts in child development are just beginning to understand the dramatic ways in which children change. Sometimes they think of the changes as "stages," but many theorists are reluctant to use the term because it implies a static resting place in development where children stay for a while before they move on. In fact, there are probably no such pauses in development. Instead, the lifespan of a human being is analogous to the metamorphosis of a caterpillar to a butterfly. Change is continuous over time and consists of many small increments that are often difficult to notice. From one day to the next, it is difficult to tell that something has changed. When enough change has taken place for experts to notice, a new developmental stage is identified. (See Flavell, 1977; Kagan, 1984.)[2]

The Role of Environment

Most changes in the developmental process are products of interactions with contexts provided by the environment; they do not happen automatically. Language is the best example of this interaction. Infants seemingly have a readiness to learn language. If language-speaking people are present in their environment, there is no way to keep most children from learning the spoken language. If infants are without access to language—either because they are deaf or because no one talks to them—they will not speak.

However, access to language alone is not enough. For instance, isolating children in a room so that they only hear tapes of Shakespearian plays would not teach them language. Language is "taught" by adults and older children interacting verbally and nonverbally with infants. According to language theorists, such "teachers" gradually program the level of difficulty so as to slowly increase the children's use of grammatic forms, vocabulary, and meaning. (See deVilliers & deVilliers, 1979; Olson, 1980.)[3]

Dialectical Theory

The environment plays an important part in shaping an individual's developmental progress, traits, attitudes, motivation, and values; because of that importance, various elements of the environment can be examined for clues as to their influences on the ways in which people change. One approach to studying development, known as a *dialectical theory*, provides an understanding of the *interactions* (dialogues) between individuals and their environment by identifying four dimensions of these interactions—two personal and two environmental (Riegel, 1976; Sameroff, 1975).[4]

Dimensions of Interaction between Individuals and Environment (Dialectical Theory)
- Inner Biological
- Individual Psychological
- Cultural-Sociological
- Outer Physical

The *inner biological dimension* refers to physiological maturational changes or health changes within the developing child. These changes are responsible, in part, for many major life changes. For example, leaving home, marrying, and having children are made possible by the biological changes associated with adolescence.

The *individual psychological dimension* concerns what is ordinarily thought of as traits or tendencies. Sociability, shyness, values, sensitivity, and artistic talent are some of the characteristics that change as one gets older. These changes help determine relations between children and parents, husbands and wives, neighbors, classmates, teachers, and students.

Changes in the *cultural-sociological dimension* produce upheavals in people's lives if they change from a minority subculture to a dominant culture. This is especially so if the new dominant culture is quite different from the original cultural heritage. Immigrants entering a country often encounter such problems. Cultural-sociological influences include religion, laws, traditions, and communities.

Finally, the *outer physical dimension* includes such phenomena as climate, natural disasters, and terrain. These factors determine what people do with much of their time—following game animals, farming, and keeping warm or healthy. Changes in these factors—a famine, for example—cause major changes in the way people conduct their lives.

Synchrony between Dimensions

The coordination and *synchrony* in the dialogues between and among these four dimensions determine an individual's behavior at any given time. When the progressions of change within one or between two dimensions are not synchronized with those in other dimensions, a crisis takes place; examples would include pregnancy before physical or psychological maturity or a forced change from elementary to middle school before psychological or physical readiness.

Crises are not necessarily negative events, but they usually do introduce upheaval as children or students struggle to reestablish some form of synchrony within the four dimensions. Thus, major events such as parental divorce, hurricanes, or serious illness can be crises in that they force children to renegotiate the dialogue they had with other aspects of their lives at the same time that they deal with the changes brought about more directly by the catastrophe.

The Inner Psychological Dimension of Development

Emphasis in this chapter is on the inner psychological dimension of change and development; and in that setting, you will look at the ways in which experience and behavior change as a result of alterations in the other dimensions. In order to study child development closely, the inner psychological dimension is subdivided into two areas that will be discussed at some length: (1) the perceptual-cognitive-moral domains of growth and (2) the social-emotional or personality domains. The first refers to the ability of children to detect, transform, manipulate, and apply information from the environment. The second refers to two types of children's understandings—their understanding of their feelings and how they act on them and their understanding of their relationships with other children and with adults.

Two Domains

Before you read the rest of this chapter, think for a moment about your own development.

- How have you changed since you started kindergarten—physically, cognitively, psychologically?
- What events or times in your life seem to be most significant in their effects on your development?
- Why were these significant?

Once you have done this, think of others who attended the same elementary and/or secondary school as you did, particularly those who were noticeably different from you. Ask the same three questions about them.

- Compare how you and those others developed and "turned out" so far in your lives. What are the similarities? What are the differences?
- Are there any individuals from your background who remind you of William and Sherry, the students described in the Snapshot?
- If so, why did you think of them in this way?

PERCEPTUAL-COGNITIVE-MORAL DOMAINS OF DEVELOPMENT

Perceptual Development

When we see things or events; hear sounds; feel surfaces, textures, or movement; smell odors; taste flavors; and detect the direction of gravity, we are involved in perception. We are noticing elements of our environment and gathering information from it. We acquire a great deal of perception.

When most adults interact with babies, they act as if the babies see the same things that they do. For example, parents usually believe that babies see faces, pets, and mobiles. Similarly, many beginning teachers believe that young school-age children see letters, words, and print and that they are aware of their own behavior, much as adults are. These beliefs are, in fact, wrong. The work of E. J. and J. J. Gibson (Gibson, 1969)[5] shows us that children's perception is initially disorganized, inefficient, and undifferentiated.

Becoming an Expert at Looking, Hearing, and Feeling

Think for a moment of the first time you looked at a night sky full of stars, examined a dental x-ray, ran your fingers over some Braille forms, watched someone communicate in American Sign Language, or listened to a symphony. At those times, you probably were in awe of someone who could distinguish constellations, read the dental x-ray, identify the Braille message, interpret the signing, or explain the symphony to you. Yet, the main difference between you and the "experts" was simply one of experience with the medium. They had already had learning experiences that you had not yet confronted. That type of learning has been called *perceptual learning*, and consists of learning to see, smell, feel, or hear. In a more technical phrase, it is "the education of attention."

For both babies and adults, the environment provides the same information. When a baby is shown the face of an unfamiliar person, that baby has available the same information available to an adult. However, the baby and the adult differ in the information they pick up. In other words, the baby and the adult differ in the ways they look at things, even though they look at the same things. E. J. Gibson (1969) has delineated four ways in which young children differ from adults, ways in which naiveté differs from expertise.

From Looking At to Looking For

First, perceptual activity, such as looking and listening, becomes more searching and less captive as people develop. The differences can be illustrated if you think of someone flipping through magazines while waiting in an office reception room. That person's attention can be said to be *captive* by the objects being looked at, that is, captured by the headlines, the graphics, and the highlighted displays. Compare that approach to looking at a magazine with that of someone who is looking for a particular quotation or statistic in a magazine. In verbal shorthand, we contrast the two approaches by thinking of the first perception as looking *at* and the second as looking *for*. This distinction is one way to characterize the difference between the novice and the expert in many areas of experience—games, sports, art, music, and classroom activities. (Chapter 2 illustrated this difference in ways of looking in its description of the difference between inexperienced and expert classroom observers' views of classroom activities.)

Systematic Searching

Second, perceptual learning consists of a change from unsystematic to systematic search. As children learn what to search for in the environment, they become more systematic in the search process. If they are given the task of looking for a word or a letter on a page, at first their eyes wander all over the page. With practice and perhaps instruction, their eyes begin to scan in a more orderly fashion, possibly from left to right and top to bottom, so that no area is covered twice while others are missed.

Detecting Details

Third, perceptual learning consists of more and more specificity of information detection. For instance, when people first see identical twins, they look for differences between the twins so that they can tell them apart. With exposure to the twins, subtle aspects of their appearance or manner seem to become more noticeable, so that after a while, the twins no longer look as much alike as they did at first. This detection of details or differences with experience is one of the changes that are part of perceptual learning.

Ignoring Irrelevant Information

Fourth, perceptual learning includes an increasing ability to ignore irrelevant information. For example, when children learn to read different styles of type and handwriting, they have learned to ignore some differences and pick out what does not vary across all examples. This is a formidable task for children who face it for the first time. They have to sort out many features of letters—straight lines versus curved lines, closed forms versus open forms, diagonals, horizontals, and verticals (Gibson, 1969).

Cognitive Development

Educators know that most children learn to think as they develop, but they are not clear about what "learning to think" involves. They are not sure what thinking is or how people learn to do it, and they are further unsure where perceptual processes leave off and cognitive processes begin. One way to think of the difference between *perception* and cognition is to define perception as the detection of information and *cognition* as the transformation and manipulation of that information. The presentation that follows uses that distinction.

Jean Piaget, 1876–1980

The study of cognition in children has been dominated by one approach for the last twenty years—the approach begun and elaborated by Jean Piaget. Piaget viewed cognitive development as a form of biological adaptation. Species adapt to their environment by changing their behavior, not just their anatomy and physiology.

Adaptation in Stages

Accordingly, as children grow, they become exposed to more of their environment; and as they perceive more of that world around them, they adapt to it by changing in certain ways. These changes occur over time as the children develop, and they occur in stages—stages that come about in response to interactions with the environment. The interchange between person and environment has two aspects—assimilation and accommodation. *Assimilation* occurs when children react to something new by finding it in something with which they are already familiar. *Accommodation* happens when children change their cognitive structure or knowledge to embrace the new facets of the encounter.

Assimilation and Accommodation

Piagetian Stages of Development

According to Piagetian thinking, assimilations and accommodations can be divided into three major types—corresponding to four major stages of development: sensorimotor, preoperational, concrete operations, and formal operations. (See Wadsworth, 1984.)[6]

> **Piagetian Stages of Development**
>
> Sensorimotor—birth–24 months
>
> Preoperational—2–7 years
>
> Concrete Operational—7–11 years
>   Decentering
>   Developing Mental Operations (representations and symbols)
>   adding and subtracting
>   ordering and sequencing
>   classifying
>   Controlling One's Behavior
>
> Formal Operational—11–14 years

Sensorimotor Stage (Roughly Birth–24 Months)

Change in Motor and Sensory Acts

The sensorimotor period is a time of change in motor and sensory acts. Sensorimotor activities begin with single acts, such as looking, sucking, reaching, and grasping, and develop toward intentional, organized, flexible actions such as the entire sequence of reaching for an object, grasping it, and bringing it to the mouth. Cognitive psychologists now believe there are four or possibly five substages in the sensorimotor period. The four substages are typically identified as follows (McCall, 1979):[7]

1. the newborn period (until about two months), in which infants respond primarily to internal systems;
2. the subjectivity period (until about eight months), in which infants more readily respond to external stimuli but fail to separate objects in the environment from their own actions;
3. the period involving the separation of means from ends (after about eight months), in which infants learn that some actions have purposes; and
4. the period involving relationships between separate entities (after about thirteen months), in which infants see objects as independent of actions that use them but also see that the two are related.

The sensorimotor period culminates with the child's ability to represent actions internally. For example, infants no longer just *do;* they also have a primitive form of knowing (McCall, 1979).

Preoperational Stage (2–7 Years)

Manipulating Symbols

The next task for children is to learn to manipulate their newly acquired *symbols* (signals, language) or *representations* (images). At this point, the world a child has experienced is disorganized—disorganized in a way that you can probably understand easily if you can remember events that occurred when you were three, four, or five years old. The memories that you still have of these years probably consist of snippets—an image of a room, a person saying something, a feeling. There are no precursors and consequences of events, no sequence to the events. These gaps in memory are not faults of memory but simply reflections of your lack of cognitive skills at the time the experiences occurred. You were not able at that time to organize the original experience so that you can now remember all its context.

Concrete Operational Stage (7–11 Years)

The next few years witness several major related but separable intellectual accomplishments: (1) decentering, (2) the development of mental operations to apply to representations, and (3) the ability to control one's behavior. Each is described below.

Decentering

The major intellectual accomplishment of *decentering* "undoes" something that is characteristic of young children's thought. When solving problems, children tend to "center," or focus, on one aspect of a problem, usually a very visible aspect. Consider, for example, what Figure 4–1 shows, the famous Piagetian liquid conservation problem:

1. Two identical glasses are filled to the same height with liquid.

2. When asked, a child will agree that the two glasses have the same amount of liquid.

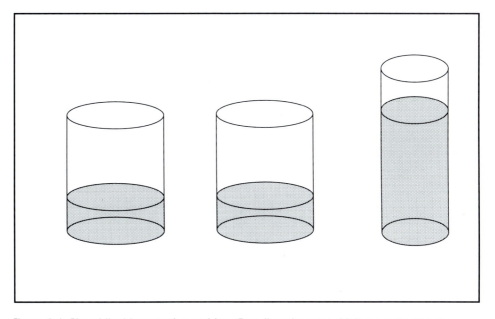

Figure 4–1. Piaget liquid conversion problem. Even though young children see liquid being poured from one of the shorter (and wider) glasses, they frequently say there is more liquid in the taller (and slimmer) glass. They do not "connect" the fact that the liquid just came from the other glass.

3. The liquid in one glass is poured into a taller, thinner container in full view of the young child.

4. The child is then asked to say whether the two containers still have the same amount of liquid or whether one has more than the other.

5. The young child almost invariably says that the tall, thin container now has more liquid. When asked "Why?" or "How do you know?", the child almost always answers that the one picked is taller. The child almost never notes that the container is also thinner.

This is an example of *centering* because the child is focused on one dimension of the problem, in this case the tallness of the second container, to the exclusion of other dimensions. Centering prevents children from considering several characteristics simultaneously because the child's attention is captured by the most salient aspect of the objects.

The ability to consider more than one aspect of a problem means that a child has begun decentering. This process is evidenced in many ways—not judging other people as all bad or all good, making judgments about whether two things—two letters of the alphabet, for example—are alike or different.

Developing Mental Operations

A second major intellectual accomplishment of the concrete operational stage, that of *developing mental operations,* allows representations (maps, symbols) to be organized and manipulated. Three such mental operations are adding and subtracting, ordering, and classifying.

The mental operations of adding and subtracting allow children to solve the conservation problem that was illustrated above with the liquid. For children to know that the tall, slender glass contains the same amount of liquid as the original glass, they must *add* to account for the new height of liquid and *subtract* to account for the new diameter. Both calculations are necessary for the child to arrive at the "no change" answer because the two calculations cancel each other out.

The addition and subtraction operations have to be learned with respect to each dimension of objects—weight, area, amount, number. Substances that are continuous, like liquids, mud, wood, clay, or paint, are subject to one set of rules—known as *conservation of continuous quantity*—while those that are discrete (countable) are subject to a slightly different set of rules—known as *conservation of number.* Part of what children must learn is the degree to which substances can be changed and still keep the same identity or the same quantity.

A second mental operation that children learn to perform during the concrete operational stage is *ordering* objects along some dimension such as height, overall size, length, and darkness. This ability is demonstrated when children can order a series of sticks or strips of paper in increasing or decreasing length. To solve these problems of series, children have to understand that an object like a stick can play two roles at the same time; it can be longer than a shorter stick and shorter than a longer stick. Understanding both roles is necessary to see how a stick fits into its proper place in a *sequence.* This ability is necessary to understanding ordinal and interval scales based on increasing amounts—age, money, inches, pounds.

A third mental operation learned during the concrete operational stage, and the last to be discussed here, is that of *classifying.* Classifying is the organization of objects and events into categories that help determine their meaning. Consider the following information made available to a young child:

Fluff is the family dog. There are lots of dogs in the neighborhood. There are also deer, snakes, cows, birds, skunks, and horses in the neighborhood. Butch is the family cat. All of these are animals. Snakes are at the zoo. Giraffes, polar bears, and lions are also at the zoo.

How can the child organize all this information? It is highly disorganized as presented here; and no particular statement has a great deal of meaning. From these randomly available statements, however, children could produce the organized hierarchy in Figure 4–2.

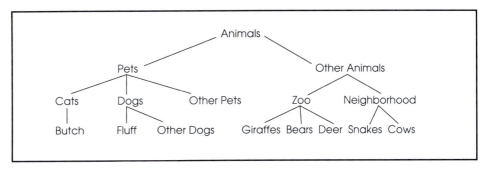

Figure 4–2. A representation of how a child might organize "animals" while using the classifying mental operation.

As a result, when a particular animal is mentioned, the whole hierarchy is part of the meaning of the word. For example, Stripes, an aunt's cat, is probably a pet that lives at her house, is not a dog but is an animal. The classification scheme helps children identify what something is *not* as well as what something *is*.

Controlling One's Behavior

A third major intellectual accomplishment of the concrete operational stage includes the ability to control one's own behavior—to tell oneself what to do and to obey that internal personal directive. This accomplishment is evidenced by children's increasing compliance to norms, by their ability to sit quietly, and by their tendencies to reflect before acting. The process of self-regulation begins, according to Vygotsky (1978),[8] in the form of commands or requests from other people—"Sit down." "Come here." "Bring Mommy her purse." Children then learn to talk aloud to themselves; and finally, the language becomes internalized and behavior appears to be self-regulated, or controlled. Self-regulation is seen explicitly when children restrain themselves from doing something in order to get a reward later and when they talk aloud to themselves while solving problems (Zivin, 1979; Berk, 1985; Trotter, 1987).[9]

Formal Operational Stage (11–14 Years)

Hypothetical Thinking

The thinking of adolescents differs from that of younger children in three ways: It can be hypothetical, it can consider several factors at once, and it can be considerably more systematic than at earlier stages. To think hypothetically means to think about possibilities—what might be. Because of the new ability to think about possibilities, adolescent thought appears idealistic and undeterred by practical considerations. Students at this stage can imagine themselves in many roles. They can create solutions to world problems. Often their images and solutions are unrealistic, however, because in the process of fantasizing them, young adolescents cannot consider the real obstacles to realizing them. For example, few know how much work it takes to become a ballerina, and almost none can understand the competing pressures involved in such political acts as peace treaties and negotiations for hostage release.

Reality gradually appears as part of adolescent thinking, as they gain more experience in the activities they are thinking about, and as they are able to take into account additional aspects of the activity. For example, they begin to realize that being an Olympic gold medalist involves not only glory but also hard work, long hours, not eating junk food, not taking trips to the beach, and not watching TV. It involves personal and financial sacrifice as well as personal commitment.

Adolescents also become capable of approaching problems through *systematic thought*. For example, in selecting answers on a test, they are able to consider one aspect of a problem at a time. If the problem requires varying two factors (for example, speed and distance), adolescents can learn to hold one constant while varying the other in order to find out how the two factors are related. The degree to which such a systematic approach carries over into other areas of adolescents' or adults' lives is not clear. At least, they have the capacity to solve problems systematically. Whether they use it in a desirable way may often be a matter of training and experience.

Development of Moral Reasoning

Just as children learn to reason about the physical environment of objects and their motion, they also learn to reason about human behavior. One of the most intriguing aspects of human behavior that children must learn about is moral behavior. Underlying moral behavior, however, are reasoning processes that may parallel general cognitive development.

If you have ever watched children learn to play games, you have probably noticed that very young children (preschool-age) seldom understand the rules of games in the same way that adults do. For young children, rules are something that can be used at will, often only if they benefit the gameplayer. They can be insisted upon, and they can easily be forgotten.

Then, sometime around the age of five, children almost suddenly begin to regard rules as sacred, written in stone, and made by some higher authority that "bestows" unchangeable rules upon a game. Indeed, to children at this age, a game and its rules are synonymous. Breaking the rules is bad, and following the rules is good. The essence of goodness, to them, is conformity and obeying rules.

At about age eight, many children begin to understand the role of rules in games and become more willing to change rules to adapt to situations. They start to see the purpose behind the rules and realize that it is important. For example, when they play scrub baseball games and pickup basketball, they adjust the rules to the situation. In other activities such as jacks, jumpropes, hopscotch, and card games, they can see that rules have variations instead of being hard and fast for all occasions.

This developmental aspect of children's exceptions of rules was first noted by Jean Piaget (1965),[10] who recognized the pattern by watching children of different ages play marbles and through interviewing them. Later, his ideas about how children view rules were expanded considerably by Lawrence Kohlberg (1970).[11] Kohlberg saw that the rules of a game could be a model of the ways in which children understand other people's behavior. In his research, he and his students read a series of stories to children at different ages and examined their responses to those stories. The stories involved someone's having to make a moral choice. A well-known example is the story of Heinz, whose wife is dying of cancer. She can only be saved by a very expensive drug. He has no money and so cannot buy the drug. One night he breaks into the pharmacy and steals the drug for his wife. After hearing a story like this, children were asked whether it was all right for Heinz to steal the drug. If so, why? If not, why not? Based on children's answers to these questions about the moral dilemmas, Kohlberg distinguished six stages of moral reasoning.

Punishment-Obedience

In the first stage (usually children under age five) children place a great deal of emphasis on punishment as a consequence of behavior. A child in this stage may say something like "No, Heinz shouldn't steal the medicine. He might get caught and be put in jail." Or, "Yes, he should steal the drug. His wife would get real mad at him and shoot him if he didn't." Note that both answers involve fear of punishment. It is also important to note that both "yes" and "no" answers are given by children. What is important in determining the stage at which the children are operating is the reasoning, the fact that children focused on punishment in their rationale.

Reciprocity-Needs

Children in the second stage begin to think of their own needs. They may give such answers as "No, he shouldn't steal the drug. If she dies, he can probably get another wife." Or, "Yes, he should steal the drug. He needs his wife to cook for him." Occasionally, children will show some evidence of awareness of reciprocal "backscratching" by answering something like "Yes, he should steal the drug. If he saves his wife, maybe she'll buy him a nice present."

Approval of Others

In the third stage (usually between ages six and ten) children show a concern for approval of others and for being "good." In answers to the question of whether Heinz should steal the medicine, children in this stage may say, "No, taking the medicine would make the pharmacist very angry." Or they may say, "Yes, he was only trying to make his wife happy."

Rules—Law and Order

Reasoning in the fourth stage demonstrates a respect for authority and duty. Children consider laws absolute; they are to be obeyed in all circumstances. Children in this stage might say, "No, he shouldn't steal the medicine because he would be breaking the law. Stealing is wrong." Alternatively, "Yes, he should steal the medicine. It's Heinz's duty to save his wife if he can."

Individual Rights and Standards

Most educated people probably reach the fifth stage in late adolescence or early adulthood. Reasoning at this stage involves the recognition of a contractual, democratic emphasis. Youth become concerned with individual rights and the general welfare of society. Responses to Heinz's dilemma might range from "No, he shouldn't steal the drug because, although he is desperate, the rights of the druggist must be respected" to "Yes, the druggist owned the drug, but his wife's need for medical care was more important."

Ethical Principles

The few adults who reach the sixth stage show concern for living up to self-chosen principles such as "the greatest good for the greatest number" or the Golden Rule. For example, those who subscribe to the belief that the value of human life is the primary value would say that only one answer leads to an assignment to Stage 6: "Yes, he should steal the drug to save her life. Human life always takes precedence over property. If he had not taken the drug, he would not have been able to live with himself."

The stages Kohlberg delineates appear to be good descriptions of the developmental sequence in thinking about moral issues. How people think does not necessarily determine their behavior, however. In the example outlined above, there are six reasons for one behavior—stealing the drug.

Kohlberg's analysis of moral development has its critics, many of whom make important points. Several point out that Kohlberg's emphasis on the reasoning behind a behavior implies that the morality of an action depends more on the reasoning than on the action. Some have ethical problems with that idea. Another criticism is that by delineating stages, Kohlberg gives a false impression that clear boundaries exist between them. In fact, the stages flow from one into another; many children will answer some questions in the pattern of one stage but answer others as they would in another stage. A more telling recent criticism comes from Carol Gilligan's widely cited *In a Different Voice* (1982).[12] She argues that Kohlberg's hierarchy may apply more to men, who are traditionally reared to be individualistic, assertive, and independent, than to women. She says that many women are more concerned than men with harmony in interpersonal relationships. For them, the maintenance of harmony and sensitivity to the needs of others are important determinants of decisions. While this focus on harmony looks like Kohlberg's Stage 3, Gilligan argues that it is in no way a lower stage of reasoning than Stage 4. Therefore, placing it at the lower level than justice implies a gender bias. She says it is a *different* kind of reasoning, but not a lower-level reasoning.

- What do you think of Kohlberg's stages of moral development? Is the reasoning behind moral behavior more important than the action itself?

- Do you agree with Gilligan that the developmental sequence may differ for men and women?

SOCIAL-EMOTIONAL DOMAINS OF DEVELOPMENT

Children not only learn to think as they mature; they also learn how to interact with other people, how to feel, and how to control their feelings in response to the actions of others. Consider the difference between a very young infant who alternates fussiness, sleep, and interest and a diplomat who reads the behavior of others and very carefully controls his or her own behavior in public so as to convey the appropriate information. At home, the same diplomat may be naturally warm and outgoing, thus demonstrating flexibility in his or her ability to monitor and control emotions. What happens between infancy and maturity that allows and encourages such complex behavior to develop? Although only a few answers to this question are known, the next section provides a survey of recent findings.

Infancy and Early Childhood

When babies are born, they already possess many personality elements, but they learn others in their early years. Parents and other caretakers are dominant figures in this learning process. This section discusses the social-emotional skills with which babies come equipped and the contributions parents can make through the preschool period.

As infants develop into the preschool period, venturing into the new world of peer relations, changes take place. These changes provide the opportunity for continued learning and development. Changes that occur during this period are determined in part by (1) what happened during infancy, (2) what the environment is like for the preschool child, and (3) the special developmental characteristics of the preschool child.

Infant Temperament

The ability to adjust to the demands of a complex world has its origins in early infancy. Babies are born with at least three different dimensions of temperament—sociability, activity, and emotionality (Campos, Barrett, Lamb, Goldsmith, & Stenberg, 1983).[13] *Sociability* is the tendency of babies to prefer to interact with adults and to do so positively. Sociable babies smile, cuddle, laugh, and use charming ways to get adults' attention. Unsociable infants are miserly with their smiles and cuddliness; they avoid interactions. Only severely handicapped infants are totally lacking in sociability, but normal infants show a good deal of variation. *Activity*, as it is used here, means simply the extent to which a child is active. Infants vary in their activity level. Obviously, some are alert and in motion more than others. *Emotionality* refers to how easily an infant is upset or angered.

Common sense tells us that parents will want to spend, and will enjoy spending, more time with sociable, moderately active, easygoing infants and that parenting is more difficult with cold, inactive, or easily upset infants. Some infants, then, place greater demands on their parents and other caretakers than others.

Social Contexts

Caretakers, in turn, vary in their willingness and abilities to interact supportively with their infants. Those who can adapt their interactions to take into account the baby's individual eccentricities while still maintaining a consistent, nurturing, and interactive environment do their share toward launching appropriately adjusted infants. In fact, such caretakers foster in infants a basic trust in the events of the world.

For instance, when caretakers engage infants in social interactions, the episodes have been likened to a *conversational dance* or to *turntaking*, and they prompt in these infants the beginnings of social understanding. For example, when caretakers talk to babies and wait for the babies to respond by cooing, laughing, or wiggling, they are teaching the babies to maintain a conversation by taking turns and attending expectantly to the adult.

When infants need to know something—for example, the meaning of an unfamiliar event, such as a visit with Santa Claus—they have a person they can look to for information about what is happening and how they are supposed to react. This dependency is a product of many caretaking events over time, such as feeding, diapering, and conversational dialogues between the caretaker and the infant. The synchrony between infants and caretakers and success of these events depends on the ability and willingness of both parties to engage themselves in the conversation. Either a sick or disturbed infant or a chronically sick or disturbed caretaker can disrupt the dialogue to the extent that the infant's intellectual and social-emotional progress is seriously impaired.

Infants who possess a sense of trust in the adults with whom they interact are better able to take on the challenges of early-childhood and preschool experiences than are children whose infancies have lacked the supportive exchange

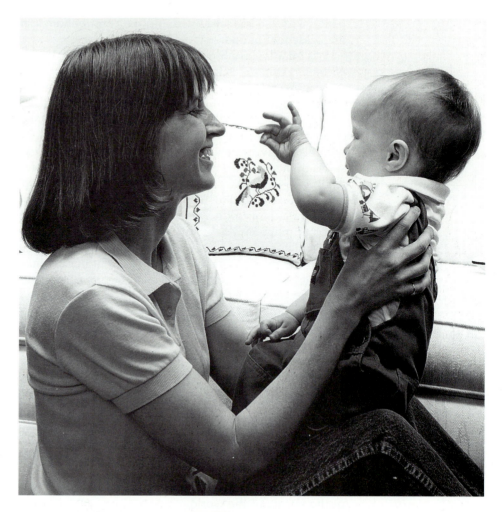

Mother and child engaged in "conversational dance."

that engenders trust. Early-childhood challenges include the broadening of the child's social sphere and the learning of the complicated rules associated with relations with peers, adults, and, perhaps, younger siblings (Dunn, 1983).[14]

Physical Contexts

At the same time social contexts expand, physical contexts also expand into new realms—daycare, birthday parties, car seats without restraining devices, grocery stores viewed from the floor rather than the seat in the grocery cart, other people's homes, nursery school, and kindergarten. Adjustment to this myriad of new experiences depends on a number of factors, but two are especially important: (1) having dedicated adults around as models and guides, and (2) the similarity of new contexts and experiences to familiar ones.

Adult reactions to situations provide information about that situation to children who witness them. Adult reactions help children interpret situations, assigning them such values as threatening, matter-of-fact, or interesting. For example, adults demonstrate a variety of responses to threat—expression, reason, flight, or passivity. They demonstrate how to behave at numerous social occasions, such as football games, formal dinners, and dental checkups. They also tell children what to feel and how to behave—to be happy at others' good fortune, not to fight at a birthday party, and to act pleased when other children receive desirable birthday presents.

Self-Control

Children internalize many of these instructions and admonitions over a period of time, thus forming the basis of self-regulatory control. Therefore, children appear at the school's doorstep with a wide variety of amounts and kinds of internalized rules and expectations. A child from a very disorganized home may not understand the need for rules and may have a very difficult time learning to follow them. "Why take turns?" "Why not shout?" "Why not run?" "Why not throw food?" "Why not hit?" "I do it at home." Also, the kinds of rules children conform to at home or in the neighborhood may not apply at school. Saying grace before meals may be common practice at home but difficult to manage at school. Water pistols may be allowed in the neighborhood but not at school. If the home and school environments are very disparate, children cannot apply what they have learned at home to the new school context. As a result some children have trouble adjusting to school.

Middle Childhood

Middle childhood, roughly equivalent to grades 1 through 4, is often thought of as a period of inertia. Already during early childhood the speed and direction of a child's development were established, and now the child is coasting. One reason for this belief is that middle childhood encompasses no apparent sudden dramatic biological changes such as birth; instead it is characterized by rather smooth transitions. However, the smooth surface belies some very important social changes in (1) social behavior, (2) social cognition, and (3) self-concept.

Social Behavior

Middle-childhood-age children experience changes in their *social behavior* for a variety of reasons and in different dimensions. The sphere, or environment, in which they live expands. They assume more and different roles within the family. They develop strong and changing gender identifications. They establish new peer relationships, and group associations and popularity become much more important than they have been to date.

Social Environment

It should come as no surprise that the social environment of children—parents, siblings, teachers, extended families—has tremendous influence on children. Directly and indirectly, these elements of the environment subtly control the course and rate of development. They do so by controlling the space in which the children act and what the children do in that space. Parents fence yards and provide toys, smile at some behaviors and scold others. Siblings expect some interactions and reject others, encourage some actions and tell their parents about others. Grandparents hug children sometimes and ignore them at others. Schools fence playgrounds and provide books and playground equipment, promote some activities, and prohibit or restrict others.

The conversational dance mentioned in the section on infants continues as children get older—but the roles given to children by parents, other caretakers, and teachers gets larger and larger. This expansion is intentional, the goal being to enable the children to think and behave independently in a mature and intelligent manner. Assignments, questions, and prompts are designed to lead children gradually toward this goal.

ZPD

Vygotsky (1978) has identified an area of growth between a child's developmental status at a particular time and what it could become with guidance as the *zone of proximal development* (ZPD). Ideally, all instruction should be aimed in this area, but in reality, such precision is difficult for caretakers and teachers, especially if they are instructing several children at different levels with varying ZPDs. William in the Snapshot at the beginning of this chapter had parents who did not carry out their interactions within William's zone of proximal development. Instead, they expected William to learn what his brother or father could master—sports, music, electronics—and he was to do it on his own. When this did not happen, his father got angry or changed the activity rather than interacting with his son in a more appropriate activity or at a more appropriate level.

Roles in Families

Children assume different roles within their families, and as they develop and interact with other family members, these roles evolve. For instance, the stereotypes of firstborn or only children as more achievement-oriented and successful than later-born children are not altogether wrong. In contrast, a second child might assume a more sociable, well-liked role; a third might be studious; another an isolate; and another an irresponsible "black sheep." (Sherry, described in the Snapshot, was a second child.) Later-borns are influenced by older siblings, and the nature of that influence depends partly on the personality and gender of the older child as well as the spacing between the siblings. For example, a young male may act more aggressive if he has older sisters, a strategy that might or might not be successful with big brothers (Dunn, 1983; Zajonic & Hall, 1986).[15]

Gender-related Interactions

The interactions of children with peers are gender related. In grade school, children prefer same-sex friendships and groups. These peer affiliations serve several functions—companionship, a conduit of new information (about sex, drugs, weapons, games), an audience for trying out new behavior (cursing, rebellion), a source for expanding one's repertoire of jokes and riddles, a source of items for collections, an environment in which to learn rules and the consequences of breaking them ("Don't tell!" "Don't be a teacher's pet."). One of the most important functions of the peer group is to reinforce gender-appropriate behavior (Huston, 1983).[16]

Peer Relationships

The status of the peer group and of a child within it depends on several characteristics of the individual child. For example, we know that physical attractiveness is one of the major determinants of status. Less-attractive children tend to have lower peer status and also more behavior problems than attractive ones. We also know that low peer status and behavior problems are often related, but we are not sure about the causes. Are both caused by the same social conditions, do the behavior problems cause the low status, or does the low status cause the behavior problems? This question is clearly analogous to the chicken-egg question. Being ugly may elicit ridicule, which produces low self-esteem, which produces problem behavior, which produces more negative reactions from peers, and so on. The cycle may continue as long as a child is in school.

However, attractiveness is not the only avenue to popularity in middle childhood. Popular children seem to have better social skills, for example, their ability to "read" a social situation before jumping into it. They are also likely to respond positively to other children who initiate contact. They are less likely than less popular children to reject others. They recognize implicitly that friendship is a long-term matter of trust and mutual understanding rather than a momentary agreement. Some of the other factors obviously involved in status are skill in

An Introduction to Teaching and Schools **141**

Elementary school students at recess who separated themselves by gender.

Social Cognition

sports, father's and/or mother's role in the community, status of siblings, and performance in school.

In addition to experiencing changes in their social environment, middle-childhood children develop *social cognition*. That is, they begin to learn rules about social relationships, a complex process that continues through adulthood. Because children are a part of the social environment of others, they affect what happens to others, and others affect what happens to them. Therefore, how children interact with these "others" is important to them. We know that the behavior of children toward other children and adults is partially a product of their knowledge of social interactions in general and their knowledge of the motivations behind a particular other's behavior. For example:

- Preschool children believe friendship is based on material things (how much candy one child gives another). Later they realize many other factors determine friendships.

- Preschool children do not understand social conventions. They do not understand why cars stay on the right side of the road in the United States. By third grade, most children believe that social conventions can be changed by majority vote. In fact, they also believe that physical laws, such as the fact that rocks sink in water, can be changed by a vote. By fifth grade, most children know more about social conventions and understand that they are different from physical laws.

- Children at age five or six do not really understand employment—for example, why a shopkeeper does what he or she does. They have no concept of economics, occupations, and what it takes to be employed. But by age eight, they begin to understand the idea of economic motivation, that a storekeeper has to pay for goods and that occupational roles, such as shopkeeper, often require particular personal characteristics.

- Twelve-year-olds are more likely to recognize psychological factors in people's behavior than younger children. When asked why people drink alcohol, five- or six-year-olds do not know or will say something like "They're thirsty." Twelve-year-olds are more likely to say, "They get depressed and want to feel better."

- In judging the goodness or badness of acts, young adolescents are more likely to put the person's intention (to help or to hurt) into the equation and give the outcome less weight than they would have done at an earlier age. When asked whether it was better to drop and break six eggs while helping your father carry in the groceries or to break three eggs while trying to sneak some cake out of the refrigerator, younger children are more likely to base their judgment on the outcome (six eggs versus three eggs) than on the intention of the actor.

Self-Concept

A third critical social change during middle childhood occurs in children's *self-concepts,* or beliefs about themselves. This change, as with the other changes, comes in response to the social environment. In short, children's concepts of themselves are also based in part on reactions of their immediate social environment to their behavior. That is, they view themselves as competent or incompetent individuals as a result of the extent to which they succeed or fail in their experiences. These experiences, in turn, help determine how willing they will be to risk failure in order to achieve success, how they will react to failure, and how persistent they will be in the face of difficulty.

Learned Helplessness

For example, in testing situations, children given easily solvable problems followed by more difficult problems will usually try to succeed with the more difficult problems. On the other hand, children given unsolvable problems to work first, followed by solvable but difficult problems, are more likely to fail at the later problems just as they did at the first. According to some investigators, this happens because children in the latter situation have learned to be helpless from their previous failures and are exhibiting a state called *learned helplessness.*

This notion of learned helplessness has been used as a partial explanation for some girls' seeing themselves as more helpless than boys in school. In a research project aimed at isolating sources of feelings of helplessness, Dweck and her colleagues (Dweck & Bush, 1976; Dweck, Davidson, Nelson, & Enna, 1978)[17] examined the feedback given to children in school. She found that early

in school, girls experience more success than boys and are criticized less. But she also found that the negative feedback that does occur is different for boys than for girls. The criticism directed at boys in those early years was mostly for conduct. In general, only about one-third of the criticism of boys was for intellectual misdemeanors.

Gender-related Expectations

On the other hand, 88 percent of teachers' criticisms directed at girls was for intellectual behavior. In other words, the criticism of girls was more focused on inadequate academic achievement and thus was more clearly a message about academic failure than the more diffuse criticism boys receive. When girls were criticized, it was because of poor thinking, wrong answers, and so forth. Dweck also found that boys were more likely to be given positive feedback for the quality of their intellectual work in the classroom than girls. These conclusions seem to indicate that many girls develop learned helplessness from negative feedback accumulated over time in the classroom and, therefore, experience declining interest in intellectual activities over the middle-childhood years.

An element in the social environment of school-age children that has a powerful effect on self-concept is the fact that they get tested. This means they face structured and obvious chances to succeed and to fail. They must adapt to the situation and cope with the threat.

Coping with Failure

A factor that contributes to the way in which children cope with potential failure involves the circumstances to which they attribute the failure. Children can attribute *failure* to bad luck, to tasks that are too hard, or to their own inadequacies. Similarly, they can attribute *success* to luck, to their hard work, to their ability, or to some combination of factors. Children who believe that effort and ability are important to success and that luck and lack of effort contribute to failure are more likely to be achievers. But we may wonder where these attributions come from. Psychologists have not yet identified all the sources, but there is a consensus that they come from the hundreds of interactions with parents, caretakers, siblings, peers, and other significant people in children's lives—including teachers.

Adolescence

Along with infancy, adolescence is one of the two periods of the most dramatic change in social and emotional development. It is especially challenging because growth rates are very uneven, and at the same time wide ranges of social behaviors are suddenly open to adolescents for the first time. Adolescents are no longer impaired by immature motor development or dependency on their parents. Society begins to expect maturity and, in turn, allows adolescents access to some of the freedoms (and related responsibilities) that adults have. But not all adolescents are equally prepared to encounter these freedoms and responsibilities.

Coping Behaviors

As adolescents face their newly available freedoms, they display various types of *coping behaviors*—among them, egocentrism, the personal fable, identity seeking—which will be discussed below. It is important to remember, however, that although the coping behaviors of adolescents follow common patterns, the individual experiences of each adolescent are quite different. Because growth is uneven during adolescence, some individuals have finished their pubescent growth spurt while others have not yet begun it. While all adolescents experience changes in sexual characteristics and feelings and are affected greatly by them, these changes appear according to a schedule that has lain latent in each individual's genes for years. Although each adolescent's changes appear in approximately the same order, the timetable is different for everyone. Of course, the social-emotional changes are related to concomitant physical changes, and the interaction of the two further complicates the whole developmental process. As a result, adolescents often face major personality-social crises (Elkind, 1970).[18]

Egocentrism

Adolescence is a period of increased self-consciousness, and people in this age range often engage in activities they never dreamed of in earlier years. The self-consciousness is often referred to as *egocentrism*, and the experimenting with different behavior is called *identity seeking*. The self-consciousness, or egocentrism, is characterized by the belief that other people are preoccupied with the adolescent's own appearance. This, then, often leads to a subsequent belief that others see the same things in individual adolescents as they see in themselves—the zits, the crooked nose, the soiled spot on the cuff of the blouse, the wrong brand name on the shoes. This imaginary audience that is believed to scrutinize the adolescent so carefully becomes all-knowing and ever present—always in judgment and always determining behavior (Elkind, 1981; Harter, 1983).[19]

Personal Fable

Consistent with this sensitivity to one's appearance is a second adolescent phenomenon that Elkind (1981) has labeled the "personal fable." The *personal fable* is manifested in the adolescent's belief that he or she has unique emotional experiences and that these experiences are important to everyone else. Unfortunate events that happen to everyone else, then, cannot happen to the adolescent. It is other people who get pregnant, have car accidents, and get caught stealing. The personal fable begins with the knowledge that unfortunate things happen to others and that those "others" are like me; but the adolescent fails to finish the equation: *therefore those things can happen to me.*

Identity-seeking young adults.

Identity Seeking

Identity seeking emerges from adolescents' growing sense of potency and independence. Many develop the idea that they can think better than adults—especially their parents and teachers. As adolescents they know what they are not, what they do not want, and that they do not want to be like the adults around them, but they often do not know what they *are* or what they *want to be*. This lack of definition results in a search for an identity or identities.

Group Affiliation

Affiliations with different groups are formed and then dissolved. They are frequently based on attention-attracting or status factors and may lead the newcomers into activities they would not ordinarily engage in (drinking beer, swallowing live salamanders, sexual experimentation) or into activities that are acceptable to their parents ("wholesome" social fellowship, respected athletic participation, health-oriented activities). These affiliations lend their identities to the novices, who can say, "I'm a Delta Phi"; "I'm a discus thrower"; "I'm liked by others"; "I'm accepted"; or "I belong." Initially, most of this sort of behavior begins as an attempt by the adolescent to be like and accepted by members of a group whose identity he or she is seeking. If such an identity involves drug or alcohol use, then drinking and drug use may take on such importance that they become the dominant force in the adolescent's life. The same is true if the identity involves team sports, running, dramatics, or church youth-group participation. At this point, think again about Sherry in the Snapshot. Might group affiliation needs explain some of her behavior?

CATEGORIES OF STUDENTS

As this chapter has emphasized, children can differ in dozens and dozens of ways—partly because they are different to begin with and partly because they encounter different experiences as they grow. So, if they are so different from one another in so many ways, how can we think of such a thing as a normal or "typical" student? The answer, of course, is that there is really no normal or typical group of students. There is, however, a *range* of typical or normal behavior among students that teachers accept, allow for in their classes, and aim their teaching toward. Unfortunately, children who do not fit within the range of normalcy often suffer in classrooms with other children who are "more typical."

You can get a feel for the difficulties involved in labeling students with the following exercise.

1. Reread the two case studies in the Snapshot at the beginning of this chapter.
2. Provide what you think would be the best possible label for each student.
3. Now think of the ways in which the labels you just thought of might convey impressions about William and Sherry that would *not* be appropriate.

Labeling Students

In spite of the potential dangers, educators often group and label students in an effort to match them to the type of instruction considered to be the most appropriate for them. In the process such educators often put a name or label on the specialized needs of some students and then group students by these labels. Although this is usually done with good intentions, many professionals object to such labels or categories because they believe the labels do more harm than good. Those who object believe that labels cause people to behave toward the labeled person in predetermined, stereotyped ways. For example, the fact that some people are labeled "retarded" may influence how other people treat them; it may also affect the way the "retarded" feel about themselves.

Nevertheless, because instruction needs to be tailored to each student, the following pages discuss several categories of students. They describe children on both ends of the intelligence continuum—"gifted" and "retarded." They also

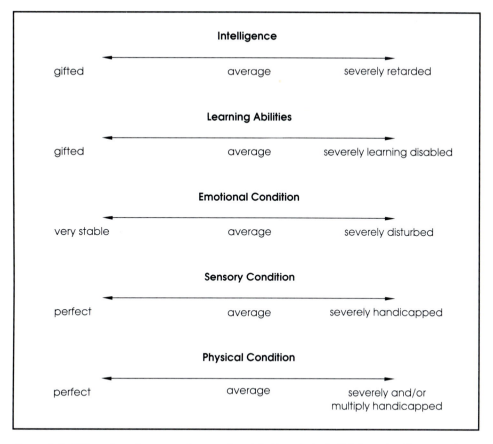

Figure 4–3. Different continua people use when labeling students. It is important to remember that students at the extremes of each continuum differ only by degree from other students on the same continuum.

discuss children who have difficulties in learning, those who are emotionally disturbed, those who are physically handicapped, and those who are called "average." Figure 4–3 shows a variety of ways in which students are grouped, emphasizing the range within each category.

Categories Based on Intelligence

Intelligence Tests

People are often described in terms of how intelligent they are, and when this happens, adjectives such as "smart," "dumb," and "stupid" are used. Interestingly enough, no one knows what *intelligence* really is. Technically, it refers to scores on intelligence tests, but even the people who have constructed intelligence tests over the years do not know clearly what intelligence is. They have opinions about which abilities are necessary to succeed in school, and they have made up tests that supposedly test those abilities. But since intelligence tests were constructed in the early 1900s, there have been many different opinions and theories about the nature of intelligence. Even as those opinions shifted, however, the old intelligence tests have continued to be used because the scores (IQs) predict success in school fairly well: The lower the IQ, the less well a student tends to do in school.

Nevertheless, if everyone in the United States were tested on one of the most frequently used intelligence tests—the Stanford-Binet and the WISC-R—half of the population would score within a very narrow range, between 90 and 110. (The average score on both tests is 100; the maximum possible is 200.) Extremely high scores and extremely low scores are very rare.

"Intellectually Gifted" Students

If children score above 145 on an intelligence test, they are considered by many to be *gifted* intellectually. Typically, these students, in addition to performing well on intelligence tests, are very creative and usually commit themselves wholeheartedly to a chosen task, whether it be music, athletics, or creative writing. A very significant study on gifted children was begun in 1921 by Lewis Terman (Terman, 1925–1959).[20] He selected 1,500 children whose IQs were 150 or greater and followed them for 50 years. (The study is still going on.) Most of the children became more attractive, healthier, and happier than average adults, and they tended to choose professional occupations.

A proposition that is often raised about the education of gifted children is something like this: If these children can do so well in typical school situations, perhaps they could do even better if their instructional environments were designed specifically for them. Many educators, parents, and psychologists who raise this point feel that "gifted" children's abilities are underutilized in most regular classrooms and that these children need intellectual challenge to keep them interested in school and out of trouble. Such a belief calls for special programs, either through placement in special classes or schools or through access to special resource rooms.

The first task in providing special programs and resources for gifted students is the identification of the appropriate children for the program. This is not easy because not all children can be given intelligence tests, and IQ is not the only index of giftedness. While most schools use some combination of teacher nomination and test scores, no identification system is perfect, and all of them will miss some gifted children. Isaac Newton, Leo Tolstoy, Frank Lloyd Wright, Albert Einstein, Pablo Picasso, Winston Churchill, and many other talented individuals either dropped out or flunked out of school.

Once gifted children are identified to participate in special programs, schools usually employ three strategies to provide the additional challenge thought to be appropriate for them: grouping the children who are selected so they can be taught separately from the others, accelerating the curriculum provided for them, and enriching their intellectual experiences in the regular classroom. The extent to which such strategies are effective in challenging these students and keeping them in school depends, in part, on the specific program, its goals, and the children themselves. (See Horowitz & O'Brien, 1985.)[21]

"Mentally Retarded" Students

If a person scores below 70 on an intelligence test, he or she may be considered officially *mentally retarded* (MR) but usually two other considerations have to be present for this designation: (1) the person has to be noticeably unable to behave normally; that is, he or she does not possess or demonstrate *adaptive behavior*; and (2) the person's condition has to have originated before age eighteen. According to present practice, retardation can vary in degree from the subcategory of *severe/profound* (IQs below 35) to *mild* (IQs from 55 to 70).

Categorizing Retardation

Schools attempt to educate retarded children by organizing their instruction to fit the different categories of students. Classification systems differ slightly, but the commonality across systems is substantial. Programs for mildly retarded

Something to Think About

Julie and Janet are identical twins who have always done very well in school and have been labeled "gifted" by the school system based on their intelligence test scores. They are completing fifth grade and their parents apply for both of them to attend the middle school for academically advanced students next year. Both qualify for admission but, because more students qualify than there are spaces, a lottery is conducted.

The twins' parents have been informed that Julie's name was drawn in the lottery, so she may attend the special school. But Janet's name was not drawn, so she may not. The parents appealed to the school board, asking that both girls be accepted. The board denied their request, saying it must stand by the policy, making no exceptions to the procedure.

A newspaper writer heard of the case and, in his column, accused the school board of being insensitive to the girls' needs and harmful to their development. He said the girls' names should have been drawn together, not separately.

- What questions does this situation raise in your mind about differences among students and ways in which school systems try to meet those differences?

- Should both twins be allowed to attend the special school? Why or why not?

- If Janet may not attend, should the parents send Julie anyway? Why or why not?

- Should the school system use a lottery to decide who attends the special school? If not, what should they do instead?

---

children may be called *"educationally mentally retarded"* (EMR) programs or *"educationally handicapped"* (EH) programs. Those for children with moderate (as distinct from "mild") mental retardation are considered *"trainable mentally retarded"* (TMR) programs. Those for children with greater retardation are simply called "severe" or "profound" programs. Because of the federal law Public Law 94–142 (the Education for All Handicapped Children Act of 1975) as amended by P.L. 99–457, all mentally retarded children must be served by schools.

Despite being classified as retarded on the basis of one, two, or three criteria, individuals who bear the "retarded" label quite often have no more in common than people with no retardation. Like everyone, they vary physically, emotionally, and by personality, disposition, and beliefs. In fact, the reasons that they are mentally retarded are varied and numerous. Some causes of mental retardation are biological—caused by genetic disorders, such as Down's syndrome, or by injury such as brain damage. Some are environmental—caused by con-

Middle school mathematics intervention class.

ditions such as extreme chronic poverty. Some involve both biology and environment.

Regardless of its type and its cause, no condition of retardation should be considered hopeless. Even the most severely retarded individuals (usually biologically caused) seem to be able to benefit from an enriched environment. The children most likely to show IQ gains after extraordinary instructional efforts are those who score in the mildly retarded range.

Unfavorable Stereotypes

Unfortunately, however, mentally retarded children often suffer from unfavorable stereotypes, probably because larger numbers of mentally retarded individuals are more likely than normal-range people to suffer from personality or behavioral problems; excessive aggression and depression are particular problems. This reaction by others simply adds a burden to the lives of retarded children, and that, in turn, often compounds the complex problems involved in educating them. It also causes some teachers to be apprehensive about having such children in their classes. (See MacMillan, 1977.)[22]

Categories Based on Learning Difficulties

"Learning Disabled" Students

Sometimes children are in the normal or higher ranges of intelligence but still cannot seem to learn. They are not retarded, do not have a sensory handicap, may be intellectually gifted; but they simply cannot learn a particular task. Usually, these children show no serious problems until they get to school, but then they have difficulty learning, especially to read or write. When this happens, it is often suspected that the child suffers from a *learning disability* (LD), which has been defined as follows:

> a chronic condition of presumed neurological origin which selectively interferes with the development, integration, and/or demonstration of verbal and/or nonverbal abilities. (For a more detailed definition, see Bryan & Bryan, 1986, p. 42.)[23]

Hyperactivity

Dyslexia

Two commonly diagnosed specific learning disabilities are hyperactivity and dyslexia. *Hyperactivity* is a label assigned to children who have difficulty sitting still and attending to classroom activities. They fidget, seemingly have no impulse control, and continually get out of their seats or other assigned spaces. In addition, some cannot attend to a task for very long. *Dyslexia* is a disorder strongly associated with reading. It is an inability to decode or interpret symbolic forms, such as printed words. Both hyperactivity and dyslexia are thought to have biological origins.

In addition to having difficulty learning at a normal pace, students with learning disabilities often become frustrated, are easily distracted, are unable to stay on task, and seem to forget easily and frequently. The forgetting, however, may be more a matter of teacher perception than of reality. Instead of forgetting, the student may not have learned the material in the first place.

Students with learning disabilities also often have problems in the social domain. They tend to have difficulties interacting with others and may be excessively shy, assertive, aggressive, and/or rude. These behavioral characteristics frequently lead teachers to stereotype learning disability students and to give up on the persistent and sensitive teaching tasks necessary to help them succeed. The characteristics try the teachers' patience and resolve at the very time when both are critically necessary if these students are to learn.

Something to Think About

Russell is in the second grade for the second time, and he is failing again. He is a mainstreamed student in the class, has slight learning disabilities, and is mildly retarded. He is a little troublesome but not really disruptive at this point. He is just older, noticeably bigger than the other students, and more aggressive.

Because of recently instituted competency testing, Russell's teacher will not be allowed to recommend that he be passed on to a regular third grade, even as a mainstreamed special student. He simply does not have the minimum test scores required for promotion.

However, because Russell's assessments indicate that he is on the borderline for placement in a self-contained special education classroom, he could be classified as mildly retarded and be put into a special education class that is not graded. But if this is done, he will probably be labeled EMR for the remainder of his elementary school years and will not be able to return to a mainstream classroom.

> Russell's teachers, the principal, the school psychologist, and his parents must meet to decide whether he should repeat second grade again in a regular class or be classified as EMR.
>
> - What do you think should be done?
> - What are the benefits and negative aspects of either action?

Various Approaches to Instruction

Teaching practices used with learning-disabled children have varied greatly over the years. Some educators advocate the establishment of highly individualized, incremental programs with close teacher supervision and guidance. Some procedures that target specific areas of functioning have been developed. Some of these are perceptual-motor training, multisensory training (an approach that uses all the senses to teach reading), language training that targets specific organic differences, and auditory-visual information processing. To date, however, data on school progress for children instructed in many of these programs are not clear or positive enough to encourage widespread acceptance and use of specific procedures. Concurrently, some special education professionals advocate greater use of behavior modification techniques with learning disabled students—including task analysis, reinforcement, modeling, and direct training. (See Fotheringham, Hambley, & Haddad-Curran, 1983.)[24]

Categories Based on Behavior Disorders and Emotional Disturbance

If a student's behavior is very bizarre but the student is otherwise of normal intelligence, the student is a candidate for the *behavior disorder or emotionally disturbed* category. There are several kinds of behavior disorders and emotional disturbances—some extremely serious, some long-lasting, some transient. The behaviors range from conditions of fearfulness, hyperactivity, withdrawal, and mild aggression to being out of touch with reality (as evidenced, for example, by hearing voices or seeing things that are not there), repetitive exaggerated movements, inordinate aggression, injuring oneself, and severe depression. Students who exhibit these behaviors in schools must be referred to specially trained professionals for diagnosis and intervention. Often special classrooms and schools are set up for children with serious behavior disorders or emotional disturbances. They are staffed by teachers and counselors especially trained in therapeutic approaches to instruction.

How do children become emotionally disturbed? Some scientists look to unhealthy home environments, while others look for biochemical problems. Still others believe that most forms of emotional disturbance have multiple causes. Currently, physical and sexual abuse are among the environmental origins being examined as causes of emotional problems in children, but much remains to be learned.

One of the most puzzling aspects of the studies of emotional disturbances in children is that some children can experience the most abhorrent treatment early in life and emerge apparently unscathed as children and adults, while others suffer significantly from less extreme situations. Until much more is known

- How do you think James' presence on the team affected the other players and the other students of the school?

Chris noticed James the first day of junior high school football tryouts. He did not pay much attention to him, however. He was too worried about himself. He wanted to make the team more than anything else in his life, and he was not thinking about the other guys.

Later that evening, as Chris reflected on the first day of practice, his thoughts turned to James. He could not see how James could make the team. Sure, he was big enough and skilled enough, but he was also deaf. How could a deaf person play football?

The next day, as Chris dressed for practice, James suited up nearby. They both finished at the same time and walked to the field side by side. Although they had attended the same schools for several years, the two boys did not know each other very well. They never communicated much. Chris always felt uncomfortable trying to talk with a deaf person.

When the two boys reached the field, a coach tossed a ball to James and told the two to warm up together. The practice involved many activities in which two boys work together, and each time Chris and James were paired with each other. This set a pattern, and they worked together every day.

James often did not understand what the coaches wanted him to do, but when this happened, Chris or one of the other boys would explain either by example or through gestures. As days went by, nearly everyone assisted James, but no one else did so as often as Chris. James was frustrated at times, but he appreciated the help.

Over the next three weeks, practice was hard and hot. Some boys quit, and others were cut. But through it all Chris and James persevered and succeeded. They also became close companions and good friends. They practiced together, showered together, and walked home together. In the process they developed their own system of hand signals to communicate with each other. Part of the system was actual sign language, which James had taught Chris, but much of it was a private code for Chris to tell James the plays and to explain coaches' instructions.

By the week before the final cut, Chris was sure he had made the team. He was practicing with the first team and doing well. James was also practicing with the first team most of the time, but Chris knew that the coaches were apprehensive about playing a deaf person. What would happen if he missed the play called in the huddle or when the quarterback checked off at the line?

The day before the final cut, the line coach called Chris aside and told him of his concerns about playing James. He also said he did not want to keep James on the team if he could not play him. He wanted Chris' assessment of how James would react to being cut. Chris said James would be devastated. He said that James felt that if he were going to be cut because of deafness, he would have been cut earlier. James knew he could play well enough.

Chris pleaded with the coach to keep James on the team and to play him. He explained the hand signals and assured the coach they would work under game conditions. It was an odd scene—a thirteen-year-old looking up to the coach with tears in his eyes pleading James' case. Chris said there was only one fair thing to do—keep James. The coach said, with unintended irony, "We'll see, but it's a shame he's deaf."

Chris did not sleep well that night. He worried: How would James feel if he was cut? How would Chris feel?

At two o'clock the next afternoon, Chris watched from a distance as the coach posted the final team roster. No one else was around. He had asked Ms. Miller if he could go to the lavatory and did so by way of the locker room. As soon as the coach left, he read the names. His name was there, but he knew it would be. Just under it was *James Haskins*. James had made the team.

Chris was waiting when James came out of his class. He flashed a thumbs-up sign, and James knew instantly what it meant. He smiled broadly but then asked, "Are you sure?" Chris nodded. "Yes!"

The two boys gave each other high fives right there in the middle of the hall. When they realized everyone was staring at them, they got embarrassed and walked sheepishly toward the locker room. Chris did not know until several days later that James would not have been on the team if he had not begged the coach.

Chris and James played football together for the next five years and were good friends all the time. The hand signals worked almost every play.

The two boys drifted apart after high school graduation, when Chris accepted a football scholarship to Vanderbilt University. He could have gone to college closer to home, but Vanderbilt had a good program in special education, and Chris had decided to be a special education teacher and coach. There were many students like James, and Chris intended to help as many as he could.

Chris played Commodore football for four years. He was a good player, and he performed even better off the field. When he graduated, he was prepared to teach special education and physical education. The other athletes elected him president of the Fellowship of Christian Athletes and in his senior year selected him for the award given to the college athlete who demonstrates the greatest concern for other people. The college faculty awarded him the Sullivan Award, given to the graduating senior who best exemplifies "a sincere interest in and concern for others."

Chris returned to his hometown as a high school teacher and football coach. He is successful and happy. His colleagues say he has a special talent for working with handicapped and "problem" students. James is a successful construction worker and painter. The two men see each other periodically, usually when James attends Chris' football games.

The Physically Handicapped Category

Cerebral Palsy

Either because of birth-related problems, inherited abnormalities, disease or injuries, a small proportion of students have *physical handicaps*. These handicaps, like hearing and visual impairments, vary in degree. Some students are so impaired that a caretaker must accompany them or a therapist must work with them. Others' handicaps may need something as technologically simple as a

Spina Bifida

brace. Major kinds of serious physical handicaps are paralysis, frequently caused by injury; cerebral palsy (CP), usually caused by oxygen deprivation during birth; and spina bifida, an opening somewhere along the spine that allows neural tissue to bulge, thus causing serious motor problems. Less frequent handicapping conditions include arthritis, muscular dystrophy, and injuries. As is the case with vision- and hearing-impaired students, the teachers must not only adjust to serve the students with physical handicaps but must also orient their classmates (Sutherland, 1984).[29]

Teachers must constantly remember that physically handicapped children are often quite skilled within or despite their limitations. They must be particularly mindful that students who have difficulty communicating may have average or above-average intellectual abilities. Even when severely impaired students cannot talk, sit, write, or type, their teachers must find ways to teach them and help them express their knowledge.

Technological Advances

In recent years technological advances have become especially helpful with special students. Devices can be designed for individual students that are sensitive to such subtle responses as gaze direction, eye blinks, and head tilts. They allow severely handicapped students a way to communicate with other people in and outside of the classroom.

Something to Think About

John is an eighth-grade student who moved recently from a rural area of Georgia to Philadelphia.[30] John's new school tracks students rather inflexibly, and he has been placed in the second-to-top academic group of the thirteen sections of the eighth grade. The placement was based on his previous school grades, his placement at his old school, and several other factors.

John is not doing well. He has failed all tests so far and is obviously frustrated. The other students think he is dumb. His teacher is convinced that the work expected of the group is above his ability and that he has not had the same background in earlier classes that the other students have had. He has asked that John be transferred to a less demanding level.

The assistant principal in charge of placing students refused to change John. He said to move John back would indicate that he is not as strong academically as reported at his old school; since John is black, he feared the school could be accused of being discriminatory. He said, "John is probably still adjusting to the new school. Let's see how he does for the rest of the year. If he doesn't improve, we can place him lower next year."

- What do you think should be done in this situation? Justify your opinions.

- What should school systems do to deal with students like John?

The Average Category

Now that some of the educational categories used to group children outside the "normal" range have been described, it is important to comment again about students considered to be "normal," or "average." The point to be made is simple. *Normal students* tend to have fewer noticeably special or exceptional characteristics than the children described above, but each of them is a unique individual. Average students might be more alike than others, but they are still not at all the same.

EDUCATIONAL RESEARCH

Using Research Data for Educational Decisions

If the world of education were perfect, educators would make decisions about the best way to teach students on the basis of a sufficient supply of research information. They would read studies conducted by others, undertake some studies of their own, analyze the circumstances that affect the situation they face, and apply whatever ideas seem to be most appropriate to their task. Then they would design a plan of action, implement it, study the results, and make appropriate modifications.

Since the world is not perfect, of course, the decision process is never that methodological or neat. Many things intrude: People do things in traditional ways and do not want to change, many have biases that they do not want challenged, information is usually incomplete, public pressure frequently requires action that is not supported by data, funds are always limited, and so forth. As a result, educational practices usually occur not because of conclusions from research but because of either (1) a desire to keep things as they are or (2) a strong enough dissatisfaction with the present situation to force a change. Sometimes the thrust of research information supports these practices, sometimes it does not.

Influence on Practice

This interplay between research and practice is illustrated below. The situation involves the question of how children who are different should be categorized and taught. The issue is whether certain students with special needs should be educated in separate special education classes and schools or whether they should attend regular classes.

During the 1960s students who were considered to have special learning problems were typically classified as having a particular type of handicap and then placed in special, separate classes, where they were taught by special education teachers. The practice seemed to work rather well even for those with mild handicaps, but over the years researchers turned up disturbing information. In 1968, after reviewing that research and analyzing current practices, one such researcher in special education, Lloyd Dunn, addressed a very pointed article to special educators which he began with the following statement:

> In my view, much of our past and present practices are morally and educationally wrong. We have been living at the mercy of general educators who have referred their problem children to us. And we have been generally ill prepared and ineffective in educating these children. Let us stop being pressured into continuing and expanding a special education program that we know now to be undesirable for many of the children we are dedicated to serve. (Dunn, p. 5)[31]

Dunn went on to say that separate, self-contained special education classes and schools for mildly retarded and other mildly handicapped students had been established for the wrong reason—to get the "misfits" out of the regular classroom so that teachers could concentrate better on the other students. He said lip service was paid to the idea that this arrangement was best for the "handicapped" student but that research reported that this was often not the case. Studies showed that special education classes were frequently composed of disproportionate numbers of minority and lower socioeconomic status students and that many students from disadvantaged homes were mislabeled as "retarded," "emotionally disturbed," "perceptually impaired," and "learning disabled."

Dunn said his reading of the data led him to believe that the process of evaluating and assessing children with learning difficulties was frequently conducted to find convenient labels for students in order to justify their removal from the regular classrooms. Often the goal was simply to get rid of them, not to formulate more appropriate educational programs for them. As a result, he stated bluntly:

> . . . we must stop labeling these deprived children as mentally retarded. Furthermore we must stop segregating them by placing them into our allegedly special programs. (Dunn, p. 6)

Dunn stated what he believed to be the reasons that such mislabeling and segregating of these children take place:

> Regular teachers and administrators have sincerely felt they were doing these pupils a favor by removing them from the pressures of an unrealistic and inappropriate program of studies. Special educators have also fully believed that the children involved would make greater progress in special schools and classes. However, the overwhelming evidence is that our present and past practices have their major justification in removing pressures on regular teachers and pupils at the expense of the socioculturally deprived slow learning pupils themselves. (Dunn, 1968, p. 6)

Research Conclusions

To demonstrate that contemporary research did not support current practice, Dunn listed the following conclusions from a number of studies of his day:

1. Homogeneous grouping tends to work to the disadvantage of slow learners and underprivileged children.

2. Retarded children make as much or more progress in regular grades

as they do in special classes, even though special classes tend to be smaller and to have more resources.

3. Diagnostic procedures frequently lead to mislabeling of students and their grouping in inappropriate homogeneous groups of children with supposed common problems.

4. Labeling children as "handicapped" reduces teacher expectations that they will succeed.

5. Disability labels hurt children's self-images, contributing to their feelings of inferiority.

6. Special class placements create problems of acceptance of disability-labeled students by the other students in the school.

In response to these findings of weaknesses in current special education practice, Dunn outlined a possible alternative approach, which he proposed for development and testing. He advocated a moratorium on what was being done *until a better way could be identified*.

> . . . it is suggested we do away with many existing disability labels and the present practice of grouping children homogeneously by these labels into special classes. Instead, we should try keeping slow learning children more in the mainstream of education, with special educators serving as diagnostic, clinical, remedial, resource room, itinerant and/or team teachers, consultants, and developers of instructional materials and prescriptions for effective teaching.
>
> The accomplishment of the above *modus operandi* will require a revolution in much of special education. A moratorium needs to be placed on the proliferation (if not continuance) of self-contained special classes which enroll primarily the ethnically and/or economically disadvantaged children we have been labeling educable mentally retarded. Such pupils should be left in (or returned to) the regular elementary grades until we are "tooled up" to do something better for them. (Dunn, p. 11)

In Dunn's view, an improved clinical approach to handling students with mild special education needs would include:

- diagnostic and prescriptive teaching in which skilled educators would evaluate students more accurately and effectively, design programs for their individual needs, monitor the results of the programs, and make adjustments accordingly;

- resource rooms and itinerant teachers that would complement regular classroom instruction and replace segregated special education classes; and

- a radically revised special education curriculum.

Dunn's demand that we discard the present way of teaching mildly handicapped students rested on substantial research findings that showed the many weaknesses of the approach. Since he made his statements, his conclusions have been further supported by recent studies. However, Dunn's alternative approach was not grounded in significant research. It was a conceptual idea, not a tested and proven model. It sounded good, but solid evidence that it would work did not exist. Dunn acknowledged this fact throughout his proposals. He felt he knew what did not work, but he did not claim that his new idea would. *He recommended only (and specifically) that it be studied and tested.*

Ironically, however, the Dunn concept quickly became the new way of doing things. School systems and states adopted some version of it without sufficient testing. In essence, they reacted to pressure to move away from the old, discredited approach, and the new concept was readily available. The new concept was called *mainstreaming*. But, even with mainstreaming, the labels and the labeling process continue.

Research Results Are Still Incomplete

As will be described in some detail in the next chapter, mainstreaming is now the dominant approach to teaching children with special needs. But, research results about its effectiveness are still incomplete and inconclusive.

CONCLUSION

Information about students such as that presented in this chapter is important to educators because it helps them make better decisions about how and what to teach. Knowing about developmental stages enables them to target their instruction at the appropriate levels for the age groups they face. Knowing about different types of learners helps them to adjust their teaching accordingly. Understanding commonalities across student developmental stages and within certain categorical groupings allows them to make common assumptions about what students can learn and do. As a result, teachers do not have to teach every student as if he or she is *absolutely* individual or unique.

Of course, as mentioned earlier, teachers must be cautious as they make these assumptions about their students. They must avoid too-sweeping generalizations about them. Although no student is unique in every way, each is highly individual.

Once educators know this about students, they can organize their schools and classrooms and design their teaching to meet the educational conditions and needs of the children and youth who come to them. This involves a process of matching student capabilities with the established educational goals.

SUMMARY

Children need to be understood if they are to be taught properly, and any attempt to understand them must include the realization that each child is similar to others and, at the same time, unique. Two of the ways children can be studied are by looking (1) at how they develop over the years and (2) at how they are alike and different from their agemates.

Dialectical theory describes development as a series of four types of interactions between individuals and their environment—inner biological, individual psychological, cultural-sociological, and outer physical. The individual psychological dimension consists of two parts—perceptual-cognitive and social-emotional development. Perceptual development involves a process of becoming less captive, more self-initiating, more systematic, more specific, and more able to ignore irrelevant information. Cognitive development, according to Piagetian theory, consists of four stages—sensorimotor, preoperational, concrete operational, and formal operational. Social-emotional development consists of four periods—infancy, early childhood, middle childhood, and adolescence. Each period has particular characteristics and events.

Because children are different, educators often categorize them according to particular characteristics, and often the categories are formulated by fitting children in somewhere along a continuum of some sort. Some categories are based on intelligence—"intellectually gifted," "mentally retarded"; some on learning ability or disability—"hyperactive," "dyslexic"; some on degree of emotional disturbance, and some on the presence of a handicap of some kind—sensory or physical. All categories include a "normal" classification or range.

Although categorizing students is often useful to teachers, they must do it with caution and sensitivity. Any categorizing involves overgeneralizing about the people involved and could be harmful.

STUDY QUESTIONS

1. Think about how your life would have changed if each of the following had taken place:
   a. Your family's income was cut off suddenly.
   b. You became seriously physically handicapped.
   c. You had to move to another country—such as Chile or French-speaking Africa—without family or friends and without knowing local customs or the language.

   What kinds of changes do these situations represent?

2. Contrast the ways in which a preschool child, an elementary school student, and an adolescent would approach this problem:

   Jim overslept one morning and found that he had only fifteen minutes to get to school. It normally takes him fifteen minutes to get ready and ten minutes to walk to school.

3. List some of the activities that students at your high school engaged in that you would consider "identity seeking."

4. What are some of the advantages and disadvantages of being in a special category of students?

BIBLIOGRAPHY

Berk, L. E. (1985). Why young children talk to themselves. *Young Children, 40*(5), 46–52.

Bryan, T. H., & Bryan, J. H. (1986). *Understanding learning abilities* (3rd ed.). Palo Alto: Mayfield Publishers.

Dunn, L. M. (1968). Special education for the mentally retarded: Is much of it justifiable? *Exceptional Children, 35*(1), 5–22.

Elkind, D. (1981). *Children and adolescents* (3rd ed.). New York: Oxford University Press. (chapter on egocentrism in children and adolescents)

Elkind, D. (1970, April, 5). Erik Erikson's eight ages of man. *The New York Times Magazine,* pp. 25–27+.

Flavell, J. H. (1977). *Cognitive development.* Englewood Cliffs, NJ: Prentice-Hall.

Gibson, E. J. (1969). *Principles of perceptual learning and development.* New York: Appleton-Century-Crofts.

Gilligan, C. (1982). *In a different voice.* Cambridge, MA: Harvard University Press.

Howley, A. (1986). *Teaching gifted children.* Newton, MA: Allyn and Bacon.

Kohlberg, L. (1970). The child as moral philosopher. In P. Cramer (Ed.), *Readings in developmental psychology today* (pp. 109–115). Del Mar, CA: CRM Books.

Miller, P. H. (1983). *Theories of developmental psychology.* New York: W. H. Freeman & Co.

Skinner, P. H., & Shelton, R. L. (1985). *Speech, language, and hearing: Normal processes and disorders* (2nd ed.). New York: Wiley.

Sutherland, A. T. (1984). *Disabled we stand.* Bloomington, IN: Indiana University Press.

Trotter, R. J. (1987, May). You've come a long way, baby. *Psychology Today,* pp. 34–45.

Wadsworth, B. J. (1984). *Piaget's theory of cognitive development* (2nd ed.). New York: David McKay Co.

Whitmore, J. R. (1980). *Giftedness, conflict, and underachievement.* Boston: Allyn and Bacon.

Zajonc, R. B., & Hall, E. (1986, February). Mining new gold from old research. *Psychology Today,* pp. 46–51.

NOTES

1. The two case studies presented in this Snapshot are based on information about students known to the authors of this text.

2. Flavell, J. H. (1977). *Cognitive development.* Englewood Cliffs, NJ: Prentice-Hall; Kagan, J. (1984). *The nature of the child.* New York: Basic Books. (chapter on connectedness)

3. de Villiers, P. A., & de Villiers, J. G. (1979). *Early language.* Cambridge: Harvard University Press; Olson, D. P. (1980). *The social foundations of language and thought.* New York: W. W. Norton.

4. Riegel, K. F. (1976). The dialectics of human development. *American Psychologist, 31*(10), 689–700; Sameroff, A. J. (1975). Transactional models in early social relations. In K. F. Riegel (Ed.), *The development of dialectical operations.* Basal: S. Karger.

5. Gibson, E. J. (1969). *Principles of perceptual learning and development.* New York: Appleton-Century-Crofts.

6. Wadsworth, B. J. (1984). *Piaget's theory of cognitive development* (2nd ed.). New York: David McKay Co.

7. McCall, R. B. (1979). The development of intellectual functioning in infancy and the prediction of later IQ. In J. Osofsky (Ed.), *Handbook of infant development.* New York: Wiley.

8. Vygotsky, L. S. (1978). *Mind in society: The development of higher psychological processes.* (M. Cole, V. John-Steiner, S. Scribner, & E. Souberman, Eds.). Cambridge: Harvard University Press.

9. Zivin, G. (1979). *The development of self-regulation through private speech.* New York: Wiley; Berk, L. E. (1985, July). Why young children talk to themselves. *Young Children;* Trotter, R. J. (1987, May). You've come a long way, baby. *Psychology Today,* pp. 34–45.

10. Piaget, J. (1965). *The moral judgment of the child.* New York: Free Press.

11. Kohlberg, L. (1970). The child as moral philosopher. In P. Cramer (Ed.), *Readings in developmental psychology today* (pp. 109–115). Del Mar, CA: CRM Books.

12. Gilligan, C. (1982). *In a different voice.* Cambridge: Harvard University Press.

13. Campos, J. J., Barrett, C. K., Lamb, M. E., Goldsmith, H. H., & Sternberg, C. C. (1983). Socioemotional development. In P. H. Mussen (Ed.), *Handbook of child psychology* (4th ed.), Vol. 2. *Infancy and developmental psychobiology.* New York: Wiley.

14. Dunn, J. (1983). Sibling relationships in early childhood. *Child Development, 54,* 787–811.

15. Zajonc, R. B., & Hall, E. (1986, February). Mining new gold from old research. *Psychology Today,* pp. 46–51.

16. Huston, A. C. (1983). Sex-typing. In P. H. Mussen (Ed.), *Handbook of child psychology* (4th ed.). Vol. 4. *Socialization, personality and social development* (pp. 387–468). New York: Wiley.

17. Dweck, C. S., & Bush, E. S. (1976). Sex differences in learned helplessness: I. Differentiation debilitation with peer and adult evaluators. *Developmental Psychology, 12,* 147–156; Dweck, C. S., Davidson, W., Nelson, S., & Enna, B. (1978). Sex differences in learned helplessness: II. The contingence of evaluative feedback in the classroom, and III. An experimental analysis. *Developmental Psychology, 14,* 268–276.

18. Elkind, D. (1970, April, 5). Erik Erikson's eight ages of man. *The New York Times Magazine,* 25–27+.

19. Elkind, D. (1981). *Children and adolescents* (3rd ed.). New York: Oxford University Press. (chapter on egocentrism in children and adolescents); Harter, S. (1983). Developmental perspectives on the self-esteem. In P. H. Mussen (Ed.), *Handbook of child psychology* (4th ed.). Vol. 4. *Socialization, personality, and social development.* New York: Wiley.

20. Terman, L. (1925–1959). *Genetic studies in genius* (Vols. I–V). Stanford: Stanford University Press.

21. Horowitz, F. D., & O'Brien, M. (1985). *The gifted and talented: Developmental perspectives.* Washington, DC: American Psychological Association.

22. MacMillan, D. (1977). *Mental retardation in school and society.* Boston: Little Brown.

23. Bryan, T. H., & Bryan, J. H. (1986). *Understanding learning abilities* (3rd ed.). Palo Alto: Mayfield Publishers.

24. Fotheringham, J. B., Hambley, W. D., & Haddad-Curran, H. W. (1983). *Prevention of intellectual handicaps.* Ontario: Association for the Mentally Retarded.
25. Gilfand, D. M., Jenson, W. R., & Drew, C. J. (1982). *Understanding child behavior disorders.* New York: Holt, Rinehart and Winston.
26. Skinner, P. H., & Shelton, R. L. (1985). *Speech, language, and hearing: Normal processes and disorders* (2nd ed.). New York: Wiley.
27. This episode is based on conversations between the Chris referred to in the story and one of the authors of this text.
28. Warren, D. H. (1984). *Blindness and early childhood development* (2nd ed.). New York: American Foundation for the Blind.
29. Sutherland, A. T. (1984). *Disabled we stand.* Bloomington, IN: Indiana University Press.
30. John was an eighth-grade student of one of the authors of this text.
31. Dunn, L. M. (1968). Special education for the mentally retarded: Is much of it justifiable? *Exceptional Children, 35*(1), 5–22.

CHAPTER 5

Equity and Excellence: Teaching All Students

INTRODUCTION

Chapter 5 builds upon information already presented in Chapters 1 and 4. It enlarges on ideas about the purposes of schools mentioned early in the text and relates them to differences among students described in the chapter just concluded. The focus of the chapter is on how American schools attempt to serve *all* students.

The first few pages of Chapter 1 describe the general purposes of American schools in terms of the nature of this country and the roles of its citizens. Because the United States is a democratic republic, its citizens need to be educated. They need to be able to understand ideas, events, and issues; to make judgments; to select leaders; to get along with others; to provide for their own economic well-being; and to be reasonably satisfied human beings. To provide the formal aspects of that education, we have schools.

Chapter 1 also describes American education of the 1980s and notes the significant changes that have occurred in recent years. Those changes shifted priorities for schools and raised new expectations about what schools should accomplish. Particular note is made of American dissatisfaction with schools of the 1980s and the desire that they increase their success in educating all children of the United States.

Chapter 4 describes how students grow and develop and how they appear to teachers on a day-to-day basis. It notes that schools categorize students in efforts to serve all of them appropriately but that those categories are artificial.

Chapter 5 puts ideas about the purposes of schools and the many differences among students together. It first steps back into history a few years to review the general purposes of American schools during the twentieth century. Then it analyzes the ways in which schools try to accomplish their goals with the students they are expected to serve.

In an effort to place the main thrusts of the chapter into perspective, the Snapshot presents short case studies of three students from different backgrounds and with different abilities and needs. All three must be served by the schools they attend.

The Analysis and Educational Research sections look at the same special effort to serve students who are often missed by schools—an alternative high school for at-risk students. You are asked to look at that effort both as a special service to students and as a research and demonstration project.

SNAPSHOT

The Snapshot for this chapter describes three students.[1] Each is different from the others, and all have different needs, but each must be served by the schools. As you read, consider the following:

- How should the schools serve each of these students so that each benefits as much as possible?

- In what ways should the instruction and instruction-related services provided for each of these students differ? In what ways should they be similar?

- How would you determine whether each of these students succeeds in school?

MARK

Mark is about to enter tenth grade in a comprehensive public high school. By most standards he is a successful student, although he is quiet and not a leader among his peers. He has solid A grades, ranks eighth in his class of more than 300, has taken most of the advanced courses available to him so far, plays second string on the soccer team; dates some of the popular girls at school, participates in several club activities, and is liked by his teachers.

Mark wants to be an engineer, knows he will go to college, and hopes to be accepted by an Ivy League university. He expects to be in the high school honors program for his junior and senior years. He will apply to be an intern in Washington, D.C., next summer.

Mark is one of three boys in a white, upper-middle-class family. Both his parents are professional educators—his mother is a college English professor, and his father teachers fifth grade. His home environment is supportive and educationally stimulating.

Mark's parents are reasonably satisfied with his schooling. He is achieving well, and they think most, though not all, of his teachers are good. They visit the school often and are active in the PTA. They frequently discuss Mark's progress with his teachers and counselors.

Sometimes Mark's parents wonder whether he would be achieving more if they had sent him to the private, academically challenging school they had considered. He would have had more stimulating classes, with students like himself. They decided to keep him in public school, however, so that he would interact with students from a variety of socioeconomic and racial groups.

JAMIE

Jamie is halfway through second grade in an inner-city, public elementary school. His performance is below grade level, but so far he has not failed a grade. He tries to do what his teachers want most of the time, but not always. He hates homework and rarely does it. His teachers say he is noisy and aggressive much of the time. He has a slight perception problem that affects his reading, and he has asthma that flares up from time to time.

Jamie knows his primary teacher cares about him and wants him to succeed. He likes her. She devotes lots of time to helping him, calls his mother regularly, and sometimes gets very upset with him. At times, she even cries when he does poorly.

What Jamie likes most about school is the track club. He is a runner, and he wins most of his races, except when his asthma is bad. The physical education teachers at five inner-city elementary schools began track clubs last year, and this year Mr. Stewart, his P.E. teacher, personally asked Jamie to join. Whenever there is a Saturday competition with any of the other four schools, Mr. Stewart picks up Jamie and takes him to the meet.

Jamie lives in a small rental duplex apartment with his mother and an older brother and younger sister. His mother is head of the household, and the family is on welfare. His father is in prison for killing a man during a holdup. His older brother is often in trouble and usually skips school. Some people say his mother is a prostitute.

Jamie thinks he will probably flunk this year. He is far behind most students, and he cannot read well. He has to pass achievement tests to be promoted to third grade, and he already has failed most of them. He does not know what he will do when he grows up, but he is pretty sure he will not quit school, at least not until high school—and not while he can run in a track club.

Jamie's mother, who quit school when she was in the ninth grade, rarely comes to school, but she always tries to cooperate if a teacher calls her. She knows Jamie is difficult to handle and that he has problems at school. She does not want him to turn out like his brother. She thinks the teachers are

good and appreciates the attention they give Jamie, but she does not really know much about teaching and schools.

SAUNDRA

Saundra is in sixth grade this year and will go to junior high in the fall, if she passes. She works hard at school but is not very bright. She has some form of learning problem but no one seems to know what type. She has already failed two grades. She is thirteen—the oldest, tallest, and heaviest student in her class. The other students make fun of her and sometimes laugh at her clothes. The teachers like her and feel sorry for her.

Saundra knows she is not very bright, and she worries about flunking again. Lots of times she just does not understand things, no matter how hard she tries. Even when teachers give her special help, she never gets more than a C. She has a very frustrating school life.

Grades are not the only frustration, of course. The other students tease her because she is so fat. They also used to criticize her because she wore the same dress all the time—the only school dress she had. But the teasing about the dress is less frequent now, since one of the teachers gave her six new dresses—not really new ones, but new for Saundra. She told the teacher it was the nicest thing anyone ever did for her.

Saundra lives with her mother, two sisters, and a brother in public housing—"the projects." Although her mother works as a maid, they must also accept welfare. Saundra does not know where her father is and cannot remember him. Saundra's mother is a strong person. She has held the family together despite adversity. The children respect her, as do the teachers who know her.

Saundra's mother knows Saundra does not do well in school, but she expects her to keep trying. She also knows the teachers are doing all that they can. She worries about what will happen when Saundra goes to junior high. The new teachers will not know Saundra as well as her present teachers do, and she is afraid Saundra will quit school because it will be so difficult for her. She knows that Saundra needs as much attention as she can get.

GOALS AND PURPOSES

Ideal Goals and the Real World

If schools were to meet the ideals set for them by Americans in general and educators in particular, they would provide an appropriate and excellent education for each of the students mentioned in the Snapshot; and they would do the same for all the other individuals who sit in classrooms across the nation. They would educate every single student to the maximum of his and her ability.

Of course, education has never met completely these ideals. These ideals and what schools can actually accomplish in the real world are very different. American schools have simply not provided an excellent education for all children, and they do not do so today. Students such as Jamie and Saundra sometimes "slip between the cracks," and those such as Mark tend to make it without focused attention. Most knowledgeable observers believe, however, that through the years, schools have decreased the gap between what is expected of them and what they achieve.

In Chapter 7 you will read about schools and teaching in the more distant American past—between colonial American times and this century—and about the ideas, events, and people before American history began who served as the early models for American schools. At this point, that history can be briefly summarized: As American schools evolved into and through the first half of the twentieth century, they increased in number, became available to more children, and expanded their instruction so that it became more useful to more students. Well before 1950, nearly every town had a school, and most rural children had access to a formal education, even if the distance to the schoolhouse was great. Nevertheless, many children did not have access to an education of appropriate quality. The children most often and most significantly slighted and neglected tended to be poor, minority, and handicapped.

Goals for Schools during the First Half of the Twentieth Century

Training the Mind

At the beginning of the twentieth century, the dominant view of the purpose of schools focused on *training the mind* and on teaching traditional academic subjects at the high school level. This view was articulated in 1892 by the Committee of Ten on Secondary Schools of the National Education Association.[2] The committee was composed mostly of college-level academicians who saw high school learning as a process of mental discipline that prepared students for college. The committee recommended that the high school curriculum consist of these nine subjects:

1. Latin
2. Greek
3. English

4. other modern languages
5. physical sciences (physics, chemistry, astronomy)
6. biological sciences (botany, zoology, physiology)
7. mathematics
8. geology, geography
9. history, government, political economy

Education for Life, for All

In 1918, another group reported on what high schools should teach, and its focus was a significant change from that of 1892.[3] The Commission on the Reorganization of Secondary Education, also of the National Education Association, looked at student needs, interests, and abilities, as well as at the needs of society, and concluded that schools of the twentieth century should channel their instruction toward seven areas of life. Their report, entitled *Cardinal Principles of Secondary Education*, called for high school instruction in the following:

1. health
2. command of fundamental processes
3. worthy home membership
4. vocations
5. civic education
6. worthy use of leisure time
7. ethical character

The *Cardinal Principles* stressed education of *all* students and for all aspects of their lives, not just college-bound students in demanding academic subjects. The report specifically mentioned that two-thirds of the students who began high school did not complete their studies and that they needed to be educated as well as those who were graduated.

The Whole Child

This emphasis on educating the *whole child* continued into midcentury. In the 1930s, the Educational Policies Commission of the NEA issued a report, *The Purposes of Education in American Democracy* (1938),[4] which, influenced by the high unemployment of the Great Depression, reflected a concern for the out-of-school lives of all citizens. It listed four broad issues of education, each of them focused on the individual:

1. self-realization
2. human realization
3. economic efficiency
4. civic responsibility

Its general theme was similar to the *Cardinal Principles*.

Life Adjustment

In 1944, another Educational Policies Commission report, entitled *Education for All American Youth*,[5] listed the *ten imperative needs of youth*. It continued the schools' focus on the whole child and the child's *life adjustment* rather than on academic preparation and mental discipline. The ten imperative needs of youth were

1. productive work experiences and occupational success
2. good health and physical fitness
3. rights and duties of democratic citizens
4. successful family life
5. wise consumer behavior
6. understanding science and human nature
7. appreciation of art, music, and literature
8. wise use of leisure time
9. ethical values
10. ability to think rationally and communicate clearly

The thrust of the report was reflected in the following quotation:

> When we write confidently and inclusively about education for all American youth, we mean that all youth, with their human similarities and their equally human differences, shall have educational services and opportunities suited to their personal needs and sufficient for the successful operation of a free and democratic society. (Educational Policies Commission, 1944)

Characteristics of the Curriculum

In essence, ideas about *how* schools should meet the needs of twentieth-century American children and youth have varied from the one extreme of teaching of college-preparatory subjects to all students, with relatively little attention to their direct application to the students' workday worlds, to the other extreme of intentionally selecting and presenting content in a protective school environment that stresses meeting individual needs, developing personal skills, and cultivating positive self-concepts.

Goals for Schools at Midcentury

Academic Quality

By the late 1950s, American policy-makers and educators began to have second thoughts about schools' emphasis on the whole child and the "less academic" ideas of the life-adjustment curriculum. Many began to feel that the schools' effort to educate everyone so broadly was resulting in an "average" education for most students at the expense of an education of true quality for anyone. They tended to assess quality, or the lack of it, in academic terms. Some noted particularly that schools seemed to be less challenging than they had been and that they apparently neglected the students who were most likely to become leaders of society. They demanded higher standards and more academically advanced instruction for the brighter students.

The Cold War

This concern developed in the context of the post–World War II and Korean conflict generation, when Americans were competing ideologically with the Soviet Union in the cold war and were intent on making America the best nation in everything. Then in 1957, Russia launched the satellite *Sputnik*. Americans were appalled. We asked, "How could the Russians do that before Americans can?" "What is wrong with our schools? Do we not have the scientists and the commitment to compete and win?" We were surprised, our national pride was hurt, and our security was threatened. We turned to the schools to fight back.

Education and the National Defense

Sputnik produced a national audience for academic critics who had been saying that schools lacked academic rigor, mental discipline, and "hard" academic subjects. The critics wanted to replace "soft" life-adjustment subjects with more serious study. They wanted the schools to narrow their goals and to stop trying to be all things to all people. They said the national interest was at stake. Political leaders listened and responded.

Because of this post-*Sputnik* pressure, the national government funneled money to schools for teacher education, curriculum development, and equipment purchases through the National Defense Education Act. Better education became a matter of national defense. The areas of mathematics, science, foreign languages, and guidance received special attention, as did programs for academically talented students.

Nevertheless, the pendulum did not swing completely away from life-adjustment education. The shift was more moderate, and the goals of educating the whole child and educating all the children were not lost. The change simply redirected educational priorities to a somewhat more balanced position between both types of goals.

Balance

James B. Conant reflected the shift and was partly responsible for its moderation. As president of Harvard University, chair of the Educational Policies Commission in the early 1950s, and author of several landmark studies of schools, he commanded much respect on school-related issues. He found in several of his studies, including *The American High School Today* (1959),[6] that although schools could be improved, they were generally not all that bad and were already able to challenge talented students and at the same time provide a comprehensive education for all students. Conant's ideas set a tone for the times.

School Organization

Ideas on how schools should be organized have also shifted back and forth through the century. Junior high schools were formed in the 1920s and 1930s to provide a transition for adolescent students between elementary school and high school. In the 1960s, middle schools replaced junior highs in many places, so that a similar close personal attention could be provided for students in transition, but this time for students in their preadolescent years.

School Size

The size of schools, particularly high schools, also has changed over the years. Small, somewhat constrained, multiple-purpose schools were replaced by consolidated county high schools with separate vocational wings and larger numbers of advanced and special courses than the small schools could provide. These, in turn, were succeeded by even larger comprehensive high schools with a myriad of courses and schools-within-schools.

Education for Individual Excellence

By the 1960s, the generally accepted mission of schools in America included a combination of thrusts. Schools were expected to educate the whole child and every child to the maximum of each individual's ability. They were to help each student to strive for and reach *individual excellence*. John W. Gardner, educator and, after 1965, secretary of health, education and welfare under President Lyndon B. Johnson, stated the idea in 1961 when he wrote the following about striving for excellence;

There is a way of measuring excellence that involves comparison between people—some are musical geniuses and some are not; and there is another that involves comparison between myself at my best and myself at my worst. It is this latter comparison which enables me to assert that I am being true to the best that is in me—or forces me to confess that I am not. . . . (Gardner, 1961, p. 128).[7]

. . . .

Our society cannot achieve greatness unless individuals at many levels of ability accept the need for high standards of performance and strive to achieve those standards within the limits possible for them. . . . If the man in the street says, "Those fellows at the top have to be good, but I'm just a slob and can act like one"—then our days of greatness are behind us. We must foster a conception of excellence which may be applied to every degree of ability and to every socially acceptable activity. . . . (Gardner, 1961, p. 131)

And we are not going to get that kind of striving, that kind of alert and proud attention to performance, unless we can instruct the whole society in a conception of excellence that leaves room for everybody who is willing to strive—a conception of excellence which means that whoever I am or whatever I am doing . . . some kind of excellence is within my reach. (Gardner, 1961, pp. 128, 131)

Current Goals for Schools: Equity and Excellence

Since the 1960s, American schools have attempted to enable their students to reach the excellence identified by Gardner. In doing so, they have sought to provide quality education for each individual child in terms of his or her capabilities. To accomplish this, they have delineated three concurrent goals for schools:

- that *all* children and youth be educated in the schools,
- that they have an *equal* education in terms of their individual capabilities, and
- that each child's education be *excellent*.

A Sampling of Diverse High School Course Offerings

A quick glance at high school course offerings usually reflects a school's attempt to serve students with different needs, interests, and abilities. A list of course titles drawn from such a set of offerings is reproduced below:

advanced placement history	data processing
honors mathematics	commercial art
general mathematics	drama III
driver training	writing fundamentals
personal mathematics	general biology

aerobics	marketing
advanced chemistry	sculpture
business practice	orchestra
carpentry	journalism
contemporary issues	calculus II
French IV	cosmetology
adapted physical education	civics
consumer economics	home economics
auto mechanics	masonry

These goals mean that all three students described in the Snapshot of this chapter—Mark, Jamie, and Saundra—would have an equally excellent education, one that would be best for each of them individually.

Accomplishing these goals is not an easy task, however, and few schools would claim to have done so. Although the reasons for the difficult nature of the effort are many, we will examine only two at this time: (1) the fact that resources for schools are limited and (2) the fact that the meaning of the concept of excellence is not always clear in relation to schools and students.

Limited Resources

Nearly all schools face significant limitations on the resources that are critical to their success. Their funds are limited, and their leaders and teachers have limited amounts of energy, time, insight, commitment, and professional skill. They cannot pay for everything they want to do. They cannot assign the best teacher to every student. They simply cannot do everything.

Trade-offs

This means schools must set priorities and make choices. They must decide which goals are most important and which are less so. In short, they must make *trade-offs*.

Equal and Excellent, Too

This need for trade-offs has led many school officials and many of those who support the schools to ask whether schools can really be equitable to all students and at the same time be excellent in all that they do. Some say they cannot. They say trying to be both equitable and excellent is too much. Some even see an incompatibility or contradiction between equity and excellence. Some go so far as to say that the two are mutually exclusive.

In fact, equity and excellence are not mutually exclusive, incompatible, or contradictory as goals for schools. They do, however, compete for attention and support, and this does result in a tension between them. But good school systems manage the tension, balance the priorities, and divide the resources rather evenly. They continue to seek both equity and excellence for their students.

Defining Excellence

How well schools provide equity and excellence for their students also depends on the meaning of "excellence." In a general sense, excellence means the best, and of course everyone wants the best—the best schools, the best education for students, the best teachers, and so forth. But for the term to be useful to teachers and other school decision makers, it must be more precise. It must be

An Introduction to Teaching and Schools **177**

made operational. Such questions as the following must be answered: Excellent in what way? Excellent by what standards?

Individual Capabilities

The statement by John W. Gardner quoted earlier provides a first step in operationalizing the concept of excellence in the context of schools. It defines *excellence* in terms of the *individual capabilities of all students*. Students are excellent if they reach the upper limits of their own potential, and schools are excellent to the extent that they enable all of their students to do this. Figure 5–1 illustrates how comparisons of excellence will vary.

A second step in operationalizing the concept of excellence involves the question, *Excellent at what?* Are students excellent because they pass the most subjects possible, because they get the best grades, because they succeed in the most demanding courses, because they get into the best colleges, or because they turn out to be very likable people? Are their schools excellent because they offer the most courses, set the highest standards, have the best teachers, or graduate the most students who go to college?

What Students Learn

In recent years, the *Excellent at what?* question has been answered most often in terms of what and how much students learn by the time they finish school. In that sense, schools are judged to be excellent on the basis of the quality or amount of learning they produce in their students. In educational jargon this is called the *quality of educational outcomes.* (For an indepth discussion of excellence, see Fantini, 1986.)[8]

Excellence—To Serve All Students Well

When excellence is thought of in this double-sided way—in terms of individual student potential and amount of learning produced in all students—the

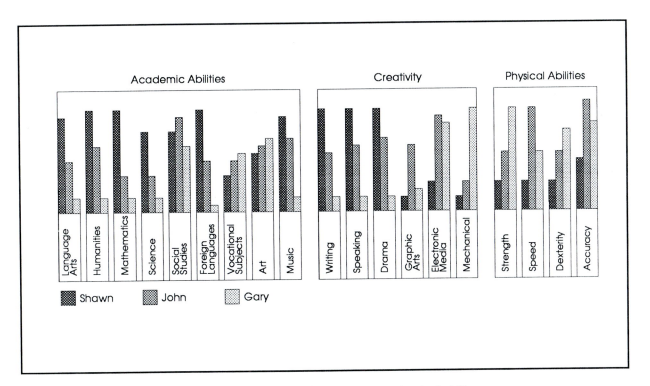

Figure 5–1. Comparison of student abilities. These graphs reflect the different levels of ability shown on teacher-administered inventories in the same classes in the same school.

Gardner's idea of excellence displayed as a banner on a school wall.

ideas of equity and excellence are not competing goals for schools. They are a single standard. The challenge for all schools is to serve all students well.

An Emphasis on Equity

In the early 1960s, a genuine and widespread concern developed in America about the plight of the poor and other disadvantaged people of this nation. American society was successful and prosperous, yet some of its citizens obviously did not share in the benefits. Political and civil rights leaders asked why this situation existed, condemned it, and called for action to change it. The Kennedy administration began an attack on poverty and was perceived to hold racial equality as a cornerstone of its agenda. When President John F. Kennedy was assassinated in 1963, President Lyndon Johnson enlarged upon and continued the effort, steering through Congress great numbers of civil rights bills, declaring a War on Poverty, and calling for a Great Society, one in which all Americans shared in the wealth of the nation, both financially and culturally. Nearly everyone felt that schools should play a critical role in this advancement of civilization.

Because of this national effort to help those most in need, because of the critical role of schools in doing so, and because poor, minority, and handicapped children were so noticeably "disadvantaged" in both schools and society as a whole, the combined equity and excellence goals for schools were somewhat skewed during the 1960s and early 1970s. Matters involving *equity* were emphasized more than those that concentrated on excellence. During the 1980s the emphasis shifted more toward excellence again, and quality of schooling is now being judged in terms of student academic achievement. However, educators in general are still committed both to equity and excellence in schools and are still trying to accomplish both at the same time.

The Legal Mandate for Equity

Much of the push for equity in the schools was part of the civil rights movement of the 1950s, 1960s, and 1970s and came from outside the schools, especially through court challenges to inequitable school policies and practices and through national legislation. The watershed year was 1954, and the key event was the United States Supreme Court decision in the case *Brown* v. *Board of Education of Topeka*.

Brown v. *Board of Education*

The *Brown* case actually involved a combination of four cases then before the courts. The issues were many, complex, and overlapping. For the purposes of this discussion, however, we will focus on only the main points that relate to the issue of equity in the schools.

Plessy v. *Ferguson*

Since the *Plessy* v. *Ferguson* decision in 1896, most United States school systems had operated racially segregated schools because the *Plessy* ruling allowed them to do so. That opinion said that "separate but equal" facilities did not violate the Thirteenth and Fourteenth Amendments to the Constitution of the United States. Those amendments eliminated slavery and protected certain individual rights, including *due process* and *equal protection* of the law.

The *Plessy* case did not arise from a question about schools. It came about when Homer Adolph Plessy sued a Louisiana criminal court judge who had convicted him for refusing to leave a "white-only" railroad car. A Louisiana law had required that white and "colored" passengers use separate public accommodations. Plessy, who was of one-eighth "African blood," had boarded a train in New Orleans, occupied a place in a "white-only" car, and refused to leave when he was ordered to do so. He was arrested, jailed, and convicted. (It is interesting to note that his action was essentially comparable to that of Rosa Parks, a tired black working woman whose refusal to move to the back of an Alabama bus in 1954 brought about a black boycott in Montgomery and ushered the future Nobel laureate, Dr. Martin Luther King, Jr., to a position of national importance.)

The *Plessy* decision said that laws requiring separation between the races could be legally enforced. Courts could not interfere. Since laws in many states segregated schools, as well as housing, transportation, and much of society as a whole, schools were affected.

In the unanimous *Brown* opinion, written by Chief Justice Earl Warren, the Court disagreed directly with the *Plessy* decision. Its two-part opinion said:

Equal Protection of the Law

1. that segregation in public schools deprived the plaintiffs in the *Brown* case of "the equal protection of the law" and

2. that schools must correct the situation.

The Court based the first part of the decision on a series of assumptions and judgments:

1. that education was a critically important part of contemporary society of the 1950s;
2. that children probably could not succeed in life without it;
3. that if states provided public education at state expense, they had to provide it equally for all children;
4. that even if most other aspects of education are equal for both races, segregation deprives minority children of an equal education because it denotes "inferiority" of the minority group;
5. that a feeling of inferiority affects a child's motivation and mental development; and
6. that this deprivation results in depriving minority children of some of the benefits they would receive in a racially integrated school system.

Therefore, the first part of the *Brown* decision said that because separating children solely on the basis of race generates "a feeling of inferiority as to their status in the community that may affect their hearts and minds in a way unlikely ever to be undone," *separate educational facilities are inherently unequal.*

Corrective Action—Desegregation

In the second part of the *Brown* decision the Court said that schools that had been legally segregated had to begin a process of correcting the situation. It said they had to

1. make a prompt and reasonable start toward desegregation;
2. carry out the ruling of the court in an effective manner;
3. proceed consistently and comply in good faith at the earliest possible date; and
4. develop local desegregation plans.

The *Brown* decision started a nationwide school desegregation process that directly affected nearly all American communities and most school students. At first, schools were most significantly affected that had been segregated by law or legal regulation—*de jure* (by right) *segregation*. Most such schools were in the South.

However, subsequent court decisions extended the *Brown* rulings to schools that were not segregated by laws requiring segregation but because of other factors—housing patterns, the locations of schools, family choice, and local custom—*de facto* (of fact) *segregation*. De facto segregation rulings affected schools throughout the nation, especially outside the South.

"All Deliberate Speed"

When school systems and state and local governments delayed implementing the *Brown* directives—as many did—complainants turned to the courts for additional help. As a result, the courts insisted a few years later that desegregation proceed with *"all deliberate speed."* School systems and states were required to develop desegregation plans with timetables, to have the plans approved by the courts, and to abide by them. Often the courts found it necessary to monitor compliance closely. School officials who persisted in delaying were charged with contempt of court. In the same year, the Civil Rights Act of 1964 authorized the United States attorney general to sue and to withhold funds from school systems that were not desegregating as expected or were otherwise discriminating by race, color, or national origin.

Swain v. Charlotte-Mecklenburg Board of Education

During the early 1970s, the courts extended school desegregation orders beyond instances of de jure segregation to cases in which schools had become segregated de facto. The most important Supreme Court case involving this type of school segregation was *Swain v. Charlotte-Mecklenburg Board of Education* (1971). The Charlotte-Mecklenburg County School District in North Carolina had technically desegregated its schools before 1971, but because of neighborhood living patterns, a number of district schools still had large concentrations of either black or white students.

Busing

In the *Swain* decision, the Court said that schools should reflect the general racial composition of the population of the whole district rather than that of specific neighborhoods. It declared that although neighborhood schools were a good idea under normal circumstances, the degree of racial imbalance in the Charlotte-Mecklenburg Schools was such that the situation was not normal. Under these conditions, desegregation was more important than neighborhood schools. It said further that although sending students to schools outside their neighborhood might prove inconvenient, transporting children by schoolbus would be an appropriate way to overcome segregation, since students already rode buses to school throughout the county.

After the *Swain* decision, the courts ruled in a number of other de facto school segregation cases, and often their decisions were inconsistent. These situations usually involved one central issue: Should serious imbalances in the racial com-

position of schools be permitted, or is racial segregation contrary to the constitutional guarantees of equality? The courts, Congress, and the executive branch of the federal government have often disagreed on how to answer the question.

Nevertheless, since the mid-1970s, the general movement of desegregation has been toward agreed-upon balances in the racial composition of schools, regardless of the cause of the imbalance. The means typically used to desegregate are those that restore balance with the least amount of disruption. However, nearly all such efforts involve a significant amount of disruption, consternation, and ideological conflict.

Desegregation, the Norm

During the thirty years following the *Brown* decision, most schools in America were gradually desegregated, and as a result minority students in general have received more equitable educations than had been the case. The most obvious effects of the process have been the elimination of legally segregated public schools and/or public schools that are transparently unequal in quality. But broader, more subtle, and probably more pervasive changes have also taken place. Most white, black, and other minority students attend the same schools, interact fairly closely with each other, and experience the same teaching. Desegregated schools have become the norm.

The Legal Mandate for Equity Applied to Students with Handicaps

In the decades since the *Brown* decision, advocates for children and youth with handicapping conditions have demanded that the same principles of equity be applied to disabled children. Their insistence has resulted in court actions and legislation that have extended those same *rights of education* to such students. As with desegregation, however, the process has not been easy, quick, or smooth.

Education: A Right for All

Although the *Brown* decision referred to the education of black children, it stated that when states choose to provide education for children, "it is a right that must be available to all on equal terms." This principle became the basis for litigation concerning the education of children with handicaps. In *Pennsylvania Association for Retarded Children* (*PARC*) v. *Commonwealth of Pennsylvania*, a landmark case opened in 1971 and ruled on in 1974, the state of Pennsylvania agreed to a consent decree stipulating that it would educate mentally retarded children at public expense. The state agreed

> to provide a free public education for all its children between the ages of six and twenty-one years. . . .
>
> to place each mentally retarded child in a free, public program of education and training appropriate to the child's capacity.

Two related court decisions extended the *PARC* case principles beyond mentally retarded children to those with other handicapping conditions. The ruling in *Mills* v. *Board of Education of Washington, D.C.* (1972) said the right of a free public education extended to children with all types of handicapping conditions. The *Wyatt* v. *Stickney* (1972) decision said children who are institutionalized also have a right to the same educational services as other children.

Public Law 94–142

These and related court decisions, as well as several laws passed in the early 1970s, set the stage for Public Law 94–142, the most significant law in U.S. history affecting the education of people with handicapping conditions. This law, passed in 1975, mandated that each state provide for the education of people with

handicaps, that it follow a set schedule in implementing the law, and that it be in full compliance by the fall of 1980. The law stipulated that children with the following handicapping conditions had to be served by each state:

- mental retardation
- hearing impairment
- deafness
- speech impairment
- visual handicaps
- serious emotional disturbance
- orthopedic impairment
- deafness/blindness
- learning disability
- multiple handicaps
- "other health impairments"

Least Restrictive Educational Environment

Individual Education Program

Public Law 94–142 specified that children and youth with handicapping conditions must be provided *a free appropriate public education* in the *least restrictive educational environment*. Under the law, the plan of education for each of these students must be developed in the form of an *individual education program* designed to meet his or her individual needs. The law also reaffirmed that the process of determining which educational services are to be provided for a specific child must be decided upon according to *due-process* procedures and with the direct participation of parents or guardians. It made states responsible for all educational programs for the handicapped and provided federal government funds to pay part of the costs. In the 1980s, Public Law 99–457 updated and reinforced the principles and stipulations of 94–142.

SCHOOLS AND DIFFERENCES AMONG STUDENTS

"The Best for Each"

As Chapter 4 showed, if schools are to serve all students equally and excellently, they cannot treat all of them in the same way. To do so would not only overlook the differences among students; it would be naive. On the other hand, schools cannot treat each student as a wholly unique individual. They do not have the resources to do so. The challenge involved in providing both an equitable and excellent education to all students, then, is to provide the *best* education for *each* student.

Categorizing Students and Targeting Instruction

To approach the task of providing the best education to each student realistically, educators often group or categorize students, and teachers then target their instruction to those groups—high ability, low ability, college prep, vocational, and so forth. They do so because they believe that categorizing helps them teach better. In fact, they categorize subject matter, activities, and materials, as well as students.

Appropriately Targeted Instruction

When educators target instruction appropriately, the process usually helps everyone. Teachers teach better, and students learn better. For example, when the students who seem to have the best writing skills are grouped together for creative writing, the teacher can focus more intently on their particular skills than when such students are scattered among poorer writers. When those reading significantly below grade level are taught together, the teacher can target their common problems more exactly than when they are in heterogeneous groups. When students are permitted to elect some of their subjects on the basis of their personal interests and goals, their motivation to learn tends to increase.

When the categorizing and targeting are wrong, however, teaching and learning are inhibited. More importantly, students are hurt. For example, when all minority students are put into segregated classes, the placement is based on stereotypes, just as is the assumption that all girls are weak in mathematics. Similarly, when children with learning problems are assumed to be mentally retarded, they are incompetently diagnosed.

In essence, categorizing students to some extent is necessary, appropriate, and helpful. But categorizing must be done carefully, must be based on multiple criteria, and must be supported by complete and accurate data. The process must be seen as complex. The students must always be seen more as unique than alike.

An Educator-imposed Process

Chapter 4 explains that students do not naturally fall into homogeneous groups. Educators categorize them, an artificial process that they impose upon the students. Even when the categorizing is done well, with student understanding and approval, with the best of intentions, and with positive results, it necessarily omits some of the qualities of the individuals involved. It is done because schools cannot meet all of the individual differences of all their students. And when they cannot make the system fit the student, they find it necessary to make the student fit the system.

Before you proceed further with this chapter, think a little about how the three students described in the Snapshot of this chapter—Mark, Jamie, and Saundra—might be classified and what specialized attention and instruction might be directed toward each of them. For each of the three students, ask yourself these questions:

- What characteristics or conditions set this student apart from more "typical" students?
- What special services and instruction should be provided to address these conditions?
- What would these efforts cost the school in terms of people, time, and money?

As you read the next part of this chapter, think of which, if any, of the categories might fit each of these students. If none would fit, why not? How can teachers serve students who are different from others in particular ways but not different enough to be placed in a special category?

EFFORTS TO SERVE ALL STUDENTS

This section of the chapter describes major efforts by schools to serve all students. Each effort focuses on a general category of students. Each is an attempt by schools to accomplish the concurrent goals of equity and excellence.

Racial Desegregation

Although the *Brown* decision said that racially segregated schools could not be maintained and, thereby, started the process of desegregation, years passed before most segregated schools were desegregated and before large numbers of black and white students attended the same classes. In some schools and for many communities of parents, teachers, and children the process is still not complete. As a result, schools, teachers, students, and our society still suffer.

An Erroneous View of Differences

Though extremely regrettable, the length of the desegregation process is not hard to understand. The tradition of racial segregation was ingrained in American society since white conquest and settlement began. Early on, our economy became a slave economy, from which resulted an erroneous view of differences among human beings. It was perpetuated by ignorance and fear and was institutionalized by economic conditions, social norms, religious justification, public legislation, and common practice. It was certainly not just a school problem. It occurred in schools because schools are a part of society which clearly reflect the values of the society.

Dual School Systems

Because state and local governments are responsible for providing public education and, therefore, decide how and to whom it is provided, it was they who established dual systems of schooling based on race. They decided when to build schools, where to build them, and how much to spend. They determined which students were assigned to which buildings, which classes, and which types of instruction. In doing this, they often made racially based judgments that were common in the society of their times. In short, segregated schools did not occur for educational reasons; they came about because of the racially biased cultural expectations of the society.

Approaches to Desegregation

In response to court orders and governmental legislation over the past three decades, school systems have tried a number of approaches to desegregation. Some of those efforts have been effective; some have not. Some have been "good-faith" responses; some have involved minimal compliance. Some have been obstructive. Among the efforts that have been effective, at least to some extent, are the following:

- *Freedom of choice, voluntary student transfer*, and *open enrollment*. Students and parents choose schools. Often, the students choosing a school outside their neighborhood are part of the racial minority of their new school.

- *Voluntary busing*. Using one of the above options, students are bused to schools outside their neighborhood.

- *Compulsory busing*. Students are assigned to schools outside their neighborhood and are required to attend that school if they attend a public school.

- *Busing across school district lines*. This involves one of the above arrangements but with the additional characteristic that the schools to which the students are transported are in different districts from those in which the students live.

- *Combining school districts*. Under this system a number of school districts are treated as if they were the same district, so that the number of minority and white students suffices to make desegregation meaningful.

- *Establishing target ratios for schools*. This involves agreements to assign students by race to specific schools in a proportion that reflects how they are represented in the community as a whole.

- *Magnet schools*. These are schools that would have a disproportionately high concentration of students of a particular race if maintained as neighborhood schools. To avoid the imbalance, educators establish in them programs with special academic foci so that students from the entire school district are attracted.

Obstructive Tactics

Obstructive tactics have included:

refusal to comply,

delays of legal actions,

closing the public schools entirely,

establishing white-only private schools, and

segregating students within schools.

(For thorough discussions of racial desegregation, see Hawley, 1981 and Rossell & Hawley, 1983.)[9]

White Flight

White flight, an interesting social phenomenon often associated with school desegregation, occurs when white people move away from neighborhoods that are in the process of absorbing additional minority group members. In the 1960s and 1970s this seemed to happen frequently as a direct result of school desegregation. When white children from one neighborhood were assigned to schools with high percentages of black students, their families moved to new neighborhoods.

More recently, however, researchers have found that white flight may be more complex than a simple negative reaction by whites toward blacks. Generally, people move to new neighborhoods for one of two reasons. When they move to "better" neighborhoods, they do so because they can afford it and because they want to improve their social and economic status in the community. When they move to less desirable neighborhoods, they do so because they are forced, usually because of economic circumstances. (See Rossell & Hawley, 1983.)

In this context, white flight is part of the mobility of families from "less desirable" to "more desirable" neighborhoods. Since white families generally tend to be economically "better off" than black families, whites more often move to so-called better neighborhoods. Frequently, blacks replace them. Of course, to the extent that people view schools with high concentrations of poor, minority students as "less desirable," school desegregation is a motivation for whites to move away.

Compensatory Education

Compensatory education is an effort by schools to provide special instruction for students whose out-of-school lives are considered to be so different from that of most students that they are at a disadvantage in the regular school program. The types of deficiencies most often addressed involve economic and social deprivation associated with poverty, family instability, and other social conditions that hinder education.

For Disadvantaged Students

Compensatory programs usually provide remedial instruction, special activities, and supplemental services intended to make instruction for disadvantaged students more effective and to produce greater achievement. Some of these are

- *Early childhood education programs for "high-risk" students,* such as Head Start and Follow Through. Head Start programs are designed to provide early intervention and special academic help to preschool students who would not be expected to succeed in the primary grades under typical conditions. It provides special readiness instruction prior to first grade. Follow Through programs continue similar special instruction through the primary grades in an effort to sustain gains made at the preschool level.

Head Start teacher and students.

- *Family intervention programs* that provide aid to children and parents of infants and preschoolers. Many of these attempt to prevent nutritional and educational handicaps from developing at early ages.
- *Basic skill instruction,* especially in reading and early language development.
- *Bilingual education,* which provides instruction in a primary language other than or in addition to English.
- *Special counseling and guidance services* for students and parents.
- *Tutoring services* for students who demonstrate areas of academic weakness.
- *Dropout prevention programs,* including alternative schools, work-study arrangements, and on-the-job training.
- *Adult literacy instruction,* which by adding reading to the student's skills can enhance quality of life and ability to get or keep jobs.
- *Job training,* which prepares students to be able to get and stay on jobs.

Federal Government Initiative

Many current compensatory education programs were initially developed at the federal government level and enacted through laws passed during the 1960s as part of the response to the civil rights movement and the federal government's War on Poverty. Those early efforts typically provided federal government momentum, guidelines, and funds but expected state and local governments to provide the programming.

As a result of federal legislation and comparable action at state levels, compensatory education is now provided for students from early childhood through adulthood. For the most part, the concept has remained strong from the 1960s

Something to Think About

The following is an excerpt from a news item in *Newsweek* (1987, June 8, p. 27). Frank Gibney, Jr. was the reporter; material used with permission.

The Gonzalez family lives in the lower Rio Grande valley in a cramped, dark and drafty three-room shack. Their home is in a *colonia* (neighborhood), an unincorporated rural subdivision. They have no heat or sewage system, and when it rains the colonia's rutted dirt roads and yards flood so badly that children must wade through a stew of water and raw sewage to get to the school buses. Even in the dry, 100-degree heat of spring kids have the wheezing cough of poverty.

That cough echoes up and down the U.S. border with Mexico, a poverty belt more desperate than even Appalachia. The heart of the squalor is in the lower Rio Grande valley, now the poorest region in the United States. In "the Valley," as it is known, Gonzalez and up to 250,000 other American citizens live in more than 400 rural slums. Unemployment in the colonias runs as high as 50 percent, water supplies are fouled and chronic diseases are rampant. Schools in the Valley's three main counties are hopelessly overcrowded. In short, the conditions in the colonias are the worst America has to offer. And the population is increasing so rapidly that studies predict it will double by the year 2000.

- How can schools provide an education for children of "the Valley" that will compensate for their living conditions?

- How would you describe or provide an "excellent" education for a child with this background?

through the 1980s; but in recent years, funding has not kept pace with inflation as the federal government, particularly under the Reagan administration, cut back on social programs in general.

Results Are Mixed

Although government officials and school leaders expect compensatory education programs to help solve the instructional needs of disadvantaged students, data from evaluation of many of those programs provide mixed results. In general, the findings do not show the gains in student achievement that have been anticipated. Unfortunately, it appears that despite tremendous efforts and much money, most compensatory education programs simply do not enable disadvantaged children to catch up with middle-class children in a significant or long-term way.

This less-than-successful history of compensatory education programs is being investigated. Some researchers fault the breadth and "scattergun" thrust of some efforts; others say that specific programs are too small and short-term in scale; some raise questions about the instructional methods used and the qualifications of the teachers; and some say the task of educating the "children of poverty" in the United States is just too complex and too difficult to be accomplished in these ways.

ANALYSIS

This Analysis section consists of excerpts from interviews of three people, a former student and two teachers, who participated in an alternative high school in a large city. The alternative school is an attempt to reach students who are "at risk"—in danger of dropping out.[10] As you read, consider:

- In what ways are the experiences described here success stories?
- What happens to students like Barbara when they do not have access to these types of programs?
- How do you think the current accountability pressures in education affect programs such as these?
- Programs such as these are usually very expensive. If you were asked for your recommendation by a school board that had to cut program budgets, would you suggest they keep this program and terminate others? Why or why not? Which types of school programs are less important to you than this? Which are more important?
- Would you want to teach in this type of alternative school? Why or why not?

BARBARA

"You can be the scum of the earth," she says, ticking off each word as evenly as a metronome, "and these people would find something good about you. If you have anything good about you, that is."

Barbara is talking about an alternative program at a large comprehensive high school, a program which enabled her to graduate from high school a year ago.

"I never thought I would graduate from high school," she says, her hands busy flicking imaginary crumbs from the table. "Not until I got into this program." With a half laugh she adds, "My parents called it a miracle."

She describes her high school experience as a progressive journey toward apathy. "I went to school freshman year, got all my credits, and got good grades, although I didn't see the point."

Her attendance became extremely sporadic her sophomore year. "In the mornings I played Frisbee and in the afternoons I played pinball."

She explains with a question. "What was the point? My teachers could[n't] have cared less."

The outwardly obliging exterior she maintained her first year of high school began to disintegrate into [that of] a defiant, sullen girl who "partied" on school grounds within eyesight of teachers who left her and her friends alone.

After her sophomore year, Barbara interviewed for admission to a new program, an alternative program designed for students in danger of dropping out of school. She says her attitude changed.

"The teachers cared so much," she says, leaning forward and stubbing out her cigarette between two slender fingers. "They told you over and over that you could do it, they knew you could. And they said they knew that you knew too, deep inside." In her intensity, her voice breaks and she looks embarrassed for a minute, but then continues. "They kept us going. The classes were so small—about 8 kids—that we had to get along. And if we didn't understand something, they explained it. We did things over and over and over until they were right."

Pinching the rim of a paper cup, Barbara says, "It was hard." She wants me to understand that this was no easy ride; there were rules and regulations, more than in the regular school. A certain number of infractions and out you went. Period.

Without preface, she mentions her daughter. "Audrey is a year and a half now. I'm nineteen. I got pregnant when I was sixteen and I had her when I was seventeen."

. . . The first person Barbara told about her pregnancy was one of her teachers. She smiles as she remembers it. "She was great. She was wonderful. I was so scared. She told me all the options, all the things I could do. She told me it was all my decision. And she didn't tell anybody else. Not one single person." She adds, "She never told anything if you didn't want her to."

Opening her wallet, Barbara shows pictures of her daughter. Her face softens, showing them. "She was completely my responsibility. I took her to a baby-sitter on my way to school every day. I mean, can you imagine how tough this program was? If you were going to be late, you had to call them. Regular high school was never like that. They didn't care what you did."

To pay for the baby-sitter, Barbara worked during the afternoons in an office, which fulfilled one of the program's requirements that students hold a job. At night her boyfriend took care of the baby and she went to her second job as a waitress.

"I did it because I knew I had to. I knew this was my last chance. There wouldn't be any other. I had to graduate from high school. I didn't want to end up sitting in a room somewhere with a baby, watching TV and waiting for my welfare payments."

. . . Barbara describes her pregnancy as a miserable experience. "Some mornings I would wake up and cry. I didn't want to go to school pregnant. The jocks would all look at me and say, 'Wow! She's pregnant.' "

Her eyes pull back and cloud over. "One day this lady on the street gave me this awful look. I was nine months pregnant and out to here"— she motions about two feet in front of her—" and I knew how I looked. But I wanted to say to her, lady, don't you look at me that way. I have a job and I'm going to graduate from high school and I'M NOT ON WELFARE.". . .

"Well, I did do it," she says. "I have a job, I graduated, I support my daughter . . ."

Her hands are finally still, clasped in front of her on the table as if she is going to pray. "Someday," she tells me, "someday I'm going to go to college.". . .

. . . as we both get up to leave, she smiles at me again. I thank her for telling me about how she got through school; I tell her she is a strong person. I want us to both leave with a feeling of optimism. Barbara is, after all, a success story.

"I'd do anything for those people," she says suddenly, as we emerge into the white sunlight of midday. She is referring to her teachers in the alternative program. "Anything. Because they did so much for me."

MIKE AND SUSAN

Barbara's teachers radiate the conviction that they are doing something worthwhile. They work with at-risk students, a population characterized by a variety of problems. But Mike and Susan are unified in their enthusiasm.

"These kids are so much more rewarding to teach," Mike says. "We find working with them to be more interesting, more creative. And the program gives us so much more flexibility and freedom. We're not boxed into a mindset that says we absolutely have to cover a certain amount of ground by a certain time, no matter if it isn't understood."

Susan chimes in. "One thing you can feel, when you work with these kids, are the rewards. When you teach in a regular classroom, as we both have, sometimes you get the feeling that those kids will make it no matter who's standing in front of them."

Susan and Mike teach in an alternative program . . . constructed around a 5-point system which governs student behavior. Each negative behavior earns the student 1 point. At the accumulation of 5 points, the student is terminated from the program. However, there are chances for redemption built into the point system. A steady week of perfect behavior results in having a point erased from one's record.

Points are meted out for "clearly inappropriate behaviors," according to Susan. "If you don't call in before school starts to say you're sick or going to be late, or if you break a window, do wheelies in the parking lot, fight with other kids—each of those constitutes a point."

Attrition is not a severe problem. "We lose about 4–5 juniors a quarter," Mike says, "but not many seniors. They can see the end in sight and can operate under the system."

What works to make these kids turn their attitudes around? Susan says, "We personalize a lot. We remember their birthdays, things like that. And we do a lot of counseling. If a kid isn't in school, we call him or her up at home and find out why not. If a kid seems depressed, we take some class time to find out what's wrong.". . .

Susan, an English teacher, gives assignments rooted in reality. "Every February when the kids think they can't go to school another day, the school boards starts talking about cutting our funding. We say to the kids: Maybe we won't be here next year. That's when the juniors write letters to the school board members."

"It's the best writing assignment I ever give, because they know how important it is to state their case carefully. They know why they have to write their letters over four times until they're perfect. We also invite people in to speak who are responsible for funding and the kids have to present their case orally. That's the very best communication instruction they could get.

Building a team spirit among the kids in the program isn't difficult, according to both teachers. "At the beginning of the year we do a lot of outdoor activities which focus on group cohesiveness," Mike says. "We take them out into the woods and present them with a situation where there's a log suspended over their heads by two ropes. We make it very immediate. Their task, for the good of the group, is to figure out how the entire group is going to get over that log. It has to be a group decision, and the kids have to come up with a plan."

"Right away you see who the leaders are. They all have to help each other; they have to touch each other and lift each other. This activity, like all the others we have them engage in, is designed so that no one can do it alone. This builds an incredible spirit among the group."

Susan responds to the notion that critics might consider their program a holding operation. "I tell the parents of my kids that they're learning more English here than in a regular classroom. I have these kids for two years and I always get excited their senior year when I see how much they've learned. I know exactly what they need to work on, what they're capable of and how far I can push them."

"Having a small class makes it possible to take difficult assignments and make sure every kid knows what to do because we are able to work one-on-one a lot . . . You wouldn't think of our kids as being shy, but a lot of them have a shyness that is based upon their negative view of themselves. They feel they're not really very good at anything. They've never been good at school and they've been in trouble at home. Shyness is a way to avoid failure."

In this program they find they can go out and have a very positive experience and get a great recommendation from an employer. Once they've gone through a couple of these experiences they start having a more positive opinion of themselves."

The team spirit among the teachers in the program is just as compelling as that demonstrated among the students. "We're supposed to meet every day for one hour," Susan says. "It always ends up being three hours. We support each other, talk to each other. It also helps that we're all full-time in the program. We don't have to split duties elsewhere in the school, so we're able to stay focused."

Mike concludes, "In general, if you ask if teachers want to work in these programs, the answer is no. But we think if they knew how great the rewards are, how positively you as a teacher can feel about what you're doing, there would be more teachers opting for an alternative program." (Turnbaugh, 1986)

Bilingual Education

Bilingual education can be thought of as a form of compensatory education targeted toward non-English-speaking students who might fall behind others in class because of a linguistic barrier to communication. Early bilingual programs were intended to teach students whose primary language is not English in their native language until they developed skills in English. The concept was enacted into law in the 1960s as Title VII of the Elementary and Secondary Education Act of 1965 and in the Bilingual Education Act of 1968. It was reinforced through subsequent legislation.

Lau v. Nicholas

Momentum for bilingual education was provided in the courts in the 1970s. In 1974, the United States Supreme Court in *Lau* v. *Nicholas* addressed questions about (1) the extent to which non-English-speaking students face a language barrier in schools and (2) what schools should do about it. The Court ruled that the San Francisco, California, schools were treating non-English-speaking students unequally when they required them to use the same materials and facilities as English-speaking students. As a result of this decision and subsequent mandates by the U.S. Office of Civil Rights, school systems must identify students whose primary language is not English and must provide language instruction for them in their primary language. They must help them learn by means of their primary language until their English is adequate.

"New-Immigrant" Students

When bilingual legislation was initially passed in the 1960s, the predominant non-English-speaking group of students in the schools used Spanish and were concentrated in California, the Southwest, and New York. Since then, many more Spanish-speaking students have entered the schools, and, more significantly, "new-immigrant," non-English-speaking families have arrived in the United States from Southeast Asia. Because of the increased numbers of non-English-speaking students and the broad array of primary languages, bilingual education took on a new significance in the late 1970s and 1980s.

Three Different Phases

In recent years, bilingual education programs have involved at least one of three emphases: (1) the teaching of English as a second language (ESL), (2) the temporary use of the primary language along with an intensive teaching of English so that students can quickly shift their primary language to English, and (3) the teaching of English with a parallel goal of helping the students retain their native language and culture. Programs that use the primary language only temporarily, until the students have learned adequate English, are called *transitional programs*. Those that strive to balance skills in both languages and cultures are called *maintenance programs* because students are expected to maintain skill in their initial language.

Generally, bilingual programs in the regular school curriculum, as distinct from those intended for adults, for example, contain elements of both transitional and maintenance approaches. They strive to teach English skills; to help the students adjust to an Anglo-dominated culture; to preserve and enhance the students' native language, cultural identities, and heritage; and to make them feel good about themselves and their cultural background.

Controversy

Since the early 1980s, bilingual education has been engulfed in controversy emanating from at least two issues. First is the question of the overall effectiveness of bilingual education programs. Do they actually help students learn? Second, educators and politicians disagree sometimes about the purpose and role of bilingual education. How strongly should it "Americanize" students from families new to the United States, and how strongly should it work to preserve the students' cultural traditions?

Central to the latter debate is the question of how long a student's primary language should continue to be used as the means of instruction in the schools. Some people stress the importance of integrating the student as quickly as possible into the use of English. Others place more value on retaining the primary language and its accompanying cultural traditions.

Multicultural Education

Melting Pot

Throughout much of American history a primary, stated purpose of schools was to provide a *melting pot* for the pluralistic population of the country. People came to this country from many countries and ethnic backgrounds, with distinct languages, and with rich cultural traditions; but they were expected to change, to become "American." They were expected to give up their language and customs

To Become "American"

and to replace them with English and "American" values. They were expected to send their children to school for socialization and acculturation, to acquire the cultural characteristics that would enable them to succeed socially and economically in the new environment. In short, the children were expected to become Anglo in speech, dress, and social demeanor; and schools, in large part, were expected to effect the transition.

Of course, cultural diversity did not disappear during those years. For a long period, new immigrants kept arriving; and as they did, they perpetuated old-world characteristics and values. Some groups—Irish Catholics, Jews, Mexicans, and Native Americans—were large enough, concentrated geographically enough, and persistent enough to preserve their identities. Some resisted the melting-pot idea to the point that they avoided sending their children to public schools.

During the 1960s and 1970s, social observers and educators alike began to question the value of the melting-pot idea in general and the melting-pot purpose of schools in particular. They began to recognize more clearly the value of cultural diversity in society. They found *forced assimilation* of students, as well as the *artificial separation* of subgroups from one another, to be contrary to American ideas of equity. They noticed negative effects on children when schools placed common cultural expectations on non-English-speaking, nonwhite, ethnically varied students. They realized that such practices stifled enthusiasm, harmed self-images, created alienation, and encouraged social exclusion among peers.

Cultural Pluralism

In response, *multicultural education* has replaced the melting pot as a major goal of schools. *Cultural pluralism* has replaced assimilation as the ideal to be sought. In this shift in ideals has also come the notion that education should provide equal opportunities for diverse students; no longer are all students to be treated as if they are the same.

Because of this new perspective, at least ideally, today's teachers try to (1) accommodate student differences, (2) teach the inherent value and respectability of all cultures, (3) inculcate in their students a belief in the importance of cross-cultural understanding, and (4) cultivate an appreciation for personal uniqueness and individuality. To the extent that they accomplish the ideal, they educate students so they can make the most of their own backgrounds and abilities and can succeed in their own way.

Student drama presentation on Martin Luther King, Jr. Day.

Gender-related Aspects of Education

When American schools were expected to provide a melting pot to make children more like each other, they taught them to understand and conform to long-accepted social norms that had become ingrained in social behavior and had served as the guides by which society functioned. People who understand and conformed to the norms were more likely to be successful and happy.

Gender Role Expectations

One of the deeply ingrained set of norms had to do with *gender role expectations*. Girls and women were expected to value and do certain things, and boys and men were supposed to value and do others. Therefore, when schools taught boys and girls how to conform to cultural expectations, those expectations were clearly different for each gender. In their extreme form they taught that boys were expected to be aggressive, tough, and mechanical; they were supposed to become medical doctors, attorneys, farmers, engineers, and industrial workers. Girls were expected to be sensitive, reserved, and caring; they were supposed to become nurses, teachers, secretaries, and homemakers.

In recent years, however, these and many other gender-related expectations in American culture have been questioned and challenged. Frequently, schools have been asked to help counteract, not reinforce, those felt to be harmful and restrictive. Generally, schools have taken up the challenge, but there has been much controversy.

Gender-related Concepts

Two aspects of gender-related issues that concern schools involve specific questions: Which gender-related concepts and values should be taught? In what ways should boys and girls be taught?

The gender-related concepts that are taught in a given school usually reflect the school's purposes, the teaching staff's perceptions, and the expectations of the broader society. In today's schools those influences tend to produce a mixture of concepts that perpetuate traditional sex-role biases and those that challenge them. At times this creates confusion for students. For example, in most schools girls are not expected to participate in sports to the extent that boys do, but they are encouraged to participate more than they would have been in the past. Fewer girls are expected to enroll in high-level mathematics classes even though they are encouraged to consider such professions as engineering. The same point holds for boys' participation in cheerleading and business education classes.

Most schools today probably teach that rigid gender-role identification and stereotypes are unfortunate and harmful. They teach students to question the validity of these ideas and to find their weaknesses. They show that gender-related roles have usually evolved from previous practice, not from biological factors or other unchangeable conditions. They encourage students to analyze these practices and to think for themselves.

Nevertheless, schools continue, often unconsciously, to perpetuate many traditional gender-related values. The roles played by males and females in the various subjects are the "typical" roles much more often than not. Textbook mothers and fathers, little boys and girls, aunts and uncles, waitresses and busboys tend to act as they did earlier in time.

Gender-related Treatment of Students

The ways in which boys and girls are treated while being taught usually follow the same pattern, sometimes reflecting old values and sometimes encouraging the new. For the most part, schools try not to reinforce the old heavily biased assumptions. They try to treat boys and girls alike instructionally. But old stereotypes and traditions continue to creep into practice. Boys have long been expected to be difficult to manage, girls to be emotional. The personal interests of students are often guided toward traditional gender classifications. Future job and career probabilities tend to carry gender-related assumptions. In short, schools today usually try to avoid gender-role stereotypes in dealing with students, but they are only somewhat successful.

Educating Students with Handicapping Conditions

Stimulated by *Brown* v. *Board of Education*, *PARC* v. *Pennsylvania*, and Public Laws 94–142 and 99–457, schools today try to educate children and youth with handicapping conditions more appropriately than ever before. Often the efforts are successful, and the targeted children benefit appropriately. But the degree of commitment, amount of activity, and attainment of results varies greatly from region to region, state to state, and school to school.

Free and Appropriate Public Education

As mentioned earlier Public Laws 94–142 and 99–457 require that all children with handicapping conditions be provided with a *free and appropriate public education in the least restrictive environment*. This means that handicapped children from ages 3 or 4 to 21 must be educated at public expense in settings as close as possible to regular or "normal" classrooms. It means that many students with handicaps can and should be mainstreamed into regular classrooms.

Mainstreaming

Mainstreaming is the practice of placing students with handicaps in regular classrooms and schools when possible. It is done so that these children can experience a "near-to-normal" classroom environment and so that they can interact with nonhandicapped peers. Usually, mainstreamed students attend some "special" classes during the day or week and receive additional services beyond those of the mainstream classroom.

Due Process

P.L. 94–142 also guarantees that children with handicaps be provided with due process of the law to assure that they are treated equally with normal students when they are identified or classified, when they are placed in a particular instructional setting, and when educational services are made available to them. This guarantee helps to keep schools from misidentifying students, placing them in inappropriate educational settings, and neglecting them outright. The law requires that each student and/or his or her parent or guardian participate in deciding what instructional plan is best.

Individual Education Plan

P. L. 94–142 also specifies that the instruction provided for each child with handicapping conditions must be based on that student's abilities and needs. It must be an *individual education plan* (IEP).

Changes that have followed Public Laws 94–142 and 99–457 represent the most significant developments in the long struggle to obtain equal education for children with handicapping conditions. In the nineteenth century, these children usually were either ignored by society or were sent to separate institutions to receive special (and segregated) instruction, often some distance from home. The burden of the costs often rested with the student's family. Sometimes these arrangements meant that the students were educated well, but often they were simply warehoused, and at times they were mistreated. Then, early in the twentieth century some communities began to allow mildly handicapped children to remain at home and to be taught in special classes in the local schools. The practice was based on the idea that these children would be better able to function as adults in the community if they were not segregated from it for their schooling. But the instruction was still typically provided in separate classes and differed in kind from that provided other students.

The 1960s witnessed an increased interest in the education of people with handicaps. Under President John F. Kennedy federal government funds were used to educate special educators and to build and expand special education facilities. By the end of the decade, millions of students who were handicapped by mental retardation, speech and hearing problems, emotional disorders, and other health-related disabilities were being served.

The federal government efforts of the sixties, however encouraging, were voluntary for state and local school systems; and as a result, the quality of services varied greatly, and many needy students were not served. It was not until the 1970s that significant numbers of states acted in accordance with federal law to expand and equalize educational services to children with handicaps.

Even today's school systems face major problems as they attempt to serve children with handicapping conditions. These problems seem to be of four types: public indifference, high costs, inadequate numbers of skilled teachers, and the difficulty of correctly identifying and classifying students.

Results Are Not Clear

At present, most schools commonly use a combination of mainstreamed instruction and supplemental special services to educate students with handicapping conditions whose disabilities are not so severe that more restrictive learning environments are necessary. But data from comparative research on the outcome of mainstreaming and segregated special education are not very conclusive. It is not clear which produces the greater learning or the better self-esteem in the handicapped student. Mainstreaming, however, does appear to improve the social acceptance of the students with handicaps by their non-handicapped peers. At this point, it may be that the benefits of any approach to educating students with handicapping conditions are best determined on an individual basis.

Educating Gifted and Talented Students

American educators, as well as the broader society, have been inconsistent about how to educate children and youth who are academically stronger and more talented than most students. At times they look at these students in contradictory ways—both as future societal leaders and national human resources who are being neglected by schools and as fortunate individuals who can succeed on their own without special help.

The special education movement seems to have convinced most educators that *something special* should be provided to serve these *special* students, but what should be done is not at all clear. Underlying this lack of clarity are at least four types of ambiguous conditions:

1. Ideas about how important it is for schools to provide special services for gifted and talented students have fluctuated over time, usually in response to shifts in the public's view of the most important purposes of schools and the availability of funds.

2. Identifying gifted and talented students seems to be as difficult as identifying those with handicaps.

3. Scholars and parents vacillate about separating gifted and talented students from their social and chronological peers.

4. The type of special instruction that is best for these students is not clear.

Priorities

When the Soviet Union sent *Sputnik* into space in 1957, Americans looked into what their schools were teaching as part of the effort to find out why America was apparently losing technological superiority to the U.S.S.R. In the process, many determined that the schools were neglecting the best minds and the most talented students. They demanded that the situation be changed and more attention be paid to the bright children.

As a result, the education of academically advanced and talented students became a higher priority of schools. New programs were developed and financed. Special sections of classes were organized for the bright students. A greater number of advanced classes was offered in various subjects. Efforts were begun to help bright students who were poor go to college.

But the momentum did not last long. In the 1960s, at the same time that questions were being raised about education for the gifted and talented, concern also developed over the education of poor and disadvantaged students. These concerns got more of the attention of the public, of politicians, and of educators than did the interests of gifted students. The poor and disadvantaged students were at more risk, and their needs were considered to be more critical. By the late sixties, the United States space program was on track, the cold war was thawing, and gifted and talented students were not so noticeably neglected as they had been.

Nearly two decades later, the educational reforms of the 1970s and 1980s swung the pendulum back a bit toward a greater interest in the education of the gifted and talented. But this time, these students were thought of more as a group that had to be educated better within the general school population, rather than as a special group of students that needed special, segregated instruction.

Which Programs and Approaches Are Best?

As with other students, it is difficult to determine which programs and classes are best for which gifted and talented students. Although these students might be classified as being alike by certain criteria, they differ in many other ways. For example, all who have exceptionally high mathematics test scores might not fit comfortably in the same advanced calculus course. Some might benefit more from individual instruction, some from additional free time to pursue non-mathematical interests, some from more time directed to other subjects, and some from the regular school program and environment.

In recent years, the instruction of gifted and talented students has been highly topical among educators, but their actions have varied greatly. Often what is done in a specific school or school system is determined by one or more of the following: the number of gifted and talented students needing attention, the influence of their parents and advocates, the priorities of the school leaders, the availability of skilled teachers, and the commitment of funds.

Educating Average Students

A Matter of Recognition

The *average* students in any school can be said to be those whose unique characteristics are not recognized as being significantly different from those of students in general. Of course, average students are just as unique as others, and often their uniqueness is recognized. Their uniqueness is just not significantly different enough to attract special attention from the system and its decision makers. Therefore, the normal or typical instructional programs and services serve them. In a sense, they fit into the normal routine of the school rather easily, so they are expected to fit in without special consideration.

Because there are more average students than there are students of any other classification, schools direct more of their efforts toward these students more of the time. Therefore, they tend to serve these students as well as, or better than, they serve any others. School decision makers have them in mind most often. Regular school operations accommodate them most easily. Teachers target their instruction and expectations toward them most consistently. Average students and the programming based on their needs are probably a main reason that so many schools look so much alike.

Likenesses and Differences among Students—A Reminder

This section of this chapter began by stating that schools attempt to serve all students by first categorizing them and then focusing somewhat different instruction and instruction-related services toward each group. It is important to remember, however, that students do not fit into the categories naturally. Despite how they are grouped,

1. students within any group are significantly *different from others in the same group;* and
2. students in any particualr group are more *like those in other groups* than they are different from them.

The categories that schools use are school developed, artificial, and arbitrary. Schools use them only because they cannot accommodate each individual student in a truly individualized way.

EDUCATIONAL RESEARCH

From Experimentation to Common Practice

Now that you have read Educational Research sections for four chapters, you should be developing insights into what educational research is and how it produces knowledge about teaching and learning. You should also realize that research findings do not explain everything and that they must be used with caution.

This Educational Research section traces in a very general way the ways in which research ideas lead to experiments and also the ways that conclusions from experiments can affect what teachers and students do in classrooms. It also outlines how you, as a classroom teacher, can be involved directly in the process.

Research

Educational research projects are tests of ideas about how to improve teaching and schooling. Generally, the process works as follows: Researchers form hypotheses (sometimes they begin as hunches) about what they think are or would be better ways of doing things in schools. They design efforts to test these ideas under conditions that will show if their ideas are correct or not. Next, they conduct the experiment, collect data, and formulate conclusions. Then they share their work with colleagues by writing about it in professional journals and making presentations at professional meetings. Other researchers react to these reports, offer suggestions, and possibly try the experiment themselves. The exchange of information and further testing eventually leads either to the rejection of the idea or to the acceptance of it in some form.

Demonstration

If an idea begins to be accepted as a better way of doing things by a number of educators, those who believe in it often develop demonstration projects to show how and why they believe it is so good. These projects also become examples of how the idea can be put into practice and how it can be refined to assure the best results. As a result, the demonstration projects are often a bridge between experimenters—who test ideas—and regular classroom teachers—who must decide whether the ideas are worth using with their students. They provide firsthand evidence about the feasibility of an idea and encouragement for local teachers to give it a try.

Common Practice

Eventually, good research ideas are gradually accepted by a broad range of educators and are adopted by increasing numbers of schools and teachers. At some point, the ideas are recognized widely as being successful and become common practice.

The idea of alternative schools for high-risk students described in the Analysis section of this chapter as well as the different compensatory education programs also mentioned are examples of ideas that are still passing through the research–demonstration–common practice process. So are the effective teaching practices identified in Chapter 3.

Unfortunately, however, except for a turnaround in the last ten years or so, research and demonstration efforts have not had the important roles in education that they should have. For a long time, many teachers taught year after year rather uncritically, much as they were taught; conversely, they jumped at untried fads with no more than a superficial analysis. The Educational Research section of Chapter 4 alludes to the latter of these situations when it described how quickly school decision makers adopted mainstreaming lock, stock, and barrel long before solid data were gathered.

Teacher Participation in Research and Demonstration

Now, educators at almost every level can participate in research and demonstration projects if they choose to do so, and it is important for the improvement of teaching and schools that they do. When they do, they not only help their own students; they also generate and spread ideas that uplift the profession of teaching generally. Teachers can become involved in research and demonstration efforts in the following ways:

- Read a few research journals regularly.

- Volunteer to participate in local experiments or demonstration projects.

- Conduct in-classroom trials of personal hypotheses, even if they seem to be unsophisticated.

- Share information about research and demonstration projects with colleagues.

As a teacher in the years ahead you, as well as all educators, will have to include experimentation and demonstration as part of the things you do to remain up-to-date with the profession. Change is occurring too fast to do otherwise.

You can begin at least thinking in these directions by:

- reading at least one professional journal regularly,

- following at least one educational research issue consistently through the remainder of your professional education, and

- monitoring general developments in teaching and schooling by reading a current education periodical such as *Education Week*.

> Other educators who have engaged in these types of activities tend to involve themselves readily in research and demonstration efforts of some kind.

CONCLUSION

Since the 1960s schools in America have attempted to provide equal and excellent education to all their students. Because those students differ and some have special needs, schools have to teach their highly varied students in a number of differing ways if all of them are to succeed. But because it is not realistic for schools to provide an entirely individualized program for each student, schools categorize students into groups and target different types of instruction and services to the groups.

The process, of course, is not perfect. Sometimes students are served well, but at other times they are misclassified, neglected, or otherwise dealt with inappropriately. However, today's educators and Americans in general recognize the need to provide equally excellent education for all students and seem to be committed to developing better ways of doing so.

Equal and Excellent Results of Schooling

Today's idea of excellence in education is not so much that of providing the same or equal services to all students. It is, instead, the idea of providing differentiated services to students, so that each of them can benefit equally well. The equality is not determined by the input (what the schools do for students) but by the results (what the students get out of it). The goal is that all student learning be excellent. If all of it is excellent, it will be equal.

SUMMARY

The goals for American schools have shifted during the twentieth century from a focus on the turn-of-the-century solidly academic coursework that trained the mind to an emphasis on life adjustment in the 1930s and 1940s and eventually to a relative balance between the two ideas since about 1960. During that time access to schools has broadened to include virtually every child, and schools have attempted to provide an equally excellent education for all. In recent decades, educators have thought of equal and excellent education as that which enables each child to learn to the maximum of his or her potential.

Court rulings and legislative mandates have required schools to provide equal education to all children regardless of race, gender, and handicapping condition. The greatest push in these directions came in the 1950s, through the early 1970s.

To try to serve all students, schools often categorize them into groups and then undertake special efforts to meet the needs of such groups. Those special efforts have been extended toward students in need of racial desegregation, compensatory education, bilingual education, multicultural education, gender-related education, mainstreaming, programs for handicapped students, and programs for gifted and talented students. Most such programs are intended to serve average students as well as those considered to be special in some way.

STUDY QUESTIONS

1. Make up a mental picture of a hypothetical student for a particular grade in school. List five ways that the student is like most students and five ways he or she is special or different from most students. Now describe ways in which that student should be treated in school that accommodate both the average and the special condition.

2. Suppose you are teaching a high school class of very successful students. The students include a number with very secure backgrounds, a lot of study help at home, and no noticeable handicaps. The class also includes:
   a. a student who is virtually blind but otherwise normal,
   b. a student from a severely deprived family background who is otherwise normal, and
   c. a student with a terminal illness who is otherwise normal.

   Suppose further that the final grade the students get in your class will help determine whether they get into the college of their choice and receive a scholarship. Would you give the students in Points a, b, or c special credit for doing the same level of work as the other students? Why or why not?

3. What would you do as a school administrator if parents approached you with the following two requests? Why would you do so?
   a. Although my daughter might not qualify for the honors group in English next year, I would like her placed there. We immigrated five years ago from Thailand, and English is not her native language. She has done very well in school despite this handicap. Being with top academic peers will be beneficial to her.
   b. Although my daughter might not qualify for the honors group in English next year, I would like her placed there. We are a professional family of long standing in the community. She has done rather well in school, and being with peers from her own social class who also perform well academically will be beneficial to her.

4. How will the decision made concerning the students described in Question 3 above affect other students in the class and school?

BIBLIOGRAPHY

Button, H. W., & Provenzo, E. (1983). *History of education and culture in America.* Englewood Cliffs, NJ: Prentice-Hall.

Butts, R. F. (1978). *Public education in the United States: From revolution to reform.* New York: Holt, Rinehart and Winston.

Commission on the Reorganization of Secondary Education. (1918). *Cardinal principles of secondary education.* Washington, DC: Government Printing Office.

Conant, J. B. (1959). *The American high school today.* New York: McGraw-Hill.

Cremin, L. A. (1961). *The transformation of the school: Progressivism in American education 1876–1957.* New York: Knopf.

Cuban, L. (1982). Persistent instruction: The high school classroom. *Phi Delta Kappan,* 64(2), 113–118.

Educational Policies Commission. (1938). *The purposes of education in American democracy.* Washington, DC: National Education Association and American Association of School Administrators.

Educational Policies Commission. (1944). *Education of all American youth.* Washington, DC: National Education Association and American Association of School Administrators.

Fantini, M. D. (1986). *Regaining excellence in education.* Columbus, OH: Charles E. Merrill.

Gardner, J. W. (1961). *Excellence: Can we be equal and excellent too?* New York: Harper & Brothers.

National Education Association. (1893). *Report of the committee on seconday school studies.* Washington, DC: Government Printing Office.

Ravitch, D. (1983). *The troubled crusade: American education 1945–1980.* New York: Basic Books.

NOTES

1. The three case studies presented in this Snapshot are based on information about students known personally to the authors of this text.
2. National Education Association. (1893). *Report of the committee on secondary school studies.* Washington, DC: Government Printing Office.
3. Commission on the Reorganization of Secondary Education. (1918). *Cardinal principles of secondary education.* Washington, DC: Government Printing Office.
4. Educational Policies Commission. (1938). *The purposes of education in American democracy.* Washington, DC: National Education Association and American Association of School Administrators.
5. Educational Policies Commission. (1944). *Education of all American youth.* Washington, DC: National Education Association and American Association of School Administrators.
6. Conant, J. B. (1959). *The American high school today.* New York: McGraw-Hill.
7. Gardner, J. W. (1961). *Excellence: Can we be equal and excellent too?* New York: Harper & Brothers.
8. Fantini, M. D. (1986). *Regaining excellence in education.* Columbus, OH: Charles E. Merrill.
9. Hawley, W. D. (Ed.). (1981). *Effective school desegregation: Equity, quality, and feasibility.* Beverly Hills, CA: Sage; Rossell, C. H., & Hawley, W. D. (Eds.). (1983). *The consequences of school desegregation.* Philadelphia: Temple University Press.
10. Excerpted from interviews conducted by Anne Turnbaugh and reported in "Newsletter: National Center on Effective Secondary Schools," School of Education, University of Wisconsin—Madison, Fall 1986. Used with permission. The school and city are not identified because the project is part of a national research effort.

CHAPTER 6

The School: A Culture
TERRENCE E. DEAL

Terrence Deal wrote the substantive sections of this chapter. Charles and Lynn Myers provided "A Close Look at Four Schools," "Analysis," "Something to Think About," and "Educational Research."

INTRODUCTION

Earlier chapters focus on classrooms and students, emphasizing how and why teaching and learning take place. This chapter steps back to examine the context of teaching and learning—the school. For many years schools have been viewed as if they were families, factories, or blackboard jungles. This chapter describes schools as organizations made up of many people and parts, all with a common purpose and common values and beliefs.

Until recent years, educators often described schools by classifying them into types based on characteristics, such as level of instruction, size, type of curricular emphasis, and location. Sometimes the typologies included affluence or its lack among the student body. Schools were labeled as primary, upper elementary, middle, junior high, high; large, small; academic, vocational, magnet, comprehensive; urban, suburban, rural; rich and poor. In at least two ways such descriptions seem to distort the view of schools. They do not capture similarities across types, and they portray schools in a rather static way.

Although this chapter addresses differences among schools, it stresses commonalities and the dynamics that most schools share. This enables you to develop a general mental image of schools everywhere, and it will also provide you with a basis for interpreting specific issues and for observing how schools change over time.

The chapter is organized around a case study of a fictive new teacher who enters a particular school culture for the first time and four case descriptions of different schools. The case study and descriptions are intended as illustrations that you can reflect on as you read other chapter sections on understanding cultures, schools as a type of organizational culture, differences among schools, subcultures within schools, and relationships between school cultures and effectiveness.

The Snapshot is a case study of the new teacher. The Analysis section presents a school observer's view of a particular high school. The Educational Research section explains and illustrates ethnographic research.

SNAPSHOT

The Snapshot for this chapter describes the experiences of Laurie Renfro, a new teacher, as she assumes her first teaching position. As you read about her initial day at Carson Junior High School, consider the following questions:

- What things seem to surprise Ms. Renfro or strike her as being unusual? Why do you think this is the case?

- What characteristics of the culture of Carson Junior High School do you notice in the scenes described during Ms. Renfro's first day?

- What conclusion can you draw about Mr. Grundig and Ms. Cohen from the brief glimpses of them presented here?

Laurie Renfro smiled as she stepped from her brand new Hyundai. "It's wonderful to think about life without exams, professors, and theories. Now *I* give the tests—whenever *I* want. From occupying the bottom rung to being the boss of my own classroom . . . I can hardly wait! And I'm even getting paid for it! Money for new clothes, a new car, a new apartment, all mine . . . almost, anyway."

Carson Junior High School looked like a friendly place, even from the outside: green lawns, well-trimmed shrubbery, and ample numbers of large lattice-paned windows. The fact that the school had been built in the 1940s seemed to add to its charm. It gave the somewhat archaic architectural lines character, something Laurie Renfro always liked in a building.

Entering the large-arched doorway, Laurie noted the familiar smell a school seems to emit in September before the students arrive. "Probably a blend of the newly waxed floors and the mustiness of being closed for the summer vacation," she mused. In fact, the custodian was still standing in the corridor admiring the floor's sheen, knowing full well that the 1,200 pairs of new shoes scheduled to arrive within the week would quickly obscure his work of art with a mosiac of scuff marks.

"You must be the new social studies teacher," the custodian observed after sighting Laurie walking down the hallway in her obviously new suit, carrying a briefcase that could not have left the shelves more than twenty-four hours ago. "I think you'll like your classes," he continued. "But I hope you're not one of those new teachers with newfangled methods that deny the absolute fact that Carson students need discipline and the fundamentals. I'll be coming by to see how you're doing when school opens."

"Which way to the principal's office?" Ms. Renfro asked politely, thinking

to herself that the custodian should stick to his floors.

"Down the hallway, two doors to the left," the custodian responded. "Oh by the way, my name is Mr. Grundig. And you must be Laurie Renfro. I heard that you went to the university. I sure hope they aren't stuffing your heads full of those three crackpots Skinner, Thorndike, and Dewey anymore. Eggheads that have never seen the inside of classrooms like Carson. My own philosophy of teaching is that . . ."

"Thank you very much, Mr. Grundig, I'd love to chat longer, but I really don't want to be late to my first appointment with Mr. Bays."

"No problem, Ms. Renfro, I'm sure we'll have plenty of time to talk once the school year begins. I'll drop by your room often. It's delightful to have a new face on our Carson team."

"Very strange," Laurie thought to herself as she moved down the hall in the direction indicated by Mr. Grundig. "He almost talks as if he's in charge here. I'll bet he'll even read what I write on the chalkboard before he erases it. We sure never talked about custodians at the university . . ."

"Oh, Ms. Renfro! We're so delighted you're here." A cheery voice greeted Laurie as she walked past the opaque glass door labeled Principal's Office. "I'm Muriel Cohen, Mr. Bays' secretary." Mr. Bays is at a superintendent's cabinet meeting right now, and he always attends the Rotary Club every Tuesday at noon; so he'll be back around 2:00. In the meantime he's asked me to introduce you to Carson. He'll continue your orientation when he returns. Let me take your briefcase, and then we'll see the school. Would you like a cup of coffee before we start?"

As the tour progressed, Laurie was amazed at how much Ms. Cohen seemed to know about the school. She knew everyone, and each teacher and staff person seemed to accord her unusual respect. She seemed able to relate easily with everyone—cafeteria workers getting their equipment ready to produce the next year's sloppy joes and tuna boats, classroom teachers busy with bulletin boards and materials. Young teachers dressed in Levis, old ones dressed in tweeds, some very old tired ones seemingly contemplating how they could survive the last year before retirement—Ms. Cohen related easily to them all.

Laurie was surprised at the variety of requests made of the secretary as she moved through the school. For questions about equipment, schedules, parents, children, and materials—Muriel Cohen had a ready answer. Many of her answers seemed to carry messages that let people know what they should be doing. Laurie also noted that Ms. Cohen asked her a lot of questions about her own background and ideas about teaching. "She seems as interested in educational methods as Mr. Grundig," Ms. Renfro thought to herself. "I wonder who really runs this school."

Finally, the two women walked up to a door with an opaque window marked 208. As Muriel Cohen opened the door, she turned to the new teacher. "This is your room for next year. What do you think?" As Laurie's eyes moved from the black bulletin boards to the metal desks arranged in neat rows on the newly waxed floors to the flag above the desk in the front of the room, her excitement rose. "Finally, my own classroom, my territory, *my* domain where I am the teller, not the told."

"It's wonderful, Ms. Cohen. I can hardly wait to get it ready for my students."

"I suspected that," Ms. Cohen said. "I'll leave you for awhile to think about what you want to do. If you need anything, see me. Oh, by the way, I noticed among your references from the university recommendations from Professors Hall and Benstran. I just thought I'd let you know that they also wrote recommendations for Lance Snelling, your predecessor who barely made it through last year. Very smart, he was. But he wasn't able to control his classes. That theory stuff seems to go over better at the university than it does here at Carson. I know you'll be different. There's a nice little place around the corner you may want to try for lunch. Just remember to be back at 2:00 for your appointment with Mr. Bays. And remember, anything that you need to know or have, come to me." With that, Ms. Cohen walked down the hall, turning her head only to acknowledge Laurie's thank you.

At lunch, Laurie mused over her introduction to Carson. The morning had been different from what she had imagined. She wondered why the custodian and secretary seemed so knowledgeable and powerful. She was surprised at the number of different people it took to run the school. She was surprised with the diversity of her colleagues in such things as age, dress, and persuasion. Each classroom seemed to have its own flavor, but even though the various subgroups seemed so different, something seemed to hold them together. Whatever it was, it made Ms. Renfro feel like somewhat of an outsider, even though the people were all friendly enough.

Maybe Mr. Bays could shed some light on all this. Maybe she should have paid more attention in last spring's sociology class. The lure of the sunshine in her senior year had encouraged Laurie to focus on beaches and parties rather than on ideas about schools as organizations. After all, she was going to be a teacher, not an employee of a corporation. If she had wanted a career in business, she would be able to afford a BMW instead of a Hyundai.

Laurie Renfro had always wanted to be a teacher. She was eagerly waiting for her first day with students in her own classroom. She was wondering about how she would fit into the school and who she would be able to turn to for advice and support. Learning the ropes might be more important and difficult than she had thought.

Not much happened at the meeting with Mr. Bays that reassured Laurie. Mr. Bays was a warm and charming man whose middle age was tempered with a dapperness and sense of humor that Laurie liked. But their conversation focused mainly on goals, objectives, district curriculum guides, school rules, discipline, evaluation procedures, and other matters that appeared to be only remotely connected to the events of Laurie's main concerns or her morning observations. Mr. Bays was clearly in charge, but the things he seemed to be in charge of seemed unrelated to many of the questions that Ms. Renfro had formulated in the presence of Mr. Grundig, Ms. Cohen, and the other people at Carson. "Oh well," she thought. "It's only my first day."

As Laurie walked out the main entrance following her meeting with Mr. Bays, her thoughts moved back and forth between getting her classroom ready and understanding what made Carson tick. The classroom thoughts brought exciting images of the year; the school itself just didn't seem to make much sense, at least not in terms of what she had originally expected.

Just as she had opened the door of her Hyundai and carefully tossed her new briefcase into the passenger seat, Laurie heard her name being called.

> Turning, she saw a small group of other teachers in the parking lot. "Laurie Renfro?" an older male teacher inquired as he walked toward Laurie extending his hand. "I'm John Welch, and I teach mathematics. Welcome to Carson. Do you have time to have a drink with a few of your new colleagues?" "Of course," Laurie responded with a pleased look.
>
> The conversation in the lounge cleared some things up and introduced still other new surprises. She liked the other teachers. They laughed affectionately when she told them about Mr. Grundig and Ms. Cohen. They asked her what Mr. Bays had covered in his meeting with her, and then proceeded to brief her, as John Welch put it, on "the way we really do things around here."

CULTURE AND CULTURES

Values a People Share

In simple terms, a *culture* is the pattern of behavior, assumptions, and beliefs that sets a group apart from others. Culture encompasses the values a people share, the common patterns among the ways they think and behave, their sense of a common history, the body of traditions they accept, and the other characteristics that hold the group together. Culture induces a feeling of belonging that helps individuals identify with the group and lets them know how to act

A Feeling of Belonging

and how to fit in. It provides a sense of security for individuals that says they are not alone. Conversely, it is the element that is missing when a person leaves familiar surroundings, travels to a distant and different world, and senses that he or she does not know "how they do things here" or "what is normally expected." It is that part of Carson Junior High that Laurie Renfro needs to absorb in order to become a part of it.

A Social Science Concept

Culture is also a concept used in the social sciences to describe the character or feel of a society; to highlight the deep patterns of values, beliefs, and traditions formed through its history; and to explain why its people do things in a particular way. This concept is an intellectual tool that observers use to interpret and explain the ideas and behavior of groups and of people within groups. It has been used to study primitive tribes, urban gangs, the country club set, yuppies, southern society, governmental bureaucracies, prisons, businesses, schools, and other formal and informal organizations.

The Culture of Organizations

Learned Thought and Behavior

Like cultures in broader society, organizations—IBM, the Catholic church, the United States Army, Harvard University, and P.S. 102 in Harlem—have their own ways of doing things, their own personality and identity. This organizational culture consists of a particular tone or feel that insiders usually take for granted but which outsiders sense strongly as they enter the organization for the first time (much as Laurie Renfro experienced her first day at Carson). Experts who study organizations label the tone or feel with such terms as "ethos," "spirit," "force," "climate," as well as "culture." It is an elusive, hard-to-put-your-finger-

This scene of villagers cooking manioc cakes at an Ivory Coast market illustrates a *culture* quite different from one that most Americans might be familiar with.

on side of an organization, an aspect that many people simply do not see or comprehend.

Symbols and Symbolic Activity

Cultures develop in organizations, as they do in the outside world, because people require symbols and symbolic activity to give meaning to their life and work. People create cultures around themselves, which then guide, define, and shape what they do and believe. The transaction is two-way—human beings create culture, and they are shaped by it. The transaction evolves continuously as long as the community, corporation, hospital, school, organization of any sort exists.

Culture in Corporate America

Since the publication of two books on the topic—Deal and Kennedy's *Corporate Cultures* (1982) and Peters and Waterman's *In Search of Excellence* (1982),[1] the concept of culture has been a preoccupation with many businesses. Firms across all sections of the economy—banks, insurance companies, hotel chains, and airlines—are now struggling to identify, revitalize, and reshape their cultures. It is difficult to attend an executive retreat, annual conference, or business seminar without hearing the term used, misused, or abused. The concept of culture in corporate America has become a powerful management tool; it is on the brink of becoming a management fad.

Understanding Cultures

A "Tribal Mystique"

Because culture is an elusive entity, special concepts or a particular language is needed to help people understand it better, especially as it applies to modern organizations and schools. One way to begin that understanding is to think of organizations as tribes cloaked in a mystique developed over many years, a mystique that includes (1) shared values and beliefs, (2) heroes and heroines, (3) rituals and ceremonies, (4) stories and legends, and (5) informal players.

Shared Values and Beliefs

For instance, every tribe has something it stands for, a special character that sets it apart from other tribes. These are the *shared values* of the culture. They are often expressed in logos, symbols, or slogans. In American society, the Stars and Stripes, the Statue of Liberty, and the phrase "America, the land of the free" represent the value that we assign to the American way. The United States Marine Corps identifies itself with the motto Semper Fidelis. The IBM Corporation anchors its business on service and dignity for the individual—values that it has adhered to since its inception. These core values are shared from the highest-ranking to the lowest-paid positions in the organization.

Heroes and Heroines

Because values are intangible, tribes also identify and recognize *heroes and heroines* who embody the essential character of the organization. Just as primitive social groups had leaders who were often heroic, companies have chief executive officers, and schools systems have superintendents. Tribes also have additional prominent figures whose collective presence represents the full range of values that are necessary for survival and success. IBM has Thomas Watson, Sr., the visionary hero who founded the company, and it also recognizes dark-suited, white-shirted marketers; unshaven, Levi-clad people who are into robotics; and the researcher who used to drive her motorcycle around the halls of one of its research and development units. In the aggregate, IBM's heroes and heroines provide role models that each person can look up to for guidance in determining how his or her behavior can contribute to the company's success.

Rituals and Ceremonies

In both primitive and modern organizations, *rituals and ceremonies* are important opportunities for individuals to experience shared values and to bond together in a common quest. The power breakfast or the afternoon gathering at a local watering hole enable people from different parts of a company to share a deeper experience than just eating eggs or drinking beer. Much as physicians and surgical teams scrub for seven minutes even though germs are destroyed in thirty seconds, people in modern corporations engage in many activities because of what those activities *express*, not for what they accomplish.

Typically, the clan members of an organization gather together once a year in ceremony to revitalize their commitment to its values, celebrate its heroes and heroines, enact its rituals, retell its stories, and fuse past and present together in a vision of hope for the future. The annual seminars held by Mary Kay Cosmetics always include the awarding of Mary Kay–pink Cadillacs and diamond bumblebee pins to its successful beauty consultants, thus reinforcing the You-Can-Do-It spirit that represents one of its core values. Each year, members of the United States Air Force come together in their "rebluing" ceremony to renew their commitment to its traditions. Annually, families gather around Christmas trees, Hanukkah candles, and other symbols to celebrate spirit and traditions that are handed down in story and legend from one generation to the next.

Stories and Legends

These *stories and legends*, in addition to being intertwined with rituals and ceremonies, have organizational significance of their own. They carry traditions,

values, and miscellaneous reflections from generation to generation and lead to the time-honored history that develops loyalty among tribe members. They help current members identify with the corporate past and, in turn, to anticipate a corporate future.

Informal Players, or Carriers

Every tribe has its network of *informal players*—the cast of "carriers" who preserve traditions, transmit organizational history, and reminisce. One of the roles of these players is to provide a powerful counterbalance to the power of the chief. They are typically older people who assure that occasions are enacted properly, that spiritual matters receive ample attention, and that history lessons are not forgotten. They are storytellers who weave the rich experience of a people into tales that transmit values in memorable ways. They are gossips who carry information from person to person, assuring that no one will be deprived of the important news of the day.

Informal players are found in all modern organizations. While the title on their business cards or office doors may not formally recognize their unofficial roles, they transact their special business day in and day out behind the scenes or outside the formal boundaries of the organization. They plan the special parties, tell newcomers how things really are, and remind everyone of the reasons for starting and preserving specific rituals and traditions. They preserve the culture and help hold the traditional elements of the organization together.

Together, all these cultural elements—shared values and beliefs, heroes and heroines, rituals and ceremonies, stories and legends, and the network of informal players—shape and give meaning to collective experience in families, sororities and fraternities, universities, armies, federal and state agencies, schools, and other organizations. They enable clan members, alumni, and workers to identify with a group that often spans time and distance. They provide a way for them to be part of the larger culture and to develop and maintain an attachment to it.

THE SCHOOL AS A CULTURE

As one thinks of the elements of culture mentioned above—shared values, heroes, and so forth—it is obvious that schools embody culture as much as any organization. School visitors can sense it as they approach a school building and can almost smell and taste it as they walk through the doors. They can see it as they observe pictures hanging on the walls, students in the halls, exchanges between students and teachers in classrooms, and in student relationships on the playground.

Organizational Saga

As early as the 1930s, Waller (1932)[2] discussed the importance of culture, beliefs, rituals, ceremonies, and values in schools; and he noted the roles portrayed by school folklore, myth, tradition, taboos, rites, ceremonials, collective representation, and participation mystiques in both the formal and informal parts of school life (103). More recently, Clark (1983)[3] discussed the idea of the *organizational saga* in colleges, which he defined as a shared mythology rooted in tradition, reinforced by a charismatic leader, and possessing a cadre of faculty supporters, distinctive educational practices, a student subculture, and an external group of alumni and other believers. According to Clark (1983), as internal and external groups share their common beliefs, this saga creates links across internal divisions and organizational boundaries in schools. With deep emotional commitment, believers (teachers, students, alumni) define themselves by their affiliation with the school and in their bond to other believers. They share an intense sense of uniqueness. They display school colors, wear school rings, attend sporting events, and willingly announce, "I'm a Cougar." In an organization that possesses a strong saga, there is the group of those who "belong" and who are set apart from others outside the chosen flock. Such an emotional bond turns the membership into a community, even a cult.

School Culture and Change

Researchers note that school culture plays a major role in school change. Sarason (1971)[4] documents the power of school culture—which he defines as behavior regularities and shared assumptions—in resisting and redefining educational innovations such as new math. Deal (1982) and Swidler (1979)[5] demonstrate the importance of culture or shared symbols in the formation and operation of alternative schools.

Deal notes that alternative schools have faced risky times because of their radical departure from conventional systems of education and because of their inability to create a new system of values and beliefs. His explanation suggests the following scenario for new alternative schools: (1) Because of appearances of deviance from conventional ideas, alternative schools violate an implicit logic of confidence and thus come under careful scrutiny. (2) Confronted with hard questions, these schools try to respond with evidence to support their virtues, failing to realize that seeing does not always lead to believing. (3) Half believing in the prevailing myths themselves, alternative school participants begin to question the legitimacy of their endeavor. (4) Lacking strong sagas to support their conventional efforts, many alternative schools revert to conventional patterns of meaning and comfort. (5) Schools that are able to survive develop strong sagas—that is, their own identity (Deal, 1982, p. 8).

Swidler's study of alternative schools supports Deal's assertions. Swidler comments, "Watching teachers and students in free schools, I became convinced that culture, in the sense of symbols, ideologies, and a legitimate language for discussing individual and group obligations provides the crucial substrate on

School Culture and Exemplary Practices

which new organizational forms can be erected." (Swidler, 1979, p. viii)

The same significance of school culture is supported by cases of exemplary schools. Effective schools are those which over time have developed a system of beliefs—a culture—that gives meaning to teaching, learning, and other school activities. Just as with businesses, these schools display shared values and beliefs, well-known and widely celebrated heroes and heroines, well-attended and memorable rituals and ceremonies, positive stories and legends, and a dedicated informal group whose members work diligently to maintain and strengthen the schools' mission.

The Exemplary Center for Reading Instruction (ECRI) Program that Fullan (1985)[6] describes is a superb example. It focuses primarily on building a belief around teaching practices. In one elementary school, for example, the introduction of ECRI created a strong consensus and sense of community. Its heroes and heroines, such as the teacher who got polyps in her larynx from teaching so enthusiastically, were well known. A unique teaching ritual was observed across different classrooms even though individual teachers varied enormously in personal background and style. Positive stories of individual students' accomplishments (for example, a foreign student whose achievement gains were especially significant in a short time span) were told repeatedly by teachers, administrators, and parents (Deal, Gunnar, & Wiske 1977).[7] These characteristics are strikingly different from patterns in less exemplary elementary schools.

School Culture and Performance

In addition to anecdotes and examples, the case for a link between culture and performance in schools can be inferred from empirical research sources. Several of these consist of school climate studies that attempt to measure the effects of social atmosphere on educational outcomes. McDill and Rigsby (1973)[8] document interesting linkages between school climate, student achievement, and student educational aspirations. Similar findings are evident in school effectiveness studies, where both climate and ethos are consistently connected to measures of performance. (For more information, see *Elementary School Journal*, 1985, January.)[9] Although clear ties between student performance in school and school climate, ethos, and culture have not been specified in these studies, it is clear that something intangible about a school style, tone, and social atmosphere is related somehow to student performance.

A Complex Human Organization

Just as school culture affects school performance, it affects the lives of the people who live within it, and the extent of the influence is particularly noticeable to new arrivals. Each year thousands of new teachers like Laurie Renfro arrive at school with expectations of what their first assignment will be like. They are excited to have their own classrooms and are filled with ideas about how they can improve education and contribute to the craft of teaching. But many of these new teachers are simply not aware that they are entering a complex human organization with its own culture. They know that they will be around other people and will have to contend with goals, a hierarchy, rules, evaluations, and other well-known aspects of the formal structure of schools. But they underestimate the political intrigue and conflict that they will encounter in schools—or in their classrooms.

School Culture and New Teachers

It is easy to imagine the uneasiness, difficulties, and surprises one would feel if first traveling to Spain, Bali, or Switzerland—the people, the languages, everything is different. The experience can be very jarring and confusing. The same thing happens when a new teacher first enters school. In a sense, he or she is a foreigner who constitutes a possible threat—unless the culture can mold the stranger into its own likeness. For the most part, schools are very successful at shaping new teachers. As Albert Shanker, head of the American Federation of Teachers (AFT) remarked:

> Ten thousand new teachers each year enter the New York City schools as a result of retirement, death, job turnover, and attrition. These new teachers come from all over the country. They represent all religions, races, political persuasions, and educational institutions. But the amazing thing is that after three weeks in the classroom you can't tell them apart from the teachers they replaced.

Organizational Dynamics and Forces

It is very important for someone like Laurie Renfro to understand the dynamics of her first days at Carson Junior High School as well as the organizational forces that will continue to press upon her and her work. Otherwise, such a teacher will be confused and hurt; eventually young teachers may long for their old universities, where to the students things had seemed to make more sense. If such a teacher never understands that many of these feelings naturally accompany everyone entering an organization for the first time, the teacher may become one of the many promising young teachers who leave the profession.

Back to Laurie Renfro

Subcultures

Had Laurie conceived of her first day at Carson Junior High as if she were a pledge entering a sorority, a long-term tourist traveling to a foreign country, or a germ entering a human body, her first day would have made more sense. She would have identified Mr. Grundig as a potential *gossip*. He shines floors but more importantly carries the word. In Ms. Cohen, she would have recognized the *priestess,* someone who would be of enormous help in her first year at Carson, enabling her to learn the ropes and avoid the traps. From both conversations, she should have noted that Carson Junior High has its ways and values that may or may not live up to those at the university. As the school secretary took her through the halls of Carson, Laurie Renfro had opportunities to note the various subcultures among the teachers and staff; for like any organization, Carson's culture hosts groups that may or may not buy into the core values of the place.

The Principal's Role

In her meeting with Mr. Bays, Laurie could have surmised that although principals are important, they are embedded in an intricate tapestry that was woven before they arrived and will remain after they leave. They may reweave a section or two, or tear a hole; and pieces of them may even become part of the mosaic. Though his meeting with Ms. Renfro may not have demonstrated it, Mr. Bays himself may realize by now that official policies often have little to do with actual behavior; that evaluation is as important a ritual as it is a straightforward task; and that his official title as principal, although bestowed by the board and superintendent, must be endorsed and augmented by his moral authority or symbolic presence. If Mr. Bays does not realize all this, the old guard that met Laurie in the parking lot will be running the school and shaping the new teachers to flesh out their concepts of the craft of teaching.

Culture of the Classroom

Laurie Renfro needs to see all this for her own comfort and survival and for one more important reason. In a week or two, thirty-three junior high school students an hour will arrive at the door of her room. Each will look as strange as many of the teachers and staff Ms. Renfro observed in her first tour of Carson with Ms. Cohen. Within the group will be small cliques, or subgroups, some planning to learn from Laurie but some already conspiring to find her weak spots and to use the class as an outlet for preadolescent attention getting. While all thirty-three students have had the summer to forget everything that their seventh grade teachers tried to offer them, unconsciously they miss old familiar Ms. Ruby and resent this new young thing who is usurping her reign. For you see, a classroom is a culture too.

Past History

Laurie Renfro will be wise if she pays attention to faculty and staff concerns about the university and if she finds out what happened to Lance Snelling, her predecessor from the university who did poorly enough that he left or was terminated. The culture of Carson will make or break Ms. Renfro's first year and each year thereafter. Over time, cultural patterns will dictate the direction and performance of the school.

DIFFERENCES AMONG SCHOOLS

In education studies, the idea of culture is rather new and not particularly popular as a concept for analyzing and understanding schools. Instead, educators tend to explain schools in terms of type or identifiable characteristic—size, academic focus, type of community where they are located, and socioeconomic status of the students. This is ironic because much of the momentum for studying culture in organizations was stimulated by research in public schools (Cohen, Deal, Meyer, & Scott, 1979; Deal, Meyer, & Scott, 1983; Meyer & Rowan, 1977).[10]

Types of Schools

Since schools are often identified by type, it is useful at this point to think of them at least briefly in this context. To a great extent, school types differ because schools exist in a variety of cultural surroundings—locations; communities; regions of the country; degrees of urbanization; social, economic, and political climates; and so forth. Influences from these cultural surroundings naturally find their way into the school and its operation. The cultural environments of mid-Manhattan, of Palo Alto, California, of the Pennsylvania Dutch country, of San Antonio, Texas, of suburban Atlanta, of Honolulu, and of rural Puerto Rico are all American but all different; and the schools in each of these locales reflect their special characteristics.

Schools also differ because of their size. More things happen in large, diverse schools of 2,000 to 3,000 students than in much smaller schools. The organizational structure, operating procedures, sense of identity, familiarity among students and teachers, and potential for getting lost in the crowd are just not the same. Neither are the breadth of course selection, the availability of advanced course offerings, the diversity of individuals, and the possibility of cross-cultural student interaction. Each type of school has its advantages and its drawbacks, and each has its distinctive elements.

Similarly, schools differ according to the age of their student body—elementary, middle, high; the focus of their instruction—academic, general, vocational, comprehensive; their type of funding and control—public, private, church-supported; the style and age of the building—old, modern, urban, brick, modular, spacious, crowded, state-of-the-art; and many other distinguishing factors. Among all these differences, however, are common elements as well—

teachers, students, administrators, a sense of purpose, an institutional identity, and many other cultural components.

A CLOSE LOOK AT FOUR SCHOOLS

The next few pages consist of brief glimpses into four different schools. Each is presented as a case study for you to consider as you think about schools as cultures. Before you read the cases, however, reflect for a moment on the schools you already know—schools you have attended, schools you have visited, and those you know less well. Then consider each of the following questions as they relate to those schools:

- What characteristics of the culture of each of these schools come to mind? Why do you think each of these characteristics developed in that school?

- In what ways are these specific characteristics common to schools in general?

- In what ways are these specific characteristics peculiar to that school?

Now consider the same questions as you read the descriptions of the four different schools. Although the schools are different—elementary and secondary; urban, suburban, and rural; public and private—they also typify schools in America today. The descriptions are necessarily brief and incomplete, so you will need to read between the lines and make assumptions beyond the observers' reports about the schools, students, and teachers.

Observation Number One: A Day at Ridgefield High

In a small midwestern town, about 1000 students go to Ridgefield High. Hundreds are deposited by bus at the front door of the two-story brick building built in the 1930s, now showing its years and lack of care. Ridgefield has cracked sidewalks, a shabby lawn, and peeling paint on every window sash. Some students walk to school; others park their cars on a gravel lot just beyond the macadam-covered spaces reserved for teachers. . . .

Inside the building there is much milling about. The halls are crowded. Students meet with friends. They noisily stuff possessions into lockers. Boyfriends and girlfriends have already met. The bell rings. The public address system warns the students not to be late for "first-hour" class.

Students at Ridgefield High are predominantly white, the families working class. For boys, normal dress consists of running shoes, jeans (without designer labels), and T-shirts (football and rock group). Some girls wear feminine versions of this "uniform." Others wear either conservative dresses or imitations of the latest fashions, too much makeup or none at all, long straight hair or bouffant curls.

The office has a pleasant atmosphere; popular music plays on the radio; lunch tickets are sold; students and teachers wander in and out. A student comes in to pick up a form from the attendance secretary and regales her with a story about seventeen busboys being fired from a nearby country club restaurant for "getting into the beer. . . ."

By now, the day's activities are in full swing. At the beginning of the second hour, the main office secretary makes announcements over the schoolwide public-address system. Her tone is informal as she runs down the schedule for yearbook pictures and promises that tomorrow's special assembly will be good, "So don't forget your twenty-five-cent admission."

Physical education classes, a favorite of most students, are going on in the gym and out back. Study hall for this hour is in the cafeteria. There, students are quiet—either sleeping or reading.

In the library, a group of students learn how to locate books, others help the librarian; still others study quietly; a few read magazines from the library's large collection (for example, *Outdoor Life, Guitar Player, Family Circle, American History*).

Down the hall, in the cramped teachers' lounge, four or five people are drinking coffee, eating snacks purchased from the vending machine, and chatting.

In English classrooms, students pick out verbs and subjects from worksheets. In history classes, they are listening to lectures on Indians, Vikings, and the religions of China. Trigonometry students work independently, solving problems in the text.

In "functional" math, several "slow" students work individually, but not seriously. They have been given packets that have catchy titles—Prime Time, Wit Kit, Math Path, Skill Drill, and Game Frame—and include equipment such as headphones, tapes, and projectors. The students, however, are not caught up in the materials. They talk and wander around while the teacher works with one student at her desk.

Biology II students listen to a lecture on the coloration of fall leaves, while Biology I students look at exhibits on an overhead projector and then have a lively debate about pollution. In Spanish class, students watch slides of the teacher's stay in Peru. Conversation in Spanish is interspersed. In home economics, students do a "seek-and-find" worksheet on sewing terms, and wait while the teacher helps one student with a sewing pattern at her desk.

In Introduction to Business, students listen and follow directions as the teacher gives step-by-step instructions, in a loud and precise voice, related to the use of a new instructional packet:

> First, put your names and "second period" on the outside of the packet, then take out every item in the packet and put your name on each of the items. [She waits.] After your names are put on all materials, put all of them back except for the booklet entitled "Instructions." Now, look at me, please. I will go slowly, and you can put what I say into your own words, but these statements are to be written inside of your instructional manual. One: These packets may not leave the classroom. Two: If absent from school, you need to come before school, during study hall, or after school, to make up for time that you've missed in class. Three: Pay attention. If you don't pay attention, you may get lost, and since we are going to be working on this for three weeks, you'll be lost for all three weeks . . . Now let's go back to page one. . . .

As students move from class to class, the routine is predictable. For the first half of the period, they mostly sit and listen, occasionally taking notes. During the last portion, students discuss material, and fill out worksheets and study guides while their teacher circulates to give individualized assistance.

It is lunchtime. Groups of students shuttle in and out of the cafeteria. There is much half-serious complaining about the food and the meager choices on the menu. Students in one small group eat hurriedly and make their way out the back door to the smoking area, where they visit with one another or smoke cigarettes or dope.

A security guard monitors the area during lunch. He does not like what is going on, but his problem is similar to that of other adults who might be upset about the use of drugs. He does not know how to stop it. A student explains: "Teachers don't like it, but what are they going to do about it? When we see them coming, we flip the joint away, and that's that." Around school, these kids are called "burn-outs"—in contrast to the "jocks" or the group called "socies."

Two boys caught fighting in the washroom are in the principal's office. Their statements are taped by Mr. Moss. All such conferences are recorded, so the affected students and parents hear the same story. The two boys spend most of the time arguing about who won the fight; each seems desperately in need of winning.

When the boys are questioned individually, John starts crying because the expected suspension means he will not be able to play football. Athletics are exalted at Ridgefield High; the jocks are the heroes of students, administrators, and parents. The coach is in on the meeting, assuring John that if he takes the punishment "like a man" he may be allowed to regain status and rejoin the team.

Lunch is over. Some Ridgefield High students take a school bus to Burr Community College to participate in a vocational program. A few leave early to work; most return to class. The corridors begin to clear.

It is two in the afternoon now. The school day is almost over at Ridgefield High. Students who have broken one rule or another are herded into the library for "eighth-hour" detention time. Usually, they are punished for coming late.

Students on athletic teams head for buses. Others take a final class or study hall before the day ends. Some linger after school for a club meeting. Still others drive around or just hang out with friends before going home.

Some students hurry off to work. Many have chores to do at home. A few are heard complaining about too much homework, but they also claim that they can get away without doing it. One student is overheard saying, "Nothing much happens here." (Boyer, 1983, pp. 11–15)[11]

Observation Number Two: George Washington Carver Comprehensive High School

George Washington Carver Comprehensive High School is in the southeastern section of Atlanta, the poorest area of the city. No matter what route you take from downtown Atlanta, you must cross the tracks in order to get to Carver. On the fifteen-minute journey from downtown, the scenery changes dramatically. Downtown Atlanta, with its bold new high rises and shiny edifices, symbolizes the hope and transformation of an emerging southern metropolis. In contrast, southeast Atlanta looks gray and shabby. Fast-food joints, gas stations, small grocery stores, and low-cost housing line the main streets. . . .

The Carver Homes crowd 5,400 people into 990 apartments. The two-story brick buildings lined up along nine streets were built twenty-five years ago as public

George Washington Carver Comprehensive High School.

housing. They do not appear as ominous and isolating as the high-rise public housing of Chicago or New York. There is something more humane about the scale of these buildings. There are stoops and porches to sit on and more possibility for neighborly contact. Yet the people here are just as poor and just as imprisoned by poverty and discrimination. What might have once been planted lawns and greenery has long since truned to gray, beaten-down dirt, and there are no sidewalks for people to walk on from house to house. Through the eyes of a northeasterner, the Carver Homes look semi-rural, even though they are part of a big-city problem. . . .

The student enrollment at Carver High School has fluctuated but seems to have stabilized at 890. As with all public high schools in Atlanta, Carver goes from eighth through twelfth grades. The five-year grade span is most vivid and visible with the boys. The young eighth-graders appear vulnerable and childlike in contrast to the tall, bearded senior boys, who seem to have suddenly shot into manhood. Except for one white boy, the students are all black. The teaching staff is predominantly black, with a small sprinkling of white faces. The white teachers are so thoroughly interspersed into the faculty that everyone I ask finds it hard to say exactly how many there are. None of the seventy-five teachers on Carver's full-time staff lives in the community. They travel several miles each morning from the more affluent middle-class sections of Atlanta and its suburbs. One teacher, who lives in a subdivision twelve miles away, is incredulous when . . . [an observer asks] him whether he lives close by. "I can't imagine living close by . . ." [he responds].

. . . The mood on campus is one of order and decorum. There is not the edge of fear or the potential for violence that one often experiences going into large urban high schools. Bathrooms are free of graffiti, hallways are swept and kept clean, and students express pride in the restored campus. Students gathered in groups do not appear ominous and threatening, but well behaved and friendly. . . .

. . . In many of the classrooms . . . very little of substance was happening educationally. Teachers were caught up in procedural directives and students appeared disinterested, turned off, or mildly disruptive. The institution has begun to emerge as stable and secure, but attention to the intellectual development and growth of students will require a different kind of focus, new pedagogical skills, and a profound change in faculty views of student capabilities. This most difficult challenge is connected . . . to the perceptions faculty hold of student futures and the place and station that students are expected to take as adults in the world beyond school.

Mr. Parrot, a slow-talking, slight man with a deep southern accent, teaches a social science course to juniors and seniors. The late-afternoon class is depleted by the absence of the seniors, who have gone off to rehearse for graduation. Five students, who have all straggled in well after the bell, are scattered throughout the large, well-equipped classroom. One has her head on the desk and is nodding off to sleep; another girl is chewing gum vigorously and leafing through a magazine; a third student stares straight ahead with glazed eyes. These three never respond to the teacher's questions and remain glumly silent during the class discussion. Two boys, Lowry and Richard, sit right under the teacher's nose and spend most of the class period being noisy and disruptive. Mr. Parrot hopes for other students to arrive, but finally decides to begin the class about twenty minutes after the bell. His opening remarks sound formal. He seems to be addressing his comments to more than the few people present. Standing behind a podium at the front of the room, he says, "Young people, let me have your attention quickly." Lowry and Richard quiet down momentarily, but the others appear to ignore his announcement. . . .

Although there are glimmers of more lively and skillful teaching going on at Carver and evidence of some sophisticated work done by a few students in biology, graphic arts, and literature, for example, the academic program seems to lag far behind the vocational training that is offered in the more than thirty shops at the school. . . .

. . . The academic side of life seems undeveloped and embryonic at the same time the vocational training feels rooted in history and clearly drawn. (Lightfoot, 1983, pp. 32–39, 52)[12]

Observation Number Three: The Ensworth School[13]

The Ensworth School is a privately financed, independent, coed day school with 460 students in grades "pre-first" through eight. It is open to all students regardless of race, religion, or creed. It began in 1958 in a former private home in one of the more prestigious sections of a large southern city. Since then, the original English Tudor residence has been expanded to include thirty-two classrooms, two art studios, two libraries, computer lab, gymnasium, exercise rooms, playing fields, tennis courts, playgrounds, and swimming pool on a well-manicured fifteen-acre campus.

Beginning at 7:30 each school morning, parents driving "hook-up" deposit carloads of bright and well-dressed children at the front porch of the school. Most students are white, but there are a few black and Asian faces. Academic entrance requirements assure that all students are of above-average ability, and virtually all are from above-average income homes, although 6 percent receive financial aid to attend.

At 7:45, several teachers gather in the lounge, where they drink coffee and discuss pollen count, soap operas, and recent student illnesses. Two secretaries answer phones and collect notes from returning absentees.

The Ensworth School.

As students in grades 3 through 8 arrive, they gather in the dining room, conversing and waiting for the school day to begin. At 7:55 Mr. Murphy, the middle school principal, dismisses them, and like a wave, they flow out the double doors, through the halls, and into their rooms. Most lower-elementary students do not arrive until 8:30 or 8:45, but some have already begun their school day in supervised free play under the direction of a P.E. or homeroom teacher.

As the day starts in Ms. Bain's first grade, work in the Sullivan programmed reading books is postponed as a student messenger delivers copies of this year's second issue of the student literary magazine. Each child receives a copy and immediately begins scanning the pages for his or her own writing and for writing of friends. Students read silently or softly to one another.

In Ms. Burgess's first grade, students sit in a circle on the carpeted floor for a show-and-tell session. Five students take their turns and share books, a poster, neon-bright shoe laces, a lost tooth, and a toy seal made of real fur. One boy questions whether a baby seal was killed to make the toy, and asks if it wouldn't be better to make toys out of old seals about to die.

Second-grade students in Ms. Kinnard's class write thank-you notes to two speakers who recently visited their classes. In Ms. McCall's class, students take their weekly spelling test.

In Ms. El Amri's third-grade class, students listen to an audiotape of the story of Amos Fortune as a culminating activity of their Civil War studies. Most students follow the teacher's suggestion and draw a related illustration as they listen; a few get so involved in borrowing crayons that they must be reminded to pay attention. The teacher periodically stops the tape and asks students factual and inferential questions. Hands go up in response—even those of students who appear not to be listening.

Across the hall in Ms. Odom's third-grade room, the class listens as one class member recounts a recent experience of appearing on a local TV show to perform a winning song she wrote and entered in a citywide song-writing contest. The class then returns to its study of Egypt. Students are assigned to write a short paper from the point of view of a person either in the Egyptian court or on an archaeological expedition that discovered an Egyptian tomb.

Students in Ms. Sterling's fourth grade spend the first thirty minutes of their regular math period making colorful tissue-paper flowers as a part of a special service project for a school for the handicapped. They then take out their math workbooks and proceed to work at an individual pace on multiplication involving two- and three-digit numbers.

At 11:30, all children in grades 1 through 4 go to lunch. Teachers lead their students down the carpeted halls in quiet, single-file lines. Students eat family style at twenty-four tables, seated nine per table—two from each grade and one adult. Students take turns being servers and runners. The day's lunch is hamburgers and French fries. Students ask one another to pass the catsup; no one argues, pushes, or grabs.

At Table 21, there is one remaining gingerbread square and four would-be takers. Since the sharing of food is the server's responsibility, the second grader in charge for the week cuts the square in half and proceeds to raffle off the pieces through number guessing. All at the table accept her decision as fair. At noon, the elementary principal dismisses the children by class. Fifteen minutes later the fifth through eighth graders observe a similar lunch pattern, but with much more chatter and a bit less formality.

After lunch, the three fifth-grade classes engage in English, geography, and math, respectively. The English class reviews for a test, and students ask questions about verb tense, verb agreement, and pronouns. Mr. Miller's geography class works in groups of two or four, creating games about the United States as a wrap-up of their studies. One group draws up rules for a Monopoly-type game in which players earn the right to buy states by correctly answering questions. Another group designs a U.S. trivia game with a map of the United States as the gameboard. In math class, students work on probability problems, projects, and games.

Two sixth-grade classes take individual oral French exams. Mr. El Amri sits at his desk with a semicircle of six students before him. The one student seated beside him shifts nervously in his chair as he labors to answer in French various questions posed by his teacher. The dozen students seated at their desks have survived their turn and either read French comic books, calculate their grade average, or engage in surreptitious English conversation.

In one of the downstairs art studios, a class of seventh graders scatters through the huge room to continue work on tempera paint, larger-than-life sports posters. Students apply careful brush strokes and critically eye their work. The posters will be the decorations for the upcoming sports banquet.

In a science lab, other seventh-grade students take a unit test on reproduction and development. Upstairs, the remainder of the seventh graders are in English, reviewing noun clauses and sentence order. Seventeen of the eighteen students listen closely as the teacher replies to questions.

The top fifteen eighth-grade math students who have been admitted to the Algebra I course take a break from their test review midway through their double-period class. As they do, one six-foot student asks the teacher if he may use the chalkboard to prove a theorem for his not-nearly-five-foot friend. Soon the board is filled with numbers and letters, and the teacher watches with amusement as the two boys use their break time to engage in academic challenge.

Other eighth-grade students leave Latin or life-studies classes for the final period of the day. As they do, they walk down the hall in boy-girl dyads and one all-girl clique. All are fashionably dressed, and many display braces as they smile. Some move toward English class, where Mrs. Sayers directs them to work in pairs to select the ten events most critical to the plot of Part III of *Watership Down* and arrange these in a time line.

At 2:45 parents driving the afternoon "hook-up" begin to line their cars in the school drive, and at 3:00 students in grades 1 through 6 spill out the double doors in a jubilant yet somewhat orderly fashion. The seventh and eighth graders stay for an additional period of P.E. By 4:15, almost all students have left the school, and all have left with books and homework assignments.

Observation Number Four: Life at Fall-Hamilton Elementary[14]

Fall-Hamilton is a modern public school in an urban location in Nashville, Tennessee. It houses 410 students from lower-middle- and low-income homes. About three-quarters of the children come from homes with poverty-level incomes and thus qualify for a hot breakfast and lunch at school. Only about one-third live in a home with both parents.

Although school will not begin for another hour, several teachers gather in the teachers' coffee room, where they discuss their weekend. At 7:15 the conversation is interrupted by a phone call, which a teacher answers. The parent on the line reports that her daughter will be late that morning. She wants the girl's teacher notified, but she does not know the teacher's name.

Ms. Tidwell, the school secretary, arrives at 7:30, turns on the easy-listening radio station, and tells the teachers that the principal will be absent today because his twins are sick. His wife stayed home from her teaching position in another school the last time they were sick, so it was his turn today.

At 7:45 eligible students who have been waiting outside the building enter the cafeteria for breakfast. They pick up their tickets and get in line. Several parents who have accompanied their children to breakfast wait for them to be served.

At the office, three substitute teachers have arrived to replace teachers who will be absent today; they sign in and are directed to the classrooms where they will teach. A mother brings a child who has had chicken pox to Ms. Tidwell to see if the child may return to school. The secretary declares the child well enough. A young student proudly shows Ms. Tidwell a wood carving he bought at the flea market over the weekend.

In the library, Ms. Ross checks the five centers she has arranged for students to use that day. Each teaches a different aspect of using the library. Her helpers

Fall-Hamilton Elementary School.

assist her by returning books to the shelves. Several other students check out books and scan the shelves. One student is writing a book report at a table.

At 8:15, Mr. Stewart, the P.E. teacher, announces over the intercom system, "We will now have our pledge." Throughout the building, students and teachers stand and recite the Pledge of Allegiance and then observe a minute of silence. Mr. Stewart announces that P.E. classes will be inside today because of the rain.

As the day starts in the kindergarten classroom, fifty children are busily engaged at various learning centers. Some are reading quietly, some painting, some doing puzzles, and some working at the computer. The two teachers are teaching basic skills to two separate small groups.

In a portable classroom at the edge of the parking lot, Ms. Henkel is teaching reading to a group of her first graders. Another group is listening to a reading tape, and the remaining class members are doing phonics worksheets individually.

The teacher of another first grade is presenting spelling words, but few of the students are listening. Several are clustered in small groups, busily chatting with each other, as she methodically proceeds from word to word down the list on the chart.

A fifth-grade class passes by Ms. Williams' sixth grade as they go to P.E. Several wave to their friends. They hear the sixth graders giving reports on apartheid in South Africa. After the reports, Ms. Williams discusses the current problems in South Africa.

At 10:45 the first class arrives for lunch. The children pass through the food line, choosing between two entrees and moving on to their assigned tables. When the entire class is seated, the teacher proceeds to the teachers' dining room, leaving the cafeteria aid in charge. As other classes enter every ten minutes, the room becomes noisy. Children talk and laugh loudly, exchange food, and scurry back to the serving area for items they forgot. The aid shouts for quiet and pounds her hand on a table with a loud slap. The children pause for a moment but quickly resume their previous behavior.

Two students begin fighting and are sent to the office. Both names are recorded on cards. It is a first offense for one of the two; he is reprimanded and sent to his classroom. It is the second offense for the other; he is talked to more sternly and told to remain sitting in the office. The principal will send home a letter describing what happened.

The students in Ms. Allen's fourth-grade classes are engaged in independent social studies projects. They are designing and painting dioramas. Ms. Miller's students are doing fractions. Some are solving problems in their workbooks, and others are doing so at the chalkboard under the teacher's guidance.

All eight children in the T-4 class listen as Ms. Ladd explains the rounding off of numbers. These students are in a "transitional class" because last year their third-grade teachers judged them unready for regular fourth grade. They are placed in a very small class in the hope that they will learn better with the close attention they receive from the teacher. Ms. Ladd writes eight examples on the chalkboard and asks each student to solve one of them. Then the class evaluates what each has done.

As the end of the day approaches, Mr. Rucks explains math problems to his sixth grade. He works a problem on the board and calls on James to explain what he has done. But James was not listening, so Mr. Rucks repeats the explanation. As he proceeds, he periodically calls on the students who seem to be less attentive. When he has finished, he asks if any students have questions. None do, so he assigns practice seatwork. As the students begin working their problems, he walks around the room monitoring their progress. As the intercom system clicks on for the end-of-the-day announcements, Mr. Rucks tells the class to finish the remaining problems on the page for homework.

Ms. Tidwell announces, "No Boy's Club activity tomorrow; the bus has broken down. LaShonda Clay, walk to Jill's house after school today. Teachers, check your mailboxes for an announcement before leaving."

Children in each class line up for dismissal. When the buzzer sounds, their teachers dismiss them, and they scurry toward their assigned exits. The building quiets down quickly. Teachers pick up paper from their classroom floors and think about their plans for the next day. A few students wait in the entrance foyer for their ride.

Before you proceed to the next section of this chapter, think about the ways in which specific elements of these four school descriptions reflect the five cultural concepts listed earlier in the chapter. Those concepts are

shared values and beliefs,
heroes and heroines,
rituals and ceremonies,
stories and legends, and
informal players.

For example, what did you learn about the shared values and beliefs of Ridgefield High? Of Carver Comprehensive High? Of Ensworth School? Of Fall-Hamilton Elementary? Even when the description does not contain enough information about a school to supply a clear answer to one of these questions, what would you infer from the information that is presented?

SUBCULTURES WITHIN SCHOOLS

Just as each school is a culture, subdivisions or groups within schools are subcultures; as with cultures, these subcultures have their own patterns of behavior, assumptions, and beliefs. School cultures can be categorized into three clusters or levels: those that come entirely or in part from outside the school, those that are almost entirely indigenous to the school and rather pervasive throughout the school culture as a whole, and those that are primarily subcultures within the broader school culture (Waller, 1932, especially p. 108).

For example, a school in New York City would be influenced by and react to different community values, expectations, and mandates than a school in rural New Mexico. But at the same time, each individual school also develops a particular set of cultural values and activities that are likely to distinguish it from others in similar circumstances. As a result, schools in the same community or only a few blocks apart have different internal cultural characteristics. Some of those characteristics appear schoolwide—a seriousness about learning or the lack of it, for example, whereas others are found only among separate subgroups, which have formed around jobs performed at school, socioeconomic status, race, academic ability, personal interests, and the like.

Subcultures are clearly evident to anyone who visits a school. Teachers, students, administrators, service workers all have their own *circles of associates*, ways of doing things, shared values, group leaders, and so forth, even though they are part of the larger school culture at the same time. Evidence can usually be seen when individuals in a school are free to choose where they spend their time. At lunchtime for example, teachers frequently cluster at a teachers' table, in a separate dining room, or in a designated lounge; students stake out their own territory in sets divided further by gender, age, race, type of personality, and friendship; and staff workers cluster with their own group in their own space.

Conversations in each of these clusters are quite different, as are the interpersonal interactions and presumptions about appropriateness of behavior. In fact, the behaviors are so distinct that nearly anyone could identify each subgroup blindfolded, simply by listening to the topics discussed and the language used.

Student Subcultures

In the general student subculture of a school, the actions and values of student leaders, or "heroes," are examples for others. These actions significantly affect the scholastic tone of a school and subsequently influence student behavior and performance (Gordon, 1957).[15] Some students who are looked up to by peers reinforce studying, others denigrate it; some stress conformist behavior, others encourage deviance. In the process they establish subgroup norms, which influence scholastic performance and educational aspirations both positively and negatively (McDill & Rigsby, 1973).

Groups within Groups

At the same time, however, the general student body of a school is not entirely cohesive. Each has its own groups within the group, and the influence of these groups within groups is also powerful. The smaller groups, or "gangs," have their own values, norms, language, patterns of dress, and informal rules for acceptable behavior. Differences among them are easily observed, especially in high schools where separate collections of "rah-rahs," "greasers," "potheads," and "brains" are clearly delineated. Here also the effect of student subculture membership on individual behavior is obvious. When subgroup norms are con-

The "Rah Rahs."

Teacher Subcultures

sistent with school goals, the behavior that is promoted supports school harmony. When the reverse is true, counterproductive individual behavior is fostered—cutting class, forming cliques, using drugs—and the school suffers.

The values, rituals, language, and beliefs of teacher subcultures are also well documented in the literature. For example, norms of autonomy and equality dictate how teachers relate to one another and may undermine efforts to introduce such innovations as peer observations, mentor teaching, open-space architecture, team teaching, or performance-based salary plans.

The teacher subculture can also directly influence teacher expectations and the amount of time teachers spend on instruction, thus influencing student performance and achievement. Some of this phenomenon was described in earlier chapters in discussions about teacher expectations and self-fulfilling prophecies. If teachers in a school expect much from themselves, most of them usually produce what they expect, and they tend to look down on those who do not. The reverse is typically true if expectations are low. Effects of this sort have been seen clearly in recent years as states have introduced career-ladder programs that attempt to distinguish between levels of performance quality.

Administrative Subcultures

The administrative subculture also has its own informal rules and procedures; and because of the position of authority of administrators, elements of that subculture permeate the school as a whole. For example, a principal's administrative style and general outlook affect the general operation of the school. If the principal is usually positive, supportive, and encouraging, teachers and students pick up the vibes and act accordingly; if the principal is too cautious, dull, and bureaucratic, they also respond to that message. At the same time,

ANALYSIS

Below is an excerpt from an observer's description of a lunchtime scene at Birmingham High School in Van Nuys, California. The report was written during the 1985–86 school year by Ben Stein, a journalist who observed in the school for most of the year. As you read, consider:

- What subcultures are reflected in the lunchtime scene? On what basis do you think they were formed?

- In what ways, does the culture of the school probably reflect the general society in which the school is located?

- What does the description seem to show about the roles and relationships associated with the principal?

> . . . A word about lunchtime at Birmingham High School. Lunch is served at 12:30. It is served in a huge outdoor space with a roof but no walls. The students eat at large tables with benches, on the grass in a giant quadrangle, along rows of outdoor lockers. In contrast to my own memories of high school, there are no fights, no pushing matches and, most of all, no smoking in secret nooks and groves.
>
> In an orderly way, the students divide themselves up into racial and ethnic groups. The blacks eat in the back of the eating room, near the soft-drink vending machine. The Mexicans eat on the grass and on benches near the grass. The prosperous white girls and boys eat nearer the center of the quadrangle or else sprawled on the cement near the student-activities room. There is also a row of blind, crippled and sad-looking students who eat by themselves along a wall of lockers near the faculty dining room, usually with a well-behaved Seeing Eye dog nearby.
>
> The different groups rarely eat together. On the other hand, individual members of each group know each other and greet each other cheerfully as they pass by to get their trays or drop off their trays.
>
> Jim Jameson, a fiftyish man who has been principal of Brimingham for about four years, walks through the cafeteria to make sure there is no butting in line and that occasional spats do not generate into anything worse. As Jameson walks by the students, they greet him and he greets each of them back, by name. Incredibly, he knows the name of almost every student among the 2,500 here. He also knows basic facts about each: "He's had a lot of trouble ever since his father died." "He's our best mathematician." "He's planning to go into the army." "She was out last week because she had a bad flu."
>
> Jameson has been voted principal of the year by the board of education repeatedly. He walks around the campus not only as if he were in charge of it, but as if it were one large child of his own. Many events at Birmingham are occasionally touching, but the rapport between the principal and his students is always moving.
>
> Seniors are allowed to leave campus for lunch. As far as I can tell, most of them do. They get into their cars—Rabbits and Toyotas and also a few Mercedes and Cadillacs—and head for the Round Table, Naugles, McDonald's and Bagel Nosh. A few go home if they live nearby and watch "The Young and the Restless."

> Generally, there is a relaxed cheerful mood around lunchtime, as if the students lived in a world from which adult concerns had been permanently banned. . . . (Stein, 1986, pp. 174–175)[17]

other subcultures in a school—for example, staff, teachers, and students—can support or conflict with that of the principal; and part of the principal's task is to make the cultures mesh.

As Wolcott (1973)[16] convincingly noted, some administrators have become preoccupied with accountability, control, and change. This in turn leads some to overmanage and second-guess teachers; they may also impose significant administrative burdens, especially in the form of paperwork. Such practices frequently put principals in direct conflict with teachers—a factor that can erode teacher motivation and effectiveness in the classroom. Principals also play key roles in encouraging or diminishing student performance. Some of their actions enhance productive activity and learning, and others hinder them. The principal's broad influence in a school culture may make teachers and students look forward to school or drive them away.

Parent and Community Values

The values and traditions of parents and the local community outside the school also affect the culture of the school and thus shape what goes on inside. For example, McDill and Rigsby (1973) show that value orientations of both teachers and the community, as well as the extent to which parents are involved in secondary schools, are linked to student performance. However, because community values differ and are championed by different interest groups or subcultures, the pressures are not consistent and often are in conflict.

Generally, subcultures of all types inside a school can play a very positive role in school performance, but they can also undermine schoolwide values, create subcultural battles, and neutralize each other. This is particularly true when subcultures, in the absence of schoolwide cultural strengths, vie constantly for supremacy and attention. For any school to perform effectively, shared values must keep various subgroups pulling in roughly the same direction. Otherwise, different subcultural influences will predominate, and both cohesion and performance will fall victim to a diversity of voices and special interests.

SCHOOL CULTURE AND EFFECTIVENESS

Culture Influences Behavior

The concept of school culture adds a particular dimension to the literature on effective schools, but that dimension has often been overlooked by many educators concerned with improving schools during the 1980s. Those who recognize the importance of the culture of schools see that beneath the well-accepted organizational characteristics of effective schools lie cultural elements that influence the behavior of administrators, teachers, and students. By influencing behavior, these cultural elements affect how well teachers teach and how much students learn. By projecting an image of what the schools stand for, they also affect perceptions and parental and community confidence. Therefore, those who understand schools as cultures realize that cultural considerations are necessary if schools are to be made more effective.

Table 6–1 outlines in two columns the characteristics of effective schools and

Comparison of Terminology Used to Describe Characteristics of Effective Schools and Characteristics of Strong Organizational Cultures

Characteristics of Effective Schools	Characteristics of Strong Organizational Cultures
Coherent ethos with agreed-upon ways of doing things; agreement on instructional goals	Strong culture with shared values and consensus on "how we do things around here"
Importance of principal as leader	Importance of principal as hero or heroine who embodies core values or who anoints other heroic figures
Strong beliefs about teaching and learning	Widely shared beliefs reflected in distinctive practices or rituals
Teachers as role models; students with positions of responsibility	Employees as situational heroes or heroines who represent core values
Staff training on schoolwide basis	Rituals of acculturation and cultural renewal
Effective meetings to plan jointly and to solve problems	Potential rituals to celebrate and transform core values
Orderly atmosphere without rigidity, guilt without oppression	Balances between innovation and tradition, autonomy and oppression
Joint participation in technical decision making	Widespread participation in cultural rituals

SOURCE: Deal, 1985, 612.[18]

Characteristics of Cultures

- shared values and beliefs
- heroes and heroines
- rituals and ceremonies
- stories and legends
- informal players

the characteristics of strong organizational cultures. A quick scan across the two columns shows similarities between the characteristics in both. However, a comparison also highlights differences between the columns, both in terminology and underlying assumptions. Effective schools research (Column 1) reflects a strong rational and technical emphasis: goals, leadership, planning, meetings, and training. The cultural approach (Column 2) shows a definite symbolic emphasis: values, beliefs, heroes and heroines, rituals. The differences are important because they represent different ways of showing the core attributes of effective schools and identifying what is needed to help schools improve.

Chapters 2 and 3 of this text provided instruction on observing in classrooms and on interpreting what happens in classroom in terms of good practice as reported in the effectiveness literature. This chapter has provided a different intellectual framework for understanding schools—schools viewed as cultures.

Look for Cultural Characteristics

Now that you have learned to think of schools as cultures, think again of the schools you know from past personal experience and from recent visits. This time, however, look for cultural concepts—the characteristics mentioned earlier in this chapter and repeated in the margin. Use them to make another assessment about what makes some schools effective and others ineffective.

SCHOOLS FROM A CULTURAL PERSPECTIVE

Questions to Ask

Having completed this exercise in a second way of looking at schools, you should now be prepared to analyze classrooms and schools from both an effective-schools perspective (that of Chapters 2 and 3) and an organizational-cultures perspective (that of this chapter). The two perspectives should be useful guides as you continue your studies and when you eventually enter your own classroom. The cultural perspective will be particularly helpful when you are in Laurie Renfro's situation—starting your first teaching job. At that point, your primary task will be to become a contributing and effective member of the school's professional staff. You will not have to give up your individuality and your own personal values and beliefs, but you will want to make what you bring to the school mesh comfortably with the culture already present. To accomplish this task, you will want to ask questions such as those suggested below for Laurie Renfro.

Laurie Renfro's Primary Task

Much of Ms. Renfro's success or failure in her first year will depend on how quickly she can learn the culture of Carson Junior High School. To do that, she should systematically consider questions such as those below. As the school year passes, she should also pose similar questions to examine the culture of her classroom. What does the school stand for? What is its history? What is its informing vision? What do its architecture and spatial arrangements say? What are its symbols? How widely shared are the core values? What are the images of the past? What are the taboos? Who are the heroes and heroines? How are mavericks treated? Are antiheroes and devils more cherished than the positive characters? What are the key rituals? What values are expressed in daily behavior? What happens in cultural ceremonies? What stories are told and retold? What are the stories about, and what do they mean? What are the sacred myths? Who are the gossips, the whisperers, the storytellers, and priests or priestesses? What are the various subcultures, and how do their values deviate from core values? How does behavior change when people enter the school? Why do people stay or leave through the years?

Carson's Primary Task

Making a School Better

As Laurie becomes an accepted member of the Carson community, she needs to join with Mr. Bays, Ms. Cohen, Mr. Grundig, and the rest of the staff to nourish, strengthen, and shape the culture of the junior high school. Her initial observations suggest that Carson already has a strong, distinctive culture. But because cultures are made up of dynamic groups of many people and elements, their members must continually work at maintaining and increasing community strengths. Here are one observer's ideas about means by which Carson could be made a better school.

1. **Recreate the history of the school.** In New York City, several elementary schools convened groups of parents, teachers, administrators, students, alumni, and retirees in sessions to recall the stories of those particular schools. In these meetings people discovered their roots and realities. By placing past and present in juxtaposition, they created a shared sense of direction and a shared vision for the schools. In the aggregate, the schools showed dramatic improvements in test scores, attendance, vandalism rates, and other measures of school performance.

2. **Articulate shared values.** What a school stands for needs to be shared.

In top-quality companies, slogans provide a shorthand means of making essential characteristics noticeable. Symbols, rituals, and artifacts represent intangible values. One school district, along with a local advertising group, made a commercial for its school. The intended audience was dual, as is often the case: Both consumers and workers were its targets. The response to the commercials was overwhelmingly positive. Efforts of teachers and students were recognized, shared, and reinforced.

3. **Anoint and celebrate heroes.** Every school has a pantheon of heroes—past, present, and future—and their anointment and celebration can provide human examples of shared values and beliefs. A recent phone call to Terry Deal, the author of this chapter, from the new principal of his old high school offers a novel example:

"We would like you to visit your alma mater," the principal said.

"Why?" Deal responded.

"Because you have done all right for yourself," she said. "And from all indicators you weren't supposed to. Your teachers remember you as a pain. Your classmates recall mischief and weren't big on your academic worth. The assistant principal notes that you spent more time in her office and the halls than you did in class. Your football coach was sure you'd end up in prison. In short, we want you on campus to show other troublemakers that there may be hope for them."

Countless other similar opportunities to celebrate teachers, students, administrators, alumni, and parents who exemplify intangible values exist in any school.

4. **Reinvigorate rituals and ceremonies.** Rituals and ceremonies provide regular occasions for special learning and celebrating and for binding individuals to traditions and values. The parents of students at a public high school recently gave a banquet for its teachers. As the teachers arrived at the school's cafeteria, they were greeted with corsages and ribbons labeled with terms such as Guru, Mentor, and Exemplar. The cafeteria tables were draped with white linen tablecloths bedecked with silver candelabra and lighted candles. Some teachers and parents sang together at a piano while others mingled, drinking wine and eating cheese. The dinner was potluck; each parent brought a dish. The program following dinner called attention to the history, values, and vision of the school. The school choir sang. The event delighted the entire audience and transformed the school.

In another such event, the principal of a large high school required his faculty to attend the annual graduation ceremony and to wear their academic robes. The district offered to pay the rental fee. Parents and students received the graduation ceremony with acclaim. The next year, attendance at graduation doubled. Student drinking and other behavior problems associated with commencement have virtually disappeared. Parent confidence in the school has gone up dramatically.

5. **Tell good stories.** Faculty at a junior high school spent most of a faculty meeting telling stories about students and each other. As a result, several exemplary students were identified, one a student who had changed from troublemaker to top student nearly overnight although he had had to overcome nearly insurmountable family and learning problems to do so. The faculty then convened an awards assembly to recognize exemplary students and to share

their stories with the other students. The student whose achievements prompted the idea was awarded a large brass eagle. The eagle award now carries the student's name and is given annually to the student who has improved the most.

6. **Work with the network of informal players.** A collection of priests, gossips, and storytellers is part of each school's culture; and their roles are important to the successful operation of the school. When changes are proposed, these people must be involved significantly, or they will sabotage the effort.

Often these roles are occupied by nonacademics such as secretaries, service workers, and custodians. Those who fill them provide important linkages inside the school and are often direct conduits to the local community. These people need encouragement. They need recognition. One school did this by naming a new patio in honor of a custodian, a man who served an important role as a keeper of the history of the school, conveying to both teachers and students its rich legacy of past exploits and glories.

Something to Think About

Ben Stein, the journalist who observed in Birmingham High School, Van Nuys, California, and whose description of lunchtime in that school appears in the Analysis section of this chapter, wrote the following quotation as part of the conclusion to his article about the school. As you read it, think of what his observations imply about the culture and subcultures of Birmingham High.

. . . Here are some things I never saw:

There was a wide variety of students in classes I visited—rich ones, poor ones, kids from famous families, kids who did not know their fathers. I never, not once, saw one student tease another about being poor or being rich or not having a car or not having the right clothes. It might have happened, but I never saw it.

There were many times when teachers were clearly aggravated and tired. I never saw a teacher sharply criticize a student or try to belittle him or her because of a mistake. I never saw or heard a teacher even address the students in an angry voice. I never saw a student leave a classroom feeling ashamed or upset or humiliated.

The teachers were all busy with their life adjustment or their teaching or with something at all times. Yet I never saw a teacher turn away a student who wanted to talk or share a problem. I never saw a teacher who was unwilling to stay after class or after school to hear a child's tale of woe.

In a word, I never saw a teacher who was not working his or her heart out either to teach or to make the children feel better. The teachers were and are onstage all day long, struggling with extremely difficult audiences. You can wonder at what they taught or did not teach, but you could not seriously question the sincerity or intensity of their efforts.

. . . The students seem to be much happier, freer and more confident than they were in 1962, when I left Montgomery Blair High School in Silver Spring, Maryland. The students are incomparably kinder to each other, far more tolerant of diversity, far less ready to pass on their parents' or teachers' prejudices except in rare instances. The students seem to me to be more comfortable with themselves and with each other.

On the other hand, the students know precious little about how their society is organized, why a free society under law is unique and why the society is worth preserving. They also know little in the way of organized thought processes or even basic ways of solving intellectual problems. They often struck me as computers without programs or any clear way to be useful, even to themselves. This is probably what the '60's education critics intended, but it is a dangerous kind of human being to entrust with the future of society. A human being who has not been taught to think clearly is a danger in a free society.

Certainly, students who leave school knowing as little of thought or facts as the students I saw are going to have difficulty maintaining either the way of life they covet or a technologically advanced society. Still, there was a winning, ebullient cheerfulness about the students that consistently blew away negative thoughts. The boys and girls were so likable, so enthusiastic, so flush with the power of youth that it seems cruel even to guess that they will not get whatever they want.

In any event, my observations are those of an adult looking in for a few hours each day on the wholly separate and distinct country of youth. As my year in their world wore on, I became convinced that high school was not so much a system of teaching or learning as a state of mind—the magic state of mind of the last, fullest measure of youth. To try to understand more than bits and pieces of high school is like trying to understand youth. It cannot be done. All I could do, in my own way, was two things; first I could take snapshots and send them home to the land of adults, where we can look at them and marvel. And there was one other thing I could do: I could and did learn to love the students at Birmingham High School as if they were my own children, to respect all the teachers I saw. . . . Whatever the shortcomings of the school and of the people in it, taken day by day and in person, they are as irresistible as youth itself. (Stein, 1986, 177–178)

- Based on this chapter's two excerpts from Stein, how would you describe the culture of Birmingham High?

- From what Stein said here and from what he wrote about lunchtime in the excerpt in the Analysis section of this chapter, how would you characterize the student subculture(s) of this school?

- What would you say are some of the basic values and beliefs that undergird the culture of Birmingham High?

CONCLUSION: CARSON JUNIOR HIGH—TEN YEARS LATER

Entering a School Culture

As John Noble stepped from his new 1999 BMW, he smiled broadly. "What a school! I'm delighted to have been selected from the long list of candidates. Just think, my own classroom, my own students, and a salary equal to my firends who opted for careers in business."

As he walked through the newly remodeled entryway of the school, he noticed a distinctive banner hanging in the center of the foyer—Carson Junior High School—Where Learning Is a Way of Life. His eyes moved toward a handsome plaque above the trophy case—Carson Junior High School—An American School of Excellence, 1996. He beamed proudly. He also noted the pictures of a Mr. Bays and a Mr. Grundig hanging among others on the wall. "I wonder who those people are? Probably important people in the history of the school," he mused. As he walked across the freshly waxed hallway floors, he admired the student artwork and class portraits on the wall.

As he entered the door of the principal's office, an elderly woman greeted him in a cheery voice. "Welcome to Carson. You must be the new social studies teacher. I'm Muriel Cohen. Our principal will be back from the superintendent's office in a moment. While you're waiting for Ms. Renfro to return, let me show you around Carson."

EDUCATIONAL RESEARCH

An Ethnographic Approach

Studying Culture

The educational research emphasized in the first five chapters of this text is rather analytical in nature—at least to some extent, it involves experimentation. But anthropologists, those who study culture, often are more descriptive than analytical. That is, they study a culture by observing people and recording what they see. Then they interpret their descriptions by comparing those of one culture to those of another, offering explanations for similarities and differences. This type of study is called *ethnography*.

Therefore, to the extent that schools are cultures, they too can be studied ethnographically. In fact, the section of this chapter entitled "A Close Look at Four Schools," consists of brief segments of four school ethnographies; when you read those four descriptions and responded to the questions that preceded and followed them, you were thinking ethnographically.

Below is a short example of an ethnographic account that was written not by an anthropologist but by a journalist. As you read it,

- Think of what terms you would use to describe the culture of Fletcher-Johnson Educational Center and its surrounding community.
- How would you compare the culture of Fletcher-Johnson to that of the four schools you already read about in this chapter?
- How would you compare it to the culture of the high school you attended?

When you finish thinking about Fletcher-Johnson in these terms, consider the three questions that follow the description.

A Journalist's Account

The account is by Marc Fisher, a Washington, D.C., journalist.[19]

On Monday mornings, when Mr. Tolson greets his ninth-grade math students at Fletcher-Johnson Educational Center, they tell him about their weekends. They tell of gun battles that interrupt their sleep, arguments that echo through the alleys, sirens and screams that are the night sounds of the projects.

"They say things that would shock your pants off," Antonio Tolson said Tuesday. "But you know, for these kids, it just seems like a normal thing."

Fletcher-Johnson, a massive brown concrete building on a hill off Benning Road in Southeast [a quadrant of the city], doesn't feel like a school in a ravaged, drug-infested neighborhood. It is a sprawling place of bright colors and the latest computer equipment. It is graffiti-free. Its halls are carpeted and quiet. In its open classrooms, teachers need not shout to be heard over other classes a few feet away.

"We are out here in the forgotten land, surrounded by drugs," said George Rutherford II, principal since 1978. . . .

Last week, when Mayor Marion Barry visited Fletcher-Johnson to teach a science class, he asked students how many of them knew someone who had been killed. Fourteen of the 19 students raised their hands.

This week, Ronnell Monroe and Bobby Goloson, ninth graders and friends from the same block at 53rd and C streets SE, thought for only a few seconds about the last person they knew who was killed.

"Oh, yeah, this lady got kidnapped and he raped her and killed her," Monroe said. "She lived across the street. It got me a little down because my mother knew her. A boy, John, also got shot. Somebody messed with his girlfriend and he bought a .22 and shot at the fella. They ran through the alley. We heard it and my mother said to click off the lights and get down, get down, get down." Monroe said he spent about 10 minutes on the floor that night. "Then all the cops came and everybody went outside," Goloson said.

"You hear shots around our way mostly all the time," Monroe said.

"The lady's friends chased that man into the house and he didn't come out until the police came," Goloson said. "He only had a .22."

Children of all ages speak almost casually of pools of blood and screams that ricochet through the projects for hours.

The stories flow easily. And they are accurate: Deputy Police Chief Alfonso Gibson confirmed most of the incidents the children related; the others, he said, "are all realistic." These are not things the children dream up. . . ."

"A dude got shot," said Jermaine Griffin, 13. "He was high and he came and messed with other people and they pushed him and shot him. I knew his name and I felt sad. I was right around the corner. I was scared when I saw the blood."

"In my neighborhood, I always got to watch for people—crazy, drunk people running from the police. And mostly I'm scared of the police. I try to get away as quickly as I can. Especially now and in the summer. That's when people really get that stuff in them and get crazy. That's what it's really about—that drugs."

"I hear the shots and I jump and run around and peep out the window and go back to sleep."

- In what ways would the out-of-school lives of the children at Fletcher-Johnson affect the in-school culture?

- How might the teachers and administrators of the school compensate for the troubled environment in which Fletcher-Johnson students live?

> • Some people would say that teachers at Fletcher-Johnson simply would not be able to compensate for the out-of-school lives of their students, that the students are doomed to failure. What do you think?

SUMMARY

One of the ways of understanding schools is to think of them as organizational cultures—dynamic groups of people who follow certain patterns of behavior, possess common values and beliefs, and pursue particular goals. Although schools vary in many ways, looking at them as cultures provides an intellectual framework that explains them more in terms of their commonalities than their differences. By using a cultural perspective, observers can look for key cultural characteristics in all schools—shared values and beliefs, heroes and heroines, rituals and ceremonies, stories and legends, and informal players.

When individuals, including new teachers in schools, enter organizational cultures for the first time, they face the task of learning how things are done in that culture. If they do not learn this, their stay in the organization is likely to be uncomfortable and unsuccessful. Frequently, they are not accepted as part of the group, and they find it difficult to mesh their personal values and goals with those of the organization.

Subcultures operate within schools, as they do in all organizations, and these affect the more general institutional culture both positively and negatively. Students, teachers, administrators, and service workers all have their cultures within the broader culture; and each of these subcultures has subdivisions within it. The extent to which all these groups work together greatly affects school effectiveness.

STUDY QUESTIONS

1. Think of one of the organizations in which you are or have been a member—fraternity, sorority, athletic team, church group, or the like. Then identify within that group the cultural characteristics of organizations that this chapter stressed—values and beliefs, heroes and heroines, rituals and ceremonies, stories and legends, and informal players. How and why do you think these specific characteristics developed as they did in this group?

2. Think again of an organization in which you are or have been a member, possibly the same one you used in Question 1. Then identify subcultures that exist or existed in the organization. Why do you think these subcultures developed in this group? In what ways was each subculture a positive and a negative influence in the organization?

3. Think of a school you know reasonably well. Then, using as your guide the six actions proposed for Carson Junior High School in the section entitled "Carson's Primary Task," propose six comparable things that people in that school could do to make the school better.

4. What are some of the things that you think Laurie Renfro probably did during her ten years at Carson that would have led to her selection as principal? Why do you think so?

BIBLIOGRAPHY

Baldridge, J., & Deal, T. (1983). *The dynamics of organizational change in education.* Berkeley, CA: McCutchan.

Cohen, M. (1985). Introduction to special issue on effective schools. *Elementary School Journal, 85*(3), 315–336.

Deal, T. (1985). National commission reports: Blueprints for remodeling or ceremonies for revitalizing public schools. *Education and Urban Society, 17*(2), 145–156.

Deal, T., & Kennedy, A. (1982). *Corporate cultures.* Reading, MA: Addison-Wesley.

Deal, T., & Kennedy, A. (1983). Culture and school performance. *Educational Leadership, 40*(5), 14–15.

Gordon, W. (1957). *The social system of the high school.* New York: Free Press.

Hamilton, S. F. (1983). The social side of schooling: Ecological studies of classrooms and schools. *Elementary School Journal, 83*(4), 313–334.

Lieberman, A. (1988). *Building a professional culture in schools.* New York: Teachers College Press.

Lightfoot, S., (1983). *The good high school: Portraits of character and culture.* New York: Basic Books.

Peters, T., & Waterman, R. (1982). *In search of excellence.* New York: Harper & Row.

Purkey, S., & Smith, M. (1985). School reform: The district policy implications of the effective schools literature. *Elementary School Journal, 85*(3), 353–389.

Sarason, S. (1971). *The culture of the school and the problems of change.* Boston: Allyn and Bacon.

Waller, W. (1932). *The sociology of teaching.* New York: Wiley.

NOTES

1. Deal, T., & Kennedy, A. (1982). *Corporate cultures.* Reading, MA: Addison-Wesley; Peters, T., & Waterman, R. (1982). *In Search of Excellence.* New York: Harper & Row.

2. Waller, W. (1932). *The sociology of teaching.* New York: Wiley.

3. Clark, B. (1983). The organizational saga in higher education. In J. Baldridge & T. Deal (Eds.), *The dynamics of organizational change in education.* Berkeley, CA: McCutchan.

4. Sarason, S. (1971). *The culture of the school and the problems of change.* Boston: Allyn and Bacon.

5. Deal, T. (1982). Alternative schools: Struggle for identity. *Changing Schools, 10*(2), 8–9; Swidler, A. (1979). *Organization with authority.* Cambridge, MA: Harvard University Press.

6. Fullan, M. (1985). Change processes and strategies at the local level. *Elementary School Journal, 85*(3), 391–421.
7. Deal, T., Gunnar, H., & Wiske, S. (1977). *Linking knowledge to schools: The process of change in six sites.* Andover, MA: The Network.
8. McDill, E., & Rigsby, L. (1973). *Structure and process in secondary schools.* Baltimore: Johns Hopkins University Press.
9. *Elementary School Journal, 85*(3).
10. Cohen, E., Deal, T., Meyer, J., & Scott, W. (1979). Technology and teaming in the elementary school. *Sociology of Education, 52,* 20–33; Deal, T., Meyer, J., & Scott, W. (1983). Organizational influences on educational innovation. In J. Baldridge & T. Deal (Eds.), *The dynamics of organizational change in education.* Berkeley, CA: McCutchan; Meyer, J., & Rowan, B. (1977). Institutional organizations—Formal structure as myth and ceremony. *American Journal of Sociology, 83,* 440–463.
11. Boyer, E. (1983). *High school: A report on secondary education in America.* New York: Harper & Row.
12. Lightfoot, S., (1983). *The good high school: Portraits of character and culture.* New York: Basic Books.
13. This observation was recorded by Alene Harris at The Ensworth School, Nashville, Tennessee.
14. This observation was recorded by Alene Harris at Fall-Hamilton Elementary School, Nashville, Tennessee.
15. Gordon, W. (1957). *The social system of the high school.* New York: Free Press.
16. Wolcott, H. F. (1973). *The man in the principal's office: An ethnography.* New York: Holt, Rinehart and Winston.
17. Stein, B. (1986, November). High school diary. *Los Angeles Magazine,* 168–175.
18. Deal, T. E. (1985). The symbolism of effective schools. *Elementary School Journal, 85*(5), 601–620.
19. Fisher, Marc. (1987, May 22). The forgotten land surrounded by drugs. *The Washington Post,* 96.

CHAPTER 7

The Schools in Historical Context: From Ancient Greece to the Twentieth Century

INTRODUCTION

Now that you have read about classrooms, students, schools, and the purposes of schooling in contemporary America, Chapters 7 through 10 turn attention to theoretical contexts within which schools and classrooms operate. Chapters 7 and 8 look at this material from the perspective of the historical and philosophical foundations of education, and Chapters 9 and 10 approach it through the perspectives of learning theory and models of instruction.

Chapter 7 reaches back into history prior to the years described in Chapters 1 and 5 and outlines the historical setting in which schools of the United States developed by describing events now considered to be the roots from which schools today have grown. Those events of the past have led to what teachers and students do in K–12 classrooms today. Schooling in Europe from ancient Greek times to the founding of the English colonies in America and American schooling from colonial times to the twentieth century are emphasized, since the roots of American schooling lie in those places and times. This general sequence is illustrated in the timeline in Figure 7–1.

This focus does not mean that early schooling in other parts of the world was not important. It was. Long educational traditions evolved in China; Japan; the kingdoms of Africa; in the Inca, Aztec, and Mayan civilizations of pre-Columbian America; and elsewhere. Those traditions, however, have not had so significant an impact on contemporary American schools as Europe and the earlier United States, and the influence they have had has not been direct.

As you read each chapter section, ask yourself the four guiding questions that follow:

- What was the purpose of schooling?
- Who was educated?
- Who did the teaching?
- What was studied?

Also look for the ideas and traditions that have molded American schools and teaching into what they are today.

The chapter Snapshot describes the schooling of an imaginary student in ancient Greece, and the Analysis section describes a colonial American elementary school classroom. The two descriptions are intended to provide historical pictures of schooling that (1) illustrate what the chapter narrative describes and (2) supply contrasts to what you see in schools today. The Educational Research section describes a historical study of secondary school teaching practices.

SNAPSHOT

The Snapshot for this chapter describes the schooling of a boy in ancient Greece.[1] As you read, consider:

- How was Alex's schooling different from yours?

- Why do you think it was different in these ways?
- How was it similar? Why do you think this is the case?
- What were the primary purposes of his schooling?
- In what ways does schooling reflect the general culture of the times?

SCHOOLING IN ANCIENT GREECE

Alex began his schooling at age six when his father arranged for a man who was a local teacher to take him into the school he conducted in his home for other Athenian boys. Alex's father had selected this particular teacher because of the subjects he taught and because his reputation as a teacher was good. Alex's father agreed at the outset on the fee to be paid and the thrust of the instruction. To some extent, the arrangement was atypical: Alex, unlike many other Athenian boys, who studied different subjects under different teachers, was to be taught all of his subjects by the one teacher.

Alex studied reading, writing, literature, music, drawing, painting, and gymnastics. Before he could read, he listened to others read Homer and Hesiod; and when he learned enough of the alphabet, he began to read on his own. When he learned to write, he recorded passages read aloud by the teacher and copied some from the scrolls hanging on the walls.

These scenes of teachers and students appear on a vase that has been preserved since ancient Greek times.

Much of his learning consisted of memorizing. At first he did not understand much of what he wrote and memorized, but gradually he understood more and more. At times the teacher and students discussed the passages, and these discussions enabled him to grasp the elements of history and geography embedded in them.

For much of the school day, the teacher sat on a chair at the front of the room, and the boys sat on backless chairs facing him. Each boy had a wax tablet and stylus for writing and a lyre on which to practice his music.

When Alex was twelve, his father contracted with another teacher to teach him at a more advanced level. The teacher had come to Athens only a few months earlier, but he had developed a good reputation quickly by lecturing at various public locations in the city. For a short time, the teacher's lectures were free because he was unknown to most of the citizens. As his reputation as a speaker, thinker, and teacher spread, more young men came to hear him and to discuss ideas with him. When he felt he was attracting an appropriate number of potential students, he rented a room, began charging admission, and changed his approach from lecturing to teaching.

In his new school, Alex studied oratory, composition, rhetoric, literature, music, history, law, arithmetic, geometry, the use of the abacus, and weights and measures. He also regularly participated in exercise and physical training. Lectures and discussions were the predominant means of instruction for certain subjects, but there was also much memorizing, writing, and calculating. Frequently, Alex and his schoolmates were expected to prepare and present speeches to their friends and families, as well as to the public.

At age 18, Alex left school to begin the two-year military training required of all boys by the city-state.

EARLY SCHOOLING—FROM ANCIENT TO MODERN TIMES

The Greeks—500–146 B.C.

Sophists

Although schooling in Europe began some time earlier, the beginning point for this historical survey is in Greece about 500 B.C. At that time, wandering teachers, called *sophists*, traveled from place to place teaching young men of important families. Their students were the future citizens and leaders of the Greek city-states. They taught about civic issues and helped their students develop communication skills, especially in speaking and writing. The teaching of Alex, described in the Snapshot, was of this type.

The purpose of this teaching was to provide the young men with the tools they needed to be effective leaders—tools that would be means to achieving political power, social prestige, and wealth. Typical subjects were rhetoric, argumentation, logic, and the Greek language.

Unlike the teachers who succeeded them, the sophists reasoned cautiously. Most did not "search for truth" in their own study and did not inculcate the idea of doing so in their students. They simply taught information their students, such as Alex, needed to know and trained them in skills needed to gain positions of leadership.

During these ancient times, two of the Greek city-states, Athens and Sparta, developed organized approaches to schooling. In both places, boys and young men attended schools for physical, moral, and civic training. But Spartan and Athenian education had different emphases. Sparta stressed training for the military, emphasizing the physical and moral development of strong, loyal soldiers. Service to the state was paramount, and characteristics of obedience, patriotism, and courage were sought and praised. Athenian schools placed more emphasis on intellectual, cultural, and aesthetic goals than did those of Sparta. But there, too, military training played a sizable part in a young man's education for citizenship.

Socrates, 470–399 B.C.

In the fourth and third centuries B.C., Athens produced three of the greatest teachers of the western world. The first of these was Socrates. Socrates traveled around Athens teaching young men and boys the same subjects as the sophists taught. But he was significantly different from the sophists, both as a thinker and as a teacher. He was intellectual, and they were technical. As an originator of ideas, he raised questions they ignored or never thought of.

Socrates.

Socratic Method

Socrates sought to find universal principles, truth, beauty, and goodness in his study. He taught his students to do the same. He urged them to seek a life of moral excellence. He believed that, as a teacher, he needed to do more than train students to gain positions of authority. He prepared them to lead their citizenry by a set of ethical ideals toward a good and morally just life. His method of teaching—a questioning of students in dialogue style—is known today as the *Socratic method.*

Guided by his principles and his search for truth, Socrates clashed with the civil authorities when his ideas conflicted with theirs. He believed that if ideas were to develop and if citizens and the state were to improve, it was necessary for all thinkers, including himself and his students, to be free to think and question.

Those in political power often disagreed and saw Socrates' social criticism as a threat to their power. Eventually, his questioning of civil authority reached a point where he was put on trial for opposing the government, found guilty, and given a choice by those in authority: Either he had to conform, or he had to die by his own hand. He held fast to his principles and committed suicide by drinking hemlock.

Plato, 428–347 B.C.

Plato, a student of Socrates, followed in his teacher's intellectual footsteps. He, too, sought truth, beauty, goodness, and justice. He believed the purpose of education was to develop the abilities of students so that those abilities could

Plato.

Aristotle.

be used to serve society. He identified *ideals,* or universal concepts, that he said existed in the abstract, serving as goals toward which all people and states should strive. He thought of people, the state, and the other elements of the known world as imperfect representations of the ideal. Education was a means to make those elements more perfect. He wrote about his concept of the ideal state in the *Republic.*

Aristotle, 384–322 B.C.

Aristotle continued Plato's teaching, particularly his idea that the purpose of education was to improve people and society. In fact, he believed that the quality of life in a city and the quality of its government were direct results of the quality of education. Education increased people's civil and humane capacities, led toward better governments, encouraged a cultivated society, and moved the city-state toward the ideal.

Aristotle was an abstract thinker like Socrates and Plato, but his teaching was more objective, practical, and scientific. He taught Alexander the Great and founded a philosophical school called the Lyceum. He wrote on many subjects, including astronomy, physics, botany, zoology, politics, ethics, logic, and metaphysics. His writings, like those of Plato, have had a powerful influence on thinkers and teachers through succeeding centuries.

The Romans—146 B.C.–A.D. 476

Rome conquered Greece in 146 B.C. Over the next century, Greek educational ideas became a part of Roman thinking, and schools became part of Roman society. As in the Greek city-states, the main purpose of education was civic in nature, with an emphasis on training new political leaders. But Roman schooling tended to be more utilitarian and practical and less philosophical and aesthetic than that of Athens.

The Romans were very much concerned with developing leadership skills that were needed to administer their expanding empire. Therefore, their more advanced schools included training in rhetoric, grammar, mathematics, law, and administration. Those who completed schooling usually entered careers in public service, as lawyers, senators, teachers, and the like.

Cicero, 100–43 B.C.

Cicero and Quintilian were among the most distinguished of Roman teachers. Cicero was a Roman senator whose educational ideas combined the practical skills of debate, argumentation, and law with the more Greek elements of a liberal education, including ethics, philosophy, history, and astronomy. For him, the purpose of education was to serve the republic. The most important tools were oratory, a command of Latin and Greek grammar, and a knowledge of history.

Quintilian, A.D. 35–92

Quintilian represented the Roman Empire rather than the republic, and he was primarily a teacher, not a political leader. He saw learning as a developmental process and outlined a sequence of education that recognized developmental stages. He stressed speaking but also believed in a broad liberal education and expected good orators to be ethical and moral people. Quintilian described his thinking on education and outlined his recommendations for Roman education in the twelve-book work *The Institutes of Oratory (Institutis Oratoria)*.

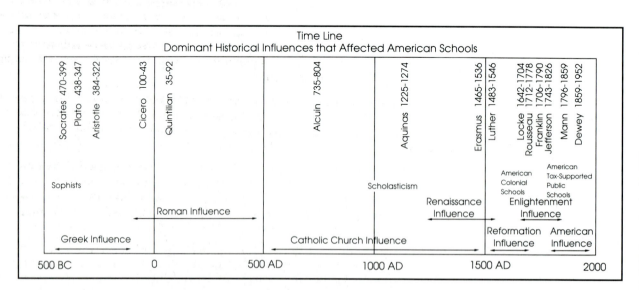

Figure 7–1. Time line of key influences on teaching and schools in Western history. The influences, ideas, and individuals listed on the time line are considered important to teaching and schools today.

The Middle Ages—A.D. 500–1500

Church Influence

By A.D. 500 the primary purposes of schooling in Europe were quite different from those of Greek and Roman times. By then, the Roman Empire had fallen, and church leaders had replaced political leaders as the main sources of authority. The primary political and social unit of society was the feudal manor or principality rather than the city-state or the empire.

Schooling was intended to train for church and military leadership and to provide for the understanding of religion and church teachings. Much of this education occurred in monastic and cathedral schools established by the church with the support of feudal lords. Separately, a second level of training, in the form of apprenticeships, taught young men the tools of the trade through long, unpaid terms of training with merchants or craftspersons.

Alcuin, 735–804

During the early centuries of the Middle Ages, Charlemagne of what is now France consolidated power in Europe by conquering many small fiefdoms and forming the Holy Roman Empire. Education in his kingdom was probably the most sophisticated in Europe at that time. Schooling was centered in his palace school and was directed by his chief advisor on education, Alcuin, a former teacher in England. Alcuin's palace school was intended to teach the children of the empire's royal class and in doing so, to train the next generation of church and political leaders.

Seven Liberal Arts

Alcuin's educational ideas and plans for schools served as models for centuries. He also is credited with developing, or at least popularizing, script writing as a substitute for printing. But his efforts tend to be overlooked by historians, who consider the Middle Ages a time of educational neglect. It was at this time, however, that education focusing on the seven liberal arts became a common curriculum. The liberal arts consisted of grammar, rhetoric, logic, arithmetic, geometry, music, and astronomy. They served as the basis of what is referred to as the *liberal arts* today.

Schooling in Europe during the Middle Ages was not limited to Charlemagne's court, however. It also occurred in the manors of many lower-level princes and in the monasteries scattered throughout the countryside. Generally, this type of schooling was very practical training for court and church leaders, as well as for craftspersons and merchants. The subject matter included a heavy religious emphasis, along with training for the students' intended station in life.

Scholasticism

By the eleventh century, a clearly identifiable type of education, called scholasticism, had developed. *Scholasticism* was an approach to study that combined faith and reason. That is, it combined a reliance on religious faith and the use of one's intellect to search for truth and meaning. It used a process of questioning, or inquiry, by which thinkers would come to understand their world and their God.

Scholasticism rested on the beliefs that God made the world knowable and that the mind is capable of discovering that meaning through deductive reasoning. A learner would gather ideas from the teachings of the church, from church authority, and from the revealed word of God. Then he would use his human mind to discover meaning in what he studied.

Thomas Aquinas, 1225–1274

Scholasticism evolved from the teaching of monks and priests, who were called *scholastics*. Saint Thomas Aquinas, a Dominican theologian, philosopher, and teacher who taught at the University of Paris, was its most noteworthy practitioner. Aquinas integrated church doctrine and Aristotelian philosophy into a means for studying the world in which he lived. He was the ideal teacher as a thoughtful scholar, an involved actor in the learning process of his students, a person knowledgeable of his subject matter and sensitive to human nature. He considered schooling as something more than the informal learning that took place as children grew up and believed it should be provided by many agencies of society. Schooling was formal, planned learning that was based on definite principles and acknowledged subject matter. It led students to draw conclusions from their study.

Scholastics used *syllogisms* both to order knowledge for themselves and as a teaching device. Their curriculum included theology, church dogma, moral philosophy, metaphysics, logic, mathematics, and science. Students of the scholastics prepared to be monks, priests, scribes, court officials, and administrators.

Universities

As scholasticism developed, the schools in which scholastic teaching occurred grew into medieval universities. Gradually, they added law and medicine to their curriculum. Over the next few centuries important universities evolved at Paris, Orleans, and Toulouse in France; at Bologna, Padua, and Naples in Italy; and at Oxford and Cambridge in England. Others were founded in Scotland, Spain, Germany, and at other European cities.

The Renaissance—A.D. 1300–1500

Classical Humanism

By the fourteenth century, a reaction had set in against the teaching of the Middle Ages. Scholars and their students grew tired of the heavy church dominance over schooling and scholarly thought. They shifted their thinking from a next-life orientation to a closer investigation of this world. Rather than relying on the revealed word of God and the church for intellectual authority, they turned more directly and more often to the writings and ideas of the ancient Greeks and Romans and to a spirit of free inquiry that they read about in the Greek classics. Gradually, their *classical humanism* replaced the thinking of the scholastics.

Renaissance thinking developed somewhat parallel to the rise of commerce in Europe. As expanding trade created centers of wealth in cities, especially those of northern Italy, the wealthy sought new learning in literature, the arts, and architecture. The wealthy commercial class began to sponsor teachers, artists, and writers, and they saw themselves as custodians of the new knowledge. As such, they became a cultural elite that could stand tall in comparison with church authority and military might.

Court Schools

To preserve this intellectual and cultural elitism, they founded court schools for their children and others of social and political position. These schools were intended to educate *courtiers*, that is, people who were learned in the classics, polished in style and elegance, and of service to the court, particularly as diplomats. The curriculum consisted of literature, especially the classics, art, architecture, and Greek and Latin grammar.

Over time, however, schooling and formal education became a goal unto itself instead of a means to a greater end of true learning. Erudition replaced substance and understanding. To know the right thing or the correct style became more important than the pursuit of new knowledge or true investigation.

Desiderius Erasmus, 1465–1536

Desiderius Erasmus of Rotterdam in the Netherlands was a noted Renaissance scholar and also its most telling critic. He was a teacher, philosopher, writer, and social critic. His most famous work, *In Praise of Folly*, satirically attacked the schooling and culture of both medieval and contemporary times. He said theologians and philosophers were more interested in showing off their intellectual egos than finding new meaning in life and the relationship between God and human beings. He said teachers stressed unimportant facts and precise intricacies of grammar rather than teaching their students meaningful knowledge.

Erasmus advocated the teaching of classical languages, history, etymology, archeology, astronomy, and the Scriptures. He also acknowledged the importance of early learning and suggested that parents begin the education of their children by teaching the children themselves at an early age. He was aware of the importance of developmental growth in students, and he recommended that teachers use certain methods of instruction.

In response to the writings of Erasmus and others, later Renaissance thinkers and teachers developed ideas that still influence education and schooling today. Those ideas involved the nature of knowledge, purposes of education, the role of schooling, specific approaches to teaching, and the place of the liberal arts in the curriculum. Probably most noticeable of the specific legacies of the Renaissance is the place that Latin has held in the secondary schools of America until recent times.

Schooling for an Elite

Although schooling during the Renaissance broadened to include more diverse students than the schooling of earlier times, it was still elitist and intended primarily for men. It was directed only to that class of people who might be expected to be able to appreciate it. It produced social critics, but not those who challenged the roles, stations in life, and importance of the powerful elite. It did not stimulate concern for the life of the peasant. It did not challenge the assumptions of the rigid social class structure or the customs and privileges that accompanied it.

To the contrary, it criticized mediocrity, those who lacked social polish and status, and the uneducated. For the people of that time, education was tied to social class because of the elitist opinion that it would be wasted on the unsophisticated. Those other classes trained for jobs but were not schooled, in the finer sense of the term.

Education of Women

Renaissance schooling was not open to significant numbers of women. Daughters of aristocrats might study certain "ladies' subjects" in court schools or with private tutors, or they might be taught in convents or convent schools, but most had no schooling at all. Those who did, studied art, music, needlework, poetry, and dancing.

The Reformation and the Rise of the Middle Class—A.D. 1500–1700

The rise of a commercial middle class, the development of modern nation-states, and the Protestant Reformation in Europe brought about a reorientation of schooling in the sixteenth and seventeenth centuries. The schools that evolved were less tied to the aristocratic classes, less bound to cities to the exclusion of the countryside, and no longer under the rules and tradition of a single church.

Education for Literacy

Schools needed to serve a variety of religious purposes. They were needed to teach as many people as possible to read the Bible, not in Latin, but in the local language—the vernacular. Whereas Catholic church leaders had considered it unnecessary for each person to read and interpret the Bible since that was the

> **Something to Think About**
>
> Some educational historians draw parallels between early European schools and select, private, boys' schools of today.
>
> - What similarities do you see between these two types of schools?
> - In what ways are they different?

responsibility of the clergy, Protestants insisted that their followers read the Bible themselves. Strict obedience to church authority was not at that time their practice. (Later, a similar split would develop among Protestants, with such sects as Baptists and Quakers among the dissenters.)

Therefore, schools were needed to instruct religious followers and to help them spread their beliefs to others. Even the lower classes had to be reached, so that they could learn their religion and live according to its precepts. Schools existed for a more serious purpose than for the more stylish reasons of the Renaissance courtiers: Reading the Bible was believed necessary for salvation.

Commerce

Economic conditions also necessitated the spread of schooling. If people were to trade and travel more, they needed to know more about other places and people. They needed to be able to write and to communicate in their own and in other languages. They needed to compute and to handle their other business affairs.

Martin Luther, 1483–1546

Protestant leaders such as Martin Luther and his early followers recommended basic schooling for children of all classes and both genders. They went so far as to urge government-supported schools. They proposed instruction in both the local language and in Latin, as well as in history, music, science, mathematics, and physical education. Schools were seen as instruments of religion, but that was not their sole purpose. There was also a civic purpose—to develop useful citizens.

In these denominational schools, teaching tended to conform to a rigid question-and-answer format and was often organized around the official catechism. The important religious denominational precepts were memorized and ingrained. As the schools spread, two levels of instruction became the norm—common "grammar" schools for all, including girls; and "classical" schools for the upper classes, those who were educated for church, civil, and commercial positions of leadership.

Schools for Everyone

The greatest legacy of schooling during this period was the concept of universal education, or schools for everyone. The schools of the first European settlers in America rested on that principle.

The Enlightenment—1700–1800

Age of Reason

In European history, the eighteenth century is known as the Enlightenment or the Age of Reason because the influential thinkers of the time emphasized the power of the human mind. These philosophers—among them, John Locke, Jean-Jacques Rousseau, David Hume, and Voltaire—believed the thinking mind could understand the universe and all in it. They thought that thinking people could develop the means to make the world and human life better. These ideas had a direct and powerful impact on all American institutions, including both the American form of government and its schools.

Scientific Method

Enlightenment philosophers saw the universe as a gigantic machine that was guided and operated by a set of constantly operating natural laws. Humans could use their minds to learn about these laws and once they did, could formulate principles that would bring all life into harmony with them. By using a pattern of thinking called the *scientific method,* they could come to understand the natural laws of the universe by forming hypotheses about all phenomena and then testing the validity of those hypotheses. Those that proved accurate could be preserved and used as tools of understanding. Those not valid could be discarded or reformulated and retested.

The Idea of Progress

Thinkers of the Enlightenment believed that the world and life in it could be made perfect and that *progress* could gradually be made toward that goal. Through the use of reason, civic leaders could improve their institutions or find better ones, could improve society, and could perfect human life. People needed only to learn enough, and the human mind would discover how to make things better. Of course, if reason and the scientific method were going to reform society and make life better, schools were a critically important civic responsibility.

The impact of the Enlightenment was much greater, however, than its influence on schools. In fact, the greatest impact of the Enlightenment was the more general effect it had on the nature and form of government and on the relationship between governments and the people they governed. In this context, the ideas of equality, human rights, and governmental responsibility to citizens were most significant.

Jean-Jacques Rousseau, 1712–1778

Jean-Jacques Rousseau was a French philosopher of the Enlightenment whose ideas concerned both education and government. He believed that humans were in their best condition when they are in their "natural state." He stated, "Everything is good as it comes from the hand of the author of nature; but everything degenerates in the hands of man." Men were "noble savages." Free men were uncorrupted, but society and its institutions corrupted them. Therefore, he believed that education should return man to his *natural state*. It should allow him to follow natural inclinations.

Rousseau believed that education was a natural process if people would not disturb it. In his eyes, young children were naturally good and needed to be allowed to grow. He did not accept the prevailing traditional idea that all humans were sinful and that education had to counter that sinful nature. He expressed his educational ideas in many works, among them a novel *Emile* (1762), about the education of a young man.

Rousseau's ideas about the nature of people and government became part of the philosophical justification for the eighteenth-century revolutions in America and France, and they molded the governments formed after them. His philosophical works *On the Origin of the Inequality of Mankind* and *The Social Contract* attacked social inequalities as artificial conditions based on property, wealth, and prestige, all of which were perpetuated by the institutions established and preserved by the powerful. He supported the revolt of the common man for a better

John Locke, 1632–1704

economic, social, and political life. He saw education as a means to bring that about.

John Locke, philosopher and scientist, was the premier thinker and writer of the British Enlightenment on both education and government. In his writings about the human mind, he stated that at birth a human being's mind is a tabula rasa, or blank slate, without any ideas. As people grow, they learn from their environment through their senses. Gradually, simple ideas are replaced by more complex ones, as the person thinks, associates, compares, abstracts, and generalizes. Locke saw learning as an active, inductive process that uses a rational, scientific method involving investigation, the gathering of information, and the formulation of sophisticated ideas. He expressed these ideas in *An Essay Concerning Human Understanding*.

Locke presented his ideas about schooling explicitly in *Some Thoughts Concerning Education*. He wrote that education begins early in life, that it should proceed gradually, and that it involves physical as well as intellectual elements. The purposes of education are a sound mind and a strong body. The environment in which a child grows up is important. The subjects that he said should be studied at an early age were reading, writing, and arithmetic; later, English, French, mathematics, history, government, and physical education were to be

John Locke.

added. His goal for schooling was an individual who could participate effectively and ethically in government and business.

Consent of the Governed

Locke expressed his political philosophy in *Two Treatises of Government*. He said that governmental authority rests on a *contract* between the people and the government and that the sources of that authority come from the people. He challenged the idea of a divine right of kings. For him, kings and all governments derived their power not from God, but from the consent of the governed. Since that is the case, the people have a right to withdraw that consent if the government does not fulfill its part of the contract. He also asserted that all people have inalienable rights of life, liberty, and property. These Lockean ideas, along with those of Rousseau, formed the basis for the American Revolution and the form of government that followed it.

> ### European Educational Thinkers
>
> A number of European educational thinkers who lived between 1500 and 1900 developed ideas about schooling that have direct influences on schools today. Four of them are described here.
>
> **Johann Amos Comenius (1592–1670)**
> Comenius grew up in Moravia (now a region of Czechoslovakia) and was a member of a small fundamentalist Protestant religious sect called the Moravians. He attended his denomination's vernacular school, a Latin school, and the very important university at Heidelberg. He served as an educator in schools in Moravia, Poland, and the Netherlands.
>
> *Developmental Stages*
>
> Comenius' philosophies of education recognized stages of readiness in children for different types of learning; he also identified four natural stages of human development—infancy, childhood, adolescence, and youth. Since these stages occurred naturally and gradually, he felt that teaching needed to be gradual and in a sequence that fit these stages.
>
> *Multiple Senses*
>
> Comenius believed strongly in universal education and stressed the importance of learning language, both the vernacular and Latin, because language was the key to further learning. His approach to teaching language involved the use of pictures and the active use of multiple senses. Because learning was a natural process, he did not subscribe to the ideas, fairly common in his day, that children were inherently bad and that corporal punishment was a frequent and necessary teaching tool. He wanted learning to be pleasant, and he sought teachers who were patient, loving, and permissive.
>
> **Johann Heinrich Pestalozzi (1746–1827)**
>
> *Supportive Learning Environment*
>
> Pestalozzi, a Swiss educator, was influenced by Rousseau's ideas about the natural good state of people and of the need that education be consistent with the naturally developing physical and emotional characteristics of the students. He was an educational reformer who insisted that the learning environment should be supportive and secure. Much of his work as a teacher was with poor and maladjusted children.
>
> *Object Lesson*
>
> Pestalozzi also believed that instruction should begin with the students' immediate environments, should use all the senses, and should progress

from the concrete to the verbal and then to the abstract. He developed a method of teaching called the *object lesson*, which used concrete objects with which students had regular contact, such as plants, rocks, and artifacts. Like Comenius, he believed learning was gradual, natural, and cumulative.

Johann Herbart (1776–1841)

Moral Education

Herbart was a German and Swiss teacher and philosopher whose primary contribution to educational ideas involved moral education. He believed that education should make people good, broaden their interests, and expand their knowledge. He thought that people who behaved in an apparently evil way did so because they were inadequately educated or misinformed.

Education, for Herbart, produced moral people because it supplied them with a reservoir of ideas and the intellectual exercise they needed to behave correctly. He divided the substance of learning into two domains: knowledge interests—mathematics, logic, music, art, and literature—and ethical interests—concern for others, social relationships, and religious sentiments.

Herbart stressed the importance of integrating and interrelating subjects taught to students. He advocated teaching specific core subjects—geography, history, and literature—and basing instruction on the previous learning of the students. He developed a five-step method of instruction that had great influence on American education in the nineteenth and twentieth centuries.

Friedrich Froebel (1782–1852)

Kindergarten

Froebel, German educator, established the kindergarten as a first step in the formal education of children. Following the ideas of Pestalozzi, with whom he studied, Froebel devised these children's gardens as planned environments in which young children learned from their surroundings as they developed naturally. In these settings, children learned and became socialized as they interacted with objects placed there, with the teachers who served as models of and guides to appropriate moral behavior, and with other children.

Maria Montessori (1870–1952)

Montessori was an Italian physician and educator, having received the first medical degree awarded to a woman in Italy. As a physician, she worked with retarded and economically deprived children in Rome, and in the process, developed a belief that these children could be helped as much through particularly designed instructional methods as through medical treatment.

Self-Motivated Learning

Teachers as Guides

In the early twentieth century, as director of a state-supported school for three- to five-year-olds in the slums of Rome, she designed an approach to instruction that characterizes young children as having especially absorbent minds and a high degree of sensitivity to sensory stimulation. Her approach stresses self-motivated learning in young children in an instructionally enriched classroom. In that setting children explore multisensory, manipulative objects that interest them. Teachers are less directive than they are in most typical classrooms and provide only subtle guidance. Montessori advocates believe this self-sufficient learning helps children

> develop sensory, motor, and mental abilities and that it is effective with all ability levels of young children.
>
> The Montessori method has influenced much early childhood and primary schooling in the United States for several decades, including movements toward open education, learning centers, and nongraded instruction. Elements of the approach are found in many nursery school through primary grade classrooms. Many private Montessori schools have been established for young learners throughout the country.

AMERICAN SCHOOLS OF THE PAST

Colonial Schools

The types of schooling established in the English colonies in America during the seventeenth and eighteenth centuries provided the foundation for schools that have developed in the United States to the present day. Those schools reflected a combination of two types of traditions: (1) the political, social, and religious traditions of the people who settled the different colonies and (2) the ideas from the Enlightenment about the makeup of the universe, human nature, government, and education. Those ideas in combination determined the purposes of schools, who attended them, what was studied, and who did the teaching.

Influence of the Enlightenment

According to Enlightenment philosophy, schools were necessary because people needed to understand the workings of the gigantic machinelike universe in which they lived. If they understood the machine and its operations, they could adjust their lives to fit its patterns. If people were in harmony with the laws of nature, life would improve.

The thinking of the Enlightenment also required schools so that people would be educated citizens led by knowledgeable government leaders. If power derived from the consent of the governed and if civic leaders were responsible to the people who selected them, then the people had to know enough to select appropriate representatives. The representatives in turn needed to be informed and skilled enough to govern effectively and honestly.

Enlightenment values also led to the expectation that schools would develop liberally educated human beings, that is, people who would be knowledgeable about and sensitive to the finer things of life. These people would be responsible for their own well-being and for the well-being of others, especially the less fortunate. They would work as partners with others in their local communities and in the broader world to make everyone's life better.

Religious Influence

Religious beliefs and traditions of the Protestant reformation that developed in England and northern Europe in the sixteenth and seventeenth centuries also made schools necessary in colonial America. According to these beliefs, people were individually responsible for their own religious faith. They had to be able to read and interpret the Bible. They had to select, follow, and understand their religious leaders. Some had to be the educated people who could serve as those religious leaders.

Because all people were considered sinful, and the devil was ever tempting, people needed to be brought up properly. They needed to be able to recognize sin and righteousness in themselves and in their neighbors. They needed to choose the correct path. Therefore, everyone needed to have at least some education, and community leaders were responsible for seeing that it was available.

New England Colonies

In the New England colonies religious influences on schooling were more dominant than the ideas of the Enlightenment philosophers because of the religious backgrounds of the people who settled there. For example, the Puritans, who began the colony of Massachusetts Bay in 1630, quickly established community schools. They did so because they believed, according to the teachings of John Calvin, that all human beings were predestined at birth for either eternal salvation or eternal condemnation. Accordingly, those selected for salvation would exhibit their status by behaving correctly or properly. To act properly, they had to read and follow the dictates of the Bible. They had to avoid being deluded by the devil. They also needed the guidance of educated ministers.

The Puritans also believed that those selected by God would expect proper behavior from all their neighbors and since their neighbors included those who were not selected for salvation, rules of behavior had to be formulated and enforced. Religious principles and civil laws were intertwined. Everyone was expected to conform. All who lived in a town were expected to abide by the laws enacted by the selectmen, to work hard enough to be productive economically, and to respect the dignity of their fellow citizens.

Common Schools

Common elementary schools were established in the towns of Massachusetts Bay to provide a basic education in reading, writing, arithmetic, and religion for all children, although girls and children from lower-class families attended less frequently than did middle-class boys. Children usually attended from about ages five or six to thirteen or fourteen.

The schools were usually one-room, wooden structures built on public land and owned by the town. The teacher typically sat at the front of the room on a tall stool behind a high desk or pulpit. A rod for discipline was always close at hand. The children sat on benches, usually studying in silence.

Hornbooks and the New England Primer

Younger children learned the alphabet and beginning reading from a hornbook, and older children read the *New England Primer*. The students spent much of the school day copying letters and sentences, practicing numbers, and memorizing religious and commonly accepted maxims:

With Adam's fall, we sinned all.

Idleness is the devil's workshop.

The idle fool is whipt at school.

While most studied silently at their seats, the teacher called children individually to the desk for recitation of the memorized lesson. Discipline was strict and corporal punishment commonplace. Laziness, idleness, and lack of learning were considered outward manifestations of the devil within, and teachers were expected to beat the devil out of students who exhibited these traits.

Usually, teachers were young men at early stages in their working life. Most intended to move on to other careers. Many were in the process of studying for

Middle Colonies

Generally, schooling in the Middle Colonies—Pennsylvania, New York, New Jersey, and Maryland—was similar to that in New England. Most children received basic instruction in the four R's and many middle-class boys proceeded to higher instruction in preparation for college and careers as ministers and government leaders. These similarities resulted from the facts that the Middle Colonies were also English in origin and that the settlers were also primarily northern Europeans who sought a new life on an undeveloped continent.

But the schools in the Middle Colonies also possessed a number of different characteristics that have been incorporated into the schools of America. The conditions that led to the differences were that (1) the people of the Middle Colonies were more religiously, culturally, and economically diverse than those of New England; (2) they settled either in the harbor towns of the coast—Philadelphia, New York, and Baltimore—or scattered throughout the farmland of the interior, rather than living in small, closely knit towns; and (3) they established their early schools about 50 to 100 years later than the first schools of New England.

The European settlers of the Middle Colonies were English, Dutch, Swedes, German, Scotch-Irish, and French Huguenot. They were Quakers, Dutch Reformed, Lutherans, Presbyterians, Baptists, Roman Catholics, Jews, and members of small Protestant pietistic sects. They were farmers, traders, bankers, and craftspersons. They immigrated to America for a greater variety of reasons than the colonists of New England.

Denominational Schools

Because of this diversity, settlers in the Middle Colonies tended to separate religion and government, and they were more tolerant than New Englanders of different religious beliefs. Communities rarely had a single government-operated town school, and they did not insist that everyone attend. Schools were more the responsibilities of the church than of the governments. The churches established denominational schools for the children of their members, as well as for children who were poor and unconverted. Middle-class parents who did not send their children to denominational schools hired private tutors.

ANALYSIS

This section consists of part of a description of a colonial American elementary school classroom written in 1750 by Christopher Dock, a teacher of German children in Pennsylvania.[5] It appeared in a document called "*Schul-Ordnung*." As you read, consider:

- What roots of American schooling that you read about so far in this chapter seem to be reflected in this description?
- What cultural and societal norms of the times are reflected?
- In what ways is the teaching you are observing in schools today different from that described here? Why does it differ in these ways?

> . . . The children arrive as they do because some have a great distance to school, others a short distance, so that the children cannot assemble as punctually as they can in a city. Therefore, when a few children are present, those

who can read their Testament sit together on one bench; but the boys and girls occupy separate benches. They are given a chapter which they read at sight consecutively. Meanwhile I write copies for them. Those who have read their passage of Scripture without error take their places at the table and write. Those who fail have to sit at the end of the bench, and each new arrival the same; as each one is thus released in order he takes up his slate. This process continues until they have all assembled. The last one left on the bench is a "lazy pupil."

When all are together, and examined, whether they are washed and combed, they sing a psalm or a morning hymn, and I sing and pray with them. As much as they can understand of the Lord's Prayer and the ten commandments (according to the gift God has given them), I exhort and admonish them accordingly. . . .

After these devotional exercises those who can write resume their work. Those who cannot read the Testament have had time during the assemblage to study their lesson. These are heard recite immediately after prayer. Those who know their lesson receive an O on the hand, traced with crayon. This is a mark of excellence. Those who fail more than three times are sent back to study their lesson again. When all the little ones have recited, these are asked again, and any one having failed in more than three trials a second time, is called "Lazy" by the entire class and his name is written down. Whether such a child fear the rod or not, I know from experience that this denunciation of the children hurts more than if I were constantly to wield and flourish the rod. If then such a child has friends in school who are able to instruct him and desire to do so, he will visit more frequently than before. For this reason: if the pupil's name has not been erased before dismissal the pupils are at liberty to write down the names of those who have been lazy, and take them along home. But if the child learns his lesson well in the future, his name is again presented to the other pupils, and they are told that he knew his lesson well and failed in no respect. Then all the pupils call "Diligent" to him. When this has taken place his name is erased from the slate of lazy pupils, and the former transgression is forgiven.

The children who are in the spelling class are daily examined in pronunciation. In spelling, when a word has more than one syllable, they must repeat the whole word, but some, while they can say the letters, cannot pronounce the word, and so cannot be put to reading. For improvement a child must repeat a lesson, and in this way: The child gives me the book, I spell the word and he pronounces it. If he is slow, another pupil pronounces it for him, and in this way he hears how it should be done, and knows that he must follow the letters and not his own fancy.

Concerning A B C pupils, it would be best, having but one child, to let it learn one row of letters at a time, to say forward and backward. But with many, I let them learn the alphabet first, and then ask a child to point out a letter that I name. If a child is backward or ignorant, I ask another, or the whole class, and the first one that points to the right letter, I grasp his finger and hold it until I have put a mark opposite his name. I then ask for another letter, &c. Whichever child has during the day received the greatest number of marks, has pointed out the greatest number of letters. To him I owe something—a flower drawn on paper or a bird. But if several have the same number, we draw lots; this causes less annoyance. In this way not only are the very timid cured of their shyness (which is a great hindrance in learning), but a fondness for school is increased. . . .

As the children carry their dinner, an hour's liberty is given them after dinner. But as they are usually inclined to misapply their time if one is not constantly with them, one or two of them must read a story of the Old Testament (either from Moses and the Prophets, or from Solomon's or Sirach's Proverbs), while I write copies for them. This exercise continues during the noon hour.

It is also to be noted that children find it necessary to ask to leave the room, and one must permit them to do this, not wishing the uncleanness and odor in the school. But the clamor to go out would continue all day, and sometimes without need, so that occasionally two or three are out at the same time, playing. To prevent this I have driven a nail in the door-post, on which hangs a wooden tag. Any one needing to leave the room looks for the tag. If it is on the nail, this is his permit to go without asking. He takes the tag out with him. If another wishes to leave, he does not ask either, but stands by the door until the first returns, from whom he takes the tag and goes. If the tag is out too long, the one wishing to go inquires who was out last, and from him it can be ascertained to whom he gave the tag, so that none can remain out too long.

To teach the uninitiated numbers and figures, I write on the blackboard (which hangs where all can see) these figures.

    1 2 3 4 5 6 7 8 9 0

far apart, that other figures can be put before and behind them. Then I put an 0 before the 1 and explain that this does not increase the number. Then I erase the 0 and put it after the 1, so that it makes 10. If two ciphers follow, it makes 100, if three follow, 1000, &c. This I show them through all the digits. This done I affix to the 1 another 1 making 11. But if an 0 is put between, it makes 101, but if it be placed after, it makes 110. In a similar manner I go through all the digits. When this is done I give them something to find in the Testament

Pennsylvania school similar to that of Christopher Dock.

> or hymnal. Those who are quickest have something to claim for their diligence, from me or at home.
>
> As it is desirable for intelligent reading to take note of commas, but as the inexperienced find this difficult, I have this rule: If one of the Testament pupils does not read on, but stops before he reaches a comma or period, this counts one-fourth failure. Similarly if one reads over a comma, it is one fourth-failure. Repeating a word counts one-half. Then all failures are noted, and especially where each one has failed. When all have read, all those who have failed must step forward and according to the number of errors stand in a row. Those who have not failed move up, and the others take the lowest positions.

Friends Public Schools

During the eighteenth century, the Society of Friends (Quakers) of Philadelphia sponsored a loose system of schools that were forerunners of American public schools. These Friends Public Schools were operated by their teachers (one per school) and were housed in rented rooms and teachers' homes at scattered locations throughout the city. Often a school would operate for only a short time, but a number of them were functioning at all times during the century. At various times, specific schools came under the sponsorship and loose control of church officials when the church subsidized their operation on the condition that they serve poor children free or at a nominal charge.

The Friends schools were intended primarily for Quaker children, both boys and girls, but other children, including blacks and Native Americans, were admitted as a matter of faith and practice. Their curriculum usually involved the four R's (reading, writing, arithmetic, and religion) and sometimes the beginning elements of commerce and agriculture. It reflected the strong Quaker commitment to nonviolence and peace, characteristics that led to criticism during the American Revolution as colonists chose sides and took up arms.

Because Quakers believed that everyone possessed an "inner light" (roughly, the conscience and inspiration) that needed to be nourished and developed and because they rejected the Puritan concept of the inevitable human depravity, they did not believe in corporal punishment in the schools. The classroom atmosphere was quite different from that of the town schools of Massachusetts Bay. (For additional information on the Friend Public Schools in Philadelphia, see Myers, 1968.)[4]

The Middle Colonies also had higher-level schools for boys who pursued schooling beyond the four R's. Most of the students in these schools prepared for college and careers as ministers and civic leaders. But as Philadelphia and the other colonial cities developed into trade centers, more students looked toward business and commerce. In response, the schools added instruction in navigation, surveying, bookkeeping, Spanish, French, and geography.

Franklin's Academy

The Franklin Academy, a Philadelphia School begun in 1751 at the urging and under the guidance of Benjamin Franklin, stressed these broader purposes. It became the prototype for the American secondary schools of the next century. Its purposes and curriculum were to prepare students for employment rather than for college. Students studied English grammar and composition, rhetoric, public speaking, classics, mathematics, science, and history. Some were also trained for specific trades, such as carpentry, shipbuilding, and printing. Before the academies, boys had received manual training through apprenticeships with craftspersons rather than in schools, a pattern begun in the Middle Ages (Myers, 1968).

Southern Colonies

Life in the Southern Colonies was significantly different from both New England and the Middle Colonies. Southern settlers usually came to North America for economic rather than religious reasons. Most came from England and were members of the Church of England rather than churches that had been persecuted back home. Many of those who arrived in the early days of the colonies came without families and expected to return to Europe after a few years. Others saw their settlements as outward extensions of the port cities of England. They intended to send their children back to England for schooling.

Through the seventeenth and eighteenth centuries, however, the economy and life-style of the Southern Colonies changed. Settlements that began as small commercial outposts for trading companies failed; and large tobacco, sugar, rice, and cotton plantations took their place. Many people scattered over the countryside rather than clustering into towns or cities. The plantations and such port cities as Charleston, which connected them to the rest of the world, became the centers of southern colonial life. That life evolved into a three-level society of planters and wealthy traders, poor farmers and craftspersons, and slaves.

Schooling was usually private and limited to the children of the wealthy. It was provided through plantation tutors, privately operated boarding schools, or schools established by Anglican missionary societies. Children of poor backcountry farmers and slaves received no formal education. No continuing system of schools developed until well after independence.

Schools of the New American Nation

Civic Purposes

The America Revolution replaced British rule with a representative democracy, and in the minds of the American founding fathers that change required a shift in the purposes of schools. Although religious purposes for schools continued, civic ones became more important. The schools of the new nation had to educate citizens. Only knowledgeable and understanding people could participate effectively in government, preserve liberty, and provide for the general welfare.

Thomas Jefferson, who was influenced by the political and educational ideas of John Locke, expressed this American philosophy of education in this quotation (it has also appeared at the opening of Chapter 1 of this text):

> If a nation expects to be ignorant and free, in a state of civilization, it expects what never was and never will be. (Jefferson, 1816)[6]

Thomas Jefferson

Jefferson believed that schooling was a state responsibility, that it had to be available to all, and that at least part of it should be provided at public expense. To implement his idea, he developed a system of education for the state of Virginia from the primary grades through college. But his ideas were too advanced for the Virginia legislature, which failed to enact them into law.

In order to teach the three R's during the early years of the American republic, towns in every state either continued community primary schools that had been founded during colonial times or started new ones. Many towns also established secondary schools much like the earlier Latin grammar schools or academies. The primary schools were often free, at least for the poor. The secondary schools usually charged tuition.

State and Local Control

Because of a particular sequence of events, schooling in America became primarily a state and local responsibility. Local community groups started early schools to serve local needs. Often they were in operation before the Revolution and, therefore, before states and the nation came into being. During the Revolution, state constitutions accepted responsibility for schools. Next, the federal Constitution, adopted in 1789, which could have claimed responsibility for schools for the national government, did not do so. Finally, the Tenth Amendment to the Constitution, the last in the Bill of Rights, reserved direct power over education to the states.

National Government–funded Territory Schools

But even in those early years, the national government demonstrated its support for schools. Shortly after the Revolution, Congress, under the Articles of Confederation, adopted a national plan to provide for schools in the territory of the west. Under the Ordinance of 1785, the land of the Northwest Territory was surveyed for development. That land, west of Pennsylvania and north of the Ohio River, was divided into townships of thirty-six square miles each. The townships were then subdivided into thirty-six sections, each one a square mile in size. When the lands were sold, the money paid for section number 16 in each township was set aside for the funding of schools. Each township was divided into sections before the federal government offered the land for sale.

"American" Schools

As the American nation grew during the early years of the nineteenth century, a distinct sense of nationalism developed. And as a result, schools were expected not only to produce educated citizens but to produce *Americans*—that is, citizens who were different from the people of Europe; who were individualists; who believed in the emerging American principles of government; who would succeed as merchants, artisans, laborers, or professionals; who could conquer the frontier; and who could demonstrate the viability, vitality, and basic rightness of the new country.

During the nineteenth century, emphasis on education for citizenship and for jobs gradually increased, while that on religious training continued to decline. Industrialization and the continuing flow of immigrants made the need for a *common* education for all as important as ever. People needed jobs. They needed to be able to get along with each other. In the minds of many, they needed to be made into true Americans.

Toward Free Public Schools

The most significant trend in education in the United States during the nineteenth and early twentieth centuries was the movement toward free public schools for everyone. Schools were quite different from state to state and community to community, and they developed at different speeds, but all seemed to be evolving in the similar directions and seemed to be following about the same three-stage process. The trend affected elementary schools initially and secondary schools later. First, communities and states passed laws that *permitted* free, tax-supported, public elementary schools. Next, the laws *encouraged* the establishment of the schools, the school boards to operate them, and the taxes to finance them. Finally, the laws *required* that schools be provided and funded. By 1900, more than half of the children in the United States between six and thirteen years of age attended elementary schools.

Nineteenth Century Academies

Secondary schools of the early nineteenth century were much like the academies of earlier decades, but they included in their curricula college preparation

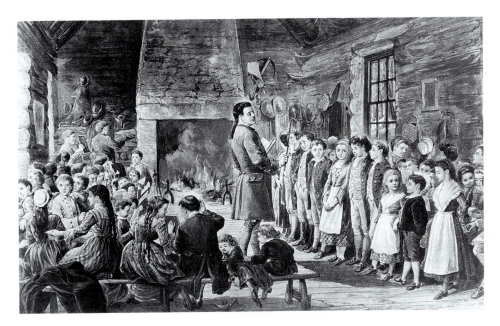

Rural nineteenth-century classroom.

as well as practical studies. They were privately funded and operated. They usually admitted many types of students, had broad and sometimes ill-defined programs of study, and were of varying degrees of quality. Usually they were run by a board of trustees or overseers and a rather strong schoolmaster. Some were partly public in the sense that they received supplemental public funds, typically to cover the cost of educating poor children.

Public High Schools

During the latter third of the nineteenth century, secondary schools spread rapidly, much as elementary schools had done a few decades earlier. In that process, tax-supported public high schools replaced the academies as the most common secondary school. The academies that continued tended to evolve into private, select, college-preparatory institutions for children of families able and willing to pay their fees.

American high schools were unique institutions. They were tax supported and free of cost to the student. They admitted girls as well as boys. They attempted to educate children for the world of work, for future college studies, and for their roles as citizens. Once the courts ruled in the 1870s that states could levy taxes for schools, most states quickly decided to do so. Not long after that, states passed laws requiring that high schools be established, rather than leaving them a matter of local choice.

Schools for Immigrants

American high schools were influenced by the people and the times of late-nineteenth-century America. That period was a time of immigration, industrialization, and urbanization. The schools were expected to Americanize and help assimilate the immigrants into the melting pot of society. They were expected

Schools for Jobs

to prepare students for jobs in the factories and in businesses. Many were expected to prepare American youths for lives off the farm and in the newly developing cities. In response, the high schools added vocational or career courses alongside college preparatory subjects. These new areas of study included clerical and commercial courses, manual and industrial arts, and home economics.

Social Integration

Whereas seondary schools in other nations focused on college preparation

Segregation

for a select few or methodically separated the academic students from those who would soon leave school to take a job, American high schools tried to accept and serve all students between fourteen and eighteen years of age. They tried to help students advance economically and socially at the same time that they served as places where youths from different cultural backgrounds could interact socially. Despite these intentions, poor and lower-class children often did not attend in large numbers.

With two notable exceptions, high schools were remarkably successful in achieving their goals. The exceptions involved racial segregation and a lack of service for handicapped people. As Chapter 5 discussed, especially in the South, black and other nonwhite students, were relegated to separate schools, usually not at all equal to those provided for white students. Physically and intellectually handicapped students were ignored.

> ### American Educational Thinkers
>
> Throughout the history of education in America, many thinkers and activists have influenced the development of schools and the way they look today. Five such people are described here.
>
> **Noah B. Webster (1758–1843)**
>
> *The Blue-backed Speller*
>
> Webster was a teacher, lawyer, and political leader in New York, Connecticut, and Massachusetts during the early years of the United States, but his most noted contributions to schools were as an author and lexicographer. His two most influential works were his blue-backed spelling book, published in 1783, and his two-volume dictionary, *An American Dictionary of the English Language,* published in 1820.[7] The speller became the first volume of a three-volume set that included a grammar and a reader. It was used in schools nationwide and continued in use well after Webster's death. Eventually, more than seventy million copies were sold. The speller did much to standardize spelling in America, and the dictionary became the standard for American English.
>
> *An American Dictionary*
>
> Webster also wrote a four-volume *Elements of Useful Knowledge*, which consisted of two books on United States history, one on world history, and one on biology. Later in life he penned an updated *History of the United States*. His influence as an educator and political leader also spread because of his frequent writings in New York newspapers.
>
> **William H. McGuffey (1800–1873)**
>
> *McGuffey Readers*
>
> McGuffey, like Webster, contributed most to American education as an author of schoolbooks. He was teacher, minister, college professor, and college president in Kentucky, Ohio, and Virginia; but his most lasting contribution to schools was in the form of readers for schoolchildren. The first of these readers was published in 1836 and, over a number of years, he and collaborators produced six of them for different elementary school grades and one for high school.[8] The McGuffey readers dominated the textbook field throughout the country for many years, and more than 122 million copies were sold. They were prized by children, parents, and teachers (and today by collectors) because of their unique combination of literary quality and American patriotic content.

Model Public Schools

Horace Mann (1796–1859)
Mann is known as the Father of American Public Education because of his advocacy and political leadership in the movement to establish public, tax-supported schools in America. As a speaker and writer, he crusaded for landmark public-school legislation in Massachusetts. As secretary of the Massachusetts Board of Education, he led an effort to upgrade the schools of that state in a manner that served as a model for other states to follow. He also pioneered a movement to improve the education of teachers through state-supported normal schools, a pattern for educating teachers that has lasted for more than a century.

Normal Schools

Learn by Doing

John Dewey (1859–1952)
Dewey was a philosopher, psychologist, educator, and probably the most influential thinker in American educational history. He developed and improved upon educational ideas and reforms that had a profound effect on educational philosophy, theory, and practice throughout the world. He stressed "learning by doing" and became the philosophical prophet of the progressive education movement, although he was often critical of progressive, as well as traditional, educational ideas.

Through his writing, teaching, and active professional leadership, he encouraged educators to inquire into the philosophy and theory that supported their educational practices. He was more than a educational philosopher, however. During his tenures at the University of Chicago, where he founded the laboratory school, and at Columbia University, he participated actively in formulating educational theory and in testing the new ideas in schools. (See the Notes section at the end of this chapter for references to selected Dewey writings.)[9]

Comprehensive Education

James B. Conant (1893–1978)
Conant was a chemist, diplomat, and long-term president of Harvard University whose major contribution to American education came through his critical studies of American public schools. Three of his most influential studies were *The American High School Today* (1959), *The Education of American Teachers* (1963), and *The Comprehensive High School* (1967).[10] Each of these included recommendations for reform that became topics of professional discussion at the time of their publication, and all were driving forces for reform. His writings stressed the importance of public education in a democracy, the need to unify conflicting views in education, the necessity of adequate education for underprivileged and disadvantaged children, and the value of comprehensive high schools.

What the Schools Taught

The thrust of instruction in public elementary schools in America did not change radically from the mid-1800s through the first half of the twentieth century. The three R's provided the focus for the primary grades, and the upper grades usually consisted of a combination of advanced basic skills and increasing amounts of science, history and geography, art, music, and physical education. Those instructional changes that were made were more often than not in teaching methods and in the updating of the specific content.

Committee of Ten

The situation was different in the high schools, however. Because the public schools had a number of purposes and attempted to serve so many types of students, high school curricula tended to be confusing mixtures of offerings. To remedy this, the National Education Association established a Committee of Ten in 1892 to recommend what high schools should teach. Charles Eliot, president of Harvard University, chaired the committee and was its major force. The committee's recommendations set the curriculum pattern that has dominated high school instruction for the nearly 100 years since they appeared.

The Committee of Ten recommended eight years of elementary school and four years of high school. It proposed a high school curriculum much like the traditional college preparation program of the past and, although it outlined four alternative tracks, it suggested that the same general type of instruction be provided all students. The members believed that similar subjects were appropriate for both college-bound and terminal students because those subjects "trained the mind." That is, they improved the ability to remember, observe, reason, and express ideas. The committee believed these capacities contributed to the students' personal well-being and to their ability to serve society as citizens, workers, and parents (National Education Association, 1893).[11]

Comprehensive Education

In the early decades of the twentieth century, as more states passed compulsory attendance laws and more students entered and remained in high school, some educators began to question the value of the Committee of Ten's high school curriculum for non-college-bound students. These people felt that the curriculum was not sufficiently comprehensive. They were less concerned about mental discipline and more concerned about the direct utility of the subject matter.

Cardinal Principles of Education

In 1918, this view was incorporated into the *Cardinal Principles of Secondary Education*, a report of the National Education Association Commission on the Reorganization of Secondary Education. The report stated that a comprehensive reorganization of secondary education was imperative at that time and proposed what that organization should be. It called for a more differentiated curriculum in which business, commercial, industrial, agricultural, and domestic science thrusts would not be overshadowed by preparation for college. The commission wanted a more truly comprehensive curriculum (Commission on the Reorganization of Secondary Education, 1918).[12]

The *Cardinal Principles of Education*, along with the earlier ideas of the Committee of Ten, established the framework for the curricula of high schools of America through the twentieth century. Although there have been shifts in emphasis and innovations added over the years, these changes have occurred within that established framework. Typically, high schools have offered four curriculum thrusts or tracks:

Academic or college prep
    English language and literature, mathematics, foreign languages, sciences, and social studies (including history)
General
    Courses with the same titles as the academic program but modified for lower-achieving students on the assumption they will not attend college

Commercial or business
> Shorthand, typing, bookkeeping, secretarial training, marketing, distribution; in more recent years, data processing

Vocational
> Industrial arts, home economics, agriculture, building trades, electronics, automotive repair, graphic arts

American Colleges and Universities

Colonial Colleges

Colleges and universities in America were established in colonial times to educate ministers and upper-class gentlemen, many of whom became political and social leaders of their communities. The colleges were organized along the patterns of the major European universities, especially Oxford and Cambridge, in England. Students studied English, Hebrew, Greek and Latin (language and literature), rhetoric, logic, mathematics, geometry, astronomy, natural and moral philosophy, metaphysics, ethics, and music. Harvard was established in 1636, William and Mary in 1693, and Yale in 1701. By the time of the American Revolution a majority of the thirteen colonies had their own colleges.

After independence and through the early decades of the nineteenth century, new colleges were established regularly throughout the states and on the frontier as the size of the population and the desires of the people required. The colleges were usually denominational but often publicly chartered, and with a liberal arts curriculum.

Normal Schools

Beginning in the 1820s and 1830s, two-year normal schools were established in many states to educate teachers. They were patterned after such schools in France as the Ecole normale supérieure, from which they got their name; and since students entered directly out of elementary school, they gave the appearance of specialized academies. At first, students prepared only for elementary school teaching. Courses in the philosophy and history of education and in teaching methodology provided the core of their curricula.

Over the years, more subjects were added, the schools began to prepare teachers for secondary schools, and subject-matter departments were added. By the early twentieth century, most normal school programs had expanded to four years, and many had begun to call themselves state teacher's colleges. At the same time that normal schools were evolving into more comprehensive institutions, state colleges and universities added teacher preparation to their purposes and opened departments of education.

Land Grant Colleges

College education in general shifted significantly toward the middle of the nineteenth century when changes in society brought on pushes for education in the mechanical and agricultural sciences, for an extension of college instruction to a broader representation of society, and for greater direct government involvement in and support for higher education. As a result, the national government passed the Morrill Act of 1862, which established land grant colleges. The act, named for its sponsor, Representative Justin Morrill of Vermont, gave each state 30,000 acres of land for each of its senators and members of congress. The income from these land grants was to be used to support one or more state colleges that would provide mechanical and agricultural education. The act immediately brought the college education to most of American society and expanded the college curricula to engineering and the applied arts and sciences.

Between the 1860s and the 1940s, the pattern of higher education remained relatively constant. Colleges consisted of denominational liberal arts colleges, state colleges and normal schools, and land grant colleges. Slowly over the years, more institutions were established as the numbers of students increased.

The GI Bill

Then, in the mid-twentieth century, the federal government passed the GI Bill of Rights to provide funds for returning World War II military personnel to attend college. Enrollments skyrocketed, and a college education became possible for a whole new group of Americans.

The Schooling of Women and Minority Group Members

Throughout much of history, women, minority group members, and handicapped people have not had the same access to education in the United States as nonhandicapped, white, English-speaking males have had. These omissions have been reflections of social and cultural attitudes of the times. Gradually, however, the exclusion and neglect of all three groups has shifted toward inclusion in the American educational mainstream.

Of the three groups, women were able to enter the mainstream first, particularly if they stayed in traditional roles. Minority children were included much more slowly, much less predictably, and much more grudgingly. Handicapped children have had regular access to schools only in very recent times.

Women

Leaders in the colonial and early national periods considered the education of girls less important than the education of boys. Some girls attended primary school, but many did not. Few continued schooling beyond the four R's and "ladies' subjects."

However, in the 1820s and 1830s, attitudes changed significantly. Academies for "young ladies," normal schools, and special women's colleges were established, and many existing boy's institutions became coeducational. Emma Willard opened Troy Female Seminary in New York state in 1821, and Mary Lyon established Mount Holyoke Seminary in Massachusetts in 1837. Both schools and others that shortly followed were essentially academies for girls. These academies offered courses in modern and classical languages, music, art, science, mathematics, and domestic science.

The high schools that replaced academies usually admitted girls, and gradually more and more parents sent their daughters along with their sons. At first, the girls studied a separate curriculum in different rooms from the boys. Then classes were integrated, and the curriculum became more common.

Except for normal schools and finishing schools, the collegiate experience for women was similar to the earlier experience for women at the high school level. First, women attended separate women's colleges; they were later admitted to coeducational institutions. Their curriculum was initially different from that for men; the differentiation gradually lessened.

Minorities

Schooling for the largest minority groups in America—black, Native American, and Hispanic—was usually neglected, or at best grossly inadequate, prior to the middle of the nineteenth century. Even after that point, improvements have been slow.

Native American Students

Colonial missionaries provided schools for Native Americans as part of their efforts to convert them to Christianity. These efforts, although often well intended, were usually patronizing (students were taught as members of a lesser culture than those of the controlling groups) and limited to the 4 R's. In the late 1800s, when the government took a serious interest in educating Native Americans, it did so in order to assimilate the tribal children into the dominant culture. But the schools available to Native American children were most often poorly constructed, inadequately staffed, and underfinanced. Frequently, the instruction was in English and based on dominant cultural assumptions. Teachers and those who hired them considered the Native culture inferior and the students deprived.

Hispanic Students

Most early American children of Spanish descent who attended school received primary instruction and the rudiments of religious training in Catholic mission schools. As towns developed over the years, Catholic parishes were established in many of them, and most parishes had Catholic parochial schools. Often these schools were more attractive to Spanish-speaking families than the public schools because of their religious focus and their Spanish and Mexican traditions. Frequently, Hispanic parents wanted their children educated in a context that preserved their religious and cultural heritage. Therefore, many avoided the Anglicizing experience of the public schools.

In more recent decades, children from Spanish-speaking families have attended integrated public schools in greater proportions. But the experience has rarely been without difficulty. Clashes between English and Spanish culture have persisted. Because Hispanic children often grew up in poor neighborhoods, the public schools available to them have often been weaker than those in the white suburbs. Their buildings tend to be worn, their teachers less experienced, and their supplies more scarce.

Black Students

Schooling for most black Americans was generally neglected or prohibited until the end of slavery and the Civil War, although black children in northern states attended school prior to that time. At the end of the Civil War, the federal government attempted a major effort to educate freed slaves and their children through the Freedman's Bureau. One of that agency's efforts was the establishment of schools for the children of former slaves, much like the town schools of early New England. But these schools were not really community schools. They had little local support. They were set apart from other schools. Their teachers were often volunteers from the North rather than people of the community.

From the period of Reconstruction through the middle of the twentieth century, the education of black students in America was primarily separate from the education of white students. Not only did black children attend segregated schools, but the philosophy of education in those schools was often different from that elsewhere. In the last decades of the nineteenth century, that philosophy was embodied in an attempt to "uplift the poor, unfortunate former slave." Later, it evolved into an educational philosophy that called for "education for work" and "education for economic security."

"Education for Work"

Booker T. Washington was the predominant spokesperson for the "education-for-work" philosophy. He believed that vocational education—for farming, manual trades, and teaching—was the most useful education for black children. He felt it was premature for blacks to hope for careers in law, medicine, and political leadership. In essence, he espoused a compromise position with the white southern aristocracy that strove to keep black people in lower social and economic positions.

While Washington's ideas fell on receptive ears, those of another black spokesperson, W. E. B. DuBois, did not. DuBois argued for an intellectually rigorous education for blacks and spoke emphatically on the need for well-educated teachers to staff black schools and colleges. He considered Washington's views to be accommodations to a repressive system of segregation.

The education-for-work philosophy, the cultural mores and laws of a Jim Crow society, and general racial prejudice determined the type and level of schooling usually available to black students. Instruction was basic and vocational. Expectations of student abilities were low. Schooling was segregated by custom and by law. In 1896, the United States Supreme Court upheld the "separate but equal" education of black students in the *Plessy* v. *Ferguson* court case. In so doing, it solidified a dual, segregated school system for America for the next half-century.

Separate Is Unequal

Pressures to change the dual system of education persisted through the first fifty years of this century, however, and they came to a head at the end of World War II. As described in Chapter 5, nine years after the end of the war, in 1954, the Supreme Court, in *Brown* v. *the Board of Education of Topeka* agreed that separate education facilities are "inherently unequal" and that they engendered "a feeling of inferiority." Since then, federal and state laws have led toward the dismantling of segregated schools, and local norms have gradually shifted toward racially integrated public schooling in America.

Students with Handicapping Conditions

Since the *Brown* case, the courts have also forced states and local communities to provide handicapped people with access to regular schools. They have said that all Americans have a right to a "free appropriate education in the least restricted environment." Therefore, schooling in the last three decades has been made available to children of school age who have physical, emotional, and educational conditions that in the past would have excluded them from receiving educational services. Today the mainstreaming of handicapped students into schools and classrooms with nonhandicapped children has become common practice and generally accepted policy.

EDUCATIONAL RESEARCH

A Historical Approach

Like anthropologists, whose study of schools and classrooms was described in the Educational Research section of the last chapter, historians also study teaching and schools. They investigate, describe, interpret, and explain events and practices of the past in an effort to provide ideas that will be useful for the present and future.

Below is an excerpt from a historical study of teaching in high schools since 1900 (Cuban, 1982). The author describes how he conducted the study, what he found, and the general conclusions he drew.

Focus of the Study

... I examined high school classrooms at the turn of the century, in the two decades between the two World Wars, and from the mid-1960s to the present. I chose these years to help me develop a series of impressions of what high school teaching was like before the Progressive movement, during the high point of the reform impulse within public schools in the 1920s and 1930s, and, finally, during and after a second effort to improve instruction that began in the mid-1960s. More specifically, for the years at the beginning of the century, I drew from both secondary and primary sources to construct a composite nationwide portrait of what teachers did in these classrooms. For the decades between the two World Wars, I focused on classrooms in Denver, New York City, Washington, D.C., and in many rural areas. For the 1960s and 1970s, I studied classrooms in New York City, Washington, D.C., North Dakota, and Arlington, Virginia. . . .

I concentrated on classrooms in the academic subjects: English, history and social studies, science, foreign language, and mathematics. I examined how classroom space and furniture were arranged, the manner of grouping for instruction used by the teacher (whole class, small group, etc.); classroom talk by teacher and students, instructional activities in the classroom (recitation, discussion, tests, lecture, film, student reports, etc.), and the amount of physical movement allowed students within the classroom. I chose these categories because they were visible signs of what happened in classrooms and could be recovered from a number of sources. Moreover, these visible signs of what occurred in classrooms coincided with varied patterns of teaching behavior that had been identified in the literature . . . At no point did I equate these visible signs of instructional activity with the complexity of what teachers do daily with children, the classroom climate and culture, the richly textured social interaction between students and teacher, or the social system of the classroom. My intent was to map out in a crude way an important part—but far from the whole—of the classroom terrain.

To collect data on classrooms that no longer existed, I examined what teachers had written, student recollections, photographs from student yearbooks, newspaper articles, reports of principals to superintendents, formal studies of classrooms, self-reports from questionnaires given to teachers, and surveys of school systems. From these sources, I collected information on nearly 2,500 different high school classrooms in the three periods. . . .

At the Start of the Twentieth Century

My information on schools at the beginning of this century had to be reconstructed from a number of sources, since no historians have examined closely what teachers did in classrooms. In slightly more than 6,000 high schools enrolling just over 500,000 students, teachers (most of whom were male) often taught more than one subject in a curriculum plainly geared to preparing young people (the majority of whom were female) to attend college. Clues about what went on in classrooms appeared in the form of rows of bolted-down desks, rooms designated for "recitation," and master schedules allotting the bulk of the instructional day to this formal activity. Using accounts from school surveys, reports from principals, and stenographic transcriptions from more than 100 classrooms, I assembled an admittedly blurred but nonetheless distinguishable portrait of what teachers did in their classes.

Generally, teachers taught their classes as a single large group. Teacher talk dominated verbal expression during the period (64% of the time, according to Romiett Stevens). Student movement in the classroom occurred only with the teacher's permission. Classroom activities clustered around teacher lectures, questioning of students, and chalkboard exercises or in-class assignments from the textbook. Science classes that included laboratory work were an exception. Expectations for uniform behavior and respect for

1920s and 1930s

the teacher's authority were demonstrated in the rows of students facing the chalkboard and the teacher's desk.

I then jumped two decades to examine what happened between World Wars I and II in Denver, New York City, Washington, D.C., and rural schools across the U.S. I chose the first two cities because of their national reputations for leadership in embracing progressive practices, [and] the other sites were selected for comparative purposes. In addition to gathering accounts of what teachers did in the various high schools, I examined national surveys and state studies of teaching practices in the 1920s and 1930s. Despite the variety of research designs, methodologies, and sources of data I studied, there was a remarkable similarity in the results.

These interwar decades displayed an explosion of enthusiasm for the project method, joint teacher/student planning, small-group work, independent study, and curriculum revision. The Eight-Year Study, for example, targeted curriculum and instruction for reform in 30 high schools that volunteered for the study. Yet, with the exception of Denver and scattered urban and rural high schools elsewhere in the U.S. (where some versions of activity programs and projects, varied classroom groups, and substantial revisions in course content occurred), few progressive practices reached the typical classroom.

Most high school classrooms showed traces of progressive ideology that had been transformed by the realities of the 30 to 40 students per class, five to six classes daily, and teachers' additional extracurricular responsibilities. There was some change in course content often in English and social studies. The stiff formal repetition of the text at the teacher's command was replaced by the less formal discussions, students leading classes, and reports or debates by students. The student-centered philosophy could be seen in greater student participation in classroom talk, occasional trips to places in the community, subject matter that touched student concerns or life beyond the school house door. But the percentage of time allocated to subjects—except for those schools that experimented with core curriculum or general education for part of the school day—remained the same. Even with the advent of portable furniture, the most common classroom arrangement continued to be that of the teacher's desk dominating the front of the room facing rows of movable table-arm chairs or pedestal desks. . . .

By the beginning of World War II, little had changed in the typical American classroom. The instructional patterns that used the entire class as the primary teaching vehicle, a question/answer format and reliance on the textbook—all of which had characterized classrooms at the turn of the century—seemed basically the same.

1960s and 1970s

By 1965 another wave of reform pumped ideas, money, and new faces into U.S. public schools. Informal education, the open classroom and alternative high schools became required reforms, especially if a district wished to be viewed as *au courant*. The reforms of the Sixties were similar in many ways to the progressive impulse of a previous generation. I examined alternative and regular high schools in various settings, including New York City and Washington, D.C., again using sources similar to those employed for the earlier period.

Although the alternative school concept became quite popular and many districts were fairly quick to create their own, most students still attended regular high schools. . . .

Hundreds of teacher accounts, interviews, student publications, newspaper articles, and numerous other sources painted a composite portrait of high school teaching during the Sixties and early Seventies that was not unlike that of the previous generation. Teachers still spent most of the class period talking to the entire class, listening to students answer their questions, and assigning portions of the textbook to the class for homework. It was the same instructional diet of meat and potatoes—occasionally supplemented by a test, lab work in the sciences, some field trips, or a film—that had been served consistently in high schools since the beginning of the century.

Finally, I examined the period after 1975, when the reform impulse had been buried under a new set of slogans about "back to the basics." In one middle-sized school district I found little change from the late 1960s and early 1970s. Two other sources included two major pieces of research sponsored by the National Science Foundation (NSF): One, a series of 11 case studies of high schools and their feeder schools; and the other, a survey of teachers and administrators on classroom practices. The case studies included many accounts of social studies, math, and science teachers. After mentioning the occasional artistry of a teacher who hooked the attention of a class and steered it gracefully for an hour, the writers noted the fundamental similarity in teaching that swept across subject matter, class size, teacher experience, or curricular group. . . .

Conclusions

What conclusions can be drawn from this quick and narrow portrait of high school teaching since the beginning of the 20th century? The overall picture is striking in its uniformity: persistence of whole group instruction, teacher talk outdistancing student talk, question/answer format drawn largely from textbooks, and little student movement in academic classes. . . .

CONCLUSION

By the middle of the twentieth century, the early goals set for schooling in America were, in fact, being practiced, and virtually all children of school age were being served. The system was still far from perfect, but nearly all children had access to schools, and the instruction provided was appropriate for most. As noted in Chapter 5, there was, and still is, a serious commitment to a quality education for all.

The education provided in today's American schools is the result of a long evolution—an evolution based in traditions that include (1) ideas from classical Greece to the present, (2) principles of Christian religious education and citizenship training, (3) Enlightenment concepts of the nature of the universe and the nature of human beings, and (4) Jeffersonian and Lockean beliefs about democracy and education. Contemporary schools, like the activities of teachers and students in them, did not develop by accident. They have a past that has made them what they are.

The Influence of History

That past guides educators when they decide who should attend school, which subjects should be taught, how students should be disciplined, which students should be enrolled in which courses, how much latitude teachers should have in deciding what they do, which teaching methods should be used, and so forth. Because of that history, the decisions that are made are slightly different for present-day American schools than they would be in other times and places.

SUMMARY

Many of the roots of American K–12 education sprang from educational ideas developed in early Europe. Ideas from the classical Greeks and Romans, and from the Middle Ages, the Renaissance, and the Enlightenment all played a part. Those ideas included religious and civic purposes for schooling and incorporated the ways in which thinkers of various times viewed the nature of the world, the needs of society, and the process of education.

Since American colonial times, schooling has been considered a community responsibility. Over the years, civic purposes for schools have gradually overshadowed religious ones; more students have attended schools; and the nature of schooling has become more diverse. In a sense, the main historical theme reflected in the development of schools in America is the realization of the idea of the common school. Schools have become almost entirely available to and largely appropriate for all children.

STUDY QUESTIONS

1. In what ways and to what extent has Thomas Jefferson's idea that a democracy needs educated citizens guided the development of K–12 schools in America?

2. Why do you think American schools have tried to serve all students when that has not been the case in most other countries?

3. It is often said that the history of schools in America is a story of schools' adjustments to the changes in American society and the needs of the people. What have you learned from this chapter that supports this idea? What contradicts it?

4. Why do Americans think the ideas of (a) a *common school,* (b) comprehensive high schools, and (c) equal education for all are so important?

BIBLIOGRAPHY

Button, H. W., & Provenzo, E. (1988). *History of education & culture in America* (2nd ed.). Englewood Cliffs, NJ: Prentice-Hall.

Butts, R. F. (1978). *Public education in the United States: From revolution to reform.* New York: Holt, Rinehart and Winston.

Cremin, L. A. (1961), *The transformation of the school: Progressivism in American education.* New York: Knopf.

Cuban, L. (1984). *How teachers taught: Consistency and change in American classrooms 1890–1980.* New York: Longman.

Cuban, L. (1982). Persistent instruction: The high school curriculum, 1900–1980. *Phi Delta Kappan.* 64 (2), 113–118.

Dewey, J. (1916). *Democracy and education.* New York: Macmillan.

Dewey, J. (1938). *Experience and education.* New York: Macmillan.

Gutek, G. L. (1988), *Education and schooling in America* (2nd ed.). Englewood Cliffs, NJ: Prentice-Hall.

Pulliam, J. D. (1987). *History of education in America* (4th ed.). Columbus, OH: Merrill.

Ravitch, D. (1983). *The troubled crusade: American education 1945–1980.* New York: Basic Books.

Spring, Joel. (1986). *The American school 1642–1985.* New York: Longman.

NOTES

1. This description of education in Athens was developed by the authors of this book from a variety of historical accounts of the period.

2. From Records of the Governor and Company of the Massachusetts Bay in New England, Vol. II, 6–7. Boston, 1853. Reproduced in Cubberley, E. P. (1920). *Readings in the history of education.* Boston: Houghton Mifflin.

3. From Records of the Governor and Company of the Massachusetts Bay in New England, Vol. II, 203. Boston, 1853. Reproduced in Cubberley (1920).

4. Myers, C. B. (1968). *Public secondary schools in Pennsylvania during the American Revolutionary era 1760–1800.* Ph.D. dissertation, George Peabody College for Teachers.

5. Reproduced in Brumbaugh, M. G. (1969). *Life and works of Christopher Dock.* New York: Arno Press, pp. 105–111.

6. Jefferson, T. (1816, January 6). Letter to Colonel Yancey. Cited in H. A. Washington (Ed.). (1854). *The writings of Thomas Jefferson* (Vol. VI, p. 517). Washington, DC: Taylor and Maury.

7. Webster, N. B. (1962, Facsimile of 1831 ed.). *American spelling book.* New York: Bureau of Publications, Columbia University; Webster, N. B. (1970, Facsimile of 1828 ed.). *An American dictionary of the English language.* New York: Johnson Reprint Corp.

8. See Lindberg, S. W. (1976). *The Annotated McGuffey.* New York: Van Nostrand Reinhold.

9. Dewey, J. (1916). *Democracy and education.* New York: Macmillan; Dewey, J. (1938). *Experience and education.* New York: Macmillan; Dewey, J. (1933). *How we think: A restatement of the relation of reflective thinking to the educative process.* Boston: Heath.

10. Conant, J. B. (1959). *The American high school today.* New York: McGraw-Hill; Conant, J. B. (1963). *The education of American teachers.* New York: McGraw-Hill; Conant, J. B. (1967). *The comprehensive high school.* New York: McGraw-Hill.

11. National Education Association. (1893). *Report of the committee on secondary school studies.* Washington, DC: Government Printing Office.

12. Commission on the Reorganization of Secondary Education. (1918). *Cardinal principles of secondary education.* Washington, DC: Government Printing Office.

CHAPTER 8

Philosophical Beliefs and Teaching: Ideas That Guide What Teachers Do

DOUGLAS J. SIMPSON

INTRODUCTION

People generally recognize that a person's philosophy of life directly and indirectly impacts individual decisions, activities, and values and results in a particular life-style. Likewise, a teacher's philosophy of life and life-style influences his or her educational philosophy and style of teaching. For instance, if people value fairness, they will not only objectively evaluate political candidates but will also objectively judge the performance of students and fairly evaluate disputes between professionals. Consequently, what people believe to be true, real, and valuable will affect the way they teach, how they interpret issues, and what they emphasize in class.

This chapter, therefore, seeks to illustrate as well as explain how teachers with various philosophical beliefs may teach; at the same time it seeks to demonstrate that stereotypical thinking about the proponents of different philosophies should be avoided. The chapter covers two main topics. The first section—"Philosophical Beliefs and Teaching"—describes the philosophy of education as a set of intellectual activities and shows how philosophy is relevant to teaching. The other major division of the chapter—"Systematic Views of Education"—describes particular philosophies of education as intellectual beliefs that affect the ways in which teachers teach.

The chapter Snapshot and the Analysis section are designed to illustrate practical aspects of educational philosophies. They demonstrate how the beliefs of teachers affect everyday life in the classroom, and they provide examples of the important questions that educational philosophies address. The Educational Research section describes one aspect of research in the philosophy of education.

SNAPSHOT

The Shapshot for this chapter describes the teaching styles of three teachers who differ in their educational philosophies.[1] As you read it, consider the following:

- How are the teaching styles similar? How are they different?
- In what ways might the different styles reflect philosophical differences of the teachers? Are some of the differences possibly the result of personality, rather than philosophical, differences?
- What strengths and weaknesses do you see in each style?
- How do the teaching styles compare or contrast with your own views of teaching?
- Why do you want to teach? How will your reasons for wanting to teach affect your teaching?

A SCIENCE TEACHER

Ms. Aycock teaches science in a private, coeducational boarding school in the Northeast. Unlike most of her colleagues, she is tolerated more than she is appreciated by the school administration and board. The reasons for the lack of appreciation are not immediately obvious. Her students do extremely well on standardized achievement tests, enjoy her classes immensely, and are awarded more university scholarships in scientific fields than students at similar schools. In addition, her headmaster and colleagues describe her as a competent teacher, well-educated person, and likable individual, even if a gadfly in meetings.

Upon talking with students and faculty at the school, a visitor soon learns that Ms. Aycock's credentials, pedagogical methods, and coverage of content are not in question. Instead, it is her *questions* that are questioned. For example, she has on various occasions asked her colleagues such questions as the following: (1) Is the government's list of priorities for scientific research a form of mind control? (2) Why do we have so few female and minority students and teachers at this academy? (3) Shouldn't the faculty and students have more input into institutional policies, decisions, and practices?

In her classes, Ms. Aycock also asks many unsettling questions; some examples follow: Is it moral for companies to build nuclear power plants and jeopardize the lives of present and future citizens? Does it make sense for the government to allow millions of people to live along the San Andreas Fault when disaster is inevitable? Should billions of dollars be spent on space exploration when millions, perhaps billions, of people in the world are poorly nourished, clothed, and educated? Is government controlled by the rich and powerful or simply by leaders who are morally insensitive to the consequences of acid rain, fly ash, and industrial waste? Why does the government allow the ruling class to exploit the masses by monopolizing natural resources, land holdings, and economic growth?

A brief visit to one of Ms. Aycock's classes illustrates her professional orientation, practice, and concerns. She begins the class by saying, "Yesterday our field trip gave us a firsthand view of some consequences of acid rain that are mentioned in the textbook. Among other things, we saw the erosion of invaluable statues and historic buildings. The absence of vegetation and fish at the dead lake may still be fresh upon your minds, too.

"Today I've invited Mr. Evergreen, an environmentalist, Ms. Cupidity, an industrialist, and Ms. Coddleston, a legislative aide, to discuss issues surrounding acid rain. After all three have spoken, you'll have an opportunity to raise questions. Tomorrow we'll break into buzz groups to discuss ways of dealing with acid rain in the various kinds of environments it affects—the ecology, the economy, government, and so on. Keep in mind the distinctions and the connections between scientific, ethical, and political matters."

Ms. Aycock's friends and detractors sometimes describe her as an iconoclast, a social reconstructionist, a Socratic questioner, a neo-Marxist, a socialist, and a communist. She usually responds, "It's obvious that you cannot recognize a Presbyterian with a social conscience when you see one."

A SOCIAL STUDIES TEACHER

Mr. Reinhold's classes think he is an exciting and stimulating history teacher. They do not, of course, always sit on the edges of their chairs, especially when he asks them to learn lists like this:

1001 Eriksson visits North America

1271 Polo travels to China

1487 Dias rounds the Cape of Good Hope

1492 Columbus voyages to the Americas

1497 Cabot reaches North America

1513 Balboa sees the Pacific Ocean

1519 Magellan starts trip around the world

He says he uses such lists to give students an overview of a period, to provide a skeleton for a cognitive framework to be developed at a later time, and to introduce students to key explorers, dates, and places.

Mr. Reinhold's major goal is to develop the rational powers of his students. He is noted for being exceptionally flexible in the way he pursues his goals. That is, he uses museums, films, libraries, lecturers, projects, computers, programmed textbooks, buzz groups, and so forth. He knows students will forget much of the information they learn in his classes, but this does not trouble him. He is more interested in their learning to think rationally and critically about the economic, political, religious, philosophical, and ethical issues humanity has faced over the centuries. He also wants his students to evaluate past ways of dealing with problems and to learn how the past affects the present and the future.

Mr. Reinhold thinks it is not only his responsibility to pursue these objectives, but it is his duty to direct students to see that there are enduring values worth passing on to each generation. If the students properly grasp these values—freedom, justice, respect, understanding, rationality, tolerance, compassion, and so on—they have guideposts that might help them change the present and direct the future.

A glimpse into Mr. Reinhold's classroom, where early white settlers and Native Americans are being studied, suggests his emphasis on these values. At the conclusion of a film on the causes of conflict between the two historical groups, he says, "Tonight I want you to discuss four points with your partner. In the morning, I'll ask you for a written summary of your conclusions. The first question: Which ethical principles are relevant to an appraisal of Indian-settler relationships during the 1500s–1700s? Second, identify particular cases of people either ignoring or adhering to these principles. Third, explain why, as far as you can determine, certain individuals followed or ignored these principles. Finally, decide which of these principles are and are not pertinent to human relationships today."

Reinhold does not feel he is alone in the educative endeavor. All teachers of basic subjects—science, social studies, English, mathematics—should have overlapping concerns. Working together, teachers can help students decide to be rational, independent thinkers, morally responsible persons, and intelligent users of the basic branches of knowledge.

Hardly anyone would question whether Mr. Reinhold is a successful teacher. Most principals, teachers, and parents would be delighted to work with him or to have him teach their children. Yet he says he does not have a philosophy of education. His colleagues teasingly tell him he is either a confused essentialistic perennialist or a muddled perennialistic essentialist.

AN ENGLISH TEACHER

Ms. Alvarez's students are seldom bored in her English classes. Her electrifying approach to life spills over into her teaching. If you can believe her students, she makes verbs vivacious, commas comical, adverbs agreeable, spelling splendid, and writing wonderful. She is a model for new teachers, the idol of her students, and an inspiration to the entire school staff. She does so many things well that it is easy to see why her friends believe she is a natural, a born teacher. Instinctively, she seems to know what to do, when and how it should be done, and the steps to take with each student.

Her first love as a teacher, however, is not teaching punctuation, spelling, capitalization, writing, and grammar. She does a beautiful job teaching these topics, but she would study literature all of the time with her students if she had a choice. Although she knows basic communication skills are valuable, she believes that the quality of life in society is enhanced by an immersion in great literature. In addition to the intrinsic value she sees in literature, she thinks the themes discussed by great writers are important social and philosophical statements. She has been known to say more than one time, "You may excel on standardized tests, win a merit scholarship, build an outstanding practice or corporation, and achieve international recognition, but you are less than successful as a human being if you are ethically indifferent to the problems around you and if you lack the courage to act on your moral principles." "Don't be a Prufrock," she quickly adds.

> When social, political, and ethical issues arise in her classes, students sometimes ask, "Aren't values personal, Ms. Alvarez?" Her most recent response is along the following lines: "*Personal* can mean at least a couple of things. First, it may mean that values are totally up to the individual and each person can do whatever he or she pleases. Second, it may also mean that values, after they have been debated and justified, must be personally decided upon and acted on if they are to have meaning. Those who subscribe to this second viewpoint think value judgments are at least partially rational, like other types of judgments."
>
> Continuing the conversation, Ms. Alvarez adds: "Is it ethically acceptable for a person to discriminate against Hispanics, Baptists, Yankees, and aliens just because it pleases her? Is it possible we are violating transcultural moral principles if we murder or rape someone? Is it fair for me to award one of you a grade of F when you have earned a grade of B?" Her questions almost always spark further discussion in an atmosphere of open reflection and respect for the autonomy of each person.
>
> When Ms. Alvarez was pursuing the M.Ed. in graduate school, one of her classmates said he thought she was an idealist. She thought for a moment and said, "If I am, please don't stereotype me and attribute all of that historical luggage to me. I'm a neoidealist with a mind of my own."

PHILOSOPHICAL BELIEFS AND TEACHING

Teaching Styles

Have you ever wondered why teachers such as the three described in the Snapshot teach differently? Is it because in their early lives they have had different role models and culturally diverse backgrounds? Is it because teachers have distinct personalities and different subject specialties, types of students, and school principals? Do the various kinds of colleges and universities that teachers attend or the types of teacher-education programs they go through partly account for the differences among them?

Similarities

No doubt these and other variables do make a difference in the way any person teaches. But other factors also seem to be involved. If teachers have both the freedom and the courage to be themselves at school in the ways that Ms. Aycock, Mr. Reinhold, and Ms. Alvarez do, their philosophies of life and resulting educational philosophies should account for some differences in their professional activities. Many teachers, of course, in spite of differing educational philosophies, teach very much alike at times. Their discussions of predicate nominatives, assignments in algebra classes, methods of teaching reading, and activities with students are quite similar. Samuel de Champlain, Francis Drake, and John Smith may appear in a social studies curriculum regardless of the teacher's philosophy. Geometry teachers may have their students study segments, angles, triangles, polygons, prisms, and pyramids even when among themselves they have radically different educational perspectives. The Milky Way galaxy, the atom, and metamorphic rocks are rather standard fare in many earth science courses. Teachers who span the entire spectrum of philosophical

Philosophical Differences

thought may use films, tapes, slides, software, and chalk. So teachers sometimes teach similarly even when their worldviews differ. Conversely, teachers whose worldviews are essentially the same teach differently at times.

Moreover, teachers as teachers do differ in many respects, and some of their differences are in part attributable to their philosophies of education. This is inevitable if one recalls Socrates, Martin Luther, Jean Jacques Rousseau, Johann Herbart, Thomas Jefferson, George Washington Carver, Maria Montessori, and some of the other major educators and thinkers they have studied. One must remember, too, that early educational institutions—Latin grammar schools, Franklin's Academy, female seminaries—and many present ones arose for different philosophical reasons. The same may be said of textbooks, laws, and statements of educational goals by professional associations. It is important, therefore, for teachers to understand what educational philosophy is and how it contributes to their professional life.

The Nature and Value of Educational Philosophy

Philosophizing

One informative way of thinking about philosophy of education is to consider it to be a set of intellectual activities that lead educators who engage in them to build a particular product. In this context, we call the set of intellectual activities *philosophizing*. The product of the philosophizing is a *personal philosophy of education*. (See Simpson & Jackson, 1984; Soltis, 1978.)[2] This philosophizing, then, might involve at least four elements: (1) *clarifying* educational discussions by mapping out concepts that make abstract ideas about education more understandable and more useful as professional guides, (2) *justifying* educational decisions by providing compelling arguments and supporting evidence for them, (3) *interpreting* educational data in order to determine their significance for educational policy and practice, and (4) *systematizing* educational discussions, decisions, and data into a coherent understanding of what education is.

Each of these activities is an important part of the broader professional life of the teacher. Each helps the teacher come to grips with two questions: What am I as a teacher? Why am I doing what I am doing in the classroom?

Clarification

"What Do You Mean?"

When teachers are encouraged to use a procedure or to pursue a goal, it is important to determine precisely what is being stated. (For more information on the activity of clarifying, see Barrow, 1981; Chambers, 1983.)[3] For example, what is the speaker encouraging when teachers are told they should meet the needs of the whole child? Are financial needs included? Probably not. What about material needs? Our answer may be slower in coming. How are teachers to be involved, if at all, in meeting the social, religious, and emotional needs of students? What is included in the concept of educational needs? Can a teacher meet all of a student's educational needs? Do priorities need to be established? Is "the whole child" a clear concept?

Any advice can confuse teachers if it—and the ideas that make it up—is not analyzed carefully. Various proponents of various educational ideas enjoin teachers to teach the basics, develop creative students, cultivate independent thinkers, pass on lasting values, pursue students' natural interests, and allow students to study whatever is meaningful to them. In some educational discussions the concepts of intelligence, indoctrination, education, learning, conditioning, self-actualization, socialization, knowledge, and authoritarianism become quite muddled.

Imagine for a moment teachers who have been instructed by their principal to make certain their students learn "the basics" by March. Understanding their local situation, the teachers might surmise that the principal used the term *basics* to refer to the material on the achievement tests that will be administered in April. Suppose further that some have just started teaching their seventh-grade class a required unit on sex education. The material in the unit does not appear on the mathematics, science, language arts, and social studies tests, but they know the reason for the new unit: Twenty-one percent of the eighth-, ninth-, and tenth-grade girls in their school system became pregnant last year. They would like to ask their principal, "Which is more basic, high scores on the achievement test or low scores on the pregnancy test? Do we discuss punctuation or impregnation?"

These situations illustrate the reason that asking "What do you mean?" is intellectually useful to teachers. First of all, raising the question helps teachers obtain a clear picture of what they are told they should or should not do. Being clear about their instructions or challenges opens the door for them to decide not only how, but whether, they ought to pursue an objective. Second, an analysis of educational language can reveal how naive some decision makers and policymakers and speakers and writers are about the educational enterprise. Often they demand the impossible and the indefensible of teachers. When a teacher knows something unreasonable is expected or demanded, the teacher may be unhappy; however, the teacher will also be better able to argue against the decision or policy. Third, an analysis of statements on teaching procedures, structures, goals, outcomes, and content may on occasion reveal naiveté or hidden values and conflicting claims. Consequently, raising some form of the question "What do you mean?" eventually leads teachers into other kinds of philosophical questions.

Justification

"How Do You Know?" Since schooling is an intrinsically value-laden endeavor, teachers may frequently raise some variation of the question "How do you know?" (For more information on the activity of justification, see Fitzgibbons, 1981;[4] Simpson & Jackson, 1984.) The teacher will want to ask, "What reasons and evidence support your views, policies, goals, and practices?" "Is the research that supports these ideas accurate and valid?" In essence, the teacher is asking for a justification of an educational idea, belief, or practice. Imagine, for instance, a school board meeting that is about to conclude. The chair praises the other members for their contributions to the new educational-excellence plan. As the board prepares to approve the plan, a member asks for a review of the list of criteria that will be used to judge excellent high schools. The following criteria constitute the list:

1. the percentage of students who pass the proficiency test on first attempt;
2. the percentage of students who score above the national average on standardized achievement tests;

3. the percentage of students who score above the national average on the ACT and SAT;
4. the percentage of students who attend a university on merit scholarships;
5. the percentage of students who graduate from a university;
6. the percentage of students who attend professional schools and become lawyers, psychologists, physicians, dentists, engineers, and business leaders;
7. the percentage of students who receive state or national recognition for outstanding accomplishments after graduation.

After the criteria are read aloud for the entire board to hear again, the member asks if the board will consider substituting an alternate list of criteria, which she proposes. Her list follows:

1. the percentage of students from low-income families who pass the proficiency test on first attempt;
2. the percentage of students from low-income families who are not arrested or incarcerated before graduating from high school;
3. the percentage of students from low-income families who score above the national average on standardized achievement tests;
4. the percentage of students from minority and low-income families who graduate from a university;
5. the percentage of female students who enter the male-dominated occupations;
6. the percentage of university graduates who eventually become teachers, clergy, social workers, nurses, and farmers;
7. the percentage of former students who contribute annually to charitable causes.

Before discussion of this new list of criteria begins, the school board member distributes a list of questions she thinks the board members need to address: Why should the board believe filling cavities, removing plaque, and attaching braces are more valuable activities than teaching science, stimulating creative thought, and challenging students to use their knowledge for the betterment of humankind? Why should the board place more emphasis on ACT scores than it does on teaching students to live by the principles of respect, freedom, and justice? How can the board justify the conclusion that people who grow food for thousands each year are less significant than those who defend a few hundred prospective criminals each year?

Much Practice Is Unexamined

Questions of this sort take the teacher to the heart of the issue of the real nature and purpose of schooling. They force thinking teachers to recognize that much of what goes on in educational circles is largely unexamined. Related philosophical questions for the teacher to consider are: Why do we require four units of English and only two units of mathematics for high school graduation? Why are mathematics, science, social studies, and language arts considered core subjects and art, music, physical education, and foreign languages considered

peripheral subjects? What are the major goals and objectives of schooling? Should schools be organized differently than they are? Why are teachers often not allowed to serve on school boards? Does the same logic apply to doctors, lawyers, and psychologists serving on professional boards?

Educators Who Think Independently

The utility of philosophizing in this realm is clear. As professionals, teachers want sound reasons for attempting to carry out their responsibilities. They want to know they are not blindly following tradition, being swept up in the most recent educational fad, or unethically pursuing even the best objectives. Educators who think independently can sometimes influence the actions of policymakers and decision makers by unearthing their underlying assumptions and, when appropriate, challenging them and their application to educational practice. Ultimately, the ideal is that teachers, by asking sensitive, probing questions about the underlying bases for educational decisions, policies, and practices, will make a difference in the processes, the content, and the outcome of schooling.

Interpretation and Systematization

Socialization

Early in life, people in all cultures are gradually initiated into a set of values, beliefs, and perceptions common to their own culture. The process is called *socialization*. The impact of socialization varies, depending upon a number of factors. Some people are so conditioned by the process that they can seldom see things through the eyes of others or even have a thought of their own. Others, for a variety of reasons, rebel against their cultural orientations. They reject their origins and become critical of their social and intellectual heritage. Still others are challenged by their cultural environments and progressively sift through their values, retaining ideas they find defensible and discarding those they believe to be indefensible. (For more discussion of interpretation and systematization, see Power, 1982;[5] Simpson & Jackson, 1984.) If the process is a rational, thinking process, the individual considers questions that rest on deep philosophical concerns—concerns about the nature of reality (metaphysics), the nature of knowledge (epistemology), the nature of values (axiology).

In each case, the socialized individual adopts and refines a set of beliefs that provides the means for interpreting and systematizing new experiences. These beliefs, in one sense, constitute an elementary philosophy of life; and that philosophy of life becomes a filter, an interpretive frame of reference, through which

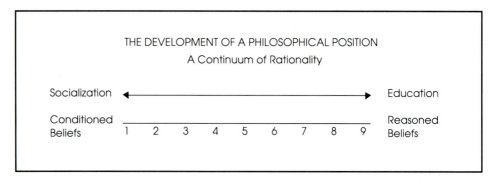

Figure 8–1. A continuum of rationality. When individuals develop their philosophical positions, they base them on influences that are derived from cultural socialization and from more purposeful education. In a sense, the two types of influences compete for dominance as the individuals decide upon their philosophical stances.

"How Should These Data Be Understood?"

the individual perceives and organizes reality. The competition of influences between cultural socialization and education is illustrated in Figure 8–1.

As an individual's philosophy of life, or frame of reference, develops, it should help the person understand future experiences and ideas, thus broadening his or her perspective. It may, however, have a restricting effect if the individual does not learn "to see with more than one pair of glasses" or at least to understand that he or she is wearing glasses. In that case, the individual does not become a philosophizing person who has learned to ask, "Am I looking at this too narrowly? Am I depending on just one viewpoint? Would some other approach help me understand this more fully?"

The Nature of Philosophy of Education

Intellectual Activity	Major Questions
Clarification	What do you mean?
Justification	How do you know?
Interpretation	How should these data be understood?
Systematization	Do these findings form a coherent pattern?

As people begin to think philosophically about life, they raise questions about their developing philosophical views, questions such as:

1. What do I mean by discrimination?
2. What reasons and evidence do I have for my values, religious beliefs, political allegiances?
3. Is this policy consistent with what I believe?
4. Do my beliefs on teaching cohere?

The result or end product of thinking in an interpretative, systematic way is a useful philosophy of life, or when applicable, of education.

When teachers philosophize about professional matters—when they ask themselves "How should this effective schooling data be explained? Why should these things matter? Is more than one interpretation possible or legitimate? If so, are they compatible? Do these new pieces of educational thought fit together with my existing ideas?"—they are essentially seeking answers to two questions: "How am I to fit these findings into my meaning system? Do these notions, theories, and data form a coherent view of education?"

"Do These Findings Form a Coherent Pattern?"

Three words—understanding, coherence, relevance—summarize the utility of interpreting and systematizing educational phenomena. To interpret educational findings and experiences is to come to understand education better, and, ideally, to become a better educator. To systematize educational phenomena is to pull together what one understands about a variety of topics into a viewpoint that promotes intelligent, consistent, professional behavior. In so doing, teachers construct their philosophies of education, which influence their entire lives as educators, including their instructional activities, curricular decisions, personnel choices, educational objectives, professional commitments, and ethical conduct.

A Hypothetical Query

The four elements of philosophizing described can be illustrated in the following questions of a newspaper reporter to a governor who just made a speech about education:

Clarification	Governor, now that you have finished your address, could you briefly tell us what you mean by "good teaching"?
Justification	Likewise, can you elaborate on why you believe many teachers are not doing a good job? And, in the light of your criticism of teachers, could you explain how it is that achievement test scores are above average across the state?
Interpretation	
Systematization	Finally, please comment on how you reconcile your views that the state has too many inadequate teachers with your proposal to allow any university graduate into the teaching profession.

SYSTEMATIC VIEWS OF EDUCATION

Present-Day Options

Teachers can study a number of philosophies of education if they wish to identify, clarify, and evaluate their own developing views on education. Thus far, no one has proved conclusively that a particular educational philosophy is true in a way that makes all competing views false. In fact, some might argue that this is nearly impossible, especially if they accept the premise that systems of thought limit as well as enhance the teacher's ability to understand educational issues.

This is not to say that all educational philosophies are equally true or reasonable. Nor is it to say that all positions offer the same degree of illumination. Some educational philosophies are based on such weak arguments and limited evidence that they merit little consideration. Others are strongly supported and deserving of considerable attention.

Any philosophy of education probably offers some value; but the ideal philosophy of education is one that is stronger than others, more reasonable than others, and more useful than others. Prospective teachers who are developing their own positions should review the competing educational philosophies.

The philosophies that are surveyed in a rather cursory fashion on the remaining pages of this chapter fall into three general categories: historical, modern, and contemporary. Each philosophy is explained from the viewpoint of a present-day educational philosoper even if a particular philosophy's intellectual heritage goes back to antiquity. The historical philosophies discussed are *idealism* and *realism*. The two modern philosophies treated are *pragmatism* and *existentialism*. The contemporary positions presented are *perennialism, essentialism, behaviorism, reconstructionism, futurism, evangelicalism,* and *Marxism*. (For more detailed analyses of these philosophies of education, see Griese, 1981, and O'Neill, 1981.)[6]

Problems to Avoid

In reviewing philosophies of education, two overlapping problems often arise. The first problem is that of *stereotyping* the adherents of a specific philosophical position. This form of stereotyping usually is based on the belief that proponents of a particular philosophy agree on every detail of their views regarding metaphysics (the nature of reality), epistemology (the nature of knowledge), axiology (the nature of values), and education (the nature of schooling). When this happens, proponents of similar positions may be depicted as mindless conformists, all doing the same thing at the same time all over the world. Thus one may erroneously conclude the following: Mary Stone is an essentialist; therefore, she believes in a, b, c, and d, teaches with goals 1, 2, 3, and 4 in mind, and utilizes methods w, x, y, and z to reach her goals.

A second, and related, difficulty results from neglecting philosophical and pedagogical similarities across the schools of thought in order to emphasize their distinctiveness. As a result, a person can be left with the impression that only Variety A teachers lecture; only Variety B teachers think values are relative; only Variety C teachers have an interest in religion; only Variety D teachers are concerned with the autonomy of students.

Because of these two potential problems in understanding philosophies of education, it is worth repeating an idea stated earlier. Teachers with similar beliefs differ, as well as agree, on a variety of matters. In like manner, teachers with different beliefs agree, as well as disagree, on issues. These two potential problems in understanding philosophies of education—stereotyping or ignoring similarities across systems—can be overcome to some degree if educational philosophical positions are viewed in much the same manner as one would view religious denomination and political party affiliations. They are convenient labels that often hinder as well as help in understanding particular individuals. They refer to some common features of adherents, but they ignore differences that are sometimes as important as the similarities.

Historical Philosophies

In the Western world, probably the oldest philosophical positions known for accompanying educational theories are *idealism* and *realism*. The intellectual roots of both reach back to ancient Greece. Present-day exponents, while connected with the past, express updated philosophical and pedagogical versions of the two positions.

mind is important, contemporary idealists do not discount educational technology and other available pedagogical options.

Great Thinkers

Likewise, today's idealists recognize that any curriculum that promotes the self-actualization of the student may be studied, and all subjects can contribute to an integrated view of reality. No bona fide subject is ignored, even though idealists have traditionally stressed the value of history, religion, literature, fine arts, and mathematics in enabling students to achieve self-understanding, self-realization, and the actualization of their intellectual, moral, social, and spiritual potential. An idealist, then, may value highly a liberal education and at the same time argue for the importance of specialized and vocational studies on very different grounds. It would be consistent with idealists' beliefs to promote, in any field of study, the emulation of great thinkers in an effort to assist students in realizing their potentialities.

The Idealist as Teacher

1. encourages students to imitate the thought of great people;
2. points out the moral and spiritual significance of ideas that are discussed;
3. attempts to model desirable qualities for students to emulate;
4. promotes independent thought in students by leading class discussions and asking thoughtful questions;
5. stresses lasting over transitory values in decision making;
6. seeks to develop both the thinking skills and decision-making powers of students;
7. directs the intellectual and moral growth of students toward a condition of excellence.

Primary Goal in Idealist's Education

Since the student is viewed as a unique person who possesses many of the qualities of the absolute mind, the idealist-teacher believes each student should be treated as an immortal, rational creature, capable of making his or her own decisions. As the student matures, the emphasis of schooling should shift from the teacher's instructing to the student's self-directed learning. The growing responsibility of the student, when supported by early instruction and training, will enable him or her to utilize personal potentialities and become a creative, autonomous person. The primary goal of schooling, then, is to develop people who understand themselves and their world and who live in ways that are consistent with the ultimate reality of a spiritual universe.

Realism

REALITY

Realism, like idealism, is a contemporary philosophical position with a rich heritage. Many think Plato and Aristotle first formalized the position. After them, a distinguished line of thinkers diversified and refined the viewpoint. Among

Material Reality

these philosophers are John Locke, David Hume, St. Thomas Aquinas, Bertrand Russell, Alfred North Whitehead, and Ralph B. Perry. Educational philosophers who have promoted the position include such diverse thinkers as Jean-Jacques Rousseau, Maria Montessori, Jacques Maritain, Frederick Breed, and Harry Broudy. (See Martin, 1982; Broudy, 1961; Maritain, 1938.)[8]

Realists can be divided into two general groups: (1) materialists, those who emphasize that reality is completely material; and (2) traditional realists, those who believe in the reality of abstract ideas. *Materialists,* the first group, think the differences detected in reality are all matter of degree, never of kind. Ultimate reality, in all of its variety, is impersonal, nonmental, and material. *Traditional realists* believe abstract ideas are not just labels, but that they describe the essential features of a group or class of things. Rather than only naming, abstractions describe the characteristics of things as they actually are; that is, the nature of specific things.

Human Rationality

While materialists radically differ with idealists over the nature of reality, some traditional realists seem close to idealists, even though they still reject the proposition that ultimate reality is spiritual. For these realists, there may be both material and spiritual reality. They agree that the ability of humans to think—their rationality—sets them apart from the remainder of known reality. And some of them add that both rationality and spirituality distinguish human beings from the remainder of reality. These realists believe that the physical world exists in its own right, just as does the spiritual world. Each realm is equally real, even though substantially different.

These two strands of thought within realism illustrate to some extent the diversity found in realistic thinking. Some of the additional diversity will be described below, as the philosophy is further clarified. For the moment, it is

A Realist Thinker

Figure 8–3. Is this illustrator's representation of a realist thinker consistent with your thinking? If not, how would you change it?

TRUTH AND VALUES

sufficient to note the differences between the two kinds of realism: one kind that consists of those who see reality as completely material and a second kind that includes those who see it as a combination of the material and the spiritual.

The position of realists on the nature of knowledge probably identifies them more frequently than any of their other positions. Realists largely agree that an objective, material reality exists and can be known. Particular things can be known and distinguished from ideas of those things. A particular item is not known, however, until its *nature* or *essence* is understood or perceived. In order to understand the essence of a particular thing, a person must first understand the class of things to which it belongs. A particular person, for example, is understood only after his or her essence, or nature, is understood. Therefore, a person cannot understand a particular human being unless that person has some understanding of human beings as a group.

Classical Realists

The diversity among realists is as apparent in the realm of values as it is anywhere. Broadly speaking, values—or at least the moral ones—may be determined in several ways. One group of realists, *classical realists*, generally think that some moral values can be arrived at by rigorous rational thought. As they see it, an agreed-upon set of ethical principles can be determined, defended, and applied to human problems in any culture, although sometimes it is difficult to do so. The principles provide invaluable guides to maintaining a just and free society.

Materialistic Realists

Other realists, notably *materialistic realists*, argue one of two positions. One opinion is that moral values are determined by the social context and are to be judged in terms of consequences upon society. Society, therefore, is free to change its values if it can verify the need. A second, and quite different, opinion expressed by materialistic realists is that just as natural order reveals natural laws, it also reveals moral law. By studying human behavior and its consequences, we can discover natural moral laws. The good moral life consists of living intelligently by these laws, experiencing the benefits of the resulting life, and avoiding the natural consequences of violating them.

Religious Realists

A third group of realists, *religious realists*, do not offer a uniform approach to ethics any more than do other realists. Some have a great deal in common with classical realists, emphasizing the role of reason in determining moral values. Others combine reason and revelation, believing that, since the absolute mind is a rational being, values are rational as well as revealed in sacred literature. Another set appear to think that natural law, reason, and scripture are all helpful in constructing sound ethical theory since God established natural law, exemplifies sound reason, and inspired scripture.

Regardless of the particular orientation of specific realists, they, along with many nonrealist philosophers, increasingly stress that there are several kinds of values and that those values need to be distinguished. They classify values, for example, as preferential (questions of taste), prudential (questions of wisdom), aesthetic (questions of beauty), and ethical (questions of morality). They say these types of values are substantively different and should not be grouped together.

PEDAGOGY

By now it should be obvious that realistic educational thought cannot easily be described. For this reason, the discussion of realistic educational philosophy will be confined to two perspectives, the educational views of present-day classical and religious realists. Other recent derivations of realism—Marxism, pe-

Cultivation of Thinking

rennialism, behaviorism—will be analyzed when we take up contemporary educational philosophies.

Classical realists believe that education is only understood when the nature of the human being is understood. The human being is believed to be uniquely a rational creature, a creature who, when fully developed, is capable not only of thinking but also of evaluating thought. Schooling, therefore, is fundamentally concerned with cultivation of thinking, regardless of the other responsibilities attributed to it by society—responsibilities such as social, physical, and emotional development.

Even though the major goal of schooling is to promote thinking (or reasoning), that goal need not be narrowly defined. *Reason* is not limited to thinking for its own sake. It is critical in understanding any subject—social relationships, emotional development, physical growth, and so on. Reason, furthermore, is necessary to thoughtful choices and independently selected ways of living, and that includes understanding values and selecting from among them.

Classical realists believe that teachers need to understand the process of thinking, need to be subject matter specialists, and need to be effective instructors. They argue that teachers cannot be effective unless they understand the rational processes involved in a particular discipline. Because classical realists are keenly interested in developing students' rational abilities and their understanding of themselves as rational creatures, the humanities, the arts, and mathematics are prime candidates for a core curriculum. A society's way of thinking are contained in these subjects.

The Classical Realist as Teacher

1. develops the essence of students as persons by focusing on their rational growth;
2. is dedicated to getting students to live in the light of a reasoned answer to the question of what kind of life is appropriate for a rational creature;
3. assists students in realizing that a commitment to reason is the way to autonomous choosing and living;
4. guides students toward finding objective rational grounds for making value and truth judgments;
5. organizes learning activities so that students will come to see that particulars belong to classes of things;
6. promotes evaluative thinking as the appropriate means to social, physical, and emotional development;
7. helps students see the differences between preferential, prudential, aesthetic, and ethical value judgments.

It would be a mistake, however, to suppose the contemporary realist is uninterested in the scientific pursuit of knowledge. Classical realists recognize that any intellectually rigorous study can develop students' rationality and, thereby, enable them to become more completely human and to search for solutions to human dilemmas. Toward this end, realists who teach employ a variety of methods to provoke thought, stimulate inquiry, and awaken the rational powers of their students. Just as with idealism, no one method is prescribed, and many can be used to good effect.

Religious realists, while common in most Western and some Eastern religions, are best known in educational circles as shapers of Catholic educational thought. Often known as Thomist philosophers, they base their thinking on the teachings of the scriptures, the doctrines of the church, and the writings of St. Thomas Aquinas (from whom they get their name). The Thomists are basically united in their belief that a personal God is the author of reality, reason, and revelation. This belief is fundamental to Catholic thought and to Catholic philosophy of education.

Holistic Education

Neo-Thomists, as some contemporary Catholic thinkers are labeled, express diverse opinions about education but are largely in agreement that the general aim of education is to develop the person as a person. In order to accomplish this aim, one must grasp the holistic nature of education. *Holistic education*, in this context, refers to a learning environment that (1) combines belief in God with giving reasons for one's faith, (2) stresses the significance of the intellect and the value of manual labor, (3) balances the spiritual and the worldly life, (4) cultivates rationality and morality, and (5) integrates non-Christian forms of inquiry with Christian truths.

Since God is author of all truth, a neo-Thomist education is appropriate for all students even though students will vary in the degree they profit from it. Included in the conception of liberal education may be both religious and vocational education, not just the traditional study of the humanities and the sciences. The integration of these fields, the Thomists believe, should assist students later in life as they seek to form a just and free society. The teacher is also to cultivate and model the virtues of faith, hope, and love.

The Religious Realist as Teacher

1. models the virtues of faith, hope and love;
2. challenges students to recognize they are the principal partners in learning;
3. teaches students to understand that God is the source of permanent values;
4. teaches students that reason and revelation are complementary ways of discovering truth;
5. seeks to develop the student as a whole person by cultivating her/his rationality, spirituality, and morality;
6. requires mechanical drills as well as memorization when they promote greater goals in education;
7. relies upon divine and human resources to transform students into complete persons.

Autonomous Humans

Students must be led to recognize that they are the principal partners in learning. They are the ones who actively learn as they are informed by the teacher and illuminated by divine grace. They are endowed with reason and freedom and must choose to utilize both their human and divine resources if they are to be transformed into complete persons. The memorization of facts and truths, while necessary, does not in and of itself bring about the goal of education. Mechanical drills by the teacher, if needed, must always be supplemented by a loving concern for the development of each child. The student, therefore, both is and must become autonomous through a liberating education.

Modern Philosophies

In contrast to idealism and realism, pragmatism and existentialism are rather new as systematic philosophies, although some of the ideas and attitudes in each of them, as in any system of thought, have been present throughout human history. Before pragmatism and existentialism, idealism and realism dominated Western intellectual circles; thus, pragmatism and existentialism marked a turning point in philosophical and educational thought. They not only changed philosophy in and of itself but also stimulated the formulation of additional and more varied philosophical and pedagogical positions.

Modern Philosophies of Education

Philosophy	Role of the Teacher
Pragmatism	To guide the development of the reflective person
Existentialism	To facilitate the development of the authentic person

Pragmatism

Heraclitus, the ancient Greek philosopher, was perhaps a seminal pragmatist, but it was nineteenth- and twentieth-century philosophers such as Charles S. Pierce and William James who commanded the attention of contemporary philosophers and educators alike. (See O'Neill, 1981; Dewey, 1933; James, 1946.)[9] John Dewey, although identified by some as an instrumentalist or an experimentalist, also contributed significantly to pragmatic educational thought and practice. Together, along with other like-minded thinkers, these thinkers exposited a new way of interpreting reality and education.

REALITY

Pragmatists have generally agreed that the universe is a natural, dynamic entity that can be partly known through human experiences and transactions. Human beings, as part of the natural universe, have evolved and become more complex than most of reality, but they are not substantively different from the rest of the universe. Humans, of course, have evolved to the point at which they can think and exercise choice; but this development, as far as can be determined, is purely natural and not supernatural. However, individual humans only partly experience reality because that which any single person knows and experiences is limited. Since a person cannot experience the whole, a general view of reality is beyond the realm of anyone's knowledge.

Reality Is Limited to the Physical

TRUTH AND VALUES

Truth Is Changeable

For the pragmatist, truth is conceptually different in a number of ways from the views proposed by idealists and realists. To begin with, there is no absolute truth. Truth, both in itself and as we know it, is changeable, never final. This is so because the knower and the universe are in a process of change. Second, truth is discovered by using the scientific method to solve problems. Thus truth is discovered by its function—its use in solving the quandaries of society. Third, knowing the truth is a process that involves a direct transaction of the knower

Figure 8–4. Does this illustrator's representation of a pragmatist thinker make sense to you? How might you portray pragmatists differently?

Knowing Is a Process of Inquiring

with sensory data. Knowing, therefore, is a *process* of inquiring, not a static state. Finally, truth is relative to the knower's experience with the available data.

Since pragmatists base their concept of values on these principles, they do not believe absolute values exist. Therefore, the Absolute does not prescribe right and wrong. Instead, the pragmatists determine values by testing hypotheses about conduct; that is, they test behavioral patterns to determine their worth. If the evidence supports the conclusion that an action is valuable, then it should be cultivated. If not, it should either be discouraged or allowed to disappear.

Some interpreters of pragmatism understand these comments to mean that one individual's view of reality, truth, and value is just as good as anyone else's. That is to say, philosophical beliefs are purely a personal matter. But pragmatists themselves generally disagree with this; they introduce an element of objectivity into their thought by determining values not through personal preference but by means of scientifically demonstrating what is socially expedient, that which leads to the growth of society. Truth, rather than being determined by individual whim, is decided by public examination of the data.

PEDAGOGY

Scientific Method

The responsibilities and goals of pragmatic teachers are extensions of their general philosophy. Their general educational goal is the development of *reflective thinkers* who employ the *scientific method* to solve personal and societal problems. Reflective thinking involves identifying a real problem, collecting pertinent data, formulating a tentative hypothesis, deducing testable consequences, and verifying actual consequences. Ideally, a solution to one's problem is discovered. If resolution of the problem is not obtained, the individual proceeds through the reflective thinking process again.

Reflective Thinkers

In order for pragmatic teachers to achieve their goal, they guide, but do not dominate, their students' learning experiences since learning is fundamentally a process that involves active problem solving. The teacher, at least at times, arranges learning situations for students around problems related to the subject matter or environment. On other occasions, students are given the freedom to select personal or social problems to study. The teacher has the freedom to allow or encourage any learning experience that has been judged to produce personal or societal growth. The teacher's focus, then, is on the *process of learning*, not the content to be learned. It is important not to misunderstand this emphasis, however; there is for pragmatists no strict dichotomy between process and content. The school curriculum, including the so-called traditional subjects, affords students the opportunity to investigate as reflective thinkers the scope of human understanding. They work as thinkers who see hypotheses to be tested in every field of inquiry.

A study of traditional subjects, therefore, may or may not be of interest at any given moment to the pragmatic teacher. If the study of these disciplines can be incorporated into activities leading to the resolution of problems, they are welcome. In fact, the resolution of many problems demands an interdisciplinary frame of reference; students therefore need to acquire information from a variety of fields if they are to solve complex problems. The pragmatist values the information, however, for its *utility* and may employ any methodology to pursue it as long as the students are actively engaged in the process.

Progressive Education

Although pragmatists contributed extensively to progressive educational thought and practice, that is, to *progressivism*, pragmatism and progressivism are separate entities. (For more information on progressivism see Knight, 1982; Kil-

> **The Pragmatist as Teacher**
>
> 1. assists students in understanding that truth in itself and as it is known is changeable;
>
> 2. trains students to utilize the scientific method to search for truth and solve problems;
>
> 3. arranges problems for students that require an interdisciplinary approach for resolution;
>
> 4. guides students' learning so that the outcomes will involve personal and social growth;
>
> 5. promotes learning activities that require the student to be directly involved in the process of inquiry;
>
> 6. involves students in value questions in an effort to lead them to develop a concern for societal growth;
>
> 7. prompts students to look for the utility of what they learn.

patrick, 1951; Graham, 1967.)[10] The progressive education movement, built partly upon the thinking of John Dewey and such pragmatists as William Heard Kilpatrick, coalesced largely around an opposition to a perceived rigidity in schooling—authoritarianism, conservatism, dogmatism, traditionalism, and absolutism. Leaders of the movement were noted for their support of pedagogical principles that were considered to be progressive: (1) a classroom centered on the child, (2) a curriculum based on interests, (3) a methodology oriented toward discovery, (4) a school focused on life, and (5) an environment shaped by cooperation. The movement eventually went far beyond, if not astray from, a rigorous pragmatism, and pragmatists were often mistakenly blamed for the excesses of sloppily practiced progressivism.

Romantic Humanism

During the middle of this century many progressive notions were incorporated into, and perhaps distorted by, the romantic humanism of such thinkers as A. S. Neill, Carl Rogers, and John Holt. (See Knight, 1982; Holt, 1967; Neill, 1960; Rogers, 1983.)[11] These individuals may also have been influenced by the existentialism of European thinkers of the nineteenth and twentieth centuries.

Existentialism

Existentialism, while treated here as a systematic philosophy, is actually a way of viewing the world (and schooling) that rejects the notion of a self-contained system of educational thought and practice. Its elements, or to state it another way, the existentialist *attitude*, can possibly be identified in the highly diverse writings of such thinkers as Søren Kierkegaard, Friedrich Nietzsche, Karl Jaspers, Jean-Paul Sartre, Karl Barth, Paul Tillich, and Albert Camus. Existentialists who have written on pedagogy include Martin Buber, Maxine Greene, and Donald Vandenberg. (See Power, 1982; Vandenberg, 1971; Greene, 1973.)[12]

8: Philosophical Beliefs and Teaching: Ideas That Guide What Teachers Do

REALITY

Existentialists are generally in agreement when they argue that reality is too complex and paradoxical and that education is too unpredictable and personal to fit neatly into a rational gestalt. Beyond that point, as with other philosophical perspectives, existential thinking varies tremendously. Two of the main streams of existentialist thought flow from the views of Kierkegaard and Sartre and others who can be roughly grouped with one or the other. These thinkers represent two quite different understandings of reality. Kierkegaard, a nineteenth-century theologian, felt that the orthodox Christianity of his day was impersonal, meaningless, and irrational. Sartre, a Nobel laureate who lived from 1905 to 1980, had significant influence over twentieth-century thought. Far from the theism of Kierkegaard (who died fifty years before Sartre was born), Sartre declared existence to be insignificant, worthless, and absurd. (It is necessary to understand that he defined all these terms in his work and did not use them as they are commonly used.) It is also important to note that Sartre found ways to justify and dignify existence and that these were not always identical even with those of his close existential friends, such as Albert Camus. Most existentialists, however, share Kierkegaard's and Sartre's feelings of initial despair and their pursuit of hope.

Religious Existentialists

Religious existentialists within Christian traditions found hope in a redefinition of the Christian—a person not noted for intellectually consenting to a set of beliefs but for a personal relationship with God. This redefinition created a new view of faith and reason. Reason provides conflicting opinions about the existence of God and may lead to atheism, but each person can reject reason to discover God by a *leap of faith*. The leap transcends reason, overcomes doubt, and secures meaning.

Nonreligious, or secular, existentialists, facing what they consider to be a meaningless, absurd, objective reality, have assumed that meaning must be found without belief in a god-like entity. If the secular existentialist finds hope, it is in the individual's freedom to choose. Each person finds meaning in deciding to be a person—a thinking, feeling, willing being. The material, objective world is radically different from the conscious, subjective person, who can create his or her essence by deciding what and who he or she wishes to be.

TRUTH AND VALUES

For some existentialists, truth is necessarily subjective. Others believe there is objective truth, as well as objective reality. The whole truth, however, is likely to be paradoxical, less declarative and more textured than that of many philosophical systems. Existentialists stress that all knowledge and perception has not been examined because it is not even available. Even if it were all open to analysis, existentialists maintain that, as traditionally understood, it would be worthless. Religious existentialists insist that truth, even the fact that God exists, is meaningless unless the individual personalizes it and is changed by doing so. Experiencing, accepting, and appropriating truth as part of one's personal beliefs is important. Passively accepting it as given is not important.

Truth Is Paradoxical

Personally Accepted Truth and Values

Values, like truth, are totally a subjective personal matter for some existentialists, whereas they are objective in part for others. In the former case, existentialists emphasize that each person creates his or her own values. In the latter, existentialists may refer to an objective set of ethical principles or criteria but once again add emphatically that intellectual understanding alone is insufficient. Values, like truth, must be personally accepted before they can be meaningful.

Among those existentialists who believe all values are entirely personal are

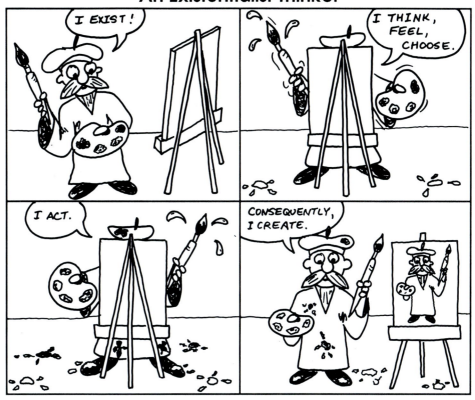

philosophers who seek to avoid a whimsical view of morality. Values, they argue, are only worthwhile if they are good for others as well as for oneself. Freedom and choice do not lead to moral anarchy but to personal and social responsibility. Thus, good is found in compassionate choice and action for others. Evil is the choice to conform—to conform to societal, familial, or peer pressures and values.

PEDAGOGY

In one sense, it makes no difference whether existentialistic teachers are nonreligious or religious, for the aim of schooling is to facilitate the development of what Sartre might call authentic people. *Authentic* people are individuals who recognize their freedom, utilize their options, and accept their responsibility. At the same time, authentic people reject an exclusively objective, impartial, rationalistic, deterministic, logical, and scientific philosophy of life. They passionately involve themselves in the selection, application, and appropriation of ideas, theories, and values. They courageously affirm the style of life that accompanies their philosophy of life.

Cultivating the Authentic Person

The existentialists have not generally addressed educational theory and practice, as their foci lie elsewhere. Existentialists are nevertheless clear on a variety of educational issues. First, their educational aim is well defined—to cultivate the authentic person. Second, the curriculum in the school is conceptualized as a tool for the student's self-realization. Perhaps most useful studies for this purpose include dialogues, discussions, and discoveries about such existential

> **The Existentialist as Teacher**
>
> 1. wants students to recognize that meaninglessness in life can be overcome by a leap of faith or by a creation of a personal meaning;
> 2. expects the student to live with the paradoxical nature of truth;
> 3. asks students to keep this question before them: "What does this idea or material mean to me?";
> 4. encourages discussions and dialogues about human tragedy, alienation, responsibility, and freedom;
> 5. nudges the student toward becoming an authentic human being;
> 6. challenges students to accept the responsibility and the results of their behavior;
> 7. strives to develop mutual respect among students engaged in the learning process.

concepts as authenticity, love, freedom, responsibility, death, values, conformity, alienation, and meaninglessness. Art, literature, religion, philosophy, history, and cognate areas may be helpful realms to examine and personalize.

Obviously, teachers are not automatons in the eyes of the existentialist. They enjoy freedom but are more concerned with their responsibility to guide their students toward an autonomous life. In nudging students toward authenticity, they value person-to-person interaction. They also internalize ideas. They challenge each student to ask, "What do these facts, ideas, and so forth mean to me? How should they affect my feelings, attitudes, decisions?" Further, they strive to see that all interaction is based upon a mutual respect by all parties. They recognize that the pursuit of truth is valuable but are always aware that the human is dehumanized if the content to be learned is considered greater than the learner.

Something to Think About

The following is a description of hypothetical teaching decisions:

Brian Lynd teaches ninth-grade social studies and science to three double-period classes of inner-city students, nearly all of whom come from very poor economic home situations. He is committed to doing all he can for his students. He realizes that knowing the content that he teaches is important to their future success and that they face end-of-year tests in order to pass on to tenth grade. He also realizes that most of his students face tremendous out-of-school problems and face great likelihood of defeat or failure in much that they do, in school and out.

Brian almost constantly faces decisions about what is best for his students—decisions such as what and how much information to cover, how to grade, what to do with students who try but still get most answers wrong, how often to allow class discussions to ramble on subjects about the out-of-school lives of the students instead of the planned topic, how much to get involved in student personal matters, and so forth. In the last week Brian had to decide the following:

- Should he allow a full-period discussion about AIDS instead of his planned science topic on nuclear waste when a student raised the issue and most of the class seemed interested?
- Should he allow Bobby to sleep all period because he had to work nights all week?
- Should he tell the students who asked that he and his fiancée live together?
- Should he give everyone in third period a passing grade on the last science test, since nearly everyone actually failed, with about equally poor scores?
- Should he skip the social studies lessons on due process and judicial review because they seem so abstract?
- Should he deal with the fact that Debbie is usually high on some substance in class?
- Should he ask Donald how his terminally ill father is and offer himself as someone for Donald to talk to if he would like?

> In what ways do you think teachers who subscribe to each of the philosophies described so far in this chapter—idealism, realism, pragmatism, existentialism—would respond to these situations?
> Which teachers who have different philosophies would respond in similar ways? Why?
> Which would have significantly different responses? Why?

After you complete the next part of this chapter, on contemporary philosophies, return to these questions and consider them in terms of those philosophies.

Contemporary Philosophies

In the earlier discussion of historical and modern philosophies of education, contemporary idealists, realists, pragmatists, and existentialists were mentioned. In fact, each of these philosophies was explained from the stance of living, contemporary, educational thinkers. Therefore, the term *contemporary*, as used here, simply refers to philosophies that are rather recent philosophical emphases. They may be seen as outgrowths of earlier idealism, realism, pragmatism, and existentialism, but they have some special features of their own. One of those

Table 8–1: Contemporary Philosophies of Education: The Role of the Teacher and Illustrative Thoughts

Philosophy	Role of the Teacher	Illustrative Thoughts
Reconstructionism	To develop builders of a better democratic world	"Teachers must address cultural crises and help build a new social order."
Futurism	To prepare students for the world of tomorrow	"Students must be taught strategies for adaptation and survival."
Behaviorism	To shape student behavior along prescribed lines	"Teachers should shape students into people who can contribute to society."
Perennialism	To produce rational beings who live according to traditional values	"The writings of great thinkers contain ideas and processes that all students need to understand."
Evangelicalism	To produce believing Christians	"All truth, including Christian beliefs, should be integrated into the thinking, choosing, and living of each student."
Marxism	To produce socialists who will build a classless world	"Teachers must break the control of the ruling class over schooling."
Essentialism	To equip students for productive life in today's world	"Students need specific competencies and information if they are to live intelligently as citizens and workers."

special features is a tendency to focus on pedagogical and/or societal questions. Another feature is that, with a few exceptions, beliefs about the nature of reality (metaphysics), the nature of knowledge (epistemology), and the nature of values (axiology) imbedded in them are implicit rather than explicit. Table 8–1 presents the contemporary philosophies and the role of the teacher under each of them.

Reconstructionism

Create a New World

Pragmatism, as a parent philosophy, has given birth to both reconstructionism and futurism. *Reconstructionism*, the older of the two, has been espoused by George S. Counts, William O. Stanley, and Theodore Brameld. (See Knight, 1982; Brameld, 1965; Counts, 1946; Stanley, 1952.)[13] Reconstructionists believe that the acute crises of the world require changes in both society and schooling. They say it is necessary to create a new world or a new order, one founded upon democratic principles and patterns of government. Failure to do so will lead up to the self-destruction of humankind.

They also demand that teachers become involved in creating this new world. To do this, teachers should show their students that it is imperative that they control their own destinies, not abandon them to the care of large corporations, which are driven largely by profits, and political officials, who may be motivated by personal ambition and guided by the principles of expediency.

For the reconstructionist, therefore, a fundamental goal of the school is to convince students that they should become eagerly involved in building a new society that includes the international community. This goal is critical, since such problems as nuclear weapons, hunger, nationalism, and racism can easily destroy worthwhile life on the planet. Individual affluence is not a goal of schooling. International cooperation and compassion are major goals.

Solve World Problems

Most reconstructionists strongly recommend studies that help students see current world problems and their potential solutions. Social studies, the social sciences, and problems courses are attractive to many of them but do not exhaust their interests. They believe scientific and technological knowledge are also necessary to help meet the needs of the world's people. If the objectives of reconstructionism are to be realized, schools need to prepare intellectually sophisticated and morally sensitive individuals.

Futurism

Strictly speaking, *futurism* is a perspective that is more inclusive than the ideas spawned by pragmatism and is in a sense a predecessor of much pragmatist thought. Throughout history, educational thinkers have been interested in the relationship of the school to the future. Only recently, however, has futurism as a movement made an impact upon educational policy and practice.

Understanding the past, controlling the present, and shaping the future are aims expressed by both pragmatists and reconstructionists. Futurists move beyond these positions to argue for another proposition, namely, that the person of tomorrow must be intellectually and emotionally capable of living in a strange new world. Since such futurists as Alvin Toffler, Harold Shane, and Robert Theobald argue or imply that the coming world and the person of tomorrow should possess certain characteristics, they are sometimes labeled *normative* futurists. (See Knight, 1982; Shane, 1973; Toffler, 1980.)[14]

Adaptation for the Unknown

Normative futurists often stipulate that schools should constitute and promote participatory democracy both through what they teach and by their example as operating institutions themselves. Rather than prepare students for a past that no longer exists or a present that is rapidly disappearing, teachers should, by their teaching and their example, prepare them to live in a democracy with many unknowns. Students, in order to live satisfactorily in this future, must acquire strategies for adaptation and survival. Adaptation, in particular, will require that students learn to think for themselves. Independent thought by the adult of tomorrow involves, among other abilities, thinking ethically, specifically, and creatively.

According to futurists, the school that cultivates independent thinking should also stimulate autonomous decision making. More than ever before, the future will belong to people who think and choose for themselves. This aim—developing tomorrow's thinkers and choosers—is partly an outcome of schooling that attempts to produce both liberally educated people and highly trained specialists. It is aided by students who recognize both the autonomy and the responsibility implied by the concepts of studying and learning. Students who learn to think independently, live democratically, choose ethically, interact tolerantly, and act wisely offer hope and promise for a preferable and promising future.

Behaviorism

Behaviorism, with its base in materialistic or scientific realism, is widely known as a system of psychology and was presented in that context in Chapter 4. The theories of past behavioral psychologists such as Ivan Pavlov, John B. Watson, Edward Thorndike, and B. F. Skinner, however, have been expanded from a philosophy of science into a worldview and, by some, into a philosophy of instruction. (See Bigge, 1982; Skinner, 1968; Watson, 1924.)[15]

Teachers as Behavioral Engineers

This instructional philosophy is based upon the premise that all behavior is caused and therefore predictable. Since teachers are commissioned to change the behavior of students, they should utilize the most effective and efficient means possible. Teachers are behavioral engineers, responsible for controlling the educational environment of students and, thereby, what students learn. Teachers are therefore key participants in building a planned, scientific, and promising society.

Reinforcement

In order to control students' learning, teachers must do several things. First, they must conscientiously identify their educational objectives and state them in behavioral terms. They must ask what student performances will demonstrate that the particular objectives have been achieved. They must break complex behaviors into small steps so that the total behavior can be learned. Second, teachers must reinforce those observable responses of students that indicate learning is occurring. They believe that rewarding correct student responses will result in those responses being practiced and that discouraging or punishing incorrect responses will cause students to abandon them. Third, teachers must carefully review the progress of each student to determine whether further goal analysis, new reinforcers, other curricular designs, and/or reinforcement schedules are needed. Since teachers cannot continuously observe each student as that student learns, they will want to consider using programmed textbooks, compartmentalized learning areas, teaching machines, computer programs, and behavioral contracts to help create desirable learning outcomes. These techniques, they believe, enable the teacher to apply the principles of a scientific pedagogy and to avoid one based upon tradition, opinion, or chance.

Perennialism

As scientific realism is a forerunner of behaviorism, so classical realism is a precursor of *perennialism*. Perennialists, especially the proponents of studying the Great Books of the Western World, have been influenced greatly by the thinking of Robert Hutchins, Stringfellow Barr, and Mortimer Adler. (See Knight, 1982; Adler, 1982.)[16] A fundamental proposition of perennialism is that education should liberate and fulfill students by developing their common essence, their ability to think and to choose.

Rational Thought and Responsible Choice

This aim is achieved by providing each person with a liberal education that cultivates rational thought and responsible choice. One method of doing this is to provide students with the opportunity to study the works of outstanding writers in all fields—art, mathematics, music, philosophy, logic, history, language, ethics, religion, and science. Through this approach, students can be introduced to the wisdom of the past and to the perennial truths and values of society. This exposure helps them learn to think critically, prepares them for life and its accompanying duties, and enables them to contribute to society as citizens.

Teachers, therefore, are accountable to some extent for their students' rational development. They are to teach reading, writing, computing, and other subjects in the lower grades; as the students mature, they are to raise provocative points, design stimulating exercises, question unexamined assumptions, discuss conflicting theories, and initiate critical analyses. They also are to focus attention on permanent values, pass on perennial truths, demand reasons for opinions, insist on evidence for conclusions, and inculcate a love for precise thinking. For the perennialist, education is therefore a cooperative enterprise that sharpens a person's rational powers and stimulates his or her potential for making good choices.

This responsibility of teachers, however, cannot readily be realized unless students choose to develop and utilize their intellectual capacities. That is, students must assume partial responsibility for their own learning. Perennialists argue that the educated person is neither an accident of socialization nor a mechanical product of education. Instead, a person becomes educated by choosing to utilize the resources of school and society to cultivate his or her intellect.

Evangelicalism

Evangelicalism, as might be expected, is built largely upon the philosophical foundation laid by religious realism. It is a diverse movement based upon a common set of Judeo-Christian beliefs that include the following: God is a personal, rational, creative being; humankind is made in the likeness of God; nature and scripture reveal truths that are otherwise impossible to know; life has purpose and meaning in the love and service of God and others; ethical principles are based upon the rational and moral nature of God; human beings are alienated from God and need to be reconciled in Jesus Christ. Contemporary exponents of the viewpoint include C. S. Lewis, Frank E. Gaebelein, Carl F. H. Henry, Ruth Haycock, and Paul Kniel. (See Peterson, 1986; Gaebelein, 1968; Lewis, 1969.)[17]

Bible-believing Students

Outside these areas of agreement, evangelical thinkers differ significantly on the purpose of schooling and the role of the teacher. Some argue that the goal of the school is to produce separated, Bible-believing Christian fundamentalists. They believe the teacher is charged with passing on beliefs such as the following: The student ought to avoid involvement in non-Christian amusements, reject ideas founded upon the theories of evolution, abstain from certain kinds of clothing, shun liberal ecclesiastical and political ideas and affiliations, and oppose practices and beliefs that stem from anti-Christian worldviews. As a rule of thumb, many fundamentalist teachers inculcate these views by quoting scripture or lecturing on specific topics. When teaching any subject, the fundamentalist works to develop in students a respect for the scriptures by indicating how they apply to particular issues, solve problems, and answer questions.

Mature Christian Thinkers

Mainstream evangelical philosophers identify additional educational goals; some even disagree totally with the ideas emphasized by fundamentalists. For many, a primary educational goal is the development of mature Christian thinkers. Mature Christian thinkers should have a liberal education that leads to an understanding of issues surrounding the reliability of sacred literature and the credibility of the Christian faith. Additionally, the mature Christian thinker should be able to apply Christian principles and knowledge from all branches of understanding to personal, social, political, and religious issues. Thus, mature Christian thinking should result in a life-style that appropriates all truth.

From an evangelical perspective, the role of teachers is vital. They believe that teachers should not only challenge students to discover honest answers for themselves but also be responsible for modeling the attitudes, dispositions, and skills of a liberally educated Christian. These may include a healthy self-image, concern for the poor, commitment to social justice, and conservation of natural resources. Ultimately, teachers provide students with a model and rationale for developing into mature Christian thinkers who act in the light of their worldviews.

Marxism

Although the impact of materialistic realism on contemporary *Marxism* is obvious, Marxism, like other contemporary philosophies, accepts and rejects portions of its heritage. Its claim that reality is exclusively material, its attention to the struggle between social classes, its belief in the inevitability of socialism, its explanation of the means of production, and its concept of the utility of truth have changed little over the years. In the field of education however, present-day interpreters of Karl Marx, Friedrich Engels, and Vladimir Ilyich Lenin, and the other early socialistic theorists push beyond the teachings of these thinkers. The writings of Samuel Bowles, Herbert Gintis, Kevin Harris, Rachel Sharp, and Michael Apple clearly demonstrate this progression (Ozmon & Craver, 1986; Bowles & Gintis, 1976; Apple, 1979).[18] These writers, however, do not ignore the Marxian view of the historical development of societies and the need to escape the exploitation of the ruling classes.

Schools Are Part of the Problem

When contemporary Marxists apply their ideas to education itself, they focus a great deal of attention and criticism on schooling. At least in most of the Western world, Marxists see schools as a part of the culture that exploits the proletariat, the class ruled over by others. The bourgeoisie, or ruling class, controls the purposes and practices of schooling—and thereby its outcomes as well.

This happens because public schools in capitalist societies are institutions controlled by the government, which in turn is greatly influenced by the ruling class, by big business, and by the interests of industry and technology. Through the schools, the capitalist ruling class sees that certain kinds of knowledge are taught, thereby legitimating its own cultural values and guaranteeing its own future and its position of control. The result is that socially, economically, and politically powerful groups continue to control all material—physical, political, educational, economic, cultural—conditions, and employment opportunities.

The role of the Marxist teacher in a capitalist society may not be immediately obvious, but several generalizations are possible. First, the Marxist teacher should awaken students to the reality that encompasses them. That is to say, the teacher should help students recognize that they have been inducted into a capitalist mindset and are blind to the real world. They have had, and continue to have, their personalities, values, beliefs, and aspirations imposed upon them. They have been convinced they are free while they live enslaved to the wishes of the ruling class.

Second, the Marxist teacher should enable students to understand that they cannot realize their own potential in a world that deprives them of the personal freedom, social justice, and material circumstances necessary to do so. Potentiality cannot become actuality without conditions that both allow and encourage development. Therefore, teachers should prepare students to counter the oppressive system.

Work for a Classless Society

Finally, the Marxist teacher can contribute greatly to the liberation of all peoples by encouraging students to work for a classless society, a people's democracy. That classless society would come about when each person is valued for his or her contribution to life in a communal environment. It would be a political entity that is governed by people who are concerned with everyone and with everyone's real needs. The teacher, then, is a necessary factor, for students must be awakened to the political ideology that engulfs them, to the material conditions essential to self-actualization, and to the type of government concerned with justice and respect for all people.

Essentialism

Common-Sense Schooling

Essentialism, unlike most contemporary educational philosophies, cannot be easily and neatly tied to a historical philosophy, although some suggest that it is at least related to idealism and realism. Others think it is simply a common-sense interpretation of schooling—a theory of education that stems from the thinking of the average intelligent person. The association of such people as William Bagley, William Brickman, Arthur Bestor, and Hyman Rickover with the philosophy may support the latter opinion. (See Power, 1982; Bestor, 1955; Rickover, 1962.)[19]

The emphases of essentialism are straightforward:

1. The teacher should be an effective instructor and disciplinarian.
2. The curriculum ought to be based upon "the basics" and other useful information.
3. The student should become a self-disciplined learner and responsible student.

More specifically, these ideas imply that the elementary school teacher is concerned with teaching the skills of listening, reading, writing, and computing. The secondary school teacher reinforces previously learned skills and passes on information from the fields of history, mathematics, science, literature, and language.

What is the desired outcome of education from an essentialist viewpoint? Answers vary, but many essentialists think schools should prepare students to live intelligently and successfully in today's society. A high school graduate should be prepared to act as an informed citizen, work as an efficient employee, and live as an informed and aware human being. In order to ensure that this outcome is accomplished, many essentialists focus their attention on the need for schools to pass on technical, scientific, and, occasionally, vocational skills and information. Still the essential teacher does not think this is all there is to schooling, for to live as an intelligent human being implies at least an introduction to the ideas, events, and people that shape the present and that offer insight into living itself.

EDUCATIONAL RESEARCH

A Philosophical Perspective

This Educational Research section asks you to pause in your study of research on teaching and schools in order to think about the interchange between educational research and philosophy—how research is affected by philosophy and how philosophy is affected by research. It describes some of the ways philosophers look at research, and it uses ideas from other Educational Research sections as examples.

Philosophers, like other specialists who study teaching and schools, examine education from a particular perspective; and this point of view influences the way they analyze and evaluate what they learn. The perspective also enables them to offer advice to other educators. For instance, philosophers warn that teachers do not adopt a teaching style, learning theory, or curricular design simply because of a research report; and researchers do not engage in a specific kind of research simply because of an idealized theoretical idea. They remind us that all individuals who work with educational phenomena begin with a cluster of philosophical beliefs that, with or without their awareness, shape their professional choices, including their selection of techniques, materials, hypotheses, explanations, and recommendations.

One cluster of beliefs that has had especially important influences on educators as they establish research agendas and interpret research data produced by others is their beliefs about human nature. For example, because theorists such as B. F. Skinner, Wolfgang Kohler, and Jean Piaget made separate assumptions about human nature, they approached their studies differently, and the elements of learning theory that they generated do not consist of a single set of coherent principles.

Recommendations about Evaluating Research

Because of this—the fact that beliefs influence research—philosophers make a number of recommendations about evaluating research. Among these recommendations are the following:

1. Educators need to understand that beliefs affect research and interpretations of research.

2. The effect of a researcher's philosophical beliefs on his or her studies should be carefully assessed.

3. The alternatives to a researcher's philosophical beliefs, hypotheses, and interpretations should be considered and evaluated.

4. The relative merits of a researcher's work should be decided in view of philosophical beliefs.

5. The knowledge gained from research should be used judiciously.

Research Data and Beliefs

A second way in which philosophers' perspectives influence their view of research can be illustrated by reexamining Lloyd Dunn's criticisms of separate special education classes, as reported in the Educational Research section of Chapter 4. Dunn, although not a philosopher, concluded that it is morally wrong to classify students and then separate handicapped students into special education classes. His rationale for concluding that the practice is wrong is related to what he saw as both the intentions of educators and the outcomes of the separation. The intention of some educators was merely to get misfits and minority group members out of "normal" classrooms. The outcomes that he considered reprehensible included the lowering of the achievement by the disadvantaged, the reduction of teachers' expectations of their students, damages to children's self-images, and an increase in inferior feelings in students.

Although Dunn concluded that the practice of separating handicapped students was not effective educationally for students, suppose for a moment that that were not the case. Assume instead that the research data had indicated that the practice significantly enhanced the learning of handicapped students. Further, assume that all of the intentions of educators had been noble. If both of these assumptions had been correct, however, the separate-class approach to educating handicapped students would still have had a bad impact upon the self-images and feelings of handicapped students. In this hypothetical situation, research would have prompted a serious conflict of values—the practice would have worked educationally, and it would have been well intended, but would it have been ethical?

Several philosophical points surface from this example. First, educators need to be concerned with the morality of educational practice, as well as with teaching effectiveness; and the morality of the practice should have priority. (Just because a practice works, does not make it right.) Second, although researchers as scientists describe what is or was, rather than what ought to be, their work frequently involves ethical issues. (Dunn argued that segregating handicapped students was morally wrong. When he did, he spoke not as a scientist but as an ethicist.) Third, the soundness of researchers' ethical positions is as important as the soundness of their research design, and both need to be analyzed. Fourth, moral issues, while partly informed by ethical principles, human intentions, educational outcomes, and related matters, are also dependent upon facts. (Without the outcomes Dunn identified, it would have been much more difficult to conclude that separate classes for the handicapped are wrong.)

A Two-Way Interaction

Although philosophy guides research and the ways in which research findings are used, the reverse is also true: Research also influences philosophy. In fact, any educator's philosophy of education can and should profit immeasurably from educational research; and educators who are so rigid philosophically that they ignore research data do so at their own peril and at the peril of their students. For example, research on communication apprehension, which is discussed later in the Educational Research section of Chapter 13, may cause teachers to alter part of their philosophy of teaching; that is, they may reject the belief isolate the unruly ones for individualized studies with programmed textbooks and teaching machines.

At first, Mr. Pavid attempted to handle misbehavior by ignoring it. Later he talked to his class about respecting the rights of others. He also reminded his students that the choices they were making were not isolated decisions but were related to their creating themselves as persons. Eventually, he experimented with a variety of techniques suggested by other teachers. Among other things, he glared at troublemakers, sent students to the principal, arranged conferences with parents, and applied corporal punishment. The most successful technique he tried, however, was the isolate-and-learn strategy.

By about the middle of his first year in the classroom, Mr. Pavid started having second thoughts about being a teacher. His views of the ideal teacher were too far removed from his everyday experience. His self-doubts caused him to question himself nearly every day. He felt that he was bouncing from one ineffective strategy or theory to another. He wondered why techniques work for some teachers but not for others, especially himself. He had tried everything he knew—including Ms. Jones's way of teaching—and nothing seemed to work.

Before the school year was over, Mr. Pavid had established a number of routines that enabled him to reach his educational goals. He also developed a reputation for being a stern disciplinarian, a wizard with programmed instruction, and an advocate of students' rights. His success, he felt, was largely due to the graduate course he had taken on behavior modification and to the survival skills he had learned from seasoned teachers at his school. While he was pleased that he had learned to handle behavioral problems and instructional tasks, his greatest pleasure was working with small groups of students on subjects they chose to study. In addition, he enjoyed talking with his fellow teachers about the rights that students, even very young ones, have.

CONCLUSION

Building a philosophy of education is a long, ongoing process. The original idealists, realists, pragmatists, and existentialists did not wake up one morning with their complete systems of thought ready for distribution. Nor did the developers of reconstructionism, futurism, behaviorism, perennialism, evangelicalism, Marxism, and essentialism hastily arrive at their destinations. To the degree that they consciously philosophized, they sought answers to fundamental questions over a period of years, if not throughout their lives. They consistently asked questions of themselves:

1. What do you mean?
2. How do you know?

3. How should these data be understood?
4. Do these findings form a coherent pattern?

Prior to their philosophizing, they groped for answers, probed for clarity, wondered about evidence, and looked for reasons.

Fortunately, most teachers also construct their own philosophies of education over time, revising them as necessary. In doing so, they draw on all of their studies and experiences. Some contribute directly and others indirectly. Studies in educational psychology, learning theory, instructional methodology, classroom management, and curriculum development are particularly informative. Also important is the contribution of teaching itself to an educational philosophy. Teaching contributes by providing fresh insights, testing suggested strategies, discrediting questionable declarations, and confirming research findings.

When you are an experienced teacher, you will quickly realize that some philosophies of education address the realities and concerns of secondary teachers more than they do those of early childhood educators. Experience will also inform you that some educational philosophies better answer the questions raised about certain types of students than do others—for example, students at different grade levels, those with weak academic backgrounds, those from affluent homes, and those in religious schools.

At the same time, as you develop professionally, you will want to engage in a concerted, focused study of educational philosophy. The descriptions of philosophies given here are intentionally phrased in as positive terms as possible, given our own biases. Of necessity, not all philosophies were included and only a limited number of viewpoints were seriously considered. The continuing search into the philosophy of education will provide you with intellectual stimulation, an element in the lives of teachers that is often missing from less challenging professions.

SUMMARY

This chapter surveyed some of the most fundamental ideas in philosophy of education. First, it noted that teachers teach differently from one another and that these differences are partially attributable to their philosophical beliefs. Educational differences are reflected, too, in various kinds of educational institutions, laws, and textbooks.

Second, the chapter illustrated educational philosophy as a set of intellectual activities that teachers do. These activities are clarification, justification, interpretation, and systematization. Taken together, these activities enable teachers to think clearly, logically, ethically, and comprehensively about educational concerns.

Third, the chapter analyzed some of the main Western philosophies and their connections to the philosophy of education. Although the historical roots of each were noted, emphasis was placed upon the ideas, especially those relating to education, of contemporary idealists, realists, pragmatists, existentialists, reconstructionists, evangelicalists, Marxists, and essentialists. The views of each group of philosophers on metaphysics, epistemology, axiology, and pedagogy were noted. All of these ideas were presented with the goal of preparing you to formulate your own philosophy of education in mind.

STUDY QUESTIONS

1. Which philosophy do you prefer at this point in your thinking? In terms of education, what is the greatest *strength* of the position you like *least*? What is the greatest *weakness* of the position you like *most*?

2. What would you do if you were told that your educational philosophy is out of place in the school where you teach? Is it ever fair to restrict the implementation or application of a teacher's philosophy of education? If so, when?

3. If you were free to organize a school completely as you desired, would you welcome teachers with different philosophies from yours? Why or why not?

4. Are school accountability efforts, teacher evaluation, and student assessment programs covert ways of manipulating schooling and imposing a particular educational philosophy on teachers and students? If so, should teachers resist such attempts? If so, when?

5. Do you find yourself combining ideas from a number of educational philosophies? If yes, why do you take this combinationist approach? What are the advantages of this approach? And the disadvantages?

6. Should teachers have a social mission? If so, what is it? If not, why?

BIBLIOGRAPHY

Barrow, R. (1981). *The philosophy of schooling.* Brighton, Sussex: Wheatsheat.

Bigge, M. L., & Reynolds, G. W. (1982). *Philosophies for teachers.* Columbus, OH: Charles E. Merrill Publishing Co.

Chambers, J. H. (1983). *The achievement of education: An examination of key concepts in educational practice.* New York: Harper & Row.

Duck, L. (1981). *Teaching with charisma.* Boston: Allyn and Bacon.

Fitzgibbons, R. E. (1981). *Making educational decisions: An introduction to philosophy of education.* New York: Harcourt Brace Jovanovich.

Griese, A. A. (1981). *Your philosophy of education: What is it?* Santa Monica, CA: Goodyear Publishing Company.

Hirst, P. H. (1983). *Educational theory and its foundation disciplines.* London: Routledge & Kegan Paul.

Howick, W. H. (1980). *Philosophies of education.* Danville, IL: Interstate Printers and Publishers.

Knight, G. R. (1982). *Issues and alternatives in educational philosophy.* Berrien Springs, MI: Andrews University Press.

Moore, T. W. (1982). *Philosophy of education: An introduction.* London: Routledge & Kegan Paul.

O'Hear, A. (1981). *Education, society and human nature: An introduction to the philosophy of education.* London: Routledge & Kegan Paul.

O'Neill, W. F. (1981). *Educational ideologies: Contemporary expressions of educational philosophy.* Santa Monica, CA: Goodyear Publishing Company.

Ozmon, H. A., & Craver, S. M. (1986). *Philosophical foundations of education* (3rd ed.). Columbus, OH: Merrill Publishing Company.

Peterson, M. L. (1986). *Philosophy of education: Issues and options.* Downers Grove, IL: InterVarsity Press.

Power, E. J. (1982). *Philosophy of education: Studies in philosophies, schooling and educational policies.* Englewood Cliffs, NJ: Prentice-Hall.

Simpson, D. J., & Jackson, M. J. B. (1984). *The teacher as philosopher: A primer in philosophy of education.* Toronto: Methuen.

Woods, R. G., & Barrow R. St. C. (1981). *An introduction to philosophy of education* (2nd ed.). London: Methuen.

NOTES

1. All three descriptions of teachers in this Snapshot are hypothetical, but the actions, characteristics, and philosophical positions presented are drawn from teachers whom the authors of this text have known.
2. Simpson, D. J., & Jackson, M. J. B. (1984). *The teacher as philosopher: A primer in philosophy of education.* Toronto: Methuen Publications; Soltis, J. F. (1978). *An introduction to the analysis of educational concepts* (2nd ed.): Reading, MA: Addison-Wesley.
3. See Barrow, R. (1981). *The philosophy of schooling.* Brighton, Sussex: Wheatsheat; Chambers, J. H. (1983). *The achievement of education: An examination of key concepts in educational practice.* New York: Harper & Row.
4. Fitzgibbons, R. E. (1981). *Making educational decisions: An introduction to philosophy of education.* New York: Harcourt Brace Jovanovich.
5. Power, E. J. (1982). *Philosophy of education: Studies in philosophies, schooling and educational policies.* Englewood Cliffs, NJ: Prentice-Hall.
6. Griese, A. A. (1981). *Your philosophy of education: What is it?* Santa Monica, CA: Goodyear Publishing Company; O'Neill, W. F. (1981). *Educational ideologies: Contemporary expressions of educational philosophy.* Santa Monica, CA: Goodyear Publishing Company.
7. Butler, J. D. (1968). *Four philosophies and their practice in education and religion* (3rd ed.). New York: Harper & Row; Brightman, E. S., & Beck, R. N. (1963). *An introduction to philosophy* (3rd ed.). New York: Holt, Rinehart and Winston.
8. Martin, W. O. (1969). *Realism in education.* New York: Harper & Row; Broudy, H. S. (1961). *Building a philosophy of education.* Englewood Cliffs, NJ: Prentice-Hall; Maritain, J. (1938). *True humanism.* New York: Charles Scribner's Sons.
9. Dewey, J. (1933). *How we think.* Boston: D. C. Heath & Company; James, W. (1946). *Talks to teachers.* New York: Holt, Rinehart and Winston.
10. Knight, G. R. (1982). *Issues and alternatives in educational philosophy.* Berrien Springs, MI: Andrews University Press; Kilpatrick, W. H. (1951). *Philosophy of education.* New York: Macmillan; Graham, P. A. (1967). *Progressive education; From Arcady to academe.* New York: Teachers College Press.
11. Holt, J. (1967). *How children learn.* New York: Pitman Publishing Corporation; Neill, A. S. (1960). *Summerhill: A radical approach to child rearing.* New York: Hart Publishing

Company; Rogers, C. (1983). *Freedom to learn* (rev. ed.). Columbus, OH: Charles E. Merrill Publishing Company.

12. Vandenberg, D. (1971). *Being and education: An essay in existential phenomenology.* Englewood Cliffs, NJ: Prentice-Hall; Greene, M. (1973). *Teacher as stranger.* Belmont, CA: Wadsworth Publishing Company.

13. Brameld, T. (1965). *Toward a reconstructed philosophy of education.* New York: The Dryden Press; Counts, G. S. (1946). *Education and the promise of America.* New York: Macmillan; Stanley, W. O. (1952). *Education and social integration.* New York: Teachers College Press.

14. Shane, H. (1973). *The educational significance of the future.* Bloomington, IN: Phi Delta Kappa; Toffler, A. (1980). *The third wave.* New York: William Morrow.

15. Bigge, M. L. (1982). *Educational philosophies for teachers.* Columbus, OH: Merrill Publishing Company; Skinner, B. F. (1968). *The technology of teaching.* Englewood Cliffs, NJ: Prentice-Hall; Watson, J. B. (1924). *Behaviorism.* New York: W. W. Norton & Co.

16. Adler, J. A. (1982). *The paideia proposal: An educational manifesto.* New York: Macmillan; Hutchins, R. M. (1968). *The learning society.* New York: Praeger.

17. Peterson, M. L. (1986). *Philosophy of education: Issues and options.* Downers Grove, IL: InterVarsity Press; Gaebelein, F. E. (1968). *The pattern of God's truth.* Chicago: Moody Press; Lewis, C. S. (1969). *The best of C. S. Lewis.* Washington, DC: Christianity Today, Inc.

18. Ozmon, H. A., & Craver, S. M. (1986). *Philosophical foundations of education* (3rd ed.). Columbus, OH: Merrill Publishing Company; Bowles, S., & Gintis, H. (1976). *Schooling in capitalist America: Educational reform and the contradictions of economic life.* New York: Basic Books; Apple, M. W. (1979). *Ideology and curriculum.* London: Routledge & Kegan Paul.

19. Bestor, A. E. (1955). *The restoration of learning.* New York: Knopf; Rickover, H. G. (1962). *Swiss schools and ours: Why theirs are better.* Boston: Atlantic-Little, Brown.

CHAPTER 9

Theories of Learning: Ideas from Educational Psychology that Guide Teaching
JEANNE M. PLAS

INTRODUCTION

This chapter examines such questions as how learning occurs and which conditions help to create good learning in schools. In part because much information about the human central nervous system and its relation to thinking and behavior is yet undiscovered, the chapter cannot present everything we need to know about learning. It describes, however, several of the important learning theories that are available to teachers today. These theories are currently guiding classroom practice; new ideas are being developed and tested for possible future use.

The chapter explores three general theories of learning—behavior theory, cognitive theory, and Piagetian theory. Further, it describes the development of each theory and the ways in which teachers use each. Chapter 10 next extends the ideas presented in this chapter by describing five models of instruction that rely upon and apply elements of learning theories in the form of rather precise approaches to instruction.

At several points during the chapter you are asked to think about applications of learning theory to classroom situations. The Snapshot provides a glimpse of an imaginary teacher from the past who had to cope without learning theories. Later in the chapter, you are asked to think again about this teacher and propose what she would have done if current theories had been available to her. In the chapter conclusion, a similar case study of a future teacher provides a contrasting situation to consider. The Analysis section describes a conversation among three contemporary teachers that illustrates how learning theory can be used to address particular learning difficulties.

The Educational Research section describes experimental research efforts as illustrations of the type of investigation often done by psychologists who study the learning process. That type of research is contrasted with the more interpretive and descriptive studies described in the Educational Research sections of the last three chapters.

SNAPSHOT

This Snapshot is about the first-year teaching experience of a teacher in 1859. As you read, ask yourself the following questions:

- Why do some children learn more quickly than others?
- Why might a child do well in one subject while doing poorly in others?
- What is the relationship of motivation to learning?
- What is the role of parents in the actual process of learning?
- In what ways does this episode illustrate a teacher's need for learning theory?

LEARNING IN THE WILD WEST

Long ago, early on a crisp and sunny morning in a small western town at the foot of the mountains, Miss Priscilla Hope gave her long skirt a couple of brisk tugs and a yank. Having made sure that no part of either ankle was visible, she sailed through the schoolhouse door with an air of quiet confidence that was not exactly false, though it surely hid from awareness such things as her sweating palms and slightly irregular heartbeat.

Miss Hope was new in town and new to her job. In fact, her job itself was new—schoolteacher for the territory's children. And what a group of children it was! There were eleven in all. Caleb, the eldest, was twelve years old and the son of the territory's richest man, the owner of Peterson's General Store. Silas Peterson wanted his only son to learn "figures and readin'" so that he could be of help in the store. In fact, Mr. Peterson had been one of those who had insisted that the territory was ready for a school and a teacher.

Little Bertram Blevins was the youngest, the seven-year-old son of the area's most successful miner. Bertram did not talk much, and his father had reasoned that learning how to read would cause the boy to speak up more often. He further reasoned that spending more than three days a week at the school would be a waste of the boy's time, and he had been quick to let Miss Hope know his opinion when he had escorted her off the Overland Stage the week before.

Sarah Finn, age nine, was in school simply because her mother adored her and wanted her, as she said "to be accomplished." The only other girl in the group, Amanda Suzette Todd, also nine years old, was there because her mother was a younger sister of Sarah Finn's mother, who had insisted that Amanda accompany Sarah. ("It wouldn't 'do' to have only one girl around

all those boys, you know.") Mrs. Finn had warned her sister not to be upset when Sarah learned faster and better than her cousin. She also had taken Miss Hope aside at the get-acquainted picnic to let her know that steps should be taken to protect hurt feelings when little Sarah outshone all the other children.

Most of the territory's children were not in school that first morning. They were helping their mothers and fathers—often taking care of young animals or young children. A couple of families thought that they might send their children over to the school in a month or two, when the weather got bad. Miss Hope planned to visit every family in the area to talk about the school and what their children could learn there.

On that first morning, she began by calling on Ephraim Brook, whose parents wanted him to preach and had let Miss Hope know that nine-year-old Ephraim was expected to learn to read the Book of Genesis before Christmas. When Ephraim was told to turn to the first page of the reader that Miss Hope had brought all the way from St. Louis, he just looked at her and began to cry. His crying scared Amanda so much that she began to cry even louder than Ephraim. Sarah became screamingly indignant at both of them, and Caleb took the opportunity to scoot out the door to hurl taunts at a passing dog. In the midst of all the confusion, not even Miss Hope was able to notice that quiet little Bertram was mouthing some of the words in the reader silently to himself as he began to hum and smile a little bit.

Eventually, Miss Hope learned much more about her students. She learned that under threat of physical punishment, Ephraim was not allowed to read anything but the Bible; Amanda was really good at spelling but could not seem to "add up" numbers at all; the adored Sarah seemed hopelessly slow in every subject; and Caleb always wanted to read the lines backward for some unknown reason. She also learned that Corey Laird, who could do nothing else with his head, was always able to get the right answer if he was measuring things or guessing at something like the amount of milk in a pail; that three of the oldest boys never wanted to come to school and so rarely did; and that little Bertram Blevins learned everything about an hour or a day before Miss Hope got around to teaching it. All in all, it could probably be said that the teacher learned more than her students.

By springtime, Priscilla Hope had decided that her three-month teaching course back in St. Louis had not really taught her a thing about what causes children to learn. And it certainly had not even addressed the issue of what makes them *want* to learn. When the spring planting began, she got back into an Overland Stage and headed out of the territories—which more or less got back to normal. Little Bertram Blevins was very quiet once more.

THE NATURE OF LEARNING

Things have changed quite a bit in American education since Miss Hope got back into that stagecoach. Teachers today have a vast amount of knowledge compared to teachers of her time, and they can apply that knowledge to what they do. Part of that new knowledge comes from the study of how learning actually occurs, and the information is fundamental in most teacher education programs. Courses in learning and educational psychology often precede or are taught concurrently with teaching methods courses.

Theories, Not Facts

However, if the issues are much clearer for today's teachers than they were a century and a half ago, it is still true that a definitive understanding of the learning process remains elusive. Today we have theories of learning to guide teaching; that is, we have a number of rather reliable speculations on the nature of learning that help direct research programs and guide practical classroom approaches to helping children learn. Nevertheless, current research findings and the practical classroom approaches that have developed from them are still based only on theories. They do not rest on solid, quantifiable descriptions of what actually constitutes learning.

It may be some time in the next century before teachers will possess definitive information on human learning processes. For now, they must be content to master one or more of the currently accepted theories of learning and its various classroom applications.

In this chapter you will read descriptions of the three most often relied-upon theories of learning available today—behavior theory, general cognitive theory, and Piagetian theory. The relationship of these theories to one another will also be addressed within a discussion of their applicability to various teaching styles. Because this text is introductory, a number of theories of learning, such as perceptual, Freudian, transpersonal, and humanistic, are not discussed, though you may study them in later courses.

Theory and Teaching Style

Just as most teachers bring to their classrooms a teaching philosophy, so each teacher brings a unique teaching personality, or style, to the classroom. Usually, that person's teaching style is more consistent with one of the theories of learning and its practical applications than with the others. Since there is no definitive approach to human learning, teachers are wise to take advantage of this situation and connect their unique strengths and habits of style to a learning theory that seems especially suited to those strengths and performances.

As you read this chapter, select the learning theory that seems to be most consistent with your own teaching personality and ideas about instruction. When you read Chapter 10, make a similar selection from any of the models of instruction that are described. After making both selections, compare your two choices and explore why you chose as you did.

Motivation

This chapter includes formal and informal considerations of the relationship of motivation to learning. The old saying that you can lead a horse to water, but you cannot make it drink has special meaning for schools and is applicable to all students. Even when we are sure of the best approach for teaching a specific subject to a specific child, that child's level of motivation can effectively retard or enhance the amount of learning that will take place. As you move through this chapter, divide your attention among three issues: the *how* of learning, the *why* of learning, and the *unique styles* of teachers and learners.

The Need for Learning Theory

Sometimes beginning teachers wonder whether it makes sense to study something if it is only a theory. Why learn something if we are not sure it is the truth?

The answer is actually rather simple. We learn theories because they are useful to us, especially in the absence of more solid information.

That principle applies to learning theory as well as theories in general. Although a clear understanding of the specific processes controlling learning are not available at the moment, teachers need guidance about how to produce or enhance student learning. In the absence of harder facts, the more important contemporary theories of learning serve as the best guides available. Therefore, it is necessary that teachers gain a working knowledge of aspects of various theories of learning that seem to have promise for the teaching situations in which they find themselves.

Theories as Guides

Kurt Lewin, an early pioneer of social psychology, once commented that "there is nothing so practical as a good theory" (quoted in Marrow 1969).[1] Through this statement he made the point that theory directs our action. A good theory prompts action, shows us where to look for trouble spots, and suggests a course of remediation. Good theory is one of the best tools a teacher can have.

The theories described below offer suggestions concerning the rules that govern learning. They also offer suggestions for action when the rules seem to be breaking down for a given child or for a given *kind* of child. Thus, these theories are tools that teachers must have access to in order to become a master professional. At some point during the translation of theory into practice, master teachers transform the science of education into the art of teaching. Table 9–1 lists the learning theories presented in this chapter, and their primary characteristics.

Table 9–1. Primary Characteristics of Learning Theories

Learning Theories	Primary Characteristics
Behavior theory	Behavior is learned and is extrinsically influenced.
Association theory	An association of events stimulates memory and behavior; learning occurs because of associations among stimuli.
Reinforcement theory	Consequences of actions reinforce behavior; learning occurs because it is rewarded.
Cognitive theory	Information-processing insight
Piagetian theory	Interaction with environment leads to adaptation, which includes assimilation and accommodation. This is both a cognitive and a developmental theory.

GENERAL THEORIES

Behavior Theory

During this century, behavior theorists have produced a great amount of work. As the name implies, *behavior theory* concentrates on the function of human behavior as people engage in their most important task—adaptation to the environment around them. There are a variety of behavior theories. Each emphasizes a somewhat different set of circumstances surrounding human behavior. Despite the differences among the various behavior theories, they all agree that behavior is learned. Thus, it is important to understand that, fundamentally, all behavior theories are learning theories. Behaviorists believe that even something as complex as personality, for example, is a learned phenomenon.

Although labels used over the years to identify types of behavior theory vary to some extent, this discussion relies on a somewhat conventional classification system that divides behavior theory into two types—*association theory* and *reinforcement theory*. The discussion emphasizes reinforcement theory because this type has greatest applicability to schools and classrooms and because it has been the one most often used within school settings. However, association theory is discussed first because it was developed first chronologically, and the later reinforcement theorists have often established their positions on the basis of comparisons and contrasts to the earlier associationist thinking.

Association Theory

Pavlov, 1849–1936

Ivan Petrovich Pavlov, a Russian scientist whose major contributions to science were in physiology, is probably best known today for a contribution that most people consider psychological rather than physiological (See Babkin, 1949).[2] Shortly before the turn of the twentieth century, Pavlov and his laboratory workers were engaged in a study of the physiological processes that control digestion. Their subjects included dogs. In that effort, Pavlov happened to notice that after the dogs had become accustomed to the conditions and routines in the laboratory, they usually began to salivate at the sight of the food keeper, rather than at the time when the daily food allotment was actually presented to them. Pavlov, although initially rather uninterested in what he saw, reasoned that the process of digestion began to occur in the dogs' bodies earlier in the chain of events he was studying than had previously been suspected.

Conditioned Reflex

Because of this phenomenon, Pavlov and his workers began to call saliva a "psychic secretion." He thought of the production of saliva in such an instance as a *conditioned reflex* and believed that dogs and other animals had no more control over salivation at the sight of a food keeper than they did when food was actually placed in their mouths.

As Pavlov pursued his study of the causes of salivation, he arranged for other things to happen at the time when the food keeper appeared or just before he appeared. For example, he rang a bell or showed the dogs a card with a circle drawn on it. After doing these things a few times, he found that the dogs salivated at the sound of the bell or at the sight of the circle. In fact, they salivated at the sound of the bell or the sight of the circle even when food was not in sight or not likely to arrive within a specified period of time.

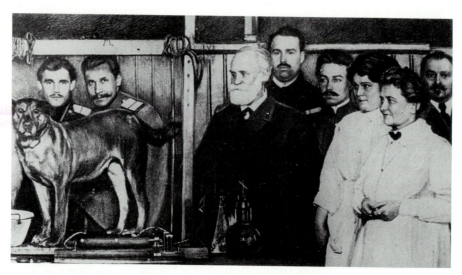

Pavlov experiment.

Pairing

Eventually, Pavlov reported laboratory results that demonstrated that dogs and other animals could, as it were, be taught to salivate at the sound of a bell or the sight of a circle on a card. All that was necessary was that the lab workers *pair* the bell or circle with food for a period of time. Soon, the dog *associated* the bell or circle with food.

Pavlov's work is thought of as an associationist theory because the physiological responses that occurred when associations between stimuli were strengthened, such as the association between food keeper and food or a bell and food were involuntary in nature. Pavlov showed that a great many physiological responses could be controlled by such associations. His studies provided the foundation for a revolution in psychological theory.

J. B. Watson, 1878–1958

During the first part of the twentieth century, an American research psychologist named J. B. Watson further developed Pavlov's associationist ideas and adapted them for use with children (Watson, 1970; Watson & Rayner, 1920).[3] Watson had an intense interest in animal psychology and believed that a thorough study of animals could teach us something about the psychology of human beings. This interest and the research work that it stimulated helped change the nature of psychology from a discipline considered to be similar to philosophy to one that was (1) heavily reliant on animal experimentation, (2) focused exclusively on behavior, and (3) oriented toward the eventual prediction and control of behavior.

Animal Experimentation

Conditioning

Watson and Rosalie Rayner conducted a classic and controversial series of studies on the *conditioning* of infant emotion. Albert B., an eleven-month-old child, was the subject of the experiment. Albert was taught to fear a variety of items that had been paired with a white rat, an object that had initially elicited playfulness rather than fear in Albert. At the beginning of the experiment, Albert did not fear the white rat; he did, however, fear an unexplained clanging noise behind him. Then, Watson and Rayner repeatedly presented the rat to Albert at the same time as they made the loud clanging noise. That is, they *associated*—

or paired—the rat and the noise. Albert rather quickly learned to fear the rat in a way that was similar to his original fear of the noise. After Albert had been conditioned to fear the rat, Watson and Rayner paired objects such as a seal coat, cotton wool, and a Santa Claus mask with the rat. The child eventually exhibited a fear response when viewing these objects by themselves, without the rat's presence.

Despite their belief that they could extinguish Albert's fear responses to the white rat and the other objects, Watson and Rayner did not do so; they did not help Albert to "unlearn" these fears. For this and other reasons, the Albert B. study has become a focal point in the literature concerned with the ethics of psychological research.

Watson and his followers believed that all emotions, pleasant and unpleasant, were learned. Indeed, they believed that all aspects of human functioning—exclusive of simple reflexes—were learned. In a well-known statement, Watson declared:

> Give me a dozen healthy infants, well-formed, and my own specified world to bring them up in, and I'll guarantee to take any one at random and train him to become any type of specialist I might select—doctor, lawyer, artist, merchant, chief and, yes, even beggarman and thief, regardless of his talents, penchants, tendencies, abilities, vocations, and race of his ancestors (Watson, 1970, p. 104).

One of the reasons for the popularity of behavioral approaches within the American public schools probably lies in the attitudes reflected in that famous paragraph. Americans have liked to think of their country as the land of opportunity, where people can become anything they choose regardless of even such factors as specific hereditary limitations. The Watsonian prescription for learning seems to contain a sense of control over destiny. It may be that others exert the control, but it is a control that promises an important amount of power over the capriciousness of natural forces.

Edwin R. Guthrie, 1886–1959

Even though the reinforcement theory presented in the next section has tended to be more popular in recent years than the earlier associationist theory developed by Pavlov and Watson, interesting and useful interpretations of associationist perspectives have continued to be developed over the years. For example, Edwin R. Guthrie (1952) is well known for his concept of *one-trial learning*.[4] Guthrie believed that people would associate and learn as a unit events that occurred together in time or space. In fact, he thought that a behavior could gain its full associative strength on the very first occasion that stimuli were paired. He argued that Pavlov's dogs learned the food-bell association the first time they were able to focus their attention on that association. The learning only *seemed* to require several pairings of those stimuli because there were competing stimuli in the environment.

Thus, Guthrie advised teachers to limit all distractions when encouraging pupils to learn. He also suggested that teachers should encourage the "inner speech" of their students in order to make sure that the important connections are actually being made. That is, students were to talk silently to themselves as they learned. In Guthrie's view, students needed "to be led to do" what they were to learn. Teachers were required to lead students toward the necessary mental connections.

> **Association Theory: Some Classroom Practices**
> 1. Mnemonic devices
> 2. Association of student hobbies and interests with course material
> 3. Like materials presented together
> 4. Associations of opposites
> 5. Rhyming exercises

Acquiring Associations

For behaviorsts such as Pavlov, Watson, and Guthrie, the associations that animals and people make as they have experiences and act are of ultimate importance. For them, learning is fundamentally equivalent to acquiring associations. In the early associationist writings geared toward education, teachers were often advised to lead the child into repetitive exercises so that the appropriate associations would be sure to be made. Recitation of multiplication tables and spelling words are examples of some of the applications of this theory that seemed useful for the classroom.

In more contemporary educational programs, mnemonic devices are strategies that are influenced by association theory. (See Biehler & Snowman, 1985.)[5] For example, music teachers often rely on the phrase, "Every good boy does fine," in order to teach that E, G, B, D, and F constitute one of the fundamental patterns of notes that must be learned in order to read music. When teachers associate a formula with something students are to remember, it is valid to assume that an associationist learning theory is guiding the activity.

Reinforcement Theory

Consequences of Behavior

While associationists concentrate on the association of events that *stimulate* behavior, the reinforcement theorists emphasize the consequences, rather than the antecedents, of behavior (Rachlin, 1970).[6] They are more impressed with the power of the events that *follow* a behavior. Their research has led them to conclude that the pleasant or unpleasant *consequences* of action help determine whether or not that action will be repeated. These theorists emphasize the Pavlov's dogs learned to salivate on hearing a bell mainly because the taste of the food that followed the bell was very good and, thus, very reinforcing.

E. L. Thorndike, 1847–1949

E. L. Thorndike (1931)[7] was the first prominent research psychologist during the initial third of the twentieth century to concentrate on behavioral consequences. He wrote of a *law of effect* that governed important aspects of behavior:

Law of Effect

> Of several responses made to the same situation, those which are accompanied or closely followed by satisfaction to the animal will, other things being equal, be more firmly connected with the situation, so that when it recurs, they will be more likely to recur; those which are accompanied or closely followed by discomfort to the animal will, other things being equal, have their connections with that situation weakened, so that when it recurs, they will be less likely to occur. The greater the satisfaction or discomfort, the greater the strengthening or weakening of the bond. (Thorndike, 1911, p. 131)[8]

Essentially, Thorndike told his readers that a behavior that is rewarded will tend to be repeated. At times, however, he shaded his interpretation of the part of the law of effect that deals with discomfort so that his readers took him to mean that punishment was ineffective in weakening a behavior—especially as compared to reward. Currently, most reinforcement theorists hold that punishment can effectively reduce the probability that a behavior will be repeated; but they recognize that other unintended consequences can also be expected to occur, among them painful emotional responses such as fear.

Law of Scatter of Effect

Thorndike further claimed that a *law of scatter of effect* also guides behavior. Those behaviors that are similar to the one that is followed by reward will also tend to be learned. For example, a child who is effectively rewarded for producing neat spelling tests will tend to produce neat arithmetic and social studies assignments as well.

B. F. Skinner, 1904–

B. F. Skinner (1974, 1977)[9] has had the most important influence of any theorist on American learning theory. In fact, in several polls during the 1970s and 1980s, Skinner was shown to be one of the most widely known American scientists, across all fields. He is most famous for the development of the concept of *operant behavior*.

Operant Behavior

Skinner was originally concerned with the effects of reward on random animal behavior. For example, in his early experiments, chickens were placed in a box; when they happened to press a bar, food pellets automatically dropped into a nearby container. This increased the chickens' tendency to press the bar. Skinner began to think of this bar-pressing behavior as being *reinforced* by the consequence of the presentation of the food. The chickens pressed the bar again because they had learned that food appeared immediately after the behavior of bar pressing.

Skinner has written that "teaching is the arrangement of contingencies of reinforcement which expedite learning" (1969, p. 15).[10] In other words, learning occurs when appropriate rewards have been presented to the learner. Teachers who alert students to approaching tests to encourage studying and who later watch student reactions as the graded tests are returned understand Skinner's point.

Schedules of Rewards

In further studies, Skinner identified several *schedules of reward* that seemed to have differential effects on behavior. For example, when chickens were placed on a *fixed-interval schedule* (the reward arrived after a specified period of time, such as five minutes), they would learn to begin bar pressing only when the specified period of time was nearly over. On an *intermittent ratio schedule* (reward occurs randomly after various numbers of behaviors have been emitted, as in slot machine gambling), bar pressing would occur continually and almost intensely throughout the time the chicken was in the box.

Those who have reinterpreted Skinnerian work on reinforcement schedules for the classroom have used the idea to explain such phenomena as student study habits. They claim that when students are aware that an examination will occur every five weeks, studying will occur most prominently immediately before the test (fixed interval schedule). When students have learned that unannounced quizzes may occur at any time, studying tends to be more consistent throughout the semester (intermittent interval schedule).

Because he has been interested in the ways that animals and humans operate on their environments, Skinner has often used the term *operant behavior* to describe the kind of animal and human activities that his research has investigated. Op-

Reinforcement and Classroom Conduct

Behavior Modification

While reinforcement theory has not been so dominant in subject-matter instruction as had been anticipated by some theorists, it has had a profound impact on the way many teachers manage their classrooms. Indeed, some teachers see themselves as behavior managers, that is, people in charge of controlling the behavior of the children while they are in the classroom and school building. The strategies that these teachers tend to use are generally thought of as *behavior modification* approaches (Premack, 1965).[13] As mentioned in Chapter 3, teachers who use behavior modification techniques systematically reinforce "target" behaviors, those behaviors that are seen as desirable for a given classroom setting.

In the most strict applications of behavior modification strategies to classrooms, a teacher assesses *baseline* behavior by counting the number of times that appropriate, or inappropriate, behavior occurs during a specified period of time. For example, a teacher might establish a baseline of target behavior for a specific disruptive child by counting over a period of time the number of times he or she raises a hand, rather than calling out during a reading lesson. The teacher then reinforces handraising by offering a social reward—smile, praise, or pat on the back—or a tangible reward—a gold star, colored paper for writing assignments, or extra time for recess. Sometimes, a token, such as a poker chip, may be given. In this case, the child adds the token to his or her collection of earned reinforcers and later exchanges a specified number of them for a major reward. The target behavior, hand raising, is assessed again after the intervention in order to see how much improvement has occurred. Such behavior modification strategies have proved to be very effective in managing the classroom behavior

Teacher rewarding student with a hug.

of problem children, and many teachers have used these techniques to shape the behavior of an entire classroom group.

The most difficult aspect of behavior modification programs involves the choice of reinforcer. Each child possesses a somewhat unique set of responses to various rewards. Some children will find only tangible things rewarding, while others will change their behavior for a smile or a hug. A sizable group of children will respond to any kind of attention as if it were a reward—even negative attention that involves scolding or some other form of punishment. Thus, it is usually difficult to decide upon a reinforcer that is simultaneously available, effective, and nondisruptive for others in the group.

Ethical Considerations

Today, literature about the classroom application of behavior modification, or at least the use of it in the strictest sense, often raises ethical issues. (See Gage & Berliner, 1984.)[14] These ethical concerns exist for some people because the techniques seem to remove control over behavior from the targeted individual and effectively change that child's behavior in a direction that primarily meets the needs of someone other than the child—usually the teacher. They feel that this creates a situation in which the development of appropriate behavior is habitually controlled extrinsically rather than intrinsically, that is, managed from outside the individual rather than from within.

Some time ago, Winett and Winkler (1972)[15] reviewed behavior modification strategies in schools and concluded that they constituted an attempt on the part of educators to make children be still, be quiet, be docile. Rejoinders to Winett and Winkler have emphasized that all classroom strategies are designed to encourage children to adopt behavior that fits with a set of common values that includes such things as consideration and cooperation. (See O'Leary & O'Leary, 1977.)[16] Whatever position one adopts on thse issues, it seems clear that a teacher's personal value system, the value system of the local institution, and that of the parents are crucial in making the decision to use behavior modification techniques. It is important that teachers who consider using one of these techniques understand the ethical issues involved.

In summary, reinforcement theory is a type of behavior theory that concentrates on the *consequences* of behavior in an effort to ensure that learning takes place. These theories hold that learning occurs because it is rewarded. In contrast, the earlier association type of behavior theory emphasizes the importance in the learning process of forming associations among stimuli. Thus, association theories concentrate on the *antecedents* of behavior rather than its consequences. The impact of reinforcement theory applications has been so great that many psychologists and educators confuse behavior theory with learning theory in general. While reinforcement theory enjoyed much popularity in American schools during the 1960s, its influence today, while pervasive, is found more often in classroom management techniques rather than in strategies designed to enhance the acquisition of knowledge and problem-solving skills.

Before you proceed to the next section of this chapter, pause for a moment to think again about Priscilla Hope, who was described in the Snapshot of this chapter. Assume she understood behavior theory and used it wholeheartedly in her teaching. As a behaviorist, what would she have done to address some of the problems she faced in teaching her students? Write down your responses on a piece of paper, and keep it until later in this chapter. You will be asked to refer to it again.

Cognitive Theory

E. C. Tolman, 1886–1959

During the 1930s and 1940s, a research psychologist working within the dominant behavioral method began to make an impact on learning theory in a way that was unusual for those times. Instead of confining his attention exclusively to behavior, E. C. Tolman (1951)[17] insisted that the *readiness* of the learner was important and that all behavior—even animal behavior—is *purposive*: Animals and humans do what they do in order to accomplish something.

Purposive Behavior

In a series of ingenious studies, Tolman demonstrated that a rat wandering about a maze evidently learns something about that maze, so that when food is placed at the end of one of the tunnels and other objects block off some of the routes toward that food, the rat seems to exhibit *insight* as it quickly and correctly chooses the only possible solution within the maze of paths. Many behavior theorists had trouble accepting Tolman's interpretation that animals engage in insight learning rather than trial-and-error learning; but despite the intense criticism, many found Tolman's work compelling, especially as the early promise of behavior theory seemed to fade. As a result, Tolman is credited with being one of the early pioneers of what has come to be called *cognitive psychology*, the scientific study of thought processes.

Cognitive theory began to develop at about the same time that computer science became important. The parallels between computer functioning and the operation of the brain were so fascinating to cognitive psychologists that another label for cognitive theory emerged—*information-processing theory*. These researchers began to think of learning in terms of sensory input, encoding, and retrieval systems, in a manner similar to that of computer scientists.

R. M. Gagné, 1916–

A classic human information-processing model was produced in 1974 by R. M. Gagné.[18] According to Gagné's model, which is illustrated in Figure

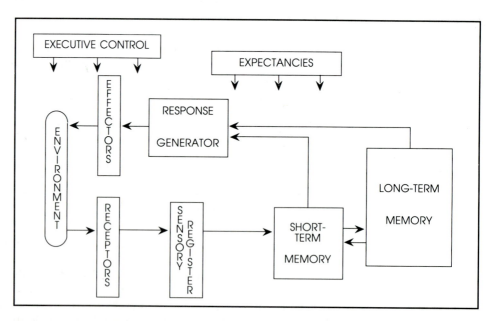

Figure 9–1. Gagné's information processing model. According to the model, humans receive stimuli from the environment and pass it on to memory. Then responses are generated, which act on the environment. (From Gagné, 1974. Used with permission.)

9–1, the environment provides stimulation for receptors located in the sensing systems (vision, hearing, and so forth). These receptors then pass on that stimulation to the sensory register. The sensory register feeds the data along to short-term and long-term memory. From there, responses are generated that guide the effectors (muscles, glands, and so forth), which act back upon the environment.

This early model has, of course, been modified and refined by other theorists, but it illustrates the basic theoretical idea accepted by information-processing specialists. It is important to remember, however, that the figure illustrates *processes*, not actual "things" that have specific locations somewhere in the body.

Many fascinating studies have resulted from the theoretical reasoning of cognitive psychologists. For example, the work of Ericsson and Simon (1980)[19] has shown that when people are asked to report verbally on the mental processes that they are using as they perform a complex task, the complexity of the total assignment seems to increase greatly. However, when they are asked to comment on *what* they are going, rather than *how* they are doing it, these same individuals find the overall demands to be far less difficult than in the first situation.

Cognitive researchers have theorized that in the first situation, there is a greater burden on short-term memory. In the second situation, the subjects were asked simply to report whatever thought came into their minds as they performed the complex thinking task. This kind of thinking out loud apparently does not overburden short-term memory and, thus, does not interfere with the ability to perform the original task.

Cognitive theorists have focused much attention on the kinds of information-processing tasks that are involved in learning and necessary for success in school. While reinforcement theorists seem to have produced more models for teachers in the realm of classroom control, information-processing scientists have produced a good many data more directly related to learning—the acquisition of the subject matter that teachers expect their students to master. These school-based information-processing models, however, tend to be very detailed, cumbersome, and difficult to understand. The terms used are usually unfamiliar to the lay public and to teachers. As a result, reading about these ideas often leads the teacher to frustration rather than enlightenment.

This is unfortunate, since cognitive psychologists have important insights to offer classroom teachers. But it is understandable when one recalls that a sizable amount of work in cognitive theory has been available for only thirty to forty years. It is reasonable to assume that, as information-processing scientists continue to learn from their research, more easily understood explanations of their ideas, as well as suggestions for classroom practice, will be forthcoming. In the meantime, a patient review of the available literature can often improve a teacher's understanding of the thinking processes that students may actually be using.

Ellen Gagné (1985)[20] has produced an excellent summary of theory and research concerned with basic skill processes in reading, writing, mathematics, and science. She reports, for example, that information-processing scientists believe that reading involves the processes of decoding, literal comprehension, inferential comprehension, and comprehension monitoring. Each of these processes, in turn, has its own subdivisions. According to this conceptualization of reading, *decoding* involves the ability to match and to recode. When students *match*, they check the pattern of a word against word patterns that have been stored in long-term memory. Matching skills result in production of a *sight vocabulary*, words that are recognized on sight, since they are matched with an already-known pattern. In contrast, *recoding* occurs when a word is sounded out. The resulting sound patterns activate the long-term memory, where the word's meaning may be stored.

> **Cognitive Theory: Some Classroom Practices**
>
> 1. Emphasizing comparison and contrast
> 2. Providing a context before introducing new material
> 3. Using prompts, such as visual images
> 4. Stimulating the use of more than one strategy for problem solving
> 5. Emphasizing synthesis of parts
> 6. Focusing on relationships between and among discrete bits of information

Several approaches to teaching these reading skills have been produced. In a common method for teaching recoding skills, sound patterns typically occurring in words are embedded in words found in a game that can be played on a microcomputer. Since sounding out words depends on the ability to group letters together within a meaningful sound unit such as "ism," "ing," or "con," cognitive theory suggests that practice at recognizing these sound units will increase the poorly skilled reader's ability to recode.

While most of the information-processing models are highly technical, some of them offer assistance at a level that many teachers would consider quite practical. For example, when discussing the skills involved in composing and writing essays, letters, and the like, Bereiter (1980), Birnbaum (1982),[21] and others have noted that goal setting is an important information-processing skill. The ultimate goal of good writers is to communicate in a meaningful way; the goal of many poor writers is simply to dump onto paper all possibly relevant ideas that are known about the topic. With this in mind, Ellen Gagné (1985) suggests that teachers should work with poorly skilled writers by teaching them to imagine an audience and to attempt to communicate to that audience.

"Input from" versus "Response to"

In summary, cognitive theory is concerned with mental processes. The development of computer science has complemented the development of cognitive theory and, as a result, many cognitive theorists think of themselves as information-processing specialists. Within this field, researchers are concerned with those mental events that occur between the person's receptive sensory *input from* the environment and his or her active *response to* the environment. Cognitive theory is based on a view of human beings as active rather than passive. The majority of research in this area uses human rather than animal subjects, since it is presumed that people do information processing in a way that is functionally different from that of animals.

An Introduction to Teaching and Schools **343**

Cognitive theory is fairly new in psychological science, and its popularity is dramatically increasing. We can expect much more useful information for teachers from cognitive researchers in the next decade.

Piagetian Theory

Jean Piaget (1952, 1967)[22] was a Swiss psychologist whose theory of learning is the best-organized and most widely respected theory of learning known today. His theory can be accurately described as both cognitive and developmental. It is a *cognitive theory* because it concerns the thinking events that are associated with learning. While Piaget believed that the environment plays an important role in learning and that behavior is an expression of learning, he was most fascinated by the thought processes that control the acquisition of knowledge.

Developmental Theory

Piaget's theory is also classified as a *developmental theory*, since it carefully considers occurrences at each stage of a child's growth and maturation as the

Jean Piaget.

capacity to learn changes. Because of this developmental nature of Piagetian theory, a detailed discussion of it was presented in the section on cognitive development in Chapter 4. Further consideration of Piaget's ideas can also be found in Chapter 10, a chapter devoted to descriptions of instructional models.

Piaget has had a great influence on education. While some of his views have been disputed, many have been found to be useful for educators, physicians, psychologists, and other experts committed to enhancing the growth of children. In fact, virtually every approach to teaching recognizes the importance of Piaget's contributions. Kurt Lewin's comment that there is nothing so practical as a good theory is highly applicable to the theory of Jean Piaget—it has proved to be important because it has been so useful.

Adaptation

Piaget believed that developing children acquire the capacity for advanced thought as a result of transactions with the environment (Piaget & Inhelder, 1969).[23] Each stage of development depends on what has occurred in previous stages, as the child and environment mutually influence one another. As this happens, the child's mental functioning results in a useful *adaptation* of the child to the environment.

Assimilation

You will recall from Chapter 4 that, according to Piaget, *adaptation* contains two complementary processes—*assimilation* and *accommodation*. When assimilating, the child changes what he or she perceives in order *to fit it into an already-existing understanding* of the way things are. For example, consider the case of a child who has learned to classify as "bike" all two-wheel machines with foot pedals. If the child should see a one-wheel apparatus with foot pedals and should call it a "bike," assimilation has occurred. That which is perceived has been assimilated into an already-existing cognitive structure. In contrast, accommo-

Accommodation

dation involves *changing existing cognitive structures in order to adjust to a new perception*. If the one-wheel machine is perceived as something other than a "bike," possibly an acrobatic apparatus, and therefore becomes part of a new thought structure called "acrobatic props," then accommodation has occurred.

Schema

The processes of assimilation and accommodation can occur simultaneously. In all cases, they are complementary forms of adaptation to the environment. Piaget referred to the cognitive structures formed through these processes as *schema*. The cognitive schema of children change as they transact with their environments. It is through this continual interplay of person and environment that learning occurs.

Piagetian Stages

Piaget identified four stages of cognitive growth: sensorimotor (birth–2 years), preoperational (2–7 years), concrete operational (7–11 years), and formal operational (11–14 years). In a fascinating series of demonstrations, Piaget showed that in early stages, children rely on their own sensations and concrete objects found in their environments as they form the cognitive schema that they use to make sense out of the world. In later stages, children are able to move from a dependence on the concrete to an ability to form schema that represent abstractions such as truth, love, and so forth. Children at the concrete operational stage learn to understand that volume remains the same despite the differences in shape of the containers that hold it. (Two ounces of water in a tall thin glass is the same amount of water as two ounces of water in an almost flat dish). Older children are able to use logic to create possibilities. Eventually, children are able to produce schema that represent what is *possible* rather than only what is *real*. Thus, adolescents can envision the creation of a new machine or a new world.

Cognitive and Developmental Theory

In summary, Piaget's theory of cognitive development has had a strong impact on many aspects of education. (For a compatible approach see Bruner, 1966.)[24] His is a cognitive and a developmental theory that emphasizes the child's need to master age-related tasks prior to moving on to the next stage. The interplay between the child and the environment creates the opportunity for learning strategies to be developed. At first, the developing human being simply relies on his or her senses. Gradually, profiting from the manipulation of concrete objects, the child forms cognitive schema. Eventually, the adolescent child learns to abandon this reliance on the concrete, and abstract thinking then emerges. Piaget's influence on curriculum development has been pervasive and will continue for many years to come.

As you did a few pages ago, stop and think again about Priscilla Hope. This time, assume she knew developmental and Piagetian theories of learning as they have just been described and that she used those ideas wholeheartedly in her teaching. Also assume that she does not subscribe to behavior theory. As a developmentalist and Piagetian, what would she have done to address some of the problems she faced in teaching her students? After responding to these questions, compare your answers to the responses you wrote when you answered similar questions at the end of the section on behavior theory. How are your two sets of responses different? Why is this the case?

Something to Think About

Reread the descriptions of William and Sherry in the Snapshot for Chapter 4. Then assume that you are a colleague of two teachers who teach these students. Each comes to you and says, "I know William/Sherry is in trouble but have no ideas about what to do." What would you suggest?

- How would you respond to each of the two teachers?

- Once you have decided what you would say, analyze the two responses in terms of what you just read about learning theory. Which elements of the various learning theories described in this chapter are you drawing upon in your replies?

- In what ways do your replies reflect your philosophy of education and your personal philosophy?

LEARNING THEORIES AND TEACHING STYLES

Inevitably, teachers' learning theory preferences are influenced by four factors: the grade level being taught, the characteristics of the students, the curriculum being followed, and the teacher's personal teaching style. Teachers need to consider all four factors as they select the learning theory or theories on which to base their teaching.

As teachers make these selections, they draw upon their knowledge of information presented in such books as this. For example, they consider what they know about student development, educational philosophy, various approaches to instruction, and curriculum patterns of organization. In a sort of executive decision making, they put all these elements together and decide what and how to teach. We can now look at four factors that affect learning theory preferences.

Grade Level

Grade level is important because some of the theories emphasize the development of learning capacities prominent at a specific age while slighting those at other age levels. Those who teach at early childhood and early elementary levels often rely on Piagetian theory, since his most detailed writing is related to the thinking of young children. Adaptations of his work are particularly good for those who teach seven- to eleven-year-old children—those at the concrete operational stage. In contrast, most of the reinforcement theory approaches have direct application to all age levels. While the majority of the information-processing instructional models are geared toward beginning readers, a growing number of information-processing studies target high school and college learners. Thus, those who teach at the upper grade levels often find themselves relying on reinforcement and information-processing theories rather than Piagetian approaches. None of these choices are wrong, or even clearly better than the others.

Student Characteristics

The unique characteristics of a classroom group sometimes require that a teacher search for approaches that differ from those that he or she has previously found useful. For example, it is not uncommon for a middle-school teacher to be presented at the beginning of a school year with a group of children who seem quite unprepared to think in abstract terms—a capacity that is usually somewhat developed within middle-school-age children. Adaptations of Piaget's work can often salvage the situation. Many remedial approaches rely on backtracking to stages of concrete manipulation before easing the child forward into abstract modes. In another case, a teacher may find a group of children of any age to be so unruly that little instruction of any type is possible. Reinforcement methods for classroom management can often help to create an environment where learning can begin to take place.

Curriculum Materials

The third consideration relates to the curriculum. Usually, individual teachers have only limited influence over the choice of the instructional materials they use. That decision is often made by supervisors or by groups of teachers who must consider such matters as the content covered, continuity across grade levels, cost, and sometimes political or religious and philosophical factors. Regardless of what influences the decision, the materials that are used of necessity reflect an emphasis on a particular learning theory or a synthesis of several theories. Therefore, most teachers are compelled to use materials that rely on a particular way of considering the learning process. It is important, then, that teachers have a clear understanding of which approach is reflected in the materials they use; they must also evaluate the degree to which they themselves find that point of view to be useful.

Teaching Style

Finally, successful teachers must understand their own personal teaching style. For example, teachers who think of themselves as powerful classroom leaders who control students and who see the learner as a receiver of presented information often prefer reinforcement learning theory because that theory emphasizes the importance of the person who passes on the information and manages the behavior of his or her young "charges." These teachers often use applications of reinforcement theory in an efficient and productive way, both with subject matter learning and classroom management.

In contrast, teachers who study the nature of the learning process in some detail and are fascinated by the ways that children think things through tend to prefer Piagetian approaches. Often, this type of teacher expresses amazement at which children say and agrees with oldtime television personality Art Linkletter that kids say the darndest things. Piagetian approaches to learning are complementary with a teaching style that includes this type of interest. Piaget himself provides a good example of this kind of style. For hours at a time, he enjoyed quiet observation of the thought processes of his children.

Those whose teaching styles include a significant need for organization might respond well to information-processing approaches. These models tend to categorize and subdivide learning processes. Step-by-step remediation strategies are sometimes available. For example, a typical information-processing approach to reading instruction will let the teacher know how many skills are involved in a particular reading task and will provide descriptions of the components of each skill.

Teachers need to rely on learning theories that complement their personal style. The adaptability of the theories increases teachers' understanding of them, as well as their utility as classroom guides. It is always true that a teacher's best teaching tool is the teacher's own self. Good teachers understand their own strengths, weaknesses, and preferences and are able to use these characteristics positively, so as to enhance their students' learning.

ANALYSIS

The teachers' lounge in a typical American school is one of the community's most important centers of action. It is here that some of the community's most important persons—teachers—relax, plan, and share. The relaxing is important, of course, because of the significant stresses that accompany every day of teaching. Relaxing seems to come naturally to those who enter. So does planning and sharing. Teachers communicate their ideas for the next class or next semester and share their views on teaching in general—their classes, the administration, the children, the parents, and issues such as whether or not the school parking lot really *does* need immediate repaving.

Listen in on the following teachers' lounge conversation that might have occurred yesterday in a typical American elementary school in a typical American town. The room is one you could—and probably will—see in many schools: about fifteen by twenty feet, vinyl-covered occasional chairs scattered with a couple of end tables and a partly filled bookcase on green asphalt tile flooring with overhead fluorescent lighting. As you read, consider these questions:

- How do you interpret this conversation and the situation with Jason?
- What factors might have been influencing Jason's behavior?

- What factors could the teacher have considered when trying to help Jason with his arithmetic study?
- Was it a good idea for the teacher to give extra teaching time to Jason? Would you have chosen the recess period as the time to give extra help?
- Based on this conversation in the teachers' lounge, do you think a Piagetian approach might have been useful?
- How would you have answered the primary-grade teacher's final question?

"Gee, Ann, you look awful today," commented Susan, a primary-grade teacher, to one of her colleagues, a fifth-grade teacher.

"I'm awful, all right, awful angry! Jason has driven me batty one more time. I've spent every recess period this week trying to teach him basic long division concepts, and we're still nowhere. Zero success. Then today I called him up to my desk when the recess bell rang, and he just informed me that he did not *want* to study arithmetic again during recess. He announced to me—to *me*—that he was not going to study during recess anymore. Then he just stormed out of the classroom. I just let him go. I knew I was so angry that if I started talking, I would just end up yelling and saying things I didn't really mean. Can you believe it? After I gave up all my afternoon breaks for four days, he has the nerve to *announce* to me that he doesn't want to learn arithmetic anyway, that he doesn't care about division, and—get this—he plans never to divide anything anyway as long as he lives!"

As Ann collapsed into a chair, her friend gave her an understanding look. Both teachers sighed.

"I can imagine that you're ready to string him up by those cute little suspenders of his, Ann. I know how much you care about him and how hard you've tried with him."

"You're darned right I've tried! And for what? So he can *announce* to me that he has no intention of studying arithmetic anymore. His mother's on the school board, you know. Maybe he can convince her to eliminate arithmetic from the curriculum altogether. Then, neither one of us will have to suffer anymore!"

Charlie, another fifth-grade teacher, joined the conversation. "What's going wrong, Ann?"

"Well," she replied, "he just doesn't get it. He's always trying to divide the bigger number into the smaller number or some other mistake like that. And when it comes to a remainder, forget it. He's just lost if a number won't divide perfectly into another one. 'Why do we always have to have something left over?' he says."

"You know," Ann," said Susan, "I used to have Jason in second grade, and I always thought his parents pushed him a lot. He's their only kid, you know. Maybe he's just rebelling or something like that."

"I've got three kids that are having a terrible time getting through this division chapter, too," said Charlie. "I'm doing the same thing with them that I did when I had trouble with the whole class last year when we came to this chapter. For one thing, Ann, you know that the textbook is particularly weak in this section—or at least, *I* think it is."

"I guess I agree with you," said Ann. "In fact, I don't think I like the whole book very much. It's too 'wordy.' There should be more pictures and more figures with problems. Jason hates the book. I have to practically twist his arm to get him to read it. I guess that's true for some of the others in my class, too. But what is it that you're doing with those three kids, Charlie?"

"I'm using one of those Piaget approaches with them. I figured out last year that my group really needed to rely on concrete objects when trying to think through the arithmetic concepts. This year, I didn't waste any time when I saw that a few of them seemed lost in the woods on this division chapter. I got out my wood bars, plastic poker chips, and that other stuff you saw me making here in the lounge right before Thanksgiving last year. They seem to get it a lot quicker if they can actually see how the problems relate to concrete things."

"Well, that's certainly true of *my* second graders," said Susan. "But they're younger. Shouldn't fifth graders be able to work the problems through in their heads?"

CONCLUSION

Teachers use learning theories to guide their teaching because research has not yet provided definitive answers to all questions about the absolute best ways to teach. The theories presented in this chapter can prove useful in guiding teachers as they attempt to meet the goals they have set for their students; becaues they are useful, they are considered good theories. But the extent to which a theory is useful may change over time. Sometimes new ideas replace or enhance present

CHAPTER 10

Approaches to Teaching: A Look at Five Models of Instruction
JANE STALLINGS

INTRODUCTION

This chapter consists of descriptions of five models of instruction, each of which is a design or plan for teaching based on a specific learning theory and intended to accomplish specific learning goals. You will notice that the models clearly reflect elements of the learning theories of Chapter 9.

Many models could be described, but these five were selected because they reflect a variety of theoretical points of view, because they have had substantial impact on instructional practice, and because they have a research base as to their effectiveness. The models that will be discussed are Mastery Learning, Cooperative Learning, Madeline Hunter's Instructional Theory into Practice, the Cognitive Oriented Curriculum, and Direct Instruction.

The chapter organization differs from that of earlier chapters. Each model is described through a vignette of teacher-student interactions, presented in the form of a Snapshot; and theoretical underpinnings and research results are provided for each model. Therefore, there are five chapter Snapshots and no separate Analysis or Educational Research sections. As you read, compare and contrast elements of the models in order to consider which instructional strategies and student outcomes are most appealing to you.

SNAPSHOT: Mastery Learning[1]

This Snapshot, like the others in the chapter, describes a segment of a lesson that illustrates one of the instruction models. As you read, consider:

- What are the essential elements of the lesson?
- Which theories of learning that you read about in Chapter 9 support this type of lesson?
- Which students might this lesson affect positively?
- Which students might this lesson affect negatively?
- What do you think about this lesson?

Situation: A first-grade class is being taught the relationship between long vowel sounds and the silent *e*.

Teacher: Today we will be studying the long vowel sounds. We will start with the long *a*. The long vowel sound says its name: ā, ē, ī, ō, ū. [The teacher laughs and points to the word *name* written on the chalkboard.] The word *name* has a long *a*. Listen for the long *a* when we say the word *name*. Say it all together: naaaaaaame.

Students: Naaaame.

Teacher: Very good. I am going to show you a rule that will help you to know when to use the long vowel to pronounce words and when to use the short one. Words are pronounced with a long vowel sound when a silent *e* comes at the end of the word. What is this word? [Writes on chalkboard.]

All Students: At.

Teacher:	Very good. Now I will add a silent *e*. The new word is a-t-e. Remember the *a* now has a long vowel sound. It says its name. What is the new word?
Four Students:	Ate.
Teacher:	Thank you Sarah, Bill, Jose and Ann. Now, everyone say the word *ate*.
All Students:	Ate.
Teacher:	Now let's look at these words and see what new words are formed when we add a silent *e*. In *hat* the *a* has a short vowel sound, but when we add an *e*, the word becomes *hate*, and the *a* has a long vowel sound. Say the new word.
Sarah, Bill, Jose, and Ann:	Hate.
Teacher:	It seems you four understand the change the silent *e* makes in words. You can do the worksheet matching the long vowel and short vowel words to the pictures.

As the four students begin working on their worksheets, the teacher talks to the rest of the class.

Teacher:	Let's look at some more words. *Mat* has a short vowel sound. What happens when we add an *e*? What happens to the sound, Cathy?
Cathy:	It becomes *mate*.
Teacher:	Good. That's correct. Let's look at the next word. What happens to *mad* when we add an *e*, Jon?

The teacher proceeds with this line of discussion until all students understand the concept being taught. As students demonstrate that they have grasped the idea, the teacher directs them to their worksheets, as she did earlier with Sarah, Bill, Jose and Ann. Then she continues with those remaining.

> The teacher also checks all worksheets to see whether everyone has learned what she intended. She plans additional instruction for those who did not.

MASTERY LEARNING

All Students Achieve

The preceding instruction took place in a Mastery Learning classroom. The primary goal of that class, as well as the primary goal of the *Mastery Learning model* in general, is to make sure that *all* students achieve the lesson's objectives and to allow each of them enough time to do so. The teachers in Mastery Learning intend to teach all of the students all of the material. In most cases this means that the material must be structured so that students can work at different paces over different lengths of time. (For additional information, see Stallings & Stipek, 1986, 742–746.)[2]

The teacher described in the first Snapshot allowed the four successful students to proceed with their independent work while she continued to help the others learn the relationship of long vowel sounds and the silent *e*. She continued to teach students about the relationship until all of them could read and pronounce the words in the day's lesson. She did this even though some children may have achieved the lesson objective in ninety minutes and others in only ten. All of them had to master the words and concept being taught in the lesson before they could proceed to the next lesson.

Mastery Learning is, in essence, a process of instruction. In its initial form, teachers organize the instruction in a precise pattern, present information and skills to the students according to the pattern, determine regularly how well each student is progressing, feed back information on that progress to the students, help students overcome difficulties through guidance and additional instruction or practice, and provide extra enrichment experiences for those who master the material quickly.

Mastery Learning

Primary Goals	*Characteristics*
• All students achieve objectives	• Common objectives for all students
• All students master material	• Common material and tasks for all students
	• Flexible amounts of time provided for different students to complete tasks
	• Students work at different paces
	• Structured lessons
	• High rates of student success
	• Close monitoring of students and frequent feedback

Educational Theory behind the Model

Rate of Learning

The underlying assumption of the Mastery Learning model was articulated in 1963 by John B. Carroll.[3] It is that nearly all students can learn the basic school curriculum, though it takes some students longer than others. To state it another way, the critical variable that determines what students learn is the *rate* at which they learn rather than their inherent *ability* to learn. Theorists of Mastery Learning describe three factors affecting learning rates: prerequisite knowledge, interest and motivation, and quality of instruction.

Benjamin Bloom, the developer of the Mastery Learning model, believes that the differences in the amount of achievement that students show on final examinations are the results of nonmastery procedures used in schools. Time, not native ability or entering achievement, explains these differences. Some students are not given enough time or enough learning experiences to learn what is expected, so they master only part of the curriculum. Therefore, since students learn at different rates, they need to be provided different amounts of time to learn. Each needs to be given the amount of time he or she personally needs (Bloom, 1968).[4]

Motivation

Motivation for learning is an important element in Mastery Learning, whose advocates note that some students come to new units of study with low motivation because of previous failure and inadequate background information. These students fall further and further behind in achievement, and their attitudes become more negative. The solution to this problem, they say, is to provide the prerequisite skills and the time needed for all students to master the content of each lesson. As the students succeed at their work, they will become more positive about it.

Prerequisite Skills

Slow Learners Catch Up

There is some evidence that students in mastery programs, after gaining the prerequisite knowledge, progress increasingly faster in their lessons when compared with nonmastery students. Bloom (1976)[5] suggests that under Mastery Learning the difference between good and poor learners in the time required to learn tends to be reduced to a vanishing point. Critics of Mastery Learning question the degree to which slow learners speed up or fast learners slow down.

The Model in Practice

Mastery Learning, as it was originally designed by Bloom and in the variations that have evolved from his original model, is a process of instruction that requires the learning of structured, hierarchical, sequential units of material. Despite these characteristics, it can be introduced into many classes without wholesale distortion of the content to be covered and without eliminating many of the other modes of instruction that the teacher employs. On the other hand, if Mastery Learning is to be pursued correctly, instructional objectives must be clear; the subject matter must be divided into short, individualized, incremental units; individualized evaluation must be provided; and individual student progress must be monitored. Teachers who incorporate the concept of Mastery Learning into their teaching can continue to teach the same information and ideas and can continue to lecture, form small discussion groups, and assign projects; but they must modify the ways they do these things in order to assure individual student mastery.

Individual Mastery

Diagnostic Assessments

Frequently administered diagnostic assessments are critical to Mastery Learning. Teachers develop and administer brief tests to determine the students' mastery of the daily objectives. Students who score 15 percent or more incorrect go over the work again until they achieve mastery. To help children achieve mastery, teachers might plan individual work, such as special reading, worksheet assignments, or computer games; they might also plan peer tutoring, small-group study sessions, or academic group games. Students who master the material quickly are given *enrichments* that enable them to study the content more comprehensively.

Grading in Mastery Learning is not competitive. When students demonstrate mastery of the information, they receive an A. Until then, they receive an I, for incomplete.

Two Formats

The two principal formats for presenting Mastery Learning material are the original Bloom format, in which teachers teach the unit to the whole class, and a variation, in which students work through the units independently at their own speed. In either case, students are given tests at the end of each unit. If they do not achieve a score of 80 to 90 percent correct, they receive more instruction and are provided more time until they can achieve a mastery grade on a retest.

The most widely followed version of the individualized format of Mastery Learning is that designed by F. S. Keller. It is called the Personalized System of Instruction. (See Keller, 1968.)[6] In contrast to the Bloom version, students in the Personalized System of Instruction use programmed materials, which they go through individually, at their own pace. Teachers monitor and assist the students individually and are not concerned about keeping the class working together. There is little teacher-led interactive instruction. As the school year proceeds, the gap between what the faster and the slower students learn expands.

Possible Problems

Both formats have some inherent problems. First, whole-group instruction requires that the teacher keep the group working on the same unit. If the teacher waits for all students to reach mastery of a unit before going on to the next unit and if some of the additional learning time comes from class time, fast learners are slowed and pay inevitable achievement costs. In the other case, when students work at their own pace, there is little time for teacher instruction for each student. For example, a fifty-minute period divided by twenty-five students allows an average of no more than two minutes per child. Obviously, some children receive more than two minutes, and others receive none at all. Also, some researchers report that children they studied using both formats of the model tended to consider finishing worksheets first or quickly as a primary desired goal of their lessons. When this happens, they become competitive and rush through the books (Buckholdt & Wodarski, 1974; Levine, 1983).[7]

Assessing the Model's Effectiveness

Programs based on Mastery Learning ideas have been embraced for about two decades by hundreds of school systems in this nation and around the world. However, as with many educational innovations, the efforts often seem to have been undertaken without serious evaluation. A significant number of those who employed the program for the first time did not carry out studies to measure program effects; and where studies were conducted, they were often poorly designed. In the mid 1970s, Block and Burns (1976)[8] summarized six studies of Bloom-style Mastery Learning efforts that were conducted in elementary schools. They report that, in general, the studies are flawed. Among the six, two had nonequivalent control groups; five had post-test scores but no pretest scores; five used criterion tests to assess mastery; and only one used standardized achievement test scores (Anderson, 1976a, b).[9] Of the five studies that used criterion tests at the end of the units, only three reported significant positive results for mastery students compared to control groups.

Mixed Results

In the one study that used standardized test scores, Anderson gathered comparative scores for eighteen classes. Of these, three mastery classes performed significantly better on the tests than did the control groups. Eight of the other mastery classes scored higher than control groups, but the differences were not great enough to be statistically significant. Three control groups scored statistically higher than the mastery groups, and four control groups scored higher than mastery classrooms, but without statistically significant differences. These findings from both criterion tests and standardized achievement tests may indicate a positive trend for mastery programs, but they certainly do not provide a ringing vote of confidence in the superiority of the performance of the mastery students.

Because the goal of Mastery Learning, at least Bloom's version, is to enable all students, especially the slow ones, to achieve and because flexible use of time is at the heart of its approach, understanding the ways in which fast and slow learners fare in comparison with each other is important in assessing the model's effectiveness. Research by Arlin (1984a, b)[10] contributed some insight to the following questions: Do the differences between fast and slow learners decrease, increase, or remain stable over time? Are faster learners held back, waiting for slower learners? If so, does this holding back increase, decrease, or remain stable over time?

In one study, students in four elementary classrooms were examined during ten consecutive lessons. Over that period, the difference between the time required by fast and slow learners to learn the intended content remained stable. The time needed to bring slower students to mastery did not lessen. Faster students were consistently held back with alternative activities while they waited for slower children to catch up (Arlin, 1984, "Times"; "Time Variability").

A second study compared all students in one school who began first grade in September 1977 and who were in the Mastery Learning program for the next four years. Results indicated that differences in the rate of learning between fast and slow learners remained stable or increased over the four years. Many of the students who needed extra time during the early years were the same students who needed extra time toward the end of the study (Arlin, 1984b).

Slow Learners Might Not Catch Up

The results of the two studies conflict with Mastery Learning theorists' claims that Mastery Learning procedures minimize achievement differences and time differences simultaneously. Arlin states, "While it was possible to minimize *achievement* differences in both studies by insuring that most students achieved at similar levels, it was not possible to minimize the differences between students in the *time needed* to achieve this mastery" (Arlin, 1984b). These results suggest that educators may be disappointed if they implement mastery programs with the expectation that the time it takes for fast and slow students to learn will equalize.

Something to Think About

> Two teachers in a faculty lounge are talking about the strengths and weaknesses of Mastery Learning. Both express themselves with conviction, the first saying:
>
> As far as I can tell, my good students are always being held back by the slow ones. The good ones are wasting time and become bored; and the slow ones are embarrassed because everyone knows they need extra time and more work to learn the same things the others master more quickly. They become frustrated. I think individualizing instruction is a better approach.
>
> The second colleague responds:
>
> As far as I am concerned, mastery learning is a godsend for my slow students. If we didn't teach this way, they would be ignored. Being put on the spot is not as bad as being neglected totally.
>
> If you were a teacher who chose to enter this conversation in the lounge, what position would you take? What would you say?

A number of investigators have raised philosophical and practical questions about how Mastery Learning is implemented. Some insist that when teachers spend sizable amounts of their time helping lower-ability students master the content, the higher-ability students are slighted and are often expected to wait for the others. Although the Personalized System of Instruction version of Mastery Learning is less susceptible to this criticism, it is criticized because it limits interactive instruction and student-to-student social interaction.

Too Rigid? Other critics suggest that Mastery Learning is too narrow, too behavioristic, too structured, and too rigid. They say that it reduces student and teacher creativity and insight; that it focuses learning on only a few rather specific sets of information and skills; that it teaches students to study only materials that will be tested; that it punishes weak students by assigning them more work; and that it is too demanding of teacher time, energy, and competence in materials development (Groff, 1974).[11]

There are additional criticisms: There is not enough general agreement among educators about specific instructional goals to formulate appropriate mastery materials. The assessment tests that are needed for evaluation of student mastery are not developed to the point that most teachers can use them competently. There are not enough efficient and appropriate *corrective* materials available for teachers to meet the needs of their students (Horton, 1979).[12]

Everyone Can Succeed The greatest vote of confidence for Mastery Learning comes from the school districts that continue to use the model and indicate that their test scores are improving. This continued positive reaction might be explained by the fact that Mastery Learning includes the expectation that most students can learn what is being taught in the classroom. That is, there is a belief that everyone can succeed—the self-fulfilling prophecy phenomenon.

SNAPSHOT: Cooperative Learning[13]

As you read the description below, consider the following questions:

- What are the essential elements of the lesson?
- Which theories of learning that you read about in Chapter 9 support this type of lesson?
- Which students might this lesson affect positively?
- Which students might this lesson affect negatively?
- What do you think about this lesson?

Cooperative learning team in middle school social studies.

Situation: A sixth-grade teacher has organized a mathematics class of thirty students into cooperative work groups. The teacher has records indicating which students have high, middle, and low mathematics scores and has formed five groups so that each group has equal numbers of students at each level. The students have been assigned seats so that low achievers are sitting between high or middle achievers.

> Teacher: This week we will have a homework tournament. Each day I'll award a point to each person who completes his or her homework. Since there are five people on each team and there are four days of homework, how many points could each team earn if everyone does the homework every day?
> Students: Twenty.
> Teacher: Right. I'll give another set of points for the number of problems correct. Remember, going too fast and getting wrong answers won't help you learn to do mathematics, so check those answers. The next thing I'll do is to give a third set of points for each group. I'll compute these from the number of correct answers on the usual Friday quiz. Remember, helping means assisting or explaining, not doing the problem for the other person. If one person on the work team does other people's problems, the people being helped too much are not likely to get right answers on the quiz. The point of these lessons is to improve your own math skills and to help each other learn to do mathematics.
> Jonathan: We want to be called the Commandos.
> Doug: We want to be Haley's Comet.
> Stacie: We're the Raiders of the Lost Ark.
> Teacher: When you have selected your name, choose a group facilitator, a record keeper, a sergeant-at-arms, and a timekeeper. Remember that record keepers check the homework in each morning and record the number of correct problems for their group on the graph on the bulletin board. The sergeants-at-arms remind people to use quiet voices during work periods. The facilitators make certain that everyone has turns to get help or share ideas during group problem-solving times. The timekeepers remind us of the time so that we continue to work and get the assigned work completed on time.

COOPERATIVE LEARNING

Student Cooperation

The preceding interaction occurred in a mathematics classroom in which the teacher followed the *Cooperative Learning model*. This model, as explained in Chapter 3, has two types of primary goals. The first is to improve student understanding and skills in the subject being taught. The second is for the students to develop cooperative group skills and to gain an appreciation for the different individuals and subcultures found in classrooms. As the students work toward these goals, they are expected to raise the value they place on academic learning and develop more positive attitudes toward people of different racial and ethnic backgrounds. (For additional information on cooperative learning, see Stallings & Stipek, 1986, pp. 746–750.)

The model works toward its goals through arrangements that require student cooperation. In some approaches, students on a given class team cooperate with each other in academic games and tournaments in order to compete effectively with other teams. Teams whose members do not cooperate rarely win.

Several cooperative learning programs have been developed during the past ten to fifteen years. The most notable ones include Student Team-Academic

Divisions (STAD), Teams-Games-Tournaments (TGT), Team Assigned Individualization (TAI), Jigsaw, Jigsaw II, and Group-Investigator (G-I). Sharan (1980)[14] identified several such models and classified them into two groups: peer tutoring and group investigation. While the models vary in structure and have different types of tasks for the students to perform, the intent of each one is to increase student cooperation while also increasing student achievement.

In some program formats, students work on a learning task as a group. This format is presumed to encourage truly cooperative learning and peer tutoring. In other formats, the task is divided, and members of the group work independently, seeking help as needed. In the end, both formats reward cooperative learning and reinforce cooperation, although the specific ways in which rewards are achieved may differ. For example, the reward or grade might depend upon a product cooperatively produced by the group, or it could be the average of the individual performances of each group member.

Cooperative Learning

Primary Goals

- Improved student understanding and skill development
- Development of skills of interpersonal cooperation
- Positive attitudes toward different individuals and cultures

Characteristics

- Assignments and tasks that require student cooperation in groups
- Group as well as individual grades
- Structured lessons and student tasks
- Peer teaching

Educational Theory behind the Model

Group Rewards

Although the above Snapshot scene on Cooperative Learning describes the forming of teams that are about to compete in homework and on a quiz, the essential activity for the students on the teams is to help each other do well in mathematics. The model was developed around this characteristic of cooperation because cooperative-learning enthusiasts believe that most classroom environments encourage competition rather than cooperation and that aside from teams in athletics, music, and drama, schools and classrooms offer few opportunities for students to develop cooperative skills. They want to change this situation because students and adults, in order to be successful in the world of work, in communities, and in families, must be able to cooperate, as well as compete, with others.

Reduce Stereotypes

Proponents of cooperative learning believe that important life skills such as speaking, listening, arriving at consensus, and problem solving can be taught through cooperative-learning experiences. They also suggest that students who have opportunities to work with students different from themselves and to experience each other as teammates will reduce some of their stereotypical attitudes regarding racial groups, low achievers, mainstreamed handicapped students, males, and females. In the process of working together, they are assumed by cooperative learning proponents to learn to appreciate each other's strengths and to develop friendships that transcend ethnic, racial, gender, and other group divisions. This, in turn, is expected to improve racial and other group relations in schools.

Achievement Gains

Proponents of cooperative learning presume that it encourages students to help and support peers in their group, rather than compete against all their classmates. As in team sports, in which individual excellence is encouraged because it benefits the whole team, team competition in the classroom results in greater student support of others' achievements. Proponents also state that students learn better from cooperative learning. For example, Robert Slavin makes the case in a 1980 study that students in cooperative work groups gain more in mathematics and reading than do students receiving more traditional instruction (Slavin, 1980).[15]

Cooperative learning theorists also believe that when students learn from each other, both high-and low-ability children benefit. As they see it, the high-ability child achieves a higher level of understanding in the process of helping slower children, and the lower-ability child benefits from the other children's assistance.

Motivation

Cooperative models are also believed to be more motivational than the individual competitive models characteristic of most classrooms because the competitive models are motivational only for those children who perceive they have a chance of winning. Studies show that many academically disadvantaged children expect to do poorly no matter how hard they try, and eventually they cease trying. They simply choose not to compete (Covington & Beery, 1976).[16]

The group reward structure is expected to increase motivation for low-ability students. Evidence suggests that simply being a member of a successful group, regardless of the child's own performance, allows the child some of the advantages of success, satisfaction, and peer esteem (Ames, 1981).[17] Group competition presumably pits groups of equal ability against each other, and consequently all groups and all students can experience winning on occasion.

The Model in Practice

As with Mastery Learning, Cooperative Learning is a process of instruction that can be implemented at various grade levels and in different subject-matter areas. Teachers simply need to understand the concept and apply it to their teaching. In order to follow specific Cooperative Learning models properly, teachers need to organize their students, learning activities, and assessments according to that model, but they have significant flexibility within those bounds, and they do not have to follow a specific formula in order to do cooperative learning. As a result, many teachers are using some form of the Cooperative Learning model without special training or direct contact with the people who developed and tested it. Thus, the model has been disseminated easily. However, it has not been easy to follow the spread of the model or to learn the ways in which it has been modified as teachers use it in their classrooms.

The general idea of cooperative learning dates back for decades, but serious research-oriented program development and testing of specific Cooperative Learning models has occurred primarily since about 1970. One such effort, and the one most carefully researched, has been conducted as the Student Team Learning Program at Johns Hopkins University under the leadership of Robert

Slavin. That program has produced Student Teams-Achievement Divisions (STADS), Teams-Games-Tournaments (TGT), Team Assisted Individualization (TAI), and Jigsaw II.

STAD

In *Student Teams-Achievement Divisions,* students are divided into four- or five-member teams so that each team contains high, average, and low achievers; boys and girls; and representatives of the racial, ethnic, and social groups in the class. Each week the teacher presents new material to the class. The team members then study and practice the material in their groups, often working in pairs. They complete worksheets, quiz each other, discuss problems, and practice exercises. Their task is to enable everyone in their group to learn the material. At the end, the teacher administers quizzes that the students must do individually.

How the teacher scores STAD quizzes is significant. The key to success is the team score. Individuals provide the best scores for their team by showing *improvement* from previous performance or by achieving a perfect grade. Because improvement is an important element in an individual's score, academically weak students can contribute significantly to the team. They are not automatically the weak team members. The teacher sees to it that weekly team scores and notable individual performances are posted.

Students who participate in STAD need to cooperate, so that everyone learns and scores highly on the quizzes. Teams without members who improve their grades and produce perfect scores do not win.

TGT

Teams-Games-Tournaments is much like STAD in that it involves teacher introduction of content, worksheets, team study, individual assessment, team recognition, and equal opportunity for success. It is different in that quizzes are replaced by tournaments between members of different teams. The process is as follows: Team members prepare each other for the tournament by studying and practicing together. The teacher matches individuals from each team with academically comparable tournament competitors and changes the matchings each week so that lower-ability students do not lose every time, individuals compete weekly, and the weekly scores are compiled and reported as team scores. Teams stay together for about six weeks.

TAI

Team Assisted Individualization (TAI) is individualized, rather than class-organized or class-paced, instruction. It was designed for use with programmed, sequential mathematics instruction. Teams are organized as with STAD and TGT, but each student works through individualized programmed units chosen to match his or her ability level.

Team members work in pairs or small groups as they complete their different exercises, but each must proceed through the materials in sequence and must complete periodic checkouts with at least an 80 percent score. When all checkouts are completed, each student takes a test over the content studied. Team scores consist of the sums of individual scores and the number of tests each team member completes in a week. The critical factor for each student's contribution to the team is his or her weekly progress.

Jigsaw II

Jigsaw II is a revision of an earlier version called Jigsaw. As with STAD and TGT, students study in teams of four or five members. Each studies the whole assignment given by the teacher but is expected to be the team "expert" on one specific element of the task. For example, each student is responsible for a particular part of a short story or a section of a textbook chapter. The most significant difference between Jigsaw II and Jigsaw is that in Jigsaw each student reads only the material for which he or she is the expert; there is no common study of the entire assignment.

When the specific assignment has been studied, the "experts" from all teams who have been assigned the same tasks meet to discuss their work and assist each other. Then the "experts" return to their own team and teach the other members about their assigned portion. On completion of the intrateam instruction, students take individual quizzes, and the individual results are compiled into team scores based on improvement, as with STAD.

Other significant cooperative learning models include Learning Together, an approach developed at the University of Minnesota; Group-Investigation, an approach developed at the University of Tel Aviv; and a variety of other approaches that require students to work together to produce a team project and/or achieve a common team grade. *Learning Together* involves four or five students in completing a worksheet assignment that results in a single grade. It is used most often in elementary grades. *Group-Investigation* organizes students into groups that prepare group projects or complete class assignments. (For references to these models, see Slavin, 1982, pp. 7–8.)[18]

Assessing the Model's Effectiveness

Because Cooperative Learning attempts to accomplish a number of goals, assessment of its effectiveness must be based on multiple criteria. The effects reported here are in terms of academic achievement, intergroup relations, mainstreaming, and self-esteem. The data are drawn primarily from a summary of research studies compiled by Slavin in 1982 and are based on rather precise and controlled implementations of specific Cooperative Learning models.

Academic Achievement

Slavin (1982) reports that the Cooperative Learning model is quite effective generally in increasing student achievement. He reviewed thirty-six studies in which students who had experienced Cooperative Learning for a significant amount of time were compared to control groups. Of the thirty-six studies, twenty-one showed significantly greater achievement for the Cooperative Learning students, ten reported no difference, and one showed a slight advantage for the controls. The studies covered grades 3 to 12; a variety of subjects; and urban, suburban, and rural schools.

In one study of TGT, Edwards, DeVries, and Snyder (1972)[19] found that TGT students in four classes of a Baltimore junior high school showed significantly more learning than control students. The groups were given pretests and posttests, using the computations subtest of the Stanford Achievement Test and a test to measure their ability to think flexibly.

In a test of STAD classes in grades 3, 4, and 6 in a Baltimore elementary school, Madden and Slavin (1983)[20] found that the STAD students learned significantly more than control students. Results were based on the changes in student test scores from pre- to post-test with intervening instruction of seven weeks. The tests covered objectives taught in all classes.

In summarizing twenty-three studies of four Cooperative Learning models developed at Johns Hopkins—STAD, TGT, TAI, and Jigsaw II, Slavin (1982) reported that seventeen studies showed significantly positive achievement gains for the Cooperative Learning students. None of the studies showed better achievement for the control groups. Generally, the positive results seem to hold for high, average, and low achievers; for boys and girls; for elementary and junior high school students; and in urban, suburban, and rural schools.

However, this is not to say that Cooperative Learning students always achieve more than others. Results of different subsections of tests are sometimes mixed, even though they might be generally positive. For example, in a study of 456 fourth and fifth graders who participated in TGT, the TGT students scored higher than control students on the Comprehensive Test of Basic Skills mathematics computation subscale but not on mathematics concepts and applications subscales (Slavin & Karweit, 1984).[21]

Research on achievement effects of Cooperative Learning is continuing, much of it seeking answers to follow-up questions about the data already reported. For instance: Do all types of students benefit academically from Cooperative Learning? Do they benefit equally? Which elements of the model are most effective—the team cooperation, the cross-team competition, or the individual accountability? Although most such questions have not yet been answered, one interesting fact has surfaced: The Cooperative Learning versions that involve the least amount of individual student accountability have been the least successful in increasing student achievement. This seems to mean that the individual student responsibilities, including individual quiz and test scores, are as important to academic achievement as the team cooperation.

Intergroup Relations

The idea that Cooperative Learning might enhance intergroup relations is derived from two research findings of earlier and more general studies. First, studies of cooperation among people indicate that people who cooperate learn to like each other. (See Slavin, 1982.) Second, research on school desegregation notes that students with different racial and ethnic backgrounds do not integrate socially just because they go to the same school. (See Gerard & Miller, 1975.)[22] If both findings are valid, Cooperative Learning that requires student cooperation across racial and ethnic groups in schools should result in students' liking each other better.

According to several studies, students who participate in Cooperative Learning do, in fact, increase their intergroup relations with other students. (See Slavin, 1982.) In most of these studies, students were asked to list their best friends before and after they participated in Cooperative Learning. The two lists were then compared to determine the number of students from other racial and ethnic groups listed each time by the same student. An increase in the number of cross-group friendships was assumed to indicate improved intergroup relations.

Mainstreaming

Several studies have also been conducted to determine the effect of Cooperative Learning on attitudes among students in classrooms containing mainstreamed handicapped students. The limited data available indicate that the experience of Cooperative Learning led to reduced rejection of the mainstreamed children, while all children in the classes gained in self-esteem and achievement. Results of this kind were found when academically handicapped students participated in STAD classes and when emotionally handicapped students participated in TGT classes (Ballard, Corman, Gottlieb, & Kaufman, 1977; Blaney, Stephen, Rosenfield, Aronson, & Sikes, 1977; Madden & Slavin, 1983; Slavin, 1977).[23]

Students who have participated in Cooperative Learning also seem to develop improved self-esteem. Studies that show these results include those of STAD,

TGT, and Jigsaw classes (Slavin, 1982). Apparently, students in these classes liked their classmates and were liked by their classmates better than control group students. They apparently also experienced more classroom success.

In summary, the Cooperative Learning model of instruction seems to produce a variety of positive results much of the time. These results include improvement in academic achievement, social relationships, cooperative work skills, and self-esteem. The results appear in a wide range of studies in different schools, at different grade levels, and with different students. The data, however, are not universally positive and are limited for the most part to controlled experimental situations. Longitudinal studies are needed to examine the long-term positive effects of cooperative work groups upon students and teachers.

SNAPSHOT: Instructional Theory into Practice[24]

As you read the account below, consider the following questions:

- What are the essential elements of the lesson?
- Which theories of learning that you read about in Chapter 9 support this type of lesson?
- Which students might this lesson affect positively?
- Which students might this lesson affect negatively?
- What do you think about this lesson?

Situation: A second-grade teacher is teaching a lesson on making inferences.

Teacher: How many of you like to try to figure out riddles? [All hands go up.] Great! Everyone likes to do that. Let's see if you can figure this one out. Think now. Don't say the answer. Raise your hands. I am going to give you some clues to help you guess what I am. I am blue, yellow, green, pink, and purple. I look like half of a circle. You can find me in the sky after a storm. Can you tell me what I am? [All hands wave.]

Teacher: Say it all together.

Students: A rainbow!

Teacher: Very good. You used the clues to guess what I was. Today we are going to learn about using clues to make inferences. *Inferences* is a new word. [Points to "inferences" on the chalkboard.] Say it together.

Students: Inferences.

Teacher: An inference is like a guess. We are going to use clues to make inferences. At the end of the period we will be able to answer *who* or *what* questions by using these clues. I will ask you what you have learned about using clues to make inferences and answering *who* and *what* questions.

Now I am going to show you the difference between making an inference and not having to make an inference. If I say, "Hank is a farmer," do you

	know what Hank is?
Students:	Yes. Hank is a farmer.
Teacher:	You didn't have to guess, did you? You know Hank is a farmer because I told you. Now look at this story on the board. We are going to use clues to find out what John is because I am not going to tell you what he is. [The class reads as a group.]

> It is early. John and his family are eating breakfast. After breakfast John feeds the chickens and gathers their eggs. The wind whistles through the tall stalks of corn in his field. John picks ripe tomatoes and green beans. He has a lot of work to do before the day is over.

Teacher:	There are many clues in this paragraph that tell us what John is. Randy, give me a *clue*.
Randy:	He feeds the chickens.
Teacher:	Good for you, Randy. Michael, give us another clue.
Michael:	Corn in the field.
Teacher:	All right, a good clue. Another one, Sonya.
Sonya:	He picks tomatoes.
Teacher:	Using the clues we have here, what do you infer John is? All together.
All students:	A farmer.
Teacher:	All right, boys and girls, I've shown you how to take something you read, find clues in it that tell you things that aren't right on the page, and then infer the answer from the clues you find. Now, take out the first sheet in your booklet. Help me find out either who or what that particular paragraph is talking about.

> The first one says, "I have a round face with numerals on it. I hang on the wall in this classroom. I make a ticking sound. When you learn how to read me, I tell you what time it is." Please put your finger on at least one clue. Be ready to tell us your clue.
>
> The teacher and students then proceed through a number of worksheet examples. For several, the teacher guides the class as a whole, asking individual students to respond to questions about clues. Later, she allows the students to work independently as she walks among them, checking with each student as she passes by. Near the end of the lesson the teacher assigns homework on looking for clues.

INSTRUCTIONAL THEORY INTO PRACTICE (ITIP): MADELINE HUNTER

Teacher Decisions

The instruction described in the ITIP Snapshot occurred in a lesson that was organized around the Instructional Theory into Practice (ITIP) model developed by Madeline Hunter, who served as principal of the university elementary school at UCLA. ITIP lessons incorporate Hunter's belief that teaching involves a constant stream of professional decisions that affect the extent to which students learn, and she has classified those decisions into three categories: those that involve the content to be learned, those that involve *how* the student is to achieve the learning—the learning activities they will engage in, and those that involve specific teacher classroom behaviors. She believes that conceptualizing teaching by these three categories of decisions provides a common frame of reference by which teaching decisions and actions can be described, interpreted, discussed, evaluated, and improved (Hunter, 1984, 1976).[25]

Seven Lesson Elements

Hunter's program provides teachers with a generic design and structure consistent with the three professional decisions, a design that prescribes seven essential elements for lessons. In practice, the elements become a formula for teachers to follow in each lesson. The lesson elements are anticipatory set, objective and purpose, input, modeling, check for understanding, guided practice,

Instructional Theory into Practice

Primary Goals

- Instruction based on teacher decisions about
  1. diagnosis of learner
  2. content to be learned
  3. how students achieve the learning
  4. specific teacher behaviors

Characteristics

- Generic structure based on teacher decisions
- Seven essential elements of lesson designs
- Lessons that follow specified "templates"
- Staff development plan
- Clinical supervision system

and independent practice, all of which are explained later in the chapter. (See Hunter, 1984.)

The Hunter model has been used widely in the United States during the 1970s and 1980s, and at times with surprising zeal, even though research on its effects on student learning and on the extent to which it changes classroom behavior has been limited. The program's appeal for teachers lies in its precise, understandable, and orderly approach to designing lessons. Its appeal for administrators lies in the fact that the program includes both a staff development plan and a clinical supervision system.

Educational Theory behind the Model

ITIP stresses the point that teacher decisions are at the core of effective teaching. Those decisions rest on what Hunter considers the two complementary aspects of teaching—the science of teaching and the artistry of teaching. She sees teaching as an applied science, derived from research in human learning and human behavior, which uses findings from the behavioral and social sciences. She says teachers make decisions about teaching based on these findings and that those decisions affect relationships with students. These teacher-student relationships, if they are successful, lead to learning.

Science of Teaching

As mentioned, Hunter believes that the key decisions teachers make are of three types: content decisions, learner behavior decisions, and teaching behavior decisions. To make these decisions, teachers must understand the science of teaching, since the science of teaching provides the intellectual base on which teachers decide. But knowing the science of teaching is not in itself sufficient for good teacher performance. Teachers must also be skilled at making and implementing the right decisions. This is the artistry aspect of teaching. Teachers become artists through a sequence of experiences—by practicing their skills while being observed, by accepting feedback from the observers, by adjusting their performance in response to the feedback, and by continuing practice. (See Hunter, 1984.)

Art of Teaching

In order to determine whether particular teachers are both knowledgeable and skilled at what they do, their performance must be compared to some examples of ideal, or at least good, performance. Hunter (1984) says that this can be done because recent educational research has generated enough data for experts to formulate several theories about teaching practice. These, in turn, have enabled model developers, such as Hunter, to formulate "examples" or "templates" for teachers to follow.

"Templates"

The Model in Practice

Teachers who use the ITIP model follow the basic lesson design and develop their lessons around planning questions that Hunter has identified. The planning questions are derived from the three types of decisions.

The Content Question

The first category of decisions concerns content to be covered. The focus is *what* the students will learn. Typically, the decision begins with the long-range goals set by the school district, by state mandates, by parental expectations, or by teachers. The teacher analyzes these goals to decide what to teach each day. That decision is based not only on goals but also on what the students know, what they are ready to learn, and what they are intellectually capable of learning. In short, the teacher decides on academically achievable content goals for the students.

The How-Students-Will-Learn Question

The second category of teacher decisions includes what the students must *do* to learn in order to reach the goal. Its focus is on *how* the students will be led to learn. Will they read, write, listen, observe, discuss, experiment, or cooperate with others? At this point the teacher must evaluate the appropriateness of planned lessons monitoring and adjusting the activities as necessary. If a student is having difficulty, the teacher must decide whether to change the task or to assist the student by using other procedures to help him or her acquire the skills necessary for successful completion of the task.

The Teacher Behaviors Question

After the teacher has made decisions about which content is to be learned and how the students are to work to achieve the learning, he or she then makes decisions affecting student motivation, the rate and extent of learning, the retention of learning, and the transfer of learning to new situations.

Lessons developed according to the ITIP model include the seven elements that are believed to be generic and basic to all subject areas and grade levels. They follow:

Seven Elements

1. Anticipatory set. The teacher does something at the beginning of the lesson that develops in the students a mental set that focuses them on what is to be learned. This move may also provide diagnostic data for the teacher. For example, in the Snapshot the teacher asked, "How many of you like to figure out riddles?"

2. Objective and purpose. In words that are meaningful to the students, the teacher states what the class is going to learn and how they will find it useful. The teacher in the Snapshot did this when she said, "Today we are going to learn about using clues to make inferences." Another example was "At the end of the period we will be able to answer *who* and *what* questions by using these clues." This lesson element increases the effectiveness of student learning because they know what they are supposed to be learning. It also helps teachers form clear and precise objectives for their lessons.

3. Input. The teacher sees that the students acquire new information about the knowledge, process, or skill they are to learn. He or she might, of course, provide the input in a number of ways—lecture, reading, student discovery, presentations by other students, observing, and so forth—but the teacher must plan the input carefully, in terms of the objectives for the lesson.

4. Modeling. The teacher provides examples of the idea, process, or skill to be learned. This is done because, when students see what the teacher means, they learn more quickly and understand more thoroughly. In the Snapshot, the teacher illustrated *clues* with the riddle about a rainbow.

5. Check for understanding. At specific points in the lesson, the teacher checks to see what the students have learned so far. He or she ascertains whether they understand what they are supposed to do and whether they have at least the minimum skills to do so. For example, the students

in the Snapshot read riddles, pointed to clues, and underlined clues. Sometimes this checking occurs simultaneously with the next element.

6. Guided practice. Students practice their new knowledge or skill under direct teacher supervision. In the Snapshot the students eventually worked silently and were guided individually by the teacher.

7. Independent practice. The teacher assigns activities in which the students practice independently what they have learned.

Assessing the Model's Effectiveness

Limited Research Data Despite the wide popularity of Hunter's model, surprisingly little systematic research has been conducted to determine how well teachers implement the model and how the model affects student achievement.

The Napa Valley Study   Stallings and Krasavage (1986) conducted one longitudinal evaluation of both teacher implementation of the model and student outcomes in two elementary schools in a Follow Through project in northern California (Stallings & Krasavage, 1986).[26] Their study describes how teachers in grades 1 through 4 implemented the model, what happened to student-engaged rates, and how the model affected student achievement in reading and mathematics. The first year of the study was devoted to gaining commitment from teachers and parents, developing a training program for the teachers, and developing the observational evaluation system. In the second and third years, the teachers attended twelve staff development meetings and retreats each year. During this time, project staff observed teachers to determine how well they were using the instructional strategies of the model and students to learn what percent of the time they spent engaged in academic work. Students were tested each year to see how much they had gained on tests of achievement in reading and math. The fourth year was a maintenance year. Project staff did not provide staff development training for the teachers, although they were available to assist principals and teachers as requested. The teachers and principals carried out the instructional program by themselves.

    The two schools selected for the study had the highest percentage of Chapter

---

Something to Think About

Frequently, a criticism of the Instructional Theory into Practice model is that it recommends that nearly all lessons follow the same format, that it is too prescriptive for teachers, and that it stifles teacher creativity. Yet it seems to have been very popular with teachers and curriculum supervisors during the 1980s, many of whom say it is one of the few realistic approaches to teacher staff development.

    Based on what you know at this point about models of instruction in general and the Instructional Theory into Practice model in particular, how would you explain this conflict of views?

I–eligible children in the district. They were selected because of the low socio-economic status of the students and because student achievement test scores were also low. Schools with populations similar to the experimental schools were chosen for comparison purposes. The selection of Chapter I schools was based on the assumption that if this program could improve the education of low achievers, it could probably work with most types of students.

At the end of the second and third years of study, teachers were found to have significantly improved their use of the ITIP model. Students had improved their engaged rate; that is, they were more on task and were doing their work more often during reading and math than before the study. Student achievement scores in math and reading improved significantly. The program was having positive effects in all areas measured.

However, during the maintenance year (the year without continued staff development training) the teachers did not use the instructional strategies they had learned as often as they had earlier. The student engaged rates in reading and mathematics were significantly lower than in the previous year. The test scores peaked in 1984 and dropped significantly from 1984 to 1985. Thus, the positive effects of the model were not sustained.

Perhaps, as in most learning, there are peaks, valleys, and plateaus. Possibly the teachers and students in this study had extended themselves beyond their comfort zone and dropped back a bit in 1985, only to continue their upward growth curve in subsequent years. In any event, this study illustrates the importance of longitudinal studies. (For a more complete description and analysis of the Napa County implementation project of the Hunter model see Stallings & Krasavage, 1986; Robbins, 1986; Porter, 1986; Slavin, 1986; Hunter, 1986; Robbins & Wolfe, 1987.)[27]

SNAPSHOT: The Cognitive Oriented Curriculum[28]

As you read this observation report consider the following questions:

- What are the essential elements of the lesson?
- Which theories of learning in Chapter 9 support this type of lesson?
- Which students might this lesson affect positively?
- Which students might this lesson affect negatively?
- What do you think about this lesson?

8:00–8:10: ARRIVAL

When the kindergarten children first arrive at school, the teacher or an aid gives them symbols (animal shapes made from construction paper), a different one for each child. Each child's symbol is taped to his or her locker. The children go directly to a small-group planning area.

8:10–8:20: PLANNING TIME

During the first fifteen minutes of Planning Time, the children plan what they are going to do in their work centers.

Teacher: José, what did you do yesterday?
José: Made this truck.
Teacher: What do you plan to do today?
José: Fix the wheels.
Each child in turn describes a plan for a project.

8:20–9:15: PROJECT TIME

Children carry out their projects independently, requesting assistance as necessary. The teacher or aid asks questions or guides the child toward solving problems.

9:15–9:30: PROJECT TIME

Children reassemble in their small groups to evaluate their projects.

Teacher: José, what did you do today?
José: I fixed the wheels on my truck.
Teacher: How did you do that?
José: I put some washers on each wheel.
Teacher: How does it work?
José: It moves easier now.
Teacher: What do you plan to do tomorrow?
José: I am going to fix the steering wheel.

9:30–10:15: INSTRUCTION TIME

The teacher has arranged big and little circles and squares cut from construction paper on the table. She holds up a large and small red circle. She holds the big one up high and asks, "Big or little?" The group answers, "Big!" This process is repeated, using different shapes and objects. The children then paste the shapes on pieces of paper—little circles and squares on one sheet and big ones on another. Either the teacher or an aid is always in the art area, eliciting oral responses from the children and encouraging conversation related to what they were doing.

In the small-motor area, children work with big and little cars and blocks. They make roads and garages with the blocks. The teacher constantly emphasizes the size relations of the objects—for example, big garages are for big cars—and encourages verbal responses from the children.

10:15–10:45: CLEANUP TIME

During a short meeting at the beginning of Cleanup Time, the children select areas they will clean up. The teacher and aid emphasize the size relations of the objects the children are putting away; for instance, two children are responsible for finding all the big blocks. Children go to the bathroom and get drinks as needed.

10:45–11:00: JUICE AND GROUP TIME

Cookies and juice are distributed to the group. There are cookies of two sizes, and each child selects one big and one little cookie. There is a brief discussion about the juice cups being full and empty as the children pour their own juice and drink it.

11:00–11:20: STORY TIME

A story is read to the group. The teacher asks interpretive questions.

11:20–11:45: CIRCLE TIME

The children go outside today to play in the playground equipment. The teacher emphasizes spatial concepts as the children play. For instance, as the children use the slide, the teacher stresses *up/down* and *high/low*.

11:45: DISMISSAL

Children go to their lockers for their coats and hats. As the children put on their clothing, the teacher and aid relate body parts to articles of clothing—for example, *hat/head*. While waiting for the bus, the children sing "The wheels on the bus go round and round," using hand motions.

THE COGNITIVE ORIENTED CURRICULUM

The classroom interaction described in this Snapshot occurred during a lesson from a cognitive development model of instruction that was developed in the early 1960s to serve children from low-income families. It was used initially at the Perry Preschool in Ypsilanti, Michigan. The program was based on the sequential cognitive development theory of Jean Piaget. (For additional information on this model, see Stallings & Stipek, 1986, 727–732; Lalli, 1977; McClelland, Smith, Kluge, Hudson, & Taylor, 1970.)[29]

Since those early days, the model has evolved significantly, and it is now usually known as the *Cognitive Oriented Curriculum*. The model rests on the assumption that appropriately designed cognitively oriented school experiences can stimulate student cognitive abilities. It acknowledges that enhancing cognitive skills is a difficult and long process and, therefore, ought to be started at the preschool level, especially for children from low-income homes whose out-of-school experiences may not be cognitively stimulating.

Children in the program start learning at the motor level, when they use their own bodies and physical experiences to explore elementary concepts. They touch, taste, smell, and manipulate things. Then they learn labels for the things and experiences they have been exploring. Eventually, they become familiar with symbols that they can use to represent the objects, events, and experiences. In short, their learning proceeds from the concrete to the abstract.

Interaction with Environment

Learning experiences are organized so that children interact actively with their environment. These experiences help them to classify things, so that they learn about size, order, and temporal and spatial relationships. The experiences also help them sort items and put them in sequence through their use of touch, smell, taste, and visual appearance. The teacher asks the children questions about specific items they encounter, questions that prompt them to think about various attributes of each item—how it looks, smells, feels, tastes, and how it can be used. The teacher also asks them to compare items for similarities and differences.

Structured Routines

Daily routines that help students manage their use of time and space and develop control over their behavior are significant program elements. These routines involve the students directly in planning, conducting, and evaluating their activities and behavior. The different segments of the class described in the Snapshot illustrate this characteristic of the program in a lesson developed in the early years of the Perry program. At that point, the program's classroom routines were rather rigid and teacher dominated, but through years of revision they have become more flexible.

Parental Contact

The program as initially conducted at Perry Preschool also contained significant contact with and involvement of parents. Students attended the preschool for five half-days each week, and program staff members visited parents in their homes for one and one-half hours a week. Staff members encouraged parents to structure home activities along the lines of the in-school pattern and to involve the children in accomplishing home tasks.

Educational Theory behind the Model

Piagetian Stages

The Cognitive Oriented Curriculum model is based on the Piagetian ideas that explain a child's intelligence, logical thinking, and development in stages according to age and experience. Piaget's ideas, which have been described in Chapters 4 and 9, are based on four cognitive developmental stages. Each is built on the previous one and requires the development of a new set of abilities.

The Cognitive Oriented Curriculum

Primary Goals

- Stimulate cognitive abilities in young children according to Piagetian stages
- Develop thinking skills

Characteristics

- Starts with concrete elements of student's physical environment and moves to the symbolic
- Includes skills of classifying, sorting, comparing
- Teacher questioning
- Daily routines
- Clearly designed curriculum, using all senses to learn

The order of stages holds true for all children, but the ages at which children progress through them depend on the child's physical and social environment.

Primary to Piaget's theory is the notion that children learn through involvement in and manipulation of the environment. This is the process by which they develop knowledge about self and objects, learn about relationships among objects, and come to categorize things and events in their own lives. Through the four stages they coordinate and integrate new knowledge with what they have learned in the past. Gradually, children develop the ability to think logically.

Piaget said that at each stage of development the child has a characteristic way of looking at and thinking about the world: Since the stages were described earlier in Chapter 4, they are only mentioned here.

Stage 1: Sensorimotor (birth–2 years)

Stage 2: Preoperational (2–7 years)

Stage 3: Concrete operations (7–11 years)

Stage 4: Formal operations (11–14 years)

Sigel Teaching Strategies

Although Piaget accumulated a persuasive body of data to support his theory of the stages of child development, it was not his purpose to implement his theory in school instructional programs. Some educators, however, have tried to put his theory into practice. For example, Irving Sigel has translated some of Piaget's ideas into teaching strategies designed to stimulate children's thinking. (See Sigel, 1969.)[30] These strategies involve prescribed sequences of teacher questions, teacher-led group discussions, precisely planned student verbal interactions, carefully selected teaching materials and classroom environments, and activities designed to enhance the students' use and interpretation of language. Each teaching strategy is intended to fit the current cognitive level of the students being taught and is consistent with the content they are studying.

The Cognitive Oriented Curriculum is an effort to formulate a precise curriculum, establish classroom patterns, and forge school-parent contacts that apply Piagetian principles and applications of Sigel's theory to the early education of high-risk children. It is intended to structure the cognitive environment of children in ways that enhance their cognitive development. It was undertaken as a type of compensatory program with the knowledge that the out-of-school environment of the typical Perry Preschool student would not be cognitively oriented. The approach is expected to teach cognitive skills to students who are not likely to learn them in their everyday lives.

The Model in Practice

Experiences That Fit Student Developmental Stages

Teachers who use the Cognitive Oriented Curriculum provide learning experiences that fit the students' current stages of development and foster development beyond that point. To do this, they prepare an environment and select or create activities that provide the children with the necessary experiences to progress through each stage. So that the instruction is responsive to the children's ideas, teachers must understand how the children in their class think and how they perceive the world. They must have a repertoire of activities that fit the students' development and must know how and when to use them.

For example, at certain developmental points, they need to provide activities that help young school children learn how to classify objects and grasp the idea of seriation. When the students understand classification and seriation, they are better able to understand number concepts, and their teachers can proceed from this point. As they proceed, students learn a sense of time, cause and effect, spatial relationships, and, eventually, more abstract mental relationships.

Teacher Guidance

The model requires teachers to assist and guide children in their learning; they do not simply tell or direct them. Teachers can guide young children by using concrete objects to help them understand new concepts and by questioning to help them understand relationships among items. Later, when the children are at the symbolic stage, the teacher presents more abstract concepts.

Learning Environment and Material

To teach according to the model's design, it is essential that the room be arranged so that the stage-appropriate learning experiences take place. Several learning centers and a wide variety of materials are necessary to achieve this. The materials and equipment can be ordinary items, but they must fit the different students' needs. For instance, a teacher might take children on a scavenger hunt across the schoolyard to gather materials. In the process, the children would fill their bags with items they find along the way: seeds, gum wrappers, sucker sticks, paper clips, a leaf, a button, safety pins, stones. Back in the classroom, individual children could arrange or classify their findings into categories according to color, shape, or whatever. Then they could play What's My Set? In this game the children take turns guessing which characteristics the others used to classify their objects. (Also see Stallings, 1977, pp. 123–166.)[31]

Every day, children plan, execute their plans, and evaluate their performances. They know what to expect of time in school—a planning session, a work period in which to carry out the plans, a clean-up time when materials are returned to permanent storage areas, an evaluation period in which small groups of children discuss their accomplishments with teachers and aids, and an activity time during which the total group engages in some vigorous play.

More Flexible in Recent Years

Over the years, the Cognitive Oriented Curriculum has moved considerably away from a tight teacher-planned structure and from teacher verbal dominance toward increased teacher reaction to student verbal cues. One observer has described the shift as a move from students responding to teachers, to teachers responding to students. Compared to the early years of the Perry Preschool program, the curriculum involves less teacher verbal bombardment of students, less teacher pushing to accelerate students' cognitive development, and more initiation of classroom interactions by students.

Assessing the Model's Effectiveness

The Cognitive Oriented Curriculum is one of the most thoroughly evaluated models of instruction. Evaluation, however, has focused tightly on the model as it has been tested by its original developers and has been used under experimentally controlled conditions. Data on how successfully it has been used by schools and teachers in less controlled conditions and with limited training are more limited.

Observation studies made by Stallings during the evaluation of the Follow Through Planned Variation Project and reported in 1974 (Stallings & Kaskowitz, 1974)[32] indicated that children in the Cognitive Oriented Curriculum model classrooms use concrete objects in their learning activities more often than children in other educational models. When working by themselves, children use objects such as weights, measures, and games to carry out their work plans.

That study also compared the effects of education models. Compared to children in classes in which a programmed-instruction model is used, children in the Cognitive Oriented model more frequently initiated conversations with adults, asked questions, and made statements to adults regarding their work.

Also, children in Cognitive Oriented model classrooms scored higher than children in Direct-Instruction model classrooms when they were compared on the Raven's Coloured Progressive Matrices Test, a nonverbal problem-solving test. The higher scores on the Raven's test seem to reflect the model's environment, where children learn relationships between items through the manipulation of materials.

Teachers' Ability to Use the Model

Because of the precise nature of the model, some educators have asked about the extent to which teachers who are not directly associated with the Perry Preschool Program can implement the Cognitive Oriented model satisfactorily. Stallings's and Kaskowitz's 1972–73 research indicated that teachers trained in this program implemented it effectively in five Follow Through locations: Greenwood, Mississippi; Fort Walton Beach, Florida; New York City; Greeley, Colorado; and Denver, Colorado.

A longitudinal study by Schweinhart and Weikart (1980)[33] followed 128 children who participated in the Perry Preschool program. By the mid-1980s, the generalization made about the academic achievement effects of the program was that the students who participated in the program were usually ahead of their primary-grade schoolmates initially, but the positive gains faded as they reached the end of first grade or during second grade. (See Stallings & Stipek, 1986, pp. 729–732.)

Gains in IQ Test Scores

Although the Perry Preschool students and the control group students with whom they were matched entered preschool with IQ test scores in the low 80s, the Perry students exceeded the controls by twelve IQ points after two years of preschool. After that, however, the differences gradually faded. At the end of kindergarten, the difference was six points; at the end of first grade, five points; and at the end of second grade the scores were equivalent. In succeeding years, neither group achieved at the level of national norms.

In the nineteen years between the time when the initial 128 students participated in the Perry Preschool program and the mid-1980s, data were collected on them using forty-eight different measures (Stallings & Stipek, 1986). Those measures were administered annually, and some continued until the students were nineteen years of age. From these measurements, indications of success in school were evident.

Other Differences

The Perry Preschool program goals were not limited to raising IQ test scores and academic achievement results. They also included improvement of student cognitive skills, personal initiative, personal planning, and personal self-evaluation. In the fifteen years of the follow-up studies on the students, school records and interviews show interesting results in several of these other dimensions (Stallings & Stipek, 1986). When compared to control groups, the Perry students were less often retained in any grade; less often referred to special education classes; more likely to have been graduated from high school; more likely to be attending college; more likely to be enrolled in training programs; more likely to be employed; and less likely to be on welfare. In the follow-up interviews, the Perry students tended to be more positive about school, more committed to schooling, and more positive in rating their own school ability. Importantly, 21 percent fewer Perry students were reported to have been arrested by age 19.

What characteristics of the model would explain these findings? Given the impressive nature of four-year-old children, it may be that a curriculum that requires children every day to (1) examine what they did yesterday; (2) decide what they plan to do today; (3) execute their plan; (4) evaluate their product; and (5) plan for tomorrow might well affect the ways in which students plan and face consequences for the rest of their lives. The aim of this program is to help children see relationships. The longitudinal research findings suggest some important program goals have been reached.

SNAPSHOT: Direct Instruction[34]

As you read the observer's description below, consider the following questions:

- What are the essential elements of the lesson?
- Which theories of learning that you read about in Chapter 9 support this type of lesson?
- Which students might this lesson affect positively?
- Which students might this lesson affect negatively?
- What do you think about this lesson?

Situation: A kindergarten teacher is working with six children on a mathematics lesson.
Teacher: Today we are going to learn to count pennies. We are going to count to five. First I am going to count to five. What am I going to do?
Students: Count to five.
Teacher: Right! You are all listening very carefully today. Here I go. One, two, three, four, five. What did I do?

Additional direct instruction on counting.

Students:	Counted to five.
Teacher:	Good answers. Now you can count to five as I drop a penny in this can.
Six Students:	One, two, three, four, five.
Teacher:	You are really sharp today. You really are. Now, Alonzo, you count to five as I drop the pennies in the can.
Alonzo:	One, two, three, four, five.
Teacher:	Good! Now you try, Maria.
Maria:	One, two, three—. [Pause.]
Teacher:	Four. Say four, Maria.
Maria:	Four.
Teacher:	Now let's count together.
Maria and Teacher:	One, two, three, four, five. [Teacher] Again, [Both] one, two, three, four, five. [Teacher] Again. [Both] One, two, three, four, five.
Teacher:	Maria, count by yourself now.
Maria:	One, two, three, four, five.
Teacher:	Good for you, Maria! We'll try it again after Beth has her turn.
Teacher:	Beth, hand me one penny and tell me how many.
Beth:	[Picks up one penny.] One.
Teacher:	Good for you, Beth.
Teacher:	Alonzo, hand me two pennies.
Alonzo:	[Hands teacher two pennies.] Two.
Seth:	I want a turn.

Teacher:	Sorry, Seth. You hand me three pennies and count to three, please.
Seth:	One, two, three.
Teacher:	Very good. You are with it today, Seth.
Teacher:	Andrea, count four pennies and give them to me.
Andrea:	One, two, three, four.
Teacher:	You are all so smart today.
Teacher:	Now, Maria, count five pennies and give them to me.
Maria:	One, two, three, four, five.
Teacher:	Hooray for Maria. You counted just right!

DIRECT INSTRUCTION

Structured Academic Program

The teacher-student interaction in this Snapshot occurred in a lesson taught by a teacher trained in the Direct Instruction model. The model evolved from a tightly structured, skill-oriented, academic preschool program developed in the 1960s by Carl Bereiter and Seigfried Englemann at the University of Oregon. That original program was targeted for preschool children from lower-income homes who lacked the language skills needed to succeed academically in school. (For additional information on this model see Stallings & Stipek, 1986, pp. 734–35, 738–40.)

The goal of the direct-instruction approach is to assist all students in gaining specific academic skills. In this approach the teacher provides a bit of information from a hierarchical structure; students are asked questions and reinforced positively for correct answers. Wrong answers are quickly corrected.

Acquire Basic Skills

The first version of the model, designed in the 1960s as a Head Start program, was called the Academic Preschool Program. The model's major objectives were to help preschool children acquire basic skills in arithmetic, develop effective use of language, and master visual symbols and basic color concepts. Developers also hoped that the children's self-esteem and self-confidence would increase as a result of their academic achievements.

The program diagnosed exactly what each child needed to succeed academically in the school and prescribed the ways in which teachers should modify the children's behavior. In this way, it differed significantly from other Head Start programs of the 1960s. Most of the other early-childhood programs were intended to develop children's social, emotional, and cognitive skills. They addressed the needs of the whole child. The Academic Preschool Program (APP) was different—cheered by behavioral psychologists and jeered by cognitive developmentalists. The latter group felt it was unwise or even inappropriate to subject young children to such narrowly focused academic training.

Assessments of Head Start efforts that compared the academic test scores of children in various Head Start models reported that APP children gained more than children in other Head Start models. (See Stallings & Stipek, 1986.) But as with the other models, the gains achieved were short-lived. By the end of first grade there was little evidence that any Head Start program, including APP, had a lasting positive effect on student achievements.

From Head Start to Follow Through

Partly because of these results, in the late 1960s the federal Office of Education called for educators to design kindergarten through third-grade programs that would build upon the Head Start programs and, it was hoped sustain the academic gains. Efforts in response to this call were designated Follow Through programs, which concentrated on stabilizing the learning of at-risk children over a longer period of time.

The Oregon Direct Intervention (DI) Follow Through model was an outgrowth of APP. The program thrived during the 1970s; by the mid-1980s more than sixty cities had adopted the model.

Direct Instruction

Primary Goals	*Characteristics*
• Develop specific academic skills in early grades	• Oriented toward academic skill
	• Tightly structured curriculum
• Improve children's self-esteem	• Behavioral

Educational Theory behind the Model

Operant Conditioning

As with other behavior modification models, the Oregon Direct Instruction model rests on the learning theories of Pavlov and Skinner and is based primarily on Skinner's operant conditioning theory. It incorporates in its curriculum and practice the belief that any healthy person can be taught to perform tasks successfully if the unit of learning is small enough and if the reinforcement offered is desired by the subject. (See Bereiter & Engelmann, 1966; Skinner, 1968.)[35]

Operant conditioning assumes that a person's behavior produces consequences, which, if pleasant to the person, reinforce the response. Therefore, if classroom students do things that the teacher reinforces that reinforcement causes them to repeat the behavior. This model accepts the premise of operant conditioning that positive reinforcement is essential to modifying student behavior and maximizing children's academic success. It also accepts the idea that a carefully sequenced curriculum and a rigidly controlled instructional process are necessary for the implementation of operant conditioning in the classroom.

Positive Reinforcement

The Model in Practice

Small, Hierarchical Steps

In the original Academic Preschool Program, Bereiter and Englemann developed sets of curricula for reading, spelling, language arts, and mathematics. The lessons were presented in small, hierarchical steps. Teachers provided a small amount of information; children repeated the information; teachers asked a simple, direct question about the information; children responded. If the response was correct, the children were praised. If the response was wrong, the teacher corrected the children, and the process was repeated until the children gave the right answer automatically. Then and only then did they proceed to the next sequence. The drill and practice was conducted at a rapid pace, with systematic and enthusiastic praise for right answers.

When the program was modified into the Oregon Direct Instruction Follow Through Program, curricular materials were prepared for reading, spelling, language arts, mathematics, science, and music for each of grades K through 3. Since the materials were to be used widely as a national model, the designers tried to make the instructional process for using the curriculum essentially "teacher proof." To accomplish this, they prepared a script for each lesson to be used by teachers and classroom aids in all parts of the country. (See Stallings & Stipek, 1986.)

Scripted Lessons

Therefore, those who use the model as it was intended to be used are required to be trained in the use of the Direct Instruction methods in their classroom and to follow a set teaching plan. According to the DI plan, children are grouped on the basis of their ability as reflected on weekly criterion tests for reading, math, and language development. The classroom teacher is usually responsible for the reading program; where available, a full-time aid is responsible for the math program; and a second full-time aid is responsible for spelling and handwriting.

Low Teacher-Student Ratio

In order for the children to receive maximum amounts of stimulation and praise during a learning session, the teacher works with eight to ten children at a time and addresses most questions and praise to the group. By addressing the group, the teacher attempts to keep all participants engaged at all times. Individual learning problems are diagnosed through the weekly testing, and each child receives the drill and practice necessary to learn required skills.

In this model, the teachers initiate each stimulus and quickly reinforce or modify each response. They control the students, keeping them on task through continuing interactions and positive reinforcement. Students and teachers share the pleasure and the excitement of correct responses.

Program Transportability

Because of the prescriptive nature of the model, it was easy for compliant teachers to implement the program. Stallings and Kaskowitz (1974) found that 90 percent of Direct Instruction teachers in five urban and rural locations implemented the model as specified by the developers. Their findings indicated that the educational model and the teacher-training program were transportable to a variety of sites.

Something to Think About

Some critics of the Academic Preschool Program as it was initially developed said it was too behavioral and at times manipulative. They said it restricted students to stimulus-response behavior in classrooms and that this was dehumanizing. Some of the responses to their criticisms include the point that the approach seems to have succeeded with high-risk students when virtually every other approach failed.

For the purpose of this activity, assume both points of view are accurate—the approach is very behavioral and manipulative, but it works. What would you do if you were a teacher whose principal asked that you use the approach for the coming school year? Explain why you would do this.

Assessing the Model's Effectiveness

Academic Achievement

Early evaluation reports for the initial version of the Academic Preschool Program indicated that after two years in the academic preschool, children made greater gains on the Stanford-Binet Test and the Wide Range Achievement Test than children of comparison groups who had not received such intensive academic training. At the beginning of first grade, the children in the experiment achieved at nearly the second-grade level in reading, arithmetic, and spelling. But as with other preschool programs, the success of the children was short-lived. At the end of the first year, there was little academic difference between the treatment and control children (Beller, 1973).[36]

Later studies of the DI version of the program, the K–3 version, looked at longer-term effects on the students who participated. Some of these compared achievement gains of these students with those of children who had participated in other Follow Through programs. In general, they reported that Oregon Direct Instruction students showed greater gains in reading and mathematics than students in other programs (Stebbins, St. Pierre, Proper, Anderson, & Cerva, 1977; Stallings, 1975).[37] But it was unclear which specific elements or characteristics of the program resulted in the gains.

Lower on Problem Solving

In at least one study, however, Oregon Direct Instruction students scored lower in nonverbal problem-solving ability than students in Cognitive Development model programs. This finding led one researcher to ask whether a program of this nature—rapid-paced drill and practice, in tightly structured sequences, without much hands-on experience in taking things apart and putting them back together or in drawing relationships—could be neglecting the development of problem-solving skills (Stallings & Stipek, 1986).

Long-Term Effects

Other studies of the longitudinal effects of the Oregon Direct Instruction model examined two important research questions: What are the long-term effects on achievement generally? Are these children who have learned in this behavioral, tightly sequenced, and teacher-directed approach to learning able later in their schooling to work and learn independently in less structured classroom settings? Answers to both questions are ambiguous.

One study by Becker and Gersten (1982)[38] tracked Oregon Direct Instruction students at five locations and their control group counterparts through several upper grades of elementary school. They found that fifth- and sixth-grade students from the Direct Instruction program scored higher than their control group students in reading decoding, mathematics, and spelling as assessed on the Wide Range Achievement Tests. They also noted, however, that the degree of difference at grades 5 and 6 was less than it had been at grade 3, suggesting the positive effect of the Direct Instruction program was eroding over time.

In a follow-up study of New York City fifth-grade students who had participated in the Oregon Direct Instruction model for four years in grades K–3, Meyer, Gersten, and Gutkin (1983)[39] found that the Direct Instruction students scored significantly higher than the control group comparison students on the Comprehensive Test of Basic Skills. Similar results were found for ninth-grade students in reading and mathematics (Meyer, 1984).[40] Other studies have shown that ninth-grade students who had the program in grades K–3 are less likely to be retained, more likely to attend school, and more likely to graduate. It appears over time that this model has also had a positive effect upon student achievement and success in school.

Other Models of Instruction

There are, of course, many other models of instruction than the five described in this chapter. A valuable description of a number of other models is provided in *Models of Teaching* (3d ed.) by Bruce Joyce and Marsha Weil (1986).[41] They divide models into four "families," and they list the areas not described above as follows:

Model	Primary Thrust
Information Processing	
Attaining concepts	To teach concepts and the ability to learn and create them
Inductive thinking	To teach information, concept building, and problem solving
Inquiry	To teach collecting and verifying information, developing concepts, and building and testing hypotheses
Learning from presentations	To increase mental activities of students through structured courses and presentations
Memorization	To teach mastery of information
Developing intellect	To teach according to stages of intellectual growth and accelerate rates of development
Scientific inquiry	To teach problem analysis and research methods
Personal	
Nondirective	To teach self-understanding, personal-goal clarification, and acceptance of responsibility
Synectics	To generate fresh ideas and solutions to problems
Increasing awareness	To increase understanding of human potential and the development of self and others
Classroom meetings	To teach in a supportive classroom environment
Social	
Group participation	To teach problem solving through collective learning in a democratic setting
Role playing	To teach the study of values, social skills, and cooperative behavior
Jurisprudential inquiry	To teach clarification of values and conflict resolution
Laboratory training	To teach interpersonal skills and ways of working together
Social science inquiry	To teach and analyze problems in social, economic, and political life

Behavioral Systems	
Learning self-control	To teach personal and social situations and appropriate behavior management
Learning from simulation	To teach through games and simulations that provide feedback about performance
Assertiveness training	To teach the analysis of communication tasks and problems and social skills to handle them

CONCLUSION

The criteria used to select the five models of instruction presented here have been noted, along with the fact that the selection of these models does not imply that they are the best or that they are representative of models of instruction in general. They are simply five examples of models of instruction.

The objectives for the chapter are to (1) acquaint you with several models of instruction, (2) to demonstrate the relationship between theories of child learning and educational practice as reflected in these models, (3) to foster understanding of the relationships between classroom practice and student growth, and (4) to encourage reflection on your own educational philosophy.

SUMMARY

Models of instruction are designs or plans for teaching; they are based on particular theories of learning, and they are intended to accomplish specific learning goals. Although there are many models of teaching, only five were described in this chapter. Those described reflect a variety of theoretical perspectives, have had impact on classroom practice, and have a research base as to their effectiveness.

Mastery Learning is designed to assure that all students achieve lesson objectives and allow each student enough time to do so. Students who do not learn as fast as others are retaught until they do.

Cooperative Learning is intended to teach students to cooperate in order to learn academically and, thereby, to learn positive attitudes toward other students in class, including those with different racial and ethnic backgrounds. Students participate in learning teams, games, or tournaments that reward cooperation.

The Instructional Theory into Practice model developed by Madeline Hunter is built around three types of teacher decisions: those that involve the content to be learned, those that concern the learning experiences in which students are engaged, and those regarding specific teacher classroom behaviors. Teachers' consideration of the three types of questions guides their actions as they develop lessons consisting of seven essential elements.

The Cognitive Oriented Curriculum, developed initially at Ypsilanti, Michigan, concentrates on the sequential development of students' cognitive abilities, beginning in preschool. Student experiences follow Piagetian developmental steps and include active use of the classroom environment, teacher questioning, and precisely designed daily routines.

The Direct Instruction model initiated as a Head Start program at the University of Oregon stresses the development of academic skills, especially language skills, in children from low-income homes, since these students often lack the language abilities needed to succeed academically in school. The instruction consists of hierarchical lessons based in operant conditioning theory.

The models of instruction presented in the chapter are intended as examples that show connections between theories of learning and philosophies of education, educational practice, and student growth. Understanding them should help teachers formulate their own philosophies and ideas about education in ways that guide what they do in classrooms and the ways in which their students learn.

STUDY QUESTIONS

1. Which characteristics of each model of instruction do you like? Which do you dislike?

2. Which underlying educational philosophies and theories of learning support each of the models? For which grade levels? For which subjects?

3. Which of the models of instruction do you prefer? How does your choice among models of instruction relate to the educational philosophy that you find most appealing?

4. How does your choice relate to the theory of learning that you find most attractive?

BIBLIOGRAPHY

Mastery Learning

Arlin, M., & Webster, J. (1983). Time costs of mastery learning. *Journal of Educational Psychology, 75*(1), 187–195.

Block, J. (1979). Mastery learning: The current state of the craft. *Educational Leadership, 37*(2), 114–117.

Block, J. H. (1971). (Ed.). *Mastery Learning: Theory and practice.* New York: Holt, Rinehart and Winston.

Bloom, B. (1981). *All our children learning.* New York: McGraw-Hill.

Carroll, J. (1963). A model for student learning. *Teachers College Record, 64*(8), 723–733.

Guskey, T. R. (1985). *Implementing mastery learning.* Belmont, CA: Wadsworth.

Cooperative Learning

Graves, N. & Graves, T. (1987). *Cooperative learning: A resource guide.* Santa Cruz, CA: International Association for the study of Cooperative Education.

Johnson, D. W., Johnson, R. T., Holybec, E. J. & Roy, P. (1984). *Circles of learning.* Alexandria, VA: Association for Supervision and Curriculum Development.

Johnson, D., Johnson, R., & Smith, K. (1985). Academic conflict among students: Controversy and learning. In R. Feldman (Ed.), *Social psychological applications to education.* London: Cambridge University Press.

Newman, F. M. & Thompson, J. A. (1987). *Effects of cooperative learning on achievement in secondary schools: A synthesis of research.* Madison, WI: National Center on Effective Secondary Schools.

Slavin, R. E. (1986). *Using student team learning.* (3rd ed.). Baltimore, MD: Center for Research on Elementary and Middle Schools, The Johns Hopkins University.

Slavin, R. E. (1983). *Cooperative learning.* New York: Longmans.

Slavin, R. E. (1983). *Student team learning: An overview and practical guide.* Washington: National Education Association.

Instructional Theory into Practice

Hunter, M. (1986). Comments on the Napa County, California, follow through project. *Elementary School Journal, 87*(2), 173–179.

Hunter, M. (1984). Knowing, teaching and supervising. In P. L. Hosford, *Using what we know about teaching.* Washington: ASCD.

Hunter, M. (1976). *Prescription for improved instruction.* El Segundo, CA: TIP.

Hunter, M., & Russell, D. (1981). Planning for effective instruction: Lesson design. In *Increasing your teaching effectiveness.* Palo Alto, CA: The Learning Institute.

Robbins, P., & Wolfe, P. (1987). Reflections on a Hunter-based staff development project. *Educational Leadership, 44*(5), 56–61.

Slavin, R. E. (1986). The Napa evaluation of Madeline Hunter's ITIP: Lessons learned. *Elementary School Journal, 87*(2), 165–171.

Stallings, J. (1985). A study of implementation of Madeline Hunter's model and its effects on students. *Journal of Educational Research, 78,* 325–337.

Stallings, J., & Krasavage, E. M. (1986). Program implementation and student achievement in a four-year Madeline Hunter follow through project. *Elementary School Journal, 87*(2), 117–138.

Stallings, J., Robbins, P., Presbrey, L., & Scott, J. (1986). Effects of instruction based on the Madeline Hunter model on students' achievement: Findings from a follow through project. *Elementary School Journal, 86*(5), 571–587.

Cognitive Oriented Curriculum

Ennis, R. (1985). Goals for critical thinking/reasoning curriculum. *Educational Leadership, 43*(2), 46.

Lalli, R. (1977). *An introduction to the cognitively oriented curriculum for elementary grades.* Ypsilanti, MI: High/Scope Educational Research Foundation.

Perkins, D. (1986). Thinking frames. *Educational Leadership, 43*(8), 4–10.

Raths, L. E., Wasserman, S., Jonas, A., & Rothstein, A. (1986). *Teaching for thinking: Theory, strategies, and activities for the classroom* (2nd ed.). New York: Teachers College Press.

Schweinhart, L., & Weikart, D. (1980). *Young children grow up: The effects of the Perry Preschool Program on youths through age 15, Monograph No. 7.* Ypsilanti, MI: High/Scope Educational Research Foundation.

Sigel, I. E. (1969). The Piagetian system and the world of education. In E. Elkind & J. H. Flavell (Eds.), *Studies in cognitive development.* New York: Oxford University Press.

Direct Instruction

Becker, W. C., & Gersten, R. (1982). A follow up on follow through: The later effects of the direct instruction model on children in fifth and sixth grades. *America Educational Research Journal, 19*(1), 75–92.

Bereider, C., & Engelmann, S. (1966). *Teaching disadvantaged children in the preschool.* Englewood Cliffs, NJ: Prentice-Hall.

Meyer, L. (1984). Long-term academic effects of direct instruction follow through. *Elementary School Journal, 84*(4), 380–394.

Meyer, L., Gersten, R., & Gutkin, J. (1983). Direct instruction: A project follow through success story. *Elementary School Journal, 84*(2), 241–252.

Miller, L., & Bizzell, R. (1985). Longterm effects of four preschool programs: Sixth, seventh and eighth grade. *Child Development, 54*(3), 727–741.

Skinner, B. (1968). *Technology of teaching.* New York: Appleton-Century-Crofts.

NOTES

1. The class segment described in this Snapshot is drawn from classroom observations by Jane Stallings.
2. Stallings, J. A., & Stipek, D. (1986). Research on early childhood and elementary school teaching programs. In M. C. Wittrock (Ed.), *Handbook of research on teaching: Third edition* (pp. 729–732). New York: Macmillan.
3. Carroll, J. B. (1963). A model for school learning. *Teachers College Record, 64*(8), 723–733.
4. Bloom, B. S. (1968). Learning for mastery. *Evaluation Comment (UCLA-CSIED), 1*(2), 1–12.
5. Bloom, B. S. (1976). *Human characteristics and school learning.* New York: McGraw-Hill.
6. Keller, F. S. (1968). Good-bye, teacher. . . . *Journal of Applied Behavior Analysis, 1*(1), 79–89.
7. Buckholdt, D., & Wodarski, J. (1974, August). *The effects of different reinforcement systems on cooperative behaviors exhibited by children in classroom contexts.* Paper presented at the annual meeting of the American Psychological Association, New Orleans; Levine, J. (1983). Social comparison and education. In J. Levine & M. Wang (Eds.), *Teacher and student perceptions: Implications for learning.* Hillsdale, NJ: Erlbaum.
8. Block, J. H., & Burns, R. (1976). Mastery learning. In L. S. Shulman (Ed.), *Review of research in education, Vol. 4* (pp. 3–49). Itasca, IL: F. E. Peacock.
9. Anderson, L. (1976a, April). *The effects of a mastery learning program on selected cognitive, affective and interpersonal variables in grades 1 through 6.* Paper presented at the annual meeting of the American Educational Research Association, San Francisco; Anderson, L. (1976b). An empirical investigation of individual differences in time to learn. *Journal of Educational Psychology, 68*(2), 226–233.
10. Arlin, M. (1984a). Times, equality, and mastery learning. *Review of Educational Research, 54*(1), 65–86; Arlin, M. (1984b). Time variability in mastery learning. *American Educational Research Journal, 21*(1), 105–120.
11. Groff, P. (1974). Some criticisms of mastery learning. *Today's Education, 63*(4), 88–91.
12. Horton, L. (1979). Mastery learning: Sound in theory, but. . . . *Educational Leadership, 37*(2), 154–156.

13. The class segment described in this Snapshot is drawn from classroom observations by Jane Stallings.
14. Sharan, S. (1980). Cooperative learning in small groups: Recent methods and effects on achievement, attitudes and ethnic relations. *Review of Educational Research, 50*(2), 341–371.
15. Slavin, R. E. (1980). *Using student team learning.* (Rev. Ed.). Baltimore: Johns Hopkins University, Center for Social Organization of Schools.
16. Covington, M., & Beery, R. (1976). *Self-worth and school learning.* New York: Holt, Rinehart and Winston.
17. Ames, C. (1981). Competitive versus cooperative reward structures: The influence of individual and group performance factors on achievement attributions and affect. *American Educational Research Journal, 18*(3), 273–288.
18. Slavin, R. E. (1982). *Cooperative learning: Student teams.* Washington, DC: National Education Association.
19. Edwards, K. J., DeVries, D. L., & Snyder, J. P. (1972). Games and teams: A winning combination. *Simulation and Games, 3,* 247–269.
20. Madden, N. A., & Slavin, R. E. (1983). Effects of cooperative learning on the social acceptance of mainstreamed academically handicapped children. *Journal of Special Education, 17,* 171–182.
21. Slavin, R. E., & Karweit, N. (1984). Cooperative and affective outcomes of an intrinsic student team learning experience. *Journal of Experimental Education, 50,* 29–35.
22. Gerard, H. B., & Miller, N. (1975). *School desegregation: A long-range study.* New York: Plenum Press.
23. Ballard, M., Carman, L., Gottlieb, J., & Kaufman, M. (1977). Improving the social status of mainstreamed retarded children. *Journal of Educational Psychology, 69*(5), 605–611; Blaney, N. T., Stephen, S., Rosenfield, D., Aronson, E., & Sikes, J. (1977). Interdependence in the classroom: A field study. *Journal of Educational Psychology, 69*(2), 121–128; Slavin, R. E. (1977). Classroom reward structure: An analytical and practical review. *Journal of Educational Research, 47,* 633–650.
24. The class segment described in this Snapshot is drawn from classroom observations by Jane Stallings.
25. Hunter, M. (1984). Knowing, teaching and supervising. In P. L. Hosford. *Using what we know about teaching.* Washington, DC: Association for Supervision and Curriculum Development; Hunter, M. (1976). *Prescription for improved instruction.* El Sequndo, CA: TIP.
26. Stallings, J., & Krasavage, E. M. (1986). Program implementation and student achievement in a four-year Madeline Hunter Follow-Through project. *Elementary School Journal, 87*(2), 117–138.
27. Robbins, P. (1986). The Napa-Vacaville Follow-Through project: Qualitative outcomes, related procedures, and implications for practice. *Elementary School Journal, 87*(2), 139–157; Porter, A. C. (1986). From research on teaching to staff development: A difficult step. *Elementary School Journal, 87*(2), 159–164; Slavin, R. E. (1986). The Napa evaluation of Madeline Hunter's ITIP: Lessons learned. *Elementary School Journal, 87*(2), 165–171; Hunter, M. (1986). Comments on the Napa County, California, Follow Through project. *Elementary School Journal, 87*(2), 173–179; Robbins, P., & Wolfe, P. (1987). Reflections on a Hunter-based staff development project. *Educational Leadership, 44*(5), 55–61.
28. The class segment described in this Snapshot is a composite drawn from classroom

INTRODUCTION

This chapter is devoted to the content taught in schools. The first section describes content as a whole, and a second part explains content in terms of three dimensions—knowledge, skills, and affective aspects of learning, such as values, feelings, and sensitivities. The skills dimension is further subdivided into thinking and other types of skills. Chapter 12 will then describe how content is fitted together in a school curriculum.

Educators today express a number of competing views about what actually constitutes the subject-matter content of schools and what that content should be. These differing views then affect the ways in which they believe content should be related to the other ingredients in classroom teaching—classroom processes, theories of learning and instruction, philosophies of education, and so forth. Because of this state of flux and because this text is designed to present you with general conceptual frameworks that you can use to understand developing ideas and trends now and in the future, the chapter treatment of content is rather historical. For example, instead of focusing on currently competing ideas about content, the chapter devotes considerable attention to the subject-matter ideas of Jerome Bruner, Hilda Taba, and John Dewey, educators who were most prominent in the 1960s and earlier. It does so because the authors believe that those ideas will provide you with useful ways of understanding how content fits into classroom activities. More contemporary issues and trends are deferred to your later study.

Although the term *content* is often thought of narrowly, as only the *information* students are taught, here it is considered in a much broader sense. This chapter uses the term to mean everything students are taught—or as a high school student once explained, "Content is all the 'stuff' teachers teach to kids."

The chapter Snapshot is an excerpt from a classic satire on what is taught in schools and its relevance to the real lives of students and society in general. The Analysis asks you to apply the ideas presented in the first two sections of the chapter by developing possible lessons. The Educational Research section looks at studies on a particular aspect of content—the teaching of history.

SNAPSHOT

The Saber-Tooth Curriculum is a satire of education in a fictional primitive society where the content taught to students was not modified as life conditions changed over time. The now-classic work was written in 1939 by educator Harold Benjamin, who used the pseudonym J. Abner Peddiwell.[1] It is paraphrased here. As you read consider:

- To what extent is the situation described similar to present-day decisions about content?

- In what ways does the content in schools you know about reflect present social conditions, past traditions, and individual priorities of public policymakers?

- What would be the most appropriate justification for each of the subjects that you studied in high school?
  In elementary school?
  In college?

- What parallels do you see between this story and the case of Dennis Littky described in Chapter 1?

According to J. Abner Peddiwell, there lived in Chellean times the world's first educational theorist and practitioner, one New-Fist-Hammer-Maker, who was known locally as New-Fist. New-Fist was a talented and educated maker of fine hunting clubs of stone. He was also a thinker and an idealist who wanted to help the people of his stone-age society improve their lives.

As a student of society and education, New-Fist often sat by the early morning fire studying how adults in his community went about meeting the basic needs of life—food, clothing, shelter, and security—and he tried to devise a way of making their work easier and their lives better.

Eventually, he thought that if the children were provided with a systematic education, they could help the tribe meet its needs in better ways. To accomplish this, he decided to teach his children three subjects:

1. fish-grabbing-with-the-bare-hands,
2. woolly-horse-clubbing, and
3. saber-tooth-tiger-scaring-with-fire.

These subjects would eventually provide more to eat, more skins for clothing, and more protection from the dangerous tiger.

As he taught these subjects to his own children, other parents followed his example. For a time, conservative tribe members objected because of religious principles, but gradually more and more parents were won over to New-Fist's ideas. Soon it became obvious that the students trained as New-Fist recommended were leading more successful lives, and eventually the whole tribe became prosperous and more secure.

If conditions in the society had not changed, New-Fist's curriculum would probably have served the tribe well forever. But conditions did change.

As a new ice age approached, a glacier crept close to the headwaters of the creek that ran through the tribe's valley. This caused dirt and gravel to be collected in the stream's water, clouding the clear creek with mud. No one could see fish in the muddy water. Even the best-educated fish-grabbing students could not catch the fish.

The additional water in the stream made the land near the village wetter than before, and this caused the woolly horses to migrate to drier land, away from the tribe. Antelopes replaced the horses, but they were more shy and speedier than the horses. They also had a keener scent for detecting approaching hunters. As a result, horse-clubbing hunters returned day after day to the village without their prey. Even those who were taught the most efficient club-hunting techniques returned empty-handed.

The dampness from the glacial conditions gave the saber-tooth tigers pneumonia, and they died. When the tigers were gone, ferocious glacial bears entered the area. The bears were not frightened by fire and could not be driven away by even the most advanced methods of tiger scaring taught in the school.

The community was in a very difficult situation. The people had no fish or meat to eat, no skins for clothing, and no security from attacking bears.

Faced with these circumstances, several of New-Fist's more thoughtful descendants devised ways to overcome the difficulties. One devised a crude net to catch fish in the muddy water. Another invented a trap to snare the swift antelopes. A third dug camouflaged pits in the bear trails to catch the threatening animals.

Fortunately, the people of the tribe learned the new techniques. They caught fish in nets, snared antelopes in traps, and killed bears in pits. The community was once again well fed, clothed, and secure.

When some thoughtful people asked why net making, trap setting, and pit digging could not be taught in school, those in control told them that such subjects were not appropriate education. After all, these sorts of things were practical, life-preserving skills, which should be taught outside school. They were not *education*; they were *training*. They did not qualify to be taught in school.

Moreover, school leaders pointed out that the school curriculum was filled with the traditional cultural subjects—fish grabbing, horse clubbing, and tiger scaring. Students needed to study fish grabbing because it developed agility. They needed to study horse clubbing because it developed physical strength. They needed to study tiger scaring because it instilled courage. Unlike more

> practical training, these subjects provided general education that carried over into all affairs of life.
>
> Some radical villagers were not satisfied. They continued to object. They pointed out that times had changed and advocated that more up-to-date activities be tried in school. They even suggested that these new subjects might have significant educational value.
>
> The elders replied, "If you had any education yourself, you would know that the essence of education is timelessness. It is something that endures through changing conditions like a solid rock standing squarely and firmly in the middle of a raging torrent. You must know that there are some eternal verities, and the saber-tooth curriculum is one of them!"

THE NATURE OF CONTENT

When most people think of the subject-matter content taught in schools, they usually think of information—the facts and ideas taught to students. But content is not limited to information. It also consists of thinking skills, a wide range of other skills, and components from the affective domain. For example, schools teach the thinking processes of comprehension, analysis, and synthesis; the skills of reading, writing, word processing, library research, speaking, and dancing; and such affective content as the values of justice and equity, the feelings of anxiety and frustration, and the sensitivities of sympathy and empathy. Therefore, when schools are successful, their students learn not only information but content of several types.

Information as Part of Content

Different from Academic Disciplines

Before devoting attention to the various dimensions of content, however, we must take a closer look at the nature of *information*. That look should clarify two persistent misconceptions about what information is and what its place in the processes of teaching and learning is. The first misconception is the confusion of information taught in schools with academic disciplines. The second is the failure to distinguish between information, which is something to be *learned by* students and which is also a device that teachers *use* to produce *learning in* students.

Often, information taught to students in schools is thought to be the same thing as the ideas studied by academic researchers. Tenth-grade biology is considered to be the same as research biology; high school algebra, the same as the content of the theoretical mathematician; and school French, the same French as that of the college French linguist. These things are simply not the same.

Selected

Information taught in schools is drawn from the scholarly disciplines, but it is not taken indiscriminately. It is *selected* by educators who have *criteria* in mind when making their selections. It is chosen to fit the students being taught, to help them learn what the teacher has in mind. Therefore, the history taught by elementary and secondary school social studies teachers is more general, more

The knowledge dimension of content is not simply a mass of small facts that are all alike and waiting to be absorbed by student brains. Although there are, of course, millions of facts to be taught and learned, some of them are more important than others, and some are more useful to student understanding. Also, the facts are not isolated or separate from each other. They are interrelated in a multitude of ways, and they can be clustered together into bigger ideas, such as concepts, generalizations, models, theories, and laws and rules.

If knowledge were only a collection of similar but unrelated facts, it would be impossible to remember and understand all of them. There would be too much to know and no rational way to approach the task.

THE STRUCTURE OF KNOWLEDGE

Fortunately, knowledge has structure—structure that people use to learn and to understand, structure that teachers use to determine what to teach and how to teach it. The structure has been developed by academic scholars as they have studied their various fields, and it has evolved over many years. As a result, knowledge is organized into categories and hierarchies, and the parts are arranged so that they have meaning.

Two views of the structure of knowledge are described below. Scholars often use the two to analyze and explain their areas of expertise; teachers use them to educate students. The first perspective classifies knowledge into fields of study or *disciplines*. The second separates knowledge into *levels of abstraction*, the layers of which are called facts, concepts, and generalizations. In a way of speaking, the first perspective places knowledge into vertical categories, and the second into horizontal layers. Table 11–1 below represents the first configuration, and Figure 11–1 shows the second.

Table 11-1. Knowledge Organized by Discipline

Humanities	Mathematics	Social Sciences	Natural Sciences
Language	Computation	History	Botany
Composition	Algebra	Geography	Zoology
Speech	Geometry	Economics	Chemistry
Literature	Trigonometry	Anthropology	Physics
Art	Calculus	Sociology	Geology
Music		Psychology	Astronomy
		Political science	

Disciplines

Its Own Content

Each academic discipline is a category of knowledge that has two main characteristics that distinguish it from other disciplines. A *discipline* has its own content and its own specialized method of investigation. For example, the *content* of physics consists of such topics as matter, energy, force, and dynamics; that of economics includes scarcity, supply, demand, and price. The *methods* of the practical training, these subjects provided general education that carried over into all affairs of life.

Some radical villagers were not satisfied. They continued to object. They pointed out that times had changed and advocated that more up-to-date activities be tried in school. They even suggested that these new subjects might have significant educational value.

The elders replied, "If you had any education yourself, you would know that the essence of education is timelessness. It is something that endures through changing conditions like a solid rock standing squarely and firmly in the middle of a raging torrent. You must know that there are some eternal verities, and the saber-tooth curriculum is one of them!"

THE NATURE OF CONTENT

When most people think of the subject-matter content taught in schools, they usually think of information—the facts and ideas taught to students. But content is not limited to information. It also consists of thinking skills, a wide range of other skills, and components from the affective domain. For example, schools teach the thinking processes of comprehension, analysis, and synthesis; the skills of reading, writing, word processing, library research, speaking, and dancing; and such affective content as the values of justice and equity, the feelings of anxiety and frustration, and the sensitivities of sympathy and empathy. Therefore, when schools are successful, their students learn not only information but content of several types.

Information as Part of Content

Different from Academic Disciplines

Before devoting attention to the various dimensions of content, however, we must take a closer look at the nature of *information*. That look should clarify two persistent misconceptions about what information is and what its place in the processes of teaching and learning is. The first misconception is the confusion of information taught in schools with academic disciplines. The second is the failure to distinguish between information, which is something to be *learned by* students and which is also a device that teachers *use* to produce *learning in* students.

Often, information taught to students in schools is thought to be the same thing as the ideas studied by academic researchers. Tenth-grade biology is considered to be the same as research biology; high school algebra, the same as the content of the theoretical mathematician; and school French, the same French as that of the college French linguist. These things are simply not the same.

Selected

Information taught in schools is drawn from the scholarly disciplines, but it is not taken indiscriminantly. It is *selected* by educators who have *criteria* in mind when making their selections. It is chosen to fit the students being taught, to help them learn what the teacher has in mind. Therefore, the history taught by elementary and secondary school social studies teachers is more general, more selective, less detailed, and less precise than the history studied in college and investigated by research historians. Similarly, the physiology taught by high school science teachers is different from that of research physiologists; and the elements of drama taught by English and language arts teachers are different from those used by playwrights or drama critics.

Purpose and Use

The difference between information taught in schools and academic disciplines derives from the *purpose* or *use* of each. Academicians and researchers use knowledge to investigate, to create new knowledge, and to organize that knowledge. Teachers use less advanced versions of those ideas, and they translate that information into terms that their students can understand. They use only part of the information, the part that they believe will help students learn and understand. Although their roles overlap, disciplinary scholars stress the probing and exploring aspects of their work, while teachers stress presenting and explaining.

Information taught in schools is also often thought of simply as the "stuff" that students are expected to know. That idea makes sense and is valid to a degree, but it is too limited. It creates the image that when teachers teach, all they do is pour information into the heads of students, whose only function is to absorb that information. Of course, teachers and students do more than this.

Device to Produce Learning

Earlier chapters have demonstrated that learning is a process of change in people. That change has many dimensions, only one of which is acquiring new ideas. Since this is the case, instead of thinking of information only as ideas to be poured into students' heads, it is more useful to think of it also as a *device* that teachers use to create the opportunity for many kinds of learning in students. With this perspective, information becomes a means that teachers use to get students *to do things with ideas*—things such as analyzing their thoughts, refining their thinking abilities, assessing their values, becoming more aware of others' feelings, and so forth. Students who do this do learn new information, but they also learn much more.

Using information in this way can be illustrated as follows:

- History teachers can use information from the American Civil War not only to teach facts about that war but also to teach the concepts of war, conflict, patriotism, slavery, sectional loyalty, tradition, militarism, human values, freedom, equality, and so on. By doing this, teachers use the content of the Civil War to produce broader, more meaningful, and more useful learning than only specific information about a specific war.

- Teachers of literature can use a novel to teach a variety of ideas, insights, and values about people in general, not just about those in that particular piece of literary work.

- Biology teachers can have students study the anatomy of a frog to teach anatomy and physiology of animals in general, including humans.

When teachers see information as a means to accomplish many educational goals, rather than only as an accumulation of ideas to be absorbed by students for their own sake, they can produce more significant and more varied potential for learning. They can make content more dynamic and learning more active.

Deciding What to Teach

Since the primary purpose of education is to change students in certain expected ways, educators select content that they believe will help them change their students in the ways they desire. When they do this, they base their decisions on a number of factors:

Subject Matter and Educational Objectives

1. the availability of content that can be taught,
2. the values of the society that the school serves,
3. their knowledge of the students they teach, and
4. their understanding of the nature of the teaching and learning processes.

For the most part, they select content that will

1. add to the knowledge, understandings, and insights that their students already possess;
2. develop students' thinking abilities;
3. enable students to attain skills that they could not otherwise use; and
4. help students develop certain values, feelings, and sensitivities in an ongoing process of development.

As the process is explained in current educational terminology, teachers choose content for their classrooms that will enable their students to reach desired *outcomes* or *educational objectives*. (For more discussion of selecting content, see Taba, 1962, pp. 1–87, 194–228; Bruner, 1960; Tyler, 1949; Klausmeier & Harris, 1966.)[2]

Chapter 12 will say more about the process of selecting content after the three dimensions of content are thoroughly explored in this chapter. As you study the rest of this chapter, however, it is important that you remember that content is not the end product of learning; it is, instead, something used by teachers to produce learning in students, that is, to change students in many ways.

Also as you read this chapter, keep in mind the message of the chapter Snapshot on the saber-tooth curriculum—content must be appropriate for the students and the community in which they live and function. In these current times of rapid change, the content students study must be revised continually, or it will quickly become dated.

KNOWLEDGE AS SUBJECT MATTER

At the beginning of this chapter, *content* was described as consisting of at least three dimensions—knowledge, skills, and affective aspects of learning. This section of the chapter looks at each of these dimensions. It focuses first on *knowledge*—the area that consists of the facts and ideas that students are expected to acquire.

The knowledge dimension of content is not simply a mass of small facts that are all alike and waiting to be absorbed by student brains. Although there are, of course, millions of facts to be taught and learned, some of them are more important than others, and some are more useful to student understanding. Also, the facts are not isolated or separate from each other. They are interrelated in a multitude of ways, and they can be clustered together into bigger ideas, such as concepts, generalizations, models, theories, and laws and rules.

If knowledge were only a collection of similar but unrelated facts, it would be impossible to remember and understand all of them. There would be too much to know and no rational way to approach the task.

THE STRUCTURE OF KNOWLEDGE

Fortunately, knowledge has structure—structure that people use to learn and to understand, structure that teachers use to determine what to teach and how to teach it. The structure has been developed by academic scholars as they have studied their various fields, and it has evolved over many years. As a result, knowledge is organized into categories and hierarchies, and the parts are arranged so that they have meaning.

Two views of the structure of knowledge are described below. Scholars often use the two to analyze and explain their areas of expertise; teachers use them to educate students. The first perspective classifies knowledge into fields of study or *disciplines*. The second separates knowledge into *levels of abstraction*, the layers of which are called facts, concepts, and generalizations. In a way of speaking, the first perspective places knowledge into vertical categories, and the second into horizontal layers. Table 11–1 below represents the first configuration, and Figure 11–1 shows the second.

Table 11-1.   Knowledge Organized by Discipline

Humanities	Mathematics	Social Sciences	Natural Sciences
Language	Computation	History	Botany
Composition	Algebra	Geography	Zoology
Speech	Geometry	Economics	Chemistry
Literature	Trigonometry	Anthropology	Physics
Art	Calculus	Sociology	Geology
Music		Psychology	Astronomy
		Political science	

Disciplines

Its Own Content

Each academic discipline is a category of knowledge that has two main characteristics that distinguish it from other disciplines. A *discipline* has its own content and its own specialized method of investigation. For example, the *content* of physics consists of such topics as matter, energy, force, and dynamics; that of economics includes scarcity, supply, demand, and price. The *methods* of the

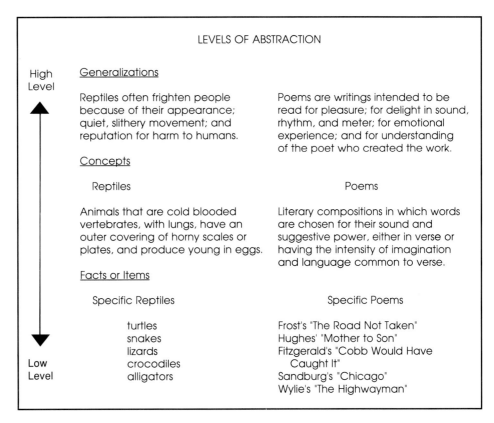

Figure 11–1. Knowledge organized by level of abstraction. Note: Although experts often disagree over the question of which are more abstract, generalizations or concepts, this text arbitrarily shows generalizations as more abstract to provide this graphic illustration.

chemist center on empirical analyses of substances under laboratory conditions; those of the anthropologist concentrate on searching for artifacts and interpreting objects and documents.

The disciplinary categories, however, are artificial. They separate data that, when found in nature, are not really separate; and they differ from each other *by degree* rather than *in kind*. For instance, although sociologists, economists, geographers, political scientists, biologists, chemists, and geologists might all study different aspects of a community, that community does not really consist of seven separate parts. The community exists as an integrated entity, and its components all overlap. The people who live there do not act sociologically in the morning, geographically in the afternoon, and biologically later in the week. They simply act.

The disciplinary scholars who study that integrated community, however, separate what they see into terms that fit their disciplines. They focus on different components of the community, stress different things, conduct different types of analyses, and form different conclusions. At the end of their studies, each individual disciplinary scholar understands one aspect of the community better than other aspects; but a reasonably complete understanding of the community develops only when those separate ideas, analyses, and conclusions are combined.

Academic disciplines serve elementary and secondary school students in ways similar to the ways they serve scholars, but obviously on another intellectual level. They help make a vast, complex, interrelated world more understandable (1) by separating it into parts that can be studied one at a time and (2) by providing a way of looking at each part that helps explain it. Because disciplines play these roles in learning, school instruction is based to some degree on them, as can be seen in a review of school schedules, which typically divide instruction into subjects that rest on disciplines—English, science, mathematics, social studies, graphic arts, and so on.

Levels of Abstraction

Basic Facts

Knowledge also consists of different layers. According to one way of looking at those layers, the lowest level is that of specific facts, things, actions, and events; for example, the parts of the human body, the capitals of states, the correct spelling of words, the dates of historical events, and the answers to simple mathematical computations. These are often referred to as the *basic facts* of a subject. They are the "fundamentals" that many traditional educators say should be "covered" for an elementary understanding of a topic.

Although individual items at this level of knowledge are less significant than those at higher levels, facts are important. They are the building blocks for the development of ideas. People cannot learn if they do not know at least some of the facts.

Concepts

Concepts are a higher layer of knowledge than facts. They are mental categories or groupings into which facts can be placed. For example, the following are concepts: human beings, animals, government, conflict, and whole number. They are general *ideas* instead of specific items. For instance, the concept *war* is a general category that includes the specific item *American Revolution,* and the concept *insect* is a general category that includes a specific *fly* on the classroom wall.

Although concepts as a group constitute one layer of knowledge, the range of difference among them is great. At one extreme are concepts that are quite narrow and precise; at the other end are very general and abstract concepts. The range begins just one step above specific facts and continues to the most general and abstract ideas people can think of.

All of the terms in Figures 11–2 and 11–3 represent concepts. Those at the bottom of each diagram are more narrow and less inclusive than the increasingly general and abstract ones higher up. As you study the two figures, remember that the nature of concepts means that any attempt to arrange hierarchies among them, such as in this illustration, is necessarily arbitrary and artificial. Which ideas are more general and more abstract than others simply depends on what different people have in mind when they think of the ideas. However, the illustration is presented here so that you can see an example of some ways in which concepts of different degrees of generalization and different levels of abstraction might fit together. The particular orders shown are the orders suggested by a group of educators polled by the authors.

Generalizations

Generalizations or *general principles* constitute a third layer of knowledge, and according to the scheme presented here, a higher level. They are valid statements that describe relationships among concepts. They are statements that people use

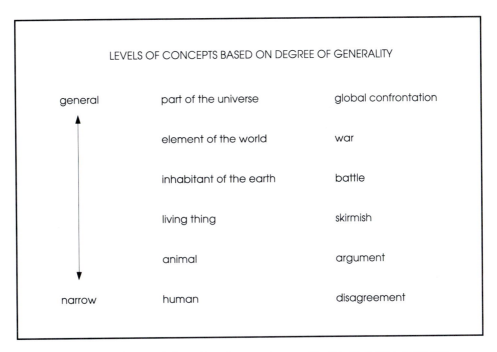

Figure 11–2. Levels of concepts based on degree of generality. This illustration shows two columns of ideas. All items in each column are labels for concepts, but the items at the bottom are less inclusive (or smaller) than those at the top. They become more inclusive (or larger) each step up the columns.

to organize concepts and facts into an intellectual system that makes sense. They look and sound like sentences that explain things.

In the following examples, the key words (those in italics) are key concepts, and the statements explain ways in which those concepts are related. If a person understands these statements and accepts them as valid explanations, he or she probably knows something more about the ideas described than a person without a comparable understanding.

- All *people* need *food, clothing,* and *shelter.*

- Under *normal environmental conditions, roots* of *plants* usually *grow* toward *water* in the *soil* and *stems* and *leaves* usually *grow* toward *light.*

- *Intelligent people* usually become better *teachers* than *stupid people.*

- *Teachers* rarely *make* more *money* than *medical doctors.*

Some scholars who study the nature of knowledge have identified other levels in addition to these three, some organize the levels differently, and many would probably say that this three-level description is much too simplistic, but it is adequte for this stage of study. The main points to remember are (1) knowledge contains a number of levels, (2) people use those different levels in their thinking, and (3) teachers can teach students best if they select different levels of knowledge when they select the subject matter they teach. (For more information on the structure of knowledge, see Taba, 1962, pp. 172–192, 211–215; Schwab, 1962, 1964; Bruner, 1960.)[3]

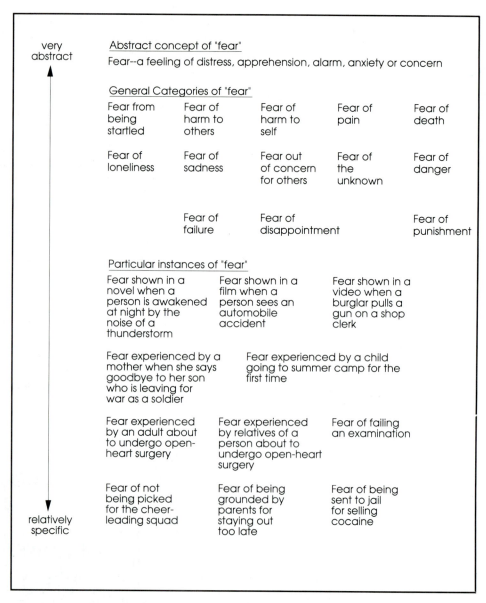

Figure 11-3. Levels of concepts based on degree of abstractness. This illustration shows instances of the concept "fear." Those at the bottom are rather specific; those nearer the top are categories of "fear"; at the top is a general definition for the term.

Teaching the Structure of Knowledge

Fundamental Structure of Knowledge

The idea of the structure of knowledge became very significant for educators of the 1950s and 1960s who were confronted with the realization that the traditional guide for what to teach—"the important facts of each subject"—was not possible or appropriate for elementary and secondary schools. The "information explosion" showed that there were just too many facts to teach, that more facts were being generated every day, and that the new information was changing some of the "correct answers" of the past. In their search for a new way of doing things, educators turned to ideas expressed in 1960 by Harvard psychologist and educator Jerome Bruner in his book *The Process of Education.*

The Process of Education crystallized thinking about how knowledge should be taught and greatly influenced the content of school curricula in subsequent years. Its main thesis is that students should be taught *the fundamental structure of knowledge* instead of a collection of basic facts and incidental information. For Bruner, this meant they should be taught

1. key concepts,
2. fundamental principles or generalizations, and
3. methods of inquiry of the disciplines.

Although there are more recent and more complex ways of thinking about knowledge and how to teach it, Bruner's ideas are presented here because they seem to be more useful than most for beginning teacher-education students. Once you understand Bruner's views, you should be able to use them as a means of developing an understanding of other ideas that you will encounter in future study.

Bruner believed that the learning of the fundamentals of knowledge would produce greater student understanding, encourage students to inquire into issues and solve problems independently, enable them to transfer ideas learned in one situation to another, and help them *learn how to learn.* He said learning to learn was critical for students who faced life in the era of information explosion. He urged teachers to make students *problem solvers* by putting them into situations in which they could use fundamental ideas to find meaning in the data they studied. He stressed that students should engage in a *process of discovery.*

Spiral Instruction

Bruner believed that students who are taught in this way could learn relatively complex concepts, first at a beginning level and later with more sophistication. As he saw it, students who possessed an initial understanding of concepts could return to them again and again in their studies, each time learning more at more advanced levels. As students proceeded through school, they could reencounter the fundamental ideas in a manner resembling a spiral.

Burner's ideas were not entirely new, of course, and the 1950s and 1960s were not the first time educators worried about which important aspects of knowledge to teach. Scholars in classical Greece, in medieval and Renaissance times, in the Enlightenment, and twentieth-century scholars dating as far back as the 1920s explored similar ideas, especially in social studies and science. But Bruner's writings were especially significant because they caught the attention of leading educators at an opportune time for change.

Because of *Sputnik,* the 1960s was a time of radical change for school curricula. School systems, states, and the national Office of Education all engaged in substantial curriculum-rewriting projects, and many of those that gained broad followings based their approach to teaching content on the ideas of structure. Many adopted Bruner's framework in total. Frequently, the projects set new directions for which content was taught and how it was taught, directions that persist until today in many classrooms. The greatest impact was at the secondary school level, particularly in science and mathematics.

Using Structure to Select Subject Matter

Since the 1960s, the idea of teaching the fundamental structure of knowledge has provided curriculum committees and teachers with ways of selecting content that stress big ideas rather than simple facts. This has freed them from the

Using Structure to Sequence Subject Matter

compulsion to cover everything and has enabled them to choose content based on how intellectually useful it is for students. It has also provided a framework on which curriculum developers can put the ideas in sequence to be taught from kindergarten to grade 12 by supplying a range of concepts and generalizations in each subject.

Teaching Information and Thinking Together

The idea of structure means that teachers can organize knowledge to introduce facts, concepts, and generalizations in the same lesson and can build on those ideas in future lessons. It means they can arrange ideas to be learned according to their complexity and degree of abstraction. In fact, they can teach information and the skill of thinking at the same time.

Ways of Thinking

When taught the structure of knowledge, students are not restricted to studying subjects just to find out what is already known. They can learn a *process of investigation* as well. They can learn the *methods of inquiry* of the disciplines and ask questions much as scholars do. They can engage in beginning levels of research, becoming young historians, linguists, biologists, and so forth. In the process, they can *learn ways of thinking* that will help them understand new ideas and solve intellectual problems throughout their lives. (See Bruner, 1960; Taba, 1962, pp. 76–83, 211–218, and 290–301; Weil & Joyce, 1978.)[4]

Something to Think About

Common Core

Which knowledge to teach has been a persistent question for educators through the ages, and answers, of course, have varied from time to time. During the latter part of the 1980s, several vocal educators said that schools were neglecting to teach students a particular *common core* of ideas and information that they need to know in order to communicate effectively as American citizens and to feel a part of American society. One of these critics, E. D. Hirsch (1987, 1988),[5] said schools need to teach more subject-matter knowledge and should return to a more traditional, fact-oriented curriculum. He said literate Americans share a certain amount of discrete information and that that knowledge makes them *culturally literate*. Students who are not taught it are *culturally illiterate* and, therefore, disadvantaged.

Cultural Literacy

Hirsch proposed that schools identify a basic core of subjects and information that all students should know and then set out forthrightly to teach it. He did not propose that this common core replace other basics such as reading, writing, thinking skills, and values. He said it should be in addition to those other efforts.

- Do you think schools should teach a common core of knowledge to all students?
- Do you think they are neglecting to do so at the present time?
- If school instruction should include a common basic core, what should be in that core? Why do you think so?

Before you continue on to the next section of this chapter, pause for a moment to think about the nature of knowledge as it has been described on the preceding pages. Compare that idea of knowledge to

1. how you would have described the content taught in schools before you started reading this chapter or before you began this course, and
2. the content of the saber-tooth curriculum of the chapter Snapshot.

EDUCATIONAL RESEARCH

Teaching and Learning History

This Educational Research section reports on an investigation into the teaching of a specific area of content—history. It describes a study (Downey & Levstik, 1988)[6] in which two history educators analyzed what other researchers have been investigating about why and how history is taught in the schools. That study asked several questions about the teaching and learning of history and reported how researchers have been answering those questions.

History was chosen as the focus of this section because the teaching of history has been debated publicly in recent years. However, the section is intended as an example of content-related research in all subject areas in general, not just history. As you read, consider what might be parallel issues and questions that concern the teaching of English, mathematics, science, foreign languages, and the other K–12 subjects.

The questions Downey and Levstik asked and their report on how research is answering these questions follow:

- How much and how well is history being taught?

  Data for the 1980s, are not available; so we really do not know the answer to this question for the past decade. Through the 1970s, however, state course requirements and student enrollments held constant for American history and declined for world history. The world history courses that were eliminated were not replaced by increases in other social studies courses or by increases in enrollemnt in those courses.

  Teachers of history rely heavily upon discussion, lecture, individual assignments, and weekly quizzes; little information exists as to how well they use these methods. One notable study reported wide variety in the quality of history instruction both across schools and in the same school.

- How central is the textbook in history instruction?

  Conventional wisdom says that history teachers rely excessively on texts, but actual studies are very limited, and two seem to question the assumption. One of these studies reports that there is little reading in history classes and that texts are used by students primarily as reference books to answer worksheet questions. The same study says, however, that many students actually avoided using texts as references by copying answers from other students and/or by completing their worksheets when the teacher reviews other students' answers. The second study reports that history teachers lecture and show films more than they rely on texts.

- How much history do students know?
Recent tests of student knowledge in history, as well as studies in the 1940s report what the test givers have called striking ignorance of history among students, but there is little agreement about what history and how much history students should know. Students who took the tests scored below the level that many people thought they should have scored, but the content of the tests and the expected level of satisfactory performance were based on subjective guesstimates made by the people who constructed the tests as much as on anything else.

- In what ways do students understand the concept of time, and how do they develop the ability to think historically?

Although research is still limited on much of this, efforts are underway, and there is evidence that students develop a variety of ways of understanding history, time, change, causation, and temporal relationships. However, the ties between age, cognitive development, historical thinking, and depth of historical understanding need much more exploration. For instance, possessing a sense of history, understanding historical descriptions, and comprehending complex historical explanations involve different levels of sophistication in thinking. One study of these areas of historical learning is particularly illustrative. According to Downey and Levstik, Hallam (1979),[7] studying students in the United Kingdom,

> found that logical structures similar to those described by Piaget could be detected in historical thinking. His students responded to questions based on narrative historical passages in ways that seemed to him comparable to Piaget's stages of preoperational, concrete operational, and formal operational thinking. However, his history students reached the concrete and formal stages considerably later than Piaget's subjects had. Hallam's students reached the concrete operational stage at about age 13, rather than at age 7 or 8 for Piaget's students; formal operational thinking began at about age 16 in history, compared to age 12 in Piaget's research. He concluded that although students develop formal operational thinking in the study of history, it happens at a later [date than in the] study [of] mathematics and science. (Downey & Levstik, 338)

In contrast to approaches like Hallam's, other investigators question whether Piagetian ideas are appropriate for describing historical learning, because Piagetian thinking was derived from research on thinking about science and mathematics. Some say thinking about history is more open and includes historical perspective, both of which, they say, make cognitive development theories inadequate for explaining how children and young people think about history. At this time, these researchers are turning to a variety of alternative explanations.

- What do studies such as these tell us about the present teaching of history?

The studies show that much practice in teaching history is not based on research and that the ways in which history is taught and learned needs to be studied more fully. To do this, research should include investigation of the relationships between child development and historical thinking as well as between historical content and the methods teachers use to teach it. It should also include close monitoring of what is happening in history classes and the documentation of effective practices.

In sum, although history has been taught for centuries, there is little evidence that proves what is good, appropriate, or poor practice. Much new information will be generated in the next few years, and knowledgeable teachers will use it to improve what they do and how well their students learn. New teachers will need to be informed.

SKILLS AS CONTENT

Skills

Skills are abilities to do things one has the ability to do. They are competencies that people possess which enable them to perform in certain ways. Skills are different from knowledge in that they require more than just knowing. They require *doing*, with some degree of proficiency.

Skills, however, are just as much school content as knowledge. They are part of what students need to learn and part of what teachers must teach. Skills differ from both knowledge and affective learning and are taught differently, but they are an important dimension of school instructional programs and are central to the reasons that schools exist.

Thinking

In at least two ways, *thinking*, which is a complex skill or combination of skills, is especially important as content to be taught in schools. First, all students must learn to think; second, the extent to which they do affects all their other learning.

When experts explain *thinking*, they usually use many technical terms. Many say it involves at least three elements—intellectual processes, mental activities, and cognitive strategies. In combination, all three help people make sense out of the information and other stimuli that they encounter in their lives and relate new information to ideas they already have. Thinking involves skills that people use to do all of the following: to impose intellectual order on disorder, to gain

insight, to predict consequences, to propose solutions to problems, and to decide what to do when faced with a decision.

A Human Trait

Some say thinking is a uniquely human trait, that it is the most significant characteristic that separates humans from other forms of life because human thinking is at a higher and more sophisticated level than that of other worldly creatures. These higher levels of thinking are described in many ways and often with highly specialized language. Some of the more common general labels are *critical thinking, systematic thinking, theoretical thinking,* and *abstract thinking*. More specific terms that define particular aspects of thinking are *conceptualizing, comprehending, computing, inferring, interpreting, analyzing, synthesizing, problem solving, generalizing, applying knowledge,* and *evaluating*.

Schools and Thinking

What actually happens inside the human mind when people think is a matter of much uncertainty, research, and debate. But despite a lack of certainty, educators and society in general believe that people need to learn to think effectively, that thinking is a skill that can be taught, and that schools should teach it. They also believe that teaching skills of thinking accelerates mental development and makes students more autonomous, creative, and productive people. (For more discussion of thinking, see Taba, 1962, pp. 211–218; Dewey, 1933; Beyer, 1985; Scriven, 1976; Norris, 1985; McPeck, 1981; Paul, 1984.)[8]

Teaching Thinking

When people think, they have to think *about something;* and when they acquire knowledge, they also develop their ability to think. In short, learning knowledge and thinking skills are interdependent and mutually reinforcing. Therefore, the effective teaching of knowledge includes the teaching of thinking and vice versa.

The two illustrations of specific types of thinking skills that follow are intended to provide more precise ideas of what thinking skills are and to show how they can be taught in schools. The two are thinking strategies that people use all the time, and they can be taught across subjects and grade levels in elementary and secondary schools: problem solving and conceptualizing. The following are examples, but they do not represent all kinds of thinking or how to teach thinking. They are only brief introductory glimpses at the thinking-skill dimension of content. (For additional ideas about teaching thinking skills, see Weil & Joyce, 1978; Parker, 1987; Chance, 1985; Raths, Wasserman, Jonas, & Rothstein, 1986; Baron & Sternberg, 1987; Costa, 1985; Sternberg, 1984; Nickerson, 1984; Copple, Sigel, & Saunders, 1984; Sigel, 1984; Joyce, 1985.)[9]

Problem Solving

Problem solving and *scientific inquiry* are terms that describe a type of thinking in which people confront new information and situations as ideas to be explained or problems to be solved. The process begins with the assumption that humans are by nature inquiring beings who seek answers when explanations for puzzling situations are not readily apparent. This natural tendency motivates them to *discover meaning* in that which they do not understand.

As people pursue this process of discovering meaning, they seem to pursue intellectual paths that have a rather common pattern and a recognizable sequence. Although experts have described the process differently over the years, they agree in a general sense on what it involves. Sometimes it is called the *scientific method*. The best-known and most traditional form of the process is probably the one articulated by John Dewey (1933) in the 1930s. The steps in the process outlined below parallel that idea.

When people solve problems, they typically do the following:

1. recognize the problem
2. analyze it,
3. propose possible solutions,
4. test consequences of those possible solutions,
5. select a solution, and
6. evaluate the selected solution.

In more pedestrian terms, they (1) face a problem, (2) gather information, (3) figure out what is wrong, (4) think of ways to fix it, (5) try some of them, (6) decide which solution is best, and (7) remember the solution so it can be used again.

People use problem solving all the time, sometimes in complex, sophisticated ways and sometimes almost automatically. For example, a TV repair person who turns on a television set and sees that nothing happens might typically do the following: turn the switch off and on a second time, wiggle the switch, push the plug tighter into the socket, check the electrical circuit, tighten possible loose contact points, replace possibly bad parts, and so forth. If the TV comes on in response to any of these actions, the problem is solved (unless more needs to be done to prevent the difficulty from occurring again). When a solution to the problem is found, the repair person uses that information to decide what to do while working on the next television set that does not work.

People act similarly in all sorts of situations—when the baby will not stop crying, when friends will not play with them, when the car will not start, when there is a detour on the road, when the roast did not taste the way it should have, and when the appliance coming off the assembly line does not work. Sophisticated experts such as nuclear physicists, engineers, medical doctors, and teachers act similarly in their work when confronted with difficulties that require interpretation and appropriate action. For them the processes might be more theoretical, complicated, and time-consuming, but the basic steps are about the same.

Teaching Problem Solving

Since problem solving is a type or thinking that involves skill, it can be learned, and people can improve through practice. Therefore, it can be taught in schools. To do this, teachers present problems to students and focus their attention on *how* the students think about the problem rather than on *what* they think. They use the students' natural desire to discover as motivation. They help students interpret the problem in a way that makes sense to them, develop guesses or hypotheses about solutions, test them, and evaluate the results. They lead their students intellectually and encourage imaginative and resourceful thinking. They guide the students as they practice the skill.

A well-known approach to teaching problem-solving thought is the Inquiry Training Model developed a number of years ago by Richard Suchman. In designing the model, Suchman (1962, 1966) analyzed how research scholars solved their problems, translated the steps they used into forms meaningful for school instruction, and developed teaching strategies for teachers to use to guide their students through the steps.[10]

Table 11–2 outlines a teaching sequence based on the Suchman model. By teaching according to this sequence, teachers guide students through classroom activities including (1) recognizing a problem, (2) searching for data appropriate to solving the problem, (3) processing the data, and (4) applying it to the situation. Then the students engage in the most important part of the whole exercise. They analyze the inquiry process they just used in order to understand what they did. By doing this, they become increasingly skilled at the process.

Conceptualizing

Conceptualizing, or *developing concepts*, is a type of thinking that involves putting things into categories or groups; people do it almost constantly. It is a basic level of thinking on which other cognitive processes depend. For example, everyone categorizes *things* in the environment into groups such as trees, buildings, vehicles, furniture, animals, humans. They group *events* in their lives into work, play, useful, silly, patriotic, distasteful, harmful, tragic. People think of *ideas* in such conceptual terms as liberal, conservative, concrete, abstract, exciting, and foolish. They divide *people* into concepts such as female, male, short, pretty, macho, bright, white, Italian.

People do this so that they can understand something about the items that they group and then make predictions about those items. For instance, even if a person never saw a specific tree before, knowing that it is a tree tells him or her a good deal about it. The same would be true about a piece of furniture, an

Table 11-2. A Lesson Sequence for Teaching Problem Solving

Step 1: Presenting the Problem

Teacher presents students with a problem that does not have an obvious answer (through observing actual situations or viewing open-ended films, pictures, or stories).

Step 2: Collecting and Verifying Data

Teacher helps students verify the nature of the problem by answering questions about information on specific objects, properties, conditions, or events of the problem; but does so only by responding "yes" or "no." (Students formulate "yes" or "no" questions.)

Step 3: Experimenting with Data

Teacher encourages students to isolate specific variables and look for relationships in the problem. Students may also begin to develop their hypotheses.

Step 4: Formulating a Hypothesis

Teacher guides students toward developing formal hypotheses or explanations for the problem.

Step 5: Evaluating the Hypothesis

Teacher points out invalid parts of the student's hypotheses and prompts them to evaluate their thinking.

Step 6: Analyzing the Problem-solving Process

Teacher helps students analyze what they did to solve the problem in order to understand the problem-solving process better and to become more skilled at using it.

This illustration is a modification of ideas described in R. J. Suchman, 1966.

---

automobile, or a dog. In the same way, knowing that a person you are about to meet for the first time is a conservative thinker, a religious zealot, a terminally ill patient, or a grouch is also helpful. When you know which groups people are generally in, you may be able to interact with them more effectively. At the same time, however, it could lead you to prejudge them and stereotype.

Conceptualizing is such a common thinking process that it occurs spontaneously. You cannot stop yourself from doing it. When you walk across campus, you think to yourself—this is the shortest path to that building; that is an expensive car; he is an attractive man; she is a pleasant person; that is an ugly sweater. When you listen to a lecture you think—that is a vague idea; his terms are too abstract; this topic is dull; none of this relates to the real world of teaching; classes like this are boring. When you see students in a school, you think—he is short; she is shy; they are black; he is slow; she is sharp; they are poor; they are trouble makers.

When people conceptualize, they engage in three mental operations:

1. They notice differences among the mass of information their senses provide for them and separate that information into discrete items or objects.

2. They look at the characteristics of the various items and use those characteristics to lump each of those items with others that have the same characteristics.

3. They put a label on that group of items.

For example, when people think about things, events, and people in their lives, they decide that some things are alive, some rough in texture, some dangerous, some unexplainable; some events are celebrations, parties, conferences, classes; and some are fun, sad, long, tedious, important, obligatory; some people are women, children, rich, socially polished, depressed, Spanish-speaking, English-speaking.

Teaching Conceptualizing

Although conceptualizing is spontaneous and people do it all of the time, some people conceptualize better than others. They conceptualize better because they have learned how to do so—they have been taught. Conceptualizing can be taught in schools at any grade level and in any subject, so long as students are engaged in thought above the recall level. Because conceptualizing is a skill, it is taught through practice. Teachers provide students with information and have them work thoughtfully and conscientiously through the steps in the process. That is, they ask them

1. to notice aspects of the information before them,
2. to group items together because of common characteristics, and
3. to propose labels for the groups.

All through the process the teacher helps the students analyze what they are doing and why they are doing it so that they refine both their understanding of the process and their skill in using it.

An approach to teaching the skill of conceptualizing called Developing Concepts has been used in schools for some time. Developed by Hilda Taba and her associates at the Taba Curriculum Development Center in California in the 1960s (Taba, Durkin, Fraenkel, & McNaughton, 1971), the approach involves a sequence of teacher questions that stimulate student thinking and discussion.[11] Those questions are outlined in Table 11–3.

Thinking about Thinking

Metacognition

For the last few years, significant attention has been devoted to *metacognition*, a rather new approach to the teaching of thinking. The concept involves thinking about thinking. The approach focuses on the process of thinking as a subject to be taught. In addition to learning and practicing thinking in a variety of subjects, students actually study a unit or take a course called Thinking. The idea is based on the assumption that learning about thinking improves thinking, and it is drawn from research indicating that a major difference between expert problem solvers and less capable ones is that the experts understand and explain their own thinking, whereas the others cannot. (For more information, see Costa, 1984.)[13]

Specific areas of metacognitive research concern one's ability to monitor and regulate thought processes. For example, research in reading comprehension and study skills shows that good readers employ a wide variety of metacognitive strategies or skills. These strategies include the following:

Table 11-3. A Lesson Sequence for Teaching the Development of Concepts

Teacher Questions	Student Responses	Student Thinking

Previous to the discussion, the teacher assigns or conducts an intake activity, one through which students learn information.

1. What are some of the things you read about in the story? or saw in the film? or found on the play ground?	Enumerate	Recall information Differentiate among items

The teacher records student responses as they are given so that they can be seen by all. He or she then cycles through the following two questions several times.

2. Which of these items can be put together in a group because they are alike in some way?	Group items	Identify similar characteristics among items
3. What labels could be used for this group?	Label group	Synthesize and generalize about groups

Throughout the discussion, the teacher asks the students to explain their thinking by asking follow-up questions, such as "Why do you say that?"

This illustration is based on discussion sequences described in Taba, Durkin, Fraenkel & McNaughton, 1971, pp. 65–70; and Myers, 1973.[12]

1. adapting one's reading behavior in a particular situation to one's purpose,
2. predicting and identifying main ideas of the text,
3. monitoring ongoing reading to make certain that comprehension is occurring, and
4. changing one's strategy (approach to the reading task) when comprehension is not occurring (Brown, 1982).[14]

Poor readers often continue their reading when they are not comprehending, and this can be a waste of time. They do not monitor and change strategies to fit their purposes and the results of their efforts. Poor performers do not plan the strategies they employ and do not assess the effects those strategies have on their comprehension. However, studies show that instruction in metacognitive skills can help these students improve their reading and studying techniques (Baker & Brown, 1984).[15]

Other Skills Taught in Schools

Skills, of course, are by no means limited to thinking. They exist in many forms—in so many forms, in fact, that it is virtually impossible to categorize them. Some are more complex than others, some are more physical than others, some are more closely tied to particular subject knowledge than others, and so on. Frequently, they overlap with each other and contain common subskills. A number of categories, each containing a list of skills, appears below. The categories are not discrete, and the lists are far from complete, but they should provide a glimpse at some of the components of this aspect of content.

ANALYSIS

This Analysis section asks you to think about teaching the knowledge and thinking-skill dimensions of content presented so far in the chapter. It directs you to select topics covered in subjects taught in K–12 classrooms and then to brainstorm how that content could be taught if you use the two approaches to teaching described earlier in the chapter. The first part of the exercise focuses on the problem-solving approach, the second on developing concepts. Both approaches combine the teaching of knowledge and thinking skills in the same lesson.

PROBLEM SOLVING

1. Select a subject taught in elementary or secondary school and a specific K–12 grade level; then identify a problem-related topic from within your chosen subject, making sure it is appropriate for the grade level you have in mind. For example, for a seventh grade social studies unit on the environment, street litter; for a high school physics class, the need to move, with limited resources, a large and heavy object.
2. Review the steps in the problem-solving approach to teaching outlined in Table 11–2 of this chapter.
3. Formulate a specific problem that you would have the students investigate, again remembering the grade level of the students you have in mind. For example, how can street litter near the school be reduced? What strategies can be applied to move the heavy object?
4. Using Table 11–2 as your guide, sketch out the six-step problem-solving lesson.

DEVELOPING CONCEPTS

1. Select a subject and grade level as you did in Step 1 above; then identify a grade-appropriate concept from your chosen subject. Refer to the earlier descriptions of concepts if you wish. For example, domestic animals from primary-level science and types of fear from a high school literature assignment.
2. Review the steps in the developing-concepts approach to teaching outlined in Table 11–3 of this chapter.
3. Devise an intake activity that will provide students with the needed background information. For example, have the primary children look

for pictures of animals in magazines, or read them a story about animals; for the high school literary assignment, assign the piece of literature to be read, or show it in the form of a video presentation.

4. Again using Table 11–3 as your guide, make a rough sketch of what your three-step concept development lesson might look like.

When you have completed both parts of this brainstorming of lessons, do three more things:

- Assess the ways in which the lessons you have sketched would teach knowledge and also ensure that the students would practice some type of thinking.

- Write how you felt as you engaged in the exercise, making particular note if you felt frustrated at times and why you think you felt that way.

- Record how you decided on the focus of the two lesson sketches, how often you changed your mind, and why you did so.

Save what you write, as Chapter 13 asks you to refer to it again.

Skills Taught in Schools

Learning/Study Skills

Reading
Listening
Analyzing data
Synthesizing data
Evaluating data
Taking notes
Outlining
Skimming and scanning
Writing

Interpretative Skills

Reading maps and globes
Interpreting charts, graphs, and diagrams
Computing scales and distances
Recognizing symbols
Interpreting timelines and calendars
Organizing events chronologically

Research Skills

Using a dictionary
Using a table of contents and an index
Identifying sources
Locating materials in library
Interpreting data from other sources
Organizing data

Communication Skills

Speaking
Listening
Writing
Observing
Giving directions
Questioning
Signing (hand signals)

Social Skills

Leading others
Interacting pleasantly with others
Conforming to rules
Controlling one's emotions
Cooperating with others
Following directions of others
Making decisions
Helping others
Acting responsibly
Assuming responsibility for actions

Motor Skills

Developing eye-hand coordination
Drawing
Coloring
Handwriting
Typing
Running
Jumping
Throwing
Dancing

Artistic Performance

Drawing
Painting
Sculpting
Singing
Playing a musical instrument
Dancing
Acting

Citizenship Participation Skills

Staying informed
Analyzing values
Formulating opinions
Stating own views
Judging opinions and actions
Making decisions
Persuading others
Leading others
Cooperating
Following others
Accepting responsibility
Voting

Skills are developmental. Students learn them over time, through a combination of instruction and practice. They typically start with little or very low levels of proficiency and gradually get better. Observers can witness this phenomenon rather easily by comparing a student's proficiency at a skill over varying lengths of time. They would normally see little difference in ability from one day to the next but would see noticeable gains from month to month or year to year.

Observers sometimes miss this developmental aspect of learning skills when they watch experts performing a particular skill. The experts perform so smoothly and effectively that their efforts appear deceptively simple. They are not simple at all, a point an observer would recognize immediately if he or she could compare the expertly performed routine with the performer's first practice session.

Most skills are more than mechanically performed habits that are learned through drill and practice. They are, instead, complex, highly organized, integrated patterns of behavior that can be demonstrated with proficiency only when the skilled person combines significant knowledge of what is involved with practice over time. In short, most skills need to be understood to be performed well.

Skills Involve Understanding

Clusters of Subskills

Some skills are so complex that experts still debate their exact nature. Reading and writing are good examples. These types of skills are really clusters of many subskills or components, and each of the components requires instruction, understanding, and practice.

Writing: An Illustration

A cursory look at how children often learn the skill of writing can serve as an illustration. In the primary grades, children learn to write letters, words, sentences, and eventually short narratives. In many programs, they begin by learning how to hold the paper and pencil correctly. Then they start actual writing by making straight and slanted lines and forward and backward circles. Next they learn and practice the correct formation for upper- and lowercase letters. After they make letters correctly, they copy short words and practice spacing those words on paper. Later they group individual words into short sentences. After much practice writing short sentences, they combine sentences into paragraphs. Eventually, they organize paragraphs into larger examples of writing, such as short essays or descriptions of events ("My Summer Vacation") or creative stories.

In the process of doing all this, students learn not only the skill of cursive writing but a vast array of writing subskills that are integrated into a complicated act called *writing*. As they continue to write, they extend and refine their writing abilities, a process that continues throughout their lifetimes.

Teaching Skills

When students learn skills well, they usually do so through planned instruction. They learn them through a process that includes instruction about the skill as well as a sequence of directed practice, assessment, feedback, and further practice. They rarely attain high-level competence automatically, spontaneously, or incidentally, as by-products of being at school.

When teachers teach skills, they supply *basic knowledge* so that students know what they are doing, and they *provide experiences* so that students can practice.

Planned Sequence

Teachers arrange information and experiences in sequences of increasing difficulty and present them one step at a time in a developmental pattern appropriate to the students' level of understanding and ability. The teaching consists of explanation, demonstration, and guided practice so that students comprehend what is done, observe how it is done correctly, and work at doing it well themselves.

Guided Practice

Because skills are learned through practice, much skills instruction concentrates on having the students use the skill under the guidance of and with explanations from the teacher. This practice makes it possible for the learner to become sophisticated at the task and to perform with greater competence, ease, and confidence. Although practice does not ensure improved performance, it provides opportunities for it. Under normal conditions teacher guidance, explanation, and encouragement helps the student improve. (For more information on teaching skills, see Taba, 1962, pp. 225–228; also, for example, see Singer, 1980.)[16]

Now that you have concluded the section on skills as content, pause for a moment to think about the skills that present-day high school graduates need. Think of how different these skills are compared to the skills that were necessary to function in society ten, twenty, or a hundred years ago. To highlight extremes, think of survival skills of the 1990s in contrast with those of a real saber-tooth-like primitive society.

AFFECTIVE LEARNING AS CONTENT

The affective dimension of the content taught in schools consists of values, feelings, and sensitivities. It includes such concepts as right and wrong, beauty, goodness, priorities, and such skills as making choices. Although it has cognitive aspects and sometimes involves skills, it differs from other dimensions of learning because of its predominant emotional and evaluative overtones.

Affective learning is part of content because schools are usually expected to teach students to "do the right thing": that is, to behave correctly according to community standards. To do this effectively, students must study the following:

1. the values espoused by their culture and others, as well as their own personal value system;
2. the feelings of others, as well as their own; and
3. the sensitivities of others and what it means to be sensitive.

Values

Values are those aspects of life to which people attach worth or esteem. They are standards that people endorse, maintain, and try to live up to. They emerge from the very nature of societies and cultures and are passed on to younger generations through the process of *socialization*. They serve as general guides for behavior. Some of the commonly accepted values important to Americans include the following:

human dignity	hard work	consent of the governed
honesty	achievement	getting along with others
equality	material success	due process of law
tolerance	interdependence	justice
freedom	freedom of expression	truth

Since values such as these are widely accepted throughout this culture, there is a fair amount of agreement about the role of schools in teaching them. However, other values are more controversial. They often at least seem in conflict with each other and/or with general cultural norms and traditions. When this happens, the role of schools in teaching them is frequently questioned. For example, schools in America are expected to teach the following apparently conflicting ideals:

cooperation	competition
honesty	avoiding hurting others' feelings
loyalty to friends	reporting of wrongdoing of others
personal success	care for the feelings and welfare of others
conforming to social norms	creativity, individuality, and personal autonomy
ethnic identity	acceptance of and respect for others
sincerity of personal religious beliefs	tolerance and acceptance of others' beliefs
freedom of political expression	patriotism and national loyalty
nationalism	peaceful cooperation among nations
nonviolence	standing up for what one believes
appreciation of diversity	rejection of deviant behavior

(See Fraenkel, 1977; Taba, 1962, pp. 68–70, 220–223; Raths, Harmin, & Simon, 1966; Kohlberg, 1975; Kohlberg, Levine & Hewer, 1984.)[17]

Feelings

Feelings are internal emotional and moral sensations that people experience as they respond to others and to events and circumstances. People acquire feelings from their interaction with their social and cultural environments. They are usually expressions of the values that individuals hold and the sensitivities they possess. Because feelings are internal and individual, we "learn" them in different ways than we learn "knowledge." We discover, generate, cultivate, extend, and, sometimes, repress them in life's experiences. Common feelings include the following:

joy	hurt	disgust	sadness
fear	belonging	alienation	anxiety
loneliness	acceptance	disappointment	admiration

(See Fraenkel, 1977; Taba, 1972, pp. 68–70, 223–225; Raths, Harmin, & Simon, 1966.)

Sensitivities

Sensitivity is the capacity to respond to others and to situations in a perceptive, humane, and empathetic way. It involves such abilities as seeing others as they see themselves, putting oneself in someone else's shoes, and communicating positively across personal and cultural barriers. It is a characteristic that runs counter to ethnocentrism, prejudice, and the rejection of values and behaviors just because they are different from one's own. Sensitive people understand the values, feelings, and aspirations of others and are able to empathize with them. (See Fraenkel, 1977; Taba, 1962, pp. 68–70, 223–225; Raths, Harmin, & Simon, 1966.)

Teaching Values, Feelings, and Sensitivities

The affective domain is part of the content taught in schools because what students need to learn in this area is too important to be allowed to develop by happenstance. Students need to be helped to understand the emotional and

evaluative aspects of their lives; to accept, extend, and modify their beliefs and feelings; and to be able to make good decisions. Schools teach in such areas by providing information and experiences that encourage values, sensitivities, and feelings to develop and appropriate choices to be made. By so doing, they help students analyze and develop their values, explore and come to terms with their feelings, cultivate and deepen their sensitivities, and practice making decisions.

Which Values?

When public groups express concern about the teaching of values and other aspects of the affective domain, invariably their concerns are not whether schools should teach values but which ones they should teach. When most of society or a local community agrees on a value, schools are expected to teach about it and either advocate it or teach that it is wrong. For example, schools are expected to support justice, equality, and honesty, and oppose murder, racial and sexual discrimination, and cheating. If a value is less broadly accepted or rejected in a community, schools may be expected to teach about it, without advocating or rejecting it. For instance, schools usually teach about but do not advocate specific religious beliefs, particular political party positions, and similarly debatable positions that have evolved from cultural traditions, such as how strict or lenient parents should be in child rearing. When communities are split on particular values or otherwise unsure what their school-age students should be taught, schools usually avoid the issue. Sex education has often been treated this way in the past, although the impact of the media and the spread of AIDS has caused society leaders and educators to have second thoughts about what to do.

Contrary to what people may think, schools have had substantial responsibility for affective learning across cultures and throughout history. Schools everywhere were established as *socializing institutions,* institutions founded by adult generations for the purpose of transmitting cultural values to younger generations and instilling in them a commitment to those values. In addition to teaching knowledge and skills, they were, and are, intended to teach *cultural expectations*—what the culture values and the behaviors that are expected of its members. (See Taba, 1962, pp. 68–70, 220–223.)

Cultural Expectations

Other Socialization Institutions

Of course, schools are not the only socializing institutions that provide affective education. Families, churches, peer groups, older generations, traditions, rituals, and print and broadcast media do as well. But in the complex and rapidly changing environment of recent times, many of these institutions have been changed, and their educational roles have become less clear than in the past. Similarly, some of these institutions, such as television, have much more strength than in the past. In response to such changes society has turned more directly to schools.

Careful Planning

Schools that provide the most effective instruction concerning values, feelings, and sensitivities plan carefully and follow patterns. They realize that providing information is only part of the task. They also know that techniques of "preaching" and indoctrinating have limited or counterproductive value in school settings. Frequently, they teach through example, case studies, and the expectations they set for their students. By doing so, they put students into situations in which they experience or witness conditions that are value-laden and emotional in content and/or response. They arrange experiences for students that require them to

- think about values, feelings, sensitivities, and choices;
- analyze and clarify their own positions, perspectives, and emotions;
- compare their ideas and emotions with those of others;
- put themselves in others' situations;
- experience the feelings involved in situations, especially those likely to be emotionally laden; and
- develop their own skills at valuing and decision making.

Second in the Planning Process

Despite careful planning, however, instruction in most subjects and at most grade levels is not usually organized initially around affective objectives. Instead, curriculum planners and teachers plan their lessons around knowledge—concepts and generalizations: then they plug into that content the affective learning they believe should take place. For instance, history teachers typically decide to teach an event from the past primarily because of the knowledge it will transmit. They then determine how they can also teach values, feelings, and sensitivities in the same process. Similarly, many language arts teachers teach a particular work because they want their students to know the work or its writer before they consider the value lessons involved in the particular work. Unfortunately, the fact that the affective education decisions frequently come second in the planning process has led some educators to think they are of second-level importance. They are not. (For more information on teaching values, feelings, and sensitivities, see Fraenkel, 1977; Galbraith & Jones, 1976; Simon, Howe, & Kirschenbaum, 1972; Brady, 1974; Brady, n.d.)[18]

Teachers use many teaching strategies to teach affective dimensions of subject matter. Some are more appropriate for certain grade levels, subjects, and teaching styles than others. Illustrations of two of these appear below. The first helps students explore feelings, and the second helps them analyze values. When teachers use either of these strategies, they actually teach three kinds of learning: (1) knowledge about feelings and values, (2) analytical skills that students can use to study their own feelings and values and those of others, and (3) the emotional and evaluative overtones of feelings and values. The two strategies are based on the curriculum development work of Hilda Taba and her associates at the Taba Curriculum Development Center in the 1960s (see Taba, 1971, pp. 76–80). They are presented here as examples because they have been used long enough to have stood the test of time in actual classrooms, are used rather widely in classrooms throughout America, and can be plugged into many different lessons across subjects and grade levels. They fit into instruction any time a classroom topic touches on feelings or values, and they work with any students who can discuss ideas in a group-discussion setting.

Illustration—Exploring Feelings

The teacher presents to the class an intake eposide that describes people in a situation involving significant feelings. Such situations as those below could be told to the students; they can also read them or see them on video.

Lesson Topic	Situation
Second-grade social studies lesson on neighborhoods	A new child arrives in the neighborhood and knows no one.
Fourth-grade science lesson on pollution	An older woman in a crowd at a zoo slips on a banana peel just tossed on the ground by a teenager.
High school literature lesson on the antebellum South	A reasonably well-meaning woman from an aristocratic family treats a slave in subhuman ways.
High school history lesson on war	A story of a family's plight after a son is killed in battle, and the mother (or another or all family members) becomes despondent.

The teacher next conducts a discussion using the following sequence:

Teacher Questions	Student Responses
1. What happened in the episode? What did _____ do?	Enumerate facts from episode
2. How do you think (the person) felt when _____?	Infer feelings

The teacher repeats the second question for each key person in the episode.

3. Do you know of a situation where something like this happened to someone you know? Would you like to tell us about it?	Describe a similar situation
4. How do you think (the person or character) felt when _____?	Inner feelings

The teacher repeats Question 4 for each key person in the student-offered episode.

5. Based on your entire discussion, what can you say about how people feel when _____?	Generalize about feelings

The teacher follows up student responses throughout the discussion by asking, "Why do you think _____ felt that way?

(This illustration is based on a lesson design developed by the Taba Curriculum Development Center. See Taba, Durkin, Fraenkel, & McNaughton, 1971, p. 78.)

Illustration—Analyzing Values

The teacher presents to the class an intake episode that describes a person or some people in a situation that involves a value-laden choice or decision. Situations such as those below could be told to the students, or the students could read them or see them on video.

Lesson Topic	Situation
Third-grade reading lesson about children who steal candy from a store	One of the children is asked whether he or she knows who stole the candy and must decide how to respond.
Eighth-grade health lesson on sexuality	A group of young teenagers is discussing supposed sexual encounters they and their friends have experienced. One of the group has to decide if he or she should admit to significantly less experience than the others report.
High school biology lesson on human physiology	A high school athlete is training for the coming football season and is afraid he is not strong and large enough to do well. He wants to use steroids. His girlfriend argues against his doing so.

Then the teacher conducts a discussion, using the following sequence:

Teacher Questions	Student Responses
1. What happened in the episode?	Enumerate facts from episode
2. Why do you think (the person) did (or decided) (the *action* or *decision*)?	Infer reasons for actions
3. If that was (the person's) reason for doing it, what do you think he (she) thinks is important?	Infer values behind reason
4. If you were in this situation, what would you do?	Predict own behavior
5. Do you know of a situation similar to this? Would you like to tell us about it? What did _____ do?	Describe a similar situation
6. Why do you think (the person) did (or decided) this (*action or decision*)?	Infer reasons for actions
7. If that was (the person's) reason for doing it, what do you think he or she thinks is important?	Infer values behind reason
8. Based on our entire discussion, what can you say about what people think is important?	Generalize about values

The teacher follows up student responses throughout the discussion by asking, "Why do you think that?"

(This illustration is based on a lesson design developed by the Taba Curriculum Development Center. See Taba, Durkin, Fraenkel, & McNaughton, 1971, pp. 81–82.)

Something to Think About

The 1980s controversy over bilingual education reflects a number of perspectives as to which dimensions of subject-matter content—knowledge, skills, affective learning—are most important for students, and each of those perspectives is tied to similar assumptions about the purposes and goals for schools. For example, consider the four statements below:

Mr. Allen: The idea of teaching children in their primary language when it is not English is critical. If young students do not understand their lessons in the early grades because of language barriers, they run the risk of never catching up.

Ms. Bates: If students are going to learn as they should in public schools, they need to be able to understand English. Teaching them in primary languages other than English slows the process. Besides, schools that try to teach in several languages cannot provide as intense and sophisticated instruction in the other languages as they can in English. Teaching in non-English languages is a disservice to students who have to compete in an English-speaking society.

Ms. Cain: When students from homes where a language other than English is the primary language are taught only in English, they are being told that they are handicapped and not as good as their Anglo classmates. This hurts their self-image and stifles learning. Of course they achieve less.

Ms. Dodge: I cannot understand why a child who learns fluent Spanish in school is considered a high achiever and one who learns fluent Spanish at home before entering school is considered deprived.

- How would you react to each statement?
- Which of the three dimensions of content described in this chapter would you say each statement emphasizes?

CONCLUSION

If schools are to accomplish all the goals set for them, they must educate students in many ways—enable them to understand new information and ideas, help them develop better skills, stimulate in them increasingly sophisticated value perspectives, feelings, and sensitivities. To do this, teachers must select several types of content to insert into their teaching in ways that truly make their students changed human beings. The task is made complex by the multiple purposes of

An Elementary Understanding

schools and by the magnitude of the content that students could appropriately learn.

Teachers can make the tasks of selecting and teaching content manageable by (1) formulating educational objectives for their classes and (2) organizing the content they teach into an intellectual framework that makes sense to them. This chapter described content in the context of a particular conceptual structure—knowledge, skills (including thinking), and affective learning—in order to provide you with a simple way of understanding what content is and how it fits into the teaching-learning process.

The particular conceptual structure of content described in this chapter is not the only one and, in fact, is not even one of the most recently developed. It has been around in rather full bloom form for at least two decades. Some educators would call it a dated system, but it seems to be especially useful to beginning teacher-education students as they start to think of content as something more than the subject labels of the courses they studied in high school and college. We hope it will enable you to come to terms with the additional ideas about content that you will confront in your future study.

SUMMARY

The content taught in schools can be thought of in many ways, one of which is to view it as having three dimensions—knowledge, skills, and affective learning. Each of these can be subdivided into facts, concepts, and generalizations; thinking and other skills; and values, feelings, and sensitivities. Content in all three areas is important for students to learn and appropriate for classroom instruction.

In thinking about content, it is useful to separate the idea of *information*—the "stuff" that students should know—from broader concepts of knowledge. When this is done, it is possible to view knowledge as facts, concepts, and generalizations drawn from numerous academic disciplines with various levels of abstraction. In this broader context, knowledge has structure, and that structure makes it understandable and perhaps easier to teach.

Skills are tasks or activities one is able to do. Learning them involves understanding and proficiency. Thinking, reading, and writing are especially important skills, but many others are also appropriate for school instruction. Values, feelings, and sensitivities can and should be taught in schools, along with knowledge and skills.

STUDY QUESTIONS

1. Think of your college academic major or subject-matter teaching field outside education and select five to ten important ideas from that subject that all students should learn before they finish high school. What criteria did you use to select those five to ten ideas? Would other students in this class agree with your choices?

2. Suppose that you are teaching all basic subjects at a fifth- or sixth-grade level and the last month of the school year is about to start. You realize that (a) you have much more than a month's amount of information to cover with your class, (b) more

than half of the students in the class are well below grade level in reading and mathematics, and (c) the class as a whole seems to be particularly prejudiced toward students who are ethnically and racially different from themselves. Knowing that you will not be able to teach everything that you would like in the remaining month, which goals or areas of content would you give highest priority? Why?

3. How would you respond if you were asked to comment on the following discussion between two high school teachers:

Mr. Johnson: I realize that most of the students read and write very poorly, but my job is to teach history, not language arts.

Mr. Smith: I disagree. All of us must teach reading and writing even if it cuts into our subject matter.

4. Should all students be required to take a knowledge and skills test at each grade level and in each high school subject before passing? If so, who should decide what each test covers? What should happen to the students who repeatedly fail?

BIBLIOGRAPHY

Adler, M. J. (1982). *The Paideia proposal.* New York: Macmillan.

Baron, J., & Sternberg. (Eds.). (1987). *Teaching thinking skills: Theory and practice.* New York: W. H. Freeman.

Beyer, B. K. (1987). *Practical strategies for the teaching of thinking.* Boston: Longman.

Bruner, J. S. (1960). *The process of education.* Cambridge, MA: Harvard University Press.

Chance, P. (1986). *Thinking in the classroom: A survey of programs.* New York: Teachers College Press.

Cooper J. (Ed.). (1986). *Classroom teaching skills.* Lexington, MA: Heath.

Dewey, J. (1933). *How we think.* Lexington, MA: Heath.

Eggen, P. & Kauchak, D. (1988), *Strategies for teachers: Teaching content and thinking skills.* Englewood Cliffs, NJ: Prentice-Hall.

Eisner, E. W. (1985). *The educational imagination.* (2nd ed.). New York: Macmillan.

Fraenkel, J. R. (1977). *How to teach about values: An analytical approach.* Englewood Cliffs, NJ: Prentice-Hall.

Gagné, R. M. (1987). *The conditions of learning* (3rd ed.). New York: Holt, Rinehart and Winston.

Hirsch, E. D. Jr. (1987). *Cultural literacy: What every American needs to know.* Boston: Houghton Mifflin.

Klausmeier, H. J., & Harris, C. W. (1966). *Analysis of concept teaching.* New York: Academic Press.

Kohlberg, L. (1975). The cognitive-developmental approach to moral education. *Phi Delta Kappan, 56*(10), 670–677.

Nickerson, R. S. (1984). Kinds of thinking taught in current programs. *Educational Leadership, 42*(1), 26–36.

Peddiwell, J. A. (1939). *The saber-tooth curriculum.* New York: McGraw-Hill. (Harold Benjamin.)

Raths, L. E., Harmin, M., & Simon, S. B. (1966). *Values and teaching.* Columbus, OH: Merrill.

Schwab, J. J. (1962). The concept of structure of a discipline. *Educational Record, 43*(3), 197–205.

Taba, H. (1962). *Curriculum development: Theory and practice.* New York: Harcourt, Brace and World.

NOTES

1. Peddiwell, J. A. [Benjamin, Harold] (1939). *The saber-tooth curriculum.* New York: McGraw-Hill.

2. Taba, H. (1962). *Curriculum development: Theory and practice.* New York: Harcourt, Brace and World; Bruner, J. S. (1960). *The process of education.* Cambridge, MA: Harvard University Press; Tyler, R. W. (1949). *Basic principles of curriculum and instruction.* Chicago: University of Chicago Press; Klausmeier, H. J., & Harris, C. W. (1966). *Analysis of concept teaching.* New York: Academic Press. All four of these were written some time ago, but they are classics in their influence on instruction.
    Also see Joyce, B., & Weil, M. (1986). *Models of teaching* (3rd ed.). Englewood Cliffs, NJ: Prentice-Hall; Martin, B. L., & Briggs, L. J. (1986). *The affective and cognitive domains: Integration for instruction and research.* Englewood Cliffs, NJ: Educational Technology Publications: Gagné, R. M., & Briggs L. J. (1979). *Principles of instructional design* (2nd ed.). New York: Holt, Rinehart and Winston. For a more contemporary general overview of subject-matter content in school curricula and teacher decisions about curricula, see Ryan, K., & Cooper, J. M. (1988). *Those who can, teach* (5th ed.; pp. 171–198, 446–448). Boston: Houghton Mifflin.

3. Schwab, J. J. (1962). The concept of structure of a discipline. *Educational Record, 43,* 197–205. Also see two chapters by Schwab in G. W. Ford & L. Pugno (Eds.). (1964). *The structure of knowledge and the curriculum.* Chicago: Rand, McNally.

4. Weil, M., & Joyce, B. R. (1978). *Information processing models of teaching.* Englewood Cliffs, NJ: Prentice-Hall.

5. Hirsch, E. D. (1987). *Cultural literacy: What every American needs to know.* Boston: Houghton Mifflin; Hirsch, E. D. (1988). Cultural literacy: Let's get specific. *NEA Today, 6*(6), 15–21. For a general overview of Hirsch's ideas see *Education Week, 6*(27), 1987, April 1. For a related perspective, also see Bloom, A. D. (1987). *The closing of the American mind.* New York: Simon and Schuster.

6. Downey, M. T., & Levstik, L. S. (1988). Teaching and learning history: The research base. *Social Education 52*(5), 336–342.

7. Hallam, R. N. (1966). *An investigation into some aspects of the historical thinking of children and adolescents.* Unpublished M.Ed. thesis. University of Leeds; also see Hallam, R. N. (1967). Logical thinking in history. *Educational Review, 19*(June), 183–202.

8. Dewey, J. (1933). *How we think.* Boston: D. C. Heath; Beyer, B. K. (1985). Critical thinking: What is it? *Social Education, 49*(4), 271–276; Scriven, M. (1976). *Reasoning.* New York: McGraw-Hill; Norris, S. P. (1985). Synthesis of research on critical thinking. *Educational Leadership, 42*(8), 40–45; McPeck, J. E. (1981). *Critical thinking and education.* New York: St. Martin's; Paul, R. W. (1984). Critical thinking: Fundamental to education for a free society. *Educational Leadership, 42*(1), 4–14.

9. Parker, W. C. (1987). Teaching thinking: The persuasive approach. *Journal of Teacher*

Education, 36(3), 50–58; Chance, P. (1985). *Thinking in the classroom: A survey of programs.* New York: Teachers College Press; Raths, L. E., Wassermann, S., Jonas, A., & Rothstein, A. M. (1986). *Teaching for thinking* (2nd ed.). New York: Teachers College Press; Baron, J., & Sternberg. (Eds.). (1987). Teaching thinking skills: Theory and practice. New York: W. H. Freeman; Costa, A. L. (Ed.). (1985). *Developing minds: A resource book for teaching thinking.* Alexandria, VA: Association for Supervision and Curriculum Development; Sternberg, R. J. (1984). *How can we teach intelligence? Educational Leadership* 42(1), 38–48; Nickerson, R. S. (1984). Kinds of thinking taught in current programs. *Educational Leadership, 42*(1), 26–36; Copple, C., Sigel, I. E., & Saunders, R. (1984). *Educating the young thinker: Classroom strategies for cognitive growth.* Hillsdale, NJ: Lawrence Erlbaum Associates; Sigel, I. E. (1984). A constructionist perspective for teaching thinking. *Educational Leadership, 42*(3), 18–21; Joyce, B. (1985). Models for teaching thinking. *Educational Leadership, 42*(8), 4–7.

10. Suchman, J. R. (1962). *The elementary school training program in scientific inquiry.* (Report 216 of Project VIII.) Report to the U.S. Office to Education. Urbana, IL: University of Illinois Publications Office. Also see Suchman, J. R. (1966). Inquiry development program: Developing inquiry. Chicago: Science Research Associates.

11. Taba, H., Durkin, M. C., Fraenkel, J. R., & McNaughton, A. J. (1971). *A teacher's handbook to elementary social studies* (2nd ed.). Menlo Park, CA: Addison-Wesley.

12. Myers, C. B. (1973). *Introduction to people in change and the Taba program in social science.* Menlo Park, CA: Addison-Wesley.

13. Costa, A. L. (1984). Mediating the metacognitive. *Educational Leadership, 42*(3), 57–62.

14. Brown, A. L. (1982). Learning how to learn from reading. In J. Langer & M. Trika (Eds.), *Reader meets author/bridging the gap.* Newark, DE: IRA. Also see Wham, M. A. (1987). Metacognition and classroom instruction. *Reading Horizons, 27*(2), 95–102.

15. Baker, L., & Brown, A. L. (1984). Metacognitive skills and reading. In P. D. Pearson (Ed.), *Handbook of Reading Research.* New York: Longman.

16. Singer, R. M. (1980). *Motor learning and human performance* (3rd ed.). New York: Macmillan.

17. Fraenkel, J. R. (1977). *How to teach about values: An analytical approach.* Englewood Cliffs, NJ: Prentice-Hall; Raths, L. E., Harmin, M., & Simon, S. B. (1966). *Values and teaching.* Columbus, OH: Merrill; Kohlberg, L. (1975). The cognitive-developmental approach to moral education. *Phi Delta Kappan, 56*(10), 670–677; Kohlberg, L., Levine, C., & Hewer, A. (1984). The current formulation of the theory. In L. Kohlberg (Ed.), *Essays on moral development* (Vol. 2, pp. 320–386). San Francisco: Harper & Row.

18. Galbraith, R. E., & Jones, T. M. (1976). *Moral reasoning.* Anoka, MN: Grenhaven; Simon, S. B., Howe, L. W., & Kirschenbaum, H. (1972). *Values clarification.* New York: Hart; Brady, L. (1974). *Do we dare? A dilemma approach to moral development.* Sydney, N.S.W., Australia: Dymock's; Brady, L. (n.d., approx. 1975). *Values taught and caught: Personal development for secondary schools.* Sydney, N.S.W., Australia: Dymock's.

CHAPTER 12

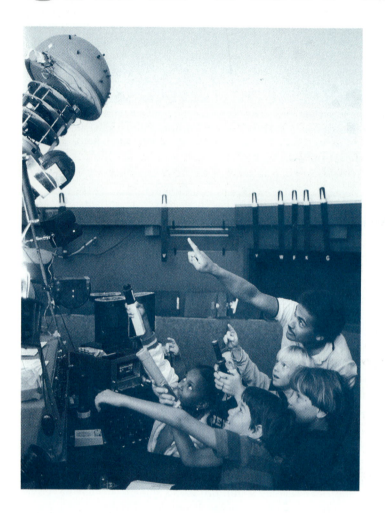

The Curriculum and Lessons: Designs for Learning

INTRODUCTION

Now that you have explored the various dimensions of content and how teachers use it to produce learning in students, this chapter turns to the ways in which content is combined with approaches to teaching, learning activities, and instructional materials into school curricula, units, and lessons. The school curriculum is the school's plan of instruction, the design of what, when, and how students should be taught; which content should be covered; and what the students should have learned by the time they graduate or finish a specific grade level. It is put together by school leaders and committees of teachers who identify what students most need to know and be able to do and how the school can provide for those needs. Units of instruction and lesson plans are both subdivisions and extensions of the curriculum. They cover segments of the content outlined in the curriculum and they elaborate more specifically on how it will be taught.

The chapter describes a continuum of action that occurs in many curriculum development efforts, from the selection of content by curriculum developers to the preparation of a single lesson. Different types of curricula are explained, and partial examples of units are provided.

The chapter Snapshot consists of weekly class schedules for four very different students. These illustrate the subject-matter components of the curriculum and the fact that the curriculum is not the same for every student. The Analysis section describes what happened when the teacher who planned the lesson described earlier in the chapter actually taught it to her first-grade students. The Educational Research section reports on studies of the effectiveness of the middle-school concept.

SNAPSHOT

The Snapshot for this chapter consists of the weekly class schedules for four students. The first is for a high school student in an academic program; the second, for a high school student in a general-vocational program; the third, for a second-grade student; and the fourth, for a middle-school student.[1] As you read, consider:

- What differences in emphases do you notice among the four programs?
- What educational priorities are reflected in the subjects studied by each student?
- How would you compare these programs with the schedules of students whom you know?

Name: William Holloway   Class: Grade 11

Period	Monday	Tuesday	Wednesday	Thursday	Friday
1	Algebra II	Algebra II	Algebra II	Algebra II	Algebra II
Homeroom					
2	English III	English III	English III	English III	English III
3	American History	American History	American History	American History	American History
4	French II	French II	French II	French II—Lab	French II
Lunch					
5	Chemistry	Chemistry	Art	Chemistry	Chemistry
6	Chemistry	Physical Education	Art	Physical Education	Art

Name: Brad Swartz   **Class: Grade 9**

Period	Monday	Tuesday	Wednesday	Thursday	Friday
1	Math I	Math I	Math I	Math I	Math I
Homeroom					
2	English I	English I	English I	English I	English I
3	Data Processing	Music	Physical Education	Music	Data Processing
Lunch					
4	Auto Mechanics	Data Processing	Auto Mechanics	Data Processing	Auto Mechanics
5	Auto Mechanics	Data Processing	Auto Mechanics	Physical Education	Auto Mechanics
6	Social Studies	Social Studies	Social Studies	Social Studies	Social Studies

Name: Kathy Wray   **Class: Grade 2**

Period	Monday	Tuesday	Wednesday	Thursday	Friday
8:00–8:30	Directions for the Day — Individual Reading ——————————————————————→				
8:30–9:00	Reading (Direct Instruction) ——————————————————————————→				
9:00–9:30	Phonics Practice ————————————————————————————————→				
9:30–10:00	Spelling	Writing	Spelling	Writing	Spelling
10:00–10:20	Language Arts Practice ————————————————————————————→				
10:20–10:30	Restroom ——————————————————————————————————————→				
10:30–11:00	Art	Music	Art	Library	Music
11:00–11:30	Math (Direct Instruction) ——————————————————————————→				
11:30–12:00	Math Practice ————————————————————————————————→				
12:00–12:30	Lunch ——————————————————————————————————————→				
12:30–12:45	Restroom/Break ————————————————————————————————→				
12:45–1:00	Story Time ——————————————————————————————————→				
1:00–1:30	Social Studies ————————————————————————————————→				
1:30–2:00	Physical Education ————————————————————————————————→				
2:00–2:30	Science	Science	Health	Science	Science
2:30–2:45	Clean up and prepare for dismissal ——————————————————→				

Name: Jill Driscoll   **Class: Grade 6**

Period	Monday	Tuesday	Wednesday	Thursday	Friday
1	Language Arts	Language Arts	Language Arts	Language Arts	Language Arts
2	World Cultures	World Cultures	World Cultures	World Cultures	World Cultures
3	Introduction to Computers	Music	Introduction to Computers	Music	Introduction to Computers
4	Mathematics	Mathematics	Mathematics	Mathematics	Mathematics
Lunch					
5	Earth Science	Earth Science	Exploratory	Earth Science	Earth Science
6	Earth Science	Art	Exploratory	Library	Art
7	Physical Education	Physical Education	Physical Education	Physical Education	Assembly

THE CURRICULUM

If students are going to learn the knowledge, skills, and affective content that teachers, school leaders, and parents expect, their instruction must be organized rationally and sensibly. It must follow a design, and the design must take into account many factors discussed in this text—purposes of schools, processes of human development, philosophies of education, theories of learning, currently accepted approaches to instruction, and the nature of content. In short, school instruction must follow a plan, and such a plan is called the curriculum. The schedules in the Snapshot of this chapter reflect how those four students' curricula are organized.

When educators design a curriculum, they decide what to teach, what to leave out, what to emphasize, what to skim over lightly. They also plan a sequence—what comes first, second, third, and so on—from year to year and from September to June. In addition, they develop ways of connecting the various elements of what is taught so that their students' instructional experiences are interrelated to some degree. Some of these connections are little more than the sequencing of lessons, but there are others—reading is related to language arts, and both are often connected with social studies; science lessons are based on an assumption that students can use certain arithmetic and mathematics skills; content from history and literature overlap and include values instruction. In good schools, formal instructional content is also tied to the social life of the school community—clubs, sports, personal friendships, and informal student-teacher relationships.

Choices at Three Levels

In making curricular choices, educators usually start with content—what they think should be covered in various subjects at each grade level. Then they arrange classes, units, lessons, teaching strategies, learning activities, and instructional materials in ways that they believe will produce the greatest amount of learning most efficiently. Ideally, similar choices actually occur at three levels—curriculum planners design curricular frameworks for schools, committees of teachers or teachers working individually use the school curriculum to formulate units, and individual teachers use the units to plan class lessons. As a result, teachers actually end up with a plan of what to do with each of their classes each Monday morning, and for the most part, that plan makes sense and is appropriate for the students they teach.

This chapter emphasizes this method of designing curricula, but the teaching world is rarely ideal. Sometimes curricula are put together haphazardly, with little thought. Sometimes there is little sequencing, coordination, and articulation across grades and subjects. In some places teachers more or less do their own thing, shifting focus when they feel like it. Some schools have no written curriculum at all.

Different Starting Points

Though the development procedure just introduced is excellent, not all good curriculum plans, units, and lessons have to start with the selection of content. It is just as important to acknowledge that teachers frequently develop good lesson plans without having access to either units or curricula. Often teachers begin planning lessons by adopting particular texts and then organize their teaching around that decision. Some start by selecting teaching strategies they want to use—lectures, small groups, seat work, discussion—or learning activities they want their students to engage in—cooperative learning, drill and practice, class reports, note taking.

The pages that follow trace the process of curriculum development from the selection of content for schoolwide curriculum frameworks to the organization of a specific lesson plan for a class. The presentation is significantly and intentionally idealized for the convenience of students just beginning their study of curriculum.

Bases for Selecting Content

Available Content

One of the factors that influences which content is taught is the pool of knowledge, skills, and values that are appropriate to be studied. In selecting knowledge to be taught, curriculum developers and teachers turn to the scholarly fields of study—the disciplines mentioned earlier. They search the disciplines for information and ideas that will be most useful, understandable, and interesting for their students. Similarly, they search for skills and value perspectives. However, because there is so much more information and are so many more skills and value positions than can possibly be taught, and because all of them are not of equal value, they must make choices.

Culture and Society

To make these selections, educators must look at criteria outside the disciplines for guidance; and when they do, these other criteria become a second influence on what is taught. One such influence involves the culture and society that the school serves and in which the students live. Educators analyze the society by asking such questions as the following: What are the traditions and long-term assumptions undergirding this society? What needs and problems does the society face? What does it expect and require of its citizens? Which values does it support? (See Taba, 1962, pp. 31–75, 179–194.)[2]

Answers to questions such as these provide teachers with ideas of two types—answers about what society expects of them as teachers and about which competencies and qualities their students will need in order to survive, participate, and prosper in the society. From such answers teachers discern what to teach and what students need to learn.

Much of Chapters 1, 5, 7, and 8 addressed these points. Those chapters describe, respectively, the current context in which schools function, the purposes and goals for schools in recent decades, the historical assumptions and traditions that affect schools today, and some philosophies of education.

Learners and Learning

The nature of learners and the learning process is a third influence on which content is taught. On a general level, this area includes ideas about the developmental stages of students, their interests, their strengths and weaknesses, their characteristics and needs, and how they learn. In a particular classroom, it also includes data about specific individuals in the class. Is this student or that average, college bound, a potential dropout, vocationally oriented, or special? Such questions direct teachers toward what to teach their students, as well as when and how to teach it. (See Taba, 1962, pp. 76–120, 132–171; also see Chapters 4 and 5 of this text.)

Chapters 4, 9, and 10 focus on these ideas. They describe, respectively, human development, theories of learning, and selected models of instruction.

The Process of Selection

Ideally, the content to be taught to a group of students depends on the educational objectives set for them. The complex process of identifying those objectives occurs at least at three levels, each described below. Although the levels presented here appear to be discrete, in reality they are intertwined. (For more thorough discussions of the process of selecting content in terms of educational objectives, see Taba, 1962, pp. 194–230; Ornstein & Levine, 1985, pp. 446–454; Kibler, Baker, & Miles, 1981; Gronland, 1978.)[3]

Broad Aims of Education

Broad aims of education, which set general directions and emphases about what is taught, are typically set at national, state, and school district levels. They reflect broad cultural values and educational philosophies, and they provide an overall direction for school programs to follow. They focus attention toward some subject matter and away from others, but only in very general terms. Usually, they are too abstract to be adequate guides for specific curricular decisions. Most are similar to the following:

- to transmit cultural traditions,
- to develop basic literacy,
- to cultivate civic responsibility,
- to provide for economic self-sufficiency, and
- to promote positive self concepts.

School-Level Goals

Somewhat more specific, middle-range educational goals are usually set at the school-district and school-building levels. These follow from the broader aims but are more focused and more specific. They describe schoolwide goals and, sometimes, student behaviors that would demonstrate that they have been attained. Goals at this level include the following:

> to develop critical thinking,
>
> to encourage participation in political activity,
>
> to enhance mathematical computational skills,
>
> to improve study habits, and
>
> to appreciate good literature.

Objectives at this level set directions for curriculum planners and teachers. They serve as the guidelines around which school programs are organized. They provide the criteria for a second-level decision in the process of content selection.

Class-Level Objectives

Objectives at an even more specific level describe learning outcomes sought at the various grade levels, in particular subjects, and for particular units of instruction. They reflect decisions made about broader aims and goals, and they fit within their scope and limits. They are more specific, however, and are therefore useful in defining what students should learn. The following are objectives of this type. The students will be able:

> to distinguish between long- and short-vowel sounds,
>
> to list the sequence of events in a story,
>
> to perform at or above the minimum standard on 50 percent of the physical fitness skill activities,
>
> to explain the process of photosynthesis,
>
> to solve quadratic equations,
>
> to write a clear, well-organized, two-page critique of a short story.

Good objectives at this level describe what teachers should teach in their classes. They tell teachers which content to cover and which ideas, skills, and values to emphasize. They also suggest which learning experiences teachers might provide, the materials they might use, and how they might assess what the students have learned. They serve as the primary basis on which teachers decide which content to teach.

Making Content Choices

Relevance

In the end, the decision on what to teach is a matter of professional judgment by curriculum planners and classroom teachers. As a matter of judgment, it involves personal choices and individual priorities. As teachers make these choices, they ask themselves questions: What is important? What is meaningful? What is relevant to the needs of the school and my students? Such questions take time to answer and frequently generate heated disagreements within curriculum committees. They are the questions that caused dissension in the sabertooth society of the Chapter 11 Snapshot. Behind them are many related and subsidiary questions: Relevant *to what?* Relevant *for whom?* Relevant *by what standard?* These are questions to keep in mind as you proceed with your studies. (For more discussion of the question of relevance, see Taba, 1962, pp. 76–79; Ryan & Cooper, 1988, pp. 218–222.)[4]

Since choices of content are rather subjective, teachers who make them have to resort to their own values and beliefs as personal guides.[5] One such guide that they are likely to turn to is their own ideas about why schools exist, that is, the general roles, functions, and purposes of schools as they see them.

Traditional Schools

Teachers who have a traditional view of schools believe that the primary purpose of school is to transmit past cultural traditions to students, to inculcate in the students a loyalty to those traditions, and to perpetuate them. They tend to select content that has stood the test of time and are more likely to stress history, classical languages, a fundamental approach to reading, and basic computational skills in mathematics rather than contemporary issues. Asian cultures, write-to-read approaches to reading instruction, and computer applications would be unlikely selections for the traditionalist. These teachers are not likely to change the curriculum frequently. (For example, see Taba, 1962, pp. 18–22; Ryan & Cooper, 1988, pp. 77–79, 84–87; Johnson, Collins, Dupuis, & Johansen, 1988, pp. 354–360, 401–402.)[6]

Schools in an Era of Change

On the other hand, teachers who have a present- or future-oriented view of schools believe that the most important task for schools is to enable students to cope with rapid social changes in modern society. They typically evaluate content in terms of its current and future utility for students and are likely to emphasize world studies, modern languages, computer mathematics, and en-

Teacher curriculum planning committee.

vironmental science. They are open to changing the curriculum to keep up with the times. (For example, see Taba, 1962, pp. 40–46, 53–75; Ryan & Cooper, 1988, pp. 79–84; Johnson, Collins, Dupuis, & Johansen, 1988, pp. 402–403.)[7]

Schools That Advocate Change

Teachers who hold a *reconstructionistic* view of the role of schools see schools as more active institutions than do the traditional or the present- and future-oriented teachers. They believe that schools should go beyond helping students cope with change and should *push for social change* to make the society better. Teachers who accept this view choose content that questions the social status quo, advocates change, and encourages students to participate in that change; they tend to support issue-oriented school studies such as human relations, civil rights, women's studies, environmental courses, and fitness education. (For example, see Taba, 1962, pp. 22–28, 65–73; Johnson, Collins, Dupuis, & Johansen, 1988, pp. 365–369, 402–403; Counts, 1932; Apple, 1982; Apple & Weis, 1983; for a critical-pedagogy perspective, see McLaren, 1989.)[8]

Schools and Other Social Institutions

In a somewhat different vein, but just as important to the decision about the content to be taught, is the concept of how schools relate to other social institutions. For instance, teachers who do not see much interaction between the functions of schools and those of families, churches, and other community institutions will have different ideas about what should be taught than people who believe that contemporary schools must fill educational voids left by changing families and churches. Normally, the first group will want schools to focus primarily on transmitting knowledge and on training in academic skills; the second group will consider the development of personal character, personality, and individual values more important. Teachers in the second group are also more inclined toward a concern for student self-concept and personal security. They see school more as a broad socializing agency than as a narrow academic one. (For more discussion on this point, see Ornstein & Levine, 1984, pp. 324–339, 345–348, 354–360.)

CURRICULUM ORGANIZATION

Patterns of Instruction

In addition to selecting content, curriculum planners arrange content and learning experiences by subject, grade level, course, unit, and lesson. When they are successful, they form patterns of instruction that cut across all dimensions of content and provide for continuous, sequential, integrated, and cumulative learning.

If the task is done well, it involves a number of steps, several of which were mentioned earlier. They include

1. defining school aims and goals,
2. diagnosing students' needs,
3. formulating educational objectives,
4. translating objectives into patterns of learning,
5. selecting and organizing content and learning experiences, and
6. choosing ways of evaluating learning outcomes.

Curriculum Framework

Units of Instruction

Lesson Plans

The effort results in three kinds of documents that guide instruction. The first is a *curriculum framework*, which arranges content in particular patterns, assigns it to certain grade levels and subjects or classes, and puts it into identified sequences. The second is usually thought of as a series of *units of instruction* for each subject or class, at each grade level. The third is the lesson plan that teachers develop and follow for each class. All three are described below.

From a student's perspective the curriculum looks like a list of sequential courses, units within courses, activities, and assignments. Different students take different courses, of course, as the chapter Snapshot illustrates; but each student follows some curriculum that is based on a set of objectives and assumptions about what that student should learn.

Curriculum Frameworks

Typically, patterns of curriculum organization are described and compared, as if they emphasize particular points on a continuum, with *subject-centered* approaches on one side and *student-centered* ones on the other. (See Figure 12–1.) Such a way of describing curricula is, of course, somewhat simplistic, but it is also useful in showing the characteristics of each pattern. The descriptions below are therefore presented in that way. Remember, however, that (1) the curricula of most schools are not exclusively of one design but a combination of patterns, (2) most programs fit somewhere toward the middle of the continuum, and (3) within any school there is variety from class to class and teacher to teacher. (For overviews of the field of curriculum, see Ornstein, 1987; McNeil, 1985; Miller & Seller, 1986; Oliva, 1982.)[9]

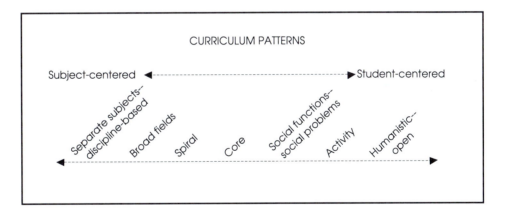

Figure 12–1. Selected curriculum patterns arranged from the most subject centered to the most student centered.

Subject-centered Curricula

In recent years, subject-centered approaches to curriculum organization have been more prevalent than student-centered ones, especially in secondary schools. Three such curriculum patterns are described below. As a group, they reflect the following directions, although they do so in varying degrees:

- Look on learning primarily as cognitive development and the acquisition of knowledge and information.
- See the teacher's main job as the provision of instruction.
- Base the subject matter to be taught on preselected objectives that include concepts, generalizations, skills, and values to be learned.
- Expect teachers to plan instruction before teaching starts and to organize it around content, separate from the conditions of the learning situation.
- Assume that certain subject matter should be taught to all students.
- Stress academic learning.

(See Ornstein & Levine, 1984, pp. 482–488, 497–499; Taba, 1962, pp. 382–393; Johnson, Collins, Dupuis, & Johansen, 1988, pp. 405–407, 411–412.)

Separate-Subjects Curriculum

The oldest and most widely followed type of subject-centered approach to curriculum organization is the *separate-subjects or discipline-based* curriculum. This pattern has two primary goals, both derived from the content to be learned by the students:

1. the acquisition of information and ideas contained in the subjects being taught, and
2. the development of the mental discipline gained from studying those subjects.

For instance, mathematics is taught so that students learn the basic content of mathematics and the ability to "think like a mathematician."

In the separate-subjects curriculum, content is divided into fairly discrete areas of study—composition, literature, history, geography, arithmetic, algebra, biology, chemistry, and so forth. Each class is separate from the rest and is taught in its own timeslot. There is little overlap across classes or time blocks.

This pattern evolved from the idea that knowledge is logically separated into a number of well-defined disciplines, such as those of the research scholars, and that it can be learned best when taught in similar units. Advocates of the pattern believe that such an approach teaches students the solid content that they should know, and in such a way as to stimulate their abilities to think and solve problems. They suggest that the separate-subjects organization helps students order and clarify the complex and conflicting ideas that they confront in their rapidly changing world.

Expository methods of instruction are used most often with the separate-subjects curriculum: lecture, assigned reading, discussion, recitation, question and answer, and written exercise. The primary resources are teacher presentations, textbooks, films and videos, and other information-giving means.

One particular group of educators who support a rather rigid view of the separate-subjects curriculum are those who advocate *basic education.* They suggest that all students should study a set of basic subjects and great books. They recommend a strong academic education, comparable to the liberal education of early Europe. Proponents of this view have included Arthur Bestor, William

Bagley, James Koerner, Hyman Rickover, and William Bennett. Mortimer Adler's *Paideia Proposal* (1982) is a description of such a curriculum and a call for its implementation in American schools.[10]

Critics of the separate-subjects curriculum say it divides content into isolated components more than is appropriate for elementary and secondary school instruction, overemphasizes the learning of factual information at a time of rapid change, slights the teaching of critical thinking, and neglects differences among students and the problems they face. They note that the real life of students is not divided into subjects. Usually they prefer interdisciplinary curriculum patterns or curricula that focus more on the students than on the content to be learned.

Because of the back-to-basics and accountability movements, the separate-subjects curriculum has been very much in vogue in recent years, as have other subject-centered approaches. School reformers and parents alike have demanded that students learn the content—and "the content" is easier to identify when it is categorized by subject or discipline. Also, subject divisions usually conform to teacher interests and areas of expertise, the coverage of separate textbooks and tests, typical organization of high school departments, and the labels under which grades are awarded. In short, experts and lay persons alike see subjects as easily recognized units of knowledge that students should know. (For more information on separate-subjects curricula, see Taba, 1962, pp. 382–393; Ornstein & Levine, 1984, pp. 484–485; Johnson, Collins, Dupuis, & Johansen, 1988, pp. 405–407.)

Broad-Fields Curriculum

The *broad-fields, integrated,* or *fused curriculum* is a second type of subject-centered approach to curriculum organization. It also stresses the acquisition of knowledge and the development of mental discipline, but it arranges content into broader, more general fields of study than the separate-subjects pattern. For example, social studies or problems of democracy classes are taught instead of separate courses in history, government, and geography; language arts instead of reading, composition, literature, and spelling; and general science instead of biology, physics, and chemistry. This type of organization assumes that broader study will provide more useful or more functional knowledge for students, both immediately and in their adult lives. Because it permits broader and more general coverage of content, it allows for, but does not necessitate or require, the elimination of some factual detail.

This pattern was developed several decades ago during a movement when educators were trying to make the curriculum more consistent with the way students naturally see the world around them. It was an effort to avoid what many saw as the unnecessary compartmentalization of separate subjects and a way of integrating studies so they would be compatible with student interests. This type of organization has been practiced more in elementary than secondary schools and, for a time, was rather common in junior high schools. It is less popular today than in the past.

Critics of the broad-fields curriculum fit into two groups—those who prefer separate subjects and those who believe it is too much like the separate-subjects pattern. Those who prefer separate subjects charge that the more generalized curriculum is often too broad, too general, and lacking in depth. They also suggest that it neglects some of the mental-discipline aspects of separate-subjects patterns. Those who dislike the broad-fields curriculum because of its similarity to separate-subjects charge that it is more tied to subjects and disciplines than to students and that it often compresses several courses into the teaching time usually devoted to one or two, and without real integration. (For more information on broad-fields curricula, see Taba, 1962, pp. 393–395; Johnson, Collins, Dupuis, & Johansen, 1988, pp. 407–408.)

Spiral Curriculum

The *spiral,* or *structure of knowledge,* curriculum is a third type of subject-centered approach. Its content is organized around the knowledge to be taught, as are the separate-subjects and broad-fields patterns; but it is different from them in at least two ways. First, as described in Chapter 11, the spiral curriculum places more emphasis on the structure of knowledge, that is, on concepts and generalizations. Second, it is designed to fit sequentially with students' developmental thinking stages.

Content taught to students in the spiral curriculum is arranged around two things—the main ideas and the methods of inquiry used in the disciplines being studied. Students are expected to learn those big ideas and to develop those ways of thinking. They study the ideas simply at first and then in subsequent classes recycle to those ideas for increasingly deeper and more sophisticated learning.

The spiral pattern of curriculum organization was developed primarily in the 1950s and 1960s, evolved from the Piagetian ideas of development, and is articulated best in the writings of Jerome Bruner (1960) and Hilda Taba (1962). Curriculum projects funded by the federal government in the 1960s in response to *Sputnik,* especially those in mathematics and science, used it extensively.

Renewed interest in it has emerged since the recent school reform and back-to-basics pushes. (See Taba, Durkin, Fraenkel, & McNaughton, 1971, especially p. 29.)

The spiral curriculum evolved in response to the criticism that most subject-centered learning was static, not appropriate for students in a rapidly changing world. As a substitute, it is expected to teach more meaningful subject matter and to emphasize thinking skills more than other curriculum patterns. Ideally, it replaces memorization of facts and rote learning with higher-level student understanding of big ideas and student inquiry into those ideas. The pattern is based on the presumption that students who learn big ideas and the skill of inquiry will be able to use those learnings to understand their world throughout their lifetime.

Advocates of the spiral curriculum argue that students taught in this way actually learn how to learn. They say that students thus better understand what they learn and are more able to use that understanding in future learning. They also note that knowledge learned in this way is not bound by subject divisions and is consistent with the cognitive development of students.

Some critics of this pattern charge that teaching ideas and methods of inquiry requires so much classroom time that many basic facts are never covered. Others say that it is still too subject centered, is insufficiently tied to student interests, and is too theoretical for many students. Some also say that it requires teacher understanding of subjects and disciplines beyond the level that many teachers, especially elementary teachers who teach a number of subjects, possess.

Figure 12–2 consists of a diagram that illustrates a structure of knowledge curriculum pattern for elementary social studies. The content focus for each grade level is listed in the spiral part of the diagram. The key concepts to be learned through the years are to the left of the spiral. The sequence of generalizations to be learned are to the right. The three arrows at the far left of the diagram indicate that the ideas studied become more general, more complex, and more abstract with each cycle.

Student-centered Curricula

Whereas subject-centered curricula emphasize the information taught to students, *student-centered curricula* focus on student needs, interests, and activities. Generally, they are assumed to be less cognitively oriented and more concerned with affective aspects of student development. Proponents say they stimulate intrinsic motivation in students.

Student-centered curriculum organizations are less popular now than they were near the middle of the twentieth century, but examples can still be found throughout the country, more of them at elementary than secondary levels.

As a group, student-centered curricula usually reflect the following directions:

- Look on learning primarily as experiences provided for students.

- See the teacher's main job as stimulator and facilitator of student activity.

- Organize learning around the needs and interests of the students rather than the content.

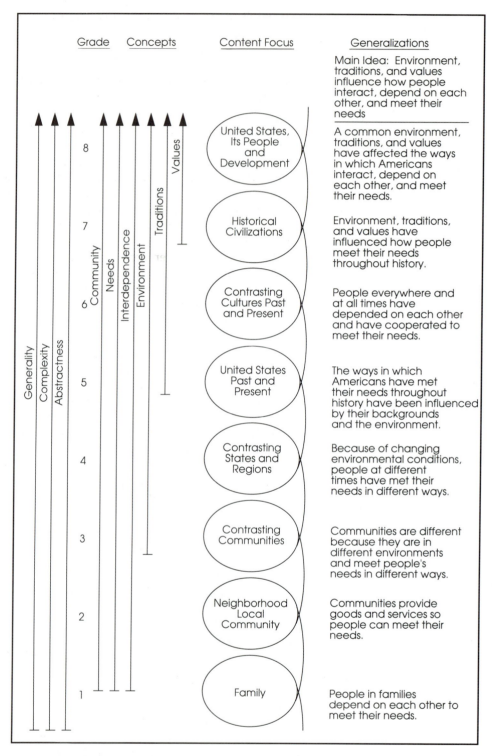

Figure 12–2. Adapted from curriculum organization patterns developed by the Taba Curriculum Development Center, San Francisco, California. See Taba, Durkin, Fraenkel, & McNaughton, 1971, p. 29.

course of completing classroom tasks. For example, teachers might plan instruction around a specific problem-solving task, such as confronting a local pollution problem; or around a research task, such as finding an explanation for a chemical reaction in a class science demonstration. In each situation, the information is woven into the tasks students perform.

Like the social functions pattern, the activity-centered curriculum was most popular before the midpoint of the twentieth century and was an outgrowth of the progressive education movement. The pattern has been used primarily in elementary schools and is still included as a significant aspect of many elementary programs. It has been followed only rarely at the secondary level and when followed, has almost always been combined with a more subject-oriented general curriculum scheme. For instance, when teachers plan the problem-solving and research activities mentioned above in science and/or social studies classes, they usually select the content in each subject before they decide on the activities.

Much of the rationale for the activities-centered curriculum is derived from the ideas and proposals of John Dewey, although many educators believe that some of what has been done in the name of activity-centered instruction is really an overextension of Dewey's recommendations. William Kilpatrick, a Dewey disciple, was probably the most outspoken advocate for activity-centered instruction. (See, for example, Kilpatrick, 1918.)[12] He stressed the need for teachers to meet student interests and to adjust their teaching when student interests changed, even if they changed rather abruptly. This would mean that lesson planning is virtually impossible and usually undesirable.

Although many versions of the activity-centered curriculum have been followed over the years, the people most critical of it usually think of its most extreme applications. In doing so, they criticize activity-centered programs as being so flexible that they lack substantive content and direction. They say that students miss necessary content simply because it does not fit with their interests at the time. They believe that instruction must be more cognitively focused and teacher directed.

The activity-centered pattern has also suffered from the same difficulties of implementation mentioned for the core curriculum—the need for broad teacher expertise, flexible school space and schedules, multiple supplemental materials; and the expectation that students need to learn certain defined content. Often teachers avoid the pattern because they prefer a curriculum that has more structure and is easier to plan for. (For more information on activity-centered curricula, see Taba, 1962, pp. 400–407; Ornstein & Levine, 1984, p. 491.)

Open Education

The *humanistic curriculum* and *open education* are as much philosophies of instruction as they are patterns of curriculum organization. Although those who espouse each would argue that they are different enough to justify being described as two separate curricular patterns, their characteristics are similar enough for them to be presented together here. They occupy an extreme end of the subject-centered–student-centered continuum.

Humanistic and open education rose to prominence in the 1950s and 1960s as reactions to a heavy emphasis on cognitive learning in the schools. Both ideas support instruction that encourages the development of student self-concepts, personal growth, feelings, and expression. Instruction that teaches students to be docile, to conform, and to follow strict school rules is not emphasized.

Ideally, teachers who follow the patterns are considered to facilitate, rather than direct learning; they are also to set expectations so that all students can succeed. These teachers encourage their students to explore ideas freely, to question openly, and to feel good about their learning experiences. They foster student self-determination, independence, self-acceptance, and consciousness development. They create a nonthreatening classroom atmosphere of trust, mu-

tual respect, cooperation, and friendliness. They accept cognitive development as an important role for schools but not at the expense of individual personal development in the affective domain.

Open classrooms are usually large, flexible spaces with movable furniture and walls. The teacher's station is often less prominent than the teacher's desk in more traditional classrooms. Students are typically free to explore at different interest centers in the area, individually and in small groups. Large numbers of books, tapes and tape recorders, and other learning materials are available. There is less direct, whole-class instruction than in more cognitively oriented classrooms.

The rationale for humanistic and open education is based on work by psychologists Abraham Maslow (1962, 1970) and Carl Rogers (1961, 1963), who see "self-actualization" and "the teaching of the total human being" as primary school goals.[13] Arthur Combs and Donald Snygg (1959), who stressed the importance of motivation and positive student self-concepts in learning, advanced the ideas.[14]

In the late 1960s, humanistic and open education were pursued enthusiastically in the British infant schools, and those efforts became examples for advocates elsewhere. Many elementary schools in the United States shifted their programs in this direction, especially at the primary grades. New school buildings were often constructed with large areas called "pods" instead of traditional classrooms in order to provide flexible teaching space and to accommodate different size classes and cross-grade groupings.

By the mid 1970s, a reaction against open education had set in in the United States. Critics considered it an inefficient way of teaching, one that neglected important cognitive goals of schools; and in the back-to-basics trends of the late 1960s and early 1980s, those views became widespread. Educators, parents, and legislators became concerned about what students were missing. They wanted more direct teaching of knowledge, more teacher-planned instruction, and less left to chance.

Although few open-education or heavily humanistic patterns of curriculum organization have survived into the 1980s, their existence in the 1970s moderated the earlier trends toward more rigid and overly cognitive approaches to teaching in most schools. Even though the pendulum has swung back and curricula in general are now more cognitively oriented than open-education enthusiasts would like, schools frequently allow for more student self-direction, more program flexibility, and more concern for student affective development than had been the case before the advent of the open education movement.

Many of the open-education programs that have continued to the present time are intended as alternative school options for particular types of students. Typically, their targets are high-risk students and students with special needs—students for whom positive self-concepts and continuing success are absolutely critical. (For more information about humanistic and open education, see Ornstein & Levine, 1984, pp. 494–497; Apple, 1983; Silberman, 1971; Berman & Roderick, 1977; Eisner, 1983, 1985.)[15]

In the Snapshot of this chapter, you were asked to analyze several student schedules in terms of the educational priorities that the schedules reflected. Refer again to those schedules and see whether you can place each of them on the subject-centered–student-centered continuum you just read about. As you do this, think about why you classify each in the way that you do.

EDUCATIONAL RESEARCH

Middle Schools

Since the 1960s advocates of middle schools have proclaimed them as a better way of educating preadolescents, but hard evidence to support the effectiveness of middle schools is not plentiful, and in fact what actually sets middle schools apart from other types of schools is not entirely clear. This Educational Research section reports on a beginning effort to identify key characteristics of middle schools and to gather evidence of their effectiveness. The study that is described is not hard research, but it provides a good example of educators asking appropriate questions that can lead to more thorough and precise analyses.

An Outlier Study

In 1983, Paul S. George and Lynn L. Oldaker conducted a survey of middle schools in the form of an *outlier study;* that is, a study that focused on the most successful examples of middle schools, rather than on middle schools in general.[16] Their look at these exemplary middle schools, or as they described them, middle schools "outside the boundaries of the mediocre," was intended to determine the characteristics and effectiveness of the best institutions. They assumed an understanding of the best middle schools would provide a basis for analyzing all the rest.

First, George and Oldaker identified 160 middle schools in thirty-four states that were listed by other studies and experts as being exemplary. Then they asked leaders of these schools to complete surveys and to supply supporting data that would describe their schools' characteristics and their effectiveness.

The study began with the assumption that true middle schools are more than buildings that house grades five through eight and are labeled "middle school." It hypothesized that they also possess a particular type of organization and philosophy and a noticeable emphasis on child development, all of which are characteristics that have been described for years in middle-school literature. The study then asked those who responded to report whether their school incorporated this organization, philosophy, and focus into what they did and if so, to describe how they did it.

At least 90 percent of the 130 schools that responded to the survey reported that their institution included the following characteristics:

- an interdisciplinary team organization of teachers who plan together and are responsible for a common group of students, who stay together for much of the school day;

- a flexible school schedule that allows teachers to adjust classes and shift students as they wish;

- a home-base, adviser-advisee arrangement that promotes close, informal, daily contact for each student with at least one teacher in a setting that enables the student to approach the teacher for personal advice and guidance;

- a curriculum focus that stresses individual personal development as well as academic achievement; and

- collaborative teacher-administrator decision making on matters affecting students.

The respondents also said that they conscientiously tried: (1) to address student self-concept and social development needs, (2) to care for the students as preadolescents, (3) to cultivate teacher and student morale and a sense of belonging to the school community, (4) to promote good rapport with parents and the community, and (5) to include teacher professional development as a central component of school operations.

Indications of Effectiveness

In terms of school effectiveness, the respondents said their schools demonstrated dramatically positive results on the following criteria: academic achievement, student behavior, school learning climate, faculty morale, and faculty participation in professional development efforts. They supplied anecdotal evidence to support these assertions. Many also reported that their move from older styles or organization and philosophies to a middle-school concept had been positive in every way, except that a number of high school teachers who taught the middle-school graduates were still somewhat skeptical.

What does this mean? For one thing, research on middle schools is only in its infancy. Those who self-reported what was happening in their 130 exemplary middle schools seemed to be happy about their efforts and convinced that they were successful. These exemplary schools were apparently following the ideas outlined in middle-school literature over the last two decades. In practice, as well as on paper, middle-school organizations and philosophies were significantly different from those of typical elementary and high schools and from junior high schools of earlier times.

However, the George and Oldaker study is only a beginning. It collected self-reported information from exemplary middle schools, and supportive evidence was limited. In a way, it asked leaders of identified good middle schools whether they thought their schools were good, and they said yes. Much of what was reported might be attributed to personal pride, to a Hawthorne effect, or to the fact that those reporting were middle-school disciples. On the other hand, the study is not insignificant. If used correctly, its information and similar information from studies like it will provide the base for continuing investigations that will add more data to the pool of knowledge about middle schools. Those data will provide the means for more research-based policy decisions of the future.

UNITS OF INSTRUCTION

Units of instruction are plans that many teachers use to organize what they do in their classes so that their students reach the objectives set for them. Teachers rely on units to arrange content, classroom activities, teaching strategies, and instructional resources into patterns of instruction. They follow them as outlines for their daily lesson plans so that they can translate school goals and the general curriculum into day-to-day classroom experiences for students.

Units of instruction vary in many ways—in form, length, amount of sophistication, degree of specificity, and so forth—but most have certain key components, including

- objectives to be achieved by the students,
- content to be learned,
- teaching strategies for the teacher to use,
- learning activities for the students to experience,
- resources to be used, and
- evaluation devices to assess student performance.

Although thorough study of units of instruction is not necessary at this point, a brief glimpse at the introductory parts of sample units should indicate the general thrusts or focuses of units and illustrate how they are used to implement the school curriculum and guide daily classroom instruction. The examples that follow include only the parts of units that show the general focus and the content to be taught. They represent various subject areas and grade levels. (Complete units would include more detail on each of the items mentioned in these samples plus detailed descriptions of unit objectives, topics to be covered, activities, materials, and education.)

Note that the skill and affective learnings listed in a number of the samples are not necessarily tied to the concepts and generalizations being taught. They have just been plugged in. Doing this enables the teacher to accomplish multiple skill and affective objectives while also teaching the intended cognitive content.

Expressive Arts — Art

Grade K
Content Focus:
    Texture
Concepts:
    texture   hard
    rough   soft
    smooth   feel
Generalizations:
    Objects have a texture.
    Sometimes objects feel different from the way they look.
Skills:
    Describing how objects feel
    Organizing objects into appropriate categories (such as hard, soft, rough, and smooth)
    Creating objects with different textures
Affective Learning:
    Appreciation of beauty in different forms
    Creativity (in creating own art forms)

Mathematics

Grade 1

Content Focus:
- Addition

Concepts:
- addition symbol set
- number equal group
- count

Generalizations:
- Addition is the joining of two sets of numbers or objects.
- Addition using numbers requires the use of the addition and equals symbols.

Skills:
- Putting items into sets
- Joining sets together
- Computing solutions to addition problems

Affective Learning:
- Cooperation (with peers in group situations)
- Honesty (in correcting own work)

Reading—Language Arts

Grade 2

Content Focus:
- Long and short vowels

Concepts:
- vowels word
- consonants word patterns
- sound long and short symbols

Generalizations:
- A word's pattern will usually determine whether the vowel sound is long or short.
- Short-vowel sounds and long-vowel sounds have different word patterns.

Skills:
- Recognizing vowel patterns in words
- Distinguishing short-vowel words from long-vowel words
- Identifying groups of words that fit into the long- or short-vowel patterns
- Locating short- and long-vowel words in printed matter

Affective Learning:
- Taking turns with other students (in reading groups)
- Respecting other students' ideas
- Perseverance (in pursuing a difficult learning task)

Social Studies

Grade 4

Content Focus:
- Physical characteristics of a community

Concepts:
- needs change neighborhood
- wants adaptation occupations

      goods   growth   transport
      services   dependence responsibility

Generalizations:
- A community is made up of people who depend on each other.
- Communities help people meet needs by supplying goods and services.
- People in the community have a variety of responsibilities, roles, and occupations.
- Communities change over time and often grow in size and complexity.
- Each community is unique.
- I am important in my community.

Skills:
- Finding information on an assigned topic (research)
- Organizing information into a report to others
- Writing reports
- Presenting oral reports
- Asking appropriate questions of guest speakers

Affective Learning:
- Acceptance of responsibility
- Cooperation with others on a group task
- Development of confidence in oneself (in preparing and presenting a report to others)
- Feeling of comfort in presenting ideas before peers

Physical Education/Health

Grade 8

Content Focus:
- Drug education—amphetamines and barbiturates

Concepts:

amphetamines	over-the-counter drugs	emphysema
stimulants	addiction	cancer
barbiturates	drug dependency	AIDS
depressants	nicotine	abuse
hallucinogens	alcohol	peer pressure

Generalizations:
- Drugs are chemical substances that speed up or slow down body activities.
- Drugs often make people feel better or happy for a limited time. They sometimes enable people to avoid reality.
- Drugs, if abused, are harmful to the body.
- Some drugs cause dependency, even if not physically addictive.
- Heavy users of various types of drugs are more susceptible to cancer, emhysema, AIDS, and other diseases than nonusers.

Skills:
- Conducting chemical experiments
- Gathering health data (research)
- Interpreting charts and graphs

Affective Learning:
- Realization that drug abuse is serious
- Desire to avoid abuse of drugs, alcohol, and tobacco

Belief that one should help those with drug problems
Willingness to take public position against drug abuse
Ability to withstand peer pressure concerning drugs

Science

Grade 9
Content Focus:
　Heat and temperature
Concepts:
　　heat　　　　　calorie
　　temperature　nutrition
　　mass　　　　　melting point
　　unit of heat　freezing
Generalizations:
　Solids, liquids, and gases expand when heated.
　Water expands when it is heated and contracts when it freezes.
　Air changes temperature faster than water.
　Gases rise when heated.
　When materials of different temperatures are mixed, the temperatures moderate.
Skills:
　Conducting laboratory experiments
　Measuring heat content of foods
　Converting Celsius and Fahrenheit temperatures
　Interpreting thermometers and other heat-measuring devices
Affective Learning:
　Cooperation (with classmates in conducting experiments)
　Realization of role of caloric intake on weight control
　Awareness of caloric content of different foods

History

Grade 10
Content Focus:
　Early commerce in feudal Europe
Concepts:
　　commerce　　manor　　　　　　manufacture
　　trade　　　　principality　　　cottage industry
　　feudalism　　militarism　　　　feudal village
　　craft　　　　the medieval　　　feudal parish
　　artisan　　　church　　　　　　Middle Ages
Generalizations:
　Feudal manors were rather self-sufficient economic communities.
　Feudalism developed because of economic needs and needs for protection.
　Princes of medieval times provided protection and economic security in return for loyalty and work.
　Medieval craft associations were early European systems of vocational education.

The feudal system combined political, military, economic, social, and religious systems or ways of living.
Skills:
Reading maps
Drawing (of trade routes)
Researching (of assigned topics in library)
Writing reports
Affective Learning:
Sensitivity to the hard life of medieval manors and towns
Appreciation of the difference between a class-based and a class-free society
Respect for the skill of craftspersons despite the perceived status of the craft
Respect for the opportunity provided by public, tax-supported education

English

Grade 12
Content Focus:
The play *Death of a Salesman* by Arthur Miller
Concepts:

symbolism	tragic hero	pride
idiom	materialism	identity
theme	competition	despair
foreshadowing	love (of family	hostility (toward
character	members)	loved ones)
traits	hope	

Generalizations:
Although people in modern, materialistic society search for personal values and identity and strive to maintain dignity, these efforts are difficult.
(as with Willy) Empty dreams of getting ahead through competition can cause a person to reject a more natural and simple life in which he or she could be himself or herself.
(as with Biff) People who live in their dreams instead of reality often fail.
People sometimes act hostilely toward people they love.
Some business cultures prize competition and images of success to the exclusion of other values.
At times people are judged by the amount of money they make and how well they are or appear to be liked by others.
Skills:
Recognizing and interpreting symbolism
Inferring feelings reflected through characters of a play
Identifying themes in a play
Analyzing characters
Comparing and contrasting playwright styles and techniques
Discussing personal literary interpretation with class peers
Affective Learning:
Greater sensitivity to the ideals of integrity, loyalty, positive human character traits

Greater sensitivity to the conditions of failure, despair, loss of innocence, denial of reality

Realization that personal success involves more than being well known and well liked

Understanding that people naturally search for things to believe in and for what they want in life

Something to Think About

One of the most difficult and complicating conditions that affects any curriculum plan and the teaching that is based on it is the fact that every student assigned to a class is not present every day. In fact, absenteeism seems to have risen in recent years and is so prevalent in some schools that high absentee rates are the norm. Yet curricula are designed as if all students are in school every day, and the teachers who follow the curriculum of any school are expected to educate all students. The new accountability demands hold them responsible for doing so.

Ben Stein, a journalist, sat in on classes at Birmingham High School in Van Nuys, California, during the 1985–86 school year and kept a diary of his observations. Two of his diary entries are as follows:

November 25, 1985

It's raining, and the students in Miss Silver's class are frantic because of the rain. There are also only about 25 out of 40 here today. I ask Jamie, sitting in front of me, why there is so much absenteeism. "Well, it's raining," she says. "Yes, but do these kids have to walk to school?" "No, but they get up in the morning and they look out the window, and it's raining, and they think it's a drag to go out in the rain, so they might as well stay in bed, have a cup of coffee, watch soap operas and then maybe get up to work at their jobs after school."

"But what about their parents? Don't their parents make them go to school?"

"No, because almost all of the parents are at work, and don't know what their kids are doing."

Class begins, and the students are. . . .

December 18, 1985

Miss Silver is in a bad mood. "It's class progress–report day," she says, stamping her foot. "I'm in a really terrible mood, so don't even talk to me today."

Outside, the sun is shining and the air is crisp and dry. The students are absent in droves. I ask Debbie, a diminutive girl with curly hair, where all the students are. "Well, it's a beautiful day, so they're probably at the beach," she says.

"But I thought they didn't come when it was raining." "I don't know," says John. "I think maybe kids don't like to be here when it's raining and also when it's sunny. Also maybe when it's cloudy, because when it's cloudy kids like to go to the tanning salon." (Stein, 1986)[17]

> - Should curricula be designed to provide for absent students such as those described in the diary excerpts? If so, how can this be done?
>
> - What should the teacher who uses the curriculum do to educate absent students?
>
> - Does the reason that particular students are absent make a difference in how teachers should adjust their planning and teaching for them? If not, which types of absence require teacher accommodation, and which can be ignored?
>
> - How accountable should teachers and schools be for seeing that students attend school? How should they deal with the problem of excessive absenteeism?

LESSON PLANS

Lesson plans are the guides or outlines that teachers develop as maps for the lessons they expect to teach. Ideally, they are developed from the school's previously prepared curriculum framework and units of instruction, but they often come from many sources, as will be explained in Chapter 13. The plans organize content, teaching strategies, activities, and materials in a format that tells the teacher what to do step by step during a designated period of time on a particular school day.

Variety of Designs

The design and format of lesson plans varies greatly from school to school, teacher to teacher, and even from year to year for the same teacher. Therefore, multiple examples of specific lesson plans, such as you would see in methods classes, are not presented here. Instead, one lesson plan is outlined, so that you can get a feel for how lesson plans in general flow from curriculum outlines and units of instruction.

The lesson plan below was developed for a primary-level class by Lynn Myers. Following the plan is an Analysis section, which describes what happened when Ms. Myers taught the lesson to her students. As you study the plan, consider the following questions:

- What knowledge, skills, and values does Ms. Myers expect the students to learn from the lesson? Which elements of the lesson teach toward each of the objectives she listed on her plan?

- In what ways does she work toward several different objectives at the same time?

- Why does she devote so much energy toward skill and affective-learning goals when the content focus is animals?

- Where on the subject-centered–student-centered continuum would you place this lesson? Why?

- How might a teacher of secondary school students plan a lesson that would incorporate similar combinations of objectives across all dimensions of subject matter?

Ms. Myers' Plan[18]

Grade 1   Topic: Animals
Content Focus:
    Differences among animals
Objectives:
    Concepts:
        Types of animals
        Kinds of animal "skin"
        Shelter or "houses" for animals
        Where animals live (land, water, air, underground)
    Generalizations:
        There are many kinds of animals, and they look different.
        Animals need food and shelter but they eat different things and have different "houses."
        Animals live in different places on earth.
Types of Thinking:
    Recognizing differences
    Making comparisons
    Combining ideas into sentences
Learning Skills:
    Reading (stories)
    Listening (to group members read)
    Writing (ideas from story)
    Spelling
Social Skills:
    Group participation
        Lead
        Follow group leader
        Share
        Take turns
Affective Learning:
    Developing a concern for animals
    Developing a willingness to share (class materials)
    Cooperating (with other students in a group)
    Appreciating the need to stay on task and complete individual work
Lesson Sequence:
1. Students sit together on mat for instruction.
2. Describe the lesson topic.
3. Tell the students they will work in groups and explain the group arrangement—6 groups of 4 each.
4. Announce to the whole class who the group leaders are.
5. Describe the contents of each book. Give one book to each group leader.
6. Tell students that each book contains a piece of paper for each child in the group that uses that book.
7. Explain that children in each group are to take turns reading parts of

their book to each other as the other group members look at the words and pictures.
8. Tell each group to discuss the story at the end of the reading.
9. Tell them to return to their desks after the discussion and individually write paragraphs about what they have learned.
10. Explain that these are to be first drafts of writing and that they will be revised tomorrow.
    Remind them about what a first draft is.
11. Give group leaders time to pick a location in the classroom for their group to meet.
12. Tell the others to join their group leaders.
13. Monitor group and individual work.
14. Collect completed paragraphs.
15. Have students begin practicing spelling as they complete paragraphs.

Evaluation:
Check for each objective through
- observing group and individual work
- questioning students individually
- reading individual responses

Resources:
Animal books
Writing paper (for each student)

ANALYSIS

This Analysis section describes what happened when Lynn Myers taught the lesson she had planned. As you read, consider:

- How closely did the lesson follow the plan, and where did it deviate? How would you explain the deviations?

- As you compare what happened in the actual lesson with the plan, what assumptions do you think Ms. Myers made as she planned the lesson? For instance, what assumptions did she make about the previous knowledge of the students, about student maturity, and about the students' ability to follow directions?

When the class enters the room from recess, the children sit on the large mat at the front as Ms. Myers picks up her materials from her desk. She sits on the chair in the midst of the students and begins,

> Today we are going to work in groups. There will be six groups with four people in each. I have already picked the groups and a leader for each one. The leaders know who they are. We will learn about animals and will practice our reading and writing skills. Listen carefully to the directions so that you know what to do.
>
> (Ms. Myers tells the class who the group leaders are.)
>
> "Each group will have one of these books. (Ms. Myers holds up six small

reading books.) They describe different things about animals—food animals eat, 'houses' animals live in, the kinds of 'skin' animals have, things animals do, special skills some animals have, and locations where animals live.

"After I finish these directions, each group leader will take a book and choose a place in the classroom for his or her group to study. Remember, leaders must see that everyone does his or her part and everyone else must follow the leader's suggestions.

"When your group is settled, the leader should start reading the book to the group, and the others should sit close enough to see the words and pictures. After a short while, the leader should give the book to someone else to read. Each person should take a turn so that everyone has an equal chance to read.

"When your group is finished reading the whole story, have a discussion about what you learned. Have the group discussion just as we usually do. Take turns, be courteous, and listen to your leader.

"At the end of the discussion, group leaders will give each person a piece of paper like this one. There are four pieces in each book. Then each person will go to his or her desk to start writing.

"When you get to your desk, put your name on the paper and write a paragraph that answers this question: 'What did I learn about animals from the book?' (Ms. Myers points to the question on the chalkboard.) If you forget the question, just look up here.

> "Your paragraph will be a first draft, or a rough copy. Who remembers what a first draft is? (Through questions and explanations Ms. Myers reminds the class what a first draft is.) I will read your paragraphs tonight and give them back to you tomorrow. Tomorrow, we will fix them up. Then you can read them to your friends, and we will put them on the bulletin board.
>
> "Remember when you are doing the first draft, you do not have to worry about the grown-up way to spell every word. If you are not sure how to spell a word, have a good guess and circle it. Tomorrow, we will take time to look up words and fix them.
>
> "When you finish writing, give me your paragraph and begin your spelling practice. The page numbers are written on the chalkboard."
>
> At this point, Ms. Myers tells the students which groups they are in, gives each leader a book, allows the leaders to pick the classroom spot where his or her group will meet, and tells the other students to join their leaders. She has assigned group membership so that each has about equal numbers of the following: high- and low-ability readers, outgoing and quiet personalities, and girls and boys. Since it is still before the mid-point in the school year, all the leaders are students with rather dominant personalities. She believes this helps the groups to stay on task. As the year progresses, she will designate less dominant children to be leaders and will help them develop leadership characteristics.
>
> As the group read the books, Ms. Myers and an aid move among them, suggesting how the children should sit so that they can see and hear, listening to what is being said, encouraging participation, managing behavior, answering questions, and monitoring group progress.
>
> As the groups complete their discussions, Ms. Myers and the aid collect the books and help each student get started writing at his or her desk. As the writing proceeds, both adults monitor and guide the writing.
>
> When individual students complete their paragraphs, they give them to Ms. Myers and begin their daily spelling practice.

THE HIDDEN CURRICULUM

Students learn more in school than the content specifically planned for them in the curriculum, and that learning outside the regular instructional program is often called the *hidden curriculum*. Although not purposely planned and often different from student to student, the hidden curriculum is, nonetheless, an important part of school learning and can affect students dramatically. It must be considered by school leaders and teachers as they decide how they want to influence the students for whom they are responsible. (For more information on the hidden curriculum, see Ornstein & Levine, 1984, pp. 492–494; Jackson, 1968; Lightfoot, 1983; Eisner, 1985.)[19]

Unintended Content

The hidden curriculum has a number of dimensions. One aspect includes the unexpected ideas, skills, and values that students pick up from their study even though their teachers had not expected them to do so. Some of these are good, and some are not. The good parts are those which are consistent with intended instruction. For example, students frequently learn new ideas in their reading that teachers thought they already knew; they gain insights from comments of other students; they learn to think better in the process of doing an assignment; and they formulate values by learning about other's views and by confronting value choices.

Unexpected school learning can also be harmful. Students can learn (or think they have learned) ideas that can be erroneous, negative, and contrary to school goals. They can overgeneralize information about particular people and create stereotypes. Some students can see values intended to be presented as negative as attractive instead. Students sometimes use shortcuts, such as plagiarism and mass-published synopses, instead of developing their own skills and completing assignments; they sometimes use such methods and attain good grades.

School Organization

A second aspect of the hidden curriculum comes from the ways in which the institutions are set up—*how* schools are organized, *how* they function day to day, and *how* teachers teach. Often these variables send unexpected messages to students, and those messages may either support or conflict with what teachers and school administrators think they are teaching. When there is conflict between this part of the hidden curriculum and what the school expects to teach, such circumstances as these can occur: Students can be forced into conformity because the school organization demands it, even though the school program is intended to encourage creativity and originality. They can find attractive role models among students, adults, or media figures that school leaders had hoped would be unattractive. They can be encouraged to compete and cheat instead of to cooperate and do honest schoolwork. Sometimes this aspect of the hidden curriculum provides students with significant practice at outwitting, outguessing, deceiving, and confronting teachers and other authorities.

School Cultures

A third aspect of the hidden curriculum is closely associated to school organization, but it has less to do with structure and rules and more to do with social atmosphere. It consists of the amorphous *school culture* and *social subtleties* that pervade a school—the traditions, rituals, peer associations, and friendships mentioned in Chapter 6. These aspects of school life, including relationships among students, among teachers and students, and among administrators and students, can stimulate personal achievement, individual responsibility, and self-confidence; or they can stifle them. They can foster a sense of belonging or instill a feeling of rejection. They can promote positive self-images or induce alienation.

Student-to-student interactions have particularly strong impact. Students who are part of the "in" group have different learning experiences from those who are not; as do those who are known as brains, those who are considered desired dates, those who have cars, and those who excel in school activities. Peer associations frequently have direct influences on school learning as a whole. Students who have close friends among their school peers and who are socially comfortable in the school environment frequently achieve in ways that their more isolated and uncomfortable counterparts do not.

Just as planned and intended school learning extends beyond the classroom and into homework assignments, out-of-school projects, and everyday applications of learning in real life, the hidden curriculum extends beyond the school walls. Uncaring comments by teachers, rigid school rules, failed tests, and unoffered and unaccepted invitations and invitations never given to the school dance are remembered for lifetimes, as are friendly words of encouragement, exceptions to the rules, academic successes, and making the team. School plays, athletic competition, club leadership responsibilities, and personal friendships are all part of school learning, as are peer rejections, disappointments, lost elections for campus offices, and the breakup of intense relationships. Often these experiences are more significant and longer lasting than academic learning and grades in courses.

Although these aspects of school learning are not part of the planned school curriculum, they are learning experiences; they must be taken into consideration by school personnel as they think about what they teach and what they want to accomplish. Although the hidden curriculum is not purposefully planned, it is part of what students learn at school, and, therefore, is content of a sort.

CONCLUSION

Curriculum frameworks, units, and lesson plans are the on-paper designs of what and how students are expected to learn in school. But there is always a difference between what those plans call for and what individual students actually learn. Sometimes the on-paper plans are simply not followed, possibly for sound reasons; even when they are, some are not as successful as the designer had hoped. Even good plans that work well with particular classes and students do not work with others.

On the other hand, effective teaching and learning rarely occur if school leaders and teachers do not design, organize, and follow good curriculum frameworks and lessons. Such a lack of conceptualization and planning leads to confusion, overlap, and oversight in the resulting curriculum.

Therefore, as you think about curriculum matters in the future, you should keep two important guiding principles in mind: Good teaching requires thorough planning, but thorough planning does not guarantee good learning.

SUMMARY

Curriculum frameworks, units of instruction, and lesson plans are devices that educators use to organize their instruction. Developing curricula involves putting together goals, content, teaching strategies, activities, and materials. The process includes setting educational objectives at three levels—the school district level, the school level, and the class or subject level.

Curricula can have various emphases and the different types of emphasis are usually thought of on a continuum that extends from those that are very content centered and subject specific to those that are very student centered and integrated. Subsections of curricular designs, units of instruction are more focused and more detailed versions. At least ideally, lesson plans are developed from units.

Students learn more than the content planned for them in the prepared curriculum and intentionally taught in teachers' lessons. Much of that unplanned-for learning comes from the hidden curriculum of schools.

STUDY QUESTIONS

1. Make a list of all the subjects you studied during the last two or three years of high school. Then consider what value each course held for you. Think in terms of its value

to you while you were still in high school, now that you are a college student, and potentially for your later life.

2. Review the five purposes for schools listed in Chapter 1. Then consider the same questions asked in Question 1 above, but this time in terms of those five purposes.

3. In which ways do different school curricula prepare students for different social and economic levels of life? In which ways do they channel students in these directions more narrowly than they might?

4. Make a list of the five or six subjects typically studied anywhere between kindergarten and grade 12 that you believe are the most important for all students. Justify each of your choices.

BIBLIOGRAPHY

Apple, M. W. (1982). *Education and power.* Boston: Routledge and Kegan Paul.

Apple, M. W. (1983). Curriculum in the year 2000: Tensions and possibilities. *Phi Delta Kappan, 64*(5), 321–326.

Counts, G. S. (1932). *Dare the schools build a new social order?* New York: John Day.

Cusick, P. A. (1983). *The egalitarian ideal and the American high school.* New York: Longman.

Gronlund, N. E. (1978). *Stating objectives for classroom instruction.* New York: Macmillan.

Jackson, P. W. (1968). *Life in classrooms.* New York: Holt, Rinehart and Winston.

Joyce, B. (1985). Models for teaching thinking. *Educational Leadership, 42*(8), 4–7.

Joyce, B., & Weil, M. (1986). *Models of teaching* (3rd ed.). Englewood Cliffs, NJ: Prentice-Hall.

Kilpatrick, W. H. (1918). The project method. *Teachers College Record, 19*(4), 319–335.

Lightfoot, S. L. (1983). *The good high school.* New York: Basic Books.

McNeil, J. D. (1985). *Curriculum: A comprehensive introduction* (3rd ed.) Boston: Little, Brown.

Miller, J. P., & Seller, W. (1986). *Curriculum perspectives and practice.* New York: Longman.

Ragan, W. B. & Shepherd, G. D. (1982). *Modern elementary curriculum.* (6th ed.) New York: Holt, Rinehart and Winston.

Taba, H. (1962). *Curriculum development: Theory and practice.* New York: Harcourt, Brace and World.

Tyler, R. W. (1949). *Basic principles of curriculum and instruction.* Chicago: University of Chicago Press.

NOTES

1. The schedules presented here are composites of typical schedules reviewed by the authors of this text.

2. Taba, H. (1962). *Curriculum development: Theory and practice.* New York: Harcourt, Brace and World.

3. Ornstein, A. C., & Levine, D. U. (1984). *An introduction to the foundations of education* (3rd ed.). Boston: Houghton Mifflin; Kobler, R., Baker, L. L., & Miles, D. T. (1981). *Behavioral objectives and instruction* (2nd ed.). Boston: Allyn and Bacon; Gronlund, N. E. (1978). *Stating objectives for classroom instruction.* New York: Macmillan. Also see

Bloom, B. S., & Krathwohl, D. R. (1956). *Taxonomy of educational objectives: Cognitive domain.* New York: McKay; Krathwohl, D. R., Bloom, B. S., & Masia, B. (1964). *Taxonomy of educational objectives: Affective domain.* New York: McKay.

4. Ryan, K., & Cooper, J. M. (1988). *Those who can, teach* (5th ed.; pp. 171–198, 446–448). Boston: Houghton Mifflin.

5. Of course, they can always turn to higher authority—the curriculum guide, the textbook, a more experienced teacher—but if they do, it is still their own choice to follow this course. When they yield to authority, they choose, in effect, to allow others to make the choice, or at least to influence it significantly.

6. Johnson, J. A., Collins, H. W., Dupuis, V. L., & Johansen, J. H. (1986). *Introduction to the foundations of American education* (6th ed.). Boston: Allyn and Bacon. Also see sections on perrenialism and essentialism in Chapter 8 of this text.

7. Also see sections on pragmatism and futurism in Chapter 8 of this text.

8. Counts, G. S. (1932). *Dare the schools build a new social order?* New York: John Day; Apple, M. W. (1982). *Education and power.* Boston: Routledge and Kegan Paul; Apple, M. W., & Weis, L. (1983). *Ideology and practice in schooling.* Philadelphia: Temple University Press; McLaren, P. (1989). *Life in schools: An introduction to critical pedagogy in the foundations of education.* New York: Longman. Also see sections on reconstructionism and Marxism in Chapter 8 of this text.

9. Ornstein, A. C. (1987). The field of curriculum: What approach? What definition? *High School Journal, 70,* 208–216; McNeil, J. D. (1985). *Curriculum: A comprehensive introduction* (3rd ed.). Boston: Little, Brown; Miller, J. P., & Seller, W. (1986). *Curriculum perspectives and practice.* New York: Longman; Oliva, P. F. (1982). *Developing the curriculum.* Boston: Little, Brown. Also see Schwab, J. J. (1969). The practical: Language for the curriculum. *School Review, 78*(1), 1–23; and Cuban, L. (1982). Persistent instruction: The high school classroom, 1900–1980. *Phi Delta Kappan, 64*(2), 113–118.

10. Adler, M. J. (1982). *The Paideia proposal.* New York: Macmillan.

11. Kilpatrick, W. H. (Ed.). (1933). *The educational frontier.* New York: Appleton-Century.

12. Kilpatrick, W. H. (1918). The project method. *Teachers College Record, 19*(4), 319–335; Kilpatrick, W. H. (1951). *Philosophy of education.* New York: Macmillan.

13. Maslow, A. H. (1962). *Toward a psychology of being.* New York: Van Nostrand Reinhold; Maslow, A. H. (1970). *Motivation and personality* (2nd ed.). New York: Harper & Row; Rogers, C. R. (1961). *On becoming a person.* Boston: Houghton Mifflin; Rogers, C. R. (1983). *Freedom to learn for the 80's.* Columbus, OH: Merrill.

14. Combs, A., & Snygg, D. (1959). *Individual behavior* (2nd ed.). New York: Harper & Row. Also see Combs, A. (Ed.). (1962). *Perceiving, behavior, becoming: 1962 ASCD yearbook.* Washington, D.C.: Association for Supervision and Curriculum Development.

15. Apple, M. W. (1983). Curriculum in the year 2000: Tensions and possibilities. *Phi Delta Kappan, 64*(5), 321–326; Silberman, C. A. (1971). *Crisis in the classroom.* New York: Random House; Berman, L. M., & Roderick, J. A. (Eds.). (1977). *Feelings, values and the art of growing: 1977 ASCD yearbook.* Washington, D.C.: Association for Supervision and Curriculum Development; Eisner, E. W. (1983). The art and craft of teaching. *Educational Leadership, 40*(4), 4–13; Eisner, E. W. (1985). *The educational imagination* (2nd ed.). New York: Macmillan.

16. George, P. S., & Oldaker, L. L. (1985). *Evidence for the middle school.* Columbus, OH: National Middle School Association; George, P. S., & Oldaker, L. L. (1985–1986). A

national survey of middle school effectiveness. *Educational Leadership, 43*(4), 790–85; George, P. S. (1981). The middle school century. *Principal, 60*(3), 11–14.

17. Stein, B. (1986, November). High school diary. *Los Angeles Magazine*, pp. 168–175.

18. Ms. Myers' plan and teaching are drawn from several plans and lessons she taught at Fall-Hamilton Elementary School, Nashville, Tennessee. The basic concept of the lesson was developed and taught initially by Margaret Duncan, Armidale City Public School, Armidale, N.S.W., Australia.

19. Jackson, P. W. (1968). *Life in classrooms.* New York: Holt, Rinehart and Winston; Lightfoot, S. L. (1983). *The good high school.* New York: Basic Books; Cusick, P. A. (1983). *The egalitarian ideal and the American high school.* New York: Longman.

CHAPTER 13

The Act of Teaching: From Planning to Evaluation

**CAROLYN M. EVERTSON
ANN M. NEELY
BRIAN HANSFORD**

An Introduction to Teaching and Schools   477

INTRODUCTION

This chapter provides a brief sketch of the process of teaching from initial planning through the actual teaching of lessons on to the evaluation of students and the assessment of the effectiveness of the lessons taught. It labels that three-part process as the act of teaching. In many ways the chapter serves as a capstone chapter for this text. As teachers prepare their lessons, they take into consideration many elements—most of them described in earlier chapters—and ideas about what works in their classrooms, goals and objectives of their instruction, the nature of students, the culture of the school, philosophies of education, theories of instruction, content, and the school's curriculum framework. Using their own style, they fit all the parts together and, somehow, make it all work. When they do this successfully, their students learn what they had hoped.

The chapter is built around a case study of an imaginary teacher who plans and conducts a second-grade mathematics lesson. Chapter sections are on planning, teaching, and evaluation. The planning section analyzes the kind of thinking teachers do as they prepare for class. The teaching section views classroom activity primarily as a process of communication. The evaluation section describes how teachers assess the effectiveness of lessons and use that information in future planning.

The Snapshot describes the planning of Ms. Rowan, the fictive teacher, as she prepares her second-grade lesson, and the Analysis section describes the teaching of that lesson. The Educational Research section reports on communication apprehension, a specific aspect of classroom communication that affects teacher-student interaction, the teaching-learning process, and what students learn.

SNAPSHOT

The Snapshot for this chapter describes the thinking of a teacher who is preparing for a week-long mathematics unit on measurement for her second-grade class. As Ms. Rowan plans for this unit, she must make many decisions based upon influences that affect her classroom—influences that result from the nature of the classroom itself, from her students, from the school, from the curriculum, and from her own style of teaching. As you read her reflections, consider the following questions:

- What influences her decisions?
- What steps does she go through as she plans?
- What type of information does she need?
- If her planning differs from what you would have expected, in what ways?

MS. ROWAN—THURSDAY AFTER SCHOOL

In the past, my second graders have had a difficult time understanding the concept of *measurement*. I think this year I will have them move into their math skillbooks more gradually. I will also give them more opportunities to work with manipulatives. This will reinforce their learning and give me a better chance to assess individual progress.

Since I have to use the standardized test to evaluate the students' growth, I need to examine the types of drawings and the problem format that will be used on the test. My examples in class can be similar to those on the test, while still being different enough to make sure the test assesses understanding rather than only memory. Sometimes, I think those tests are written in ways so foreign to my students that they are penalized because of test format when I *know* they understand the material!

What manipulatives would be most helpful to this group of students? I can introduce the idea of measurement to the entire class on Monday as I begin the unit. How can I make sure everyone is able to see what is being measured? I think I should use the overhead projector. I need to make a note to check it out of the media center on Friday. I can put items on the projector and shoot the image on the empty wall over the chalkboard. I think that even David will be able to see the examples then!

Before I talk about inches, I will help them understand the concept of units of measurement. I can use paper clips as the *units*. I will first measure a pencil. I will put the pencil down on the projector surface and ask Susan how many paper clips she thinks would be as long as that pencil. Then I will ask others (who look as if they need to be brought into the lesson) to guess. Since Jim sits near the projector, I will have him come to the projector and line up the paper clips alongside the pencil. I will need to make sure the row is straight!

Since the children will need several examples, I will have a piece of chalk, a short ruler, a string, and my stapler ready to put on the screen. I will need to ask questions about measurement so that all the children are paying attention and thinking about measurement. Otherwise, I will lose the attention of those who need to listen the most.

So that the children can practice by themselves, I will arrange their written work for Monday just like the group work. Each student will need a sheet of paper with ten lines of different lengths drawn on it. They will measure the lines with paper clips. Will ten lines be too many? Maybe I should just draw eight lines. I better put ten paper clips in a separate plastic bag for each child ahead of time. That way, I will be able to use two helpers to pass everything out quickly.

Before they do that, I will need to give the class directions, or they will not listen after they receive the materials! As they do the worksheets, I will walk around and help those who need it. I will need to check to see what I need to explain to the class in more detail.

What will I do with those who finish first? They can connect their units together into a paper-clip chain. What about those having problems? They can measure the pencils in our pencil holder with a partner and then do an extra practice sheet. The class should need about ten to fifteen minutes to do the worksheets. Since they go to phys ed right after math, they will need to start the worksheets by 10:15 at the latest.

We will begin on Tuesday by measuring other items with the chains of

Sarah Rowen often plans as she does her daily walking.

clips. On Wednesday, we will change units. That clear plastic ruler will show up on the overhead. We can repeat measurements using inches. I can divide the class into small groups to measure different items and record their measurements. Then they should be ready for their math skillbooks on Thursday.

On Friday, I will give my own test. This will help me know which students still need practice. I will need to make up the test Wednesday night.

Even though I have plans worked out for the entire week, I may have to change things as we go along. I have not used many of these activities in this way before. I hope it will help them understand and remember the concept of measurement better than last year's class.

PLANNING

Mental Images

The planning described in the Snapshot is typical of the thinking Ms. Rowan does for lessons for her second graders. She envisions what the classroom will be like as the lesson is being taught. She forms *mental images* of her lessons. The Snapshot reflects her own thinking about the lesson, not a conversation with another person. She thinks about her students, the goals they all need to accomplish, her past teaching experiences, the content the class must cover, and the material she will use. Gradually, she fits all the components together.

As teachers think about future lessons and plan their work, their thoughts are usually somewhat random; they also occur at various times, both in and out of school. Teachers do not limit planning time to the thirty minutes scheduled during the school day or to the time they set aside for work in the evenings. Lesson plans are often made in rush-hour traffic, at the grocery store, at the health club, or in the early morning. A student teacher once said, "It seems as if I'm always planning for my class. I'll be at a party, having a conversation, and in the back of my head I'm thinking of how something will fit into a lesson."

Written Plans

Following the thinking described in the Snapshot, a teacher would translate his or her mental images of the lessons into written lesson plans. In Ms. Rowan's case, the written plan is merely a set of brief notes that follow her thoughts on the lessons. It is simply an outline of her thinking and a reminder of the decisions she has made for the lessons. It is not very sophisticated or detailed, and it does not fit a precise format. But since she has years of experience that help her elaborate on her notes, it works for her. Ms. Rowan's written plan might look like this:

Sketch Plans for Math Lessons

Math—Measurement   Date: October 19–23
                        Time: 9:50–10:30

Monday

Introduce measurements—25 minutes

Discuss "units"

    Overhead projector (Check out Friday.)
    250 paper clips—Have Jenny put in sandwich bags on Friday.
    Pencil, chalk, ruler, string, stapler
    Ditto of lines of different lengths—10–15 minutes
    Have pencil holder ready with pencils of different lengths.

Tuesday

Review use of units of measure—5–8 minutes.

Ask how we could make using units easier—chain together.

Examples on overhead—15 minutes.

Ditto of pictures of objects to be measured—10 minutes.

Class check—10 minutes (correct own papers).

Wednesday

Review—5 minutes

Introduce ruler, inches—15 minutes.
    26 plastic rulers.

Review—Remeasure lines on Monday's ditto—10 minutes.

Math skillbook—p. 25.

Thursday

Review inches, ruler—8–10 minutes.

Small-group measuring—20–25 minutes.

> 6 groups (plan these Wednesday)
> Sheets describing what is to be measured (sticks, books, etc.)
> Bags of items
> Rulers
> Check groups' measurements—10 minutes.

Homework—skillbook, pp. 26–27.

Friday

Review—5 minutes.

Check homework—10 minutes.

Informal check—questions, 5–10 minutes.

Measurement test—15–20 minutes (make this up Wednesday).

Approaches to Planning

Goals and Objectives Goals and objectives serve as guideposts that keep lessons focused on specific activities and outcomes. Skilled teachers must have them in mind for the lessons they develop and communicate them to students. Chapter 12 described the nature of goals and objectives and how they are typically developed, and it is important to remember that goals and objectives are necessary for effective lessons. They are not simply made up on a teacher's whim; rather, they are derived from what school leaders, the community, and other teachers expect to happen in classrooms.

Although goals and objectives are critically important points of reference for all planning, the extent to which they dominate, or should dominate, planning is a matter of debate among educators today. That debate is reflected on the next few pages, as two approaches to planning are described—the rational-choice approach and the lesson-image approach. These two approaches are not the only ways teachers go about planning, but they are the two that have been most prominent in educational literature in recent years. They also seem to be the two used most widely by teachers and curriculum leaders.

The Rational-Choice Approach to Lesson Planning

Much of the research on teacher planning in recent decades has focused on the *rational-choice model* of planning originally developed by Ralph Tyler (1950) and adapted later by Hilda Taba (1962) and James Popham and Eva Baker (1970).[1] It has become the approach taught most consistently in colleges of education and used most often in statewide teacher evaluation programs. The rational-choice model uses four steps to effective planning:

1. specifying behavioral objectives,
2. identifying students' entry behavior (knowledge, skills, and value perspectives),
3. selecting and sequencing learning activities so as to move students from entry behavior to the objectives, and
4. evaluating the outcomes of instruction in order to improve planning.

This approach is a logical and organized way to plan for instruction. Teachers who use it set goals and then identify paths to reach them. They often start with long-range goals, outline the course for the year or semester, develop units, and gradually subdivide the plans until they focus on what they want to happen on a specific Monday morning. In engaging in this process, they select and manipulate all the instructional devices and classroom elements available to them—content, activities, materials, their own instructional skills, and so forth; at the same time, they avoid, moderate, or adapt to potential hindrances to reaching the goals—student misbehavior, time limits, different ability levels, and interruptions. The main task, as in all planning, is in making things fit together so that students reach the goals set for them.

The Lesson-Image Approach to Lesson Planning

Cyclical Process

Despite the facts that the rational approach to planning seems to make so much sense logically and that it is stressed in teacher-preparation courses, most experienced teachers seem not to follow it. Instead, they plan more often as Ms. Rowan did, by jotting down ideas from their mental notes that describe the activities they will use. For example, Clark and Yinger (1979), who studied elementary schoolteachers' planning, found that many of the teachers in their study did not begin their planning with goals and objectives.[2] Instead, their first concern was about the activities they would use, the content they would teach, specific student needs, and the materials or resources available. They also used information gained from evaluating their previous lessons. Clark and Yinger also found that teachers' written plans usually took the form of an outline or list of topics to be covered (similar to Ms. Rowan's sketch plans shown earlier). The Clark and Yinger study showed the teachers' planning was mainly a mental process, not committed to paper.

Zahorik (1970), another researcher, concluded some time ago that the rational-choice model for planning should be expanded if it is to be an effective model for most teachers. He suggested that it be changed as follows:

> . . . retain the goals-experiences-evaluation type of planning . . . but add it to a plan that focuses directly on teacher behavior. That is, along with the typical learning, develop a teacher plan that identifies types of teacher behaviors to be used during the lesson. . . .[3]

Elementary teachers in the Clark and Yinger study (1979) described the types of planning that they did along with the constraints, rationales, and considerations that affected their plans. The teachers indicated that the act of planning itself served two functions: the first and most obvious one was that planning was a means of organizing instruction, and the second, less obvious, function was that it served as a psychological resource, a source of confidence, security, and direction.

Planning as Problem Solving

Studies have also focused on the thinking and decision making that teachers engage in as they plan (Morine, 1976; Peterson, Marx & Clark, 1978; Yinger, 1977; Yinger, 1979; Yinger & Clark, 1981).[4] Among these, Yinger (1977) examined teacher thinking while the teachers actually engaged in planning. Based on his findings, he concluded that teachers see the planning process primarily as a task of solving problems. The problem is the need for the students to learn; the solution is a realistic sequence of activities that will produce that learning.

Morine (Morine & Vallance, 1975) found that teachers' written plans rarely reflect the teachers' comprehensive planning activities.[5] She described the outcome of these planning activities as "lesson images." These images contain the details that are seldom recorded in written plans but which teachers visualize and plan for specifically.

The Effect of Experience

It appears that beginning teachers tend to rely more on the rational-choice approach for their planning (Neely, 1985, 1986);[6] but as they gain experience, they shift more to the use of lesson images and to varied and personal ways of planning. This shift might occur, at least in part, because experienced teachers have more knowledge to draw upon and feel more secure in planning without detailed written plans. They realize that they must take into consideration a multitude of factors that will influence what they actually do in the classroom and how successful the lessons will actually be.

Factors Affecting Teacher Planning

As the research just reported implies, most teachers develop lessons around mental images, and many factors affect their decisions. Those factors are listed below and later in Figure 13–1. They are organized into five categories, and each category is based on a type or source of influence that affects teachers' thinking. Those five sources of influence are teacher influences, external influences, organizational influences, student influences, and curricular influences.

Influences on Planning

Teacher Influences	*External Influences*
Experience	Predetermined goals
Organizational style	Accountability
Teaching philosophy	Community and parent pressure
Knowledge of content	Traditions
Goals for lessons	Specific circumstances
Teacher expectations	
Feelings of security and control	

(continued)

> **Influences on Planning (*continued*)**
>
> *Organizational Influences*
>
> Schedules
> Time available
> Type of planning
>   (long-range/short-range)
> Class size and
>   student numbers
>
> *Student Influences*
>
> Physical needs
> Psychological needs
> Academic needs
> Motivational levels
> Student cultural characteristics
> Group characteristics
> Student expectations
>
> *Curricular Influences*
>
> Subject matter
> Teaching strategies and
>   methods
> Materials available

Before, during, and after the Lesson

Before describing the factors, however, it is important to note that all that affect the planning process—either as mental images and written lesson plans—do not occur only before a lesson starts. Some intervene at two later stages: at the implementation stage, when the teacher is actually teaching the lesson; and at the assessment stage after the lesson has been taught. As a result, teachers can only rarely carry out a lesson entirely as planned. They must anticipate what is likely to happen as they teach their planned lessons and must make accommodations as they proceed.

This need to plan ahead and replan as the lesson proceeds is not surprising. Good teachers expect to adjust their plans as they go along, and they plan alternatives so that they are prepared to do so. The old pros seem to do this intuitively, but in reality what appears to be intuition is actually a combination of forethought, insight, experience, and common sense. It rests on a set of teacher capabilities that include intelligence, keen perception, confidence, flexibility, decision-making skill, and practice.

However, the fact that most plans must be modified cannot be used as an excuse to avoid thorough initial planning. Few teachers can wing it, and when they do, the quality of their instruction nearly always suffers. Planning establishes a proposed course of action that serves as the teacher's guide, from which appropriate deviations can be made. Without such a guide, both the teacher and students frequently get lost.

In a way, planning for teaching is much like planning for a trip. Studying maps and marking routes set directions for the journey, providing assurance that the trip will end where the people plan to go. When this planning is done, the trip can be undertaken with confidence. Although there may be detours and adjustments to make, the driver keeps in mind a general sense of direction that provides guidance throughout the trip.

An Introduction to Teaching and Schools   **485**

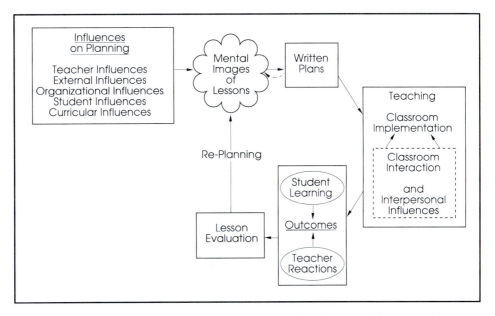

Figure 13–1. Steps in lesson planning and replanning. Teachers form mental images of lessons based on a number of influences. Then they write plans, teach the lesson, assess outcomes, evaluate the lesson, and replan.

Assessing Results

The part of the planning process that continues after the lesson has been completed involves teacher assessment of at least two major outcomes. The first outcome is what the students have been able to learn and how it reflects upon the success or failure of the lesson as taught. The second outcome is the teacher's perception of the lesson in terms of what he or she expected. Taken together, these two outcomes determine the teacher's lesson evaluation. The teacher then plans or replans subsequent lessons. In the process, the outcomes of the earlier lesson become another influence on the mental images for the planning of those that follow. (See Clark & Peterson, 1986, pp. 260–268.)[7]

Teacher Influences on Planning

Experience

The amount of *experience* teachers have with teaching and with children is one of the important factors that influence planning decisions. To state the point simply, past experiences help enrich mental images of lessons. Because experienced teachers have more previous experiences, their initial lessons tend to be more on target and generally require less adjustment.

Because beginning teachers lack experience, they must often compensate by planning to a greater extent than might be necessary. As they gain experience, however, the continued planning is *replanning,* rather than *initial* planning. Each experience influences the next.

Organizational Style

A second influence on teacher planning is the teacher's personal *organizational style,* which, in turn, is shaped by that person's need for structure, planning routine, planning format, and style of problem solving. Teachers vary in the

Amount of Structure

amount of structure needed in order to feel comfortable with a plan. Some teachers

Fitting all the pieces together into a coherent plan requires organizing skills.

need to write very detailed notes about the lesson to be taught. For others, a brief list, similar to the written plans in the Snapshot, adequately triggers an elaborate mental plan, which may never be written on paper.

Planning Routines

Another matter of organizational style is *planning routine,* or how a teacher approaches the planning task. Some teachers begin planning by asking themselves questions: How should I introduce this concept? How will I check for learning? Will anyone have difficulty with this material? Other teachers begin planning by brainstorming for a time, then recording ideas, and then gathering resources. Others search for resources first and plan around those that are available. Still others start with an organization such as that presented in a specific text or teacher's manual, structuring the lesson around the content. Others select a variety of class activities first and plan from those points. Regardless of which planning routine they follow, however, all teachers translate the guidelines they use into mental images of their lesson.

Planning Format and Sequence

Another part of organizational style is the *planning format* that teachers use—not just the format on paper but also that in their heads. Some teachers think rather chronologically—they think of each step of the lesson in the order in which they occur in the lesson, and their plans look like a sequence of personal directions, beginning with the gathering of materials well before the class starts and ending at the lesson ending or even after its evaluation. Others think of goals or results of lessons first, then develop the parts of the lesson, and later fit the parts together in a logical sequence. The Snapshot plan reflects the first approach more than the latter.

Style of Problem Solving

Teachers' planning routines and formats are frequently determined by their *style of solving problems.* For instance, the challenge a teacher faces in determining how the class will reach the intended learning outcomes can be viewed as a problem the teacher must solve. Teachers may learn to identify the problem, determine possible solutions, and select the solution most appropriate for a particular class.

Teaching Philosophy

In addition to experience and organizational style, a third influence on the types of lesson plans a teacher devises is the teacher's own *teaching philosophy*—the teacher's view of teaching and learning in general. Such philosophies usually begin developing during preservice teacher-preparation years and continue to be developed and refined as teachers gain experience with students and teaching. Teaching philosophies are, of course, not limited to how the teacher views teaching and learning but are part of that teacher's general makeup as a person.

Knowledge of Content

The teacher's *knowledge of content* is a fourth important influence on planning. Teachers obviously cannot plan content they do not know, but it is extremely rare that a teacher gets into the position of having to teach a complete unknown. However, it is not unusual for a teacher's knowledge of content to be limited enough to affect both planning and teaching. In such an event, planning is necessarily restricted and usually less creative than it might be. The teacher must also undertake additional study, thus making the planning task more time-consuming and burdensome. Teachers who know their content, of course, usually can plan more varied and flexible lessons because they can readily use and arrange information.

Content Knowledge and Flexibility of Planning

Depth of Understanding

Teachers' knowledge of content has at least two dimensions. One dimension is obvious—the extent to which they know the information that they must teach their students. The second is the extent to which they know the information *in depth.* This requires a sufficient understanding of the content to provide explanations and illustrations, analyze student perspectives, and answer student questions. Such an understanding enables teachers to think on their feet during lessons.

Teachers who feel their knowledge of some particular content is inadequate tend to avoid teaching it, or they may teach it superficially or only in an expository style. They often lecture, so that students do not ask questions. Beginning teachers who are still insecure about their knowledge of content often develop plans that are dominated by content-related information.

Knowledge of content also affects the ways in which teachers determine the goals for their lessons. As they plan, they must be able to answer questions: What should the students know when they are finished? Where am I going with this lesson? The answers provide direction for the lesson, and that direction would be slight or absent if the teacher were uncertain of lesson goals.

Goals for Lessons

In themselves, the *goals* that teachers set for their lessons significantly influence planning. Goals and objectives are targets that teachers set for their teaching. They represent the desired student achievement or mastery that would follow a successful lesson in which students had learned the intended knowledge, skills, and value perceptives. Correctly used, goals become a dominant influence on planning.

Teacher Expectations

The *expectations* that teachers set for their classes, for student learning, and for their own teaching also influence their planning and lesson images. If they have high expectations, the plans and envisioned lessons are demanding. If their assumptions are more restricted, the lessons may be less rigorous. Typically, teacher expectations are set early in the school year, or possibly before school starts; the teacher continuously revises as the year proceeds. These revisions result from teacher assessments of lessons taught and of the reactions of students, parents, administrators, and other teachers.

Feelings of Security and Control

Finally, general *feelings of security and control* about teaching play an influential role in the planning process. This point was mentioned earlier in terms of teacher knowledge of content, but that is only one aspect of the phenomenon. When a teacher feels secure in all dimensions, including content, ability to control students, teaching methods, and intended outcomes, teaching plans tend to be less rigid. When this is not the case, teachers are inclined to be more structured and to plan in greater detail.

Actually, the relationship between planning and a sense of security for teachers is cyclical. Teacher confidence in plans promotes feelings of security as lessons are implemented, and successful lessons promote more confidence in future plans.

External Influences on Planning

As teachers plan and teach, they face constraints that are external to themselves and their individual classrooms. Often these constraints emanate from decisions by school administrators, from public pressures, and from traditional practices and assumptions that have been in place for some time—the way it is done here. In recent years, external influences have placed ever-increasing pressures on teachers and have affected what they plan and how they do so.

Predetermined Goals

One form of external pressure on teacher planning involves the *goals and expectations established by school systems*. School systems establish objectives that teachers are to pursue and students are to reach. Although teachers often have considerable autonomy, their teaching must be consistent with these goals; thus they are not wholly free to teach anything they want. This influences planning and teaching.

Often school-system goals and expectations have been in place for a long time and are rather traditional, though this is not always the case. In recent years, for example, many school systems have required that such subject matter as the contributions of minority groups to American culture, substance abuse, teenage pregnancy, death, and safe sex be taught—topics that only a few years earlier were unusual, if not directly excluded from the curriculum. When such topics become official additions to school programs, teachers must, of course, plan their teaching to include them.

Accountability

Increased pressure for teacher and school *accountability* is another external influence on the process of planning. One effect of this pressure is that teachers' plans are expected to be more precise than in the past and to reflect specific intended learning outcomes. Although many teachers have reported for years that they decide early in the planning process exactly what they want students to learn, many have rarely stated these goals in behavioral terms or have committed them to detailed written form. Now, however, teachers are frequently required to write formal behavioral objectives for lessons. Often the requirements specify that lesson objectives be exact statements of what students are to learn, how the learning will be evaluated, and the level of learning that will be accepted. In some cases, these objectives are then used as measures of the teachers' performance. The following examples of behavioral objectives might be written for the lesson described in the chapter Snapshot:

Behavioral Objectives

- Given a teacher-made test of lines to be measured, students will measure accurately to the nearest inch at least seven of the ten lines.
- Given five measurements, students will draw accurate lines of at least three of the lengths.

When school systems require this type of planning, many teachers plan more exactly. Many also shift some of the emphasis of their teaching toward content that is easier to state as behavioral objectives and assess on objective tests than content they might otherwise have used. For example, they may feel a pressure to teach and assess knowledge of information that can be recalled instead of values and skills that cannot be recorded in multiple-choice fashion.

Observers

A second effect of teacher accountability pressures comes from *observations* of teachers and classrooms by principals and supervisors, who are frequently required to observe classrooms and evaluate teaching. This is an old truth, but when these observations are scheduled, teacher plans are influenced by the teacher's perceptions of the observer. The mental image of the lesson includes this individual's presence. Even when teachers try to ignore these influences, they invariably plan a lesson that seems to be likely to please the observer, and they take fewer risks.

Testing

Standardized achievement tests, now given yearly in many school districts, and other forms of *system-wide testing* are other examples of the influence of teacher accountability on planning. Test scores are often used to determine the achievement gains for individual students and classes as a whole. Sometimes they are the critical factor in determining whether students pass to the next grades. They are also considered a clear reflection of teacher performance.

If test scores receive a great amount of attention, teachers often prepare their students to take the tests. This situation has raised concern among educators who believe many teachers feel forced to let standardized tests dictate too many of their planning and teaching decisions. They believe teachers, to be effective, must retain the authority to make planning decisions that reflect their teaching situation and capable personal judgments.

Community and Parent Pressures

Community and parental pressures also have their impact on teacher planning, and the pressures push two ways. Sometimes teachers are expected to include certain topics, materials, or teaching techniques, and at other times they are expected to exclude them or treat them with extreme caution. Topics that have been pushed for both inclusion and exclusion are sex education, drug education, child abuse, AIDS education, and numerous local issues that involve values and emotions in controversy. At times, certain texts and other student-used materials become controversial in local communities, raising the potential for censorship of books, materials, and teachers. At other times, parents question teachers' use of classroom strategies, such as values clarification and open discussion of value-laden issues.

Traditions

Traditions—the ways things have been done in schools and communities—also influence teacher planning. For example, teachers have to plan for at least some of the following events: sport rivalries (football and basketball take time when there are big games or tournaments), Columbus Day, Thanksgiving, end-of-semester exams, Christmas break, snow days, Martin Luther King Day, prom, spring break, spring fever, and senior cut day. Most also have to turn in grades by deadline dates and have to see to it that a sufficient number of grades has been recorded for each report-card grading period.

Other External Influences

Other external influences on planning include such conditions as student absenteeism and interruptions. Teachers must adjust to and even anticipate both. Students who miss work must be able to catch up as much as is possible, and teachers must replan lessons that are delayed or seriously disrupted. Sometimes these interferences are fairly minor and not difficult to accommodate, but persistent and large-scale absences occur in virtually all classes, and special assemblies, field trips, and pull-out programs are common in most schools.

Organizational Influences on Planning

All teachers function within organizational structures and procedures. Some of these are based at the school-system level, some at the building level, and some at the classroom level. At the classroom level, teachers organize time, space, materials, the curriculum, and the use of students' time. They also manage student behavior. Similar structures, processes, and routines exist for entire schools and for whole school systems. Each imposes constraints on teacher planning and influences teachers' lesson plans.

Schedules

The schedules that school systems establish for schools, that schools establish for activities in the building, and that teachers establish for classes are one type of organizational influence that affects planning. The yearly calendar determines when students are in school, and daily schedules determine what happens within each day. Examples of such schedules for elementary and secondary students are shown in the Snapshot of Chapter 12.

When teachers plan and develop images of their lessons, they must fit their instruction within these schedules. They must provide for lunch, recess, resource classes, pull-out programs, music, physical education, pep rallies, unexpected changes in schedules, and so forth.

Available Time

The *time available* for instruction also greatly influences the planning process. Secondary school teachers usually have firmly set amounts of class time for the entire year and must plan their lessons within those limits. Class periods are just so long, and there are just so many of them. Elementary school teachers have somewhat more latitude; but they also face time expectations, at least as guidelines. Within these limits teachers determine the amount of time to be devoted to specific lessons and topics. This determination rests on teacher predictions of the amount of time needed to complete lessons successfully. Teacher plans, therefore, reflect a matching of time available with the time needed to teach lessons effectively. Figures 13–2 and 13–3 show typical teacher schedules.

The planning process is not just a matter of fitting self-contained lessons into isolated hours, days, and weeks. Lessons must fit together, and learning must be incremental. As a result, teachers plan with different lengths of instructional time in mind—daily, weekly, and longer-range—and how they conceive of these periods of time also influences the plans they develop. The goal of all

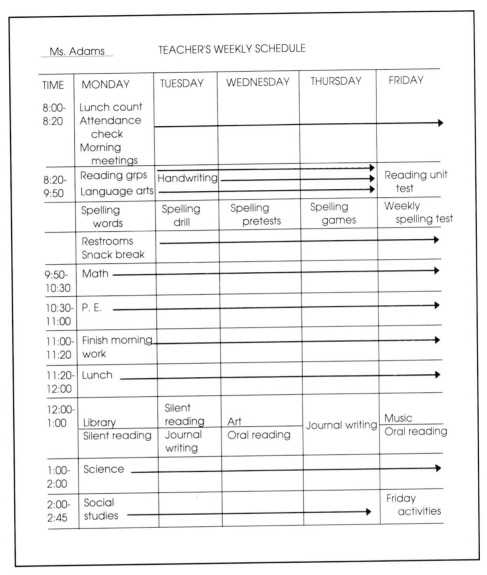

Figure 13–2. An elementary teacher's weekly schedule.

Type of Planning

planning is that students receive an intellectually meaningful education, in whatever timespans are available.

Interestingly, another organizational influence on planning involves an aspect of the planning process itself—that is, the type of plans teachers develop affects both the written plans themselves and the teachers' mental images of the lessons they describe. Teachers who think first of specific, daily, and short-term plans and only secondarily consider longer-term ideas plan different kinds of lessons than those who think first in terms of longer time sequences.

The most effective teachers usually plan by thinking of long-term and short-term plans at the same time. If teachers neglect to follow semester goals or to create long-range plans, their lessons often lack direction and continuity. On

	Ms. Brown		TEACHER'S WEEKLY SCHEDULE		

TIME	MONDAY	TUESDAY	WEDNESDAY	THURSDAY	FRIDAY
8:00–8:20	Home Room	Home Room	Home Room	Home Room	Home Room
8:25–9:15	English Lit II	English Comp I (Sect. a)	English Lit II	English Comp I (Sect. a)	English Lit II
9:20–10:10	AP English	AP English	AP English	AP English	AP English
10:15–11:05	English Comp I (Sect. b)	English Comp I (Sect. c)	English Comp I (Sect. b)	English Comp I (Sect. c)	English Comp I (Sect. b)
11:10–12:00	Preparing Marking	Preparing Marking	Preparing Marking	Preparing Marking	Preparing Marking
12:00–12:40			LUNCH		
12:45–1:35	English Comp I (Sect. a)	English Lit II	English Comp I (Sect. a)	English Lit II	English Comp I (Sect. a)
1:40–2:30	English Comp I (Sect. c)	English Comp I (Sect. b)	English Comp I (Sect. c)	English Comp I (Sect. b)	English Comp I (Sect. c)
2:35–3:25	Debate	Debate	Debate	Debate	Debate

Figure 13–3. A secondary English teacher's weekly schedule.

the other hand, if they neglect short-term plans, their lessons may lack clear development. Figure 13–4 depicts graphically the influence of long-range plans on daily and weekly planning.

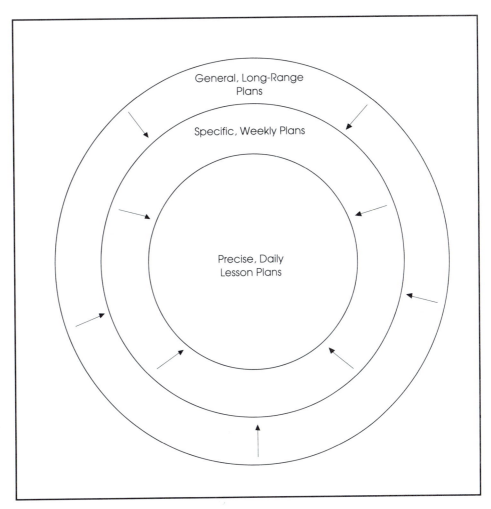

Figure 13–4. The effect of long-range plans on daily and weekly planning. Where a teacher expects the class to be instructionally several weeks ahead in the school year impacts what that teacher plans each day.

Class Size and Student Numbers

Another important influence on teacher planning is the combination of *class size* and the total *number of students* the teacher instructs. Understandably, teachers with large classes and large total numbers of students plan differently from those with fewer students. They think of the numbers of students they expect to teach and design lessons that they believe will serve those students best—as a group and as individual learners. Some activities work well with small numbers, and others do not; the same is true for large groups.

Some activities are more demanding of teachers than others, and teachers are more likely and more able to pursue the more demanding ones if student numbers are small rather than large. For example, teachers with a large number of students may find thorough evaluation of a large number of writing assignments impractical. (Note that the teacher whose schedule appears in Figure 13–4 teaches three sections of English composition and, presumably, has three sets of compositions to mark regularly.) Similarly, large numbers of students might require more copies of reading materials than are available.

Even when teachers have average numbers of students, they often find that to instruct all students effectively and to provide for individual needs, they must plan several simultaneous activities. They frequently plan to divide their larger classes into smaller groups in order to conduct multiple activities at the same time. This, of course, adds complexity to the planning process and to teaching.

Student Influences on Planning

Physical Needs

Student needs affect teachers' plans in significant ways. Because each student is different, those needs are quite varied, and they change over time. Students come to school with various *physical needs* that cannot be ignored. Those who are hungry, tired, or sick are unlikely to benefit very much from even the most exciting lesson. They are likely to need rest, and they withdraw psychologically. Students with physical handicaps or who are vision or hearing impaired also have particular physical needs, which may range from special seating requirements to the use of high-tech equipment.

Psychological Needs

Students also come to school with a wide variety of *psychological* and *emotional* needs that affect their classroom performance. Students who need greater self-esteem, increased peer affiliation, and security may be difficult to involve in lessons. Students who are easily bored require challenges and variety. Other students may be especially anxious and fearful of taking risks in the classroom. They may need reassurance and encouragement before they try a classroom task and risk embarrassment. Still other students dominate and have to be kept busy. Often students with special needs require a great deal of guidance and refocusing if they are to accomplish any task at all.

Think about how the teacher in the Snapshot of this chapter planned the sequence of activities for her unit on measurement and how she accommodated the needs of her students. She thought of alternate plans to occupy those who would finish early. She considered the questions she would ask students during the measurement demonstration in terms of involving them in the lesson. She planned specifically for several individuals. She gave herself time to walk around the room and attend to those who need extra help or encouragement.

Academic Needs

A great deal of educational research has focused on determining effective strategies for teaching students with varied academic abilities and different *academic needs*. Studies have demonstrated, for example, that effective methods for teaching high- versus low-ability students can be quite different, that low-ability students can often benefit academically from teaching strategies that provide for a slower pace and divide content into small steps with ample opportunities for practice and that higher-achieving students may require a faster pace, more challenge, and opportunities for discussion and interaction about the task (Brophy & Evertson, 1976; also see Brophy & Good, 1986).[8]

Motivation

Motivational levels relate directly to the time and energy required to capture students' attention and focus their energy on learning tasks. Slower students may lack motivation because of past failures whereas boredom may be the issue with faster students. In either case, lessons must challenge and provide variety. Recent research on motivation focuses on a theory that the effort a person is willing to invest in a task is determined by the degree to which the person (1) expects to be able to succeed and (2) values either participation in the task or access to the rewards that successful completion will bring. In other words,

Something to Think About

> Earlier chapters of this text contain several case studies describing particular students with special needs. Remembering those individuals, consider the questions below. The case studies and the pages on which they can be found are as follows:
>
> | | |
> |---|---|
> | William, Sixth Grade | page 122 |
> | Sherry, Eleventh Grade | page 124 |
> | James | page 155 |
> | Mark | page 168 |
> | Jamie | page 168 |
> | Saundra | page 170 |
> | Barbara | page 190 |
>
> (When thinking about Barbara, picture her in a regular class before she entered the alternative school.)
>
> - How would the presence of each of these students influence the mental images of lessons being planned by their teachers?
>
> - In what ways will the teaching of lessons be more complicated because these students are in class?

students do not invest effort in tasks in which they do not believe they will succeed or in tasks in which they do not value. (See Ames & Ames, 1984, 1985 for reviews.)[9] Planning effective lessons therefore requires that teachers be aware of students' perceptions and values of the tasks they are asked to complete.

Student Cultural Characteristics

Students' *cultural backgrounds* may affect how they can be expected to react to both content and methods of presentation, and teachers must plan accordingly. For instance, some cultural norms consider challenging a teacher's statement and looking a teacher in the eye as disrespectful. Other cultures deemphasize competition, especially among peers. Students whose cultures have strong sanctions against competition may not be willing to participate in team competitions, number facts drills, and other activities that require them to stand apart from their peers.

Cultural characteristics are very likely to affect students' inclinations or freedom to participate in classroom activities. Teachers who teach children from cultures other than their own will not succeed without careful planning.

Group Characteristics

Teachers often remark that each class has its own personality, a synergistic combination of unique individuals—which can often be altered by the addition or subtraction of only one individual. Some classes abound with cooperation and enthusiasm; others do not. Some classes seem to catch on quickly; others need much more instruction, direction, and review. Such characteristics of class groups naturally influence the planning of lessons and the ways teachers imagine them as they plan.

Also students in a class, like all persons in groups, play certain roles, and these roles affect classroom dynamics. Successful teachers plan with these students in mind and use them to accomplish their instructional goals. For example, nearly everyone remembers from their own schooldays the students who assumed the roles of "court jester," "brain," "goody goody," "troublemaker," "crazy," and "picked on" (Smith & Geoffrey, 1968; Damico & Purkey, 1978; Davis, 1972).[10] As teachers plan, they know that the ways they interact with these different personalities affect how well their lessons progress.

Student Expectations

Student experiences with schooling, with other teachers, and with the norms of the community in which the school sits lead them to expect certain things from their teachers. As a result, teachers take these expectations into consideration. Typically, they act very much as their students expect them to. For example, students often have common understandings about what school is supposed to be like. Nash (1976) found that students expected their teachers to "teach" them rather than leave them on their own to learn, to "keep order," and to keep other students from being too disruptive or interfering with lessons.[11] Other researchers (Carter & Doyle, 1982) found that when assignments increased in ambiguity, students pressed to "routinize" them and make them more predictable.[12]

Curricular Influences on Planning

Subject Matter

As discussed in Chapters 11 and 12, the content or subject matter taught also influences teacher plans and images of lessons. For example, English composition, mathematics, laboratory science, and history are different enough to necessitate different teaching approaches and classroom activities. Even within a subject such as English, planning varies with the level of instruction—advanced placement, general level, or remedial—and when the content emphasis for the day or the unit are different—grammar, literature, and reading-skill development. Teachers know that what they teach determines to a great extent how they teach, and this affects how they design their lessons.

Teaching Strategies and Methods

As teachers plan, they select the *teaching strategies and methods* that they believe will be most effective in promoting learning in their students, and the mental images and written plans for those different plans vary greatly. For example, planning for a discovery lesson requires a very different mindset than does planning for a lecture.

Materials and Resources

Teachers' plans are also influenced greatly by the materials and resources that are accessible and available to them. For instance, in order to plan a reading and language arts class that is integrated in a whole-language approach, a teacher must have a large number of books that interest children. Similarly, a science teacher who wants students to conduct experiments must have the necessary equipment. When such resources are lacking, teachers may be prevented from planning lessons they would most like to implement. Alternatively, they may be especially creative and industrious about finding materials that will work. In either case, they must plan in advance, and the planning is more difficult than when resources abound.

ANALYSIS

The episode below portrays Ms. Rowan as she is in the process of teaching the lessons based on her planning, which was described in the Snapshot at the beginning of this chapter. It is Wednesday, the third day of her unit on measurement for her second-grade students. As you read, consider:

- What adjustments to her original plans does Ms. Rowan seem to make?
- What additional information does Ms. Rowan now have that she did not have when she developed the plans?
- How might Wednesday's mathematics lesson have been different if Ms. Rowan had not planned as she did in the Snapshot?
- Next week, Ms. Rowan will begin a science unit on planets. What mental images do you think will occur to her as she plans the lesson? What will her written plans look like?

Ms. Rowan arrives at school at least thirty minutes before the children arrive. Upon entering the room, she looks back over her planbook, which triggers the earlier mental images for today's lesson. She refines these images and adds new ideas appropriate for the day.

First, Ms. Rowan looks at her plans for math. She thinks about the activities she has described for a few minutes, then gets out the materials she needs for the measurement lesson plan. She has brought with her rulers for each child, plus two extras in case one gets broken or a new student arrives.

Ms. Rowan also has a bundle of newly sharpened pencils to give to the children for the writing lesson. They will be able to use these when they work on recording the measurements they make and when doing page 25 of their math skillbooks.

Ms. Rowan collects the materials she will need for the review of the unit thus far. She puts on her table a paper-clip chain used in the lesson from Tuesday. She checks the overhead projector again, since the bulb flickered several times yesterday. She decides that the bulb should be replaced and does so.

Ms. Rowan checks her "helpers" board and notes that since it is Wednesday, Sheila will be the student in charge of passing out supplies to each of the tables. She makes a mental note to remind Sheila of this a few minutes before the math lesson.

Thinking back on Tuesday's class, Ms. Rowan remembers the children had problems getting into the lesson. She feels that during transition between language arts and math, many of the highly distractable children wasted time and did not settle down. She makes a note on her lesson plan to remind the students of the class rule about going to their seats quickly and quietly. She also decides to let the collecting and passing out of materials overlap. Realizing that Sheila will need help with this chore, she decides to ask Jimmy to collect the language arts work.

> Ms. Rowan locates the dittos of the lines she used Monday. She had run sixty of these last week and saved thirty to be used today. She remembers the children who had difficulties with the written work on Monday and Tuesday and plans to use the seatwork time to circulate among them to monitor their work. She jots their names on a small piece of notepaper. If she notices these students having problems again today, she may assign them partners for some of the measurements.
>
> Immediately after math the class goes to physical education, so Ms. Rowan usually plans the closure of the morning work for that time. She remembers, however, today is the day to collect money from the children ordering books from the book club. She knows that she may have to shift her usual schedule and have the students do the math skillbook assignment when they return from P.E. and are waiting for lunch. She revises her original plan and jots down a note in her planbook.
>
> Ms. Rowan then turns to her language arts and reading plans for the day. She expects the reading lesson to be rather straightforward since it follows the guidelines in the district-adopted Reading Skills Framework, but she wants to be sure she has not overlooked something. She also anticipates no difficulty with language arts. Every student did well in the lesson yesterday. She wants to think about it one more time even so.
>
> The students are about to arrive. Ms. Rowan will review her plans for this afternoon's science and social studies lessons while they are at physical education.

Conclusions about Planning

By this point, it should be obvious that the act of teaching requries substantial planning, that planning is a complex process, and that many factors influence how and what teachers plan for their lessons. Approaching lesson planning in a rational way that starts with goals and objectives seems logical, and such a beginning is particularly recommended for new teachers because it puts in focus what students will have learned when the lesson is successful. This focus then becomes a guide for lesson development. But because teaching is so multifaceted and because so many factors influence teaching and planning, a strict rational-choice approach to planning is not realistic for most teachers. As a result, most experienced teachers plan around their images of classes. The process they use is intricate and may appear confusing; for success, it demands skilled, perceptive, and intelligent classroom experts.

More will be said about the skills required of effective classroom teachers in the next chapter. Before that, however, let us look at what happens as teachers implement their plans with their classes.

TEACHING

Teaching as Communication

After planning comes teaching, obviously too complex a subject to be analyzed thoroughly in a chapter or a book. This chapter therefore examines teaching

An Introduction to Teaching and Schools 499

from one point of view, as a process of classroom interaction and communication. That particular perspective is presented because it shows classroom activity as a dynamic process with many parts, it provides a useful view of teaching for beginning education students, and it is consistent with much recent research into classroom processes. The perspective should supply an initial way of looking at teaching that will also serve as a useful comparison for other ideas.

Even on the most preliminary levels, this perspective shows a number of facets of the complex process of teaching. For example, when several researchers examine communication in the classroom, a number will concern themselves with the functions of verbal and nonverbal communication, others will analyze formal and informal talk, and still others will focus on the directions of classroom talk—student-to-student, teacher-to-student, student-to-teacher, and competitive talk among students. (For a survey of this information, see Hansford, 1988.)[13] Regardless of the approach, observers see classrooms as busy places, and this is reflected in the amount and diversity of communication that takes place.

Classroom communication is complex for a number of reasons—because of the nature of communication itself, because of the nature of instruction, and because both take place among human beings. Communicating in classrooms is much more than an exchange of information from teachers who present content to students who listen, understand, and learn. Therefore, it is never certain what will occur in any given class on any day.

Nevertheless, classroom communication has at least three common elements that can guide us at this point. First, instructional messages transmit more than just factual information. The values, attitudes, and perceptions of teachers and

Physical education teacher and students.

students are also involved. Second, what teachers and students communicate in classrooms is not necessarily interpreted and understood in the way it is intended. *Misunderstandings and misinterpretations,* either deliberate or unintended, occur; and when they do, they can cause problems. Third, in every class students vary greatly, and teachers must keep those variations in mind. Even if students in a classroom are of a similar age, they are not the same physically, emotionally, socially, and psychologically, and teachers must try to engage them all.

Teachers as Decision Makers

As the people in charge of classroom communication, teachers are expected to provide structure and meaning for what goes on. They do this by deciding what should happen and by communicating with students in ways that bring about what they want to happen. As decision makers, teachers must consider many questions: which activities to pursue, how to present material, who will answer questions, what standards of behavior are acceptable, when praise is appropriate, whether students will participate in the development of class rules, how much homework is appropriate, and whether to report instances of misbehavior to the principal. Those decisions must be followed up by the necessary communications with students, who must be told what to do and how to do it. In fact, some researchers associate successful teaching with the extent to which students understand teacher communication and believe it to be appropriate and fair. (For more information, see Hansford, pp. 154–161.)

Maintaining Pace and Balance

In the rapid-paced interactions that typify classroom communication, teachers must balance instructional responsibilities with management, encouragement, advice, direction, interest, and concern. It is the maintenance of this balance with continual decision making and constant interaction that makes teaching productive, demanding, and rewarding. Teachers may say something like this when they are communicating along the lines just listed:

> Get in your seats. Let's be quiet. Open your books. Who knows the answer to number one? John, read the first one. That's close! Who has a different idea? Why do you think so? Is he right? Why do you say that?

The Teacher's Challenge

Pause for a moment to think of Ms. Rowan, the second-grade teacher whom we have followed as she prepared to teach the lessons she has planned. Her initial planning is now over. Ms. Rowan has given considerable thought to what she will do in the classroom, she is confident about her knowledge of the ideas she will present, she understands the students, she believes herself to be well organized, and she thinks she has designed appropriate activities. Only one thing remains, the actual teaching. Ms. Rowan hopes her lessons on measurement go well, and for them to go well, she must foster and maintain a classroom environment in which learning can flourish.

Every Student Learning

Among the most important classroom variables that make teaching so challenging is the fact that she must communicate with so many different individuals at the same time (Jackson & Lahaderne, 1967; Jackson, 1968).[14] There are usually twenty or more (sometimes many more) students; and although they may live in the same area of town, travel on the same buses, be the same age, and sit in the classroom together, they are also unique, and this uniqueness is represented in many ways. They probably differ in levels of intelligence, and some achieve more quickly than others. They come from a number of cultural backgrounds and diverse home environments. To meet their needs and her expectations, Ms. Rowan must engage all her students in learning. She must try to stimulate every one of her students so as to produce learning, at the same time being sensitive to their intellectual and emotional needs. In particular, she must interact with them so that all feel like integral participants in the classroom process.

TEACHING AS COMMUNICATION

During lessons such as those presented by Ms. Rowan to her grade 2 class, many events and circumstances affect what the students learn. A few categories of those types of things are described below. Knowing these categories helps the understanding of all sorts of classroom activity.

Verbal Communication

A critical factor in teaching is the important verbal communication processes among teacher and students. Teachers rely heavily on their capacity to transmit information and directions to students via the spoken word; similarly, students generally use the same medium to respond to teacher comments and seek additional information. Because this is so, the extent to which teachers use and understand verbal communication greatly affects their classroom effectiveness.

Amount of Talk

Anyone who observes classroom behavior or just stands outside a classroom for a few minutes can easily verify that an immense amount of talking occurs in classrooms. This raises a number of questions for teachers to think about. For example,

- How much talking is occurring?
- Who is talking?
- Is all the talking relevant to the subject?
- Do all students share in talking?

(The text discusses each of these topics. For a more detailed survey of classroom verbal communication, see Hansford, pp. 77–111.)

Teacher Verbal Dominance

Studies of classroom interaction indicate that teachers often dominate classroom talk. They talk to instruct, to give directions, and to control student behavior. They tell students what to do, how to do it, when to start, and when to stop. As a result, it is not unusual to find that about 60 to 80 percent of classroom talk is teacher talk, and this dominance appears to suggest that many of us believe that learning occurs when teachers talk and students listen.

Some observers suggest that a large amount of teacher talk is bad, but that is not necessarily true. There are times when teachers should lecture, give directions, and explain ideas; and these tasks require a significant amount of talking. Teacher talk is probably appropriate if it is consistent with the purposes of the lesson and if the teacher is aware of the amount and type of talking that is occurring.

Teacher Awareness

On the other hand, studies have reported that teachers are frequently unaware of the extent to which their talk dominates classes and that they often do not know whether their talk accomplishes what they want it to do. One aspect of this ambiguity is the teacher's ability (or lack thereof) to assess and control the relevance of talking to the subject be to learned. Is it consistent with lesson objectives? Is it producing learning? Is any of the conversation off task?

Formal and Informal Talk

Classroom verbal communication consists of *types of talk,* as well as amount and speaker. One way to analyze classroom talk is to divide it into *formal talk,* which is generally associated with instruction, and *informal talk,* which is usually designed to assist interpersonal relationships. (See Hansford, pp. 77–111.) Even with formal acts of instruction teachers will be uncertain as to whether all students understand their instructions, directions, and explanations. As a consequence, they may try to increase the chances by repeating what they say, sometimes several times. They rephrase explanations, redirect questions, and reinforce directions. Although in such cases the teacher's intention is to clarify, repetition can cause problems. For instance, when a teacher repeats a point with multiple illustrations (because some students might not understand), the danger of disenchanting and boring those who grasped the idea quickly is strong. Also, the subtleties of each illustration may confuse rather than clarify, especially for the very perceptive students.

Communication Overload

Ignoring Students

On the other hand, teachers frequently talk only to the students who seem to be catching on quickly, in the process virtually ignoring those who need more explanation (Brophy & Good, 1974).[15] Teachers usually initiate verbal contact with students, watch for positive responses, and react to those responses. Frequently, the rest of the class gradually fades from teachers' focus even though they intend to interact with all students in the classroom. Bright, verbal students are inevitably inclined to involve themselves in classroom talk, and teachers find it difficult to slow them down or ignore them in order to draw others into the conversation.

Zone of Action

In some classroom settings the *zone of action*, the area that is likely to involve the most teacher-student interaction, has particular significance (Adams & Biddle, 1970).[16] In a formal classroom of traditional rows of desks, the zone of action typically includes students sitting in front and in the center rows. (See Figure 13–5). Students seated in these seats tend to be in the teacher's direct path of vision and perhaps for that reason are more likely to be talked to directly, called on to answer questions, and asked to carry out tasks.

A question related to the zone of action is the extent to which students are aware of it. Do they know that where they sit in the clsssroom influences the frequency with which they have contact with the teacher? In classrooms where students can select their seats freely, do those who want to have contact with the teacher know or sense where the highly interactive locations are? Do those who want to avoid contact know where to sit? Do some students know how to play this seating game, while others do not? If you were behind in mathematics,

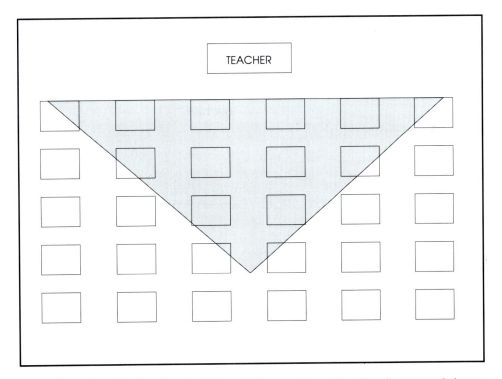

Figure 13–5. Zone of action. The shaded area is the area in most traditionally arranged classes that typically gets the most teacher attention.

Perceptions of Students

had failed the last test, and had not completed your homework, would you sit in the middle of the front row under the direct gaze of the teacher?

Classroom verbal interactions are also influenced by teacher perceptions of students and by students' self-perceptions and perceptions of each other. The effects seem to flow three ways: Perceptions affect expectations, and both perceptions and expectations influence verbal interactions. For instance, perceptions and expectations are sometimes tied to the gender of students. In one study, boys received more teacher verbal contacts than girls in a number of classrooms, and many of these contacts varied in type as well as frequency (Brophy & Good, 1974). The teacher verbal comments to boys frequently contained a rather high proportion of controlling or critical statements: Don't do that. Come out here. I told you not to push others. Put that book away. Another study reported that although girls seemed to receive fewer verbal contacts, more of the contacts they receive deal with instructional content than with directions or behavior control (Brophy & Evertson, 1981).[17]

Inequalities of Contact

Teachers, aware of their responsibility to treat all students fairly, naturally make substantial efforts to interact appropriately with students regardless of how talkative the students are, where they sit, and what their gender is. But on a busy day and in a very demanding interpersonal setting, teachers may not be aware of how much interaction they are having with certain students. In fact, teachers who have been observed and informed of the inequalities of contacts that occur in their classrooms frequently express surprise (Brophy & Good, 1970).[18] A good example of this is the contrast in time a teacher allows after directing a question to a particular student and while ascertaining whether an answer is forthcoming. Teachers tend to wait longer for students they believe to be bright (Brophy & Good, 1970).

Teacher perceptions and expectations of students are of course not always negative factors in the process of classroom communication. Teachers must have some expectations of student performance in order to decide on content, methods, materials, and so forth; and they need expectations to target the level of their presentation and to frame their questions. But those same expectations, if used unskillfully, can be misleading and can inhibit classroom interaction.

Expectations

Think again of Ms. Rowan. As she plans and begins teaching her lessons, does she have preconceived expectations regarding her students? Are those preconceptions accurate and fair? Might she think as follows? "The new girl, Jane Newcomer, does not seem to know much about mathematics. In three lessons she has not answered one question. She may need help, but I need to keep the lessons flowing and active to keep most students involved." Might she early in the lesson ask Jane a question and, on failing to receive a quick response, shift the question swiftly to Tiffany Bright, who, as usual, answers immediately? In such a process the teacher's expectations could be reinforced, and a self-fulfilling prophecy might be confirmed.

Nonverbal Communication

Some years ago studies of what actually happens during acts of teaching focused almost totally on verbal communication, but educators are now much more aware of the importance of nonverbal communication—the gestures, facial expressions, body movements, general appearance, changes in vocal pitch and tempo, and so forth that accompany or substitute for spoken words. In fact, the effectiveness of lessons such as Ms. Rowan's lessons on measurement may well depend not just on *what* teachers say to students but also on *how* they say it and what they do as well as say (Woolfolk & Brooks, 1983). (For more information, see Hansford, 1988.)[19]

Manipulated Nonverbal Communication

It is possible to divide nonverbal communication into two broad categories—manipulated and spontaneous. *Manipulated nonverbal communication* takes place when the teacher or students *knowingly* use a particular nonverbal cue, such as a facial expression or hand gesture, in an endeavor to supplement, modify, or perhaps contradict spoken words. For example, Ms. Rowan may find Karl Pest's interruption quite amusing, but she puts on a very stern face that tells him to raise his hand when he wants to say something in class. Similarly, students who are not much interested in measurement as a topic still know it is appropriate to look at the teacher, smile, and nod. On the other hand, students who are interested in the subject but who fear negative peer pressures if they show too much enthusiasm may slouch in their chairs, write notes, or look above it all. In other words, teachers and students all use or manipulate nonverbal cues purposely.

Spontaneous Nonverbal Communication

Spontaneous nonverbal communication is that which occurs *naturally*, without specific intent. It happens all the time in classrooms, where there is a great deal of smiling, laughing, loud talking, whispering, waving of arms, walking around, touching, pushing, frowning, and tapping of pencils. In fact, each person in a classroom transmits a considerable amount of spontaneous nonverbal communication, and although it is not intentional, it is observed and interpreted. Students act upon what they think the teacher *really* meant because of nonverbal behavior such as the tone of voice, the look on the teacher's face, or the teacher's hand and body movements. Similarly, teachers interpret the level of student understanding or interest on the basis of comparable nonverbal cues.

Kinesics, the study of posture, movement, gestures, facial expressions, and eye behavior, provides valuable information for observing nonverbal classroom communication. Observers who use it can recognize a variety of nonverbal behaviors, such as emblems, illustrators, and regulators (Hansford, 1988, pp. 118–122). *Emblems* are gestures that have a direct verbal translation and are usually used instead of spoken words. They are often performed by hand movements. For example, teachers may use emblems to transmit messages such as "Come here" and "Be quiet." Students use them to transmit "I would like to answer that question" and "I need your help." *Illustrators* are used to amplify a spoken message; teachers and students accompany terms such as *large* or *small* with hand movements to do this. *Regulators* are used to control discussions and movement between persons. Hand signals, head nods, eye movements, smiles, and frowns inform students that it is their turn to speak, to slow down, or to be quiet.

Like verbal communication, nonverbal communication is transmitted in multiple directions. Teachers not only direct nonverbal communication toward students but also receive it from them, and students send and receive it among each other. Effective teachers observe and monitor nonverbal student messages in order to determine whether students are listening, whether they understand, and whether the lesson is progressing at a reasonable speed. They also watch for it to determine what students are "saying" to each other.

Impeding Classroom Communication

A number of factors frequently impede the process of classroom communication; and when they do, even the best-planned lessons carried out by the most skilled teachers are not as effective as they might be. Two such factors—*noise* and *barriers*—are described below. (For additional discussion, see Hansford, 1988, pp. 10–11, 23–32.)

Noise

Normally the term *noise* is limited to physical sounds heard by human ears, but here we use a broader meaning. We extend the word *noise* to include *all sensory distractions* that impede classroom communication. This broad definition is necessary because classroom communications are not limited to sounds. For example, just as the sounds created by other students whispering, the physical education class on the athletic field outside the window, people running in the hall, passing trucks, and band practice interfere with classroom communication, so do distracting sights passing school windows and open classroom doors, hot or cold room temperatures, stuffy rooms, and bad odors.

Internal and External Noise

Classroom noise of this broader type can be divided into two types—external and internal. *External noise* comes from outside the people affected by it and includes all of the illustrations just mentioned. *Internal noise* comes from within people themselves. It includes elements such as the thoughts and feelings of teachers and students. For example, when teachers are worried or ill, their capacity to communicate effectively with students will likely be reduced. When students are daydreaming about life beyond the classroom, under pressure at home, or having difficulty with their peers, they probably will not provide responses or initiate interactions as well as their teachers hope.

Semantic Noise

In addition to sensory distractions, another kind of noise, called *semantic noise,* also influences the flow of classroom communication. This type of noise concerns aspects of the actual language used in classrooms. Instruction relies heavily on the capacity of teachers to interpret reality and then transmit this interpretation by means of appropriate verbal and nonverbal symbols. Unfortunately, the symbols used to transmit messages do not always create the same images or meaning in the minds of all people. Such things as incorrect use of words, words that have multiple meanings, and complex sentence structures can be sources of semantic noise.

Some form of noise exists in all settings where humans interact with each other. The challenge that faces teachers as classroom managers of communication is not to eliminate this noise but to recognize it and teach accordingly. Thus, it is only natural to expect that external, internal, and semantic noise will have substantial influence on the teaching-learning process.

The process of classroom communication is also impeded by *barriers,* something that gets between the flow of communication and the people involved. Four prominent classroom types are discussed below: filtering, wandering, masking, and communication apprehension.

Filtering

When people talk, one or another will sometimes *filter* out much of what is being communicated, so that they hear only what they want to or can bear to hear. They may reject information that is not in accord with their systems of belief. They hear selectively. Teachers are selective in both which and how they convey information to students. They are also selective in how they respond to students. Sometimes the selectivity is conscious and at other times unintentional. Some parts of a lesson may be covered very generally or not explained at all, and sometimes particular student comments are ignored or responded to ambiguously.

Students also filter or select from the ideas and information provided by the teacher those elements that they want to retain or believe to be of greatest value to them. For example, when Ms. Rowan reviews the material covered in her measurement lesson as she prepares the students for a test, she will find considerable differences in the amount and nature of information retained. Of course, some of the differences will reflect what students have forgotten, but students may have filtered out ideas and explanations they did not understand in the first place. Nearly every teacher has heard students who are having difficulty with a particular problem say things like these: "I just don't get it, so there is no use spending more time trying." "I didn't like that topic, so I skipped it!"

Wandering

As students enter their classrooms, they frequently bring with them concerns, thoughts, and emotions that cause their minds to wander. This, of course, inhibits communication and challenges teachers to ensure that students pay attention so that they can learn. They must motivate, challenge, and involve students with high-quality, on-task learning activities. But teachers' thoughts also wander; and when they do, ideas seem to get lost in midsentence, lectures slide off the topic, student questions go unanswered, and explanations are not as clear as they should be.

Masking

Teachers and students often present to each other facades that hide inner thoughts and feelings. The phenomenon is called *masking*, or *impression management*, and may result from endeavors to conform to expectations, create special effects, portray oneself in a favorable light, or engage in some act of deception. When this happens a lot, the real student or teacher is obscured, and the other people in the conversation are misled. For example, students who tell teachers they understand something when they do not may not get the remedial attention that they need, whereas those with obscured emotional or physical problems may be labeled as lazy.

To an extent, some masking occurs all of the time and should be expected. Teachers do not need to know everything about their students and should not expect to. Some matters are just not the teachers' business. On the other side, teachers have the same rights of privacy. However, the line between privacy and deception, between being nosy and knowing enough about the other person to communicate effectively, is sometimes hard to determine.

Communication Apprehension

Communication apprehension is a state in which individuals are anxious or fearful about being involved in oral communication with others. Some individuals experience it in such high levels that they try to avoid being involved in or withdraw from situations where they might be expected to speak. Some students, as well as teachers for that matter, are highly apprehensive about being required to answer questions, offer opinions, lead discussions, speak before a group, take part in a play, or interact orally in a general way. Research indicates that high communication apprehension among students may affect their attitudes toward school, which seats they select in classrooms, how they feel about themselves, and their capacity to perform well academically (Hansford, 1988, pp. 148–153). Communication apprehension is difficult for teachers to detect and even more difficult to do something about.

As a point of illustration, think of Ms. Rowan's class and assume that the class includes a student named Julia Quiet. Julia rarely says a word. How does

Some insecure students are uncomfortable with close monitoring of their work.

Ms. Rowan determine whether Julia Quiet is experiencing unduly high levels of communication apprehension? If she is, what is causing it, and what should Ms. Rowan do about it? A number of children are simply quiet by nature. Others have teachers and parents who emphasize the virtues of quietness. When children such as these find themselves in classrooms where teachers foster interaction, they may feel confused or threatened. When teachers force these students to participate in discussions, debates, and plays in an effort to help them overcome their shyness, they may intensify the apprehension.

EDUCATIONAL RESEARCH

Communication Apprehension

This Educational Research section reports on information about communication apprehension, only one specific barrier to effective classroom communication. It does so for three reasons:

1. So much information is available on classroom communication that only a focused review is practical in the space available here.

2. The concept of communication apprehension is not widely understood among teachers.

3. Active participation in classes is so important for student success that those who experience difficulty speaking out are frequently slighted in many classes.

We hope this focus on communication apprehension will demonstrate it as a matter of teacher concern and at the same time will illustrate in one area the extent to which many of the other elements of classroom activity are being investigated by educational researchers.

The following research summaries briefly examine the relationship between communication apprehension and self-concept, attitudes toward school, preference for particular types of educational experience, and teacher expectations.

Self-Concept

- For many years educators have believed that the way students feel about themselves plays an important role in both academic and social development. In fact, positive beliefs and feelings about oneself tend to be associated with high levels of school performance. (See Hansford, 1988, pp. 54–71, and earlier sections of this text.) As a result, many teachers spend a considerable amount of time fostering a classroom environment that enhances positive self-images and feelings.

   A number of studies, especially those by McCroskey, Daly, Richmond and Falcione (1977), have shown a consistent relationship between self-esteem and communication apprehension.[20] In simple terms, these studies tend to show that individuals experiencing high levels of communication apprehension have relatively low levels of self-esteem. Although research is unclear whether high communication apprehension *causes* low self-esteem or vice versa, it is clear that teachers encounter some students who try to avoid classroom communication and also have poor or negative images of themselves.

Attitudes toward School

Pupils with positive attitudes toward schools in general and toward specific subjects in particular tend to achieve good grades at school, or at least good grades in the subjects they like. (See Wittrock, 1986, pp. 298–302.)[21] At the same time, a number of studies report that attitudes toward school are related to levels of communication apprehension. For example, McCroskey (1977a), McCroskey (1977b), and McCroskey and Andersen (1976) suggest that as communication apprehension increases, attitudes toward schools become increasingly negative.[22]

Preferences for Educational Experiences

Research studies indicate that students who are apprehensive about involving themselves in classroom oral communication express a preference for particular types of instructional experiences. For instance, Burgoon (1976) reports that highly apprehensive students prefer to (1) complete written assignments rather than participate in discussions; (2) attend lectures rather than class discussions; (3) be tested in written, rather than oral, form; (4) be graded on test performance rather than class participation; and (5) have their grades based on written rather than oral presentations.[23]

Teacher Expectations

Researchers have also focused attention on the relationship among communication apprehension, teacher expectations, and the manner in which students are treated in classrooms. A study by McCroskey and Daly (1976) indicates that teachers expect students with high levels of communication apprehension to have lower levels of achievement than less apprehensive students, rather poor futures in education, and rather inadequate relationships with peer group members.[24]

It is clear that students experiencing high levels of communication apprehension are sometimes perceived as lacking in intelligence and, as a consequence, are treated in a manner that inhibits their potential development. Sensitive, aware teachers may be able to minimize the hurt and life impediment experienced by apprehensive students, but to do so they need to recognize communication apprehension and respond accordingly. In some cases, they may find it necessary to seek professional assistance for these students.

Conclusions about Teaching as Communication

Organizing Communication

Although there are many ways of looking at what happens during classroom lessons, the perspective presented in this chapter is that of classroom activity as a process of communication intended to produce learning in students. This view casts teachers both as communicators and as organizers of the communication process. They talk, listen, direct conversation, and so forth; and they do so among many different human beings and under an enormous variety of conditions. To be successful, they must plan, understand their purpose and function, and be skilled for the tasks. They face a number of impediments to effective classroom communication, but dealing with those hurdles is part of the job of teaching.

Planning Influences and Potential Difficulties

Of course, the impediments to effective teaching are not limited to the few described above, all of which interfere directly with classroom discourse. There are problems, complications, and intrusions of many kinds, and they come from many sources. Some of these were described earlier in this chapter among the influences that teachers consider in their planning. To understand this point more clearly, reconsider the descriptions of influences on planning early in the

Some students are more verbal than others.

Outside Intrusions

chapter, this time looking at those influences as potential *difficulties* teachers face as they conduct their lessons.

Other problems and complications that affect teaching should also be mentioned. Some intrude from outside the classroom—fire drills, assemblies, shortened class periods, announcements, lost films and videos, the big game, students' and teachers' social lives, broken legs, headaches, the flu, and so forth. Each of these makes teaching harder than it might be, makes planning more important than it might otherwise be, and confounds the best-made plans. Good teachers, however, seem to take them in stride and think of them as annoyances rather than as real problems. One such teacher is known to have two special files for plans affected by situations such as these. The file labels read It Should Have Worked and Just a Lousy Day.

EVALUATION

The third step in the act of teaching, after planning and the actual teaching of lessons, is lesson evaluation. The teachers assess how well they have succeeded in accomplishing what they had set out to do. As in Figure 13–2, they compare what happened with what they expected to happen, and they determine whether the students learned what the teachers had anticipated. This assessment helps them decide whether anything needs to be retaught, what should be taught next and how it should be taught, and what should be done differently next year.

We do not present a detailed explanation of lesson evaluation here, but we refer you once again to Figure 13–2 for close study. Note where lesson evaluation fits into the continuous process of lesson planning and how it influences the next planning cycle. As you study the illustration, try to think of lesson evaluation not only as an event that follows teaching but also as a task that precedes the next stage of planning.

First and Last Step

Several key points about lesson evaluation are in order. First, for good teaching, lesson evaluation is necessary and must be taken seriously. It is a central component of teaching. Second, lesson evaluation involves informal, unwritten reflection about lessons as well as more formal analyses of how things went. Third, as your review of Figure 13–2 should have indicated, lesson evaluation is not only the *last* major step in the process of teaching lessons that have been completed; it is also the *first* step in planning future lessons. It is part of the bridge between lessons that helps hold lessons together and enables teachers to continually improve their work.

The Analysis section earlier in this chapter described Ms. Rowan as she prepared for the third day of her five-day lesson on measurement. During the first two days, she made adjustments in her original plans in response to classroom events, and she was anticipating other modifications as she approached day three. It is logical to assume that she continued this reflection-adjustment style of operation for Thursday and Friday and that she conducted a more thorough analysis of all five days after completing the whole lesson at the end of the week.

CONCLUSION

Teaching is more than standing before students and telling them what they need to know or are supposed to do. It is a complex, multifaceted process that begins with thorough planning and ends with lesson evaluation. Good teachers take each step in the process seriously, and the streamlining that experienced teachers do in no way undercuts that critical responsibility. Beginning teachers commonly need to devote more time and effort to assure consistently positive results than do old pros, but all successful teachers plan and evaluate.

Because of the complexity of these and other tasks, teaching can be analyzed from a number of perspectives. The prospectives described in this chapter emphasize planning as the building of images of lessons, teaching as a process of communication, and evaluation as a reflection on how well a lesson went. These ways of looking at planning, teaching, and evaluation should provide some intellectual framework for understanding what teachers do in classrooms, particularly how they make everything fit together and lead toward productive student learning.

SUMMARY

Teachers draw on all elements of education described earlier in this text and put them together in a personal way in order to produce desired learning in students. To do this effectively, they plan, conduct, and evaluate lessons. Good teachers engage in all three steps knowledgeably, skillfully, and conscientiously. They know what to do, are able to do it well, and take the responsibility seriously.

Although the rational-choice approach to planning has been stressed in recent decades as the way teachers should plan lessons, many teachers use a different approach, the lesson-image approach. They plan by formulating mental images of their lessons. In so doing, they think about what they want their lessons "to look like" and put all the pieces together in their own individual ways. It seems, too, that they do this almost all the time, not just at school or during their planning time.

Because it involves so much, the teaching of lessons can be described in many ways. One way that seems to be useful to beginning students of teacher education and that also has received substantial recent attention from educational researchers is to view teaching as a process of communication. This perspective portrays teaching as a dynamic process, stresses the interaction that takes place among teachers and students, and focuses on the many roles teachers perform in the classroom.

Lesson evaluation is a necessary and integral step in the act of teaching. Teachers assess their lessons to determine whether they successfully taught what they intended and to start the process of planning future lessons.

STUDY QUESTIONS

1. Think about teachers you had in elementary and secondary school and select the one who you think probably planned his or her lessons most thoroughly; also select the one who you think probably planned the least. What evidence did you consider in making each selection? How was the teaching of the two individuals different in style, effect, motivating quality, and so on?

2. Below are several analogies that have been used to describe the function(s) of classroom teachers. In your judgment, how is each accurate or inaccurate?
   - teacher as orchestra conductor
   - teacher as traffic director
   - teacher as driving instructor with twenty-five or thirty beginning drivers, each in a separate car but all being instructed at the same time

3. Assume that when Ms. Rowan finished her lesson on measurement, she gave a test, and most of the class missed more than half of the test questions. What should she do? Why?

4. Select a subject, a grade level, and a topic for a lesson you would want to teach to a class of elementary or secondary school students. What types of things would you need to know in order to develop useful mental images of that lesson?

BIBLIOGRAPHY

Barker, L. (Ed.). (1982). *Communication in the classroom.* Englewood Cliffs, NJ: Prentice-Hall.

Brophy, J. E., & Good, T. L. (1974). *Teacher-student relationships: Causes and consequences.* New York: Holt, Rinehart and Winston.

Brophy, J. E., & Good, T. L. (1986). Teacher behavior and student achievement. In M. C. Wittrock (Ed.), *Handbook of research on teaching: Third edition.* (pp. 328–375). New York: Macmillan.

Brophy, J. E., & Evertson, C. M. (1981). *Student characteristics and teaching.* New York: Longman.

Dick, W., & Reiser, R. A. (1989). *Planning effective instruction.* Englewood Cliffs, NJ: Prentice-Hall.

Good, T. L., & Brophy, J. E. (1987). *Looking in classrooms* (4th ed.). New York: Harper & Row.

Goodlad, J. I. (1984). *A place called school: Prospects for the future.* New York: McGraw-Hill.

Hansford, B. C. (1988). *Teachers and classroom communication.* Sydney, Australia: Harcourt Brace Jovanovich.

Jackson, P. W. (1986). *The practice of teaching.* New York: Teachers College Press.

Neely, A. M. (1986). Integrating planning and problem solving in teacher education. *Journal of Teacher Education, 37*(3), 29–33.

Neely, A. M. (1985). Teacher planning: Where has it been? Where is it now? Where is it going? *Action in Teacher Education, 7*(3), 25–29.

Seiler, W. J., Schuelke, L. D., & Lieb-Brilhart, J. C. (1984). *Communication for the contemporary classroom.* New York: Holt, Rinehart and Winston.

Stein, B. (1986, November). High school diary. *Los Angeles Magazine,* pp. 168–178.

NOTES

1. Tyler, R. W. (1950). *Basic principles of curriculum and instruction.* Chicago: University of Chicago Press; Taba, H. (1962). *Curriculum development, theory and practice.* New York: Harcourt, Brace and World; Popham, J. W., & Baker, E. L. (1970). *Systematic instruction.* Englewood Cliffs, NJ: Prentice-Hall.

2. Clark, C. M., & Yinger, F. J. (1979). Research on teacher planning: A progress report. *Journal of Curriculum Studies, 11*(2), 175–177.

3. Zahorik, J. A. (1970). The effect of planning on teaching. *Elementary School Journal, 71*(3), 143–151. (The quotation is on pp. 150–151.) Also see Zahorik (1975). Teachers' planning models. *Educational Leadership, 33*(2), 134–139.

4. Morine, G. (1976). *A study of teacher planning.* (Technical Report 76-3-1, Beginning Teacher Evaluation Study.) San Francisco: Far West Laboratory for Education Research and Development; Peterson, P. L., Marx, R. W., & Clark, C. M. (1978). Teacher planning, teacher behavior, and student achievement. *American Educational Research Journal, 15*(3), 417–432; Yinger, R. J. (1977). Unpublished doctoral dissertation, Michigan State University. *A study of teacher planning: Description and theory development using ethnographic and information-processing methods;* Yinger, R. J. (1979). Routines in teacher planning. *Theory into practice, 19*(2), 163–169; Yinger, R. J., & Clark, C. M. (1981, July). *Reflective journal writing: Theory and practice.* East Lansing: Institute for Research on Teaching, Michigan State University. (ERIC Document Reproduction Service No. 208 411.)

5. Morine, G., & Vallance, E. (1975). *A study of teacher and pupil perceptions of classroom interactions.* (BTES Special Report B.) San Francisco: Far West Laboratory for Education Research and Development.

6. Neely, A. M. (1985). Teacher planning: Where has it been? Where is it now? Where is it going? *Action in Teacher Education, 7*(3), 25–29; Neely (1986). Integrating planning and problem solving in teacher education. *Journal of Teacher Education, 37*(3), 29–33.

7. Clark, C. M., & Peterson, P. L. (1986). Teachers' thought processes. In M. C. Wittrock (Ed.). *Handbook of research on teaching: Third edition.* (pp. 255–296). New York: Macmillan.
8. Brophy, J. E., & Evertson, C. M. (1976). *Learning from teaching: A development perspective.* Boston: Allyn and Bacon; Brophy, J. E., & Good, T. L. (1986). Teacher behavior and student achievement. In M. C. Wittrock (Ed.). *Handbook of research on teaching: Third edition.* (pp. 328–375). New York: Macmillan.
9. Ames, R., & Ames, C. (Eds.). (1984). *Research on motivation in education: Vol. 1. Student motivation.* Orlando, FL: Academic Press; Ames and Ames, (Eds.). (1985). *Research on motivation in education: Vol. 2. The classroom milieu.* Orlando, FL: Academic Press.
10. Smith, L., & Geoffrey, W. (1968). *Complexities of an urban classroom: An analysis toward a general theory of teaching.* New York: Holt, Rinehart and Winston; Damico, S. B. & Purkey, (1978). Class clowns: A study of middle school students. *American Educational Research Journal,* 15(3), 391–398; Davis, J. (1972). Teachers, kids and conflict: Ethnography of a junior high school. In J. P. Spradley & D. W. McCurdy. *The cultural experience: Ethnography in complex society* (pp. 103–119). Chicago: Science Research Associates.
11. Nash, R. (1976). Pupils' expectations of their teachers. In M. Stubbs & S. Delamont (Eds.). *Explorations in classroom observation* (pp. 83–98). New York: Wiley.
12. Carter, K., & Doyle W. (1982, March). *Variations in academic tasks in high and average ability classes.* Paper presented at the annual meeting of the American Educational Research Association, New York.
13. Hansford, B. (1988). *Teachers and classroom communication.* Sydney, Australia: Harcourt Brace Jovanovich.
14. Jackson, R., & Lahaderne, H. (1967). Inequalities of teacher-pupil contact. *Psychology in the Schools,* 4(2), 204–208; Jackson, P. (1968). *Life in classrooms.* New York: Holt, Rinehart and Winston.
15. Brophy, J. E., & Good, T. L. (1974). *Teacher-student relationships: Causes and consequences.* New York: Holt, Rinehart and Winston.
16. Adams, R. S., & Biddle, R. (1970). *Realities of teaching: Exploration with videotape.* New York: Holt, Rinehart and Winston.
17. Brophy, J. E., & Evertson, C. M. (1981). *Student characteristics and teaching.* New York: Longman.
18. Brophy, J. E., & Good, T. L. (1970). Teachers' communications of differential expectations for children's classroom performance: Some behavioral data. *Journal of Educational Psychology,* 61(5), 365–374.
19. Woolfolk, A. E., & Brooks, D. M. (1983). Nonverbal communication in teaching. In E. W. Goodwin (Ed.). *Review of Research in Education,* 10 (pp. 103–149). Washington: American Educational Research Association.
20. McCroskey, J. C., Daly, J. A., Richmond, V. P., & Falcione, R. L. (1977). Studies of the relationship between communication apprehension and self-esteem. *Human Communication Research,* 3(3), 264–277.
21. Wittrock, M. C. (1986). Students' thought processes. In M. C. Wittrock (Ed.). *Handbook of Research on Teaching: Third edition* (pp. 297–314). New York: Macmillan.
22. McCroskey, J. C. (1977a). Classroom consequences of communication apprehension. *Communication Education,* 26, 27–33; McCroskey, J. C. (1979b). *Quiet children and the classroom teacher.* Falls Church, VA: Speech Communication Association; McCroskey, J. C., & Anderson, J. E. (1976). The relationship between communication apprehension and academic achievement among college students. *Human Communication Research,* 3(1), 73–81.

23. Burgoon, J. K. (1975). *Teacher strategies for coping with communication apprehension.* Paper presented at the annual meeting of the Speech Communication Association, Houston.

24. McCroskey, J. C., & Daly, J. A. (1976). Teachers' expectations of the communication apprehensive child in the elementary school. *Human Communication Research, 3*(1), 67–72.

CHAPTER 14

The Professional Teacher: The Life and the Work

14: The Professional Teacher: The Life and the Work

INTRODUCTION

Although many people believe they understand the lives and work of teachers because of their years in schools as students, they often know less than they think. When we went to elementary and secondary schools, we were very young. We had only our perspective as students, and being the lesser part of the partnership inevitably biased us in many ways. We had only a few teachers, whom we mainly saw only at school. Peers, parents, and gossip could prejudice us. In short, people who think they know about teaching because they have been students have only a limited understanding of teaching, and they have no experience of the emotions that go with the job.

Therefore, this chapter presents a view of teachers as practicing professionals. It analyzes in succession the job of teaching, the needs of students that teachers address, the conditions under which teachers work, the rewards they accrue, and the standards they are expected to meet. The chapter concludes with a glimpse at teachers as part of a professional group.

The chapter Snapshot and Analysis are teachers' reflections on their experiences. The Snapshot is a letter by a teacher who is well satisfied in her career. The Analysis contains comments by beginning teachers about incidents in their own teaching. The Educational Research section reports on a survey of teachers' perceptions of their job.

SNAPSHOT

This Snapshot is part of a letter written by Margaret Metzger about her professional life in teaching.[1] She wrote it to a former student who had just completed college and was considering a teaching career. As you read, consider:

- Would this letter sway you toward a career as a teacher? Why or why not?

- In what ways do you think Ms. Metzger's experiences and attitudes are representative of teachers in general?

- What do you think might be some negative aspects of Ms. Metzger's work that she does not mention?

- Think of your own contacts with teachers. Which aspects of their professional lives appeal to you? Which do not?

Dear Clare,

. . . By mid-August I start planning lessons and dreaming about classrooms. I also wonder whether I'll have the energy to start again with new classes. Yet after September gets under way, I wake up in the morning expecting to have fun at work. I know that teaching well is a worthwhile use of my life. I know that my work is significant.

I am almost 40 years old, and I'm happier in my job than anyone I know. That's saying a lot. My husband, who enjoys his work, has routine days when he comes home and says, "Nothing much happened today—just meetings." I never have routine days. When I am in the classroom, I usually am having a wonderful time.

I also hate this job. In March I want to quit because of the relentless dealing with 100 antsy adolescents day after day. I lose patience with adolescent issues. I think I'll screech if I have to listen to one more adolescent self-obsession. I'm physically exhausted every Friday. The filth in our school is an aesthetic insult. The unending petty politics drain me. Often I feel undermined on small issues by a school system that supports me well on [something as major as] academic freedom.

Like all jobs, teaching has inherent stresses. As you know from student teaching, you must know how to discipline a roomful of adolescents; you need to have a sense of purpose about what you are teaching; you need to cope with the exhaustion; and as an English teacher you must get the paper grading under control. I am always saddened by the number of excellent teachers who leave teaching because they think these difficult problems are unsolvable.

A curious irony exists. I am never bored at work, yet my days are shockingly routine. I can tell you exactly what I have done every school day for the past 18 years at 10:15 in the morning (homeroom attendance), and I suspect I will do the same for the next 20 years. The structure of the schoolday has changed

little since education moved out of the one-room schoolhouse. All teachers get tired of the monotonous routine of bookkeeping, makeup assignments, 22-minute lunches, and study-hall duties. . . .

. . . To most people, I am "just a teacher."

But this is the outside reality. The interior world of the teacher is quite different. Although you have come to some terms with the outward flatness of the career, I want to assure you that teachers change and grow. So little research has been done on stage development of teachers that the literature recognizes only three categories—intern, novice, and veteran. This is laughably oversimplified. There is life after student teaching; there is growth after the first year. You will some day solve many of the problems that seem insurmountable during your exhilarating student teaching and your debilitating first year.

Sometimes I am aware of my growth as a teacher, and I realize that finally, after all these years, I am confident in the classroom. On the very, very best days, when classes sing, I am able to operate on many levels during a single class: I integrate logistics, pedagogy, curriculum, group dynamics, individual needs, and my own philosophy. I feel generous and goodnatured toward my students, and I am challenged by classroom issues. But on bad days, I feel like a total failure. Students attack my dreams about going to Aruba, but I go to the next class.

I keep going because I'm intellectually stimulated. I enjoy literature, and I assign books I love and books I want to read. I expect class discussions and student papers to give me new insights into literature. . . .

To me, teaching poses questions worthy of a lifetime of thought. I want to think about what the greater writers are saying. I want to think about how people learn. I want to think about the values we are passing on to the next generation. Questions about teaching are like puzzles to me; I can spend hours theorizing and then use my classroom as a laboratory. . . .

And then there are all the difficult, "normal" situations: students and parents who are "entitled," hostile, emotionally needy, or indifferent; students who live in chaotic homes, who are academically pressured, who have serious drug and alcohol problems. The list goes on and on. No school of education prepared me for the "Hill Street Blues" intensity and chaos of public schools. I received my combat training from other teachers, from myself, and mostly from the students. You will too. . . .

Ultimately, teaching is nurturing. The teacher enters a giving relationship with strangers, and then the teacher's needs must give way to students' needs. I want to work on my own writing; instead, I work on students' writing. My days are spent encouraging young people's growth. I watch my students move beyond me, thinking and writing better than I have ever done. I send them to colleges I could never afford. And I must strive to be proud, not jealous, of them. I must learn generosity of heart.

I am a more compassionate person because I have known teachers and students. I think differently about handicaps because I worked with Guy, who is quadriplegic from a rugby accident. Refugee problems have a human face because I've heard Nazmul tell stories about refugee camps in Bangladesh, and I've heard Merhdad tell about escaping from Iran, hidden in baggage on a camel. I have seen the school social worker give suicidal students his home phone number, telling them to call anytime. I have seen administrators bend all the rules to help individual students through personal crises. Every day I hear stories of courage and generosity. I admire other teachers.

Facing every new class is an act of courage and optimism. Years ago, the courage required was fairly primitive. I needed courage to discipline my classes, to get them into line, to motivate them to work. But now I need a deeper courage. I look at each new class and know that I must let each of these young people into my life in some significant way. The issue is one of heart. Can I open my heart to 200 or more adolescent strangers each year? Put bluntly, can I be that loving?

I hope to love my students so well that it doesn't even matter whether they like me. I want to love them in the way I love my own son—full of respect and awe for who they are, full of wanting for their growth, full of wonder at what it means to lead and to follow the next generation.

Clare, when you consider a life's work, consider not just what you will take to the task but what it will give to you. Which job will give self-respect and challenge? Which job will give you a world of ideas? Which job will be intellectually challenging? Which job will enlarge you and give you life in abundance? Which job will teach you lessons of the heart?

With deep respect,
Margaret Metzger

PROFESSIONALS WHO EDUCATE

About the same time each weekday morning between September and June, 60 million American children, adolescents, and teenagers crawl out of bed, nibble breakfast, gather belongings, and stumble off to school. With varying degrees of anticipation or reluctance, they either walk to the neighborhood school, board school buses, or slide into cars. Within a short time all arrive at school. The pattern is usually routine and occurs with little fuss and confusion. It is what they expect to do.

The Students

At the end of this daily procession, students enter classrooms where they pass the next six to seven hours of their lives under the control and responsibility of one or more teachers. The community expects it; the law requires it; and the students, whatever their personal feelings may be, normally conform to these expectations without serious question.

Once in classrooms, students engage in learning experiences that are designed and conducted by their teachers, experiences intended to transform them into more informed, better skilled, and increasingly sensitive human beings. For many, those experiences taken as a whole are the most significant and most challenging of their lives. And so they should be. Teachers are judged by the extent to which the experiences they provide students are successful in educating them.

Assumed Competence

But because of the routine nature of schooling, few people actually consider what teachers do to educate their charges. Instead, they tend to think without much evidence, that teachers know what they are doing, are well intentioned, and are competent. They choose to believe that teachers' classroom activities are good, effective, and appropriate for each individual in the class. Typically, parents and others from outside the school get involved only when something appears to be wrong or when it is so unusually good that it deserves special notice.

In the course of their K–12 schooling, most students spend about 15,000 hours under the direction of teachers, no matter what they might prefer to be doing, regardless of how much they are or are not learning, and perhaps without considering how skilled and informed those teachers happen to be. Except for sleeping and playing, that amount of time takes up more hours than any other discrete activity those students engage in. By comparison, most children, adolescents, and teenagers spend more time with teachers than they do with any other group of adults besides their parents; and for many the time spent with teachers is also longer than that spent with parents. (See Jackson, pp. 5–6; Csikszentmihalyi & McCormack, 1986.)[2]

Images of Teachers

Diverse Individuals

Generally, teachers are like most educated Americans. They come in all sizes, shapes, colors, and personalities. They function with varying idiosyncrasies, degrees of physical and mental health, and levels of personal satisfaction. Not all are as satisfied as Margaret Metzger, but many are. Most are above average intellectually when compared with the population as a whole. They have diverse political, social, philosophical, and religious beliefs but seem to cluster toward the middle point on most continua. Just over 40 percent say they are Democrats, about 25 percent say they are Republicans, and almost one-third claim to be independent of political party affiliation. A few belong to minor parties. (See National Education Association, 1983a, 1987; Educational Research Service, 1987; Kottkamp, Provenzo, & Cohn, 1985. For the public's attitudes about teachers see Gallup & Clark, 1987.)[3]

More Women Than Men

As noted in Chapter 1, about two-thirds of K–12 teachers are women. Just under 90 percent are white, 7 percent are black, 2 percent have Spanish surnames, 1 percent are Native Americans, and 1 percent have Asian or Pacific Islander family origins. Their average age is in the low forties. Over three-fourths are married, and of those not married one in ten has been married previously. Most spouses of teachers work outside the home (National Education Association, 1983a; 1987).

Experienced

The average teacher in a K–12 public school in recent years has been teaching for fifteen years or more and has spent about twelve of those years in the same school system. On average, elementary teachers teach 24 students in a class, and secondary teachers face between 100 and 150 students in a typical five-period teaching day. About two-thirds belong to the National Education Association, 8 to 10 percent to the American Federation of Teachers, and 15 to 20 percent do not belong to a union (National Education Service, 1983a; Educational Research Service, 1987).

In 1989–90, the average school-year teaching salary was about $31,200 (*Education Week*, 1989, September 6, p. 2).[4] A sizable number of teachers, especially male teachers, also hold second jobs in the summer, on weekends, or in the evening.

In spite of the fact that teachers are about as diverse as the American population in general, there are several patterns of behavior or roles that teachers as a group are perceived to follow. Sometimes these perceptions are accurate, but not always. Teachers are thought to be outgoing, widely read, well traveled, emotionally balanced, caring and sincere, and active in social and governmental

An Introduction to Teaching and Schools 523

Teachers at lunch.

Middle of the Road

affairs. They are assumed to be more "middle of the road" than the general population on most issues, more conservative in their ideas and actions, and more moral and ethical. They are expected to demonstrate models of behavior for children to follow. They are considered to be dedicated to an improved social order, but also preservers of past traditions and the status quo (National Education Association, 1987).

Middle Class

In appearance, dress, life-style, and housing, teachers are thought to be middle class. To some extent, especially in traditional communities, they are assumed to be religious. They are considered to be less likely to do far-out or extreme things in- and outside the classroom. As a parent of elementary school children once said, "The teachers in this school might 'do' drugs and have very active sex lives but we do not want our children to think of them in those ways."

Knowledgeable

In the classroom and in their other school-related contact with students, teachers are supposed to transmit knowledge, develop skills, and instill values. Therefore, they are expected to be intelligent—at least more intelligent than most "average" people—knowledgeable of the subject matter they teach, and skilled in teaching methods. They should know content, teaching techniques, psychology, and the general things that intelligent people know. They also should know how to discipline students and motivate them to learn. They should be able to assess students and guide their learning toward appropriate obtainable goals. (See, for example, Gallup & Clark, 1987; Clark, 1987.)[5]

Substitute Parents

Especially at the elementary school levels, teachers are often expected to be substitute parents. This involves a whole range of roles—service provider, authority figure, judge, nurturer, confidant, counselor, caring supporter, defender, arbitrator, and so forth. The roles vary in importance with different students

> ### Something to Think About
>
> Think for a few minutes about your own image of a teacher. For instance, write the title The American Teacher at the top of a blank sheet of paper. Then draw a human figure to fit the image you have in mind. (Put clothes on the figure that fit your image, and so forth.) After you have done that, consider these questions:
>
> - Why did you draw the figure you did?
> - Did you have a particular person or people in mind when you drew the figure? If so, why do you think that person or those people came to mind?
> - In which ways is your image of Ms. Metzger, from the chapter Snapshot, similar to and different from the figure you drew? How do you account for this?
>
> Compare your figure with those drawn by other students in this class.

and from time to time, and they have changed in recent years. Modeling behavior and setting expectations are now major responsibilities.

Beginning Teachers

Responsibilities

For beginning teachers, the professional expectations, roles, and responsibilities of teaching are sometimes overwhelming. In fact, the first year of teaching has often been described as an emotional roller coaster, but it is probably no more difficult or less rewarding than the first year of other professions that involve significant responsibility for the lives of others. It is intense, involves unexpected demands, includes troublesome worries about the welfare of students, and causes bothersome second thoughts about actions already taken—actions that sometimes affect students seriously and can hurt deeply.

Satisfied

But by the end of the first year on the job, most new teachers are satisfied with what they have done and, in fact, are quite proud of themselves. They often admit they have learned more than they expected and sometimes realize they had known less than they thought. More importantly, they have learned how responsible and rewarding the job of teaching is and realize that no one can really understand all the facets of the life of a professional teacher without being one.

Reasons for Teaching

Why do people become teachers? The motives, of course, are many, and they range from very idealistic to very practical. However, when contemporary teachers are asked about their motives, they often mention a desire to work with young people, a liking for a particular subject, an interest in doing things they see teachers do, and a desire to perform a valuable public service. They also believe teaching provides status, job security, good retirement benefits, free time in summers, work schedules compatible with raising a family, a good "first career" while they prepare for a second, and a career that is easier to prepare for than other professions. (See Ornstein & Levine, 1984, pp. 4–17.)[6]

Older teachers and those who have recently retired also mention two other reasons for teaching that no longer apply. Many men who entered teaching between the end of World War II and the early 1970s did so because teaching positions were available, and teaching was a step up the professional ladder from the work their fathers performed. Because they were military veterans, the government paid them to go to college, which was something they would not normally have expected to do. They were often the first in their family to attend college, and teaching was frequently the only profession they thought they knew. Teaching seemed less mysterious than the work of medical doctors, lawyers, and engineers.

During the same time, many women and minority group members entered teaching because it was one of the few professions open to them. They were not expected to be physicians, lawyers, and engineers and were often excluded from those fields. (For more discussion of teaching as a profession, see Ornstein & Levine, 1984, pp. 38–48; Gallup & Clark, 1987.)

THE JOB OF TEACHING

The next several pages describe some of the aspects of the job of teaching by looking at what teachers do in several different contexts:

- in classrooms
- with students
- in the general school environment
- among professional peers
- as employees
- with parents
- behind the classroom door

However, as you read, remember that teaching involves more than the brief sketches presented here and that the various roles are intertwined.

In Classrooms

Classrooms are teachers' workplaces—where teachers practice their profession of instructing students and where they succeed or fail professionally. They are different from the workplaces of any other professional group. To begin with, classrooms are populated primarily by young people rather than adults and are designed with that in mind. They have a particular purpose, recognizeable physical characteristics, and a *feeling* that sets them apart.

Physical Characteristics

When compared with each other, classrooms have similar general characteristics but are different in detail. Most have walls, but those walls look different. All involve instruction, but it is never the same. All are controlled by a teacher, but no two teachers are exactly alike. (For more discussion on classrooms, see Jackson, 1968; Doyle, 1986; Doyle, 1981; Hamilton, 1983; Brophy, 1983.)[7]

Classrooms tend to have a typical size and shape. Except for open education pods, they are built like boxes along long hallways, behind doors which teachers close to separate their work from the intrusions of the outside world—doors with small windows that are often covered with paper. Classrooms contain desks, chalkboards, bright lights, books, a flag, audiovisual equipment, paper supplies, a trash can, a pencil sharpener, and a closet.

This sameness in the physical aspects of classrooms is illustrated in the writing of Philip W. Jackson (1968, pp. 6–7):

> . . . School bulletin boards may be changed but they are never discarded, the seats may be rearranged but thirty of them are there to stay, the teacher's desk may have a new plant on it but there it sits, as ubiquitous as the roll-down maps, the olive drab wastebasket, and the pencil sharpener on the window ledge.
>
> . . . Even the odors of the classroom are fairly standardized. . . . If a person stumbled into a classroom blindfolded, his nose alone, if he used it carefully, would tell him where he was.

Crowded Places

Classrooms are crowded places in which to work. They are not very large spaces for twenty, thirty, or more people, even if the people are often small in size; and they contain lots of furniture, equipment, and supplies. There is constant activity, and people frequently bump into each other (Doyle, 1986; Jackson, 1968; Berliner, 1983; Brophy, 1982).[8] Few other workplaces are so cramped, and few involve the same level of hustle and bustle. Teachers not only work in this congested environment, they are personally responsible for its smooth, productive operation.

Social Contexts

Classrooms also have particular and consistent social contexts. They are youth dominated and learning oriented, with an adult in charge. Under normal conditions, all activity is set to serve the learning needs of the students. Desks, teaching stations, learning centers, individual study alcoves, bulletin boards, electronic equipment, and so forth are all strategically located for that purpose. Verbal interactions are structured to accomplish it. (Doyle, 1986, esp. pp. 403–409; Berliner, 1983; Doyle, 1981).

Social Conventions

Classroom environments include a number of common social conventions. Some would say they are ritualistic. For example, the teacher sets the pattern of behavior, establishes standards, and gives directions. The students normally follow. The arrangements are so common that substitute teachers can take over without ever seeing the regular teacher, and nonteaching visitors can tell when something is wrong (Jackson, 1968). Most of the time someone is talking, and, more often than not, it is the teacher. Chalkboards are erased nightly, bulletin boards changed monthly, and desks straightened as often as needed. In tightly ordered rooms, loose paper is picked up from the floor at the end of each period. A corner of the board is used for assignments, reminders, and the posting of infractions. A hook near the door or in the top drawer of the teacher's desk holds a hall pass.

Routine Patterns

Classroom events follow regular routines and patterns. Schedules, periods, assignments, special activities, and pull-out programs are all arranged to fit with one another, and most are planned during the summer before school starts. One year's instruction follows developmentally those before it. Subjects are sequenced through the schoolday. Art, music, and physical education are planned so that the one or two specialists in the building can see all students for about equal amounts of time each week. Nearly everything is scheduled around a few immovable events, particularly the bus schedule and lunch.

Even activities that teachers arrange within their own classrooms follow set patterns, and although teachers could make changes, they rarely do. Most think their job is more manageable if events occur predictably. Certain subjects are taught at the same time each day. For example, in elementary schools, reading is typically taught in the morning, when students are most alert. Lecture, recitation, seatwork, guided practice, individual study, enrichment, and assessment follow a consistent sequence. (See, for example, Doyle, 1986, pp. 395–403.)

Prescribed Rules of Behavior

Both students and teachers perform their duties according to prescribed rules of behavior that everyone is expected to understand and obey. These are thought to be necessary because the students, regardless of their age, are not adults. They need direction to stay on task and to avoid classroom chaos. For example, students are to be in their seats when the bell rings, they are not to interrupt others, they are to look only at their own papers, they are not to run in the halls, they are not to smoke on school property. Teachers are expected to dress appropriately, speak correctly, treat everyone equitably, punish wrong behavior, assign homework, and have a positive attitude. Students and teachers who follow the rules are considered good.

Many Things at Once

For a variety of reasons, teachers need to do many things at once, a point already discussed in Chapter 3. This, in turn, means teachers must be skilled planners, organizers, and directors of all that occurs in their rooms. (See Brophy, 1983; Chap. 3 of this text; Smith & Geoffrey, 1968.)[9]

Rapid-paced Interactions

A major aspect of the many-things-at-once classroom is rapid-paced, teacher-led interactions. For example, all of the following might happen within seconds of the middle of a lesson: A teacher asks a question and glances toward John. John looks away because he does not want to be called on. Then he frowns in embarrassment as he peeks out of the corner of his eye toward his girlfriend. As he suspected, she is looking at him and knows he does not understand. Both blush. She looks away, hiding her feeling of sympathy for him. The teacher sees all this and calls on another student but makes a mental note to return to John shortly with an easier question so he can save face.

The magnitude of the task of managing classroom activity can be illustrated with a comparison to the work of other professionals. Physicians usually treat one patient at a time, with the assistance of a nurse, a laboratory assistant, a receptionist, a pharmacist, and other support staff ready to respond at a moment's call; meanwhile, patients wait their turn, sometimes for hours, in rooms away from the physician. Specialists, even more buffered, await referrals. Engineers tackle individual phases of projects in sequence, without a need to monitor the behavior and thoughts of other people at all; they can take a break when they feel like it without disrupting others. College professors teach more mature and patient students who are less demanding of attention, more likely to be motivated, and who may be in class by choice. College students also meet classes only a few times weekly; the teacher-student interaction is not a day-long routine.

Studies have found that teachers engage in as many as one thousand significant interpersonal interactions each day (Jackson, 1968, p. 11). In the process of instruction, they communicate constantly with whole classes of individuals verbally and nonverbally, sometimes interacting differently with several students at the same time—listening to Janet respond, while motioning to Amy that her turn is next, watching Jill and Sarah whisper, nodding to Bill that he may sharpen his pencil, and nudging Jim's feet back under his desk.

Interruptions and Delays

Interruptions, disruptions, and delays are facts of classroom life. Students prompt some of these with unexpected questions, extraneous comments, inattention, misbehavior, and procrastination. Visitors, public-address announcements, special events, principals, and other teachers also intrude. But in spite of it all, bells ring as planned, and school ends on time.

In order to be happy and productive, teachers must want to work in the unique environment of the classroom. They must be accepting of the crowded physical space, the routines and rules, the pace, and the multiple interactions. They must like coordinating the myriad of facets of classroom life so that all fit together and somehow foster learning. (For a review of research findings about classrooms and the teaching skills needed to handle them well, see Jackson, 1968; Berliner, 1986.)[10]

With Students

Cultivating Relationships

The best standard by which teachers are judged is the extent to which they succeed in helping students learn. To succeed in this way, teachers cultivate positive relationships with students. After all, teachers are in classrooms by choice, and when they agree to take a class, they accept the responsibility to teach every student regardless of individual abilities, motivations, state of cleanliness, personality quirks, and parental support. Students, on the other hand, have to be there. Their presence is not voluntary. Most cannot even choose their own teachers.

Relationships between teachers and students are complex professional associations between superiors (teachers) and subordinates (students). They are dominated by the teacher's authority and enforced by custom and law. Students usually comply with teachers' wishes, rely on their help, and cultivate their support and favor. They do so publicly, before their peers, and with the threat of embarrassment and failure (Jackson, 1968).

Although these relationships are significant, often close, and sometimes intense, they are not as personal or as emotional as family relationships and friendships. They are also not as permanent. They are typically limited to certain hours in the day and for a school year.

Teacher Authority

Because teachers possess authority over students, they usually control the relationships and, therefore, must accept primary responsibility for them. They need to use their power carefully to establish, maintain, and cultivate positive associations. If they fail to do so, they often jeopardize student success, and teaching becomes less pleasant than it should be.

The authority that teachers have over students is characterized by Philip W. Jackson (1968, pp. 30, 32) as follows:

> . . . Seated at his desk the student is in the position to do something. It is the teacher's job to declare what that something shall be.
>
> At the heart of the teacher's authority is his command over the student's attention. Students are expected to attend to certain matters while they are in the classroom, and much of the teacher's energies are spent in making sure that this happens. At home the child must learn how to stop; at school he must learn how to look and listen.
>
> . . . When students do what the teacher tells them to do, they are, in effect, abandoning one set of plans (their own) in favor of another (their teacher's). At times, of course, these two sets of plans do not conflict and may even be quite similar. But at other times that which is given up in no way resembles the action called for by the teacher. . . . (p. 30)

Many Personalities

Probably the most challenging aspect of the relationships between teachers and students is the fact that each class consists of many individual student personalities with which teachers must interact. Some students enjoy being in school, in particular classes, and with specific teachers; others do not. Some are secure and find learning easy, others are threatened and have difficulty. Some have personal styles that are compatible with the teacher's, some clash. Some are middle class, polite, clean, and neat; others are "at risk," rough, gruff, and dirty. Some are turned on, others are tuned out. In spite of it all, good teachers—

such as Ms. Metzger who wrote the letter in the Snapshot of this chapter—interact warmly with all students.

Student Dislike for School

Many of the students who dislike school seem to fall into two groups—those who find their school experience to be frightening and embarrassing and those who are bored by it. (See Jackson, pp. 41–61.) Those in the first group often fail and frequently suffer publicly and painfully before their peers. Those in the second tend to endure in sleepy silence. In either case, much alienation seems to derive from what teachers do or have done to and with those students. When these students turn up, other teachers are the only ones who can make the classrooms nice places again.

Many Roles

Although teacher-student relationships revolve primarily around instruction, what teachers do in other roles also has an important impact on their students. As noted earlier, besides being instructors in a strict sense, teachers are substitute parents, managers of behavior, confidants, advisers, arbitrators, role models, protectors, and evaluators. At critical times throughout every school year, what teachers do in these other roles has a greater effect on some students than their instruction. Virtually every adult remembers such instances from his or her own schooldays—a pat on the back, an enthusiastic congratulation, a forgiving glance, a patient ear, a confidential bit of advice, a discouraging frown, a moment of ridicule, a disappointing lack of interest, a public condemnation.

In recent years, teachers have not been as sternly expected to function as substitute parents as in previous decades, but they still shoulder many of those responsibilities. They are supposed to make students do the right thing, to correct them when they do not, and punish them if they do not listen. They are expected to be forceful if the situation warrants it.

In this regard, parents expect teachers to set standards of acceptable conduct and to punish those who transgress—to stop fighting, to prevent harrassment, to prohibit the use of foul language, and to require proper dress and manners. They often want to be informed about their own children's inappropriate behavior and want other children's parents notified as well. When violations are serious, they want legal authorities notified, except, perhaps, when the culprit is their own child. (See, for example, Zitkel & Reichner, 1987.)[11]

Guidance and Advice

Students frequently turn to teachers when they need guidance, advice, and affirmation. They do so partly because teachers are readily available, respected adults who usually can help or know someone who can and because they are not so emotionally involved with the students as parents and relatives. Such requests vary with maturity and age, and they range from the simple and common to the complex and profound. For example:

Should I hit Betty back?

Should I smoke?

Is it okay to have sex with my boyfriend?

I'm an alcoholic. Will you help me?

My father is sexually abusing me. What should I do?

I'm pregnant. Will you help me get an abortion?

My parents threw me out of the house. Can you help me find a place to live?

Most teachers see questions such as these as part of the territory. When students need help, they try to provide it, even if their actions might be criticized and second-guessed. They believe that to ignore questions such as these is to neglect students whom they are pledged to serve.

Being Protective

Teachers are frequently called on to step into situations in order to protect students who are unable to protect themselves. For example, they are asked to shield students from physical injury by stopping fights, from embarrassment before their peers, by cutting off accusatory dialogues, from discrimination, and from other forms of mistreatment. They are expected to protect them against their own actions as well as those of other students, teachers, and the system. Sometimes they have to do so in spite of the rules and potential harmful consequences.

Evaluating

In a role that seems at times to contrast with several already described, teachers also evaluate their students. They set standards for student performance, encourage students to strive to meet them, test periodically, and fail those who do not measure up. In addition to academic achievement, they assess personal characteristics and qualities such as motivation, intellectual ability, behavior patterns, and potential. Like it or not, they separate students into good and bad on a number of criteria. For many teachers the role is a burden, but it too comes with the territory. (See Doyle, 1983.)[12]

As was illustrated in the Snapshot about Leonard Rucks in Chapter 1, recent education accountability movements emphasize the teacher's evaluative role and shift thinking on the subject away from that of the 1960s and 1970s, a time of flexible standards and softened expectations. The teachers of the 1990s are expected to enforce strict academic performance standards for students; if they shy from the task of evaluation, they may be considered weak or contentious.

To be satisfied with a job in teaching, teachers must like interacting with students and building relationships with them. They must understand student youthful behavior, tolerate their weaknesses, and want to devote time and energy to serving their needs. They must believe they can help them and be committed to trying. Of all the things that keep teachers in the profession, relationships with students are probably the most sustaining.

In the General School Environment

Child and Youth-oriented Environment

Because schools are child- or youth-oriented, they have different cultural environments than other workplaces. (This was indicated earlier in the section about classrooms.) Schedules, rules of conduct, dress regulations, standards of language usage, disciplinary procedures, degrees of formality, types of cafeteria food, and size of furniture are all decided upon because of the students. Rules are plentiful, restrictions tight, and administrative directives inhibiting. Compliance is expected. (See Chap. 6 of this text; Jackson, 1968; Doyle, 1986; Hamilton, 1983; Berliner, 1983.)

Although expectations are different for teachers than for students, teachers are caught up in the regulatory milieu. They are expected to model appropriate behavior and to follow school norms. They do not smoke in the halls, wear their most beat-up casual shoes, call each other by nicknames in the presence of students, or use the time-honored explitives they might express at home.

To be happy, teachers need to like working in these student-oriented conditions. They must be willing to listen to incessant talk about sports heroes, rock music, and dates and appear interested. They must be open to—and expect—juvenile banter, student council, debates, athletic competition, assemblies, dances, and pep rallies.

Heartaches

As with any work environment that includes a large number of people, schools have their share of disappointments, pains, and sadness; and when they occur, teachers, sometimes more than anyone else, feel the effects. Sometimes those sad occurrences happen directly to teachers; but more often than not, they happen to students, and the pain transfers to the teacher.

Realistic teachers must accept the fact that students sometimes fail, get hurt, and die. Some do not achieve as much as teachers hope or expect because they lack ability, motivation, or support from home. Some become hooked on drugs. Some are physically, emotionally, or sexually abused. Some are so alienated that they cannot be reached. And for students, even though they are young and deserving, life is often unfair.

Among Professional Peers

Isolation

Unlike most other professionals, teachers usually practice their profession in relative isolation—each in his or her own classroom out of the sight of colleagues. They rarely communicate with each other about professional matters of substance. Granted, they share ideas about teaching strategies and information on students, and they sometimes gossip. But they do not watch each other teach, critique each other's work, or purposely advise each other on how to teach better. Doctors, lawyers, businesspeople, and engineers all do this regularly.

Flat Profession

One group of researchers into professional interactions among teachers (Glidewell, Tucker, Todt, & Cox, 1983) describes teaching as a *flat* rather than a *hierarchical* profession.[13] They note that teachers think of each other as equally skilled and knowledgeable rather than dividing themselves into expert, average, and novice performers. They are uneasy when observed closely by peers and reluctant to act as if they know more or less than the others. Teachers who know more than their peers and display that knowledge openly tend to be disliked rather than respected, and those who admit they do not know enough are considered to be weak.

Although there has been some change in recent years, most school systems generally have not arranged for skilled, experienced teachers to help those recently hired. All are expected to work competently and alone from the first day. Other teachers, even principals, are not expected to intervene and often do not. Those who frequently ask for help are looked down upon.

Professional Differentiation

A significant thrust within educational reform movements of recent years is targeted toward making teaching more hierarchical. Most plans divide teachers into ranks based on regularly scheduled evaluations and label them accordingly. Those at higher ranks are considered more skilled and are assigned to help those lower on the scale. They also receive higher levels of pay.

Although these schemes are becoming common, most run counter to tra-

ditional professional norms among teachers. Their introduction has usually prompted teacher objection and has forced teachers to look differently at their professional relationships with colleagues. As a result, mentoring, cross-class observing, and peer counseling are all growing parts of teachers' professional lives.

In the eyes of most teachers, the traditional isolation from peers has had both advantages and drawbacks. Although it frees teachers to do things their own way and avoid direct criticism, it also denies them support and makes the seeking of advice more conspicuous. It establishes a norm in which giving and receiving advice about classroom performance is not routine.

Socially Active

This is not to say that teachers do not interact socially with each other or with other professionals. They probably do so as much as those in any profession, and the extent to which they do probably depends more on individual personality than on anything else. Those who find each other compatible and like the same things tend to become friends and do things together in school and out.

Contrary to images of long ago, teachers tend to be outgoing and active socially. They dress fashionably, party, drink, and vacation at exciting locations. Despite what some small children think, teachers do relax, act silly, and get married—just like normal people.

As Employees

Principals

Teachers work for many people—students, parents, school boards, communities—but those with the most direct influence over them and their jobs are their building principals, whose impact is usually followed in importance by department chairs, curriculum supervisors, and central office administrators. Principals are the most immediate supervisor and the de facto school leaders.

Of course, principals and other superiors have different philosophies, personalities, styles of operation, idiosyncrasies, and habits; and each of these traits affects the job conditions of the teachers under them. Sometimes they cause problems for certain teachers; but good, experienced teachers usually size up their supervisors and act accordingly. They fit in most of the time, accommodate differences when they need to, and manipulate situations to their liking when they can. In a sense, they use the principal and other administrators to support their own professional goals. Usually, new teachers admire the skill, perception, and ease with which the old masters do this.

Fitting In and Manipulating

Cultivating Support

Like officials in all bureaucracies, principals and supervisors play many roles. In their work with teachers, good ones encourage, provide support, gather and disperse ideas and materials, facilitate normal operations, stimulate new efforts, manage crises, mediate disputes, and absorb blame. They also protect teachers from intrusions, criticisms, and abuse. As middle managers, they try to serve their superiors as well as their teachers and, when necessary, provide a buffer between the two. Because of multiple responsibilities and conflicting expectations, they are easy to disagree with and dislike. Smart teachers, however, see them as leaders whose support is invaluable, and they cultivate it.

Autonomy without Neglect

Principals and supervisors rarely question teacher decisions unless someone complains—test scores are low, the classroom is noisy, someone hits someone, there is too much homework or not enough. In fact, recent proponents of accountability complain that school administrators tend to be so unintrusive that they know little about the quality of their teachers' performances.

This may be a problem, but good principals do not neglect their teachers. They check on beginning teachers rather closely and often advise them. They also look out for teachers with difficulties. If the teachers are doing well, they manage subtly. They see their main role with teachers as that of providing the conditions in which teachers can practice their skills to the maximum of their capabilities. A prophetic principal once said, "Good teachers teach well without direction from managers; good principals make it possible for them to do so."

With Parents

Teachers interact with parents less often than most people think. In fact, when things run smoothly, there is likely to be little or no contact at all, especially for secondary teachers. When contact is made, the teacher usually initiates it, and it typically marks an exceptionally proud moment or a significant problem. Some teachers like the situation this way and see parents as complicating elements in the education of their children; others seek parental involvement even in normal times.

Parental Confidence

In any event, the job of teaching includes interacting with parents—informing them of progress and difficulties, consulting them on decisions, cooperating with them on matters of mutual responsibility, asking their help, and responding to their requests. Good teachers consider serving parents part of their job, and they conscientiously keep the channels of communication open. They understand parents' concern about their children's welfare. They want the parents' confidence.

Of course, different parents devote varying amounts of attention to the education of their children. Of those involved the least, some are overwhelmed with other pressures—family matters, sickness, their own work; some are just normally busy; some do not understand school operations and are intimidated by teachers; some feel superior to teachers; and some just do not care. Those involved the most are normally helpful to teachers. They share information about their children, support teacher decisions at home, volunteer at school, and raise money. Some, however, are more bother than help. They want unfair amounts of attention for their children, think they always know what is best, publicly criticize teacher actions, and love a dispute. Even if their intentions are good, they are bothersome.

Cultivating Relationships

For their students' sake and to accomplish their own professional goals, good teachers cultivate positive relationships with all kinds of parents. They inform them of their priorities, philosophies, and expectations and convince them that they are intelligent, caring, and skilled professionals who will be beneficial to their children. They win their support. Similarly, they try to understand parents because that understanding helps them teach the children.

Honest Communication

Successful teachers usually interact well with parents. They possess good communication skills. They are honest and direct when things are not going well, as well as when they are. They praise parents with sincerity when they can, challenge their actions when those actions hurt their children, and report them for child abuse when necessary.

To do all this, teachers need to remember that parents do not pass tests to have children. They possess widely different levels of competence and perceptions about themselves, their children, the school, and the teacher. They range from highly intelligent to mentally retarded, from emotionally secure to nervous wrecks, from socially stable to drug addicts. Some have their children under control, others have no hope of that. Some understand their children's strengths and weaknesses, and others' perceptions of their children are absolutely invalid. Most love their children, but some do not. All, however, believe, or at least hope that teachers will make their children better and more successful human beings. (For an interesting perspective about involving parents in schools, see McLaughlin & Shields, 1987.)[14]

Behind the Classroom Door

When teachers close the classroom door, they are in charge. They set the agenda, direct the instruction, decide what to cover, and choose whom to praise and reprimand. Few other adults know what teachers do with their classes day to day and minute to minute. Even fewer would intrude on their authority. Most trust teachers to do the right thing and assume they are capable enough to do so. In a sense, the classroom is the teacher's palace. This amount of autonomy

Something to Think About

> Below are a number of comments that various teachers have heard over the years from parents. Each reflects a different perspective about the teacher-parent aspect of teaching.
>
> I asked that Marsha be assigned to you because you're the best teacher in the school.
>
> My husband left me last year, and I'm at a loss. I can't cope well, and Johnnie is devastated. His school work deteriorated in grade 8, and he's been in trouble with the law. Please help him this year. He needs it so badly, and I have no one else to turn to.
>
> I'm sorry to say this, but Mike is a rotten kid. I can't do anything with him. Please don't call me about his school problems. I can't help.
>
> I was never good at school, so I can see why my children have problems. But I am interested in how they do, and they better behave. Let me know how I can help. I always work at the school fair and bake cakes.
>
> I used to be a teacher, and your teaching style is different from anything I was ever taught.
>
> William did well last year for Ms. Miller. I don't know why he has so many problems since you became his teacher.
>
> You seem to be an intelligent and capable teacher. The kids love you. Would you consider working for me in my business? I need a person like you. I'll pay you a heck of a lot more than you'll ever make as a teacher.
>
> You must have been teaching a long time. When do you retire?
>
> - What do you think might have motivated each of these comments?
> - If you had been the teacher to whom each of the comments was made, what would you have said or done?

Freedom with Responsibility

is not characteristic of most other types of employment, especially not of work that involves similar responsibility.

Most successful, experienced teachers like being their own boss and do not want interference, but autonomy has its burdens as well as its benefits, particularly for new teachers. If beginning teachers do not have the pressure of supervisors looking over their shoulder and do not have to justify their actions to them, they must also make most of their own decisions and live with the consequences. Although they have more professional freedom than people in other professions, they also have more personal responsibility.

Why teachers have so much autonomy is not clear, but they have had it for a long time—probably since the one-room schoolhouse. It is so ingrained that present teachers protect it as a matter of principle. They assume that they know what is best for their students and that outsiders can do no more than offer advice. They believe that outsider dictation about what and how they should teach, as well as close evaluation of their teaching according to external criteria, destroys classroom spontaneity and hurts children (Jackson, 1968, pp. 129–133).

This idea of classroom autonomy is reflected in the following statement of a cooperating teacher to his new student teacher:

> When I close that door, it's the students and me. What we do determines how much they learn. There are policies, guidelines, and a curriculum; and I try to abide by them as much as is practical. But in reality, few other adults walk through that door while I am teaching. My students learn what they are supposed to learn and they like me. No one bothers me. I'm free to do what I think is best.

ANALYSIS

The episodes in this section consist of firsthand comments by teachers about personal experiences during their first years on the job. They reflect some of the aspects of teaching described on the preceding pages. As you read, consider:

- Do the comments reflect the job of teaching as you see it?

- In what ways do the comments highlight the noninstructional aspects of a teacher's job?

- Of the elements of teaching that are highlighted, which would you want changed? Why? How could those changes be accomplished?

- Which of the elements of teaching that are highlighted require adjustments in the ways you have thought about your teaching?

IN THE CLASSROOM:

Teaching seemed so easy when I observed classrooms as a college student. Then it seemed so complex when I had to do it in student teaching.

Questioning was especially difficult at first. I could not think of the right questions or phrase them so that the kids understood. Even when I did, I didn't listen to the answers. I must have agreed to lots of really stupid answers. Once I said "Correct!" when a student told me he didn't know the answer. You have to do ten things at once. Thirty sets of eyes looking at you. Thirty mouths ready to talk. All that energy needing direction. Sometimes I felt like an orchestra conductor, and all the musicians were ignoring me.

One day class was really going well. A discussion was flowing smoothly; everyone was into it. Then, within five minutes two kids left for a band trip, the secretary interrupted on the public-address system, Mary from next door asked to borrow a book, a parent showed up at the door, and the fire drill bell rang. We never did get back on track.

WITH STUDENTS:

When I started, the other teachers said, "Be firm" and "Don't smile until Christmas," and I tried to follow their idea. I'm glad I did. It felt uncomfortable at first, but I was strict, not mean. I liked the kids and they could see that. They tried to test me but found that I was serious when I said our top priority was learning. We could have fun but only if we also learned.

I remember a boy asking me why I was not "soft" like other first-year teachers and a mother telling me that my reputation among her daughter's friends was "hard, serious, and friendly." I was proud of both comments. One day, I overheard one of my students talking to a new student about me. He said, "He's little, but don't mess with him. Do what he says. He means it. But he's okay. He's the best teacher I have. If you have a problem, he's the one to talk to." After hearing this, I would have taught the rest of the year without pay. My motto when it comes to students is be firm, friendly, fair; and care.

AMONG PROFESSIONAL PEERS:

When I first started, I felt so alone. Everyone was busy getting school started with his or her own classes. They were friendly but did not have time to reassure a scared new teacher, and I was also very busy. I saw other teachers only in the halls, at lunch, and in the parking lot. When I had control problems, I

Lynn Myers and Sarah Rowen sixteen years later, still discussing teaching.

> couldn't turn to anyone, and I didn't want anyone else to know.
>
> Then Sarah sat down and talked with me. She sensed I was unhappy and befriended me. She became a source of support in every way. She knew what to say even when I didn't ask. Sarah got me through the first weeks and over the hump. She became my best friend and still is. About the third week of school, Sarah took me to Friday afternoon happy hour with the faculty. We were the noisest group in the tavern, probably sounded like kids at lunch. I quickly got to know most of the other teachers socially. They are a fun group, and they welcomed me openly. But you know, I know them well socially, and we all teach in the same school, but I have never seen most of them teach, nor they me.

THE NEEDS OF STUDENTS

The purpose of teaching is to serve the educational needs of students, and students have many needs. The next few pages describe some problematic aspects of students' lives that create needs that teachers must face. Because the purpose of this section is to draw attention to the elements of student lives that have significant impact upon what teachers do, the problems presented are those that severely affect students rather than more normal and commonplace conditions.

Average Students

Although teachers never face the ideal class of academically hungry students who have no worries, weaknesses, or personal problems, most classes do consist of a preponderance of students who look like the stereotypical average school-age student. These students vary in intellectual ability but are friendly, possess middle-class values, attend school regularly, are comfortable with their lives and their learning, and like their teachers. They come from average homes, have enough to eat, dress appropriately, handle their personal problems adequately, and appear to be reasonably well adjusted.

But many students are not like this. They face conditions and crises that are great and sometimes long lasting—conditions that present special challenges for their teachers. Some of those conditions are poverty; discrimination; physical, emotional, and intellectual disability; family trauma; child abuse; neglect and alienation; drug and alcohol abuses; vandalism, delinquency, and violence.

Poverty

Although nearly all teachers in America are middle class, many of their students live in poverty. Some of these have only the very basics of life, if that. They live from day to day, often with insufficient food, inadequate clothing, and substandard housing. Some have never slept in a bed of their own or seen a pediatrician or family doctor. Some move among migrant labor camps and have no permanent place to call home. Some do not know of a single family member who holds a job or expects to get one. Insecurity and psychological strain are facts of life.

Because of conditions such as these, America began a national War on Poverty in 1964; it was intended to break the *cycle of poverty* that trapped so many children. Schools played a major part in the effort (as described in Chapter 5). But so far,

Teachers—A Way Out

the war has failed many families and children. Poverty is still present in the lives of children in most schools. In fact, according to recent statistics, the gap between the middle class and the poor in America is widening rapidly, and the lives of some children are getting worse. (For more information about family conditions, poverty, and other demographics about children, see Hofferth, 1987; Cardenas & First, 1985; Ekstrom, Goertz, Pollack, & Rock, 1986; also see "Here they come, ready or not.")[15]

Teachers must serve poor children as best they can, and that means devoting extra effort to them. They must help them compensate for the burdens of their disadvantaged position in society and enable them to learn anyway. They must reach them instructionally no matter how difficult they are to reach, provide them with the academic and other coping skills they need to succeed, give them hope, and ease the pain. The task is enormous and failures frequent, but teachers find despair the worst enemy; they cannot afford it. For some students, teachers are the best hope of making it out of poverty, and many of those who do make it say that at least one teacher was critical to that success.

Something to Think About

The following case study of a poor child is not atypical:[16]

Gerry is fifteen and in the eighth grade. He does not like school. He flunks most tests and is frustrated all the time. He plans to quit next year. Most of his friends already have.

No one in his family has finished high school. His mother stopped in the tenth grade, when she became pregnant. His father never returned after he was sent to reform school during ninth grade. His brother dropped out last year, supposedly to look for a job, and his sister, a sophomore, rarely attends and is flunking every course.

Gerry is never encouraged to study at home. No one else ever did, and there is no quiet place to do it even if he wanted to. His parents would not be able to help him if he got stuck, and he would not embarrass them by asking. No one else at home reads anything but occasional newspapers and magazines.

His parents have not visited the school since he was in fifth grade. They are uneasy about talking to teachers. He knows his teachers think his parents do not care about his education, but he is sure they do. They just do not know how to help. They are as frustrated as he is.

Gerry knows that some of his teachers want to help him but cannot. They talk about things he does not understand, go places he will never see, and own things he cannot get unless he steals them. They live in a different world. They do not understand.

- What could teachers do to be successful with Gerry?
- What would constitute success in this situation?

Discrimination

Many students suffer from discrimination of one form or another—because of race, ethnic or religious background, gender, or handicapping condition. For many, discrimination is direct, personal, current, and continuing. For others it is the result of past injustices inflicted upon them, their ancestors, or the group with which they identify. In either case, the experience is painful and produces economic, social, emotional, and sometimes physical scars. Frequently, it makes learning difficult and causes students to be behind in school in comparison with their more fortunate counterparts.

Confronting Discrimination

To be successful with these students, teachers must confront the effects of discrimination, teach in ways that succeed in spite of the scars, and provide the knowledge and skills that enable students to achieve despite the burden. In addition, since serious prejudice is displayed in behaviors at school, teachers must watch for it and root it out. They must stand above the crowd and avoid being caught up in subtle bias and prejudicial assumptions that could cause them to discriminate themselves. They must not only fight the problem, they must be ever vigilant against becoming part of it.

Although some political and educational leaders of recent times, particularly those of the recent Reagan administration, have advocated the teaching of victims of discrimination just as others are taught, compensatory instruction and extra effort seem to be necessary. Teachers need to do *more* for and with these children if they are going to achieve at the same level as their relatively unscarred classmates.

Until now, however, broad-scale attempts at compensatory instruction for victims of discrimination have not been very successful. For example, studies show that black and other minority students still perform below the level of whites on academic criteria, and more of them fail to graduate from high school. Also, minority students are disportionally assigned to special education classes and identified as problem students (Ekstrom, Goertz, Pollack, & Rock, 1986; Edmonds, 1981; Graham, 1987).[17]

Individual Concentrated Help

But there is hope. Concentrated work by individual teachers with individual students helps significantly, and such efforts occur in every school every day.

Physical, Emotional, and Intellectual Disability

Like students who suffer from poverty and discrimination, students with disabilities, even if they are not discriminated against, have conditions and needs that are out of the ordinary and require special teacher attention. Some have handicaps severe enough to require specially arranged instruction and consideration, while others have less serious conditions—such as diabetes, epilepsy, dyslexia, mild retardation, chronic illness, and controlled emotional disorders—and require only limited adjustments.

Compensating for Handicaps

Whatever the specific handicapping condition or the severity of its effect on student learning, students who live with handicaps deserve to be educated to their fullest, and teachers are responsible for providing that service even if it is difficult or inconvenient. They must help students with handicapping conditions learn in spite of their condition and aid them in dealing with the complications caused by it.

Family Stress

If sometime in the romantic past virtually all students came to school from stable, secure families with two knowledgeable, skilled, dedicated parents living in the same house and with one parent at home most of the day performing services for the rest of the family and waiting at the door when the children returned from school, that time no longer exists. Nowadays, students come from all sorts of homes. Some are strong and supportive, but many are under stress, on the verge of collapse, or already shattered. When there are problems at home, students are affected at school, and the circumstances must be of concern to teachers.

Working Parents

During the last few decades, the American family has undergone enormous change, and schools and teachers have not always kept up with the times. For example, single-parent homes are the norm for many schools. And in 60 percent of American families with two parents, both parents now work outside the home, an increase of more than 20 percent in only twenty years. (See Hodgkinson, 1985; Hofferth, 1987; Cardenas & First, 1985; Stern & Williams, 1986; Bureau of Census, 1985; Office of Civil Rights, 1984.)[18] Parents are at home less and busier and more fatigued when they are at home. Many are less able to concentrate

on traditional, middle-class, one-parent-at-home parenting functions such as reading to the children, enforcing homework time, monitoring television, talking over milk and cookies, and participating in family outings.

Latchkey Children

Therefore, more children and school-age youth are on their own more of the time. They arrive home on their own schedule, choose their own detours in route, have their own key, watch their own soap operas, and hang out away from home for much of their out-of-school time. Some younger children spend more time with baby-sitters than with either parent.

Isolated, Transient Families

Families live more isolated existences in more impersonal, urban environments than previously. They have less contact with extended family members, and they move more often. Schoolchildren typically change neighborhoods and schools several times during their thirteen years of schooling.

A rather extreme illustration of contemporary, urban family life for a class of elementary school children is portrayed in the case study reported below, which reports on a class taught in the mid-1980s by Lynn Myers:

> Of the 27 first graders, 21 lived with neither or only one of their own parents. Several lived with grandparents, rarely saw their mother, and did not know their father.
>
> Approximately one-third lived in a home that included an adult male who was not their father and was not married to their mother. They usually referred to him as "uncle" or "momma's boyfriend." His presence was considered to be temporary.
>
> One child came from a home of five children who had the same mother but five different fathers. None of the fathers currently lived with the family, but a grandmother did.
>
> During that year, nine children moved and transferred away from the school. Eight children transferred in. One child moved away and back again three times during the nine months, while her mother persistently tried to reconcile (unsuccessfully) with her alcoholic husband, who physically abused her and the child.

Contemporary teachers must constantly remember that at any given time one or more of their students are probably suffering under some form of significant family stress that affects how those students learn and function in school. They must tailor their teaching to help those students learn as best they can under the circumstances.

Child Abuse

The *battered child syndrome* is well known in American society today. In populated areas, cases are reported in the media constantly. Those reported, however, are only the worst cases and the ones known to authorities. Many more occur, and most of the victims go to school. With all of their physical and emotional scars, they sit before teachers who are pledged to teach them.

The abuse can be physical, sexual, and psychological. It is always emotional. It can occur as an isolated incident or be repeated frequently over long periods of time. It can show up as highly visible injuries and scars or be almost hidden. But in all its forms, it is traumatic.

A Need to Act

Most teachers knowingly confront child abuse sometime during their career, and some face it regularly. When they do, they are often the first people in positions of authority to notice it, and that fact places them in unique situations of responsibility. They must do something. If they do not act, they allow current abuses to continue, and they neglect a child who needs special treatment.

Often teachers want to shy away from child abuse situations. They are heart wrenching and messy. Intrusion could make the child more vulnerable. Accusations could open the teacher to threats, physical attack, and legal challenges. But as responsible adults, they cannot avoid action. They must step in, notify authorities, and stop the abuse.

Teachers' responsibilities, however, are not limited to the reporting of child abuse. They must teach the victims and, at the same time, help them succeed in spite of the circumstances. They must care for them emotionally as much as they can, help them cope, and protect them from further pain as much as possible.

Drug and Alcohol Abuse

Alcoholism and drug abuse are rampant in American society among adults and students. Majorities of high school students drink alcohol, at least occasionally, and apparently similar numbers use street drugs or abuse medicinal ones. At least one in twenty teenagers is already an alcoholic. Even elementary students are "hooked," sometimes from birth because of prenatal usage by their mothers. Drug and alcohol abuse is so prevalent in some homes and neighborhoods that it is the expected thing to do, even for children. (For more data on drug and alcohol abuse among students, see, for example, Hawley, 1987; Shannon, 1986; Cody, 1984.)[19]

Children of the Drug Culture

In recent years, children of the drug-culture parents have appeared in the primary grades of some schools. They have already suffered from parental usage and withdrawal. Some cannot concentrate or remember, are hyperactive, cannot hold their hands still, and in the worst cases are noticeably brain damaged. Their conditions make normal learning impossible.

Many children and youth who do not abuse drugs and alcohol themselves still suffer from the consequences. When parents, siblings, and other relatives and friends are hooked, all close to them suffer. The impact is at least distracting, clearly emotional, and sometimes devastating.

Under the circumstances, teachers must face the reality that some of their students suffer because of alcohol and drug abuse, and they must act accordingly. They must be especially observant, understanding, and sympathetic toward students already suffering or at risk. They must intervene to try to stop harmful repercussions. They must teach about the harmful effects of alcohol and drug use. And they must adjust their teaching to compensate for alcohol- and drug-related handicaps that affect learning.

Another Need to Act

As with child abuse situations, teacher involvement in alcohol and drug abuse matters has its professional risks. The circumstances are personal, private, and messy. They almost always include family situations that are embarrassing to all and not normally a teacher's concern. Nevertheless, if they are harmful to their students, teachers who do not act are negligent.

Vandalism, Delinquency, and Violence

Today's students are often victims of violent behavior. They may suffer directly, suffer under the threat of harm, or suffer from the repercussions of harm inflicted on those close to them. The harm might be physical or psychological. It might occur at school or in their out-of-school lives. They could be participants, perpetrators, or victims.

A Violent Society

In the out-of-school world, thousands of people are attacked, intimidated, harassed, and otherwise harmed each day. Thousands more are frightened by what might happen. And that atmosphere of violence spills over into schools. Some students hurt, steal from, and extort money from others. Some badger, threaten, and assault teachers. Some vandalize school property and teachers' and other students' cars.

Violence in Schools

The causes of this behavior are diverse and often obscure. Modern society is large, complex, and impersonal; and schools are often the same. Society, in and out of school, is competitive and sometimes harsh. Whatever the causes, however, the conditions interfere with learning and disrupt teaching. They do not go away if ignored.

Therefore, teachers and school administrators must confront violence in schools and the effects of violence that intrude from outside. They must stop the abuse and remove the fear. They must make schools as safe and the lives of their students as secure as they can. They must protect potential victims, report perpetrators, and head off trouble before it starts.

Sometimes teachers have to step in physically to stop violence as it is occurring and get emergency help to do so, but more often teachers' roles are more subtle. They can counter a propensity toward violence by the way they manage students, by the behavior they model and expect in their classrooms, by how they reach out to potential troublemakers and victims, and by what they teach—especially in the values aspects of their instruction. These efforts do not always work, but they do help much of the time.

In addition to confronting trouble, teachers must also prevent it from pulling them away from their primary task. They must continue to teach effectively, whatever the conditions. Even in troubled schools, the students must continue to learn.

Addressing Student Needs

Helping with Problems

This section began with the warning that it stresses problems in the lives of students, problems that are severe enough to intrude into classrooms and complicate what teachers do. It was presented in this way to emphasize that the job of teaching involves more than instructing students under ideal conditions. Teaching also involves meeting the broader needs of students. It does so for two reasons: (1) because those needs impinge upon what students learn and (2) because teachers are expected to address student needs beyond those that are narrowly academic.

JOB CONDITIONS

Teachers teach under all kinds of conditions, from ideal to intolerable, but most teaching situations are fairly close to the midpoint between those extremes. Individual teachers usually see both good and bad aspects in what they do, but for the most part, they take conditions into account, balance them out, and teach successfully.

Generally, teachers like their work. They usually find their goals achievable, the expectations of their superiors reasonable, limits on their freedom acceptable, responses from students stimulating, and feedback on their performance encouraging. They tend to fit comfortably into their classroom and school environment. They find their interactions with other people to their liking and the results of their efforts rewarding.

Although most teachers can easily find something legitimate to complain about, usually those situations are eventually corrected or gradually forgotten. In general, job conditions are on a par with those of most comparable professions and not much different from that which most beginning teachers expect from the start.

That is not to say that teaching is easy or that job conditions are always as they should be. Teaching is a hard, stressful, and sometimes burdensome occupation; and anyone considering it as a career should face that fact realistically. Some specific negative work conditions are unavoidable, and others take time to correct. The next few paragraphs describe some of the positive and negative aspects of teaching.

EDUCATIONAL RESEARCH

Assessing the Condition of Teaching

This Educational Research section presents selected findings from two efforts in 1988 to assess the current condition of teaching. The two reports include demographic data, teacher perceptions of school conditions and problems, and researcher conclusions about these data. Because this is the last Educational Research section in this text, the data are presented in rather raw form and you are asked to draw your own inferences from them. As you read the information presented, consider what the data may mean to you as a potential teacher. Do any of the data surprise or disappoint you?

The report *The Condition of Teaching: A State-by-State Analysis, 1988* presented demographic information about public schools as well as the results of a survey of 22,000 public school teachers about their perceptions of working conditions and the students they teach.[20] The information reported was on public schools as of 1988 and included the following:

Demographic Data

- There were 40,123,808 public school students in 1988, a decrease of 2.1 percent from 1980–81 but an increase over more recent years.

- There were 2,275,209 public school teachers, a 3.4 percent increase from 1980–81.

- The average public school teacher salary was $28,031. (This increased to $31,200 in the next two years.)

Feeling of Satisfaction The feeling of satisfaction is illustrated poignantly by Philip W. Jackson in *Life in Classroom* (1968). One of his illustrations follows:

> When you see a child that has suddenly caught on and is enjoying reading or is going ahead to be an independent worker, you can't help but have satisfaction and know that you have done something for this particular child. You know that you aren't going to do wonders with every child. . . . But when you do see a child bloom, it's gratifying. (1968, p. 138).

Doing a Good Thing The belief among teachers that they are doing good, useful, prized, and respected work rests on the assumption that teaching improves students' lives and the well-being of the entire community. These two quotes from anomymous teachers illustrate the idea:

> I think of teaching as missionary work. I have always wanted to serve others, and this is my way of doing it. I believe my work is important.

> By teaching, we help young people, and that helps everyone. We contribute to society and make people's lives more fulfilling.

Other Positives Other positive aspects of the job that teachers frequently mention follow:

- The constant reinforcing feedback from students who are enjoying what the teacher is doing—"You can tell they like it by the smiles and attention."

- The openness and informality that teachers and students have with each other—"You do not have to perform like an employee performs for a boss. You can be yourself with students; they certainly are themselves."

- The autonomy—"When you close that door, you're the boss, at least until someone complains."

- The spontaneity of the classrooms—"Sometimes students say or do things that you would never expect and you change directions in response. It reminds you that you are working with active human minds. I find it exhilarating."

- A daily schedule and yearly calendar that are compatible with those of children—"Of course I have to work a lot after hours at home, but those hours are flexible, and I can be home most of the time that my children are there."

Salary Although teacher salaries are not as high as they should be and do not attract many people to teaching from other careers, they are the primary external reward for teachers, and in the recent years of educational reform they have been getting better. (More on salaries appears in the next chapter.)

Other Benefits Other extrinsic benefits that teachers normally receive are

- job security (although enrollment declines in the 1970s and 1980s caused layoffs);

- annual salary increments;

- secure and adequate retirement benefits;

- adequate benefits, such as health insurance and leaves of absence;

- opportunities for additional paid assignments such as coaching, club sponsorship, curriculum development, and summer teaching;
- free time in the summer.

(See, for example, Jackson, 1988, pp. 115–155; Educational Research Service, 1987; National Education Association, 1983b; Kottcamp, Provenzo, & Cohn, 1986.)[22]

The Negatives

While the positive aspects of teaching, satisfaction and compensation, for example, tend to be general in nature—things that happen to teachers because they teach—the negative aspects tend to be more specific conditions of work. Some of those conditions are, of course, simply a part of teaching—working in crowded classrooms, among young people, within bureaucracies, under strict time pressures, surrounded by noise and confusion, and with the expectation that student achievement will improve—but other negative work conditions are specific irritants that sometimes can be modified or adjusted. Points that teachers complain about most often follow:

- set bureaucratic procedures;
- insensitive, impersonal, and impractical regulation;
- inadequate supplies and resources;
- too many students and too large classes;
- too little planning time;
- old and worn-out facilities;
- demanding and insensitive administrators;
- lack of student discipline;
- unprofessional colleagues;
- too much paperwork;
- criticism from parents and community groups; and
- stress.

Teachers also express concerns about more specific conditions, such as

- lack of adequate feedback and appreciation;
- inadequate pay;
- declining family interest in education;
- lack of support from parents;
- being held accountable for conditions they cannot control;
- increased student testing;
- students' refusal to do homework;

- abuse from students;
- censorship and challenges to academic freedom;
- vulnerability to legal liability action;
- denial of due process in employment matters;
- sex discrimination;
- loss of tenure rights;
- testing to prove their competence; and
- limited opportunities for professional advancement.

(See, for example, National Education, 1983b; Kottcamp, Provenzo & Cohn, 1986; Frymier, 1987; McLaughlin, Pfeifer, Swanson-Owens, & Yee, 1986.)[23]

Bothersome Rather than Disruptive

Negative conditions such as these are usually bothersome rather than defeating for most teachers, but they are matters of concern nonetheless, and they do impinge upon teacher performance. When they go on for long periods of time and occur in great numbers, frustrations build up, and teaching is not as enjoyable as it should be.

Teaching—On Balance

The extent to which individual teachers see their job in positive or negative terms depends on a number of things, including

1. the relative balance between positive and negative conditions that actually exist,
2. the perspectives and attitudes of the teacher facing the conditions, and
3. the standard against which the conditions are being judged.

In some circumstances, the rewards outweigh the trials and tribulations; in others the negative conditions are too numerous, intense, and frustrating to be balanced by the positive. Some teachers are so satisfied and proud of what they do that they take the negative conditions in stride and succeed happily despite them, while others are so troubled by bad conditions that the good never compensates for them. Sometimes teachers judge their job conditions against the way they should be, while others think of how much worse they could be. In any event, most teachers who remain in the classroom consider their work worthwhile and satisfying.

TEACHERS AS A PROFESSIONAL GROUP

Like any group of professionals, teachers have much in common. They do the same kinds of work, have similar professional responsibilities and goals, experience comparable successes and frustrations, and confront common pressures. Some people say teachers even think alike, have similar life-styles, and select their friends from among other teachers.

A Group of Professionals

Collectively, teachers and other professional educators have professional power that they can, and do, use to affect the direction of American education. They help select political officials, direct public policy, shift educational priorities, and sway public decisions; insist that students be educated appropriately and treated fairly; and demand that they themselves be compensated adequately, treated justly, and consulted regularly. They also influence curriculum decisions, teacher evaluation standards, teaching procedures, and all sorts of matters that affect what and how they teach.

In the past, many teachers were reluctant to use their collective power. They tended to see themselves as rather passive, do-gooder public servants. During recent decades, however, they have become more outspoken on educational matters and have been more forceful as advocates for children and better schools. They have also become more visible proponents for their own welfare.

Influential Organizations

Organizations through which teachers and other educators wield influence include the following national groups:

- National Education Association (NEA)
- American Federation of Teachers (AFT)
- National Association of Secondary School Principals
- National Association of Elementary School Principals
- American Association of School Administrators
- National School Boards Association
- National Congress of Parents and Teachers
- Council of Chief State School Officers
- Association of Teacher Educators

Many of these groups have state and local affiliates or counterparts.

Unions

The two major national teachers' unions—the National Education Association and the American Federation of Teachers—along with their state and local affiliates, are the largest and most influential teacher bodies. Both exist to advocate for improved education and to represent the interests of teachers. Their main activities include:

- negotiating and collective bargaining for their members;
- influencing legislative and regulatory bodies;
- supplying information to members;
- protecting teachers against legal action and unfair outside pressures;
- setting standards of professional practice;
- providing personal support services (such as stress management consultation and financial advice); and

- providing auxiliary membership services (such as insurance, investment programs, travel packages, and book clubs).

Both unions have significant political clout, especially as official bargaining agents and lobbyists. They actively support and oppose legislation and the election of candidates, and their actions are often very effective. For example, both have helped pass local and state education bond issues and tax levies over the years and have fought budget cuts for education. The NEA was particularly influential in the election of President Jimmy Carter in 1976 and the primary force behind his establishment in 1979 of the U.S. Department of Education. Both unions have also been vocal in support of desegregated schools and programs that improve the welfare of students. They have opposed using public funds for private schools and for religious education.

Because of their power and large constituencies, the two organizations were represented on most major education reform commissions of the 1980s, and their influence continues. Most observers believe their concurrence with proposed reforms in the future is going to be necessary if the reforms are to have a lasting impact. Currently, both unions are directly involved in efforts intended to change the ways in which teachers are evaluated, certified by states, and prepared by colleges.

NEA

The National Education Association is the oldest and largest teachers' union. It was begun in 1857, and in 1988 had approximately 1,800,000 members—about three-fourths of all practicing teachers. It includes administrators and supervisors as well as teachers.

In addition to its bargaining and political activities, the NEA is active in teacher staff development and curricular matters. It also gathers data about schools, students, and teachers, which it disseminates to its members. Teachers use the data to improve their teaching; association affiliates use them to further their advocacy work. For example, the affiliates use comparative information on salaries, fringe benefits, negotiation arrangements, and job conditions to convince legislatures and school boards to be more supportive of their schools and teachers.

The NEA has been especially active in the move to place teachers in control of their own profession through the establishment of state professional standards boards that contain a teacher majority. In its view, these boards should control standards for teachers, police their own ranks, and monitor the conditions under which teachers work. They should operate similarly to the medical boards and bar associations established by doctors and attorneys.

AFT

The American Federation of Teachers was begun in 1916, is an affiliate of the AFL-CIO labor organization, and currently has about 600,000 members, many of whom are employed in major U.S. cities, including New York, Philadelphia, Boston, Washington, D.C., and Detroit. It does not admit administrators or supervisors.

The AFT focuses its energies more narrowly on teacher employment concerns than NEA (as different from curricular matters, for example) and because of its AFL-CIO ties is more influential in national political matters that affect other school employees and union workers in other areas of employment.

Through its longtime national president, Albert Shanker, the AFT is a supporter of national standards and testing for teachers. Shanker has been outspoken in favor of making entry to the teaching profession more rigorous. He also advocates a national professional standards board controlled by teachers.

Specialized Professional Organizations

In addition to unions, many teachers also join professional organizations that identify more closely with their specific teaching specialties or with a particular group of children and their specialized needs. They do so because these groups advocate for issues they believe in and because they are a means of communication on such matters. Because the groups can speak on behalf of and with the support of their members, they, too, enhance the power of their teacher members. Organizations of these types include:

Specialty Groups

- American Alliance for Health, Physical Education, Recreation, and Dance
- American Association for Asian Studies
- American Association for Gifted Children
- American Association of Workers for the Blind
- American Council of the Teaching of Foreign Languages
- American Industrial Arts Association
- American Montessori Society
- American School Health Association
- American Speech-Language-Hearing Association
- American Vocational Association
- Association for Childhood Education International
- Association for Children with Learning Disabilities
- Association for Education in Journalism
- Convention of American Instructors of the Deaf
- Council for Exceptional Children
- International Reading Association
- Modern Language Association
- Music Educators National Conference
- National Art Educational Association
- National Association for Bilingual Children
- National Association for Creative Children and Adults
- National Association for the Education of Young Children
- National Business Education Association
- National Council for the Social Studies

- National Council of Teachers of English
- National Council of Teachers of Mathematics
- National Rehabilitation Association
- National Scholarship Service and Fund for Negro Students
- National Science Teachers Association
- Rural Education Association

Teachers and Group Membership

Teachers, like all professionals, benefit from professional group membership. Through it, they develop contacts, friendships, and a feeling that they are not alone in their job. They get to know people like themselves who do the same things, gain the same satisfactions, and suffer the same frustrations. Those other people are available to them when needed to share excitements and provide support.

Pride of Membership

In addition, professional group membership provides individual teachers with a general group identity—a sense of belonging that comes when one says, "I am a teacher" or "I am going to be a teacher." That sense of belonging makes a person part of a professional community, and being part of such a community carries with it a certain amount of professional respect, status, and pride. To outsiders, the person has special credentials.

Of course, if the profession is not well respected, the status attributed to it and its member is not very high. Most observers would say that teaching is respected more than many professions, but not as much as some. Therefore, those who contemplate joining the group called teachers have at least two questions to consider:

- Do I want to be called a teacher?
- Will my work as a teacher add to the professional respectability of the group?

CONCLUSION

Comparing Professionals

When people try to assess teaching as a career, they often compare teachers with other professionals. In doing so, they consider the work the different groups do, job conditions, compensation, degree of satisfaction, status, and so forth. Then they try to decide whether teaching is better or worse than the other jobs by determining the extent to which teaching measures up against the others. The process helps people decide whether they want to be teachers, but it is admittedly artificial for several reasons:

1. Professions differ in enough significant ways to make some comparisons artificial.
2. Professions change so rapidly and radically that comparisons quickly become dated.

556   14: The Professional Teacher: The Life and the Work

3. Comparisons of this type do not place enough emphasis on the personal values and priorities of the people who are facing the career choice.

Personal Goals and Priorities

Probably a more useful way of determining whether teaching is a career for you is to ask yourself questions that compare teaching as you know it with what you want for yourself—your personal career goals and priorities. The four questions that follow might start that process for you.

- What do teachers do in their jobs?
- What are their professional lives like generally?
- Do you want to do that?
- Do you want to live like that?

This chapter is intended to help you raise questions such as these and to provide you with sufficient information to develop some responses to them. If it has been successful, you now have a basis on which to formulate further questions and answers as your study continues. In the years ahead, you will be able to balance the pluses and minuses of teaching within your own value system.

The Snapshot that opened this chapter presented Margaret Metzger's thoughtful assessment of why she is and remains a teacher. You might want to return to that letter again to stimulate your own thinking at this point. You might also want to consider the following incident:

> Professor Mark Shannon had just finished observing Tim Johnson, one of his social studies student teachers at John Overton Comprehensive High School in Nashville, Tennessee. As he approached his car in the parking lot, he noticed a note under the windshield wiper. It said,
>
> Dear Professor,
>
> Just a note to let you know what a great teacher Mr. Johnson is. We all respect him and learn a great deal from him.
>
> Yours truly,
> The Students of John Overton High School
>
> Tim Johnson was hired as a regular teacher in that school the next year.

SUMMARY

Although teachers are a diverse group of human beings, they are similar in having common professional goals and performing comparable work. Most are middle class, have served in classrooms for at least a few years, seem to be relatively middle of the road on most issues, and are thought to be knowledgeable about what they do.

Beginning teachers soon realize that teaching is a complex job. Most seem to adjust quickly, however, and express satisfaction with the way they handle their first year in the classroom.

The job of teaching revolves around a number of contexts within which it takes place, including the nature of classrooms and schools as workplaces; the characteristics of the students being taught; the relationships developed between teachers and their students; the interactions that occur between teachers and their peers, their principal, and parents; and the roles and responsibilities assumed by teachers when they close the classroom door. The job is also greatly affected by the needs of the particular students each teacher faces. Students who experience particularly harsh living conditions—such as poverty, discrimination, abuse, and alienation—have special needs and present special challenges for their teachers.

Job conditions of teachers vary greatly, but most teachers seem to balance out the good and the bad. Typically, teachers list a feeling of doing worthwhile and respected work as the most positive aspect of teaching and mention day-to-day frustrations and specific deterrents to doing their work as the most persistent negatives.

Teachers join professional groups to share common concerns, marshal professional power, and influence educational and political decisions at local, state, and national levels. The National Education Association and the American Federation of Teachers are the two national teacher unions.

STUDY QUESTIONS

1. Make a list of ten to fifteen circumstances or conditions that teachers often face in a given day or week on the job, being sure to include about equal numbers of positive and negative items. Then rank the items from the most positive aspect to the most negative. Which items would cancel out items at the other end of the ranking?

2. Which types of teacher work conditions would be most likely to drive you out of teaching? Which aspects of the job would be likely to keep you in the classroom despite the negatives? Justify your thinking on each response.

3. Which types of issues and situations should have highest priority for attention by teacher unions? Why do you think so?

4. How involved should teachers get in out-of-school problems of students?

BIBLIOGRAPHY

Berliner, D. C. (1988, February). *The development of expertise in pedagogy.* Paper presented at the American Association of Colleges for Teacher Education, New Orleans, Louisiana.

Berliner, D. C. (1986). In pursuit of the expert pedagogue. *Educational Researcher, 15*(7), 5–13.

Brophy, J. E. (1982). How teachers influence what is taught and learned in classrooms. *Elementary School Journal, 83,* 1–13.

Csikszentmihalyi, M., & McCormack, J. (1986). The influence of teachers. *Phi Delta Kappan, 67*(6), 415–419.

Doyle, W. (1983). Academic work. *Review of Educational Research, 53*(2), 159–199.

Doyle, W. (1981). Research on classroom contexts. *Journal of Teacher Education, 32*(6), 3–6.

Ekstrom, R. B., Goertz, M. E., Pollack, J. M., & Rock, D. A. (1986). Who drops out of high school and why? Findings from a national study. *Teacher College Record, 87*(3), 356–373.

Good, T. L., & Brophy, J. E. (1984). *Looking in classrooms* (3rd ed.). New York: Harper & Row.

Hodgkinson, H. L. (1985). *All one system: Demographics of education—Kindergarten through graduate school.* Washington, DC: Institute for Educational Leadership.

Jackson, P. (1968). *Life in classrooms.* New York: Holt, Rinehart and Winston.

LeCompte, M. D. (1987, May 13). The cultural context of dropping out. *Education Week, 6*(33), 21, 28.

Lortie, D. C. (1975). *School teacher: A sociological study.* Chicago: University of Chicago Press.

National Education Association. (1986). *Status of the American public school teacher: 1985–86.* Washington, DC: National Education Association.

NOTES

1. Excerpted from Metzger, M. (1986, March 4). Reflections on a career in teaching. *Education Week, 6*(23), 28, 36.

2. Jackson, P. (1968). *Life in classrooms.* New York: Holt, Rinehart and Winston; Csikszentmihalyi, M., & McCormack, J. (1986). The influence of teachers. *Phi Delta Kappan, 67*(6), 415–419.

3. National Education Association. (1983). *Teacher opinion poll: Demographic highlights.* Research memo. Washington, DC: National Education Association; National Education Association. (1986). *Status of the American public school teacher: 1985–86.* Washington, DC: National Education Association; Educational Research Service. (1987). *Educator opinion poll.* Arlington, VA: Educational Research Service; Kottkamp, R. B., Provenzo, E. F., & Cohn, M. M. (1986). Stability and change in a profession: Two decades of teacher attitudes: 1964–1984. *Phi Delta Kappan, 67*(8), 559–567. Also see Gallup, A. M., & Clark, D. L. (1987). The 19th annual Gallup poll of the public's attitude toward the public schools. *Phi Delta Kappan, 68*(1), 17–30; Harbaugh, M. (1986). Who will teach the class of 2000? *Instructor, 95*(2), 31–35.

4. *Education Week, 9*(1), 2.

5. Clark, D. L. (1987). High school seniors react to their teachers and their schools. *Phi Delta Kappan, 68*(7), 503–509.

6. Ornstein, A. C., & Levine, D. U. (1984). *An introduction to the foundations of education* (3rd ed.). Boston: Houghton Mifflin.

7. Doyle, W. (1986). Classroom organizations and management. In M. C. Wittrock (Ed.), *Handbook of research on teaching: Third edition*, pp. 392–431). New York: Macmillan; Doyle, W. (1981). Research on classroom contexts. *Journal of Teacher Education, 32*(6), 3–6; Hamilton, S. F. (1983). The social side of schooling: Ecological studies of classrooms and schools. *Elementary School Journal, 83*(4), 313–334; Brophy, J. E. (1983). Classroom organization and management. *Elementary School Journal, 83*(4), 265–285. Many characteristics of classrooms are also mentioned in slightly different form in Chapters 3 and 12 of this text.

8. Berliner, D. C. (1983). Developing concepts of classroom environments: Some light

on the T in classroom studies of ATI. *Educational Psychologist, 18*, 1–13; Brophy, J. E. (1982). How teachers influence what is taught and learned in classrooms. *Elementary School Journal, 83*, 1–13.

9. Smith, L. M., & Geoffrey, W. (1968). *The complexities of an urban classroom: An analysis toward a general theory of teaching.* New York: Holt, Rinehart and Winston.

10. Berliner, D. C. (1986). In pursuit of the expert pedagogue. *Educational Researcher, 15*(17), 5–13.

11. Zirkel, P. M., & Reichner, H. F. (1987). Is *in loco parentis* dead? *Phi Delta Kappan, 68*(6), 465–467.

12. Doyle, W. (1983). Academic work. *Review of Educational Research, 53*(2), 159–199.

13. Glidewell, J. C., Tucker, S., Todt, M., & Cox, S. (1983). Professional support systems: The teaching profession. In A. Nadler, J. D. Fischer, & B. M. DePaulo (Eds.) *New Directions in helping: Allied research in help-seeking and -receiving* (Vol. 3, pp. 198–212). New York: Academic Press. Instead of the term "flat," these researchers use a "norm of equality."

14. McLaughlin, M. W., & Shields, P. M. (1987). Involving low-income parents in the schools: A role for policy. *Phi Delta Kappan, 69*(2), 156–160.

15. Hofferth, S. L. (1987). Implications of family trends for children: A research perspective. *Educational Leadership, 44*(5), 78–84; Cardenas, J., & First, J. M. (1985). Children at risk. *Educational Leadership, 43*(1), 4–8; Ekstrom, R. B., Goertz, M. E., Pollack, J. M., & Rock, D. A. (1986). Who drops out of high school and why? Findings from a national study. *Teachers College Records, 87*(3), 356–373; Here they come, ready or not. (1986, May 14). *Education Week, 5*(34), 13–37. Also see LeCompte, M. D. (1987, May 13). The cultural context of dropping out. *Education Week, 6*(33), 21, 28; and news articles such as Shalala, D. E. (1986, October 29). It just makes sense to help poor children. *Chronicle of Higher Education, 33*(9), 96; Feistriteer, E. (1987, July 7). Children at risk, and more to come. *Wall Street Journal*, p. 28. For background information on social class and schooling, also see Ornstein & Levine, 1984, pp. 364–396.

16. This case study is a composite based on information about several students known to the authors of this text.

17. Edmonds, R. (1981). Making public schools effective. *Social Policy, 12*(2), 56–60; Graham, P. A. (1987). Black teachers: A drastically scarce resource. *Phi Delta Kappan, 68*(8), 598–605. Also see reference to Dunn, 1968, in the Educational Research section of Chapter 4 of this text.

18. Hodgkinson, H. L. (1985). *All one system: Demographics of education—Kindergarten through graduate school.* Washington, DC: Institute for Educational Leadership; Stern, J. P., & Williams, M. F. (Eds.). (1986). *The condition of education: A statistical report, 1986 edition.* Washington, DC: Center for Educational Statistics. United States Printing Office; Bureau of Census. (1985). *School enrollment—Social and economic characteristics of students: October, 1984.* (Advance report.) Washington, DC: United States Printing Office; Office of Civil Rights. (1986). *Elementary and secondary civil rights survey, 1984. National summaries.* Washington, DC: Office of Civil Rights.

19. Hawley, R. A. (1987). School children and drugs: The fancy that has not passed. *Phi Delta Kappan, 68*(9), K1–K8; Shannon, J. (1986). In the classroom stoned. *Phi Delta Kappan, 68*(1), 60–62; Cody, B. (1984). Alcohol and other drug abuse among adolescents. *Statistical Bulletin of Metropolitan Insurance Companies*, (January–March), 4–13.

20. Carnegie Foundation for the Advancement of Teaching. (1988). *The condition of teaching: A state-by-state analysis, 1988.* Princeton, NJ: Carnegie Foundation for the Advancement of Teaching.

21. *The Metropolitan Life survey of the American teacher, 1988: Strengthening the relationship between teachers and students.* (1988). New York: Metropolitan Life Insurance Company.
22. National Education Association. (1983b). *Nationwide teacher opinion poll, 1983.* Washington, DC: National Education Association.
23. Frymier, J. (1987). Bureaucracy and the neutering of teachers. *Phi Delta Kappan, 69*(1), 9–14; McLaughlin, M. W., Pfeifer, R. S., Swanson-Owens, D., & Yee, S. (1986). Why teachers won't teach. *Phi Delta Kappan, 67*(6), 420–426.

CHAPTER 15

Teaching the Next Generation: Is It for You?

INTRODUCTION

The last chapter surveyed key aspects of the professional work of contemporary teachers. It was intended to provide a brief glimpse at what teachers do and the situations they face day after day as practicing professionals. This chapter builds on that material. It extends current conditions and trends that affect schools and teaching into the next generation in order to provide a look at teaching during the 1990s and beyond. It ends by asking you to consider this question: If that is what teaching will be about in the years ahead, do you want to be a teacher?

The chapter begins with a look at the ways in which educational reform agendas described earlier in this text are likely to be played out during the next decade or so, and it comes to focus on the central importance of the teacher. Next, it surveys key employment matters for beginning teachers—supply and demand, ideas about where to teach, and salary and compensation. It then describes several professional and societal conditions that are expected to have great impact on teaching through the turn of the century. Finally, it asks you to consider whether K–12 teaching is the career for you.

The Snapshot and Analysis are different from those of previous chapters. The Snapshot asks you to take an instant picture of yourself, now, and to make an assessment of what you see. The Analysis asks you to place that picture into the landscape in which teachers can be expected to work in the near future. Together, the two exercises should help describe what a teaching career would be like for you.

SNAPSHOT

Instead of providing you with a Snapshot picture of teachers, students, schools, or events that affect teaching, as in other chapters, this Snapshot asks you to take a picture of yourself—to look at yourself as a person preparing to make a career decision. It suggests points you should consider and also recommends that you add to the list. Proceed as follows:

1. Look at yourself honestly in terms of the points listed below, as well as those that you add to the list.

2. Write a description of what you see.

3. Analyze that description as it relates to teaching.

4. Keep the description for use again at the end of the chapter.

Be careful. Do not draw a picture of a teacher who might be you. Record an honest picture of you, and *then* ask: Is this a picture of a teacher?

Points to consider:

- your personal strengths,
- your weaknesses,
- things you enjoy,

- things you dislike,
- attachments and associations that are important to you,
- ways in which you relate to others,
- things you aspire to do and achieve,
- things you value,
- where you expect to live,
- the life-style you expect to follow,
- the type of professional career you envision for yourself,
- activities in which you anticipate engaging in your work,
- activities you anticipate outside your professional work, and
- other points that occur to you as being relevant.

EDUCATION REFORM EXTENDED

The basic premises of the education reform movements of the 1980s were (1) that students were not learning as much as they should in school and (2) that schools and teaching had to be changed to correct the situation. Therefore, numerous efforts, described earlier in this text, were initiated to bring about change. The first stages of those initiatives are now in place, and early data about their impact are being collected, but clear results are not yet available. They will accumulate gradually during the next decade.

The stages of the reform efforts that have been completed so far are probably the easiest to accomplish. They aroused interest, mobilized energy, put on pressure, provided tentative directions, and raised some resources for change; but they did so on a very general level. Laws were written and regulations changed. Educators were told to do things differently.

Results

Now individual schools and teachers must implement the directives and follow the new ways in their classrooms and with their students. They must turn the ideas and plans into results. They must improve student learning.

The situation can be illustrated by a military analogy. The alarm has been raised. The apparent enemies have been identified. The nation has been mobilized. The general battle plan has been developed. Some of the supplies have been secured, and supply routes have been designed. A new type of soldier (teacher) has been envisioned. Now the conflicts of reform must proceed in the trenches (classrooms). Teachers and school building administrators will determine whether the war will be won—whether students will learn as much as society expects.

Pursuing Reform: The Next Steps

Because much of the work of schools and teachers in the 1990s and the early twenty-first century will involve continued implementation of education reform agendas, teaching in the next generation needs to be understood in the context of reform. That context can be understood if education reform is thought of as five interrelated agendas, as described in Chapter 1:

1. back to basics and accountability,
2. greater professionalization of teaching,
3. more effective schools and teaching,
4. more equitable education (not just equal amounts of education), and
5. changing the content or subject matter taught. (See Finn, 1987; Pipho, 1986.)[1]

Responsibility for reform in education has now shifted from legislatures and policy-makers to schools and teachers. School leaders and teachers are now deciding what students need to learn and how they should be taught so that they learn it. Once teachers do this, they undertake the teaching and if all goes well, produce the learning desired. As this happens, students are assessed to see whether the process produces the results expected. Data from assessments will indicate how successful the schools and teachers have been. Those results, in turn, will indicate appropriate future directions.[2]

Changing Professional Environment

As teachers do all of this, they continue to teach students much as teachers have done for years. But all is not the same. The professional environment is changing. In fact, it is already significantly different from that which teachers faced in the early 1980s in many ways, including the following:

- Student achievement data are collected and compared statewide and nationally.
- Teachers are assessed and compared on a national basis through newly developed instruments.
- State and national professional standards boards are beginning to oversee teaching.
- Poor, minority, and nonachieving students are the focus of great attention (but effective ways of reaching them have still not been identified).
- Questions about content are being debated. (See, for example, Hirsh, 1987, 1988; Benninga, 1988; Ryan, 1986.)[3]

Toward a Nation's Report Card

The collection and comparison of student achievement data are based on the assumption that schools and their teachers are accountable for what students do and do not learn. Those data and the tests that produce them are used as yardsticks against which teachers, schools, school systems, and states will be judged. They will increasingly influence what is taught and enable everyone to see how the local students do in comparison with others.

Educators at all levels use the results either as justification for what they are doing or as guides for how to improve. Doing better on next year's test becomes an implicit goal, and the criteria for deciding how to improve becomes the anticipated content of that test. Those whose results are not good promise that their students' scores will get better, and teachers teach more directly for the tests.

If current trends continue, either the National Assessment of Educational

Progress or instruments similar to it will, in effect, serve as a national blueprint for education. Unlike the way these instruments were used in the past, data from the assessments in the form of student scores in certain core subjects will be reported comparatively as a nation's report card. As a result, school curricula can be expected gradually to conform to the areas of knowledge assessed on the tests, and those who want their area of interest included in the curriculum will push to have it covered on the tests. Some semblance of a de facto national curriculum will emerge. (For more information on this shift in the use of National Assessment data, see *The Nation's Report Card,* 1987; McLarty, 1986; Olson, 1987, March 25; Comments of the Assessment Policy Committee, 1987; Rothman, 1987, June 17; Chiefs Urge . . . , 1987.)[4]

National Criteria for "Good Teachers"

The development of national assessments for teachers means that what is thought to constitute good teaching will be made more defined and more explicit. Those developing the instruments have already been deciding what effective teachers need to know and be able to do. They are using those decisions to set assessment criteria. Teachers who are assessed have to do well in terms of those standards. (See, for example, Shulman, 1987.)[5]

Because the assessment data are being compared in a traditionally competitive society, individual teachers, the colleges that prepared them, and the school systems that hire them want to appear to be better than those with whom they are compared. Because they want to improve their test results, they set their priorities in terms of test content. As a result, there will be increasing agreement on what constitutes good teaching. This, in turn, will pressure teachers to show their competence in certain prescribed ways.

Teacher Standards Board

The push for state and national boards to set standards for licensing teachers and to control entry into the profession of teaching is affecting many aspects of education—who becomes teachers, the qualifications they possess, the college programs that prepare them. Advocates for such boards say they should be controlled by teachers; set higher and more relevant standards than in the past; end emergency licensing; and be willing to suspend, revoke, withdraw, and deny licenses and program approval. (See Rodman, 1987, April 29; Olson & Rodman, 1986, September 10; Olson & Rodman, 1987, February 18; Wise, 1986.)[6]

Moves in this direction shift more of the control and responsibility over teachers from public and community officials to teachers themselves. They put teachers in charge of broader educational policies, and that changes the nature of the profession. They put teachers in the position of deciding who can be certified to teach, who can be hired by school systems, and what should be done when no qualified teacher can be found for a position. Local and state school boards of education have been making these decisions until now.

Focus on Poor Students

The continued concern about teaching poor and minority-group students and the special challenges involved in doing so will dominate teaching throughout the next generation. Schools and teachers will keep struggling at the task of teaching these students more effectively, but noticeably successful approaches will probably continue to be elusive. Americans will continue to believe that education can overcome poverty, and they will retain the hope that teachers will find a way to make it happen.

Although more will be said about this later in the chapter, it is important to note that studies consistently report that poor and minority students are achieving less and dropping out of school in greater proportions than students as a whole.

Schools are still not succeeding anywhere close to the level that they should with the following student groups: blacks, Hispanics, those from lower socio-economic families, those from single-parent families, those from large families, those living in large cities, those in the South, and those with weak self-concepts. Other studies report that people such as these who do not achieve in school are not likely to do so in the adult world. (For further discussion on several of these points, see Graham, 1987; Shalala, 1986; Snyder 1987, pp. 22, 86–91, 195; Here they come . . . , 1986; Ekstrom, Geortz, Pollack, & Rock, 1986.)[7]

Changing Content

Questions about the content that should be taught will change the school curriculum during the 1990s, although some of the directions of that change are not clear and may not be clear for some time. Teachers will be expected to teach certain prescribed common core subjects and to do so with more adherence to set norms and demonstrated success than in years past. They will be expected to provide the basics, to make students culturally literate, to teach students to think, and to inculcate the correct values. Student test results will be checked to see if teachers successfully achieve this.

In a sense, this means that schools and teachers will gradually become more accountable for *what* students learn as well as for how much and how effectively they learn. Teachers will be less able to slide over a topic on the basis of their own professional judgment or because students are not interested in it. Students will need to know the prescribed information and to develop the prescribed skills and values. Those items will be covered on the test. There is an irony here. Teachers will have more decision-making authority in many ways, but they will also have to teach more of what others want and do it with a degree of conformity and do it more successfully.

Something to Think About

Some critics of education reform say that two conflicting reform pressures on teachers—to be more accountable to others and to be more professionally responsible for their own classes—are incompatible, unfair, and impossible for teachers to meet. These critics say that teachers cannot be scrutinized more closely against standards set by politicians, school boards, and commissions and at the same time be held accountable personally for the lack of success of their students. They also say that if teachers are not trusted to set the direction and standards for the education of their students, they should not be responsible for the results.

- Do you see a significant contradiction as these critics do?
- If so, what do you think should be done to avoid it?

Different Kinds of Professionals

As teachers continue teaching through the changed education environment of the 1990s and at the same time assume the additional responsibilities that reform has thrust upon them, they, in fact, will gradually become different kinds of professionals than teachers of the past. They will be caught up in a nationwide process of rethinking what schools should accomplish and how schools and teachers should operate. This means that as teachers of the next generation take on more responsibility in a more complex educational world, they will have to be

1. *executive-like managers* who select priorities of instruction and oversee the running of their schools;

2. *decision makers* who decide what and how to teach, in what depth, to which students, at which times, and for which tests;

3. *subject-matter scholars* who understand the content they teach well enough to manipulate it so that it can be learned by their students;

4. *abstract thinkers* who can pull together ideas from various subject areas, taught in the school sociology, child development, and learning theory and bring these to bear on what they do in the classroom; and

5. *infinitely skilled practitioners* who can make all this work.

(For more discussion on these points, see Berliner, 1986, 1985, 1988; Wise, 1986.)[8]

Different Kinds of Schools

Much of each of these aspects of teaching is not new, but the level of complexity involved in each is. The pleasant, dedicated, caring teachers of past times who continue to function as artisans will not be adequate in the future. Successful teachers of the 1990s and beyond will have to be more intelligent, better informed, more insightful, and more highly skilled than most of their professional predecessors if the dreams of education reform are to be attained.

Schools will also have to be different, not only in what occurs in them but also in their governance and organization. Much as the Carnegie Task Force on Teaching as a Profession (1986) suggested,[9] schools will need to be places where skilled teachers *decide* and *do* what is necessary to produce appropriate student learning rather than places where they follow the dictates of tight curriculum frameworks and rigid, status quo–seeking managers. These changes will be especially threatening to many—to communities and parents who want to run the schools so tightly that they prescribe what is taught and how to teach it, to principals who want controlled and orderly schools, and to teachers who want administrators to tell them what to do and how to do it.

If the reform agendas are to come to fruition, dramatically different kinds of teachers will staff classrooms. Their day-to-day work will be startlingly more sophisticated. The demands on them to show success will be more persistent. Their roles and responsibilities will be more complex. Their levels of competence will have to be much higher. Many of the people who used to pursue successful careers in teaching would no longer be capable of doing so.

THE IMPORTANCE OF TEACHERS

Virtually everyone who has studied contemporary education in America agrees that teachers are the critical variable in the education process. They also agree that the extent to which student learning will improve in the years ahead depends directly on the abilities of the teachers available to teach those students. As a critic of schools during the 1980s stated, "Nearly everyone agrees . . . that America's schools are only as good as their teachers and that teachers aren't as good as they should be" (Stipp, 1986).[10] In light of this consensus, it is useful at this point to reflect again about the characteristics that seem to make contemporary teachers influential and effective with students and then to itemize some of the competencies that teachers for the future should possess.

Teacher Influence on Students

The most significant characteristics of influential teachers seem to be their attitudes toward teaching, toward the subject matter, and toward student success in learning. Influential teachers show that they believe learning what they are teaching is worth the time and effort. Students often describe learning under these teachers as follows:

> You learn a lot because it doesn't seem like work; it's something you really *want* to do. (Csikszentmihalyi & McCormack, 1986, p. 419).

(See Chapter 3 of this text; Csikszentmihalyi & McCormack, 1986; Clark, 1987.)[11]

Effective Teaching

Teacher effectiveness researchers say that in addition to the points just made, the most effective teachers are those who prepare thoroughly, organize their work carefully, provide a variety of involving activities, use time efficiently, and have high expectations of their students. They also manage student behavior well, keep students engaged in academic pursuits, and teach for understanding. They are good in terms of specific teaching techniques such as withitness, overlapping, wait-time, questioning, and the use of praise. (See Chapter 3 of this text.)

Competencies of Future Teachers

Much of this information about influential and effective teaching, as well as that reported in Chapter 3, has been generated during the last two decades. Before then, efforts to try to identify the precise competencies that characterize good teachers and good teaching had been difficult. Not much information was available, and much of that seemed vague and contradictory. Good teachers did different and even conflicting things, but somehow they seemed to work—students liked their studies and learned well. Others teachers did many of the same things, but their students failed.

Identifying Critical Characteristics

As a result, for a long time the concept of good teaching was very general. People said they could identify good teaching when they saw or experienced it but could not define it or list its critical characteristics. Many even said teachers were born, not made, and were artists whose abilities were too abstract to be isolated and labeled.

Statements such as these are no longer accepted. Regardless of how artistic teaching might be or whether teachers are born or not, experts believe that characteristics of good teaching can be identified with greater assurance, and

many are in the process of doing so. The data being generated are making the elements of teaching more understandable.

Finding the Experts

At this point, however, there is a lot more to be learned. Both the criteria and expertise to identify good teaching are still inadequate. David Berliner, a leading researcher into the characteristics of expert teachers, suggests that most teacher-of-the-year competitions are so superficial and unscientific that they are insulting. He notes that judges of Olympic competitors usually have twenty to thirty years of prior experience; judges of teachers have comparatively little. Cattle show judges must train more intensively or have more experiences as unofficial judges than many of those who evaluate teachers (Berliner, 1986, pp. 8–9).

Areas of Competence

Nevertheless, we know enough to identify areas in which teachers of the 1990s and beyond have to be more competent than their predecessors. These areas of competence have been alluded to earlier in this book and are a direct result of changing conditions also already mentioned—the changing priorities of education, the evolving society in which schools operate, and the developing nature of the teaching profession. These areas of necessary competence for future teachers include the following:

Knowledge

Teachers have to know more information and understand it better. They still need to be well versed in the tricks of the trade, but more importantly they need theoretical knowledge—ideas from pedagogy, history, psychology, sociology, philosophy, subject-matter disciplines, and so forth—that will help them answer questions as yet unraised. They need knowledge that is deep and sophisticated enough to be applied in all kinds of classrooms, all of them bombarded by the multitude of changing circumstances and pressures already described. For example, they need to have enough background knowledge and depth of understanding to grasp the concept of cultural literacy, to decide whether it is as significant to teaching as its proponents say, and to determine what it means for their own personal teaching. They need to be able to evaluate regularly as other popular new concepts surface throughout their teaching careers.

Intelligence and Insight

Teachers have to be able to think flexibly, abstractly, and conceptually. They must simultaneously process all sorts of information. They must constantly take in new and competing ideas, use them to reconfigure what they believe, and apply them to what they do with students.

For example, when educational theorists suggest that teachers should rely less on stimulus-response techniques to motivate students and should base their teaching more on student intrinsic motivations, teachers need to be able to understand the point, assess its validity for their own teaching, and modify their classroom strategies accordingly. It is simply no longer adequate to teach by doing things the way Mr. Washington or Ms. Jones always did them, the way a college professor suggested, or the way they are outlined in the teachers' guide.

Organizing Ability

Because more than ever before seems to be happening in and around classrooms these days, teachers have to be especially competent organizers, planners, and managers. They need to arrange such things as ideas, classroom events, subject-matter content, developmental skills, student strengths and weaknesses, and their own teaching strategies in ways that bring meaning to what they do. They need to have a clear idea of what they intend to accomplish so that they can balance everything. They need to formulate and pursue routines and procedures that enhance, rather than stifle, teaching and learning.

Technical Skills

As always, teachers have to be skilled in the technical aspects of their jobs—to formulate objectives, motivate students, diagnose difficulties, correct or reinforce behavior, vary activities, utilize equipment, evaluate materials, sequence lessons, pace instruction, monitor student progress, provide feedback, ask questions, manage time, keep students on task, assess performance, and so forth. They have to do all this and make it lead to demonstrable student learning.

Confidence

Teachers have to be secure and confident professionals who are convinced that they know what they are doing, that it is the right thing to do, and that they can do it. Teaching nowadays is too complex for the cookbook teacher who might have survived in the past, too demanding for the unsure and the marginally qualified. Even the experts strain at times to keep up.

Ability to Handle Complexity

Interwoven among all of the above is the fact that teachers face a more complex set of tasks and more complex circumstances than their predecessors. Students, social conditions, expectations for schools, teachers themselves, and the very act of teaching all seem to be more complicated than what we remember of the good old days. The teacher of the one-room schoolhouse (such as Priscilla Hope, described in Chapter 9) simply could not cope with the current multutide of teacher roles and the magnitude of present conditions; but teachers today must be able to succeed in that environment.

Of course, none of these areas of competence is really new to teachers. Good teachers have possessed the abilities noted and have performed ably under similar circumstances for years. Now, however, the needs seem to be more pressing, and the level of competence required seems to be more difficult to achieve.

Here is a critical question: *Can America attract to teaching enough people who possess the capabilities it wants in its teachers?* One skeptic described the situation this way:

> Since about 1983, Americans have said they want teachers comparable in ability to leading business and industry executives. But they are willing to pay them no more than they pay assembly line workers; moreover the working conditions of schools are more like the plant floor than the board room. (Myers, 1986)[12]

Others are more positive and those who are say that current changes and reform-generated improvements support their position.

TEACHER SUPPLY AND DEMAND

Effects of the 1960s and 1970s

During the 1950s and early 1960s, Americans had babies in record numbers, and the baby boom swelled K–12 school enrollments greatly through the 1960s and early 1970s. Then the boom turned to bust. The boomers completed school, their parents were beyond childbearing age, and they were not yet old enough to have school-age children of their own in great numbers.

These demographic trends had a direct effect on the need for teachers. At first, the need outstripped the number of teachers available, and school systems were forced to hire almost anyone with a college degree who was willing to teach. When news of the demand spread, more college students pursued teaching. Gradually, the supply caught up to and eventually passed the demand.

When the bust hit schools about 1973, the supply of qualified teachers suddenly outdistanced the demand in most teaching fields and regions of the country. Fewer students attended K–12 grades, but large numbers of boomers were still being graduated from college, and many of them still wanted to teach. Again, the news spread, and this time fewer college students chose careers in teaching. (For more information on teacher supply and demand, see Olson & Rodman, 1987, June 24; Carnegie Foundation, 1986; Feistritzer, 1987.)[13]

Older Teachers

The impact of the shifts in the numbers of teachers hired in the 1960s and 1970s was not limited to those years, however. Because many teachers were employed before 1973 and few between 1973 and the mid-1980s, the average age of teachers crept up each year. As a result, a disproportionate number of teachers either retired in the 1980s or will retire in the 1990s. An illustration of the phenomenon was reflected in 1984 in a high school in upstate New York, where no teacher in the building had been teaching for fewer than seventeen years, that is, since 1967.

Increased Demand

Now the supply-demand situation has changed again. Since the mid-1980s, student enrollments have been increasing as children of the baby boomers enter elementary school and move through the grades and as the birthrate among certain population groups remains high, especially among Hispanic Americans. The need for teachers is expanding again.

During the last years of the 1980s, the general demand for teachers across the nation and in all fields increased by about 4 percent a year, although different grade levels, subject areas, and regions of the country experienced higher demands than others, and some still had oversupplies. The higher demand is expected to remain for some time, and the reasons given include the following:

1. The bulge in school enrollments caused by baby-boomer children will continue for a number of years as those children pass through the system. (See Figure 1–1 in Chapter 1, Bickers, 1987, pp. 2, 5, 8, 40, 43, 45; and Snyder, 1987, p. 33.)[14]

2. Birthrates among Hispanic and black Americans are expected to remain high, and many women in those groups are in their childbearing years (Bickers, 1987, esp. p. 33).

3. Many school systems are reducing teacher-student ratios. (See Figure 1–3 in Chapter 1; Snyder, 1987, p. 33; and *Education Week*, 1988, October 19, p. 17.)

4. Large numbers of current teachers are approaching retirement and will need to be replaced.

Increased Supply

What this increased demand will do to the supply of teachers in the next two decades is not clear. Surely, the supply will increase to some extent, but the important question is whether the increase in supply will be great enough and strong enough to prevent a shortage of teachers. An important parallel question is if the supply of *skilled* and *competent* teachers will increase enough to avoid deterioration in the quality of new teachers.

Quality

Factors that will influence the answers to these questions include the following:

1. Will the increase in students in teacher-preparation programs during recent years continue?

2. Will people trained as teachers in the past who did not get teaching jobs take the positions that are becoming available?

3. Will better salaries and working conditions attract more people to teaching?

4. How will higher standards for entering teaching effect the numbers?

5. Will women and minority-group members turn to teaching even if offered better paying positions in other fields?

A more detailed picture of the teacher supply and demand situation is reflected in data reported below. Those data include information on school enrollment, the supply of teachers, teacher quality, and influences that affect supply and demand equations.

Enrollment

School enrollment in the United States has gradually increased since 1984 and will continue to do so for a number of years. One of the reasons for this is that there has been a rather large number of women of childbearing age in recent years, and even though some of them are having fewer children per family than earlier generations, their total numbers are higher. (See Figure 1–2 in Chapter 1; Here they come . . . , 1986; Rist, 1986; Snyder, 1987, p. 33; Montague, 1987, June 3.)[15]

Teacher Numbers

The number of new college graduates who *completed teacher-education programs* with a bachelor's degree was 89,421 in 1959–60. That number rose in 176,641 in 1969–70, 194,229 in the peak years of 1972–73. Then it fell to 87,221 in 1985–86. In percentages, the proportion of college graduates who completed college in teacher education was 21.1 percent in 1973 and only 8.9 percent in 1986. (See Figure 15–1; Carnegie Foundation, 1988a, p. 27; Snyder, 1987, p. 204; Kane, 1987; Berger, 1988, May 6, p. A1; Rothman, 1987, January 14, p. 55.)[16]

The percentage of college freshmen who said they *intended to become teachers* declined between 1968 and 1982 from 23.5 percent to 4.7 percent; then it rose to 8.8 percent in 1988. (See Figure 15–2; Astin, Green, Korn, Schalit, & Berz, 1988, December; Astin, Green, Korn, & Schalit, 1987, December, and 1986, December; Astin, Green, & Korn, 1987, January; Rothman, 1987, January 14, pp. 12, 18; Rothman, 1986, November 5, p. 7. Also see National Education Association, 1986, pp. 56–60.)

The number of people *employed as new teachers* averaged about 138,000 per year between 1972 and 1985 and rose to an average of about 190,000 between 1986 and 1988. It is expected to remain above 210,000 through the first part of the 1990s. Of these hired during the 1980s, only about half remained in the classroom longer than five years, and in some systems the attrition rate approached 40 percent in the first two years. (See Olson & Rodman, 1987, June 24.)

High percentages of current teachers are expected to retire or leave teaching for other reasons before the year 2000. As a result, the decade of the 1990s will have a high turnover rate and a greater number of new teaching jobs available than in the recent past. (See Olson & Rodman, 1987, June 24.)

Of course, general teacher supply-and-demand statistics and trends do not present an adequate picture of real supply-demand situations. Teachers are not interchangeable parts, and the need for teachers is not equal across fields and in all regions. As of the late 1980s, this country needed more elementary teachers than secondary. Science, mathematics, and special education teachers were in

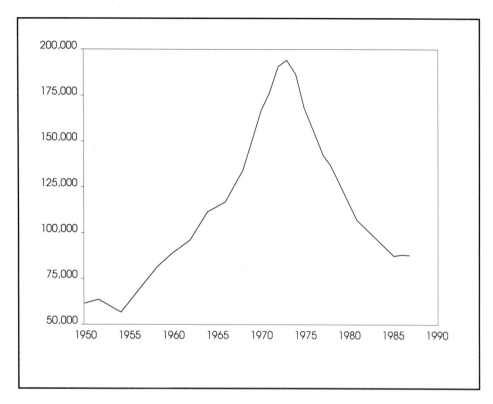

Figure 15–1. Bachelor's degrees earned in education, 1950–1986. (Sources: Snyder (1987), p. 204, 14; U.S. Department of Education.)

great demand. Inner city classrooms lacked sufficient numbers of qualified practitioners, while suburban schools had more qualified applicants than they needed. Enrollments in the South, Southwest, and California increased while they stabilized or declined elsewhere.

Teacher Quality

Teacher capabilities and quality are also critical in assessing supply-and-demand conditions. School systems will probably always be able to find someone to stand before nearly every class of children, but that is not the issue. The issue is whether schools can attract enough people who are good enough to do what teachers must do and what children deserve. If children are expected to learn more, they deserve especially qualified teachers.

Recent data about the people who are becoming teachers are enlightening, but much progress still needs to be made. For example, in 1973, the average SAT score for college freshmen who said they intended to teach was 59 points below the national average. By 1982, it had dropped to 80 points below the average, even though the average SAT itself declined (Carnegie Foundation, 1986, p. 27). Although the gap closed slightly by 1985, the average of intended teachers that year was still below all other college majors except four—agriculture, ethnic studies, home economics, and trade and vocation fields (Carnegie Foundation, 1986, p. 27).

The same uneven pattern is reflected in the credentials of some groups of practicing teachers. For example, in some states one-third or more of high school science and mathematics teachers do not possess minimum state qualifications

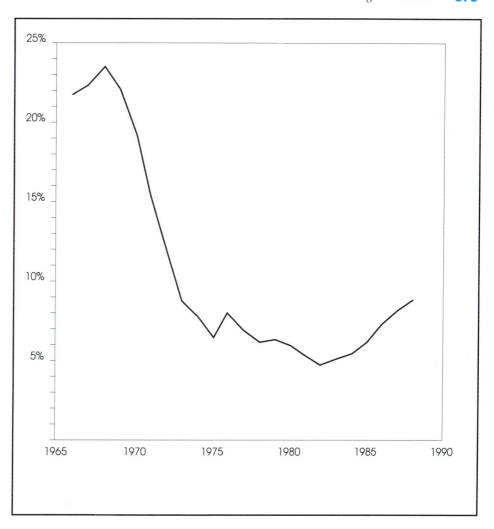

Figure 15–2. College freshmen saying they plan to teach, 1966–1988. (Sources: Astin (1987, January); Astin (1986, December); Astin (1987, December); Astin (1988, December).)

for their positions. Several states that set minimum-level basic skills standards for teachers in the middle of the 1980s have since lowered them to allow less-qualified practicing teachers or teacher applicants to qualify into the qualifying arena. For example, in 1985, Louisiana reduced its National Teachers Exam cutoff scores because of teacher shortages in math and science; and Georgia and Alabama reduced test score standards when sued by practicing teachers who challenged the tests in court (Darling-Hammond & Berry, 1988, p. 23; Rodman, 1988, March 9).[18]

Influencing the Equations

Two developments that are expected to influence teacher supply-and-demand conditions substantially over the next decade are increased school system efforts to recruit high-quality teachers, including those from nontraditional sources, and general efforts to further professionalize teaching.

A number of school districts and several states have developed plans to attract to teaching people from other careers—people with liberal arts degrees and little teacher training and older people who prepared to teach in the past but either never did so or have not done so for some time. Some of the plans are primarily recruiting efforts and flexible training arrangements that make teacher preparation possible for these people but retain the same expectations and quality checks as more traditional programs. Some substitute alternative criteria for the more traditional checks, and some drop most entry standards. The extent to which these plans attract high-quality teachers who remain in the classroom will not be known for several years, but if they do succeed, they will greatly affect supply-demand situations.

Reform efforts at further professionalizing teaching—such as those recommended by the Carnegie Forum on Education and the Economy, the Holmes Group, the National Governors' Association, and the Education Commission of the States—propose the setting of higher standards for selecting teachers and assume that this will result in a higher public regard for teachers that would in turn make teaching more attractive. (See Chapter 1 of this text.) These efforts call for intellectually sophisticated, inquiring teachers who challenge students with ideas and thought-provoking questions, who run their own schools, and who are the executive decision makers described earlier. (See Berliner, 1986.) They envision a more select group of teachers with more status and power and better compensation (Darling-Hammond, 1987; Wise, 1986).[19] If and when these things happen, the teacher supply-demand picture will be quite different from what it is today because the nature of the teaching force itself will have changed.

Minority Teachers

Probably the most acute teacher supply-and-demand challenge ahead for schools is the need to attract more minority-group members to teaching. Today, a significantly lower percentage of minority-group members teach than attend school, and the situation will worsen. The problem was described in 1987 by Patricia Albjerg Graham, dean of the graduate school of education at Harvard University:

> Simply stated, the problem is that, as minority enrollments in the public schools are rising, the number of minority teachers, especially black teachers, is shrinking. This is the case because proportionately fewer blacks are going to college than a decade ago and, of those who do go to college, fewer are choosing to become teachers and, of those seeking to become teachers, too few are passing the new teacher tests, especially in the southern states, where about half of the nation's black teachers are prepared. Throughout the seventies and into the eighties, blacks constituted about 8 percent of public school teachers, roughly half the proportion of black children in the schools. Today, however, blacks make up less than 7 percent of the teaching force, and that percentage is expected to decline even further by the end of the decade [1989], when black enrollments may well be substantially higher than the current level of about 16 percent. (Graham, 1987, pp. 529–600)

While minority teachers are in great demand, two factors work against more minority-group members' entering teaching. Those who perform well in college are in such demand for jobs in other fields that school systems cannot compete for them. Those who do not do well in college also perform poorly in terms of the new academic standards for entering teaching. Of course, the latter group would not make good role models in the classroom where majority and minority

students need to interact with intelligent, articulate, and academically successful minority teachers. (See Rodman, 1988, February 3; Graham, 1987.)[20]

Something to Think About

> In recent years school systems seem to have struggled to hire minority teachers, but there have simply not been enough qualified minority-group members to fill the positions available.
> - What strategies should be used to attract more minority-group members to teaching positions?
> - What are the advantages and disadvantages of each?

A Look Ahead

Although it is hard to predict precisely what teacher supply-and-demand conditions will be like in a decade or so, the following estimates seem to be reasonable:

- School systems will strain to attract good teachers and compete with each other to do so. The more affluent districts will get the better teachers.
- Good teachers will be in demand in most parts of the country, at most grade levels, and in most fields.
- As long as qualitative standards remain in place, teacher numbers will not expand to satisfy the demand to the extent that they did in the 1960s.
- Women and minority teachers will be in particularly short supply.
- Teacher turnover will be high.
- Marginally qualified and unqualified teachers will be hired by school systems that cannot get better ones.
- The less-qualified teachers will be teaching poorer students whose parents lack political clout.

Sellers' Market

In summary, the next decade or two will be a sellers' market for highly qualified prospective teachers, although there will be regional variations. But the people most in demand will also be sought by other professions. Some will never teach; others will be attracted away after teaching only a short time. School systems will compete for the best, but many of them will have to settle for less.

WHERE TO TEACH

To the extent that qualified new teachers enter a sellers' market in the next generation, they will make decisions about where to teach; and all teaching positions are not equal. Conditions vary greatly, and jobs that appeal to some will not appeal to others. A number of varying circumstances that teacher applicants will want to consider as they look for jobs are noted below.

However, two parts of the question of where to teach are not addressed directly. First, the general characteristics and circumstances of teaching have already been treated in earlier chapters of this text. Second, the attractions or detractions of a specific job are too individually variable to be described usefully at this point. Therefore, comments included here are directed toward three points: teaching in different regions of the country, in different types of communities, and in different types of schools.

Regions of the Country

Personal Preference

Probably the prime considerations about which part of the country prospective teachers find most attractive have more to do with personal background and preferences than regional ways of life or teaching conditions. Factors such as where a person grew up, location of relatives, jobs of spouses, climate, proximity to cultural events, and so forth should not be undervalued. Prospective teachers will regret choosing jobs that require them to live where they will not be happy.

Regional Enrollment Trends

On the other hand, teaching and schools in different regions of the country are, in fact, different. School enrollments will increase most in the South, the Southwest, and California. They will increase most in urban schools with high percentages of minority and poor children. Enrollments will be more steady in the Northeast and the upper Midwest and will decline in rural areas. These trends will affect the number and types of teaching positions available and the financial resources for schools. They will affect teaching jobs and job conditions.

School Improvements

The states of the Southeast, where schools have been weakest historically, seem to have made serious commitments recently to doing better and have shown the greatest gains. In most of these states, tax increases have provided more money for schools, and many quality-improving reforms are underway. Yet, because of where they started, even these special efforts might not be enough to bring conditions to a par with more advanced states. Even where there are great gains, the reform energy and state funds will run out.

Urban Conditions

In all regions, many urban schools will have monumental problems. They will experience the biggest barriers to success, the greatest limits on resources, and the students with the greatest need. Their teaching jobs will be the easiest to find and the most difficult to perform. For talented, committed teachers with the right predilections, those jobs will be the most satisfying, as well as the most demanding.

Variations

Generally, experts predict that schools as a whole nationally will get better for the next decade or two, although many see urban schools as an exception to the trend. Some areas and states will advance faster than others, at least for a time. Those that develop fastest at one point will eventually slow and be passed by others. In any event, there will probably be more variation in teacher employment and conditions in schools within regions than across them.

Specific Considerations

College graduates considering teaching positions in different regions of the country should first consider where they would like to live, but more specific considerations are probably best left to the time when applicants are in the midst of their job search. Decisions made too early can exclude good options and may be based on conditions that are likely to change. Like most contemporary American professionals, those who begin teaching in the 1990s and do well will be less tied to one position than their predecessors. They will have the opportunity to change jobs during their career. If conditions in one locale turn out to be less than optimal, they will be able to look around in the sellers' market.

Types of Communities

Because communities vary greatly and because schools are an extension of the communities in which they are located, prospective teachers should think carefully about the locale in which they anticipate teaching and living. Rural, suburban, and urban areas have different types of social environments, life-styles, and atmospheres in which to work. They vary, for example, in basic, important matters such as cost of living, how close one lives to school, how one travels to and from work, and how long it takes to do so. A short walk, a long drive through heavy traffic, or a subway ride are three significantly different ways of starting the day. Teachers who like living and working in one environment may not enjoy doing so in the others.

A thorough discussion of the benefits and burdens of living and teaching in various community settings is not necessary here, but it is important to acknowledge that teaching involves daily interaction with students, administrators, peers, and parents who are influenced by the culture in which they live; as a result, teachers cannot separate their work in the schools of a community from the community itself. Those who try to do so seem to complicate their jobs unnecessarily. It seems only logical that those who take jobs in communities where they fit in comfortably have a greater chance of enjoying their work.

Greatest Need

As with decisions about regions of the country, whether a person teaches in an urban, suburban, or rural community is primarily a matter of personal preference. However, if prospective teachers are motivated to teach because of a desire to do good, they should seriously consider urban positions, simply because urban students need good teachers most desperately. Besides, younger teachers usually find city life more exciting and have fewer family responsibilities of the sort that make city work and life impractical for others. Both authors of this book have spent nearly all of their K–12 teaching careers in urban schools and recommend teaching there.

Types of Schools

Differences

Within communities, schools vary as much as they are alike, and those variations affect the experience of teaching in each. Some of the basic differences are:

- age and grade level of students,
- comprehensiveness of curriculum,
- proportional numbers of students with different social and economic backgrounds,
- number of at-risk and special-needs students,
- educational philosophy,
- tightness of administrative regulation,
- style of school leadership,
- level of expectations for student performance, and
- degree to which academics are stressed.

Public or Private

Of course, private, religious affiliated, and public schools differ greatly and in many ways.

Because Chapter 6 has discussed differences among schools, we need no further description here. However, prospective teachers need to remember that the general nature and day-to-day activities of any teaching position depend greatly on the environment in which that teaching takes place—the school atmosphere, the students, teaching peers, administrators, secretaries, custodians, and the less tangible accompanying circumstances. All these affect the job. They make it exciting, pleasant, tolerable, burdensome, or horrible.

A Matter of Choice

Different teachers evaluate schools by different criteria. Some like working where others would fear to tread. And, of course, things change over time. People who are considering a teaching career need to assess teaching positions in terms of their own preferences and predilections, both on the basis of what they see in the school and what they expect it to be like some years ahead.

SALARIES AND COMPENSATION

Although teacher salaries are not as high as people may believe they should be and do not attract significant numbers of individuals away from other professions, they are the primary external reward for teaching. For years, teacher salaries have been below the average salaries of most other professions that require four years of college preparation, but they have been getting better in recent years. As a result, they are less of a handicap than they once were.

Generalizing about teacher salaries is difficult because (1) they change each year; (2) they vary from state to state and district to district; (3) they are adjusted for years of service, extent of professional study, career ladder category, and type of assignment; and (4) they can be supplemented by performing extra duties. Comparison with other occupations is also complex because (1) those other salaries change and vary; (2) most teachers are paid for nine or ten months work a year without paid vacations; and (3) teachers rarely receive on-the-job training within the schoolday and at school expense, a typical benefit in other fields.

Nevertheless, general data about teacher salaries are presented below. Those data show recent average salaries for beginning teachers and for all teachers in each state. They also reflect trends in recent years and as projected for several years to come.

Average Salary

The average teacher salary for *all* public school teachers in the United States for the school year 1989–90 was about $31,200. That amount compares with $4,995 in 1959–60; $8,635 in 1969–70; $15,970 in 1979–80; and $25,313 in 1985–86. So in the thirty years between 1959–60 and 1989–90 average teacher salaries rose more than six times. They almost doubled in the ten years between 1980 and 1990. (See Figure 15–3; and *Education Week,* 1989, September 6, p. 2; Carnegie Foundation, 1988b; Snyder, 1987, pp. 61–62; Sedlak and Schlossman, 1986, p. 6; also see National Education Association, 1986, pp. 65–70; The Forgotten Message, 1988, April, p. 5.)[21]

The average salary of all *beginning* teachers in the United States in 1988–1989 was $19,510. It was $8,063 in 1974–1975, $11,676 in 1980–1981, and $16,692 in 1985–1986. The percentage increases as of 1987 were about 175 percent since 1976, over 50 percent since 1981, and nearly 33 percent since 1985. (See Figure 15–3; The Forgotten Message, 1988, April, p. 5; *NEA Today,* 1989, April, p. 8; Snyder, 1987, p. 293; American Federation of Teachers.)

These figures are distorted, however, by at least two factors—inflation and the fact that the average age of teachers has been increasing in recent years. As a result, the average teacher salary in 1990 is for a teacher with more years experience than the average salary a number of years earlier, and dollar-for-dollar it does not buy as much. Several studies report that recent salary increases have had the effect of only restoring teacher buying power to a level comparable to what it was in the early 1970s. (See, for example, Darling-Hammond & Berry, 1988, esp. pp. 38–49.) In any event, real gains are now being made again.

When compared with the first-year twelve-month salaries of bachelor's degree recipients in other professions, first-year teachers salaries in 1987 compared as follows:

Teaching	$17,500	Engineering	$28,512
Business	21,324	Sales/marketing	20,688
Computer specialist	26,172		

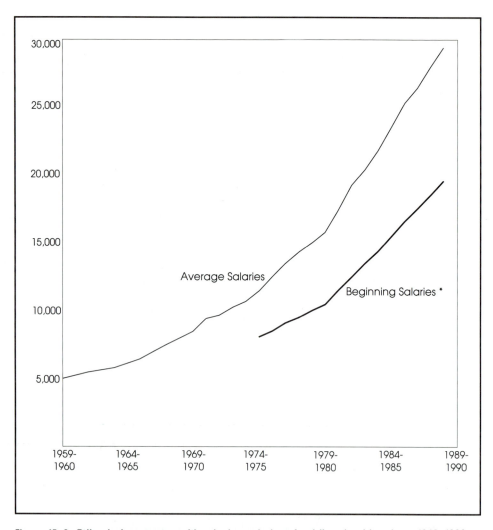

Figure 15–3. Estimated average and beginning salaries of public school teachers, 1960–1988. (Sources: Average salaries—Snyder (1987), p. 293; *The Forgotten Message*, p. 5; *The Condition of Teaching* (1988), p. 2; *NEA Today* (1989, April), p. 8. Beginning salaries—American Federation of Teachers, based on data compiled from various reports of Educational Research Services.)

(For more detailed comparisons, see Figure 15–4; The Forgotten Message; 1988, April, p. 5; Snyder, 1987, p. 293.) If teaching salaries are considered to represent only nine months' work, as some people insist, the twelve-month equivalent of the $17,500 in 1987 was $23,333, an amount more than the average yearly salary for business and sales/marketing.

Averages, of course, obscure variations in salaries within the teaching force, and those variations are quite extensive. Table 15–1 shows salaries by state. (Snyder, 1987, p. 62; *Education Week*, 1987, September 9, p. 20.) Table 15–2 below is an example of a typical teacher salary schedule for 1989–90. It reports on salaries for each year of service based on traditional increments—years of teaching experience and amount of college education.

Salary Schedules

New Bases for Increments

However, recent reforms have introduced other bases for awarding differiential salaries—career ladder ranks, incentive pay plans, and merit awards. Most

An Introduction to Teaching and Schools **583**

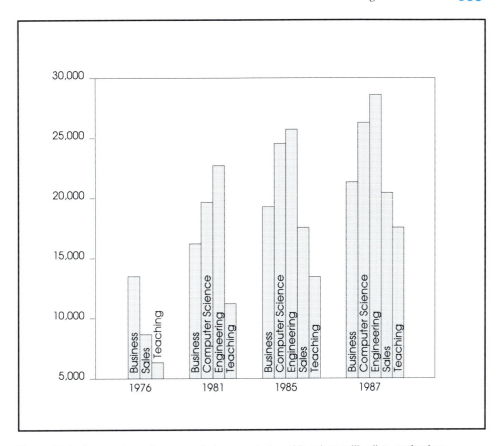

Figure 15–4. Comparison of average first-year salaries of teachers with other professions. (Sources: Snyder (1987), p. 293; *The Forgotten Message*, p. 5.)

Table 15-1: **Average Teacher Salaries by State***

State	Salary	Rank	Percent of U.S. Average
Alabama	$25,190	37	85.2
Alaska	41,693	1	141.0
Arizona	28,684	23	97.0
Arkansas	21,692	50	73.4
California	35,285	5	119.3
Colorado	29,558	17	100.0
Connecticut	37,339	3	126.3
Delaware	31,605	11	106.9
District of Columbia	37,504	2	126.8
Florida	26,648	30	90.1
Georgia	28,038	25	94.8
Hawaii	30,778	15	104.1
Idaho	22,860	44	77.3
Illinois	31,195	13	105.5
Indiana	28,664	24	96.9

cont.

Table 15-1: (Continued)

State	Salary	Rank	Percent of U.S. Average
Iowa	25,884	33	87.5
Kansas	27,401	27	92.7
Kentucky	24,920	40	84.3
Louisiana	22,470	45	76.0
Maine	24,933	39	84.3
Maryland	33,700	8	114.0
Massachusetts	31,670	10	107.1
Michigan	34,419	6	116.4
Minnesota	31,500	12	106.5
Mississippi	22,036	47	74.5
Missouri	25,981	32	87.9
Montana	24,414	41	82.6
Nebraska	24,203	42	81.9
Nevada	28,840	22	97.5
New Hampshire	26,703	29	90.3
New Jersey	32,923	9	111.4
New Mexico	25,205	36	85.2
New York	36,500	4	123.4
North Carolina	25,650	34	86.8
North Dakota	22,249	46	75.2
Ohio	29,152	20	98.6
Oklahoma	22,000	48	74.4
Oregon	29,500	18	99.8
Pennsylvania	30,720	16	103.9
Rhode Island	34,233	7	115.8
South Carolina	25,060	38	84.8
South Dakota	20,480	51	69.3
Tennessee	25,619	35	86.6
Texas	26,513	31	89.7
Utah	23,023	43	77.9
Vermont	26,861	28	90.8
Virginia	29,056	21	98.3
Washington	29,176	19	98.7
West Virginia	21,904	49	74.1
Wisconsin	31,046	14	105.0
Wyoming	27,685	26	93.6

* From *NEA Today*, 1987, April, p. 8.

of these are intended (1) to reward teachers who are believed to be performing noticeably better than their peers, (2) to compensate more for teaching in areas of greatest need, and (3) to attract more and better qualified people to teaching.

For example, in 1986 the state of Tennessee began paying teachers between $1,000 and $7,000 more than their base salary if they underwent successful career ladder evaluations. Houston (Texas) Independent School District's Second Mile Plan provides extra stipends of $2,000 per year for teachers of mathematics, science, and special education, and to those who teach in certain low-income area schools.

Table 15-2: Sample Teacher Salary Scale, 1988–89, DeKalb County, Georgia*

	Bachelor's Degree			Master's Degree			Specialist's Degree			Doctor's Degree	
	Annual	Monthly		Annual	Monthly		Annual	Monthly		Annual	Monthly
(1)	$23,100	$1,925	(1)	$24,660	$2,055	(1)	$26,976	$2,248	(1)	$29,496	$2,458
(2)	23,100	1,925	(2)	24,660	2,055	(2)	26,976	2,248	(2)	29,496	2,458
(3)	23,400	1,950	(3)	24,960	2,080	(3)	27,276	2,273	(3)	29,796	2,483
(4)	23,700	1,975	(4)	25,404	2,117	(4)	27,792	2,316	(4)	30,396	2,533
(5)	24,000	2,000	(5)	26,172	2,181	(5)	28,632	2,386	(5)	31,308	2,609
(6)	24,660	2,055	(6)	26,976	2,248	(6)	29,496	2,458	(6)	32,256	2,688
(7)	25,404	2,117	(7)	27,792	2,316	(7)	30,396	2,533	(7)	33,240	2,770
(8)	26,172	2,181	(8)	28,632	2,386	(8)	31,308	2,609	(8)	34,260	2,855
(9)	26,976	2,248	(9)	29,496	2,458	(9)	32,256	2,688	(9)	35,292	2,941
(10)	27,792	2,316	(10)	30,396	2,533	(10)	33,240	2,770	(10)	36,348	3,029
(11)	28,632	2,386	(11)	31,308	2,609	(11)	34,260	2,855	(11)	37,452	3,121
(12)	29,496	2,458	(12)	32,256	2,688	(12)	35,292	2,941	(12)	38,592	3,216
(13)	30,396	2,533	(13)	33,240	2,770	(13)	36,348	3,029	(13)	39,744	3,312
(14)	31,308	2,609	(14)	34,260	2,855	(14)	37,452	3,121	(14)	40,944	3,412
(15)	31,308	2,609	(15)	35,292	2,941	(15)	38,592	3,216	(15)	42,156	3,513
(16)	31,308	2,609	(16)	36,348	3,029	(16)	39,744	3,312	(16)	43,296	3,608
(17)	31,932	2,661	(17)	36,348	3,029	(17)	39,744	3,312	(17)	43,296	3,608
(18)	31,932	2,661	(18)	36,348	3,029	(18)	39,744	3,312	(18)	43,296	3,608
(19)	31,932	2,661	(19)	37,080	3,090	(19)	40,536	3,378	(19)	44,160	3,680
(20)	32,556	2,713	(20)	37,080	3,090	(20)	40,536	3,378	(20)	44,160	3,680
			(21)	37,080	3,090	(21)	40,536	3,378	(21)	44,160	3,680
			(22)	37,800	3,150	(22)	41,328	3,444	(22)	45,024	3,752

* From DeKalb County School System, DeKalb County, Georgia

Two of the most interesting developments concerning teacher salaries in recent years are state efforts to extend teacher employment through the summer with additional pay and to raise teacher pay to match salaries of occupations that require similar amounts of academic preparation. Some of the recent plans for extended teacher contracts provide up to 25 percent more pay annually for the extra work.

In 1985 the state of Georgia commissioned a study of beginning annual salaries of graduates from Georgia state colleges who entered professions such as business and engineering for the purpose of comparing those amounts to beginning teacher salaries. Then the state set a goal of raising teacher salaries to match those in the other fields. The extent to which they will be able to keep pace in doing this, of course, remains to be seen and depends on future available revenues.

In summary, teacher salaries have been increasing faster in recent years than in the past. There are sincere state efforts to increase them further, to make them comparable to those of other fields, and to tie them to performance criteria. The key questions for the years ahead are whether the commitments in these directions will remain strong enough to bring about permanent improvement and whether there will be enough money to finance the efforts. In any event, it seems logical to predict that teachers of the 1990s will be paid comparatively better than those of the 1980s and earlier. On the other hand, most teacher salaries will still be lower than many people believe they should be.

CONDITIONS AHEAD

Now that you are nearing the end of this text, this section of this last chapter describes five very general societal conditions that many experts think will be among the significant situations and circumstances that schools and teachers of the next generation will have to address. The conditions described represent trends already begun, and all have been mentioned to some degree earlier in this book. They are presented here not as new information, but as ideas to stimulate your thinking about the challenges of teaching in the 1990s and beyond—the time when you will be in the classroom if you continue into teaching. The first is tied directly to teaching itself; the others are more truly societal in scope. After the five conditions are described, the authors state their personal views of how schools and teachers will face the challenges noted.

The Continued Professionalization of Teaching

Optimists believe that teaching will continue to evolve to a higher level of professionalism in the years ahead. They expect to see teachers of recognized quality and status who inspire public confidence and respect. Their scenario includes high standards of accountability for students, teachers, and schools, as well as the means to attain those expectations. As one prognosticator expressed it, "Teachers will be doing significant, high-quality work; they will be respected; and they will be compensated at a level that more closely approximates what they deserve."

Implemented Reforms

This expectation involves implemented reform in teacher education, induction, and certification—bachelor's degrees in liberal arts, fifth-year training in professional education, year-long supervised internships, tests in professional knowledge and teaching subject matter, sophisticated ongoing teacher evaluation, and higher standards at each checkpoint. It also includes greater selectivity and a restricted supply of teachers, even though more people will seek credentials. Many who wish to enter teaching will be rejected because of lack of qualifications. All of this should lead to even higher pay, better working conditions, and greater attractions to teaching for better qualified people.

Selectivity and Restricted Supply

Teachers in Control

In this view, teachers will be intelligent, abstract thinkers who have high expectations for their students and themselves; they will set high standards for their colleagues and drive out the weak; and they will decide how and what to teach, control their own curricula, and manage their own schools. Their job will be more complex and more demanding than only a few years ago, but they will be prepared to handle it.

Less optimistic observers believe that some of these predictions will occur, but they anticipate fewer successes. They also say that teachers cannot become more professional if they are consistently held to tighter accountability standards imposed by lay-person-dominated school boards and other political bodies. However, even the doubters think the profession of teaching is moving toward a higher, more complex, more demanding plane; and they consider much of the evolution irreversible, at least for the next generation.

America and International Competition

Schools—Problem and Solution

Much of the current driving force for change in education has surfaced in part because of the traditional American belief that the United States is the best and most powerful nation on earth. But, in the 1980s, many Americans began to have doubts about that position of prominence. When this happened, they looked to schools to see what went wrong and to determine what to do to make things better. In short, Americans saw schools both as a major cause of the problem and as a potential part of the solution.

Nation on Top

At the start of the 1990s, Americans still believed that the United States was "on top" on most matters of national importance. For example, no political system was as stable as that of the United States. Japan might be considered stronger economically, but not militarily. The Soviet Union might be about equal militarily, but was less developed politically, economically, and socially.

Fixing

So, as of 1990, the fixing that Americans thought to be necessary to make America stronger was considered doable. Many of the problems that had developed resulted from neglect, not from inherent flaws in basic ideas or conditions. A little more attention to neglected areas, including the major one of schools, was expected to stabilize the country again.

During the 1990s and beyond, the idea of an invincible American nation will be severely challenged internationally. Competition of all types—of ideas, of economic systems, of military might—will not always end in apparent American wins. For example, it is probably safe to assume the following:

Not Really Invincible

- The United States will continue as a debtor nation, with poor balances of trade and under the financial control of foreign investors.

- Segments of its major industries will be unable to compete internationally.

- Middle Eastern oil will not be a reliable or convenient resource.

- Consumers will continue to reject American products because they are not as good as those of international competitors.

- Americans will lose Olympic and other international athletic competitions, perhaps more than formerly.

- Minority-group members and those already poor will become comparatively poorer.

- American military troops will not be able to stop the spread of aggression in every nation of the world.

- Skirmishes in places like Nicaragua will add to the "loss of innocence" begun in Vietnam.

- More nations will question America's righteousness and reject its leadership.

Shaken Faith

As Americans realize that these things are happening, their sense of national pride will be shaken, and they will experience forms of national self-doubt. That, in turn will disturb their faith in their institutions, including schools. What all this will mean for schools is, of course, a matter for conjecture; but as it happens, schools will face a different national environment and psychological atmosphere from that of most of the 20th century.

Changing Technology and the Media

Much has been written about changing technology and its expected impact on American lives in the years ahead. Technological changes are making life more complex, communication instantaneous, skilled jobs more difficult, and teaching more complicated.

Lost Personal Touch

People used to get credit at the store because the manager knew and trusted them, but few managers know their customers any more. There are too many customers, and managers change jobs too often. The decision as to who gets credit is based on computer data and company regulations, not personal, face-to-face judgments. The personal touch is lost. Computers record information on every one, and God help us when the computer is wrong or the data are lost!

Instant Communication

Radio and television report world events in living rooms within minutes, maybe seconds, of their happening—events that require an education to understand. The telephone relays family problems across distances for others to share the anxiety, when in the past the difficulty would have passed before they could know about it and begin to worry. Americans view athletic competition on television from the other side of the world and watch participants they do not know competing in events they may not understand; yet often they develop instant favorites, especially if their uniform is emblazoned with a symbol of their own country.

Baffling Information

People are sometimes bombarded with more information than they can understand or would even care to know. The weather report takes ten minutes when all the listener may want to know is whether it will rain or not. Financial news may absolutely baffle many of us, but somehow it affects personal bank accounts. Two politicians can argue endlessly over a moral issue, and both may appear to be right. Teachers may teach children content beyond the comprehension of parents, but it sometimes sounds important.

Electronic Transactions

Paychecks can be deposited directly into the bank, loan payments automatically withdrawn, purchases electronically charged, overdrafts approved, and interest deducted without the people involved ever seeing the money. Some people find themselves hopelessly in debt without realizing what happened. They know they are in trouble when the bank balance on their television screen says so, or when they get nasty letters that some computer wrote them.

Lots of People

Commuters get up at six in the morning to sit in traffic jams in order to get to the office by eight. They arrive at home late and grouchy because the traffic reporter in the radio helicopter told everyone to use their route home because of an accident on the freeway. When they arrive, dinner is burned because the children put it in the oven at the 5:15 commercial break as directed, and there was no way to countermand the directive from the car in bumper-to-bumper traffic. A car phone may be a necessity. Some people have it even worse. They get stuck in underground commuter trains because the grid system computer says there are too many trains on the same track because a door got stuck on car 33 on the Red Line.

Work, as we have often said, is becoming more complicated, as reflected in this 1987 news article:

Complexity at Work

Ypsilanti, Mich.—Lavester Frye works at an assembly table eight hours a day building automobile horns, setting a metal plate on a metal dish with one hand, adding a tiny ring with the other.

In the 22 years he has worked at the Ford Motor Co., it never really has mattered that he didn't finish high school. He always has had jobs like this one, jobs that depend more on his hands than his mind.

But Frye has been told that his job will become more complicated. To improve productivity, the company is phasing in an intricate statistical system of quality control.

The news made Frye feel nervous and unprepared, and when he looked at the charts he would be expected to keep under the new system, he was even more troubled by what he saw: decimal points. "A long time ago at school, I had decimals, but it faded out of my mind," he said.

On this factory floor, amidst the assembly lines the huge hulking furnaces and the din of metal on metal, the ability to put a decimal point in the proper place suddenly has become a ticket to a job.

Like thousands of other workers across the country, Frye is experiencing firsthand the transformation of the American workplace in pursuit of competitive advantage. He also sees—and feels, painfully—that, in this race to keep up with other countries, a critical and often missing factor is education. (*Washington Post*, 1987, April 14, p. A1.)[22]

Biological Engineering

Biological scientists are making breakthroughs almost daily. They can make infertile couples fertile, artifically inseminate women, find out when fetuses are defective, correct some defects before or after conception, recommend abortion when risks are high, and in essence engineer the conception, prenatal development, and birth of babies. Some say these discoveries are wonderful, others say they are immoral. Either way, they create choices for prospective parents that did not exist a few years ago.

TV—The "Third Parent"

Television is often called a third parent in contemporary American society—the children's friend, source of values, attractive picture of the world, and fantasy. It tells children that life consists of excitement, violence, personal confrontation, and Rambo-like physical conflicts—but that in the end (after thirty to sixty minutes) problems are solved and goodness prevails. It also shows a world of physical attraction and sexuality, in which few are lonely or neglected and in which life is routinely easy and families supportive. Television has become so powerfully intrusive in the lives of many children and youth that in their minds it has replaced the real world. (See, for example, Stein, 1986.)[23]

Poverty

Much has already been said in this text about poverty in America and its implications for schools and teachers; the main points made earlier that project into the future are repeated here:

- Many schoolchildren are very poor.
- Their numbers are increasing.
- The gap between poor and middle-class children is widening.
- Schools are and will be expected to educate these children out of poverty.
- So far, schools have not been able to do this.

As of 1985, 15.6 percent of American children and 43.1 percent of black American children lived in poverty. In 1987, 46 percent of black American children under age 15 were classified as poor (U.S. Bureau of Census, cited in *Education Week*, 1986, May 14, p. 27.) The figures have not improved since.

Lack of Education

The relationship between poverty and lack of education surfaces all of the time. For example, in 1987 California social-services officials responsible for establishing a new work-training program for unemployed welfare recipients found that 60 percent of the applicants could not read, write, or do the arithmetic necessary for the lowest-level jobs available. Many who had completed high school read below the sixth-grade level. Although jobs were available, these people could not handle them, and the state had not provided the millions of dollars necessary for remedial education (Montague, 1987, May 13).[24]

In a 1986 speech Donna E. Shalala, president of Hunter College of the City University of New York, described the situation this way,

> Walk down any city street or into any public school, visit a shelter for the homeless or the maternity or pediatric ward of any public hospital, and you'll see that poor children are in desperate trouble. They are living on welfare, going without proper medical care, and dropping out of school. They are going hungry—in rural communities as well as on the streets of big cities. And they are experimenting with drugs.

School Dropouts

The facts are tragic . . .

In education, the statistics are staggering. The school dropout rate is 25 percent overall and more than 50 percent for blacks and Hispanics. Of the small number of children who go on to college, many need remedial help to succeed there.

There is no question that children are now by far the most impoverished group in the United States. As Senator Daniel Moynihan has said, "We may be the first society in history of which it can be said that the children are worse off than their parents." Clearly, an article of faith that was at the very foundation of our nation is in grave danger.

We Americans have always believed that each succeeding generation would outreach the one before. . . .

Twenty, thirty, forty years hence we will need our children to work, to be the teachers and the doctors—even the lawyers—for future generations of children, to say nothing of paying the Social Security taxes that will make our retirement possible.

Future Adults

Our destiny as individuals, as families, as a nation is tied to the destiny of children, all of them—black, Hispanic, Asian, and American Indian, as well as white. As educators, we must convince America that all children, rich and poor, deserve an equal opportunity to grow and learn. That is the challenge as we approach the next century. (Shalala, 1986, p. 96)

Something to Think About

A number of educational thinkers question the extent to which schools can and should be expected to enable poor children to overcome the conditions in which they live. They usually say that poverty involves too much that needs to be overcome for the schools to succeed at the task and that other agencies and elements of society must be involved in the effort more than some people think. Some say poverty is endemic to American economic and social conditions and that it will not be overcome without radical changes in the American way of life.

- Do you think schools can and should be expected to play the dominant role in helping poor children overcome the conditions in which they live? If so, how should they do this?
- What should other agencies and other elements of society do for poor children?
- What should *not* be expected of schools in this regard?

Changing Families

Because the changing conditions in American families were described earlier, only a few statistics are noted here as reminders.

- Three out of every five children in elementary school during the 1990s will live with only one parent before reaching age 18.
- Two-thirds of married women with children of school age are in the workforce.
- One-half of all children between ages 5 and 14 change residences at least once in five years.
- The largest age group of poor Americans is children, who are six times more likely to be living below the poverty line than people over sixty-five years of age.
- About 20 percent of all births are to teenagers, most of whom are poor, undereducated, and unmarried.
- Each day in America 40 teenagers give birth to their third child.

In essence, many families in the 1990s and beyond will be unable to fulfill the supportive and educative functions of real or idealized families of older times. Other institutions may try to fill the void and compensate for the neglect. Schools and teachers will continue to be expected to shoulder much of the burden.

Teaching in the Years Ahead—As We See It

The conditions just listed for the 1990s and the next century will pose formidable challenges for schools and teachers. They will require competence and commitment in big doses. But teaching will still provide the satisfactions and rewards that past teachers have enjoyed and will probably supply them more generously. Of course, teaching will be difficult, but teachers will be up to the task.

Educating Future Generations

Nothing will change the fact that children of future generations deserve to be educated at least as well as children of the past. They deserve it in their own right; but besides that, our future national well-being depends on them as effective, educated participants in society. One statistic alone illustrates the point. In 1945, twenty-seven workers supported the American social security system for each retired person who drew from its reserves. In 1995, that ratio will be three workers for every retiree. One of those three workers will be nonwhite, and most will have grown up in poor, unstable family circumstances. America simply cannot afford a large undereducated population.

Of course, it is unrealistic to rely on schools to cure all societal ills. On the other hand, it is only logical to expect schools and teachers to do their part. That is why schools were established. That is why we have teachers.

DO YOU WANT TO BE A TEACHER?

Obviously, you have considered the question of whether you want to be a teacher often—before you ever took this course or began reading this text, during your time in the course, and again now. Of course, you will continue to raise it many times again in the future, especially if you continue toward a teaching career. If you become a teacher, you will then often ask, "Should I continue teaching?"

The Analysis that follows is intended to focus your thinking toward the future and to help you search methodically for an answer. Before you begin that exercise, however, you might want to reflect on what you have learned so far about teaching and schools and compare your presently held ideas with those you had when you first considered teaching as a career.

- Do you see teaching differently from the way you saw it before? If so, in what ways?

- Do these differences mean that a career in teaching would be different than you thought earlier?

- Would these differences make teaching more or less appealing to you?

ANALYSIS

Now that you are about to finish this text, it is time to project ahead, to think about teaching in the next generation. This Analysis section asks you to develop your own description of teaching in the future by doing several things in succession:

1. Imagine a teacher, a school, and a class of students ten years after the year you expect to take your first teaching job. Pick the grade level, type of school, and type of community that you would most likely teach in, but do not be selective in any other way.

   Make the scene realistic based on what you have learned in this course and your other studies. The teacher is not necessarily you. He or she is simply a realistic representation of a teacher for that time, school, class, and community.

2. Write down what you see.

3. Compare what you have written with the Snapshot description that you wrote about yourself at the beginning of this chapter.

4. Ask yourself whether that person from the Snapshot fits into this scene.

SUMMARY

The impact of education reform will continue in teaching and schools for the next generation, but the most significant activity will occur in classrooms and with teachers and students rather than in state legislatures and among policy boards. The continuing reform will include agendas such as (1) back to basics and accountability, (2) greater professionalization of teaching, (3) more effective teaching and schools, (4) more equitable education, and (5) changes in content.

Virtually everyone who understands teaching sees teachers as the most critical variable in the education process. Because of the increasing complexity of teaching, teachers in the future will have to be more competent in more diverse ways. It will be difficult to find enough capable teachers. Attracting qualified minority teachers will be particularly hard.

Deciding where to teach is a personal decision for most teacher candidates and depends on personal preferences and values. Some of the main considerations for most people are region of the country, type of community, and type of school.

Teacher salaries have always been low in comparison to those in other professions, but they have increased in the last few years. Some states have pledged to make teaching more attractive by improving compensation and working conditions.

Teaching in the next generations will be influenced by many professional and societal conditions, including the continued professionalization of teaching, international competition, changing technology, poverty, and the changing nature of the American family.

STUDY QUESTIONS

1. If a high school student who is thinking about becoming a teacher asked you what you think are the positive and negative aspects of teaching, what would you say?

2. In what ways will teaching in the year 2010 be significantly different from today? In what ways will it be the same?

3. Which aspects of today's teachers' jobs do you think most need to be preserved without change in the years ahead?

4. What is the most important reason that you are considering (or might consider) a career in teaching? What is the greatest deterrent to your doing so?

BIBLIOGRAPHY

Because this is the last chapter in this text and because the thrust of the chapter has been on teaching in the next generation, there is no bibliography. Rather, the text authors suggest that you keep up with conditions and circumstances that will affect teaching and schools in the years ahead by reading four types of periodicals:

- a general periodical about teaching and schools, such as *Education Week,*

- a general professional journal on issues that affect teaching and schools, such as *Phi Delta Kappan,*

- a professional journal in your educational area of interest, such as a publication of one of the specialty organizations listed in Chapter 14, and

- a general weekly news magazine, such as *Newsweek.*

NOTES

1. Finn, C. E. (1987). The two new agendas of education reform. *Independent School, 46*(2), 5–13; Pipho, C. (1986). States move reform closer to reality. *Phi Delta Kappan, 68*(4), K1–K8.

2. Some say these changes will assure more competent teachers and that this in turn will produce greater respect. Others, however, say such scrutiny and rigid standards have the opposite effect—they deprofessionalize teaching.

3. Hirsch, E. D. (1987). *Cultural literacy: What every American needs to know.* Boston: Houghton Mifflin; Hirsch, E. D. (1988). Cultural literacy: Let's be specific. *NEA Today, 6*(6), 15–21; Benninga, J. S. (1988). The emerging synthesis in moral education. *Phi Delta Kappan, 69*(6), 415–418; Ryan, K. (1986). The new moral education. *Phi Delta Kappan, 68*(4), 228–233.

4. *The Nation's Report Card.* (1987). Washington, DC: U.S. Department of Education; McLarty, J. (1986, November 5). On making NAEP a national "blueprint" for education policy. *Education Week, 6*(9), 22; Olson, L. (1987, March 25). Bennett panel urges major expansion of NAEP. *Education Week, 6*(26), 1, 8–9; Comments of the Assessment Policy Committee on The Nation's Report Card. (1987, June 24). *Education Week, 6*(39), 22–23; Rothman, R. (1987, June 17). NAEP's policy board endorses redesign plan, with reservations. *Education Week, 6*(38), 6; Chiefs urge changes in NAEP by 1990. (1987, April 1). *Education Week, 6*(27), 7.

5. Shulman, L. S. (1987). Assessment of teaching: An initiative for the profession. *Phi Delta Kappan, 69*(1), 38–44.

6. Rodman, B. (1987, April 29). N. E. A. pursues its plan to establish state boards controlled by teachers. *Education Week, 6*(31), 1, 20; Olson, L., & Rodman, B. (1986, September 10). Teachers' unions vie for professional status, back national board. *Education Week, 6*(1), 12–13; Olson, L., & Rodman, B. (1987, February 18). Thorny issues face planners of board to certify teachers. *Education Week, 6*(21), 1, 28–29.

7. Graham, P. A. (1987). Black teachers: A drastically scarce resource. *Phi Delta Kappan, 68*(8), 598–605; Shalala, D. E. (1986, October 29). It just makes sense to help poor children. *Chronicle of Higher Education, 33*(9), 96. Also see Snyder, T. D. (1987). *Digest of educational statistics, 1987.* Washington, DC: Center for Educational Statistics, Office

of Educational Research and Improvement, U.S. Department of Education; Here they come, ready or not. (1986, May 14). *Education Week, 5*(34), 12–37; Ekstrom, R. B., Goertz, M. E., Polluck, J. M., & Ruck, D. A. (1986). Who drops out of high school and why? Findings from a national study. *Teachers College Record, 87*(3), 356–373.

8. Berliner, D. C. (1986). In pursuit of the expert pedagogue. *Educational Researcher, 15*(7), 5–13; Berliner, D. C. (1985). Laboratory settings and the study of teacher education. *Journal of Teacher Education, 36*(6), 2–8; Wise, A. E. (1986). Three scenarios for the future of teaching. *Phi Delta Kappan, 67*(9), 649–652.

9. Carnegie Task Force on Teaching as a Profession. (1986). *A nation prepared: Teachers for the twenty-first century.* New York: Carnegie Forum on Education and the Economy.

10. Stipp, D. (1986, November 11). Teaching teachers: Schools of education try to assure Johnny a decent instructor. *Wall Street Journal,* p. 1.

11. Csikszentmihalyi, M., & McCormack, J. (1986). The influence of teachers. *Phi Delta Kappan, 67*(6), 415–419; Clark, D. L. (1987). High school seniors react to their teachers and their schools. *Phi Delta Kappan, 68*(7), 503–509.

12. Myers, C. B. (1986, November). "Social studies teacher education in an era of "Haves" and "Have Nots." Paper presented at the annual meeting of the National Council for the Social Studies, New York, November.

13. Olson, L., & Rodman, B. (1987, June 24). Is there a teacher shortage? It's anyone's guess. *Education Week, 6*(30), 1, 14–16; Carnegie Foundation for the Advancement of Education; (1986). Future teachers: Will there be enough good ones? *Change, 18*(5), 27–30; Feistritzer, C. E. (1987, February 17). There's no shortage of good teachers. *Wall Street Journal,* p. 34.

14. Bickers, P. M. (1987). Indicators of future school enrollments. Arlington, VA: Educational Research Service.

15. Rist, M. C. (1986). The baby boomlet has begun, but it's more (and less) than you bargained for. *School Boards Association Journal, 173*(4), 35–40; Montague, W. (1987, June 3). Districts scramble to cope with building needs. *Education Week, 6*(36), 1, 19–20.

16. Carnegie Foundation for the Advancement of Teaching. (1988a, July/August). The rise and fall of education as a major. *Change, 20*(4), 27–32; Berger J. (1988, May 6). Allure of teaching reviving: Education school rolls surge. *New York Times,* p. A1; Kane, P. R. (1987). Young teachers: Who comes? Who stays? Who leaves? *Independent School, 46*(3), 43–46; Rothman, R. (1987, January 14). More college freshmen note interest in teaching as career. *Education Week, 6*(16), 12, 18.

17. Astin, A. W.; Green, K. C., & Korn, W. S. (1987). *The American freshman: Twenty year trends, 1966–1985.* Los Angeles: Cooperative Educational Research Program, The Higher Education Research Institute, UCLA; Astin, A. W., Green, K. C., Korn, W. S., Schalit, M., & Berz, E. R. (1988). *The American freshman: National norms for fall 1988.* Los Angeles: Cooperative Institutional Research Program, The Higher Education Research Institute, UCLA and similar reports for 1986 and 1987; Rothman, R. (1987, November 5). Raise status of teaching, colleges told. *Education Week, 6*(9), 7; also see Harbaugh, M. (1985). Who will teach the class of 2000? *Instructor, 95*(2), 31–35; Kemper, R. E., & Mangieri, J. N. (1987). America's future teaching force: Predictions and recommendations. *Phi Delta Kappan, 68*(5), 393–395; Woodring, P. (1987). Too bright to be a teacher? *Phi Delta Kappan, 68*(9), 617–618.

18. Darling-Hammond, L., & Berry, B. (1988, March). The evolution of teacher policy. RAND; Rodman, B. (1988, March 9). Georgia, N. E. A. settle suit on teacher testing. *Education Week, 7*(24), 1, 17.

19. Darling-Hammond, L. (1987). The educational reform dilemma. *Basic Education, 31*(6), 2–5.
20. Rodman, B. (1988, February 3); The fiercest competition. *Education Week, 7*(19), 1, 13.
21. *Education Week, 9*(1), 2; Carnegie Foundation for the Advancement of Education. (1988b). *The condition of teaching; A state-by-state analysis, 1988.* Princeton, NJ: Carnegie; Sedlak, M. and Schlossman, S. (1986). *Who will teach?* RAND; National Education Association. (1986). *Status of the American public school teacher: 1985–86.* Washington, DC: National Education Association; The forgotten message: Excellence costs. (1988, April). *NEA Today,* pp. 4–5; *NEA Today* (1989, April); for more up-to-date statistics also see recent issues of *Education Daily*.
22. *Washington Post.* (1987, April 14).
23. Stein, B. (1986). This is not your life: Television as the third parent. *Public Opinion, 9,* 41–42.
24. Montague, W. (1987, May 13). "Workfare" applicants said to lack skills. *Education Week, 6*(33), 5.

APPENDIX

The Teacher-Student Interaction Observation System

An Introduction to Teaching and Schools **599**

This appendix consists of a second classroom observation system, which is intended for use by students who have completed Chapter 2. It supplies an additional analytical way of looking at classroom instruction and reinforces ideas and skills covered in the chapter. It is organized just like the Student On-Task/Off-Task System in Chapter 2 and can be pursued independently from class instruction. The Analysis section of the material provides an opportunity for practicing the use of the system, and after you have completed it, you should be able to use the system when observing in real classrooms.

The Teacher-Student Interaction Observation System supplies data on the oral interaction, or verbal exchange, between the teacher and individual students. It lists the times a teacher talks to each student and the form of that communication—statement, question, praise, reprimand, and so forth. The form on which the observer records the data is called the Teacher-Student Interaction Seating Chart. As with the off-task instrument, it is an observer-designed seating chart appropriate to the arrangement of the class being observed. If the class is organized with traditional rows of seats and the teacher plans to talk with the whole group at once, the chart might look like Figure A-1.

EXPLANATION

The purpose of the Teacher-Student Interaction System is to record each time the teacher speaks to individual students. The data are collected continuously throughout a class period. The instrument is intended to be used primarily in classes in which there is a pattern of teacher-student verbal interaction, such as direct instruction, recitation, drill, and teacher-led discussion, rather than when students are studying individually, reading silently, watching a film, or taking a test. When teacher comments are directed to the class as a whole, the observer notes the symbols in the teacher box.

DIRECTIONS

1. Prepare for the observation by developing a boxlike seating chart similar to that in Figure A-1. The boxes need to be large enough for several entries to be made in each.

2. Enter the teacher's name, school, date, and the beginning time of the observation on the form.

3. As soon as the teacher begins the lesson, record each teacher question or statement. Note particularly those that are directed to a specific student. Record continuously until the end of the lesson or until you have observed for the length of time you had planned. Record each continuous teacher-student interaction in a single line in that student's box, and start a new line if the teacher returns to that student later.

4. Record the time when you stop.

5. Note that when the teacher directs a student to respond rather than asking him or her a question, the comment is still recorded as a question because its purpose is to prompt a student answer. (See "Allen, take Number 1," in the first teacher comment in the Analysis that follows.)

TEACHER-STUDENT INTERACTION SEATING CHART

Teacher: _____ School: _____

Date: _____ Time: _____ to _____
                                        (beginning)   (end)

(front of classroom)

Teacher

[Seating chart grid with 20 empty boxes arranged in 5 rows of 4]

CODES:

- ? = Asks a direction question
- ⓘ = Asks an open-ended question
- ⸮ = Checks for understanding
- ✓ = Makes a general or social comment or response
- + = Praises or supports a response
- C = Corrects a response
- G = Corrects and guides a response
- − = Reprimands behavior
- * = Student initiated comment

Figure A–1. Teacher-student interaction seating chart. (Source: Jane Stallings, Houston Center for Effective Teaching, University of Houston.)

An example of a completed observer seating chart appears in Figure A-2.

DATA RECORDED AND CODES

? Teacher asks a student a direct question or directs the student to respond: "Sam, What is the spelling of the word 'voyage'?" "Frankie, spell #4."

- ⑦ Teacher asks a student an open-ended, thought-provoking question: "Karen, what do you think might happen if the girl in the story does that?"
- ✓? Teacher checks for understanding: "Maria, you said, 'photosynthesis.' Tell us in your words, Maria, what photosynthesis means."
- ✓ Teacher makes a social comment or response: "Tracy, your hair looks nice today."
- + Teacher praises or supports a response: "Very good, José; 'forty-two' is the correct answer."
- C Teacher corrects a student's response: "That is not correct, Jack. The correct answer is 'Mark Twain.'"
- G Teacher corrects *and guides* a response: "Donna, that is close. Try spelling the word one letter at a time, according to how it sounds, and see if you can figure it out."
- − Teacher reprimands behavior: "Mary, be quiet."
- * Student initiates a comment or raises a question when he or she has *not* been called on.

ANALYZING THE TEACHER-STUDENT INTERACTION SEATING CHART DATA

In Figure A-2, you will notice that the number and types of comments that the teacher made to each student are recorded. The sequence of interaction with each student is also discernible.

It is also clear that several elements of teacher-student interaction are not recorded. For example, the chart does not report the overall sequence of the teacher's comments. The teacher might have talked with one student five times in successtion or might have interspersed those five comments with interactions with other students. The chart does not indicate how long each teacher comment was; nor does it note how long the pauses between comments were. The chart does not report when students were off task, and it contains no information about nonverbal teacher-student interaction.

With the data that are reported, however, the observer can determine the following:

1. how many students the teacher spoke to,
2. how many times the teacher addressed particular students,
3. the types of teacher communication with each student,
4. the frequency of each type of communication, and
5. whether the place where students sat reflects a pattern in the interaction.

The data in Figure A-2 can be summarized by completing a summary chart like the one shown in Figure A-3. To do this for the information recorded on the seating chart in Figure A-2, complete the summary sheet in Figure A-3.

Appendix

TEACHER-STUDENT INTERACTION SEATING CHART

Teacher: __Mr. Smith__   School: __Fall-Hamilton__

Date: __March__   Time: __2:15__ (beginning) to __2:50__ (end)

(front of classroom)

		Teacher ✓✓✓		
Tracy ✓ ?G+	Marla ?+ ?+	Betty ⊙+ ?+ ? ?G+	Joe ✓ ?+	
Jose ⊙?+ ?+	Susan ⊙?+ ?+?G+ *	Robert * ?C ✓	Dora ⊙?G ?+	
Ursula --	Daniel ⊙G+ ?C	Ellen ? ?⊙+ ?+	Bill ?GC?+	
Sharon -- --	Jack ?+	Lee ?C?+ --	Mary	
Thomas	Sarah	Andrew	Calvin	

CODES:

- ? = Asks a direction question
- ⊙ = Asks an open-ended question
- ? = Checks for understanding
- ✓ = Makes a general or social comment or response
- + = Praises or supports a response
- C = Corrects a response
- G = Corrects and guides a response
- – = Reprimands behavior
- * = Student initiated comment

Figure A–2. Partially completed teacher-student interaction seating chart. (Source: Jane Stallings, Houston Center for Effective Teaching, University of Houston.)

After you have completed the summary chart, answer the following questions:

- Which students did the teacher speak to most often? Where were they sitting?
- Which students did the teacher speak to least often? Where were they sitting?

```
              Summary Sheet
        Teacher - Student Interaction

How many students were in the class? _____
How many students were spoken to? _____
Where was the student or students most spoken to sitting? _____
Where were the students not spoken to sitting? _____

Number of direct questions asked _____
Number of open-ended questions asked _____
Number of checks for understanding _____
Number of teacher non-questioning comments _____
Number of praises _____
Number of corrections _____
Number of guides _____
Number of reprimands _____
Number of student-initiated comments _____

Were there any patterns to the interaction? _____  If so, what were they?
```

Figure A–3. Teacher-Student Interaction Summary Chart. (Source: Jane Stallings, Houston Center for Effective Teaching, University of Houston.)

- Which students did the teacher reprimand? Where were they sitting?
- What was the ratio between numbers of direct questions, open-ended questions, and checks for understanding?

As we pointed out earlier, the analysis of teacher classroom behavior on the basis of inadequate data collected by inexperienced observers is usually inaccurate and often unfair. However, in order to illustrate how the above data could be used, you will be asked to speculate on the information gathered above by answering several questions. Suppose that you are an experienced classroom observer with significant background experience to draw on and that you have observed a teacher a number of times and have consistently recorded data such as those on the seating chart in Figure A-2, and on the summary sheet in Figure A-3.

- What significant findings do you infer from these data?
- What explanation would you offer for the findings and patterns you see?
- What recommendations would you make to the teacher?

ANALYSIS

Now that you have learned about the Teacher-Student Interaction Observation System, analyze the teacher-student interaction from the transcript printed below. The transcript reports all teacher-student oral interactions for ten minutes of a teacher-led, whole-class discussion involving the same English teacher and students described in the Analysis in Chapter 2. The time is now two days later.

1. Make a Teacher-Student Interaction Seating Chart as in Figure A-1. The students are seated as they were for the Analysis in Chapter 2. You will need to refer to this section to make an accurate seating chart.
2. Fill in the boxes of the seating chart based on the transcript.
3. Make and complete a summary chart as in Figure A-3.
4. Respond to the questions.

INTERACTION TRANSCRIPT

Teacher: Let's begin the grammar assignment I just handed you. As I call on you, please read the adverb phrase you find in each sentence. Allen, take Number 1.
Allen: Beside the base.
Teacher: Good. How do you know that phrase is an adverb and not an adjective?
Allen: It tells where the player stood.
Teacher: So it would modify which word?
Allen: Stood.
Teacher: Yes. Hope, take Number 2.
Hope: With a spin.
Teacher: How do you know *with a spin* functions adverbially?
Hope: Because it tells how he threw the ball.
Teacher: And it would modify what word?
Hope: Threw.
Teacher: Right. Charlie, do the next one.
Charlie: For the winning point.
Teacher: Good. And how would you prove that phrase is an adverb?
Charlie: It is an adverb because it tells—uh—how?
Teacher: Think again. Efram, please put all four of your chair legs on the floor.
Charlie: Well, I think it modifies *batted,* and I guess it tells why.
Teacher: Yes. Felicia, Number 4.
Felicia: In the red hat.
Teacher: Oops. I'll agree that's a prepositional phrase, but is it adverbial? Look again.
Felicia: With his left hand.
Teacher: Good. And how do you know that is an adverbial phrase?
Felicia: [Stares at paper but makes no response.]
Teacher: Louise, can you explain it?
Louise: It has to be adverbial because it tells how he threw the ball.
Teacher: Exactly. Now look at *in the red hat.* Who can explain that phrase? Allen?
Allen: It's an adjective phrase pointing out which boy.
Teacher: You're so right. Class, continue working on this sheet for the

next few minutes. Raise your hand if you need help.

[Students work as Ms. Lloyd walks from desk to desk, looks over shoulders, and comments to students.]

Teacher: Patty, let's make a deal. The classroom is really not the place for personal grooming. If you won't comb your hair in class, I won't brush my teeth here. Okay? [Patty giggles and puts her comb away, and the teacher moves on.] Good work, Quillen. Rosa, your penmanship is improving, and I'm pleased with your efforts. Sam, look again at Number 8. Tara, please put your shoes back on.

Nan: I need help with Number 8.

Teacher: Where are the subject and the verb? [Nan points to them.] Yes, good. Now *think*. Does any phrase tell how, when, where, or why?

Nan: This one here? [Points again.]

Teacher: Yes, you've got it.

Hope: I need help telling adjective and adverb phrases apart.

Teacher: Hope, you must look at what the phrases *do* in the sentences; that determines what they are. What can an adverb do?

Hope: An adverb can tell *how, when, where, why,* and *to what extent.*

Teacher: You're right. And if a prepositional phrase does any of those, then it is an adverbial phrase. Okay? [Nan nods.] Efram, the number of chair legs touching the floor should always be four. [Efram shrugs and sits up straight.]

Teacher: All right. Is everyone finished through Number 8? [All students nod.] Good. Put this sheet in your folder and finish it for homework tonight. [All students comply.] Now let's change gears and focus on last night's literature assignment. What words or phrases come to mind when you hear the name *Rip Van Winkle?* Gary?

Gary: I guess *a long sleep* and also *henpecked.*

Teacher: Why do you say *henpecked?*

Gary: Because Dame Van Winkle was always fussing at him.

Diana: The word *lazy* comes to my mind, and I think his wife had good reason to nag!

Teacher: How so?

Diana: Well, if I had a husband who never worked or helped around the house but went around playing with kids and fixing broken fences for other women, you can bet I'd say something!

Teacher: You definitely have a point there. Let's go back to the idea of a long sleep. Just suppose you went to sleep tonight and woke up twenty years later. What are some things you think really might be different.

Efram: You can bet the cars would sure be different.

Teacher: How, so, Efram?

Efram: Well, probably they'd use some fuel besides gasoline.

Teacher: Can you think of any general effect that might have on life?

Efram: Hmmm. Well, maybe it wouldn't pollute the air so much, and

	people could breathe better in the cities.
Teacher:	That's an interesting idea.
Sam:	In twenty years there would be a whole lot more people.
Teacher:	Can you think of any ways that might affect life in general?
Sam:	You'd probably have to stand in lines longer at Disney World.
Teacher:	Could well be. Patty, this is not the place to file your nails. [Patty returns the file to her purse.]
Mary:	I think movies and television would be different, probably all 3-D and maybe with smells, too.
Teacher:	Interesting.
Quillen:	Everything would be computerized and then some.
Teacher:	How might that make life different from what we know now?
Quillen:	Well, it might save a lot of time on things. Maybe there would even be a computerized homework machine. Or maybe a computerized teacher. Ms. Lloyd, do you think you could be replaced by a computer?
Teacher:	Not this year.

Glossary

Academic discipline. A category of knowledge that has an own identified conceptual focus and method of inquiry.

Academic engaged rate. The ratio between the amount of time students are actually engaged in academic learning tasks and the total time they are in class.

Academic learning time. The time in class during which students are actively engaged in academic tasks and are succeeding at a high rate.

Accommodation. The process of changing one's patterns of thinking in order to incorporate newly learned information and ideas.

Accountability. Being held responsible for one's actions and the results of those actions.

Accountability techniques. Teaching techniques that hold students responsible for their learning.

Act of teaching. A specialized use in this text to mean the three-part process of planning, teaching, and evaluating lessons.

Active teaching. Teaching during which the teacher is actively interacting with students who are engaged in learning tasks.

Activities curriculum. A curriculum arranged around the types of activities planned for the students and in which the content coverage is often quite flexible.

Adaptation. Changing one's ideas and/or behavior as a result of interacting with the environment.

Adaptive behavior. Learned behavior derived from accommodating to one's environment.

Affective domain. The area of educational objectives that focuses on values, feelings, and sensitivities.

Affective learning. The learning of values, feelings, and sensitivities, as opposed to cognitive learning.

Age-grouped societies. Subgroups within broader society divided primarily by age.

Age of reason. A time in the development of Western education that roughly parallels the eighteenth century, characterized by a strong interest in science and empirical investigation; also called The Enlightenment.

Alerting of students. Teacher techniques of classroom presentation and questioning that keep students involved in learning tasks.

"All deliberate speed." An order of the United States Supreme Court that schools be desegregated in a prompt and timely manner.

Allocated time. The time provided in class for students to be engaged in learning tasks.

Analytical observation. The purposeful viewing of a situation with particular attention to its component parts and essential features.

Analyzing values. A specific set of teaching strategies that are used to teach students to think about their own and others' values.

Anticipatory set. Something a teacher does at the start of a lesson that helps students develop "mental sets" about the instruction to follow, one of the seven elements of a lesson in the Instructional Theory into Practice model of instruction.

Assertive discipline. A specific counseling-based approach to behavior control that includes guides for teachers to follow as they formulate their personal discipline plan.

Assimilation. The process of integrating newly formed ideas with one's current patterns of thinking; the integration of cultural traits as different cultural groups intermix.

Association theory. Theory about behavior and memory that says that learning occurs because the mind makes associations, or mental connections, between certain items and events.

At-risk. A condition under which a person, family, nation, or other entity is particularly vulnerable.

Authenticity. The quality of being one's own person; genuine, reliable.

Authentic people. Those who believe in their own freedom to think and act, utilize their own ideas, and accept their own responsibility.

Axiology. The study of the nature of values; a branch of philosophy.

Barriers. Things that impede the flow of communication.

Baseline behavior. The behavior measured or assessed before learning takes place or before an experiment starts.

Basic education. A view of education that emphasizes the study of basic academic subjects such as English, history, mathematics, science; stresses literacy and the study of great literary works.

Basics. Subjects that many consider essential, usually including reading, writing, English, mathematics, science, and social studies.

Behavior disorder. A condition in which students exhibit problem behavior.

Behavior modification. The use of conditioning to change behavior.

Behavior theory. Theory that says that behavior is learned and extrinsically influenced.

Behavioral objectives. The anticipated result or product of instruction, usually stated in terms of the behaviors that teachers expect students to be able to exhibit as a result of instruction; also called educational objectives and instructional objectives.

Behavioral research. Investigations that focus on analyzing how and why people and groups act as they do.

Behaviorism. The belief that all behavior is caused and, therefore, predictable and susceptible to modification.

Belief. The acceptance of an idea or proposition as true or that a situation or object actually exists.

Brisk classroom pace. An instructional tempo that maintains momentum and student motivation and helps students stay on task.

Broad-field curriculum. A type of subject-centered curriculum arranged around broad, integrated subject areas such as social studies and language arts.

Career ladder. A system of job classification that contains successively higher levels of responsibility and salary through which employees, such as teachers, can advance by means of evaluation, training, and/or experience.

Carriers. Individuals in a tribe or organization who tell the stories and legends and pass on the traditions.

Chapter I. An abbreviated reference to Chapter I of the Education Consolidation and Improvement Act of 1981, which provides federal government aid to programs for low-income families.

Checking for understanding. A technique of instruction in which the teacher monitors student responses and practices to determine if and how well they understand, rather than just recall, the ideas to be learned; often done through questioning and written assignments; one of the seven elements of a lesson in the Instructional Theory into Practice model of instruction.

Citizenship education. A purpose of schooling that gives students the knowledge, skills, and values to be effective political, economic, and social participants in society.

Class-level objectives. Objectives established for instruction at particular grade levels, often set for each subject taught.

Classification. A group or category; the act of grouping or categorizing.

Classifying. Organizing things into categories and assigning labels to each category.

Classroom climate. The physical, psychological, social, and interpersonal atmosphere of a classroom.

Classroom culture. The values, belief systems, and norms present in a classroom.

Classroom ecology. The physical aspects of a classroom environment.

Classroom effectiveness. The degree to which classroom conditions enhance effective teaching and learning.

Classroom milieu. The interpersonal atmosphere, or "feeling" aspect, of a classroom environment.

Classroom structures. The procedures, routines, and rules of a classroom as established by the teacher's management plan.

Classroom verbal interaction. Interaction in a classroom through the use of words.

Cognition. The process of knowing, learning, and/or thinking.

Cognitive. Of or pertaining to the processes of knowing, thinking, or learning.

Cognitive behavior modification systems. An approach to behavior change, based on behavior theory and cognition, that emphasize the students' role in their own behavior change.

Cognitive domain. The area of educational objectives that focuses on information, ideas, and thinking.

Cognitive learning. The learning of information, ideas, and thinking skills, as opposed to affective learning.

Cognitive research. Investigations into how people know and learn, often with a particular focus on thinking.

Cognitive theory. Learning theory that says learning is a process of information acquisition that includes perceiving, encoding, and retrieving from memory; also called information processing theory.

Common schools. *Either* schools of American colonial times established by towns to provide rudimentary education to the town's children *or* schools of the nineteenth century established through state authorization and tax supported.

Communication apprehension. Anxiousness or fearfulness about participating in oral communication.

Communication overload. A phenomenon in which students are confused because too much is being communicated at a given time.

Compensatory education. Educational efforts intended to make up for social, economic, and educational deficiencies in students' out-of-school lives.

Concept. A category or representation into which or under which specifics are grouped.

Conceptualizing. A thinking process that involves categorizing things or putting things into groups, also referred to as developing concepts.

Continuous progress. A characteristic of instruction that enables large numbers of students to progress continuously with high rates of success and a minimum of confusion.

Conversational dance. Communication and social interactions between infants and caretakers that prompt the beginnings of social understanding; also referred to as turntaking.

Cooperative Learning. A method of instruction that uses a specific type of classroom group organization to foster student peer interaction, cooperation, and understanding.

Coping behavior. Actions whereby individuals deal with difficulties, stress, and conflict without relinquishing their goals.

Core curriculum. A curriculum organization that combines both subject-centered and student-centered characteristics; one that is arranged around broad, integrated fields as well as student needs, interests, and experiences.

Courtier. One in attendance at the court of a prince or king.

Criterion tests. Assessments that compare scores or performances against an identified standard.

Cultural expectations. What a culture values and the behaviors that are expected of its members.

Cultural literacy. The possession of a common set of knowledge about one's culture, which advocates such as E. B. Hirsch suggest should be known by all who expect to function competently in contemporary society.

Cultural pluralism. The recognition of diverse cultural, language, and ethnic groups and heritages in American society.

Culture. The patterns of behavior, values, beliefs, traditions, and norms that characterize a group.

Curriculum. A plan of instruction for a school system, school, or area of subject matter; the design of what, when, and how students should be taught; a plan of what content should be taught at which grade levels.

Curriculum framework. A document that outlines the plan of instruction for a school system, school, or area of subject matter.

Cycle of poverty. The phenomenon that children who grow up in poverty conditions tend to accept poverty as a permanent way of life and continue to live under similar circumstances as adults.

Decentering. The ability to see something from more than one perspective, particularly from perspectives other than one's personal point of view.

Decoding. Translating a coded message into an uncoded one or into one that is more readily interpretable.

De facto segregation. The forced separation of people because of conditions and practices other than those enacted by law.

De jure segregation. The forced separation of people by legislation and other legal means.

Denominational schools. Schools sponsored by churches, prevalent during American colonial times and the early nineteenth century.

Diagnostic assessments. Tests intended to assess student prior knowledge and abilities so that appropriate instruction can be provided.

Dialectical theory. A concept of development that focuses on the interaction between individuals and their environment.

Differential instruction. Teaching that accommodates differences among individual learners.

Discipline-based curriculum. *See* separate-subjects curriculum.

Due process of law. Legal procedures designed to assure that people are treated fairly in terms of the law.

Educational equity. The goal that schools provide an equally high-quality education for every student.

Educational objectives. The anticipated result or product of instruction, usually stated in terms of the behaviors that teachers expect students to be able to exhibit as a result of instruction; also called behavioral objectives and instructional objectives.

Educational outcome. The result or product of instruction, usually stated in terms of what students learn.

Egocentrism. Self-centeredness.

Emblems. Nonverbal communication actions that have direct verbal translations and are often used instead of spoken words.

Emotionality. Possessing and/or exhibiting emotion.

Emotionally disturbed. An emotional state or condition outside of the normal range.

Engaged time. Time during which students are actually involved in purposeful classroom activity.

Enlightenment. A time in the development of Western education that roughly parallels the eighteenth century, characterized by a strong interest in science and empirical investigation; also called the Age of Reason.

Enrichments. Supplemental instructional experiences provided for students beyond that offered normally to enable them to study more comprehensively or in greater depth.

Epistemology. The study of the nature of knowledge; a branch of philosophy.

Equal protection before the law. A right guaranteed in the fourteenth amendment to the U.S. Constitution that protects individuals from biased or discriminatory treatment.

Equality of input. The idea of equity in education that stresses equal amounts and quality of school services for all students.

Equality of results. The idea of equity in education that stresses the providing of different amounts and quality of school services in order to enable students with different abilities and backgrounds to learn as much as all students in general.

Essentialism. The belief that truth and knowledge consist of an identifiable and indispensable common core of information and ideas.

Ethnographic research. Investigations that study people, groups, or cultures primarily though observation and the analysis of descriptive data.

Ethnography. The study of people, groups, or cultures primarily through observation and analysis of descriptive data.

Ethos. The fundamental characteristics, spirit, or "feel" of a culture or group that informs its beliefs, customs, and practices.

Ethos of achievement. An underlying sentiment or attitude of a school or classroom that promotes accomplishment.

Ethos of a school. An underlying sentiment of a school that is built upon the school's values, customs, and practices.

Evangelicalism. The belief that truth and knowledge rest on the Christian gospels and their teachings.

Excellence in education. The goal that schools provide the best possible education for each individual student.

External motivation. The stimulation of student learning that comes from the offering of rewards or threats of penalties from outside the students themselves.

Existentialism. The belief that what is true and real is tied to personal existence rather than abstract principles, and that individuals are totally free to act and are responsible for their actions.

Experimentalism. The belief that experience and scientific experimentation are adequate sources of knowledge.

Exploring feelings. A specific set of teaching strategies that are used to teach students to think about their own and others' feelings.

Feelings. Internal emotional and moral sensations that people experience as they respond to others, to events, and to circumstances.

Filtering. The process of selective listening that impedes communication.

Fixed-interval schedule of reward. A reward schedule in which the reward occurs after determined and consistent periods of time or numbers of responses.

"Flat profession." A characterization of the teaching profession as being nonhierarchical; that is, not having novice, experienced, and expert levels as many other professions; a view that virtually all teachers are comparably knowledgeable and skilled.

Follow Through Project. A federal government program intended to help high-risk children maintain academic achievement gains through grades K–3, intended primarily to extend support provided for younger children by Head Start.

Formal talk. Classroom discourse that is associated, at least generally, with instruction.

"Free appropriate public education." A stipulation incorporated into Public Law 94–142 and other legislation that requires schools to educate handicapped children and youth on the same basis as they do nonhandicapped children.

Fused curriculum. Similar to a broad-fields curriculum but with the subject matter divisions even less noticeable; also called an integrated curriculum.

Futurism. The belief that individuals need to prepare intellectually and emotionally to live in a somewhat unknown world of the future.

Gender-role expectations. The belief or assumption that men and women possess or follow expected values, abilities, and roles.

Generalization. Valid statements of relationship among concepts; a general conclusion.

Gestalt. The idea that a whole is more than a mere sum of its independent parts.

Gestalt psychology. The line of thinking within psychology that says that experience consists of integrated structures or patterns that are more than the sum of their individual elements, and that organisms react to situations as a whole rather than to their specific elements.

Gifted. Possessing unusually high levels of ability.

Guided practice. Student use of new ideas or practice of recently learned skills under the direct supervision of the teacher; one of the seven elements of a lesson in the Instructional Theory into Practice model of instruction.

Handicapped. Possessing an impairment that limits one's activities.

Heroes and heroines. Prominent members of a tribe or organization that embody the essential character of the group.

Hidden curriculum. What students learn from the school environment other than the content intentionally planned for them.

Hornbook. A type of primer used in American colonial schools, consisting of a sheet of parchment mounted on a wooden board and covered with a thin transparent horn, often containing the alphabet and other information to be learned.

Humanistic curriculum. A curriculum that emphasizes the development of student self-concepts, personal growth, and expression.

Hypothesize. To make a thoughtful prediction about something based on prior knowledge and relevant generalizations.

Hypothetical thinking. Thinking that considers possibilities rather than that tied to established facts.

Idea of progress. A belief characteristic of Enlightenment thinking that the world can be made better through the use of reason and scientific investigation.

Idealism. The belief that what is true or real is a matter of perceptions that are based on ideas of the mind rather than on physical objects.

Idealist. One who believes that reality consists of perceptions of the mind rather than physical objects.

Ideals. Universal ideas that embody perfection.

Identity seeking behavior. Behavior associated with a developing sense of potency, independence, and experimentation; usually seen in adolescents.

Illustrators. Nonverbal communication actions used to amplify a spoken message.

Independent practice. Student application and practice of what has been learned without close teacher supervision; one of the seven elements of a lesson in the Instructional Theory into Practice model of instruction.

Individual education plan. A written plan of instruction designed to meet the needs of an individual student and to accommodate his or her specific abilities.

Incentives. The offering of rewards to students by the teacher to encourage learning or good student behavior.

Influences on planning. Factors that affect teachers' thinking about the lessons they plan and how they plan them.

Informal players. Individuals in a tribe or organization who preserve tradition and transmit the group's history and reminiscence; at times, informal players counterbalance the power of the chief.

Information processing theory. *See* cognitive theory.

Input. Supplying information and ideas for students to learn, such as through lecture or assigned reading.

Input-output research. Investigations that compare data at the beginning of a process with data at the end of the process, for example, how well students can perform addition at the start of the school year and at the end of the year.

Insight. An apparent sudden and unexplained realization or clear understanding of something.

Instructional objectives. The anticipated result or product of instruction, usually stated in terms of the behaviors that teachers expect students to be able to exhibit as a result of instruction; also called behavioral objectives and educational objectives.

Instrumentalism. The belief that the mind and ideas are instruments to be used by individuals to plan actions and to adjust to their environment.

Integrated curriculum. Similar to a broad-fields curriculum but with the subject matter divisions even less noticeable; also called a fused curriculum.

Intellectually gifted. Either an intellectual ability reflected in scores of over 145 on the Stanford-Binet or WISC-R intelligence tests, or intellectual ability well above the norm.

Intermittent ratio schedule of reward. A reward schedule in which the reward occurs randomly.

Interventions. Techniques that teachers use to stop or correct student misbehavior.

Intrinsic motivation. The stimulation of student learning that comes from personal needs or internal drives, such as enjoyment of learning and a sense of satisfaction or the belief that the learning is valuable.

Kinesics. The study of body language as forms of nonverbal communication, including posture, movement, gestures, facial expressions, and eye behavior.

Knowledge base of education. The ideas and information about teaching and schools that make up the core of what professional educators need to know to understand their field.

Latch-key children. Children who arrive home from school to a house without an adult present and who, therefore, carry their own house key.

Law of effect. Principle within association theory that says intellectual associations are strengthened through success and rewards but not weakened through negative consequences.

Law of scattered effect. Principle within association theory that says behaviors that are similar, although not exactly the same, to behaviors followed by a reward also tend to be learned.

Leap of faith. A way of discovering meaning or God that relys on a belief that transcends reason and that is not provable intellectually.

Learned helplessness. A condition in which individuals come to believe they cannot succeed, usually a result of persistent failure.

Learning disability. A condition that makes learning more difficult than would normally be expected.

Learning theory. A set of assumptions or generalizations about the nature of learning that are supported by philosophical and scientific principles and that suggest the direction of further investigation about how learning takes place.

"Least restrictive environment." A belief and legal stipulation that handicapped students be educated in classes and other instructional settings as close to those provided for nonhandicapped students, as their handicapping condition will allow.

Lesson plans. Teacher's plans about how they will provide instruction for specific classes on particular days, usually involving step-by-step directions for a period or particular length of time.

Levels of abstraction. The successive layering of facts, concepts, and generalizations from specific facts to the broadest of generalizations.

Liberal arts. Subjects or branches of learning that served as the foci of education during the Middle Ages; grammar, logic, rhetoric, arithmetic, geometry, music, and astronomy.

Longitudinal study. A study that follows the subjects for an extended period of time.

Mainstreaming. The process of integrating students with handicaps into programs and classes with nonhandicapped peers.

Maintenance bilingual program. Instruction provided in a non-English-speaking student's native language with the purpose of helping the student retain the native language as he or she also learns English.

Manipulated nonverbal communication. Intentional nonverbal communication.

Marxism. The belief that reality is material and that social classes have struggled over time to control the means of production.

Masking. Sending false or inaccurate communications by verbal or nonverbal means.

Mastery Learning. A structured approach to instruction that enables all students to learn the material intended through the completion of designed learning tasks, flexible allotments of time, and frequent assessment and reteaching.

Master teacher. An experienced teacher whose classroom performance is considered to be an example others should follow.

Materialist. One who is more concerned with material things than with spiritual, intellectual, or cultural values.

Mental images. A mental picture of what a situation that has not yet been confronted would be like, such as how a lesson that is being planned will actually occur.

Mental linkages. The intellectual connecting of new ideas to previously learned knowledge and past experience.

Mentally retarded. Either an intellectual ability reflected in scores of under 70 on the Stanford-Binet or WISC-R intelligence tests or intellectual ability well below the norm.

Metacognition. Thinking about how one thinks.

Metaphysical. That which deals with the nature of reality.

Metaphysics. The study of the nature of reality; a branch of philosophy.

Middle schools. Schools designed for teaching adolescents, usually for grades five or six through seven or eight, typically organized around interdisciplinary teams of teachers with flexible schedules so that teachers can maintain close contact with individual students.

Moral development. The idea that as people grow and learn they pass through stages associated with what they believe is right, good, and just.

Mnemonic. Having to do with intellectual associations that learners use to memorize or remember information, such as familiar words, letter patterns, sayings, and jingles.

Modeling. Demonstrating or acting as one wants others to act; providing examples of ideas, processes, or skills that students are to learn; one of the seven elements of a lesson in the Instrumental Theory into Practice model of instruction.

Models of instruction. Particular approaches to teaching that are based on specific learning theories and intended to accomplish selected learning goals.

Motivation. The stimulation and sustaining of action.

Multicultural education. Instruction that recognizes cultural differences and the contribution of different ethnic, cultural, language, and social groups and heritages in American society.

Natural laws. Assumed principles that govern the way the universe, including humans, operates.

"Noise." A special use of this term to mean any sensory distraction (not only sound) that impedes communication.

Nonverbal communication. Communication without the use of words.

Norm of autonomy and equality. A value generally found among teachers that assumes that individual teachers are free to teach as their personal professional judgment suggests and that one teacher's professional judgment is as good as another's.

Normal schools. Schools for the training of teachers.

Normative development. Development consistent with normal expectations.

Object lesson. A method of teaching that develops lessons around objects with which the students have direct contact.

Observation system. A specific approach or set of techniques used to view a situation for the purpose of collecting valid data about that situation.

Off-task rate. The ratio between the number of times students are off task compared to the number of times they could have been off task.

On-task behavior. Student behavior that is consistent with that which the teacher expects.

Open curriculum. A curriculum that emphasizes student self-development and is especially flexible so that teachers can fit the content to student needs and interests.

Operant behavior. Principle within behavior theory that says behavior is learned because of the consequences of actions rather than because of the stimuli that elicit them.

Oral communication. Transmitting information through language.

Organizational style. The way different people arrange their thinking about tasks they face as well as the various elements of the task in order to complete the task or solve a problem.

Optimal error rate. The ratio between correct and incorrect student responses that leads to the greatest student achievement.

Ordering. Arranging things methodically, often placing them in a sequence.

Organization. A group or association of people drawn together for the purpose of accomplishing some end or work.

Organizational saga. The shared mythology of an organization.

Overlapping. The ability of a teacher to be engaged in more than one teaching task at a time.

Overlearning. Learning that results from a teaching technique in which the teacher conducts drill or repetitive practice for a longer time than is necessary for initial learning of ideas or skills being taught; the technique is used to prompt quick recall or to enable students to recall the ideas or to reuse the skills a long time after the learning has taken place.

Perception. The process of becoming aware of something, usually through the senses.

Perennialism. The belief that truth and knowledge are universal, permanent, and not subject to change or cultural evolution.

Personal fable. A feeling or belief that an individual's emotional experiences are both unique to the person experiencing them and important to everyone else; usually associated with adolescence.

Personal idealism. The belief that reality and value are centered in a personality, a supreme being, God.

Phi pheononemon. The illusion of movement when no movement is actually taking place, created when two or more stimuli occur in rapid succession and in close proximity to each other; such as blinking neon signs.

Philosophizing. The intellectual process of thinking something through in order to form a conclusion or make a decision.

Piagetian theory. Learning theory that combines cognitive and developmental theory, attributes learning to interaction between individuals and their environment, and acknowledges that learning occurs over time and in stages; developed primarily by Jean Piaget.

Planning as problem solving. An approach to lesson planning that begins with the idea that there is a problem to be solved. The "problem" is that the students need to learn certain information, ideas, skills, and so forth.

Planning routine. The particular approach that a person, such as a teacher, uses in developing plans.

Pragmatism. The belief that what is true and real is known through human experience and inquiring thought.

Prerequisite skills and knowledge. Skills and knowledge that students must possess in order to profit from the instruction about to be provided.

Problem solving. A process of thinking in which one who confronts unexplained information or a problem situation is able to formulate an appropriate explanation or solution.

Process of investigation. The manner in which investigators raise questions about their areas of study and the way they conduct their research.

Process-product research. Investigations that compare instructional processes or activities (processes) with results or outcome (products).

Professional standards board. A body of professionals such as teachers that sets standards of acceptable practice and assesses how well individual members of the profession meet these standards.

Professionalization of teaching. A movement toward making teachers more expert, holding them more responsible for the results of their teaching, and giving them more control over their professional decisions.

Prompts. Subtle teacher suggestions that guide and encourage student responses or remind students of previously learned ideas and information.

Public schools. Either community operated, tax-supported schools of the nineteenth century or common schools of American colonial times, which were public in purpose but not tax supported.

"Pull-Out" programs. Special school programs that require the students who participate in them to leave their regular class for extra instruction.

Rational-choice approach to lesson planning. Planning lessons thoughtfully, beginning with the establishment of behavioral objectives and moving sequentially from that point.

Readiness. The willingness, desire, and ability to engage in a given activity, such as a particular learning experience.

Realism. The belief that what is true and real rests on substantial entities and objects, apart from the mind's consciousness of them.

Realist. One who believes that the universe consists of real, substantial entities that can be known and, when known, can provide principles that guide individual actions.

Reality. A concept of being that engages the question, "What is real?" The answer one supplies for the question depends on that person's philosophy or metaphysical position.

Reconstructionism. The belief that society can be improved and that individuals and institutions have a responsibility to encourage the process.

Reconstructionistic. A philosophical view of the role of schools that sees schools and teachers as agents for making society better.

Redundancy. A technique of instruction that includes repetition in the teaching of main points and key concepts to be learned.

Regulators. Nonverbal communication actions used to control discussions and movement among people.

Reinforcement theory. Theory that says the consequences of actions encourage or discourage behavior and that learning occurs because certain behaviors are rewarded or punished.

Relevance. Pertinent; having to do with that which is important or meaningful.

Representation. A configuration, drawing, painting, photograph, model, or image intended to resemble something or someone.

Retarded. Delayed in development; slower than or below normal rates or levels of development.

Rewards. Positive teacher actions that encourage and reinforce good student behavior.

Rituals and ceremonies. Events at which members of a tribe or organization have an opportunity to experience shared values and to be bonded together in a common quest.

Self-concept. An individual's image of himself or herself as a person.

Schema. Organized mental structures that enable an individual to interpret new information in terms of existing knowledge.

Scholasticism. An approach to study during the Middle Ages that combined reliance on religious faith and reason to search for truth and meaning.

Scholastics. Christian teachers of the Middle Ages who subscribed to scholasticism.

School culture. The values, belief systems, and norms present in a school.

School-level goals. Statements of purpose or guidelines around which school instructional programs are organized.

Scientific inquiry. Thinking that proceeds though steps like those described as the scientific method.

Scientific method. An approach to research and investigation and a pattern of thinking that involves the steps of identifying a problem, gathering relevant data, formulating a hypothesis, and testing the hypothesis.

Self-fulfilling prophecy. The idea that teacher expectations actually cause students to perform above or below the level of achievement at which they would normally be expected to perform.

Semantic noise. Impedance in communication because of different meanings of words.

Sensitivities. The capacities to respond to others and to situations in a perceptive, humane, and empathetic way.

Sensory handicap. An impairment of one of the senses, for example, hearing or sight.

Separate-subjects curriculum. A type of subject-centered curriculum arranged around specific content disciplines such as English, history, or mathematics; also called discipline-based curriculum.

Seriation. An arrangement of items in a sequence; the act of arranging items in a sequence.

Setting the stage for teaching. Planning and organizing all elements of instruction ahead of time to ensure that teaching will occur as intended.

Shared values and beliefs. Ideas and principles that a tribe or organization stands for.

"Should do" statements. Policy statements that prescribe what teachers and schools should do.

Skill. The ability to do something with proficiency.

Sociability. The ability of people to communicate and interact positively with others.

Socialization. The gradual initiation of children and youth into the values, beliefs, and assumptions of a culture.

Socializing institutions. Institutions established for the purpose of transmitting cultural values to younger generations and instilling in them a commitment to those values.

Social behavior. A person's actions as a member of a group or of a society; often behavior approved by the dominant cultural group.

Social cognition. The learning of rules and patterns of interpersonal relationships.

Social conventions. Common practices or assumed ways of behaving that develop within cultures and organizations; established standards and patterns for how things are usually done.

Social environment. The aspect of one's surroundings made up of other people and interactions with them.

Social-functions curriculum. An integrated curriculum plan arranged around social activities or life situations that students face or will face as adults.

Social system of classrooms. The formal and informal rules that guide interpersonal actions and relationships in classrooms.

Sociolinguistic research. Investigations that focus on the interactions of language and social structures.

Socratic method. A method of teaching developed by Socrates that uses questioning of students in dialogue style.

Soft imperatives. Subtle but firm teaching techniques used to stop or correct student misbehavior.

Sophists. Teachers of ancient Greece who travelled from place to place.

Spiral curriculum. A curriculum arranged around a hierarchy of concepts that are taught several times through the years, each time with added sophistication and depth; also called structure of knowledge curriculum.

Spiral instruction. Teaching concepts and skills in a somewhat repeating fashion in which the concepts and skills are returned to often but taught with increasing sophistication and depth each successive time.

Spontaneous nonverbal communication. Nonverbal communication that occurs naturally without specific intent.

Sputnik. The first manmade satellite to orbit the earth, launched by the Soviet Union in 1957.

Stories and legends. Miscellaneous reflections that are passed from generation to generation in a tribe or organization and carry the groups traditions and values.

Structural routines. Tightly drawn patterns of action that occur regularly without modification.

Structure of knowledge. The manner in which knowledge is organized into disciplines and levels of abstraction.

Structure of knowledge curriculum. *See* spiral curriculum.

Structuring of lessons. The planning and organizing of lessons into predetermined sequences.

Structuring the learning experience. Precise planning and organizing of the lesson sequences that students will experience.

Student-centered curriculum. A curriculum arranged around the needs, interests, and experiences of students.

Subculture. A small group within a larger group that has its own values, beliefs, and patterns of behavior.

Subject-centered curriculum. A curriculum arranged around organized fields of knowledge such as English, language arts, history, mathematics, science, or social studies.

Symbol. A representation of something; a configuration, signal, word, or other representation that stands for something not intrinsically suggested by its form.

Symbolic activity. Actions that people and groups engage in to give meaning to their life and work.

Systematic study. Planned investigation that follows a purposeful sequence.

Tabula rasa. The idea expressed by John Locke that the human mind is a blank sheet at birth and that all knowledge is learned though the senses.

Teacher as ringmaster. The idea that teachers are similar to circus ringmasters because they have so many things to do to manage classrooms and produce learning.

Teaching effectiveness. The degree to which teacher behavior produces student learning.

Teacher effectiveness training. A specific therapy-based approach to behavior control that focuses on analyzing interpersonal conflict situations.

Teaching as communication. The idea that teaching is primarily a process of communication between the teacher and students.

Teaching as a craft. A concept of teaching that thinks of the act of teaching as a set of behaviors and skills that are best learned by watching experienced "master" teachers teach and by practicing the techniques of those masters.

Teaching effectiveness. The degree to which teacher behavior produces student learning.

Teaching functions. Types of teacher behaviors that researchers have discovered as they have analyzed classroom practice.

Teaching routines. Classroom patterns planned and established by the teacher and followed by students so that classes can be effective.

Template. A pattern or mold to be followed by those who want to produce pieces of work that are exactly alike.

Theory. An assumption or generalization supported by philosophies and/or scientific principles that support hypotheses, explain phenomena, and suggest appropriate action or the direction of further investigation.

Therapy-based behavior control systems. Approaches to behavior control based on ideas from counseling and psychotherapy.

Time on task. The time during a class period when an individual student is engaged in the tasks the teacher expects.

Trade-off. Prioritizing goals and exchanging those of lesser value for those of greater value.

Tradition. A belief, custom, practice, or convention that is passed from generation to generation.

"Training the mind." An approach to teaching based on a belief that students learn to think better though practicing hard thought problems.

Transitional bilingual program. Instruction provided in a non-English-speaking student's native language for a temporary time while the student is also taught English and with the expectation that English will replace the native language.

Trial and error learning. Learning in which the learner tries various responses somewhat randomly until one response or a combination of responses results in success, satisfaction, or a reward of some type.

Tribal mystique. The idea that tribes and other groups possess distinctive shared values and beliefs, heroes and heroines, rituals and ceremonies, stories and legends, and informal players.

Turntaking. *See* conversational dance.

Underclass. The social and economic stratum consisting of people who are poor, undereducated, and of low social status.

Unit of instruction. A plan of instruction that many teachers develop for a class, so that the students reach the objectives set for them, usually involving lesson sequences that coordinate content, activities, teaching strategies, and resources.

Value. The idea that something possesses worth; the attachment of worth or esteem to something; standards that people endorse, maintain, and try to live up to.

Verbal communication. Transmitting information through language.

Wait-time. The time after teachers ask a question and before they call on a student to respond, when the students in the room do not know who will be responsible for answering.

Wandering. Allowing extraneous thoughts, concerns, and emotions to impede communication.

White flight. The migration of white people away from an area, usually from areas with increasing high rates of minority population.

Withitness. The ability of a teacher to know what is happening in the classroom all the time and to anticipate what is about to occur before it does.

Zone of action. The physical area in a classroom that is likely to involve the most teacher-student interaction.

Zone of proximal development. The area of growth from the point at which a child stands developmentally at a particular time to the state of development he or she could be expected to reach with guidance.

Index

Accreditation, school, 26
Adaptation in stages, 129, 344, 382–384. *See also* Cognitive development theory
Affective learning
  representative lesson, 431–432
  selecting content to be taught, 427–430
  teaching strategies, 429–430
  values, ideals, feelings listed, 426–427
AFT (American Federation of Teachers), 553
Alcuin, 251
Alternative high schools, 215
Aquinas, Thomas, 251–252, 298
Aristotle, 249, 297
Assertive discipline, 101
Assimilation/accommodation, 129, 344
Association theory
  classroom practices, 333–334
  proponents, 331–333

Behavior theory
  educational goals, 312, 333–334
  proponents, 312, 331–333
Behavioral/emotional disorders, 152–153, 541
Brown *v* Board of Education of Topeka, 179–180, 197, 276
Bruner, Jerome, 411

Certification, teacher, 33
Classrooms
  characteristics, 89–90
    differences/similarities, 52, 90
    elementary classrooms, 51–52
    secondary classrooms, 52
  effectiveness, 88–105
    importance of communication, 509–510
    learning time, academic, 91–92
    teacher expectations, 510
    unknown aspects of, 114–116
    wait-time, 93–94
  organization
    climate, 94–98, 525
    grouping students, 85–86, 104–105
    learning centers, 5

Classrooms (*cont.*)
  and management, 94–108
  structuring space, 98, 526
Cognitive development theory, 129–134, 340–345
  assessing the effectiveness, 385–386
  classroom practices, 342, 381–382, 384
  goals/characteristics listed, 383
  representative lesson, 379–381
Colleges and universities
  colonial times, 273
  curriculum, 273–274
  establishment of, 252, 273
  GI Bill of Rights, 274
  land grant colleges, 273–274
  teacher education, 273
Comenius, Johann Amos, 257
Communication, classroom. *See also* Research, educational: communication apprehension
  formal/informal talk, 502
  impediments to, 506–508, 528
  involving all students, 500–501, 503–504
  maintaining pace and balance, 500, 528
  nonverbal, types of, 505
Compensatory education programs, 88
  alternative high schools, 190–193
  bilingual education, 193–195, 433
  case studies, 190–193
  disadvantaged students, 188–189
  federal government initiatives, 188–189, 541
  gender-related education, 196–197
  multicultural education, 195–196
Comprehensive education, 271–272
Conant, James B., 271
Concrete operational stage, 131–132, 383
Conditioning, 335, 389
  conditioned reflex, 331
  of infant emotion, 332–333
  operant behavior, 335, 389
Content. *See* Curriculum
Cooperative learning, 105, 366–373
  assessing the effectiveness, 371–373
  goals/characteristics listed, 368
  models in practice, 369–371
  representative lesson, 366–367

Cooperative learning (cont.)
　supporting educational theories, 368–369
Culture
　organizational
　　characteristics of, 211–214, 233
　　examples in broad society, 211–214, 233
　　primitive forms of, 213
　　socialization of members, 291–292
　in schools, 13–15, 95, 531
　　administrative subgroups, 230, 232
　　affecting new teachers, 207–211, 216–218, 234, 237–238
　　enhancing effectiveness of schools, 216, 230, 232–233
　　ethnography used to study, 238–240
　　the hidden curriculum, 471
　　influenced by school location, 218
　　organizational saga concept, 215
　　personal, social development, 15
　　societies, age-grouped, 14
　　strengthening and maintaining, 217–218, 234–236
　　student subgroups, 14, 217–218, 229
　　teacher subgroups, 230
Curriculum. *See also* Education, historical perspectives; Knowledge, structure of; Lesson planning; Thinking process, developing the.
　affective learning, 426–432, 215
　based on educational objectives, 443–446
　based on learning theory, 346
　college preparatory, 12–13, 261, 264, 272
　contemporary shifts, 13, 175–178, 566
　criteria for selection, 403–405
　general studies, 12–13, 272
　the hidden curriculum, 468, 471–472
　kindergarten, 12, 258
　middle schools/junior high, 12
　preschool, 188, 258–259
　purposes for, 404
　reconstructionist perspective, 446
　sample class schedules, 439–441
　satire, of primitive society, 400–403
　student-centered organization, 451–457
　　activity-centered curriculum, 454–455
　　core curriculum, 453–454
　　humanistic curriculum, 455–457
　　social functions curriculum, 454

Curriculum (cont.)
　subject-centered organization, 447–451
　　broad-fields curriculum, 450
　　separate-subjects curriculum, 448–450
　　spiral instruction, 411, 450–451
　universities, 252, 273–274
　upper elementary grades, 12
　vocational studies, 13, 273

Development emotional/social
　adolescence, 144–146
　infancy/early childhood, 136–139
　middle childhood, 139–144
Developmental theory. *See* Cognitive development theory
Dewey, John, 271, 302, 305, 417
Dialectical theory, 126
Direct instruction, 386–391
　assessing the effectiveness, 391
　goals/characteristics listed, 389
　model in practice, 389–390
　representative lesson, 386–388
　supporting educational theories, 389
Discipline
　behavior modification systems, 100, 338–339
　by development stages, 101–103
　in colonial American schools, 260, 265
　prescribing rules of behavior, 527–528
　specific interventions, 99
　therapy-based systems, 100–101
　violence in the schools, 545

Education, historical perspectives, 171–175
　ancient Greece, fictive account, 245–246
　colonial American schools, 259–265
　　classroom organization, 260
　　economic, gender segregation in, 260–261
　　influenced by locality, 260, 263–265
　　public schools, formation of, 261–263
　　religious training, 259–260, 263, 265
　democratic, republican foundations, 6–7
　the Enlightenment, 254–257
　European educational thinkers, 257–259
　Greek philosophers and teachers, 246–249
　the Middle Ages, 251–252

Education (*cont.*)
  liberal arts, foundations of, 251
  scholasticism, 251
  the Reformation and literacy education, 253–254
  Renaissance, 252–253
  Roman influence, 250
Egocentrism, 144
Employment outlook for teachers
  areas of greatest need, 580
  older teachers, 572
  public v. private schools, 580
  reasons for increased demand, 572–573
  regional trends, 17–18, 578–579
  shortage of competent professionals, 572–574
Enrollment, student trends
  demographic changes, 11
  by economic background, 11
  by ethnic origin, 10
  family structure, 11
  by gender, 10
  gradually increasing, 573
  private and parochial schools, 9, 10
  racial percentages, 10
Environment
  classroom climate, 94–98
  role in growth and development, 125–126
  social, 139
Equality of education. *See also* Handicapped students; Segregation reforms
  diversity of offerings, 175–176
  and individual excellence, 175–178, 203
  legal mandate for, 179–184, 197–198
  new emphasis on, 178–179
Erasmus, Desiderius, 252–253
Essentialism, 315
Evaluation, lesson
  to modify future lesson plans, 497–498, 511–512
  setting performance standards, 531
Evangelicalism, 313–314
Existentialism
  educational goals, 307–308
  nature of reality, 306
  proponents, 305
  truth and values, 306–307

Formal operational stage of development, 133–134, 383

Froebel, Friedrich, 258
Future predictions for teaching, 36–38
  graduates ill-prepared technologically, 589
  higher performance standards, 586
  impersonal electronic society, 588
  intrusion of media, 590
  more student dropouts, 591
  prevalence of poverty, 590–591
  role in international competition, 586
Futurism, 311

Gagné, R. M., 340. *See also* Cognitive development theory
Gender-related aspects of education, 196–197
Gestalt psychology, 352–354
Gifted and talented students
  designing education for, 148, 199–200
Guthrie, Edwin, 333

Handicapped students
  equality of education, 182–184, 197–199, 270, 276, 368, 541
  Individual Education Plan, 183–184, 198
  mainstreaming of, 198, 372
  Public Law *94-142*, 182–184, 197–198
Herbart, Johann, 258
Holistic education, 301
Humanism
  classical, 252
  and open education curriculum, 455–457
  romantic, 305
Hunter, Madeline, 375–379

Idealism
  educational goals, 296–297
  proponents, 295
Information-processing theory. *See* Cognitive development theory
Input-output research designs, 40, 74
Instructional models, 392–393
Instructional theory into practice (ITIP), 373–379
  assessing the effectiveness, 378–379
  goals/characteristics listed, 375
  model in practice, 376–378
  representative lesson, 373–375
  supporting educational theories, 376
Instructional units
  key components, 460
  representative outlines, 460–465

Intelligence, categories based on, 147–150
  gifted students, 148
  mentally retarded students, 148–150

Knowledge, structure of
  levels of abstraction, 408–410
  methods of teaching knowledge, 410–413
  organized by discipline, 406–408

Labeling of students
  affecting group dynamics, 496
  to determine instruction, 146–154, 157, 184–185
  efforts to reduce stereotypes, 368
  results of, shown by research, 158–161
Latchkey children, 543
Learning disabilities, 150–151
Learning theories. *See also* Association theory; Behavior theory; Cognitive development theory; Piaget, Jean; Reinforcement theory
  characteristics of various, 330–345
  futuristic case study, 352–354
  need for, 329–330
  and teaching style, 329, 345–347
Learning time, academic, 91–92
Lesson planning. *See also* Evaluation, lesson
  curricular influences, 496
  developing written plans, 480–481
  external influences, 488–490, 510–511
  forming mental images, 477–480
  influencing factors, listed, 483–484
  lesson-image approach, 482–483
  organizational influences, 490–494
  rational-choice approach, 481–482
  representative sample, primary level, 467–468
  students' influence on, 494–496
  teacher's own influence, 485–488
Locke, John, 256–257
Luther, Martin, 254

Mainstreaming students, 198, 372
Mann, Horace, 271
Marxism, 314–315
Mastery learning, 359–365
  assessing the effectiveness, 363–365
  goals/characteristics listed, 361
  possible problems, 363
  representative lesson, 359–361
  supporting educational theories, 362

McAuliffe, Christa, 15
McGuffey, William H., 270
Mentally retarded students, 148–150
Merit schools, 27
Misbehavior. *See* Discipline
Montessori, Maria, 258–259, 298
Moral reasoning, development of, 134–136, 258

NEA (National Education Association), 172–173, 553

Observation. *See also* Student On-Task/Off-Task Behavior Observation System; Teacher-Student Interaction Observation System
  of classrooms
    analytical observation systems, 64–73, 599–603
    analyzing videotaped classes, 63–64
    collecting, coding data, 59–62
    cultural case studies, 219–228
    formulating questions, 59
    input-output research designs, 40, 74
    interpreting data, 63
    organizing data, 62
    practice exercises, 71–73, 603–606
    process-product investigation, 75–77
    researchers' perceptions of, 54–55
    role of perceptual development, 128
    systematic processes, 56–73
    teacher accountability pressures, 489
    value of, 57–58
  of schools
    year-long journalistic study, 231–232, 236–237, 465–466
Organizations, professional, of educators, 552–555
  intrinsic rewards, 555
  ones influenced by members' involvement, 552
  for specific teaching specialties, 554–555
  unions, 552–553

Pavlov, Ivan Petrovich, 331–332. *See also* Association theory
Peer relationships
  importance of group affiliation, 145–146
  social interaction among teachers, 533, 539

Peer relationships (*cont.*)
  among students, 140–141, 155–157
  teachers uneasy with comparisons, 532
Perceptual development, 128–129
Perennialism, 312–313
Pestalozzi, Johann Heinrich, 257–258
Philosophies related to teaching. *See also* Behavior theory; Essentialism; Evangelicalism; Existentialism; Futurism; Idealism; Marxism; Perennialism; Pragmatism; Realism; Reconstructionism
  contemporary, 309–315
  historical, 294–302
  modern, 302–309
Philosophy, personal, of teachers
  clarification of concepts, 288–289
  examination of accepted practices, 290–291
  fictive case studies, 283–287, 308–309, 318–320
  influencing lesson plans, 487
  integration and practical application, 318–320
  interpretation of data, 291–293
  need for justification, 289–290
  personal factors influencing, 287–288
  problems to avoid, 294
  systematization of beliefs, 291–293
Physical handicaps, 154, 157
Piaget, Jean, 129–134, 343–345, 382–383
Plato, 248–249, 297
Plessy *v* Ferguson, 179–180, 276
Pragmatism
  educational goals, 304–305
  nature of truth, 303–304
  proponents, 302
Preoperational stage of development, 130–131, 383
Process-product investigation, 75–77
Programmed instruction, 336–337
Progressive education, 305
Public Law *94-142*, 182–184, 197–198
Public schools, establishment of, 261–263, 268–270
Purposes, general, of schools. *See also* Education, historical perspectives; Segregation reforms
  academic achievement, 8
  citizenship education, 7–8, 246–248, 264, 268
  college preparation, 9

Purposes (*cont.*)
  equality for all students, 7, 175–184, 254
  historical perspectives, 171–175
  individual excellence, 174–178
  Jeffersonian view, 6–7, 267
  literacy education, 253–254
  national defense, 174
  personal, social development, 9
  redefined, 34, 445
  religious training, 263, 313
  vocational preparation, 8, 254, 269, 275

Realism
  educational goals, 299–302
  proponents, 297–298
Reality therapy, 101
Reconstructionism, 310–311, 446
Reform, educational, 5, 23–29. *See also* Equality of education
  in *A Nation at Risk*, 23–26, 28, 30–31
  "back to basics" movement, 28–29, 448–449
  Carnegie Foundation report, 33–34
  for increased professionalization of teaching, 586
  for international prominence, 587
  Holmes Group report, 33–34
  notable American activists, 270–271
  RAND Corporation report, 32
  in salary schedules, 582, 584–585
  subject-centered curriculum, 447–451
  teacher education programs, 33
  "waves" of reform and subsequent changes, 25–29
Reinforcement theory
  and classroom conduct, 338–339
  and learning, 336–337, 389
  proponents, 334–335
Research, educational
  classroom effectiveness, unknown aspects of, 114–116
  communication apprehension, 509–510
  development of research projects, 201–203
  and educational philosophy, 316–318
  ethnographic studies, 238–240
  general nature of, 39–41
  Gestalt psychology, 352–354
  middle school effectiveness studies, 458–459

Research (*cont.*)
  secondary schools, historical study of, 277–279
  survey of teachers' perceptions, 546–548
  teaching and learning history, 414–416
  using research data for educational decisions, 158–161
  what we know about studying classrooms, 74
Rewards and academic achievement, 110–111
Rousseau, Jean-Jacques, 255, 298

Salaries and compensation, teachers'
  comparisons with other fields difficult, 581
  new bases for increments, 582, 584–586
  state averages, 581–586
Scholasticism, 251
Schools. *See also* Students; Classrooms
  current issues facing, 19–20
  differences among
    effects of cultural surroundings, 218
    ethnography used to study, 238–240
    factual case studies, 219–228
  general perceptions of, 20–22
  organization of grade levels, courses, 12–13, 174
  prevalent problems
    dropout rates, 591
    drug use, 21
    efforts to minimize, 96–103
    lack of discipline, 22
    recent public poll, 22
Scientific method, 304
Segregation reforms
  in early public schools, 270
  by ethnic minority, 274–276
  by gender, 253–254, 274
  handicapped students, 182–184, 276
  racial, 179–182, 185–187
  social and economic, 252–253
Sensorimotor stage of development, 130, 383
Sensory handicaps
  hearing-impaired students, 153–157
  visually handicapped students, 154
Skills taught in schools. *See also* Thinking process, developing the
  categorized and listed, 424
  teaching methods, 425–426

Skinner, B. F., 312, 335, 389. *See also* Reinforcement theory
Socrates, 247–248
Spiral instruction, 411, 450–451
Sputnik, influence on education policies, 173–174, 199–200, 411, 450
Student On-Task/Off Task Behavior Observation System, 64–70
  calculating off-task rates, 70
  coding off-task behavior and activities, 64–67
  practice exercise, 71–73
  summarizing data, 69–70
  visual sweeps, 67–68, 71–73
Students. *See also* Enrollment, student trends
  in cycle of poverty, 537, 540, 565–566, 590–591
  diverse personalities, 529
  dropping out of school, 591
  grouped, in classrooms, 85–86, 104–105
  home life of, 592
    abused children, 543–544
    delinquency, vandalism, 544–545
    drug and alcohol abuse, 544
    transient families, 543
    working parents/latchkey children, 542–543
  influenced by teachers, 86, 88, 337, 512, 522, 529–531, 568
  relationship with teachers, 529–531
  violent behavior, 545

Taba, Hilda, 420–421, 430
Teacher effectiveness training, 100
Teacher-Student Interaction Observation System, 599–603
  analyzing data, 601–603
  coding interactions, 599–601
  practice exercise, 603–606
Teachers. *See also* Teaching, profession of
  application of learning theory, 347–349
  characteristics of, 55–56
    age, median, 18, 522
    education level attained, 16, 522
    gender, 16, 522
    minority teachers, 576–577
    political ties, 522
    racial/ethnic, 16, 522
    union affiliation, 522, 552–553
    years experience, 16, 32, 522

Index **629**

Teachers (*cont.*)
   as classroom managers
      autonomy in the classroom, 536–537
      in charge of classroom communication, 500
      formulating rules and procedures, 96, 527
      routines, teaching of, 96, 527
      student accountability techniques, 97
   competencies needed in future, 568–571
   critical criteria for success, 569–571
   effectiveness
      active teaching strategies, 105–107
      characteristics of, 85–86, 568
      development of national criteria, 565
      judged by students' tests, 564–565
      setting goals and expectations, 108–110, 487–489
   as employees, 534
   expectations regarding student performance, 108–109
   relationships
      cultivating parents' support, 534–535
      influence with students, 86–88, 337, 512–522, 529–531, 568
      peer relationships, 532–533, 539
      relationship with principals, 534
   serving many roles, 523, 530, 567
   societal perceptions of, 15, 21, 521–523
   teaching prescribed content, 566
Teaching, profession of, 586–593. *See also* Future predictions for teaching; Teachers
   attracting professionals from other fields, 576
   attraction to other fields, 17, 19, 32
   becoming more hierarchical, 532
   beginning teachers' responsibilities, 524
   changing professional environment, 564
   evaluation of teachers, 538, 565
   hiring trends, regional, 17–18, 578–579
   historical view, 56

Teaching (*cont.*)
   increasingly complex profession, 567, 571
   making career decisions, 555–556
   negative work conditions, 550–551
   one's personal suitability for, 562–563, 593–594
   positive aspects, benefits, 548–550
   ratios, student-teacher, 18
   reasons for teaching, 524–525
   salaries and working conditions, 32, 522, 581–586
   shortages, supply-demand imbalance, 17, 32, 571–577
   special challenges
      abused children, 543–544
      confronting discrimination of students, 541
      delinquency, vandalism, 544–545
      drug and alcohol abuse, 544
      indigent students, 537, 540, 565–566, 590–591
      research results, 547
      student dropouts, 59
      transient families, 543
      violence in the schools, 545
Testing, student
   as basis for student promotion, 26
   indicating teacher effectiveness, 564–565
   as indicators of risk, 31
   influence on lesson planning, 489
   intelligence tests, 147–150
Thinking process, developing the
   conceptualizing, 418–420, 422
   levels of complex thinking, 416
   metacognition, 420–421
   problem solving, 417–418, 422
Thorndike, E. L., 334. *See also* Reinforcement theory
Tolman, E. C., 340. *See also* Cognitive development theory

Visual sweep, 67–68, 71–73

Watson, J. B., 332. *See also* Association theory
Webster, Noah B., 270
ZPD (zone of proximal development), 140